Testimony

The Minnesota Supreme Court in session, 1980

Testimony

Remembering Minnesota's Supreme Court Justices

Minnesota Supreme Court Historical Society

St. Paul, Minnesota • Minnesota Supreme Court Historical Society • 2008

On the cover: *Main stairway to the Minnesota Supreme Court, Minnesota State Capitol, St. Paul (from a post card, ca. 1905)*

On the back: *The bench of the Minnesota Supreme Court, Minnesota State Capitol* (Janet Marshall photo)

Illustrations in the text are from the photo collection of the Minnesota Supreme Court unless otherwise noted as following:

Courtesy of the Minnesota Historical Society (used by permission): front cover, pp. 193, 210, 258, 265, 268, 276, 282, 293, and 295.

In the public domain: From 4 *Green Bag*: pp. 4, 20, and 30; from *Men of Minnesota*, 2d ed. (St. Paul: R. L. Polk, 1915): pp. 204, 219, 223, 230, 235, 244, 247, 252, 280, and 285; from Hiram F. Stevens, *History of the Bench and Bar of Minnesota*, 2 vols. (Minneapolis: Legal Publishing and Engraving, 1904): pp. 1, 6, 11, 13, 18, 42, 46, 50, 54, 60, 66, 80, 83, 89, 96, 102, 110, 124, 132, 139, 142, 144, 161, 173, 176, 182, and 201.

Editing and design: E. B. Green Editorial, St. Paul
Indexing: Barbara L. Golden, Minnesota State Law Librarian
Printing: Sexton Printing, Inc., St. Paul
Binding: Muscle Bound Bindery, Minneapolis

Supported in part by The Roger L. and Agnes C. Dell Charitable Trust

Contents

Foreword

Gentlemen, I have endeavored briefly, I know with imperfect success, to express what . . . survivors on the bench think and feel in regard to our departed associate. Your eloquent and appropriate memorial shall be entered into records of the court, there to remain as a testimony so long as those records shall be preserved.
—Chief Justice Gilfillan, June 10, 1881

In this sesquicentennial year of Minnesota's statehood, the Minnesota Supreme Court was excited to encourage the creation of a new organization to collect, study, and disseminate the history of the Minnesota judiciary. The result—the formation of the Minnesota Supreme Court Historical Society—will provide the citizens of Minnesota the opportunity to better understand and celebrate the contributions that the judiciary has made to the security, prosperity, and well-being of our state.

From the days when the three justices of the territorial supreme court also comprised the entire trial bench for Minnesota Territory, we have indeed come a long way. Our judiciary is now made up of seven justices of the state supreme court, 19 judges of the court of appeals and 288 judges of the district court, the latter distributed through 10 judicial districts. The dramatic increases in the size of the judiciary have been necessary to keep pace with ever-increasing caseloads. Each year, more than two million new cases enter at the district court, with at least 200,000 of them requiring substantive judicial attention. The court of appeals reviews about 2,500 of those cases, and the supreme court considers providing discretionary review in more than 600 of them. In addition, the Minnesota Supreme Court has mandatory jurisdiction over all appeals from first-degree murder convictions, appeals from the tax court and the workers' compensation court of appeals, lawyer discipline matters, and certain election cases.

That the first major project of the newly formed Minnesota Supreme Court Historical Society is the publication of this volume of memorials to justices is fitting. Perhaps more than in any other branch of government, the legacy of members of the judiciary lives on in their decisions, to which we give great deference particularly as we interpret and shape the common law in Minnesota. For example, in recent terms, the supreme court determined that the common law prohibition of the corporate practice of medicine is rooted in a 1933 decision authored by Justice Loring, built in turn upon a 1930 *per curiam* decision.[1] And its recent decisions on common law immunity for government officials continue, to some degree, the dialogue contained in the majority and dissenting opinions of Justices Todd, Scott, and Kelly in the 1970s and 1980s, which built on a 1962 decision authored by Justice Otis, abrogating the common law doctrine of governmental immunity.[2] We regularly use and rely upon the words and the reasoning of our departed colleagues.

In years past, the Minnesota Supreme Court, working with the Minnesota State Bar Association, commemorated the justices in open court. On one of the last of these occasions, on May 31, 1966, the court assembled to hear the memorials for three deceased chief justices—Henry M. Gallagher, Charles M. Loring, and Roger L. Dell. The following excerpt from the memorial for Roger L. Dell describes the dedication to the work of the court that typifies so many justices: "Judge Dell was blessed with innate ability and keen legal mind, but these assets were abetted by a tremendous capacity for work. Time meant nothing to him in the preparation of his files and in representing clients. He was an indefatigable laborer in all phases of his profession. And when he became a member of this court he brought all of those rare qualities with him, and immediately the court and its functions became the object of his all-consuming interest and pride."

This volume completes the memorials for all deceased justices to this date. I am pleased to announce that the Minnesota Supreme Court, working in conjunction with the new Minnesota Supreme Court Historical Society, will resume the practice of receiving memorials at sessions of the court for all future deceased justices. These will be available immediately on the judiciary's website; future generations of members of the historical society will no doubt publish them in volume 2.

—Russell A. Anderson, Chief Justice
Minnesota Supreme Court

References

1. See, e.g., *Isles Wellness, Inc. v. Progressive Northern Ins. Co.*, 725 N.W.2d 90, 93 (Minn. 2006) [citing *Granger v. Adson*, 190 Minn. 23, 250 N.W. 722 (1933), and *In re Otterness*, 181 Minn. 254, 232 N.W. 318 (1930) (*per curiam*)].

2. Compare *Schroeder v. St. Louis County*, 708 N.W.2d 497 (Minn. 2006), with *Hage v. Stade*, 304 N.W.2d 283 (Minn. 1981), *Cracraft v. City of St. Louis Park*, 279 N.W.2d 801 (Minn. 1979), and *Spanel v. Mounds View School Dist. No. 621*, 264 Minn. 279, 118 N.W.2d 795 (1962).

Preface

And now the Minnesota State Bar Association, in obedience to a custom hallowed by time and consecrated by gratitude and esteem, directs that this memorial be made to perpetuate an example which, if forgotten, would leave an ellipsis in the history of the birth and development of our state.

—Martin J. Severance

This volume memorializes 74 justices and two commissioners who served on the Minnesota Supreme Court during 150 years of statehood and on the territorial court established in 1849.

For many years the court, working with the Minnesota State Bar Association, commemorated departed justices at special sessions. Starting with the death of territorial Associate Justice Andrew G. Chatfield in 1875, such proceedings were transcribed and published in Minnesota Reports, the official reporter for the decisions of the Minnesota Supreme Court. After honoring 47 justices, including three of the ten territorial justices, and two commissioners, the publication of such memorials ceased, in 1966. From statehood, only Justice Thomas Canty (inexplicably) was missed.*

This volume collects those published memorials for the first time. Ranging from about 1,500 to 13,000 words, some memorials provide detailed biographical information while others only generally recognize a justice's accomplishments and the high regard of his peers. Collectively, they put a human face to the court, with stories and fond reminiscences from people who personally knew the justices they eulogized, providing a wealth of biographical and institutional history found nowhere else.

A word of explanation regarding the inclusion of the two commissioners, Edward Lees and Myron D. Taylor, who were memorialized in Minnesota Reports and are included in this volume: The court appointed these commissioners under the authority of a legislative act, 1913 Minn. Laws, ch. 62, to relieve the work of the justices of that time. The commissioners had the same qualifications, duties, tenure, and salary that justices had; only the method of their appointment differed. All the appointed commis-

sioners authored opinions published in Minnesota Reports.

The office of commissioner was intended to exist only until a constitutional amendment increased the state supreme court from five to seven justices. Three proposed amendments (in 1914, 1916, and 1926) failed. Not until 1930 did voters approve 1929 Minn. Laws, ch. 430, and the two incumbent commissioners become justices. Five people served as commissioners: three continued service as justices.

Myron D. Taylor was one of the first commissioners, appointed in 1913; he served until 1930, when he resigned to retire to California, shortly before approval of the amendment. Edward Lees, appointed a commissioner in 1918, served until he resigned in 1927, shortly before his death. The memorials of these two commissioners are part of the institutional history of the court and thus included here.

Twenty-seven new memorials, written specifically for this volume, commemorate the remaining territorial justices, Justice Canty, and all those justices who have died since the publication of memorials ceased. The particular author is credited at the end of each of these.

The memorials appear in the order that the justices came on the court, rather than alphabetically or chronologically by date of birth or death. This approach provides context for their place in the court's history and in that of the state. To assist readers in determining a particular court's makeup, the table of succession, found at the back of this volume, lists every justice to the present. This is the most complete and correct table currently available.

The authors consulted many sources, including friends and relatives of the justices. The following books and articles were particularly helpful:

Books

Minnesota State Bar Association. *For the Record: 150 Years of Law & Lawyers in Minnesota.* Minneapolis: The author, 1999.

Gunderson, Russell O. *History of the Minnesota Supreme Court.* St. Paul, Minnesota: Minnesota Supreme Court, 1937.

Stevens, Hiram F. *History of the Bench and Bar of Minnesota.* 2 vols. Minneapolis: Legal Publishing and Engraving, 1904.

Articles

Elliott, Charles B. "The Supreme Court of Minnesota," 4 Green Bag 113 (1892).

Heiberg, Robert A. "Social Backgrounds of the Minnesota Supreme Court Justices: 1858–1968," 53 Minn. L. Rev. 901 (1968–1969).

Sheran, Robert J., and Timothy J. Baland. "The Law, Courts, and Lawyers in the Frontier Days of Minnesota: An Informal Legal History of the Years 1835 to 1865," 2 Wm. Mitchell L. Rev. 1 (1976).

Memorials previously published in Minnesota Reports have been edited minimally. The earlier memorials include some historical error, as well as attitudes (for instance, in descriptions of the Dakota Conflict of 1862) reflective of their time but not of present-day sensitivities. Spellings and sentence constructions also remain as originally published to preserve the flavor of their period. But for easier reading, punctuation has been modernized and *that* substituted for *which* where appropriate. Most of the text reflecting the court proceedings (such as "May I address the court?") has been omitted. The memorials recently written have been edited according to modern standards and for consistent style.

An alphabetical index lists the names of the honored justices and the attorneys, judges, and persons of political importance mentioned in the text, as well as the authors of the memorials. Relatives, unless they belong to the categories mentioned, and the authors of quotations (some of whom were not cited) are not included. Italicized page numbers indicate the beginning pages of the memorials, all but two of which include an image of the honoree. Despite an extensive search, we were unable to locate photos of territorial Chief Justices Jerome Fuller and Henry Z. Hayner, who resided in Minnesota only briefly.

Much appreciation goes to Ellen Green of E. B. Green Editorial for her invaluable assistance in preparing this manuscript. I commend the work of the Minnesota Supreme Court Historical Society Publications Committee, cochaired by William Hart and Kate MacKinnon, for its dedication in producing this volume in time for the Minnesota sesquicentennial celebration. Special thanks to former Justice Sam Hanson for initiating this project.

—Barbara L. Golden,
Minnesota State Law Librarian

---

* This volume includes memorials only for those who have served on the Supreme Court. Minnesota Reports also published memorials for: William Sprigg Hall, Judge, Ramsey County Court of Common Pleas (20 Minn.); Charles H. Berry, Minnesota Attorney General (79 Minn.); Cushman K. Davis, U.S. Senator (81 Minn.); Martin J. Severance, District Judge (102 Minn.); William Lochren, Judge, U.S. District Court (119 Minn.); Albert F. Pratt, Attorney General (173 Minn.); and William D. Mitchell, U.S. Attorney General (246 Minn.)

Testimony

Remembering Minnesota's Supreme Court Justices

Aaron Goodrich

1807–1887
Chief Justice, Territorial Supreme Court, 1849–1851

On March 19, 1849, President Zachary Taylor named the three men constituting the first supreme court of Minnesota Territory—David Cooper, Bradley Meeker, and Aaron Goodrich, the latter as first chief justice. Little could the president have anticipated that controversy swarming his selection would lead to Goodrich's unceremonious removal from office. And little could he have known the unique character of the man he chose to preside over the court.

Aaron Goodrich was born in Cayuga County, New York, on July 6, 1807. His family, of Welsh origin, for generations subsisted by farming in New England before moving to New York. In 1815, Goodrich's father moved the family west to settle in Erie County, New York. One of eight children, Goodrich split his time between work on the farm with his father and his lessons in small country schools.

At about age of 19 or 20, Goodrich tired of farm life and moved to Buffalo, New York, where he worked as a traveling agent for the Isaac W. Skinner Iron Foundry. During this time, Goodrich gained his first experience in the law under the tutelage of Samuel Wilkeson, a lawyer at a Buffalo law firm. After a time in Buffalo, Goodrich rejoined his family, which by then had resettled in Michigan Territory. There, many members of his family found success— one brother later became a justice of the Michigan Supreme Court, and two others were elected to the state senate. While in Michigan, Aaron helped his family manage its family-run bank, which failed in 1838—likely setting Goodrich on the path toward his appointment as chief justice.

Following the failure of the Goodrich Bank, Aaron moved to Dover, Tennessee, where he served in the 93rd Regiment of the state militia and married a Michigan woman, Celinda Fay. While in Dover, Goodrich finished his legal studies; he began practicing law in the fall of 1841. Six years later, Goodrich ran for a seat in the Tennessee Legislature. When the election count was returned, Goodrich, a Whig, had lost by a mere two votes to his Democratic opponent, Abithel Wallace. Not one to accept defeat by such a tiny margin, Goodrich challenged the result, and Wallace subsequently withdrew from the race. On October 18, 1847, Goodrich, the only Whig ever to represent his district, took his place in the legislature.

In Tennessee, Goodrich gained a particularly powerful ally: Zachary Taylor. Following his own "election," Goodrich traveled across the state to speak in favor of Taylor's bid for the presidency. Shortly after Taylor's election, the president named the first justices of Minnesota's territorial supreme court. Based on recommendations of Goodrich as a man of "high character and integrity" and out of gratitude for his support, Taylor tapped Goodrich for a four-year term as first chief justice of the infant territory.

Following his appointment, Goodrich departed Dover and traveled down the Cumberland River to Paducah, Kentucky. From there he proceeded to St. Louis, where he took the steamboat *Cora* to St. Paul, arriving on May 20, 1849. Goodrich made the journey alone, having sent his wife home to Michigan.

When Goodrich arrived, the territory was divided into three judicial districts, each assigned a single supreme court justice to serve as district judge. The territory's first district court was called to session in Stillwater in August 1849. There Aaron Goodrich presided. Nearly 20 lawyers, each with a strong preference for the particular rules and procedures of his home jurisdiction, attended. It is no surprise that only one of the ten indictments returned during that term—one for assault with intent to maim, another for perjury, four for selling liquor to Indians, and four for keeping gambling houses—went to trial. The others were held until the next spring.

That lone trial, the first in the new territory, was notable in that the defendant was none other than William D. Phillips, the first district attorney of Ramsey County. Phillips was accused of assault with intent to maim, based on an altercation in which he drew a pistol on another man. Even more unlikely was his explanation: Phillips claimed that the gun was not loaded, explaining that he carried crackers and cheese in the pocket in which he kept his pistol and that a crumb lodged in the muzzle, making the gun appear to be loaded.

The environment of the first sessions of the court reflected the rough and rugged state of the early territory. Goodrich presided over one session in Mazurka Hall in St. Paul. The roof of the building had been thoroughly fireproofed but not waterproofed, and umbrellas were necessary to shelter the courtroom occupants from a sudden downpour.

The first term of the territorial supreme court opened at the American House in Saint Paul on Monday, January 14, 1850, its business concerning only housekeeping matters with no cases heard. Over the course of three days, the court appointed its clerk, admitted 19 individuals to the bar, and promulgated the rules of practice for the territory—personally drafted by Goodrich. Not until July 7, 1851, during the second session of the court, were substantive issues addressed. During that session, the court heard 15 cases, the first of which was *Gervais v. Powers*, an action of trespass concerning a cow.

Although *Gervais* was the first case, the first case published was *Desnoyer v. L'Hereux*, an appeal of a decision Goodrich had rendered as a district judge. Such a strange arrangement, in which the justices reviewed the cases over which they had presided as district judges, was economically necessary. The territory simply lacked the funds to support three additional judges. Goodrich, of course, dissented from the reversal of his decision and thus rendered the first dissent in the first published opinion of the supreme court.

Goodrich was a unique presence on the court, his interest in law paling in comparison to his interest in the study of literature and archaeology. Reflecting the

era in which he practiced, Goodrich was a firm believer in a flexible common-law system as described by Sir William Blackstone, and he considered statutory codes excessively costly to maintain. His disdain for statutory law was perhaps most evident in Goodrich's contribution to a commission tasked with compiling a code derived from territorial law. Instead of compiling the laws of the territory, Goodrich drafted a code all his own, with one provision stating simply: "If any question shall arise, civil or criminal, which is not provided for in this revision, the ancient statutes shall prevail in regard to it." Not surprisingly, Goodrich's code was never adopted.

The premature end of Goodrich's term as chief justice had little to do with his judicial philosophy. When Millard Fillmore succeeded the deceased President Taylor, the chief justice's fate was likely sealed—Goodrich had made a personal enemy of Fillmore during his youth in New York. That Goodrich never endeared himself to the people of Minnesota only contributed to his downfall. One particularly important individual—territorial Gov. Alexander Ramsey—had come to believe very early that the chief justice lacked knowledge of the law and had "utter incapacity for his place." One group of settlers made an early attempt to remove Goodrich from office, and later, a number of Minnesota attorneys presented a petition to President Fillmore accusing the justice of improprieties both on and off the bench. The petition was likely the straw that broke the camel's back; President Fillmore removed Goodrich from office on October 22, 1851. Goodrich challenged his removal, claiming he was a member of the federal judiciary, whose office lasted during good behavior, an argument cut short when he was struck from the government payroll.

Though Goodrich's career as a justice was over—he never served as a judge again—he stayed in the public eye. Following his removal from the court, Goodrich continued to practice law and he became a charter member of the Minnesota Historical Society. On one notable instance, he represented on appeal a Native American named Zu-ai-za, who had been convicted of murder. Unable to pronounce his client's name, Goodrich referred to him by the biblical name Ahasuerus during arguments, which failed; his client was later hanged, in the first execution performed under Minnesota law.

In 1861, President Abraham Lincoln appointed Goodrich secretary of legation in Brussels, Belgium, a position he held until 1869. While in Europe, Goodrich wrote a book entitled *A History of the Character and Achievements of the So-Called Christopher Columbus*. Published in Philadelphia in 1874, it sought to show that Columbus's real name was Criego and that the explorer was formerly a pirate. When his time in Brussels came to a close, Goodrich returned to Saint Paul, accompanied by a 19-year-old girl to whom he had extended protection on her journey from Paris. Goodrich subsequently divorced his wife, who from all accounts never joined him in Minnesota, and married his young charge. The former chief justice made his home in St. Paul until his death on June 24, 1887.

Aaron Goodrich was a unique representative of "American sturdiness and of the peculiar American intellectual ambition developed under the rough conditions of primitive life in a new country." Described by some as a man who presided over his court while nursing a glass of liquor and chewing a wad of tobacco as big as an orange, as a man "full of stories and broad fun," and as a "stormy petrel" of the territorial bench, Goodrich influenced the court in a way that will never be replicated.

—Jonathon D. Byrer

David Cooper

1821–1875

Associate Justice, Territorial Supreme Court, 1849–1853

A brilliant legal mind, a swift rise in his profession, an eccentric personality, a brief tenure as justice that coincided with the seminal moments of the Minnesota judicial system, and a tragic end—such was the life of Associate Justice David Cooper of the first Minnesota Territorial Supreme Court.

David Cooper was born in Brooks Reserve, Frederick County, Maryland, on July 22, 1821. Ten years later, his family moved to Gettysburg, Pennsylvania, to further the legal ambitions of his brother, James. David Cooper briefly attended Pennsylvania College and then studied law at his brother's Gettysburg office. In 1845, at the age of 24, he was admitted to practice and moved to "Louistown," Pennsylvania. By the time he was 28 years old, he had a thriving practice and was attracting notice in both law and politics.

In 1848, Zachary Taylor was elected the last Whig president of the United States. Both David and his brother, U.S. Senator James Cooper, had supported Taylor's campaign. As a result, in 1849, President Taylor appointed David Cooper, still 28, as one of two associate justices of the supreme court of the nascent Minnesota Territory. His colleagues were Chief Justice Aaron Goodrich and Associate Justice Bradley Meeker.

Minnesota Territory was born by act of Congress on March 3, 1849. The organic act provided that the judicial power of the territory was vested in a supreme court consisting of three justices, each of whom would also serve as the district court judge in one of the three judicial districts. This system boasted the peculiar feature, criticized even at the time, that the justices of the territorial supreme court would routinely review their own orders from below. The organic act entitled each justice to an annual salary of $1,800. It also provided for the erection of public buildings and a library.

Minnesota Territory in 1849 was a rough wilderness, sparsely populated, and in large part still under Native American control. Along with the other two justices and a few other luminaries, Cooper was present for Gov. Alexander Ramsey's May 27, 1849, proclamation declaring the territorial government duly organized. On June 11, Ramsey divided the territory into three judicial districts, the boundaries of which changed several times during Cooper's four years on the court. He was assigned the Third District, seated at a trading company warehouse in Mendota. He called the state of territorial law "a mess of incongruous imperfection."

Cooper presided over the first court session in his district; on August 27, 1849, he addressed the first grand jury impaneled there, providing it an elaborate and inspiring charge. The eloquence of his speech was largely lost on the members of the grand jury as only three of them could speak English. Still, the local newspaper later reported his words.

Also on that day, Justice Cooper admitted several attorneys to practice. He implored them to observe the rules of "courtesy and gentlemanly bearing":

> It will be my object to see that those rules are esteemed and respected, and painful indeed would it be to me to be under necessity of punishing their willful infractions. It shall likewise be my object never to be harsh, petulant, or oppressive but to observe towards you a strict impartiality, a kind and courteous manner. This is due from the court, as well as from the bar . . . That I shall frequently err, I doubt not; that is but human, and older, more experienced men than I am have often erred in the construction of laws. But whenever I do err, I shall not hesitate to retrace my steps, if possible, or to give to those who feel themselves aggrieved every facility in my power to have a hearing before a higher tribunal.

The first term of the Minnesota Territorial Supreme Court began on January 14, 1850. The court dealt solely with administrative matters and heard no cases.

Justice Cooper presided over the territory's first murder trial in February 1850. A boy had shot his 13-year-old companion and was convicted of manslaughter. In the absence of any penitentiary, he was sentenced to 90 days in the Fort Snelling guardhouse, forced to subsist on bread and water for the first two and last two days. The local newspaper observed that Justice Cooper dispensed justice in "homeopathic doses."

In its second term, beginning July 6, 1851, the supreme court heard its first argument, pertaining to the trespass of a cow. Lacking a courthouse or a state capitol, the court resided in Methodist Episcopal Church. (The court moved into the new capitol building in 1853.)

Like many in positions of power, Cooper faced his share of media and public relations problems, brought on both by his irascible temper and the vast differences between him and the people he undertook to serve. Although indisputably industrious and probably the finest legal mind of the three original justices, he was extremely stubborn and became irate when anyone dared to disagree with him. According to Judge Flandrau, one of his successors, "He so fully identified himself with the cause of his client that fair criticism from opposite counsel of the merits of the case would be construed into a personal affront, and he never forgave a judge who decided against him. With all these peculiarities, the judge had a very genial nature." His adherence to one side of any argument likely proved problematic for a justice reviewing his own opinions!

Cooper was something of a dandy. Despite his youth, he affected the fashions of earlier years, including a brocade coat with cambric ruffles at the neck and lace cuffs. His eagerness to portray himself as an aristocrat might have attracted notice even back east, but to the rough frontiersmen of territorial Minnesota it appeared foppish and ridiculous. James Madison Goodhue, founder of St. Paul Pioneer and Public Printer, referred to Justice Cooper as a "profligate vagabond," mocked his dress, manners, and "punctilious and ceremonious" deportment, accused him of absenteeism and indebtedness, and impugned him for being "so certain and set in his views that he could not endure opposition to them."

Matters came to a head when Goodhue published yet another scathing and colorful critique of Cooper: "He is not only a miserable drunkard, who habitually gets so drunk as to feel upward for the ground, but he also spends days and nights and Sunday playing cards in [saloons]. He is lost to all sense of decency and respect. Off the Bench he is a beast, and on the Bench he is an ass, stuffed with arrogance, self conceit and ridiculous affectation of dignity."

Although Justice Cooper was out of town at the time, the screed so enraged his brother Joseph that he and Goodhue confronted one another in the public street. Joseph Cooper stabbed Goodhue twice with a Bowie knife, and Goodhue shot Joseph Cooper. Goodhue died of related infections a year later. Joseph Cooper was crippled for life.

At the beginning of his administration in 1853, President Franklin Pierce removed all the justices and replaced them with men of his own choosing. Justice David Cooper's term ended on April 7, 1853. He practiced law in St. Paul for the next decade or so, eventually relocating to Nevada. The details of the rest of his life are scant and sorry: he died in an inebriate asylum in Salt Lake City.

David Cooper left a limited legacy in terms of precedent and judicial opinion. His significance to the history of the Minnesota Supreme Court lies more in the fact that he was present for its formation, for its first cases, for the beginning of what became a noble tradition. His life offers a snapshot of a moment in history as the frontier shifted westward, the East Coast elite colliding with the western wilderness and forming the beginnings of a civilization premised on the rule of law. Justice Cooper stands at the head of a long line of men and women who have worked to fulfill the promise of that first rough court in a warehouse.

—Elizabeth Hanson

Bradley B. Meeker

1813–1873
Associate Justice, Territorial Supreme Court, 1849–1853

Bradley Burr Meeker was born on March 13, 1813 in Fairfield, Connecticut. He was the second of eight children born to Joseph and Rhoda (Nichols) Meeker. Although they were descendants of Robert Meeker, who established the town of Fairfield in 1650, Bradley Meeker's parents were poor and therefore unable to provide their children an education. After years of struggling, Meeker attracted the attention of Connecticut's Gov. Gideon Tomlinson, who took an interest in the young man. Under Governor Tomlinson's patronage Meeker took the opportunity to enroll in Weston Academy and subsequently at Yale College, from which Tomlinson had graduated in 1802.

After leaving Yale, Meeker moved to Richmond, Kentucky, where he supported himself by teaching school while he studied law. Meeker entered practice in 1838 and worked in Richmond until 1845, at which time he moved to Flemingsburg, Kentucky. There he focused on building a career in law. He became involved in the movement to organize a convention to revise the state's constitution. At the same time, Congress was establishing a new territory that would change Meeker's career—and life—forever.

On March 3, 1849, an act of Congress creating the Territory of Minnesota granted broad powers to the governor and established a judicial system including a territorial supreme court and district and probate courts. In this era, judicial appointments were largely political. Upon the urging of prominent Kentucky figures such as John Bell, on March 19, 1849, President Zachary Taylor appointed Meeker an associate supreme court justice for the new territory. Meeker left his home in Kentucky to join Chief Justice Aaron Goodrich of Tennessee and Associate Justice David Cooper of Pennsylvania on the newly formed Minnesota bench. There he quickly became known as the least controversial of the three.

Historical reports suggest Meeker was above average in ability, although he did not have extensive practice at the bar at the time of his judicial appointment. In what might seem unusual by today's standards, the organization of the territorial court system resulted in each supreme court justice serving simultaneously as a district court judge. Minnesota Territory included three judicial districts, and the opinions of the district court judges were subject to review by the supreme court, sitting *en banc*, with any two justices constituting a quorum. For a supreme court justice to participate in the review of his own lower court decision was not uncommon. Meeker fulfilled his district court duties by holding court in the old government gristmill on the west side of the Mississippi River, just below the Falls of St. Anthony in Minneapolis. Records suggest that in his role as a district court judge, Meeker entered no guilty judgments.

Although appointed in 1849, Meeker's arrival in Minnesota was delayed until 1851, and he missed the first term of the court held in January 1850. Because the court rarely met *en banc*, Meeker's first opportunity to participate in the highest territorial court came on July 7, 1851, its second official term. The justices heard arguments at the Methodist Episcopal Church, which resulted in the court's first recorded opinion. During his tenure on the bench, Justice Meeker authored seven opinions and no dissents. The lack of a large number of written opinions, however, does not directly reflect upon the importance of Justice Meeker and his fellow members on the court. In this day, a large amount of legal business was rendered without written opinion, and some of the records are thought to have been lost.

6

Meeker's service on the court ended in 1853 with the election of President Franklin Pierce, who replaced all three territorial justices with political appointments of his own. Despite his short term, Meeker remained an outspoken member of the Minnesota political landscape. He was known as a man of conviction who had the courage to maintain his position, popular or otherwise. Meeker firmly believed that the new presidential administration had no power to remove territorial judges, and he threatened to take the question to the U.S. Supreme Court. While Meeker eventually abandoned this idea, he continued to participate in the discussion of the process by which judges were selected. In 1857, as a member of the Democratic wing of the Minnesota Constitutional Convention, Meeker held firm to his advocacy of an appointed judiciary and declared, "I contend the judges who are elected, are elected by parties, and are the mere buglemen of caucuses; the best tricksters or the best managers of caucuses are just as likely to be the nominees of the party as the most learned men in the nation."

While Meeker never returned to the practice of law, he left his imprint on the culture of Minnesota through other activities. He served as one of the first regents of the University of Minnesota (1851–1857), he was a member of the territorial legislature, and he was a charter member of the Minnesota Historical Society. In 1856, Meeker County was created and named in his honor.

After leaving the bench, Meeker focused on real estate investment. He purchased a large tract of land on the Mississippi River below St. Anthony, including the area now known as Meeker Island and extending eastward. In 1857, Meeker organized a group of Minneapolis businessmen to construct a lock and dam below the Falls of Anthony to bring river traffic into the heart of the city and allow for navigation upriver from St. Paul to Minneapolis. While the project was delayed by the financial panic of 1857 and later by the Civil War, in 1868 Meeker succeeded in getting congressional support for the dam through a large grant to the State of Minnesota. Not until 1894, more than 20 years after Meeker's death, did Congress authorize the construction of two dams (Ford Dam and Meeker Island Dam). Construction of the Meeker Island Dam, just above the Lake Street Bridge between Minneapolis and St. Paul, began in 1899, and it was operational eight years later. The first vessel, the power boat *Itura*, passed through on May 19, 1907. The Meeker Island Dam was later demolished, but some of its remains are still visible. The ruins were added to the National Register of Historic Places in 2003.

Meeker died in Milwaukee, Wisconsin, in February 1873 at the age of 59, while passing through the state on his way east. His remains were taken to Connecticut for burial. A bachelor his entire life, Meeker did not leave any direct descendents in Minnesota but instead left his mark on the state by helping to lay the foundation for the judicial framework that continues to govern Minnesota today.

—Tammera R. Diehm

Jerome Fuller

1808–1880
Chief Justice, Territorial Supreme Court, 1851–1852

Of those who served on the Minnesota Territorial Supreme Court, Jerome Fuller, the second chief justice, is unique in that he has been largely lost to history. In stark contrast to his contemporaries, little record concerning him remains, perhaps for the simple reason that in the most technical sense he was never a chief justice at all.

Jerome Fuller was born in 1808 in Litchfield, Connecticut, and reared in Brockport, New York. Little is known of the years before Fuller's appointment to the territorial court, except that he served as a New York state senator for the 27th District from 1848 to 1849. During his time as a state senator, Fuller appears to have been an opponent of slavery; he once argued that state officials should be forbidden from aiding in the enforcement of the Fugitive Slave Law of 1793. Fuller changed his views on the subject, however, and became a strong critic of the antislavery views of those such as William H. Seward, who later served as secretary of state to Abraham Lincoln.

President Millard Fillmore appointed Jerome Fuller in 1851 to replace the recently removed Aaron Goodrich, chief justice of Minnesota Territory. Shortly thereafter, Fuller arrived in St. Paul to begin his term with the court. Months later, word reached the territory that the U.S. Senate had rejected his appointment. In all, Chief Justice Fuller served on the court from November 13, 1851 to December 16, 1852, during which time he authored only three opinions, all of which may be found in the first volume of the *Minnesota Reports*.

Although Fuller's time with the court was brief, he left a lasting impression on the fledgling territory. As a public figure, Fuller became known as a man who gave freely of his time whenever asked to give public speeches and lectures. The members of the legal profession with whom he dealt quickly came to regard him as a model adjudicator who conducted his court in an exemplary but strict manner. On one representative occasion, while sitting as a district judge in the first judicial district—a common practice for justices of his time—Fuller found 57 cases on the court calendar, none of which were ready for trial. To excuse this fact, the offending attorneys tried to explain that no cases in Minnesota *ever* were tried on the first day of court. Fuller, however, was unimpressed and simply informed those attorneys that they were to be ready for trial on the scheduled day, lest they be subject to the imposition of costs.

Following his short time with the territorial supreme court, Fuller returned to New York, where he was elected district judge of Monroe County. Fuller eventually made his home in Rochester, New York, where he remained until his death on September 2, 1880. He was subsequently laid to rest in the Old Brockport Cemetery in his hometown of Brockport.

That Fuller's tenure was cut short for what appear to have been purely political reasons with no relevance to his skill as a lawyer or jurist is unfortunate. By all accounts, he was an intelligent and honorable man; that he was not given a greater chance to make his impression on the laws of the newly founded territory is nothing less than tragic. That is not to say, however, that his impact was negligible. When this territory and its laws were in their infancy, Fuller gave his time to help ensure that the rule of law reigned supreme. By the contributions of such individuals, who gave selflessly of their talents, Minnesota was able to grow from a wild backwater territory into the proud state it is today.

—Jonathon D. Byrer

Henry Z. Hayner

1802–1874

Chief Justice, Territorial Supreme Court, 1851–1852

The 112 days that Henry Z. Hayner spent as territorial chief justice were a mere hiccup in time, for him and for Minnesota. He never wrote a published supreme court decision, though he did declare a liquor law unconstitutional and may have imposed Minnesota's first death sentence. Nevertheless, the New Yorker adored Minnesota. Probably few Minnesotans knew him, but easterners certainly admired Hayner, a principled and energetic man who abhorred slavery, volunteered for the Civil War at age 59, and was known to President Abraham Lincoln. Hayner's tenure as Minnesota's chief justice was just a small part of who he was.

Henry Zachariah Hayner was born September 18, 1802 in Brunswick, New York, the son of Zachariah and Eve (Clum) Hayner. After tilling the family farm and attending local schools, Henry attended preparatory academy in Hadley, Massachusetts, before entering Yale College as a sophomore in 1823. Upon graduating in 1826, he studied law with the Hon. David Buel in Troy, New York, and in 1830 established a practice in that upstate city near the capital. Henry Hayner remained committed to his alma mater. When much of Yale College's operating fund disappeared during an 1831 bank failure, he was among alumni who amassed a $100,000 replacement.

During his life, Hayner married three times and had three sons and two daughters. He enjoyed a successful career and was counsel of record in more than 30 published New York decisions between 1838 and 1850. Seven years into his practice, he was at the center of a widely reported insurance-coverage dispute. As agent for North American Insurance Company, Hayner had accepted a premium from a storeowner but failed to provide him immediately with the policy documents. Hours later, the store burned. North American denied coverage on grounds that it had revoked Hayner's agency authority. A jury found in the insured's favor, and the Supreme Court of Judicature of New York affirmed.

Hayner did not limit himself to commercial matters. He was among a minority in Troy who advocated for slavery's abolition, and he represented his community at the American Anti-Slavery Society's annual meeting in New York City on May 12, 1835. Hayner's abolitionist views were tested on June 2, 1836, when a mob attacked philanthropist Theodore D. Weld during an antislavery speech at a Troy church. The congregation intervened as Weld was dragged from the pulpit, and Hayner, as if he were Atticus Finch in *To Kill a Mocking Bird*, shooed the mob and delivered the orator to safety. A Troy historian wrote that the incident "created intense excitement throughout the city and doubtless strengthened the ranks of the local abolitionists."

Hayner's human rights interests extended to landlord-tenant law. By 1845 he was among New York's leading spokespersons for tenants' rights. He also had established himself in the Whig Party, and he was elected to the New York Assembly for 1846. The next four years were busy for the litigator. New York reports contain eight published decisions involving Hayner from 1848 and several more from 1849 and 1850.

Most historical accounts limit Hayner's Minnesota chief justice tenure to the period from December 16, 1851, to April 7, 1852. He assumed the post only because the U.S. Senate rejected President Millard Fillmore's first choice, Jerome Fuller, in August 1852. That Hayner never presided over a court term is undisputed. News of the Senate's rejection did not reach St. Paul until after Fuller had presided over the last term of 1852, and President Franklin Pierce named William H. Welch chief justice before the first term of 1853 began.

When and in what capacity Hayner came to Minnesota Territory are not clear. Apparently he served some judicial role before December 1852. He is described as having imposed Minnesota's first death sentence after native resident Yu-Ha-Zee was convicted of murdering a German immigrant near Shakopee on October 27, 1852. According to Minnesota author-historian J. Fletcher Williams (*History of the*

City of St. Paul, 1876), the sentence came within days of the slaying. "Justice, those days, was speedy (to Indians, that is)," he wrote. Edward D. Neill, in his *Concise History of the State of Minnesota* (1887) told a more vivid tale and confirmed that it was Judge Hayner who imposed the penalty:

> On the day of his trial, [Yu-Ha-Zee] was escorted from Fort Snelling by a company of mounted dragoons in full dress. It was an impressive scene to witness the poor Indian half hid in his blanket, in a buggy with the civil officer, surrounded with all the pomp and circumstance of war. The jury found him guilty. On being asked if he had anything to say [as to] why the sentence of death should not be passed, he replied through the interpreter that the band to which he belonged would remit their annuities if he could be released. To this Judge Hayner, the successor of Judge Fuller, replied that he had no authority to release him; and ordering him to rise, after some appropriate and impressive remarks, he pronounced the first death sentence ever pronounced by a judicial officer in Minnesota.

Hayner also struck down a territorial law on constitutional grounds, again perhaps before he was chief justice. The law, which the territorial legislature passed on March 6, 1852, made it a penal offense to manufacture, sell, or possess liquor. Because the legislature directed that the measure be put to a vote throughout the territory, however, Hayner declared the law unconstitutional because the legislature had improperly delegated its power to the electorate.

Williams and two other author-historians of Minnesota—W. H. C. Folsom (*Fifty Years in the Northwest,* 1888) and Judge William P. Murray (*Recollections of Early Territorial Days and Legislation,* 1904)— wrote that territorial residents voted on the law on April 5, 1852. Williams and Folsom both identified Hayner as the judge who invalidated the provision, as did pioneer educator Harriet E. Bishop (*Floral Home, Or, First Years of Minnesota,* 1857). Because the law likely was challenged without delay, Hayner probably acted before December 1852.

Hayner stayed in Minnesota for a time after losing the chief justice seat. He clearly liked the territory. In a June 22, 1853, letter he wrote from St. Paul, Hayner boasted of a "happy" and "peaceful" Minnesota that welcomed "the hardy sons of New England and the down-trodden masses escaping from tyranny." There was "no country," he wrote, "better adapted to the confidence of western tradition than Minnesota."

Eventually, Hayner returned east to practice law in New York City. But on November 1, 1861, at age 59, he answered President Lincoln's call for Union Army volunteers and became a major aide-de-camp assigned to Maj. Gen. John E. Wool. Hayner's son Herrick, a fellow Yale graduate, also served in the Civil War and was killed.

Major Hayner was no minor player in the war effort. On June 19, 1862, he was entrusted with accompanying seven Confederate officer prisoners from Baltimore to Fort Delaware. President's Lincoln's correspondence contains a few references to the former chief justice: "Please send Major Hayner over now," Lincoln wrote in a September 25, 1863, telegram. In 1864, Hayner distinguished himself by serving under Maj. Gen. Lew Wallace.

Lincoln's assassination likely left Hayner crushed. On April 25, 1865, Major Hayner was among the honor guard when Lincoln's remains were on view at New York's City Hall. According to the *New York Times,* Hayner had the Tenth Watch, from six o'clock until eight o'clock in the morning. Then the war ended, and Hayner was honorably discharged just weeks before turning 63.

Hayner was neither eager nor willing to retire. After the war, he worked to secure mineral-land titles for New York capitalists and helped organize mining operations in the West. Kidney disease drove him to Florida with hopes that a southern climate would provide relief. It did not. A Yale University obituary states that Hayner returned to the East Coast in "feeble health" and died of "Bright's disease" on March 31, 1874, in New York City. But Hayner had made his mark—a tiny one in and on Minnesota and a substantial one elsewhere.

—Steven P. Aggergaard

William H. Welch

1805–1863

Chief Justice, Territorial Supreme Court, 1853–1858

William H. Welch served as the chief justice of the Minnesota Territorial Supreme Court. By all accounts, he was a capable, respected, noble, and loyal citizen and public servant.

Welch was born in Litchfield, Connecticut, on June 17, 1805, the son of Capt. John Welch, an officer who served with distinction in the Revolutionary War, and the former Rosanna Peebles. Welch received an undergraduate degree from Yale College and a law degree from Yale Law School. He was the first chief justice of the Minnesota Supreme Court to graduate from law school.

After graduation, Welch moved to Steubenville, Ohio, to practice law. About that same time, in 1830, Welch married Henrietta Edwards, granddaughter of American theologian Jonathan Edwards. The Welches had eight children: John, William Henry, Abraham Edwards, Henrietta E., W. Henry, Edmond P., Irene, and Garrett P. Six children grew to adulthood, William Henry and Irene having died in infancy.

The Welches moved to Kalamazoo when Michigan was yet a territory. In addition to practicing law there, Welch was a member of the convention that formed the first constitution of that state. Welch must have been a well-respected and upstanding citizen of Kalamazoo, as the "Welch Addition" was named for him.

In 1849 or 1850, about the same time Congress passed the Organic Act, which created the Territory of Minnesota from land that had previously been part of the territories of Iowa and Wisconsin, the Welches moved to St. Anthony, Minnesota. At St. Anthony, Welch practiced law and served as a justice of the peace, hearing and considering a wide variety of matters. In 1852, Welch was elected judge of probate of Ramsey County. In 1853, after Presidents Zachary

Taylor and Millard Fillmore made three short-term and largely failed appointments of chief justices, President Franklin Pierce appointed Welch chief justice of the Minnesota Territorial Supreme Court. President Pierce and the infant territory found in Welch a capable leader, who served a term of years without controversy. Welch, who already lived in the territory and had graduated from law school, commanded the respect of the legal community and presided over the three-member court with sound common sense. At the expiration of Welch's four-year term, President Buchanan reappointed him chief justice. Welch performed in that role until the state entered into the Union in 1858.

During his years of service on the bench, Welch authored only seven majority opinions (no dissents). Arguably the most important case before Chief Justice Welch and the territorial supreme court arose from the expansion of the railroad in Minnesota.[1]

The facts of that case date to 1854, when, as part of an effort to encourage settlement and development of the new territory, the territorial legislature passed a law incorporating the Minnesota and Northwestern Railroad Company and purporting to vest the company with title to all lands that the federal government might thereafter grant to Minnesota for railroad use between St. Paul and the northwest shore of Lake Superior. Indeed, on June 29, 1854, Congress granted approximately a million acres of land along this stretch for this purpose. The bill was drafted so that no currently existing corporation could obtain rights to it. But before the bill passed, the wording was somehow changed so that it could be interpreted to allow the company to take title to the entire million acres. Congress was not pleased with this outcome and voted to repeal the land grant on August

4, 1854. The railroad company pressed on with its claim that the Act of June 29 had immediately vested the right to the land in the company.

In the fall of 1854, a trespass action was filed against the company for cutting trees on a section of the land that was part of the land grant, and the court heard and decided the case—*United States v. Minnesota and Northwestern Railroad Company*—in 1854. Writing for the court, Welch, who had already heard and decided the case below, ruled that because the Act of June 29 constituted a present grant of the land to the territory and the territory had given the lands to the railroad, the land could not be taken from the railroad without violating the U.S. Constitution, which prohibits the taking of land without just compensation.[2]

By 1858, the Welches had become residents of Red Wing, Minnesota. During their time in Red Wing the Civil War began. William Welch, always patriotic, encouraged those who enlisted. Despite his brave front, however, the war concerned Welch on a personal level, for the Welches' son Abraham Edwards was one of the first in the state to volunteer his service. While serving as first lieutenant in the First Regiment of the Minnesota Volunteer Infantry, the younger Welch

was wounded and taken prisoner at the First Battle of Bull Run. After he was paroled and had recuperated at his parents' home, he served as major with the Third Regiment of the Minnesota Volunteer Infantry during an "Indian disturbance" dubbed the "Dakota conflict" in 1862. Again he received a serious injury and spent time at his parents' home recuperating.

During this time William Welch fell sick. His family determined that his illness was a "nervous fever" caused by the long months of civil unrest and his concern and despair for his son. Welch died in Red Wing on January 22, 1863.

—Susan Peterson

References

1. Carol Chomsky shared information about *United States v. Minnesota and Northwestern Railroad Company* from pages 30–33 of her "The Frontier of Justice: The Early Years of the Minnesota State Courts," an undated unpublished manuscript on file with the Minnesota State Law Library.

2. After another similar case and several appeals, the U.S. Supreme Court reversed, holding that the Act of August 1854 was a valid repeal of the land grant and that the company therefore had no claim to the land.

Andrew G. Chatfield

1810–1875
Associate Justice, Territorial Supreme Court, 1853–1857

The Honorable Andrew G. Chatfield, Judge of the District Court for the Eighth Judicial District and formerly an Associate Justice of the Supreme Court of the Territory of Minnesota, died at his home in Belle Plaine on October 3, 1875. A meeting of the members of the bar of the state, in attendance at the term of the Supreme Court then in session, was held at the capitol on October 8, and the resolutions then adopted were presented to the court by Hon. Charles E. Flandrau on October 9.

In presenting the resolutions, Judge Flandrau addressed the court as follows:

The committee of the bar of Minnesota, to whom was intrusted [*sic*] the preparation for a memorial on the death of one of our much esteemed brethren, the late Andrew G. Chatfield, has appointed me to present their report to this court and move that it be entered upon its record. In performing that duty, I shall only preface the same by saying that the memorial embraces the heartfelt sentiments of the bar and their committee and that we all rejoice in the fact that, after a long and well spent life of usefulness, our brother calmly yielded his spirit into the hand of Him who gave it, breathing out his last sigh upon the bosom of her who had been the partner of his joys and sorrows for nearly forty years and in the midst of his family and friends.

I now have the honor of presenting the memorial to your honors.

The bar of Minnesota, in convention assembled at the capitol of the State to record their sorrow at the loss of one of their members, Andrew G. Chatfield, late Judge of the Eighth Judicial District of this State, declare:

That in the death of Judge Chatfield the profession has lost one of its most learned, cultivated, honored and distinguished brethren; that the Judiciary of the State has been deprived of an able, just and admirable judge; that the commonwealth loses a citizen whose services, both public and private, have greatly contributed to its present prosperity and advancement; and that society mourns the loss of a distinguished ornament.

Judge Chatfield, nearly a quarter of a century ago, adorned the supreme bench of the Territory of Minnesota. In that early and rude period of our history, his learning and integrity, and firm and impartial administration of the law, did much to mould the judiciary of the present, of which we are so justly proud.

His genial, social characteristics endeared him to all who enjoyed his acquaintance. His generous hospitality will long and gratefully be remembered by the wanderers on the frontier in early days.

Judge Chatfield was too intellectual a man ever to become an accumulator of much wealth. He spent his young life in public services, which added more to his fame than to his fortune. His professional labors for many long years were arduous in the extreme and largely devoted to charitable objects; and like many of the zealous members of his profession, his reward was an overtasked mind, which became the active cause of an enfeebled constitution. We can truthfully say of him:

'Twas thine own genius gave the final blow,
And helped to plant the wound that laid thee low.

At an advanced age, Judge Chatfield was again called to the bench, and for several years shed the light of his ripened wisdom upon the judicial affairs of the state, but we were not long to enjoy the benefit of his services. The hand of the destroyer was upon him, and on the third day of this month, he passed to his final rest, mourned by all who knew him.

He was a man of pronounced political conviction formed in early life and adhered to consistently to the end. He was a christian [*sic*] gentleman, bigoted in nothing, tolerant in everything. He died, as he lived, a true man: true to himself, true to his convictions, and true to his fellow men. He was a modest and unassuming man. His good works were done without ostentation or display; they were felt in the world rather than seen. They were like rills through meadows, "that with a livelier green betray the secret of their silent course."

The words of the Psalmist well and truly characterize our beloved and departed brother: "Mark the perfect man, and behold the upright; for the end of that man is peace."

We point to his career and virtues as an example to the men of the present day and to those who are to come after us, and our heart-felt sympathies go out to his much bereaved family.

Hon. Aaron Goodrich, the first Chief Justice of Minnesota, then addressed the court as follows:

It has been suggested that it were meet that I, who have known the deceased for so many years, should make some observations on the present occasion. "I come not to speak at Caesar's funeral" but rather by standing in your presence silently to testify my respect for the memory of the dead.

With the personal relations that have characterized my intercourse with him whose loss we now mourn, neither history nor posterity can be largely concerned; suffice it to say that these were ever pleasant. Possessing a form and features cast in a mould that would have been satisfactory to an Angelo, adorned by a bearing and manners reaching the standard of a Chesterfield, with a mind stored and marshaled by days of toil and nights of study, guided, whether in the forum or upon the bench, by unswerving devotion to his convictions of justice and fidelity, Andrew G. Chatfield naturally occupied a prominent position in the estimation of his fellow men.

He has finished his course; his work is done; and now, at this mournful and contemplative season of the year, when the primeval forest, crowning the hills which look down on the beautiful plain of his choice, is tinged with "the sear and yellow leaf" and time has set a frosty seal upon his brow, he is gathered to the tomb. And it seemed to me, as I aided neighbors and friends in consigning his remains to the narrow house, most fitting that the soil upon which he so oft and so lovingly trod while living should brood over him when dead. Verily,

> The race of man is like the waves of the ocean;
> Like the leaves of woody Morven,
> They pass away in the rustling blast,
> And other leaves lift their green heads on high.

[Court note: Judge Goodrich was one of the pallbearers. The place of burial had been selected by Judge Chatfield. It is near his late residence and upon grounds owned by him when all in sight was yet an unbroken prairie.]

Hon. John L. Macdonald, of Shakopee, then addressed the court as follows:

When a few days ago I announced to this court, and the bar of the state, the death of Hon. Andrew G. Chatfield, I performed a most painful duty. With a proper appreciation of the worth and character of the deceased and the respect due to him and his position in life, this court, upon that announcement, suspended business and adjourned, and the bar of the state, represented by the members then present, met to pay fitting tribute to his public and private virtues.

The result of that meeting is the resolutions now presented to this court; and while I am oppressed with a sense of my inability to do justice to the subject of them, I would do violence to my feelings and prove false to the memory of one of the kindest and best friends I ever had, did I fail to offer a few words in support of them. Honoring and loving him while living, and revering his memory when dead, I cannot be silent on this occasion.

I first met Judge Chatfield in the year 1855, then in the enjoyment of remarkably robust health for a person of his years. He was then an honored associate justice of the Supreme Court of the Territory of Minnesota and *ex-officio* judge of the third judicial district. He was associated with Judges Welch and Sherburne, both of whom have preceded him in the passage from earth to eternity. In April 1857, he retired from that position, having occupied it from

April 7, 1853. Upon his retirement, he resumed the practice of his profession at his home in Belle Plaine, in this state, and through his well-known ability as a jurist and advocate was soon engaged in an extensive practice. It was in the latter part of the same year that I became a student under him, and I remained in his office, as student and attorney, until 1861. I will not detain you by attempting to describe the interest that he took in me and the fatherly care and solicitude that he manifested towards me in the prosecution of my studies, until upon his own motion I was admitted to the bar and stood in the ranks, a member of that profession of which he was so bright an ornament. The memory of those many acts of kindness will be cherished in silence as a sacred thing. I need only say that it was his goodness of heart and nobility of character exemplifying itself. Nor did his kindness and friendship terminate with my becoming a member of the legal profession. To the time of his death, he was the same kind and considerate friend and adviser, and I always enjoyed his confidence and esteem. Is it then to be wondered at that I should wish to join with the more eminent members of the profession in doing honor to this eminent citizen and good man?

He continued in the practice of his profession until 1870, when he was elected judge of the eighth judicial district, which office he filled and adorned with his dignity of character and urbanity of manner until death took him from us, leaving our district to mourn the loss of one who was known but to be loved and praised.

With his career, prior to his coming to Minnesota, I am only acquainted through the same sources that you are, but we know that it was an honorable one and is a part of the history of the Empire State. As the associate of such men as Silas Wright and William H. Seward, he occupies no secondary position to them in the legislative and political history of New York during the period he was in public life in that state.

During the time that he was not upon the bench in this state, he was the recipient of many marks of confidence from the political party of which he was an honored member. His nomination at different times for the several offices of Chief Justice, Attorney General, and Member of Congress prove the esteem in which he was held by his political associates and were honors worthily bestowed. In his political views, as in all

other matters, he was earnest in his convictions; yet he was noted for his impartiality and freedom from bias in the discharge of his official duties.

He was emphatically a gentleman of the old school. He seemed to belong to a race that is of the past and fast becoming extinct. He was a marked man in any body of men. In personal appearance, as well as in point of ability, he would be singled out as a distinguished exception. Aside from his conceded ability as a jurist and his statesmanlike qualities, there were few who possessed finer literary tastes or were more familiar with the standard authors. In his every-day intercourse with his fellow citizens and neighbors, his geniality and frankness coupled with his unaffected simplicity endeared him to all. While recognizing his eminent position, the humblest citizen knew that at all times he would be received as cordially as if he were the most distinguished citizen in the land. But pre-eminent above all this was his singular purity of life and character. When we consider the many opportunities that an extensive practice and the political arena offered him to accumulate wealth [would] he but resort to practices that though popular in a measure he would not indulge in, we can pronounce no grander eulogium upon him and his character or furnish no more convincing proof of his purity than to state the fact that he died a poor man. I would that it were otherwise, and I would not mention it, but I believe it to be due to his memory that (in this age and time, when fortunes are so often rapidly accumulated by questionable means) this suggestive fact be stated, even if in so doing I trespass upon the privacy of his condition and circumstances.

But, your honors, it was in his home life that Judge Chatfield displayed his most endearing qualities. He had to be known there to appreciate him in his character. A loving husband, a kind and indulgent parent—it would be utter folly to attempt to describe the grief and desolation that his death has produced in that once happy home. We leave its inmates to the care of a kind Providence and pray Him to extend to them that consolation which He alone can give. Especially may He lighten the burden and smooth the pathway of her who has been the partner of his joys and sorrows for so many years, enabling her to bear up beneath the great weight of her affliction, as she, in her declining years, pursues her journey alone, to meet him who we hope is "not dead, but gone before."

Such, in brief and as I have endeavored to describe him, was Judge Andrew G. Chatfield as I knew him, and I knew him intimately and well. As we take leave of him, and drop affection's tear over his memory, let us hope that his life and character may be imitated by those growing up around us. And we who have reached the age of maturity, and even those passing from manhood to old age, can find in his exemplary life many traits of character to emulate.

Hon. L. M. Brown, of Shakopee, then addressed the court, as follows:

I should not feel justified in omitting to pay a humble tribute of regret on the present occasion to the memory of one with whom I have been so long acquainted and professionally associated. In the month of September 1855, I made application to the Supreme Court of the Territory of Minnesota, then sitting at what is known as the old court house in this city, for admission to practice as an attorney in the courts of the territory. At that time the bench was occupied by Chief Justice Welch and Associate Justices Sherburne and Chatfield, of the last of whom we now meet to make a memorial. From that time my acquaintance with those men commenced, and it continued until the death of each, Judge Chatfield being the last survivor. The third judicial district comprised (I believe) all that portion of the then Territory of Minnesota lying west of the Mississippi river. To that district Judge Chatfield had been previously assigned. I had, before my admission to the bar, located in Shakopee, in Scott county. My practice, therefore, was for a considerable time confined to that district and before Judge Chatfield. From him, therefore, I learned my first lessons in the practice under the code. Perhaps I may be partial to my first teacher, but I must say that I have always regarded him, in many respects, and particularly upon questions of practice, as the best judge before whom it has been my lot to practice. He was possessed of a remarkably clear mind, and oftentimes when he decided questions against me, he was able to explain the matters involved with such comprehensiveness and clearness that I felt entirely satisfied with his rulings. One thing

I think I may say of Judge Chatfield, which will never be truly said of any other judge in the state: He held the office of judge of the supreme court of the late territory for four years. During that time he held the district courts as far north as Hennepin county, and as far south as Winona (and perhaps farther) and as far west and southwest as Blue Earth, and tried a large number of cases, involving large amounts of property and valuable legal and equitable rights, and only one case ever came to the territorial or state supreme court for review, by appeal or writ of error. That one was the case of *Converse* v. *Burrows*, reported in 2 Minn. 229. The case was tried before Judge Chatfield and a jury in Nicollet county, and a point relating to the measure of damages recoverable upon a breach of contract was ruled upon at the trial in the charge to the jury. Upon a motion for a new trial, the judge came to the conclusion that he had erred in his charge and thereupon ordered a new trial of the case. From this order an appeal was taken to the supreme court of the territory, but [it] was not heard until after the state had been admitted into the Union. Upon the organization of the state courts and at the December term, 1858, the appeal was heard and the order granting a new trial was reversed, a majority of the court as then constituted holding that the ruling at the trial had been the correct one.

The case of *United States* v. *Gideon,* 1 Minn. 292, was tried before Judge Chatfield, and upon objection made by defendant to the sufficiency of the facts stated in the indictment to constitute a public offence, Judge Chatfield expressed great doubt but finally held the indictment good for the purposes of the trial, and upon conviction of the defendant, he suspended sentence and reported the case to the supreme court for review, where the objection was sustained. These two cases are the only ones ever brought up for review in any manner from the third judicial district during the judicial administration of Judge Chatfield as a member of the territorial supreme court. These facts, of themselves it seems to me, are sufficient to establish for all time his great learning and ability as a judge.

As a lawyer practicing at the bar, he was earnest, diligent, and zealous in protecting and serving the interests of his numerous clients. In fact, if Judge Chatfield had any fault as a lawyer (which I do not aver), it was that of over-zeal for his clients and for the protection of their rights and interests. He always, as a judge and a lawyer, proceeded upon the theory that there was a remedy for every wrong, and his mind was ever searching for that construction of the law which would accomplish that end, prevent the wrong, and vindicate the right.

As a citizen, a husband, a father, or an associate, he was, in my judgment, as nearly faultless as any man with whom it has ever been my fortune to be associated in this life. I do not believe that in the whole twenty-two years that I have known Judge Chatfield he has ever knowingly done a wrong to any person or been guilty of a single dishonest intent. It is proper, therefore, when such a one disappears from among us and we are to see his form no more, that a proper memorial be made, not only for the sake of recollections of the living but as a guide and pattern for those who are to follow. I sincerely regret, together with his brethren at the bar, that so valuable a life should have terminated so soon.

Gen. W. A. Gorman then addressed the court as follows:

It was in March or April 1853, when, on the appointment of the President, Andrew G. Chatfield and myself came to Minnesota, he to exercise the judicial duties to which he had been assigned and I as the executive of the territory. It is, therefore, most fitting that I should pay my tribute to his memory. Andrew G. Chatfield was truly a remarkable man, possessing, in my opinion, not a single element subject to unfavorable criticism. He was not [word omitted], as is often the case with men of superior attainments and possessing quick, active minds. Rather he had an unusually logical mind and was also singularly wise and just in all his acts. In fact, his was one of those physical and mental formations that needed but the opportunity to have placed him on the very summit of the ladder of fame, alongside with Seward and other great minds, among whom the days of his early active life were passed. When he came to the state, the bar will bear me out, he bore himself as the peer of all. He was just. He had a marked will, which gave him strength. He early selected his residence in a retired spot on the Minnesota river, in its quiet and beauteous surroundings characteristic of and in keeping with his peculiarly quiet, refined mind. He was not rich. Such men seldom are. His life was a continuous lesson for good to the younger generation and an honor and credit to the profession, the recollection of which will ever shed lustre upon its history in this state. He had a mind above all small, mean things—a mind that reveled in the pure and discarded all that was calculated to lower and debase. It has pleased the Divine Providence to take him from among us to that home whither we are all tending. His example should not be lost upon us, but it should encourage us to so live as to do honor to his memory and make us worthy of the companionship in the future of Andrew G. Chatfield. [21 Minn 543]

Moses Sherburne

1808–1868
Associate Justice, Territorial Supreme Court, 1853–1857

By the time 45-year-old Moses Sherburne took his seat on the supreme court of Minnesota Territory in 1854, he already had a remarkable career as a lawyer and as a public servant in Maine. By the time of his death barely 15 years later, Sherburne left a lasting mark on the territory and state of Minnesota.

Born at Mount Vernon, Maine, in January 1808, Moses was the oldest of five children of Samuel and Lucy Carson Sherburne. He first attended public school in Mount Vernon, where he distinguished himself as a high achiever. Sherburne's academic success resulted in his enrollment at the Academy of China, Maine, a local institution of renown in the first half of the 19th century. After his graduation from the academy, Sherburne entered the study of law at the Farmington, Maine, law office of Nathan Cutler—then the acting governor of Maine—under whom he studied for two years.

Sherburne gained admission to the bar in 1831 at the age of 23. He immediately opened a law practice in Phillips, Maine, and quickly became a prominent and successful lawyer. Sherburne's indefectible integrity, imposing presence, and commanding eloquence attracted clients locally and from surrounding counties.

One year later, Sherburne married Sophia Dyar Whitney. Although the family history is sketchy, we know that the couple had several children, among them Sarah, Moses T., and James.

Sherburne did not seek office in his early years of practice, but his popularity and public stature attracted, if not demanded, such service. In 1837, at age 29, Sherburne was appointed to the modest position of postmaster in Phillips. Just seven months later, he received the first of seven gubernatorial appointments—from five different governors. Gov. Edward

Kent made the first appointment, tapping Sherburne as the Franklin County attorney. Soon thereafter, Sherburne entered elected politics, gaining a seat in the lower house of the Maine legislature. He served one term there and then gained a seat in the Maine senate, where he served two terms. During this same period, Gov. John Fairfield commissioned Sherburne as eighth division inspector for the Maine Militia, with the rank of lieutenant colonel. Two years later, Governor Fairfield promoted Sherburne to major general with the same division.

In late 1840, Sherburne received his first of four judicial appointments. Governor Fairfield appointed Sherburne as justice of the peace and of the quorum for Franklin County, a minor judicial position with a seven-year term. Sherburne distinguished himself as a judge, prompting Gov. Hugh Anderson in 1845 to elevate him to judge of probate for Franklin County, a position of high dignity. Again Judge Sherburne distinguished himself, this time prompting Gov. John Dana in 1847 to appoint him as justice of the peace and of the quorum for the entire state.

In 1850, Gov. John Hubbard appointed Sherburne bank commissioner of Maine. At about the same time, Sherburne received his party's nomination for U.S. Congress. Unfortunately, it was the Democratic Party, and Sherburne's congressional district was strongly Whig. He was defeated. But Sherburne's eloquence on the campaign trail earned him the acquaintance of another lawyer and Democrat, New Hampshire attorney Franklin Pierce. They became close friends. Pierce secured a dark-horse presidential nomination on the 49th ballot at the 1852 Democratic National Convention, setting the scene for Sherburne's final judicial appointment.

That scene had first started to unfold in December 1846, when the territorial delegate from Wisconsin introduced a bill into Congress for the creation of Minnesota Territory. This so-called Organic Act did not become law until early 1849, on the eve of Zachary Taylor's inauguration. The act called for a territorial supreme court consisting of a chief justice and two associate justices, each of whom would also serve as a judge of the district (lower) court. Territories being creatures of the federal government, the justices were to be appointed by the president of the United States.

Just 16 days after the bill became law, and 15 days after Taylor became president, Minnesota received its first territorial supreme court. Sherburne undoubtedly knew little, if anything, of these events. But Taylor, a Whig, died less than two years after taking office, and his successor, Vice President Millard Fillmore, was not the Whig Party nominee in 1852. This left the door open for dark-horse Pierce, who trounced the Whig candidate by a 6–1 margin in the electoral college. In April 1853, President Pierce appointed his friend Moses Sherburne, the able and eloquent lawyer and public servant from Maine, territorial supreme court justice in the distant land of Minnesota. In Maine, a local newspaper applauded the appointment, stating: "The President could hardly have selected a man better suited to this honorable and responsible position."

Justice Sherburne brought his family to Minnesota that fall and took his seat on the court in January 1854. He served until 1857, when James Buchanan became president. During his time on the court, Justice Sherburne wrote 17 majority opinions and no dissents, all of which can be found in volume 1 of Minnesota Reports. A case of particular note is *Freeman v. Curran & Lawler*, 1 Minn. 169 (1854). The case's notability lies not in the substance of the parties' dispute, but in the court's search for its independent voice in the making of Minnesota's common law. One of the attorneys proposed that the decision of a New York court should decide the outcome. Justice Sherburne announced the view that Minnesota courts must decide matters of law independently, with guidance only insofar as was consistent with sound policy and settled legal principles, a view still followed some 150 years later: "The Judge making this [New York] decision is probably a very respectable lawyer, but we know nothing of him, except from the ephemeral report of this decision. A decision made by any Judge of New York or any other State, when supported by good sense, and showing evidence of its adherence to well settled legal principles is, of course, entitled to high respect, otherwise it is entitled to no more regard than the opinion of any other lawyer." *Id.* at 174.

Justice Sherburne fulfilled his role in the lower courts with equal integrity and high regard for the rule of law. One story recalls him presiding at the sentencing of a criminal defendant. The defendant, a Mason, provided to the judge a letter of support from a fellow Mason. The defendant undoubtedly knew of Justice Sherburne's enthusiastic support for the Masons, having previously founded the Blue Mountain Lodge of Masons in Phillips, Maine, and risen to the position of grand master of the Grand Lodge of Masons for Minnesota Territory. Perceiving the letter as an attempt to influence his judicial decision, Justice Sherburne indignantly shredded it and passed a full sentence upon the defendant.

When his appointment expired in 1857, Justice Sherburne stayed in Minnesota and returned to the private practice of law. The same reputation for integrity and commanding eloquence that attracted clients in Maine did the same in Minnesota. Indeed, his reputation as an advocate earned him the title "the old man eloquent." In addition to his successful law practice, Sherburne was instrumental in guiding Minnesota into statehood. He was an influential member of Minnesota's constitutional convention in 1857, and he served on the 1858 commission that delivered to the nascent legislature the first code of laws for the new State of Minnesota. His service to Minnesota, and the high regard in which he was held, are reflected in his namesakes—Sherburne County, Minnesota; Sherburne Avenue, St. Paul; and Ashton and Sherburne's Addition, St. Paul. Justice Moses Sherburne died on March 29, 1868, leaving a legacy of integrity and service.

—William M. Hart

Rensselaer R. Nelson

1826–1904

Associate Justice, Territorial Supreme Court, 1857–1858

On the afternoon of December 14, 1904, at the court room in the building then used as the State Capitol, Honorable Edward C. Stringer, President of the Minnesota State Bar Association, in its behalf addressed the supreme court, then in session, and presented the memorial that on the preceding December 6 had been presented to the United States District Court for the District of Minnesota, Lochren, J., presiding, the state judges of the District Court for Ramsey County sitting with him. Before reading the memorial he made use of the language in which he had addressed Judge Lochren:

In behalf of the committee appointed by your Honor to draft a Memorial on the death of the Honorable Rensselaer E. Nelson, who for forty years served his country in the capacity of judge of the federal court of this state, I beg leave to present a Memorial to this court and to these courts on his death. It is fitting, and I think desirable, that a brief record of the life of Judge Nelson be perpetuated for future generations by the entry thereof in the record of the courts of this state. And for that reason it should be recorded that Judge Rensselaer R. Nelson came of English and Irish parentage and was born at Cooperstown, New York, May 12, 1826. His father, Samuel Nelson, was for many years Chief Justice of the Supreme Court of the state of New York and was from 1845 associate justice of the supreme court of the United States, until his resignation in 1872, one year prior to his death.

Judge Nelson was graduated from Yale College in the class of 1847, was admitted to the bar in 1849, commenced the practice of law in Buffalo, New York, the same year. In 1850 he came to St. Paul, and here engaged in the practice of his profession. Shortly after, he removed to Douglas County, Wisconsin, and in 1854 was elected district attorney for that county. Two years later he reached St. Paul, and in 1857 was

appointed territorial judge of Minnesota by President Buchanan. When Minnesota was admitted to the Union in 1858, Judge Nelson was appointed United States District Judge of Minnesota, his appointment being immediately confirmed by the Senate without the customary reference to a committee. This position he held until his voluntary retirement in 1896, on the seventieth anniversary of his birth. The committee thus appointed, your Honors, desire to present the following memorial:

The Bar of the state of Minnesota desires that a Memorial be spread upon the records of the courts of our state, expressive of its keen sense of loss to the state and to our profession in the death of the Honorable Rensselaer R. Nelson, who died at St. Paul, Minnesota, October 15, A.D. 1904, expressive also of its full appreciation of the sterling qualities of mind and heart that he possessed.

Nearly half a century of his well-spent life was passed in the highest calling of our profession, and at the time of his voluntary retirement from the office of Judge of the United States Court for the District of Minnesota, he was the oldest federal judge in point of continuous service in the United States. Before Minnesota was admitted to the Union of states, he presided over her territorial courts. He neither sought nor would he accept political honors; he made the law his mistress and the bench the acme of his ambition. He was no common man but was a prince among gentlemen. No sordid or mean trait marred his character. The stream of his life was pure and undefined, and the purity of his thought was equalled by his high sense of honor. He never wittingly wronged a human being. Sensible of the frailty of humanity, he tempered Justice with Mercy. A close student of human nature, endowed alike with keen perception and clear judgment, insensible alike to fear or favor, he held the scales of Justice on an even beam. His eminent fitness for the position he held so long, and whose arduous duties he discharged so faithfully and with marked ability, was recognized by all.

Judge Nelson was an honorable, just, capable, and upright judge. His long period of service on the bench withdrew him somewhat from the activities of life other than judicial; his judicial robes aside, he was ever a social, genial, entertaining, and delightful companion; in the discharge of his official duties dignified, courteous, high-minded, he maintained at the level of his own lofty conception the honor and dignity of the bench.

Monuments erected by the hand of man soon crumble and decay. But there are those that defy the ravages of time. Of these is a judicial record "without spot or blemish, or any such thing"—imperishable so long as the records of our courts exist. Such a monument have the life and work of Judge Nelson erected to his memory.

Deeply sensible of our loss in his death that has taken from us an honored and revered brother, we respectfully ask that this Court spread upon its records this brief expression of our regard for his memory.

>Edward C. Stringer
>Thomas Wilson
>J. M. Gilman
>Wm. W. Billson
>C. D. O'Brien
>Austin H. Young
>Greenleaf Clark
>Martin J. Severance
>George W. Bachelder
>George N. Baxter

Charles W. Farnham, Esq., Secretary of the Minnesota State Bar Association, then read the addresses that had been delivered before the United States District Court, as follows:

Mr. John M. Gilman said: When I came to this city on September 10, 1857, Judge Nelson was territorial judge. In May 1858 the state was admitted to the Union, and soon thereafter Judge Nelson was appointed United States district judge by the President. He held that position for thirty-seven or thirty-eight years. Besides his duties as district judge of this state, he was also clothed with the judicial powers of circuit judge. I knew Judge Nelson intimately from the time he was appointed district judge until he retired from that position some eight years ago. I had considerable business both in the state court and in the United States circuit and district courts.

Judge Nelson, as district judge, also had jurisdiction of criminal cases under the federal statutes, which consisted chiefly of indictments under the national currency and Indian laws. When he became judge we had a large number of Indian tribes, the Sioux and Pottawattomies having large reservations in the western part of the state. Both of those tribes became belligerent, and in 1862 the Indian war broke out. The Chippewas, who had large reservations in the northern part of the state, were not engaged in that rebellion. At the time that war broke out we had six regiments at Fort Snelling ready to go south to engage in the Civil War. The Indian outbreak deterred those men from going to the South. General Sibley was appointed commander and immediately took charge of these six regiments and pursued the Indians as far as the Missouri river. He did not, however, overtake them. The Indians were in a starving condition, and when General Sibley returned, they followed and ultimately surrendered to him. Many were indicted and tried, and some thirty of their number were simultaneously executed at Mankato. Those facts I well remember. Bear in mind that within twenty-four hours after that outbreak the Indians had murdered some eight hundred of the male population of the state and Northwest. [Modern estimates place the total white dead in the whole course of the Dakota Conflict closer to 450.] The country northwest of Minneapolis and St. Paul was then very sparsely settled, and the entire male population was practically wiped out. The women and children, when relieved, came mostly to St. Paul, and all the private houses in the town were filled with these unfortunates. While this trouble lasted, Judge Nelson was holding court and protecting the Indians from violence, under the federal laws.

In addition to his duties as district judge in criminal matters, Judge Nelson also acted as judge of the federal court under the bankruptcy law, which was enacted, I think, in 1867. This work kept him on the bench daily for many years. He also assisted the circuit judge and frequently completed the term business of that court. He was, therefore, constantly engaged in district and circuit court duty. I had a great many cases before Judge Nelson as district judge in bankruptcy matters and also as circuit judge and can say with confidence that a fairer, better judge never occupied a bench in this state. I can endorse everything that was said in that Memorial.

For thirty-five years I had business before him at every term of court and know as well as any man what his qualifications, disposition, and character were as a judge and jurist. He was never worried or annoyed by counsel; he never showed any favors to counsel that he liked or animus to those he disliked. He was always ready and willing to listen to counsel and never intimated what his decision would be until counsel were through. If the case involved important legal questions and he had time, he would adjourn court until he could confer with the circuit judge, who was holding court in another room, but if he could not take time to confer with the circuit judge, he would dispose of the matter according to his understanding of the law. And he would always state the reasons for his decisions. His opinions were always accepted with grace, even by the defeated party. Under all circumstances Judge Nelson was disposed to do his duty faithfully. I never knew him to take offense at the manner in which his decisions were reviewed by a higher tribunal. If a case that he had decided was reversed or modified, he never complained, never had any fault to find, but accepted the decision as conclusive upon the question; and upon a retrial of the action he was always disposed to follow closely the decision of the higher tribunal.

I recollect very well having a case that involved a large amount of real estate. I was for the defense and interposed a demurrer to the complaint, which Judge Nelson sustained. It went to the U.S. Supreme Court. I engaged Senator Davis to look after it until it came on for hearing, when I would be present. Senator Davis took no part in the argument. I supposed, from what took place at the hearing, that the case would be decided in my favor. Justice Gray delivered the opinion of the court and to my surprise reversed Judge Nelson on

the theory that the statutes of Minnesota favored that view of the Law. Senator Davis, who was very friendly with Justice Miller, asked how the court came to decide that way. Judge Miller said, "The decision is all wrong; there is no doubt about that, but Judge Gray was very positive in his views, and I didn't think best to quarrel with him; I knew the case would come out all right, and therefore I didn't make any objection." This decision necessitated the taking of testimony and another hearing before Judge Nelson, and in determining the matter he followed the decision of Judge Gray just as far as possible, never complained that the supreme court was wrong, never complained that he had been overruled or anything of the kind, but said he had nothing to do but to follow that decision. And that was his way in every case that went up on appeal from his decision. I never knew him to complain of being overruled by the higher court, but on the contrary, he accepted the decision of that court as conclusive. He never made any distinction as to persons and never showed partiality.

Judge Nelson was not only disposed to follow the decisions of the higher courts on any question that had gone up from his decision but always took great pains to find out the principle upon which it had been rendered; and when he ascertained it, he would follow it. That was one great characteristic. I think he attempted to do exactly what was right in everything that came before him. He never, to my knowledge, had a word to say outside of court about any case that had been before him. He always delivered his opinions from the bench; and never outside of the bench or disconnected with the court did he have anything to say.

Judge Nelson had not only a fine judicial and discriminating mind, but aside from his legal and judicial attainments, he was a gentleman of the very highest order. For twenty years I lived in a house adjoining Judge Nelson's home, saw him daily, and had an opportunity to form a correct opinion in regard to the character, quality, and genius of the man, and [I] never found anything in him that was not perfectly just and right. He knew exactly how to treat his neighbor. There were many matters that we were both concerned in with reference to our adjoining properties, and I knew he was just and correct in his views and disposed to carry out in every respect what he considered just and right. I might relate many incidents that occurred between us regarding our property but will pass those by. However, I desire to say that I heartily endorse everything contained in the Memorial that has been read, and if it were possible that anything could be added, I would gladly concur in that.

I recollect a certain case before Judge Nelson when he was acting as circuit judge, where one of the attorneys referred to and read a decision in the federal court in which Judge Nelson's father, Samuel Nelson, had delivered the opinion of the court. I recall that he repeated the name of Samuel Nelson with a great deal of emphasis: "This is the opinion of Samuel Nelson, one of the judges of the highest court in this country." I then thought, and still think, he was trying to impress the name of Samuel Nelson on R. R. Nelson, in order to control the opinion of R. R. Nelson in the particular case then being argued. However, when R. R. Nelson came to decide the case, he decided it according to the decisions of the Supreme Court of the United States without reference to that case at all.

This simply shows Judge Nelson could not be prejudiced one iota by any attorney who might appear before him or by any party that might be interested in the case; he would not listen to anything that would tend to prejudice him from laying down the law as he understood it in the particular case. That was Judge Nelson's character throughout, and every lawyer that practiced before him was satisfied of that fact.

Hon. M. J. Severance then said:

Well might I have urged my own infirmity as a plea in bar to my appearance here today, but I should have been disloyal to the promptings of my heart had I shunned this occasion and failed to pay my tribute, though it be nothing but the widow's mite of the life of one devoted to the exaltation of our race.

When we look for the highest proof of the universal recognition of duty performed, we shall find it in the disposition of all the living to embalm the memory of the worthy dead. It is not a privilege, but it is the duty of those who survive to rescue from oblivion any noble example and weld it into the endless chain of virtue that should run commensurate with human existence. The future is entitled to all the treasures of the past, and with them it continues to maintain and build higher the fabric of social and national integrity. It is

the myriads of lives devoted to the primitive conceptions of duty but that history disdains to notice that send down their countless rivulets to fill the reservoirs of national development. It is the inspiration flowing from such considerations as these that directs my voice whilst speaking in eulogy of Judge Nelson today.

I am not speaking of a pampered child of fame. I am only speaking of one who, in the ordinary walks of social, civil, and judicial life illustrated those higher qualities of heart and mind that the world approves and conscience demands.

Judge Nelson was the worthy son of a noble sire, and his ancestry imposed on him the duty of bearing its standard in the vanguard of distinction and success, and that standard he never deserted in life. He was cradled in the lap of luxury and reared amid aristocratic surroundings. But of aristocracy he brought nothing to his western home save its culture and decorum. He dismissed all of its pride, except such as adheres to the gentleman. Thus endowed with a generous habit of mind, fraternal in all his instincts, he would not chafe or fret in the company of that simple, uncultured democracy that always lays the foundation of a state.

When speaking in memoriam I never cast a name for any man's religion or politics. If I find that he had a controlling desire to live in harmony with the purposes of his Creator and suffered that desire to color all the activities of his life, then he answers my conception of true religion no matter whether he drew his inspiration from Plato, Buddha, or the Greater Nazarene. If I find that in civil life he subordinated every selfish motive to the common weal and exalted political rectitude high above the conquests of party, then he answers my conception of patriotism and civic duty, no matter whether he drew his inspiration from the tomb of Lincoln or the shades of Monticello. Believing that the life of Judge Nelson fell within the boundaries of these conceptions, I revere his memory and commend his example to all the living.

Judge Nelson was conservative by nature, but he was not so conservative as to balk in the pathway of progress, for he was willing to explore any new conception that had any basis other than a mania for mere speculation. He came to Minnesota, as Webster said of the Pilgrim Fathers, "to settle on bare creation." Only the smoke of a few log cabins indicated to him that he had any companions here. He stood on the lowest and highest rounds of the ladder that measures the heights of Minnesota's development. Yet in his whole career, the wild life of the pioneer never even dimmed the burnish of his character.

In every phase of our social, civil and judicial life, he was an actor and participator, and in all this did he so well bear his part and demean himself that the voice of censorious criticism never assailed him. In social life he was not an autocrat bidding all others be silent; but urbane, benignant, and considerate of the feelings of others, he gave to every occasion the ease and confidence of social equality. He never chilled social communion by making his own the standard of another's excellence. Piquant, lively, and radiant in conversation, he wooed the friendship of all around him. No one ever left his presence shivering, but all left it aglow with the warmth of mutual esteem. The life of such a man always removes a segment from the social circle that can never be restored except by another of equal endowments.

In civil life he was attentive and alert to every movement that concerned his city, state, or nation, and he never deserted the forum or the assembly as long as either was held in debate. He wore the toga of a citizen with a full comprehension of all of its duties. He saw his state ascend to its proud position in the empire of liberty, and he believed that he had seen the dawn of the day. And he said to me a few months before he died, "If all the signs of the times were not all delusive and Christianity did not trail its banners and admit its defeat, the reign of universal equity would soon come when men shall beat the sword into plowshare and the spear into the pruning hook." And it seemed to give him infinite delight to believe that the time was approaching when the nations "would learn war no more forever." He never did believe that training for human slaughter was the only exercise that could give virility to human government but did believe that it is the virility of national conscience, not of physical power, for which the world has longed in all the ages of its grief. When The Hague catches a few more strains from Calvary, then we may expect that all civilized nations will deride the horrors of war; then the Shekinah, in all its glory, will hang over the dedication of the Temple of Peace.

He saw the jealous ruler over the forest sullenly retire from this very spot. He saw this city develop under genial civilization, until it held within its walls every institution that gives culture and grace to the mind and those other institutions born of a Christianized civilization, all throbbing with love for the unfortunate of our race. And when his eyes were closing on Time I feign would believe that their last lingering glance rested on yonder Parthenon where the heart of Minnesota is beating amid the trophies of her patriotism.

As to his judicial career I hesitate to say anything, lest I dilute the phrases of the Memorial. The great Plutarch, familiar with the pomp and abuse of Roman office through the reign of all the Caesars, said, "It is the man that gives dignity to the office, and not the office that gives dignity to the man," and this truth has no higher illustration than in the life of Judge Nelson. With a thorough literary education, deeply studied in the law, with an honest purpose in every act, he could but distinguish the office he held so long. He did not consider his office a badge of nobility but only a trust whose duties he was bound to perform. Though presiding in a court representing the power of the nation, he did not hold it as the sword of Damocles over other courts of lesser jurisdiction, but in a spirit of amity and judicial courtesy he permitted them all to revolve harmoniously in the orbit of the nation's economy. He never exercised an offensive dominion over the members of the bar. He did not claim to be the oracle of Delphi but only a co-worker with them in the labor of unravelling the problems of the law. He was willing to listen, anxious to be convinced, and he delighted in nothing more than in the certainty of truth. He never joined that restless and mistaken throng that rails at the technicalities of the law, for he would not sacrifice the syllogisms of a thousand years to that eager haste that would dispose of life and liberty at a single bound. He presided over his court with that dignity born of labor—a dignity that is never arrogant but always more than fraternal. Always lovable, always courteous, always self-poised, he attracted to himself the friendship of all and never provoked a sneer, for he never inflated his office with the hydrogen of personal conceit. Add to these graces the effluence of a sensitive and an enlightened conscience, and you find Judge Nelson as he was. Fortunate it was for him and for his fame that he left so few ellipses in his career, and fortunate indeed it is for us that he left his unsullied judicial mantle to fall on one who will never dishonor its folds.

He lived long beyond three score years and ten, and this overtime the Psalmist (petulant and morose in view of his own troubled life) has filled with all the spectres of discontent, "labor, and sorrow." But Judge Nelson never fell under the shadow of this curse, for a constant interchange of the amenities of life banished all the gloom of his age. Though years and years ago the unkindly hand of Death smote her the Ivy that entwined, yet this did not embitter his life, for he was ever buoyant in the belief that he had only to cross the river to renew a tie that eternity would never dissolve.

Human life, like Nature, has its Indian summer, and it often comes in this "overtime," when the frost of age has killed the deadly nightshade of passion and painted the foliage of life with the radiance of its setting sun. It was during this period, when Judge Nelson was reviewing the past and rounding out his life with remaining beauties, that the bow was drawn that sent the arrow to his heart. But it was not premature, for so smoothly, considerately, and justly had he run the current of his life that he trespassed on no one and left no enemies behind him unless, such as Aristides had, those provoked at virtue.

If I had omitted all I have said and simply said that Judge Nelson from the beginning to the end of life walked aright before God and man, I should have said everything that human eulogy can bestow upon the dead. All else is nothing but the desire of friendship or the ambition of rhetoric to leave no virtue untinted.

Something I see around me here to-day inspires me to speak for a single moment, perhaps beyond the proprieties of this occasion. I plead the license of that friendship I would not dare to plead before any other court on earth. Speaking for myself and presuming to speak for the Judge upon the bench and for half a score of others I see around me, all frosted with age—and all of whom saw the North Star burst from the twilight and blaze for the first time in the firmament of the republic—we know that when Judge Nelson left the world he did not close the door behind him but left it standing ajar for us. Death cannot much longer riot in our sanctuary. When a few more have gone, the casket holding Minnesota's first generation will be closed forever. But we are not dismayed at the prospect that lies before us. Neither do we shrink from the common lot. When the Marshal of Death shall serve his summons on us, undaunted and serene we will embark on that ocean that has no further shore; and when our bark swings out into the waves we will turn to those we leave behind us, and, pointing through the mist to the flag of the Republic, we will commit it to their hands and then bid them a cheerful and final adieu.

Hon. A. H. Young then said:

I esteem it a privilege to be permitted to say a few words on this occasion. Only a short time ago, on an occasion similar to that which brings us together today, Judge Nelson in speaking of an honored member of the bar just laid to rest said, "May we during our lives emulate his virtues, so that when our time comes to pass away from earth we may leave a name honored and respected."

It is only in exceptional cases that the services of a single life, however worthy, will be so marked as to give to the person a place above and distinct from that of his fellows. In the main we stand in this life shoulder to shoulder in our respective places in the contribution we make to the progress of the world, but to each is given the ability to live a life worthy of emulation. I believe it was the controlling purpose of Judge Nelson to live such a life and to leave to the world a name, as a private citizen and as a public officer, worthy to be honored and respected and so has his expressed desire been fully realized that he has left a name that we by this memorial service honor and respect, and it will be honored and respected by all who knew him in his years of service.

It was not my privilege to have an intimate personal acquaintance with Judge Nelson, but for well-nigh forty years I had known him as a judge upon the bench and entertained for him as a man the highest respect and for his judicial ability and probity the greatest confidence.

It is much to be able to say of one occupying a position charged with judicial responsibilities that by his life and service he won the confidence of the public whom he served. The public are critical, litigants are selfish, and to be able to so adjudge between contestants as to retain the confidence of all for impartial fairness calls into exercise qualities of wisdom and of justice. It is not in a spirit of adulation that we ascribe to Judge Nelson such qualities. He was a wise man; he was a just judge. During all the years of his service upon the bench large responsibilities were laid upon the judiciary—to so interpret and administer the law as to hold in cheek an element restless and impatient of legal restraint and so to safeguard the rights of the people. His natural qualities of mind, taken in connection with his legal training and high sense of justice, constituted Judge Nelson a sane and valued judicial officer. Removed as he was from any inducement to seek political preferment, his aim was to walk uprightly before the world and to justly interpret and apply the law in all cases brought before his jurisdiction.

We are too little given to praise men while engaged in the active discharge of public duties; we are more inclined to criticize than to praise, but when a life has been completed and active service is closed, it is both pleasant and profitable to speak in fitting terms of a noble life and make an enduring record, not of deeds—for they will live in their fruit—but of our appreciation for a life of valued service, a life full of years well-rounded and complete.

In his life Judge Nelson was ever worthy the esteem of all who knew him personally, and in the discharge of his duties as a public officer he made for himself a record that any man might well covet, that of an able and just judge. Up to the limit of his three score years and ten he faithfully performed the work given him to do in a public office than which there is none more honorable. And then when by long service he had earned for himself the right to lay aside the judicial ermine, which by law was his for life, he quietly and with dignity handed back the robe of honor and responsibility and patiently abided the call to a higher and to a more enduring service. What honor and dignity crown the life of such a man! It is such lives that constitute the true measure of human greatness. He did not seek for fame. The trust with which he was charged was too sacred in its nature to admit of applause for even the most faithful servant. He simply sought to execute with fidelity the trust committed to him and so by a life of virtue and faithful service

to leave a name that should command the honor and respect of those he left behind, and we who here today participate in this service do ourselves honor by causing to be placed upon the records of this court a Memorial expressive of our appreciation of the faithful life and service of our friend and brother.

Mr. George W. Bachelder then said:

I had the honor to be appointed upon this committee. I was unable to attend the meeting of the committee for the purpose of framing the Memorial to be presented to this Court, but I have heard it read here today and can endorse all that it says. If I could repeat the Memorial it would be a good deal more than I myself could say of Judge Nelson.

I cannot claim to have been a particular comrade of Judge Nelson; I had not the experience that some of my brethren who have spoken here had with him in matters in court and of business. And yet I do not think any one who had lived in Minnesota forty years would be unacquainted with Judge Nelson. I first became acquainted with Judge Nelson in 1857, some time after he had been appointed a judge of the territorial court, when he held a term of court at Faribault. Shortly before I met Judge Nelson I had met Judge Flandrau, who was also judge upon the same bench and was holding a term of court in Owatonna. I enquired of him about the new judge who was going to hold our term of court. This was the second term of court that was held in Rice county, Judge Chatfield having already held one term. Judge Flandrau, after extolling him highly as a lawyer and a jurist, concluded by saying: "And one of the best fellows that you ever met." This was a characteristic expression of Judge Flandrau, and, as I always found, a saying worthy to be made of Judge Nelson. I should not have remembered it so well, probably, if I had not been reminded of it at all times when I met Judge Nelson.

The term of the court was very short, lasting only a few days. Of course the business was very light. There were not a great many attorneys in this state at that time. Oscar F. Perkins, John M. Berry, and myself, as far as I recollect, constituted the bar of Rice county. The portly and dignified manner of Judge Nelson in presiding over the court at that time and his cordial affable disposition shown both on and off the bench impressed not only the attorneys in attendance but the jurymen and all others who had the pleasure of being present on that occasion. I attended another term of court, in St. Paul, at which Judge Nelson presided as territorial judge. Judge Nelson, I soon learned, was a man whose acquaintance could be very easily made and very easily kept. His conduct while judge of the district court was of the same even character: always affable off the bench, always dignified on the bench, and always bent upon doing exact justice.

But it was on the federal bench that Judge Nelson's character and reputation seem to have been largely made. He was admirably adapted to the position. During an experience of thirty-eight years as judge of that court, he enjoyed the good opinion and confidence of the bar of the whole state and of the community in which he lived. He established a character and reputation of which any man might be proud. Judge Nelson, in my opinion, was not a very ambitious man. He did not, so far as I know, aspire to higher than those that were given to him. He seemed to be entirely satisfied.

I always looked upon Judge Nelson as a remarkably fortunate man, not only in his personal traits and in his ability as a presiding judge, but the environments of his youth had been everything that he could wish. Notwithstanding his agreeable surroundings, which frequently are regarded as a bar to final success, Judge Nelson never buried his talents in the earth but built upon and improved them and made of himself a distinguished lawyer and jurist.

The career of Judge Nelson upon the federal bench was very long, very distinguished, and, I have no doubt, very useful. He was blessed with great length of years, beyond what most men are permitted to enjoy, and during his whole life he maintained the good qualities that have been spoken of by those who have preceded me and continued to be the same good judge and refined gentleman so long as he lived. Rarely do we find a man who, at the close of his life, has so completely finished his work as had Judge Nelson. I believe he accomplished all he aspired to accomplish. And when he began to feel the finger of Time in the declining years of his life, he gracefully withdrew from his position on the bench, undoubtedly not caring longer to listen to the discussions of the attorneys in court or to be burdened with the responsibility of deciding and settling the disputes of litigants. His work had been done and well done. He retired to private life, no doubt intending to enjoy the ease, comfort, and quietness of that life. No doubt during the last eight years he had more enjoyment than he had even when upon the bench. His work was all done and well done, and we trust that he is now meeting his reward.

Hon. E. C. Stringer then said:

Many have been kept from attending this service by engagements that could not be broken, and there are also some without the state who have expressed themselves as desirous of paying a tribute to the memory of Judge Nelson. With the permission of the Court I will read a portion of a letter expressive of such desire, written by the Honorable Eugene G. Hay, in which he says:

I very much regret my inability to attend. As a practicing attorney in the United States District and Circuit Courts of Minnesota during a part of Judge Nelson's long career as presiding judge and for a little more than four years as an officer of this court, I learned to know Judge Nelson intimately and to honor, love, and respect him. Of all the official or professional relations of my life, none were to me more pleasant than those sustained with Judge Nelson during the time I occupied the position of United States attorney for Minnesota. He was at all times an upright and painstaking judge, jealous always that exact justice should be meted out in his court and those who were so fortunate as to know him intimately will, I believe, join me in saying that he was one of the most lovable of men. As an administrator of the law in the pioneer days and through the years of Minnesota's growth and development, he contributed very largely to the fabric of government that now clothes that splendid commonwealth. I deeply mourn his death and will always revere and honor his memory.

At the conclusion of these addresses Judge Lochren made the following response:

The memorial that you present sets forth with clearness and brevity the Manly virtues, ability, and amiable traits of character of Judge Nelson that endeared him to the bar and won and held the esteem and veneration of the people of our State. It will, as is most fitting, be entered of record in these courts, where he presided so ably and worthily during thirty-eight years of his vigorous manhood.

Called to this bench in his youth, his life work was here; and the records of these courts disclose the character and extent of that work and bear witness to the learning, ability, integrity, and industry with which that work was performed. These records contain his decisions, which his successors will consult for their guidance, fortunate to have such helps in their efforts to emulate his usefulness. His amiable personal and social characteristics, which attached to him all who came within the range of his acquaintance, have been referred to by many of you who knew him intimately. He also possessed that quiet, natural dignity with nothing of coldness in it, which compelled decorum in his presence.

I will conclude by quoting words that he himself spoke of another on a like occasion and that as aptly apply to himself: "No judge ever was influenced by purer motives or surrounded by a higher moral atmosphere . . . He was learned in the law, which he administered wisely and thus won confidence and esteem."

Associate Justice Lovely said:

During the last twenty-four years of Judge Nelson's judicial service I was engaged in the trial of many causes in the court over which he presided, and as we became quite intimate in our personal associations I enjoyed the valuable privilege of his friendship. He had reached the meridian of life when I first appeared in his court in 1876. From then on until the end of his service I was in attendance at all of the district or circuit courts of the United States held either at St. Paul or in the southern divisions at Mankato or Winona, where the ablest lawyers of the state appeared in the transaction of professional business, very many of whom have since passed before to their rewards.

He was the first federal judge of the District of Minnesota, appointed in 1858 upon its admission into the Union, and from that time until his voluntary retirement in 1896 at the age of seventy he had served uninterruptedly through what must be regarded as the most important period of the development of the jurisprudence of the country in the extension of federal

jurisdiction of the national courts arising from the constitutional amendments adopted immediately after the Civil War. He went upon the bench very early in life and remained there until he reached the allotted age of three score and ten. The labors imposed upon him were often exceedingly difficult. Our state was developing in commercial importance, and property interests of the highest magnitude were continually presented for judicial investigation.

While his professional experience before his appointment must have been necessarily limited, he had through legal training considerable general culture and much knowledge of the world. He was exceptionally free from narrow prejudices, possessed of a catholic disposition towards his fellow men, and always inclined to apply the golden rule of the Gospel to the affairs of life. He was learned in the procedure under the old rules of equity and the common law though never constrained by their useless restraints, for he was progressive and displayed an anxiety to adapt the capacities of the law to the demands of modern times. When I first met Judge Nelson he had become through study and experience an able and learned jurist, trained in the precedents of his forum and possessed of a comprehensive grasp of the general principles of jurisprudence. He disliked technicalities and looked upon the rules of practice as a means to forward rather than retard the enforcement of justice. His duties exacted unremitting attention to his work during the entire thirty-eight years of his service on the bench, but it was not observable to me that it ever tried his equanimity or disturbed a serene composure that seemed natural to the man, becoming to a judge, and most gratefully appreciated by those who were called to present their contentions in his court while his forbearance was often put to the proof; he was equal to the emergencies of each situation, and the lawyer who went into his court for the first time, coming often at a distance from rural localities, perhaps with prejudice against a forum with which he was not familiar, left his presence with the pleasant impression that he had to the fullest extent his day in court and would be kindly welcomed again; and if mistakes were made by counsel, the generous and sympathetic disposition of Judge Nelson seemed to overlook them, and the younger members of the bar came to regard him with paternal respect. He was a sincere friend, transparently honest in all things; his thoughts were fashioned on his tongue but restrained in expression by the courteous gentility of the old school of which he was one of the best examples.

The breadth of his humanity and his love of justice were well illustrated in his exercise of equitable jurisdiction. He entered upon the trial of cases submitted to the court with a determined purpose to subordinate all pride of opinion if it existed, which I doubt, to a mastery of the facts and the application of the obligations of truth and right. Recognizing the value of authority and the aid that the learning and ability of the bar could give, he was an attentive listener so long as argument could possibly aid in the investigation of the cause at bar. As a result I doubt if the record of any federal judge will present fewer reversals than those submitted on renew from his judgments during the extended period of his continuous services on the bench. I always believed that he was peculiarly fortunate in the aptitude and capacity he displayed as a presiding judge in common-law actions. He found the jury system in the constitution; he believed in it and recognized its value as a potent instrument in the administration of justice, always willing to give full latitude and scope to its functions. Where suitors asked redress for wrongs to their person or property in this tribunal he insisted that the jury should exercise the full measure of authority, and in the admission of evidence, if there was doubt, he resolved it in favor of the most liberal rules of evidence. So too it may be said that in a court whose jurisdiction was the continued subject of controversy and the Federal authority supreme in that question, the possession of this power excited no desire on his part to display it or deny recognition to the jurisdiction of the state courts. Whenever doubt existed in this respect, he declined to entertain the cause. The arbitrary element had no place whatever in his character, for he possessed that most essential quality of his station, a judicial humility that tempered his judgments with a sweetness that went far to reconcile the unsuccessful practitioner to the result of adverse judgment.

He had a very keen appreciation of the ludicrous and was at times capable of exquisite humor but re-

served the manifestation of this inclination for his private and social relations rather than for exhibition on the bench. Here he was always the poised and kindly self-respecting man, firm in the conduct of the business in hand. Apparently the most unobtrusive of judges, his courteous demeanor and complete self-control secured that obedience to the exercise of essential authority his duty required him to maintain. I have seen him preside over several troubled controversies at the bar where the zeal of counsel expressing the feelings of their client engendered opposition that well nigh reached the limits of propriety and toleration, but on all such occasion Judge Nelson never lost his self command; above the jarring factions he presided with dignity and held the balance even.

> Calm as the patient planets gleam
> That walk the cloudless skies.

Judge Nelson's judicial career was almost phenomenal. The recorded decisions that he delivered display ability of a high order, but his purpose was to be right rather than brilliant, and in this aim he was more than successful.

At the end of a long life of usefulness he retired from the bench to enjoy in his days of rest the solace of kind friends and the ministration of a daughter. During this period he was a genial companion whose society was enjoyable to the young and old alike. He has at last laid down life's burden without fear or dread, reposing in the confidence of a Christian that the services to the humblest supplicants for justice would entitle him as a reward to the fulfillment of the promise, "Inasmuch as ye have done it unto the least of these, ye have done it unto me."

The highest compliment that will be paid to his public service is that his judicial record deserves to be the object of emulation by those upon whom his mantle has fallen.

His righteous life yields a lesson that will not be forgotten. It is a valuable possession of his country and this commonwealth. It will long be referred to with respect and commendation, for "The actions of the just smell sweet and blossom in the dust." [93 Minn. xxi]

Charles E. Flandrau

1828–1903

Associate Justice, Territorial Supreme Court, 1857–1858, and Minnesota Supreme Court, 1858–1864

On the afternoon of October 6, 1903, in the court room at the State Capitol, Hon. [Martin] J. Severance, in behalf of the State Bar Association, addressed the Supreme Court, then in session, and read the following memorial:

On the ninth day of September last Charles Eugene Flandrau closed his book of life at the city of Saint Paul and now he rests with his fathers. Though three quarters of a century spanned his life, yet the wheels of time in their ceaseless roll had left no visible trace on his body or mind. An angry shaft from the quiver of Death smote him whilst he had the tread of a giant, and he fell to rise no more forever. With his death a star fell from the firmament of Minnesota's history, but its lingering luster will continue to illumine the memory of those who loved or admired him. . .

It is not the purpose of this memorial to gild an idol existing only in the caprice of fancy but to trace with historical accuracy the activities of one whose career exalted his profession and reflected an imperishable honor upon his race, society, and state. It is not the gift of a bounteous nature that inspires just panegyric, for disloyalty to that may invoke the unutterable contempt of mankind, but it is the self-wrought nobility of character and action perceiving and advancing the highest purposes of human life that renders the name of any man welcome to the casket of endless memory.

Charles Eugene Flandrau, the subject of this memorial, was born on the fifteenth day of July 1828, in the city of New York, and his ancestral line runs back to the Hugenots of France, expatriated by the revocation of the Edict of Nantes. At the age of thirteen, attracted by the mysteries of the sea, he went before the mast on different revenue cutters in the United States service, and on these and some merchant vessels he performed the duties of a common sailor for the period of three years. After the expiration of that period and before he was nineteen years of age he attended private schools in Georgetown and Washington in the District of Columbia for two or three years, where he received his chief preparatory education. At the age of nineteen he went to Whiteboro in Oneida county, in the state of New York, the residence of his father, who was a lawyer of high repute, and studying law in his office was admitted to the bar in 1851 and remained in practice with his father until he came to Saint Paul in November 1853, where he entered upon the practice of the law with Horace R. Bigelow, under the firm name of Bigelow & Flandrau. In October 1854, he removed to Saint Peter and became a deputy clerk of the District Court of Nicollet county and was afterwards in the same year elected District Attorney for that county, a position he held for more than a year. In 1855 he was a member of the Territorial Council of Minnesota, in which capacity he served for one year and then resigned. On the sixteenth day of August 1856, President Pierce appointed him United States Indian Agent for the Sioux of the Mississippi, a position he held for one year and then resigned. In 1857 he was a member of the Constitutional Convention that reared the fabric of our organic law. In July 1856, he was appointed by President Buchanan an Associate Justice of the Supreme Court of the Territory of Minnesota, which office he held until the territorial government was superseded by that of the state.

On the thirteenth day of November 1857, he was elected Associate Justice of the Supreme Court of the State of Minnesota for the term of seven years, but he resigned his office on the first day of June 1864. In 1858 and while he was Associate Justice of the Supreme Court of the state, by appointment of Governor

Sibley he held the office of Judge Advocate General of the state, a position he filled during the administration of Governor Sibley. In 1864 he removed to Carson City, in the territory of Nevada, where he practiced his profession for a year. In the spring of 1866 he removed to Saint Louis, in the state of Missouri, and practiced his profession with Richard Musser for a short time. In 1867 he removed to Minnesota and practiced his profession with Isaac Atwater at the city of Minneapolis. In March 1867, he was elected City Attorney of that city, which office he held for one year. In 1870 he removed to Saint Paul and associated with Horace R. Bigelow and Greenleaf Clark in the practice of law, under the firm name of Bigelow Flandrau & Clark, and afterwards he was the senior member of the firm of Flandrau, Squires & Cutcheon, in which firm he remained until his failing health required him to lay down his heaviest burdens. After that he practiced his profession alone in the city of Saint Paul as his strength permitted and doing historical work until he was compelled by his progressive decline to lay his armor aside.

In the varied life and career of Judge Flandrau many incidents that embellish his character must be omitted here, as they belong more properly to the domain of general history than to the records of this court. This memorial is more concerned with his achievements as a man, lawyer, and judge. Nothing in his eventful life will be overlooked when the story of which is written to be placed in the archives of the state.

The power of environment in fashioning a plastic mind endowed by nature with high moral aims may be easily detected all along the current of his life. There was more than the trace of chivalry in his nature. Perhaps there came throbbing down the arteries of time from the realm of the troubadours an invisible, silent impulse that gave a tinge of romance to his life and made adventure a passion with him. This would easily lead him out into untrodden paths where primitive nature disdained the conventionalities of a ripe civilization. Then it is no wonder that he came in his youth to this virgin land to sit by campfires of those who heard the roar of Saint Anthony's waters before they were enslaved by the mill wheel and subjected to the industrial dominion of man. To be a pioneer and lead the vanguard of new discovery and new creations would be the natural trend of his mind. To stand where civilization and barbarism were chafing against each other would be enchantment for him.

When we look for the sources of his unchallenged manhood that left its impress on every act of his public, professional and judicial career, we may remember the fact that he was schooled in the District of Columbia, the heart of this republic, where the very air was resonant with the utterances of the architects of our greatness. This was the forum of the nation, adorned with the trophies of her victories, where its orators and statesmen spoke for all coming generations under the flag that symbolized our power and where the Areopagus of America sat expounding national and international law. All this would add dignity to youth only waiting for the toga of manhood. But more potent is the fact that his legal education was had in the office of his father, an acute and celebrated lawyer who mingled in the tutelage of his son lofty professional pride with ardent parental solicitude. Add to this the radiance of a distinguished family on the maternal side, and you behold the influences that crowded upon a receptive mind.

Without the burnish and scholarly discipline of a college education, he drew from the necessities of his serious practical labors all the elements of learning until an exact literary taste with all of its graces lent its charm to his manifold accomplishments; and he left behind him a history of his state couched in admirable style and paraphrase, which at once ranks him among the eminent historians of this country.

Judge Flandrau in every walk of life wore the mantle of courtliness—a courtliness not too rigid or unbending and not bespeaking personal pride or hauteur but only a conscious gentility everywhere radiating a decorous demeanor. He will be missed in the social circle and at the festive board where his memory, pregnant with reminiscence, gave life and piquancy to idle hours.

So facile were his talents that he turned from one department of duty to another with all the ease of a universal student limited by no special education. Civil administration, judicial requirements, and military strategy—all fell within the range of his powers. So far-reaching was his comprehension of progress that the [fetish] of an unstable tradition would not prevent him from keeping step with the march of experience in every domain of life.

As a lawyer Judge Flandrau rose to a full conception of the dignity of his profession; to chafe and wrangle in peevish encounter was foreign to his taste and abhorrent to his view of a duty commissioned only to discover and establish the truth.

With the sensitive character of a cavalier he bore himself in forensic debate, giving and parrying a thrust without a tinge of personal hostility. It was the good fortune of Judge Flandrau in his whole professional career to be associated with lawyers of eminent attainments, and his dread of inferiority would suffer no relaxation of his powers. He was pre-eminently a trial lawyer, dexterous in the management of a cause, allowing no advantage to escape him, and all the time adhering to his logical diagnosis of the case. Fluent but not redundant and foaming of speech, he was direct and incisive in his diction, disdaining the tawdry floridity of mere rhetoric and scorning the argument *ad hominem* as an ignoble play upon the chords of prejudice and bias. He would stir the intellect, but he would leave the emotions to play their part in the realm outside of the domain of abstract justice. In his life and in the practice of his profession he observed the golden rules of honor and the sublime ethics of integrity, and this gave him the advantage of an impervious character before courts and juries, where he could consistently assail the lapses of others with nothing to condemn in himself.

With profit may the Bar of Minnesota heed the lessons of his life, for it will find his footprints all in the path of duty leading up to an honorable distinction. The Bar of this state cannot but deplore the loss of one who so long bore its standard with more than knightly devotion.

Before Charles E. Flandrau arrived at the age of thirty years he became a member of our Territorial Supreme Court and in a year after a member of this court, and he wore the ermine of a judge with credit to himself, with honor to our territory and state, and laid it aside with no stain of dishonor upon its folds.

He stood at the helm of our judiciary in the formative period of our legal practice, and with a discernment and maturity of judgment phenomenal in one of his age, he played a conspicuous part in laying the foundation of a system on which has been reared our stately judicial fabric. He hailed with delight the dawn of that day when reason descended in her royal robes to assume her empire over the human mind and hurl the ordeal of chance into the abyss of dishonored superstition. He would rear the law on the pedestal of intellectual certitude and crown it with the diadem of eternal justice. A view of his written opinions spread on the records of our courts, perspicuous in phrase, correct in the enunciation of legal principles, and tolerating no compromise with partial justice, will place his name high on the tablet of Minnesota's judicial fame. If untiring application, honesty of purpose, and innate love of justice are the chief qualifications of judicial equipment, then all of these abound in Judge Flandrau in an eminent degree the conspicuous elements of his mental and moral economy.

Finally, gratitude and humanity demand the recognition of this memorial. For the services that Judge Flandrau rendered in the interest of human life where savage fury swept the homes of Minnesota with the besom of destruction, his name will be interwoven with the story of every fireside as long as the world shudders at beastial atrocity. In 1857, when the settlers of southwestern Minnesota felt secure in their humble homes, supposing that the Indians had disowned the instincts of the brute, Ink-pa-du-ta, an incarnate fiend, with his band of remorseless demons descended upon scores of happy homes, and the gleam of the scalping knife that for many years had rested in its scabbard again presaged havoc, torture, and death, Judge Flandrau, then Indian agent for the Sioux, by an energy of action unsurpassed, stayed the slaughter of the defenseless settlers after forty-two had fallen before the tomahawk and the rifle. The female captives that survived the riot and carnival of lust, by an adroit diplomacy, he rescued from the clutches of their tormentors and restored them to all there was left of their homes, desolated by barbaric cruelty.

Again, in 1862, when the Lower Sioux revolted to regain the empire from which they had sullenly retired, he met them in battle array at New Ulm with his bands of volunteers, routed them, and broke the cyclone of savage vengeance that was sweeping down the valley of the Minnesota. History, justice, and truth will declare with due deference to the bravery of others that to a moral certainty had it not been for the presence of Judge Flandrau at the battle of New Ulm with his dauntless courage, his knowledge of Indian strategy, his ability to command, his fertility of resource, and the inspiration of his example, New Ulm would have fallen, and twelve hundred hapless men, women, and children would have been added to the thousand then rotting on the prairie, and the torrent of blood would have rolled on down the valley. [As noted previously, modern estimates place the total figure for the Dakota Conflict closer to 450.]

When the billows of smoke lurid with the glare of burning homes were rolling and breaking around him; when the Alaric of the Dakotas was raging along the tightening circles of the naked, painted, yelling demons, hungry for sack and pillage, urging them to closer and deadlier conflict; when the wail of women and children shrinking from the clutch of savage monsters filled the darkening air with dismal sound; and when to many all seemed to be lost; Judge Flandrau with the withering scowl of utter contempt repelled every suggestion of retreat. To any who would leave their post in despair of further defense Judge Flandrau said: "Do it if you will, but if you do, Minnesota will be eternally too hot for you." Met and baffled by heroism like this, the Indians at last skulked away to the horrid orgies of their distant camp, where a hundred women were praying for the relief of death. And so New Ulm was saved. Chivalry never crowned a head more deserving than that of Charles Eugene Flandrau.

The story of his domestic life is written on the hearts of his home, and this memorial will not invade that sacred precinct.

(Signed)   A. H. Young
         R. R. Nelson
         John B. Sanborn
         W. E. Hale
         M. J. Severance,
                 Committee

In the absence of Hon. Isaac T. Atwater, the following tribute prepared by him was read by his son, John B. Atwater, Esq.:

On the occasion of this memorial meeting in honor of Judge Flandrau I have desired to present some slight tribute to the regard and esteem that I have had for him during his life. As my physical infirmities prevent me from being personally present at this time, I can only send a brief and imperfect testimonial to my departed friend, partner and fellow associate in the Supreme Court of this state.

I first met Judge Flandrau shortly after his arrival in the territory of Minnesota—in the year 1853, if I recollect right—but my intimate acquaintance with him dates from our association together in the first Supreme Court of this state. Judge Flandrau's early entry into the territory was an important addition to the legal force of the then-infant commonwealth. His natural abilities as a lawyer, combined with his attractive presence, his open and frank countenance, and his genial and engaging manners, at once won for him the respect and affection of those with whom he was brought in contact. His influence in the affairs of the territory was soon felt, and in 1856, as I remember, he was appointed by President Buchanan District Judge of the United States Court for the Fourth Judicial District. In this position he displayed those judicial qualities that afterwards won for him an enviable reputation in the wider field of the Supreme Court of this state, and he then laid the foundation for that popularity that later enabled him to gain this high honor. I attended the first court that he held in Minneapolis at the old Court House on Fourth street, and I can still remember the universal encomiums that were then given to his ability and fairness as a presiding *nisi prius* judge. Although most of the lawyers and litigants who attended that court have now passed away, I have often at that time and since heard Judge Flandrau spoken of as being one of the best judges who ever held court in Hennepin county.

At the election in 1857 Judge Flandrau together with Lafayette Emmett and myself were elected justices of the first Supreme Court of the state of Minnesota. At this election politics were largely in a transition state. The Whig party was about being dissolved; new parties were being formed; the new Republican party was rapidly coming to the front, but the old Democratic party was the most coherent and best organized. The Democratic party was generally successful in this contest, although long years elapsed before it again succeeded in electing many of its candidates at a state election.

The early sessions of the first Supreme Court were held in a room in the north wing of the old Capitol Building. There was at that time no law library for the use of the judges, and we were necessarily much hampered in our work by the lack of that facility. Often we would have brief references to decisions that might be of controlling weight upon a case under consideration, but it was impossible for us to obtain any full report of these decisions. Many cases came before us, especially in real estate and railroad law that were of first impression, and we were obliged to struggle with the questions presented with practically no aid from the text-books or prior precedents. The court, however, was assisted by a bar, the abilities of which I cannot but feel were the equal of any that have followed it, and perhaps their ingenuity and logical acumen in presenting a case were heightened by the lack of those precedents, the mass of which often seems to overwhelm a modern lawyer in the argument of a legal question. Nearly all the lawyers who in those early days appeared most prominently before us are now out of the active practice of their profession, but their names and fame will live in the reports of cases, often important and quite often very novel, that they so forcibly argued before us. At that time the salary of the Justices of the Supreme Court was $2,000 each per year, and this was rarely, if ever, paid in cash. If a judge had any pressing need of money he was obliged to sacrifice from ten to twenty per cent of his warrants in order to have them discounted. We had at that time no consultation rooms, and most of the consultation work outside of the Court House was done either at Judge Emmett's house in Saint Paul or at my home in Minneapolis. In our mutual work upon the bench, which brought us very closely together, I have nothing but praise to say of Judge Flandrau. He was quick to grasp and analyze the legal points that were decisive of a litigation, but he always looked to the real equities involved and gave them full consideration in his final determination. He was patient in his weighing of a case, slow to come to a final decision and, when our opinions differed, was always ready to give full value to the arguments of his colleagues and was open to conviction until the last moment. I do not know just what early advantages he had had in the study of law, but he certainly demonstrated that he was a natural-born lawyer, and the high reputation that he won on the Supreme bench is now the fair heritage of his family and his State.

After several years spent on the Supreme bench, both Judge Flandrau and myself resigned and for a few years practiced law as partners at Carson City, Nevada. For several years thereafter Judge Flandrau and myself were partners in the practice of law at Minneapolis, until Judge Flandrau went to Saint Paul and became a member of the firm of "Bigelow, Flandrau & Clark." In our family relations we have always been close friends.

The tribute that I can now pay to him I feel most inadequate. I can but touch on the relations in which we lived and worked together, and I have not even spoken of the record that he made as a gallant soldier in the war against the Indians and the undying love that his services in that terrible time won for him in the hearts of the people to whose assistance he came. I have known Judge Flandrau as intimately as any man during my life in Minnesota, and I know him to have been a true man—brave, generous, just, and kind. As a father, husband, and friend, as a citizen, judge, and lawyer, in every position in which he has been placed, he has met the test of honesty, loyalty, and worth. In expressing our farewell to him, we can each of us say, without exaggeration or adulation, that we could wish no fairer record than the one that he has left behind him.

Hon. R. R. Nelson then addressed the court:

When distinguished judges and lawyers die, we take notice of the event before the courts with which they were associated. Judge Flandrau was an honored member of this court at an early day in the history of Minnesota and after he left the bench continued as an active and earnest advocate before the court until his health failed. His death was a public loss; it was a painful wound to me although at the time not unexpected. It was a personal loss. We emigrated more than a half century since from the state of New York, where we lived in adjoining counties. There was a bond of sympathy between us from the start, and our friendship survived a lifetime. Flandrau was a strong and forceful character, of good executive ability, and a born leader of men. In every enterprise in which he was engaged he always was found at the front. If public services outside of his profession engaged his attention, he discharged the duties honestly and fearlessly. He had great personal courage, was self-reliant to an eminent degree, and possessed no mean military ability. Perhaps his training as a sailor before the mast in the navy contributed to this. In 1857 Mr. Buchanan, then president of the United States, appointed William Welch of Minnesota, Chief Justice of the Supreme Court of the territory, and John Pettit of Indiana and R. R. Nelson of Minnesota, Associate Justices. For some reason Pettit declined the appointment. At that time Flandrau was agent of the Sioux Indians, located in the valley of the Minnesota River, and on the advice and at the solicitation of friends resigned the office and was appointed in Pettit's place, a position more congenial to his tastes. He served as an Associate Justice during 1857 and until he was elected and qualified a Justice of the Supreme Court of the state. He was unable to sit *in banc* with the other judges at the term of the Territorial Court held in 1857, but you will find in the first Minnesota Report at the end of an opinion I wrote in a case decided at this session, "I concur, Flandrau, J." His name appears for seven years and in the succeeding reports of the Minnesota Supreme Court until he resigned.

Flandrau was fond of a good story and inimitable in telling one. When he approved of the opinion just referred to he said it reminded him of the story of a trial before an ignorant justice of the peace in New York. One of the lawyers cited a case and claimed it was on all fours with the one before the justice. He read the opinion in full, which was signed "Jones, Judge," and asked for judgment. When he sat down, the lawyer on the other side arose and said he was astonished that his learned opponent had attempted to deceive the justice, that the court deciding the case consisted of five judges, and the opinion read was that of one judge, Jones, and if his opponent had finished the citation it would be found that "a majority of the judges conquered" (concurred). And Judge Jones' opinion did not prevail. The justice, not appreciating the difference between "concurred" and "conquered." so decided.

Judge Flandrau lived near Saint Peter in the Minnesota valley and before he had official duties to discharge practiced in the Territorial courts and before the United States Land Office. It was not unusual for him to walk across the country from his home to Winona, where the land office was located. He told me that the happiest experiences of his professional life at that time were when the court was held at places where there were no law books and no musty precedents could be cited. Counsel had to rely upon their knowledge of legal principles and grasp the salient points as the cause progressed. Flandrau was a wise lawyer and a formidable adversary; he possessed the elements necessary to success. He was intelligent, had a robust constitution and great vitality, was genial and social in disposition, which endeared him to all with whom he came in contact. He was urbane, courteous, and remarkable for good judgment, sound common sense, and quick perception, and withal a healthy moral tone pervaded his professional career. He spoke ill of no one. Although of strong convictions, he was not opinionated, and I never heard an unkind word against anyone pass his lips. He sustained his views of public policy by logical arguments and did not resort to vituperation of those who disagreed with him. When [he was the] Indian agent he was confronted with the execution of a very difficult and delicate duty. Among the desperate characters in the Sioux nation at that time none were more lawless and treacherous than Chief Ink-pa-du-ta and his band. This chief made a raid upon the sparse settlement in Minnesota near Spring Lake, Iowa. Hideous atrocities and massacres were committed, and several female captives were held for ransom. Judge Flandrau undertook their release and succeeded in securing it. A graphic description of this undertaking, written by himself, can be found in the archives of the State Historical Society. In order to procure the ransom, he obtained the necessary money by issuing, as he said, the first bond of the commonwealth of Minnesota, pledging the payment of the amount required, and the legislature recognized the obligation and appropriated money to redeem the bond. That he had military ability the defense of New Ulm during the Indian massacre bears testimony. On the bench Judge Flandrau was calm, patient, courtly, and dignified. His decisions are distinguished for practical justice and conspicuous for the right application of legal principles to the cases presented to the court.

These occasions, as said by another, "bring home to us the great truth that we are destined to pass away from the earth, leaving no trace other than the memory retained by those who loved and esteemed us." Our friend has gone to that "undiscovered country from whose bourne no traveler returns." He has crossed the river to the Great Beyond. May we during our lives emulate his virtues, so that when our time comes to pass away from the earth we may leave a name honored and respected.

Hon. William E. Hale then addressed the court:

It is said, "There is nothing innocent or good that dies or is forgotten; that no stream from its source flows seaward, how lonely soever its course, but that some land is gladdened; that no star ever rose and set without influence somewhere; that no life can be pure in its purpose and strong in itself, and all life not be purer and stronger thereby."

The life of Judge Flandrau, as he lived it in this city, in this state, and among all its people, now belongs to the bench, to the bar, and to the public. It is a beautiful picture of a long life well spent.

In 1851, the governor of the then territory of Minnesota, in his message to the second legislative assembly, said: "That the fertility of our soil, the salubrity of our climate, our forests, our fisheries, our mines, our inexhaustible water-power, furnish elements that will attract hither a large and steady immigration and secure a growth both vigorous and rapid cannot be doubted." The population of the territory was then about five thousand. Three years after this general invitation, young Flandrau came to Minnesota to help in a large way to make it one of the foremost states of the Union. He defended it in war and contributed much towards shaping and enforcing its laws. Always public spirited, he was ever ready to give his time and his talents to all public questions that concerned the welfare of his state and his city. Had he belonged to that political party that has been in power most of the time since 1861, he could, and probably would, have occupied a place among the highest and most influential of its counsellors. What a dignified, graceful, and able representative of his country would he have made at any of the courts of Europe.

He ranked exceedingly high as a lawyer and a judge, and for thirty years or more he had no superior in this state as a trial lawyer. Fairness, manliness, and uprightness characterized the conduct of his cases, and he won the confidence and admiration of both courts and juries. The most complicated entanglement of facts and law was always reduced to harmony and simplicity under his skilful handling. He was a lover of truth for truth's sake. His ideas of life and of the duties of a lawyer were exalted. It was impossible for him to stoop to, or in any form countenance, a low or mean act. He was, indeed, a superb character, both in appearance and in action. He was a most genial spirit, affectionate and kind to his friends, and magnanimous to his enemies, writing their injuries and faults on the sand.

Death comes to us all alike and makes us all equal when it comes; but it is not the good fortune of many to have lived so useful a life to his state and its people as was the lot and opportunity of Judge Flandrau. The history of this state cannot be truthfully written unless his life, his acts, and his deeds are shown to have had a prominent influence upon its formation and development.

Hon. C. D. O'Brien then addressed the court as follows:

The great poet has said, "The evil men do lives after them, while the good is oft interred with their bones." The custom of the bar that we practice today preserves the good done by men whose services in the profession are eminent and whose lives have passed the censorship of their associates at the bar. The life of which we speak today contained no evil; all that was in it, to my observation, was good and exceedingly good. To attempt to add anything to the tributes that have been paid to the memory of Judge Flandrau by such men as Judge Severance, Judge Nelson, his associates, and my friends who have preceded me would be upon my part perhaps exceedingly presumptuous. But a man who has lived his life has the right to summon, even from the humblest ranks, witnesses to the good he did and the virtues that he practiced while among us.

There are two classes of men at the bar who may be spoken of upon an occasion of this kind: The first are those who, preeminent in their ability and industry, at an early period in their lives rise far above the ordinary practitioner and their names are inscribed upon the tablets of fame and the work that they do is enduring because of its benefit to the profession. The other class of men are those in general practice who seek no professional advancement, who live their lives in energy, industry, and in the honorable pursuit of their profession, doing that which comes to hand according to their best capacity and keeping always before them the obligation to their profession, their clients, and the courts. Such a man was Charles E. Flandrau. It has been well and truly said that the history of Minnesota, from territorial days down to the present time, would be wanting unless his career was read into each one of its pages.

His singular attribute was his devotion to duty; capable, honorable, and truthful, he took his duty as it came to him in every capacity of life, without any personal ambition to signalize himself beyond his fellow-citizens merely for ambition's sake. When public duties were presented to him he performed them and then passed the office to another. His professional duties were executed in the same way. His ear was ever open to the call of the humble and the oppressed; no man's cause was too small and no man's station too humble to receive from Judge Flandrau the very best and most complete consideration. He waited for no corporate retainers; he waited for no engagement in cases that would add to his fame. Always willing, always ready, he did his duty, as I said before, as it was presented to him, and it was complete in each case.

It has been well said of him by the learned Justice Nelson—and I concur from my own experience in the expression—that no man ever heard him make an unkind criticism or say an unkind word of any man.

To my mind Judge Flandrau was the most useful model to the ordinary member of the profession. In his career at the bar as well as upon the bench, he always was a model. His opinions, rendered in the early territorial days under the circumstances adverted to by Judge Atwater in his memorial, stand to-day as the law of this state, and at the present term of this court they are being cited in the briefs of counsel as the principles of law applicable to cases that are being presented to your Honors.

When I came to the bar of this state, Judge Flandrau was of course a senior member. He was a model then to the young practitioners, and the singular beauty and usefulness of his life were that during his entire career; and to myself since my admission to the bar in 1870 he was a model, and I always felt assured that in following his footsteps I was doing my duty to the courts, to my clients, and to my profession. May it please your Honors, the rain falls to-day softly and gently upon the grave of a man who all his life was just, and true, and honorable, and who carried out in his daily life and in everything that he did the new and great commandment of our Saviour: "Love ye one another."

Associate Justice Lovely said:

At a time when the Twin Cities were outposts on the confines of civilization and the great river at their feet that carries the commerce of many states upon its waters was the boundary of an unknown land, the subject of this memorial, richly endowed with the best learning of the schools of literature and law of the Empire State, sought the wilderness and here established his permanent home. He left behind him the blandishments of society, the association of cultured men and women among whom he could forecast a successful career, to gratify the independent aspirations of the pioneer, to build upon a new soil under new conditions a new commonwealth where the land of adoption should surpass the land of nativity as the place of liberty, fraternity, and equality, protected by the sanctions of justice and law. A half century has passed, and the dream of the pioneer has been eclipsed by reality. The wilderness has become a land of plenty, rich in the realization of the brightest hopes of the founders of the state, richer still in the golden opportunities for the future whose limitations no one may yet fix with certainty. It is now in the retrospect the distinctive merit that the subject of this memorial gave his services to secure these results to which his ability, energy, and character have largely contributed.

He chose the vocation of the law for his field of endeavor and was a faithful servant at her altar to the end. He held during the many years of his life various positions of public trust, but his best ideals were professional. Here his position was at once conceded and easily maintained while on the bench and afterwards during many years at the bar and until a few months before his death, when physical weakness forbade excessive labor that greatly taxed his strength and made his retirement a necessity. He went upon the bench of this court at its organization very early in life, at a time when many lawyers of his years were contending for recognition at the bar, and ably filled the position from 1838 to 1864, when he resigned.

The superior excellence of his opinions cannot now be questioned. They are a part of the judicial history of this country, displaying no unnecessary effort at embellishment, are clear, lucid, and erudite. At times they displayed a richness of imagination and warmth of feeling that made them eloquent, particularly where the rights of the person and the domestic ties were the subject of consideration.

Judge Flandrau was to some extent in after years inclined to speak lightly of his early judicial efforts, but a much higher judgment will be placed upon his accomplishments as a jurist by his critics, and without any detraction to his associates it must be said it was fortunate for the highest bench of this state that he was one of its earliest members.

A careful perusal of the decisions of this court while Judge Flandrau was on the bench cannot but excite the pride of the lawyers of the state who have occasion to refer to the precedents then established for future guidance. A new state with a new constitution furnished problems of difficulty that required independence of judgment, exalted ideals of duty permeated by a necessary judicial humility that should inspire the just judge. Judge Flandrau fulfilled these requirements and during this period on the bench exhibited these qualities to an eminent degree. Many of his opinions are still quotable and quoted to illustrate application of constitutional rights to legislative action and the restriction that the judicial power imposes in the adaptation of a new people to the progressive principles of jurisprudence.

If Judge Flandrau had not from experience acquired those resources that only long continued study and acquaintance with the authorities will bring, he was to an eminent degree possessed of a genius for judgment, the love of right, the consciousness that law was made for man, and that the men to whom it was to be applied and adapted were around him and devoted to new conditions and aspirations that could not be hampered or controlled by restrictions and limitations that had become effete and inappropriate to modern life.

When he retired from this court, he entered upon a long successful professional career that continued for many years. I first met Judge Flandrau in 1870, when I had occasion to appear in the Federal Court of this district and formed an acquaintance that continued until his death and was the recipient of many tokens of kindness that were so characteristic of himself and other members of the bar of the Capital City. As a lawyer he possessed a keen analytic mind, a painstaking capacity for research, and as a jury advocate he had no superior.

His considerate and courteous treatment of his opponents and associates at the bar when engaged in active practice was a part of the very nature and habit of the man, observed and appreciated by all. He was a paragon for imitation in this respect. His sterling integrity, his unblemished honor, were not and could not be questioned. His candor with the court was never affected by his zeal and earnestness as an advocate. He did much to establish the early reputation of the bar of the Capital City for its courteous and kindly treatment of the country lawyer, and his long service as a lawyer full of honor will be remembered with many kindly recollections by many of us who are past the meridian of life.

I do not think that Judge Flandrau ever said an unkind word of any man. He was firm in his convictions of political and moral duty, but he bestowed that charity upon the opinions and views of those with whom he differed that was characteristic of the great and generous heart that possessed the man and dictated his conduct.

The members of this bench cannot but feel deeply impressed by this occasion. The declining years of Judge Flandrau with the necessary results of his arduous labors had injured his health and made it necessary for him to retire from active practice two years before his death. The last occasion when he appeared in this court was at the close of an extended argument that he presented to the court; he then paused and said, "This is all I desire to suggest with reference to this case. I crave the indulgence of the court to refer to another matter. I have now been connected with this court as a member and practitioner at its bar for nearly fifty years, but my physician admonishes me that I must cease my active work in my profession. I have come to the stopping place. This is my last case. I give you my best wishes and bid a kindly good by."

It was an affecting occasion, unexpected but decidedly impressive and brought to every member of the court a feeling of deep and sincere regret. He then turned and left the room with that courtly air that always abided with him. We shall treasure his good wishes with unfeigned respect.

This was but a few short months ago, and now that he has gone to be numbered with the silent majority, we can truthfully say that his record is written in gold, not only upon the history of our court but in the hearts of its members and all good citizens.

He will surely receive his reward, and blessed be his memory.

Associate Justice Collins said:

The territory of Minnesota was noticeably fortunate in its pioneers, and of these, few there were who attained a higher place in the estimation of its citizens than Charles E. Flandrau. Coming to the territory in the year 1853 a young lawyer well educated in his chosen profession, his intellectual and moral worth and ability were so pronounced that they commanded immediate recognition first in Saint Paul and then in the valley of the Minnesota River, wherein he had subsequently located. He became at the outset one of the most prominent lawyers of that section, a representative citizen, and a noted political leader. In the fall of 1856 he was designated by the president as agent for the Sioux Indians, a tribe then occupying more or less of the southern half of the territory—a position of great trust and responsibility. May I become reminiscent enough to say that the first time I saw him was soon after this appointment, when with some twenty or more of his Indian wards mounted on ponies he rode into the little village in Dakota county in which I then resided. It was a particularly attractive body of men, clad in the rough garments of the frontier, buckskin shirts and leggings, bright colored handkerchiefs about their necks, gaudy sashes about their waists, some wearing slouch hats, but the greater number without head-covering except that provided by nature (always in abundance among the Indians). I remember that Agent Flandrau was browned by exposure to wind and sun to such an extent that he could hardly be distinguished from others of the party, some of [who] had white blood in their veins. But there was the magnificent figure, the intelligent face, and the courteous manner, always distinctive and attractive wherever he was placed. It is almost unnecessary to say that he was a very popular official with the Sioux and that his career as an agent was exceedingly satisfactory to the authorities at Washington.

But his term of service in this capacity was brief, for on the first Monday in June 1857, he was elected as a delegate to the constitutional convention, authorized, by congress to meet at Saint Paul in July following. It will be remembered that, upon meeting, the members of this body separated on political lines and that two conventions were held. In the Democratic, Judge Flandrau became a prominent factor in committee, in consultation, and in debate. These two bodies finally united and submitted but one constitution to the voters, which was adopted at an election held October 13. At the same time he was elected as one of the two associate justices of the Supreme Court for the new state, but pending formal admission of Minnesota into the Union, May 11, 1858, a vacancy occurred in the Territorial Supreme Court, and he was appointed to the place by President Buchanan. As an Associate Justice he presided once or twice in District Court—then a part of the duties of the Justices of the Supreme Court—but if he wrote any of the opinions of the court last mentioned they were not published. All of the work of that tribunal is found in the First Minnesota Report and the last opinion, being in the case of *Foster v. Bailey,* page 310 (436), was written by Associate Justice R. R. Nelson. To it Judge Flandrau added a few words of concurrence, his first and last utterance in that volume. His first opinion was a dissent from the conclusion reached by a majority of the state court in *Minnesota & Pacific Railroad Company v. H. H. Sibley, Governor,* 2 Minn. 1. It may not be necessary to remind those present that this case grew out of a difference of opinion between Governor Sibley and the railroad companies as to the requirements of the amendment of 1858 to section 10 of article 9 of the Constitution, authorizing the old bond issue. Two of the three Justices then composing the court determined that the deed of trust to the state to secure the payment of bonds to be issued by the companies need not give to it priority of lien upon the roads, lands, and franchises of the various companies for which the state became surety, while Justice Flandrau ably and forcibly expressed himself to the contrary, agreeing with the governor. His last opinion is found in the case of *Sons of Temperance v. Brown*, filed February 6, 1864, and reported in 9 Minn. 141 (151). His style of writing was vigorous and concise, and it is proper to say that the manner in which he performed his work is worthy of imitation, and he expressed his views clearly and lawyerlike, so that his opinions are models in style of composition.

In estimating his worth as a citizen and a public man and in assigning to him a place in the history of the territory and of the state, the fact that he was a pioneer in his youth must not be forgotten. The opportunities for all professional men were limited in the early days, and the higher standard that has since been reached was impossible. Social functions were of the free and easy style, and the daily life of the early settler was not always above just criticism. There was a tendency to conviviality—usually attractive to the young—and he who escaped contamination when confronted with such influences is to be congratulated and commended. Such a man was the subject of these remarks, and one who passes through years of such a life and emerges without stain or reproach as did Charles E. Flandrau must be of good fibre; he must be conscientious, fearless, honestly ambitious, and possessed of superior mental faculties. Not many men in the territory stood the test of frontier life as well as he did, and very few were accorded the sincere respect and esteem that were his—the tribute of all classes of men. He possessed the rare faculty of obtaining the good will and great esteem of all who knew him, without yielding to the vices, big and little, that prevailed in nearly all of the small communities then within our borders and that composed a population in the state of less than 173,000 in 1860.

He knew how to follow his own line of deportment far separated from that of many men with whom he associated without giving offense or securing their ill will, and this faculty was his all through life. His course of conduct from the first was of the highest type, independent but never perverse, dignified but always modest, courageous but never combative.

His literary ability was of a high order, but the demands of a large and successful law practice prevented its development to any great extent. He contributed several valuable papers to the Historical Society pertaining chiefly to his own experiences in Minnesota, and their worth will be the better appreciated as time passes on and with it his associates in laying the foundations of our state. I think his most pretentious work was a history of Minnesota that he dedicated as follows: "To the Old Settlers of Minnesota, who so wisely laid the foundation of our State upon the broad and enduring basis of freedom and toleration, this history is most gratefully and affectionately dedicated."

Not many of those referred to in those dedicatory words are entitled to more credit for their wisdom and work than was the author himself.

Reference has been made to his military life and service at the time of the Sioux outbreak in 1862. Although not under his command in those days, I personally knew of his courage and resourcefulness and here record my belief that of all the citizens who took up arms in defense of our frontier Charles E. Flandrau stood pre-eminent. It should also be recorded at this time, as a somewhat remarkable circumstance, that of his two associates in the Territorial Court in 1858—one, the Hon. R. R. Nelson, is still living and with us here today, while the two gentlemen who served with him in the State Supreme Court from May 1858 to July 1864, Chief Justice Lafayette Emmett and Associate Justice Isaac Atwater still survive, the former a resident of New Mexico, the latter of the city of Minneapolis.

Finally, let me say that a well conducted life, adorned by those deeds that are benefactions in all communities, abounding in honors and blessed to an unusual degree by the great affection and unbounded esteem of our citizens, has come to an end, and there has gone out into the Unknown a beloved citizen, an upright and capable public official, and a gracious and graceful gentleman. We know that the eternal Peace that is assured to God's noblemen is his.

Chief Justice Charles M. Start then said:

Some one has said: "The worth of a civilization is the worth of the man at its center." If this be true, and it is, then it is also true that the greatness of a state depends very largely upon the character of her pioneers. Minnesota, in this respect, was exceptionally fortunate. Her pioneers were as a rule masterful men who believed and practiced the gospel of self-reliance and honor. They were self-sacrificing and patriotic. They heroically struggled with the savage and the wilderness to build upon broad and enduring foundations a commonwealth dedicated to the cause of liberty and justice for all men. They wisely organized and faithfully fostered the educational and charitable institutions of the state. They sowed the seed that we might reap. Theirs was the toil, ours the fruitage. What manner of men they were you may judge from the venerable few who are still with us, loved and honored by all.

Judge Flandrau in this great work of building the state bore a conspicuous and honorable part. He was one of the great leaders in the work, and the political, military, and judicial history of the state cannot be impartially written without a record of his life and public services. In his death the state he loved and served so well mourns the loss of a well beloved and most illustrious citizen. [89 Minn. xxi]

Lafayette Emmett

1822–1906
Chief Justice, 1858–1865

On the afternoon of December 4, 1906, in the court room at the State Capitol, Hon. Thomas Wilson addressed the Supreme Court then in session and said:

The undersigned, committee of the members of this bar, beg leave to present the following memorial and to ask that it be accepted by this Court and incorporated into its minutes:

The Honorable Lafayette Emmett, the first Chief Justice of this Court, died at Santa Fe, New Mexico, on the tenth day of August last and was buried at Faribault in this state on the twenty-ninth day of October. He was born in Ohio in 1822 and lived in that state until he came to the Territory of Minnesota in 1851. He was admitted to the bar in the State of Ohio in 1848 and entered upon the practice of his profession in the City of Mount Vernon, where he was married in 1849 to Elizabeth Ball. His wife died while he lived in Faribault as below stated, and of the nine children born to them but two are living—Mary, the wife of John C. Pichon, who resides in Boston, Massachusetts, and Carrie, the wife of Miguel Otero, of New Mexico, who resides in and for two terms was Governor of that Territory. Soon after Judge Emmett came to Minnesota, he formed a partnership with the late H. L. Moss for the practice of the law and as a member of that firm continued to practice his profession in this city until he was elected Chief Justice in 1857. He held the office of Chief Justice until 1865. He removed from St. Paul to the city of Faribault in 1872 and lived in the latter city until 1878, when he removed to Ortonville in this state. From Ortonville about the year 1885, he went to New Mexico, where he continued to live until the time of his death.

He was a man of good character, good education, and of exceptionally fine presence and engaging manners, and, as the reports of his judicial opinions show, of much more than ordinary ability. Nature endowed him with those attributes that would have enabled him by diligence had it been his ambition to take a very high stand in the practice of his profession.

Thomas Wilson
W. P. Murray
Harvey Officer

Judge Wilson also said:

I have very little that I wish to say. I had the pleasure of knowing Chief Justice Emmett, as I was a little while on this bench with him. I knew him then and knew him for a little while after. Soon after leaving the bench he ceased to be much known in this state as he did not take much part either in the practice of his profession or publicly at all. He was a man of a great deal more than ordinary ability, and, as this paper says, a man of very exceptional attractive characteristics and personality. The only comment adverse to Judge Emmett that could be made would be that he was a little inclined to be indolent. Had he done his best he would have been a man of mark. He was, however, a man of mark, taking into account his personality, his accomplishments, and his ability.

Hon. Harvey Officer then said:

I was introduced to Lafayette Emmett and to Henry L. Moss, his then law partner, by Capt. Alexander Wilkin, in the month of June 1855; and from that date until Judge Emmett left the state, my professional and personal relations with him were close and intimate.

From 1855 until Judge Emmett became Chief Justice of this Court in 1858, he was recognized and esteemed as one of the leaders of the bar of this Court and of Ramsey County, successfully competing with such lawyers as William Hollinshead, Horace R. Bigelow, John B. Brisbin, George L. Otis, Henry J. Horn,

M. E. Ames, John M. Gilman, John B. Sanborn, and many others of marked ability and reputation.

As a lawyer Judge Emmett was neither aggressive nor forceful, excelling rather as a counsellor in the office than as an advocate in jury work; but whether before the court or jury, he was always calm, self-possessed, deliberate and scholarly, commanding the respect of the court and winning the love of his associates at the bar by his uniform courtesy and his most attractive personality.

Judge Emmett was a man given to hospitality in its largest sense. His old home still stands on West Seventh Street in this city; it was one of the mansions of Territorial days. While he was Chief Justice, on Monday of each alternate week during the winter session of this Court and the session of the Legislature, he and his family opened their home to all their many friends without formal invitation; and all comers were received with a hearty and generous welcome. Such entertainments were possible in those days, but would not be practicable now under existing conditions; and they were occasions not to be forgotten by the few surviving old residents of the state.

The later days of Judge Emmett's residence in St. Paul were clouded by the long continued sickness of certain members of his family, but he always retained the love and respect of his many friends as an accomplished and upright gentleman.

I owe to him and his then associates on the bench my appointment as Reporter of this Court; and I esteem it as a duty, as well as a privilege, to second the motion to spread the memorial offered by your Committee, on the records of this Honorable Court.

Justice Jaggard, in behalf of the court, then said:

It accords with recognized propriety and honored custom that your memorial should become a public record.

On February 26, 1857, Congress passed an act authorizing the Territory of Minnesota to hold a constitutional convention. The election of members for that convention, held on June 1, 1857, resulted in so close a division of votes between the Republican and Democratic delegates that each party held a separate convention. By means of conference committees, however, they united in one document. That constitution was submitted to the vote of the people October 13, 1857, and was adopted almost unanimously. The constitution thus adopted was approved by the federal congress May 11, 1858. Section 16 of article 15 of that constitution provided for an election of all state officers at the time of voting upon the adoption of the constitution.

Lafayette Emmett was the logical candidate of the Democratic party for chief justice of the supreme court. He had been the attorney general of the territory from 1853 to 1858. He had appeared in the interests of the city of St. Paul in the litigation consequent upon the act of Joe Rolette in disappearing with the enrolled bill changing the place of government to St. Peter. Judge Nelson, then on the second circuit, had issued a writ of mandamus to Governor Medary and the territorial officers to compel their removal to St. Peter, at the instance of A. F. Howes, president of the St. Peter Land Company. Judge Chatfield appeared for the complainant, Emmett for the officers. Judge Nelson held that the law on file, not being the original bill, was invalid, and St. Paul remained the territorial capital.

Judge Emmett's nomination for chief justice, occasioned by these and other political and personal circumstances, was largely due to the active part he had taken in the debates and proceedings of the Democratic branch of that convention. He was there recognized as a man of broad opinions in harmony with prevailing views and with a capacity for their forcible presentation. More particularly the controversy whether the judiciary should be elective or appointive was prolonged and lively. The report of the committee on the judicial department provided that the governor should nominate and, by and with the advice and consent of the senate, appoint the supreme judges. Mr. Emmett moved a substitute, providing for the election of the judges of the supreme court by the electors of the state for the term of seven years. Mr. Sherburne actively opposed the elective judiciary. He was supported by Mr. Meeker, who said, inter alia: "I contend that the judges who are elected are elected by parties and are the mere fuglemen of caucuses. The best trickster or the best manager of caucuses is just as likely to be the nominee of the party as the most learned man of the nation." Mr. Emmett, replying, said inter alia: "We hear a great deal of talk about an independent judiciary. The phrase is in everybody's mouth. What does it mean? Independent of whom? Independent of what? Independent of the people? Sir, I say to the gentleman who was last up (Mr. Meeker) that out of his own mouth I propose to condemn him . . . Sir, if the people are incapable of selecting their judges, they are also incapable of selecting the man who is to appoint the judges. I think the facts will show that the people are much better qualified to select your judges than is the governor. The governor always selects men belonging to his own political party, while the people often select them regardless of parties." The principle of his amendment was adopted.

On May 24, 1858, all state officers elected in the previous October entered upon their respective duties as the first officers of the State of Minnesota. The first supreme court of the State of Minnesota was composed of Lafayette Emmett, chief justice, and Isaac Atwater and Charles E. Flandrau, justices. In 1864, Justices Atwater and Flandrau resigned. S. J. R. McMillan and Thomas Wilson were appointed to fill the vacancies. Chief Justice Emmett served until January 10, 1865, when he was succeeded as chief justice by Thomas Wilson.

The first opinion of Chief Justice Emmett was in *Minnesota & Pacific Railroad Co. v. Sibley,* 2 Minn. 1 (13), granting an application to the court for a writ of mandamus requiring the governor, Henry H. Sibley, to issue state bonds in aid of railways. This beginning of this historic litigation received the sanction of a bare majority of the court. Judge Flandrau dissented. The last opinion of Chief Justice Emmett was *Armstrong v. Hinds,* 9 Minn. 341 (356),

The court as originally constituted prepared opinions in the following number: Flandrau, 217; Atwater, 158; Emmett, 112. After the retirement of the other justices, Chief Justice Emmett handed down twelve more opinions. He dissented in thirty-six of these cases, in twenty-six instances without opinion. Judge Flandrau dissented nine times, and Judge Atwater eight times. In the seven years of the chief justice's services he handed down 124 opinions, or about 17 in one year. It is interesting, in this connection, to note the growth of the work of this court. Its maximum was probably reached in 1895, when the number of cases amounted to 695, or 139 to each judge. During the nineteen years of Judge Mitchell's service, he wrote more than 1,500 opinions and averaged approximately eighty opinions in a year, about the number of opinions now prepared each year by each member of the present court. That is to say, Justice Mitchell wrote about as many opinions in a year and a half as Chief Justice Emmett in seven years.

His opinions were marked by the same sound common sense that in his first opinion in this court he recognized as the basis of the interpretation of legal instruments. Of necessity they rested upon principle rather than upon authority. Not only were library facilities limited at a time antecedent to the present plethoric growth of legal literature, but also many of the questions were new in themselves. The reports of this period abound in cases of first impression. The municipal code of the state was in its literal infancy. A very large proportion of his decisions, in some volumes amounting to seventy-five percent, were made without the citation of any authority whatever. For example *Camp v. Smith,* 2 Minn. 131 (155), established the right of a pre-emptor to transfer his interest in land. This principle, now so familiar and indisputable, was determined purely upon principle and without reference to any adjudication.

With the embryonic condition of the laws and of all state constitutions at that time, we are all familiar. It is, however, somewhat of a surprise to have occasion to realize how young, indeed, was the entire nation. For example, at that time, in the city of St. Paul, Judge Emmett's brother, as the author of both words and music, directed the singing for the first time of a song that has become the national hymn of a great part of this republic; that song was "Dixie."

The historical record here made serves in a measure to preserve alike the personal worth and the public services of those great men who laid the foundations of this commonwealth. To such statesmanship, the judgments of all men have always without dissent accorded high praise. The philosopher and historian Hume has thus expressed that universal opinion: "Of all men that distinguish themselves by memorable achievements, the first place of honor seems due to . . . the founders of states who transmit a system of laws and institutions to secure the peace, happiness and liberty of future generations." The founders of the government of this state are, however, entitled to peculiar honor because of the circumstances under which they labored, of the spirit of devotion to duty with which they wrought, and of the merits of the results they attained.

They were confronted by all the difficulties arising from diverse factions and opposing local interests usual in the beginnings of any government. They were also face to face with problems peculiar to sparse populations, newly scattered through primeval forests and unbroken prairies, where they were exposed to a severity of climate more merciful than the malignant enmity of valiant, persistent, and cunning aborigines. Moreover, this was at a time when the destiny of the entire nation was unfixed and unknowable and when the certain vision of the tragedies of the approaching crisis fitted them least for the cold deliberation and clear thinking so essential to their titanic task. The chronicles of the struggles of opposing parties contain no record more honorable in itself nor involving a nobler subjection of partisan advantage to public weal than is to be found in the production by two hostile political conventions of one constitution embodying the highest principles of both factions of honest and intense men and providing a just basis for the jurisprudence of this state for all time to come. With the abiding efficiency and practical excellence of their colossal work, the unrealizing world is daily made familiar, but it is prone to forget the self sacrifice, the prescience, the faith and the patriotism, the unswerving worship of ideals and the exalted wisdom and virtue of the pioneer founders of this state.

Accordingly, with a due appreciation of the gratitude due to lofty and unselfish achievements of the founders of this state and of the justice of your tributes to the one-time member of this court, "the door of whose mind has been closed on earth to open to the dawn beyond the tomb," it is now directed that your memorials be inscribed on the records of this court, there to remain as a lasting annal of his worthy life and public usefulness. [97 Minn. xxvii]

Isaac Atwater

1818–1906
Associate Justice, 1858–1864

On the afternoon of April 3, 1907, in the court room at the State Capitol, Hon. Daniel Fish, in behalf of the Minnesota State Bar Association, addressed the Supreme Court, then in session, and said:

The thirteenth day of October next will be the fiftieth anniversary of the election whereby the people of Minnesota Territory adopted a constitution preparatory to admission into the Union. On the same day they chose from their number three eminent citizens to constitute the first supreme court of the new commonwealth. Today, near the close of a half century of statehood, the bar of that court presents, for incorporation in its records, a brief commemorative notice of one of those pioneer justices, the last to pass from earth of a distinguished triumvirate. But three and a half years have elapsed since a like service was performed for the first of them, Judge Flandrau, when an eloquent tribute to his memory was read at this bar from the pen of the last survivor whose death we now deplore. In the meantime Lafayette Emmett, the first chief justice, departed this life, and he, with Justices Clark and Buck of later times and Judge Nelson, the first occupant of our federal bench, have all been commemorated here. And now George B. Young, once a member of this court and but yesterday the peerless leader of our bar, has passed away. Of the six former chief justices but one survives, Thomas Wilson, still in full practice. Of fourteen associate justices (not counting Judge Wilson who served in both capacities) but four remain and they of the more recent. All the territorial justices are gone and nearly all of the earlier practitioners.

Fifty years are but few in the life of a state, yet already the age of tradition is upon us; the story of our bench and bar begins to take on the soft haze of antiquity.

I am asked to read the following inadequate sketch of Judge Atwater's career and to move that it be entered in the minutes of the court:

Born at Homer, Cortland County, New York, Isaac Atwater, son of Ezra and Esther (Learning) Atwater, grew up amid the wholesome conditions of a farmer's life. Both parents were natives of Connecticut, the father certainly, and probably the mother also, being of English extraction. The rural schools of the neighborhood until the age of sixteen, afterward a seminary at Cazenovia and the academy at Homer, prepared their son for college. Entering Yale at twenty-two and supporting himself there mainly by his own efforts, he was graduated in 1844. After a year of teaching and eighteen months of study in the Law School at Yale, he went to New York. There pursuing a further course of preparation, he was admitted to the bar, beginning his practice in that city in 1848. The following year he was married to Permelia A. Sanborn, of Geddes, New York, and with her removed soon after to St. Anthony, now a part of Minneapolis, settling there in October 1850. His wife and three of the four children born of the marriage preceded him to the grave. John B. Atwater, Esq., of the Hennepin bar, is the surviving son.

Judge Atwater was very prominent from the beginning, not only in professional life but in all that concerned the interests of his adopted home. He edited and for a time owned the "St. Anthony Express," the first newspaper of his town and the first to be issued in the territory outside of St. Paul. As member and secretary of its first board of regents, he helped to establish the University of Minnesota. He delivered the first Independence Day oration, lectured in the early courses given by the Library Association, and was the first initiate member of the local Masonic lodge. In 1852 he was an incorporator of the company that erected the first bridge that ever spanned the Mississippi and later joined in the formation and management of the Minneapolis & St. Louis Railroad Company. He was among the first to acquire land west of the river, where the main city of Minneapolis now stands, and was one of the first aldermen of that city and a member of its first board of education. He reported the decisions of the territorial supreme court rendered in 1852 and in 1853 was elected prosecuting attorney of his county. For many years he was president of the local board of trade and always was a leader in the affairs of the Episcopal church, in whose faith he lived and died. Thus in all the activities of those formative days, Isaac Atwater discharged to the full every duty of citizenship.

It was but natural that a trained and successful lawyer who had evinced also great capacity and zeal in public affairs should be chosen by the people, at their first opportunity, to high judicial office. A self-governing community is best studied in its laws and in the character of the men selected to construe and apply them. Minnesota was most fortunate in that the foundations of her jurisprudence were laid by such men as Emmett, Flandrau, and Atwater—men of the people familiar with their struggles, in sympathy with their aspirations, yet instructed in the mistakes of the past and in the principles whereby like errors may be shunned. For more than six years, viz: from May 34, 1858, to July 6, 1864, Judge Atwater sat in this honored tribunal, meagerly compensated, money wise, excluded from the activities so alluring to one of his ardent nature, often misunderstood of course, yet patiently, justly, and wisely fulfilling the exalted duties of an appellate judge in a new commonwealth destined to have a large part in the nation's history.

The opinions written by him, 158 in number, appear in volumes 2 to 9, inclusive, of the Minnesota Reports, the last in *Martin v. Hurlbut*, 9 Minn. 133 (142). Most of these were cases of first impression, and nearly all have been cited many times. They exhibit easy command of legal principles, remarkable facility and dignity of expression, sound judicial reasoning, and a keen sense of justice. The bar of today can with difficulty appreciate the careful labor that settled the practice and procedure now so familiar, the thoroughness of that pioneer work which enables the present court to dispatch its vastly increased business; nor, indeed, do we often realize how completely in this jurisdiction the reproach of "the law's delay" is obviated.

Impelled by the need of ampler incomes, the two associate justices resigned their seats in July 1864 to resume the practice. For a short while they were partners at Carson City, Nevada, but Judge Atwater did not remove his family thither nor give up his residence here. Both returned in the fall of 1866 and continued their partnership in Minneapolis. Upon the removal of Judge Flandrau to St. Paul in 1871, the senior remained and with associates and alone conducted for many years a lucrative practice. Gradually his private concerns and his unceasing interest in the public welfare came to afford him sufficient employment. Fortunately he was able to retire seasonably from exacting professional labors. But he was never idle. Hours that to other men would have been hours of leisure were devoted by him to the preparation of a full history of his town and county, volumes that no one else could have written, source-books for later annalists. Advancing age brought on the inevitable infirmities. His last years were years of bodily weakness, but his mind was alert to the end. Bereaved of wife and children, he yet remained genial, interested, hopeful; bent by the weight of nearly ninety years, he peacefully laid down a life filled with good works.

This scant memorial but faintly suggests the value of such a life or our sense of loss in its passing. We can only hope that in future times some appreciative eye scanning the page on which it is inscribed may discern therein more than is formally set down.

Daniel Fish

Henry G. Hicks

Harvey Officer

Hon. Harvey Officer then said:

I am glad of the privilege of seconding the motion to spread the Memorial on the minutes of the court, and I am glad to join in the memorial on behalf of Judge Atwater not only as a representative of the State Bar Association and one of its committee but also as a member of the bar of Ramsey county. For in the time between 1855 and 1858 and before Judge Atwater was elevated to this bench, his was a familiar figure as well in the territorial supreme court as in the district court of Ramsey county. In fact his circuit might be said to extend from St. Cloud on the north to Winona on the south, throughout the then central part of the territory.

While he was on the bench it was the duty of the reporter of this court to prepare the syllabi of its decisions, but those syllabi, before they went to print, were always submitted to the judge who wrote the opinion for his correction and revision, to the end that they might reflect in as few words as possible the gist of the decision. This duty was always performed by Judge Atwater with the greatest care, and that work established between the members of the court and its officer, the reporter, that personal relation that necessarily must exist between the court and its reporter.

After Judge Atwater returned from Nevada and resumed practice in this state, he was well known in this court and in the lower courts of that state. There are two cases in particular to which I might call attention that reflect his ability as a lawyer. I refer to the two cases of *Atwater v. Russell,* reported in the Forty-ninth, the one involving the construction of the will of Mr. Martin, the old-time friend and client of Judge Atwater, and the other involving the construction of a trust deed executed by Mr. Martin, both of which documents, as I understand, were the professional work of Judge Atwater. Both involved the construction of devises and legacies for charitable purposes, a grant under the deed of trust for similar purposes, and in that connection the construction of the then somewhat crude law of the state on the subject of uses and trusts. If the court will notice those two cases of *Atwater v. Russell,* it will find that there were very few notations of cases in the supreme court of this state. There are only five or six cases noted, among them the case of *Simpson v. Cook,* but the inspiration of the attorneys involved in the discussion of it and of the court was necessarily derived from the decisions of the English Court of Chancery and from the decisions of the courts of New York and Massachusetts and the older states. Therefore those two cases may be called the initial cases involving the construction of chari-

table gifts under deed or will for charitable purposes in this state and in cases of that class that have arisen since they have generally been quoted and referred to with approval, notably in the recent case of *Watkins v. Bigelow*, reported in the Ninety-third.

Judge Atwater as a lawyer, as well on this bench as in the district in which he practised and in Ramsey largely, always commanded the confidence and the respect of the court, and his genial manner endeared him to his associates at the bar.

For ten or twelve years prior to his death I was closely associated with him in certain classes of church work. For several years past that work was necessarily done at his office, where he had to be carried in a push-cart. We met him at his office when he was able to be there, or if he possibly could not be there by reason of his physical infirmity, we met him at the bedside in his hotel. He was always present at an appointment of that kind, always alert, active, and intelligent in the discharge of his duties.

While acting with him I became aware of the generous gifts that he made in a most unostentatious way, not only to the church of his choice but to other benevolent associations and corporations and to individuals in the city where he lived. Very few knew of the nature and the extent or the generosity of his benefactions in that direction.

His was an inestimable character worthy of emulation as a lawyer by all the bar and as a high-minded, noble gentleman. I second the motion.

Associate Justice Elliott [in behalf of the court] then said:

The Memorial that has been presented by your committee expresses in appropriate form the virtues, abilities, and traits of character of Judge Atwater that entitle him to the respect of the bench, bar, and people of this state, and they will be spread upon the records of the court in which he served with honor to himself and to the state. Although but recently deceased, Judge Atwater belonged to a generation that has about passed into history, a generation that founded the commonwealth of Minnesota. It is fitting and proper that we should honor in all appropriate ways these pioneers in jurisprudence and state building. Their work was well done and will endure while the records of history are preserved. I think it is generally conceded that Minnesota was fortunate in the character of its early judges. They were, without exception, men of character, ability, and adequate learning in the law. May we always and on every proper occasion acknowledge the debt we owe to the men who laid the safe foundations upon which their successors have erected the great state of the present time.

Judge Atwater was the last survivor of the original supreme court of the state. He left the bench of that court in 1864 and retired from active life nearly a generation ago. I doubt whether he was personally known to any of the present members of the court, but his judicial record is well known and appreciated. It is found in Volumes 2 to the Reports and compares creditably with that of his associates and successors. In the building of the Temple of Law Judge Atwater had an honorable part. His work bears the stamp of industry and care and is marked by an evident desire to do justice between the litigants. He took his high duties seriously and sought to fulfill them in the spirit of the just judge of whom it was said: "When he goeth up to the judgment seat, he putteth on righteousness as a glorious and beautiful robe to render his tribunal a fit emblem of that eternal throne of which justice and mercy are the habitation." [99 Minn. xvi]

Thomas Wilson

1827–1910
Associate Justice, 1864–1865; Chief Justice, 1865–1869

On the afternoon of June 10, 1910, in the court room at the State Capitol, Charles W. Bunn, Esq., chairman of the committee appointed to draft a memorial of Honorable Thomas Wilson, a former Associate and Chief Justice of the Court, addressed the Supreme Court, then in session, and presented the following memorial with the recommendation for such disposition thereof as is customary.:

The Hon. Thomas Wilson, once Associate Justice and the second Chief Justice of this Court, died in St. Paul on the third day of April last. His eminent services to the people of Minnesota, as a justice of the Court, as a legislator, and as a lawyer, make it fit that a record be made of those services.

Judge Wilson was born in County Tyrone, Ireland, May 16, 1827. When twelve years old he emigrated with his parents, who settled on a farm in Venango county, Pennsylvania, where Thomas lived, alternating working on the farm and attending the common school until he was twenty. He then entered Allegheny College, graduating in 1852. Then commencing the study of law in Meadville, Pennsylvania, he was there admitted to the bar in 1855. Two months later he removed to the territory of Minnesota, where he commenced his professional life at Winona. He was a member of the Constitutional Convention of 1857 and in the fall of that year became District Judge of the Third District, which office he held for six years. He was appointed by the Governor an Associate Justice of this Court and in the subsequent autumn, 1864, was elected Chief Justice. This office he held for four years and a half, resigning in July 1869 to resume practice. He was a member of the House of Representatives of the State in 1880–1881 and of the State Senate in 1883–1885. In 1881 he was the Democratic nominee for United States Senate and declined a nomination to Congress in 1884. In 1886 he was elected to Congress, where he served one term. In 1890 he was the candidate of the Democratic party for Governor of Minnesota.

In the autumn of 1892 Judge Wilson was appointed General Counsel of the Chicago, St. Paul, Minneapolis & Omaha Railway Company and thereafter lived in St. Paul, active in professional duties up to the very day of his death. In 1891 he received the degree of LL.D. from Allegheny College and the same degree from Macalester College in 1892.

For fifty-five years he was prominent in the affairs of Minnesota, standing in the foremost rank of the legal profession of the state. During much of this time he commanded an unsurpassed clientage and was engaged in much of the most important litigation. A sound constitution and abstemious habits extended his active and useful life beyond the ordinary. Exemplary living preserved his health and physical and mental faculties unimpaired to the end. And without exaggeration it may be said that every day of his long life in Minnesota produced fruits of his unflagging industry.

Good mental and physical equipment was in Judge Wilson supplemented by remarkable industry, capacity for work, tenacity of purpose, and loyalty to his clients. But he was more than a judge and lawyer; he was a loyal and generous friend, a good neighbor, and good citizen. He was more than a student of the law and an advocate for his clients; he was a lover of justice, considered much the public good, and stood for that even against the interest of clients.

Charles W. Bunn
L. L. Brown
W. W. Billson

William D. Mitchell
John Lind
William E. Hale
Charles C. Willson
James B. Sheean,
                    Committee

William D. Mitchell, Esq., then addressed the Court and said:

An intimate friendship for over half a century between Thomas Wilson and those near to me gave me the privilege of a close association with him. That association was of as intimate a nature as is possible where great disparity in age exists, and while my own capacity to truly judge his qualities has been limited to the closing period of his life, I feel that the lifelong and beautiful friendship that endured between Judge Wilson and the late Justice Mitchell makes fitting that some expression should be made by a member of my family.

The final impression left by Judge Wilson is that of distinct individuality. He was a most unusual man, unusual in more separate respects than any man within my knowledge. He belonged to none of the types in which we are accustomed to classify our acquaintances, and those who knew him best will agree that they have never known and do not expect to know any man who remotely resembles him.

It is appropriate that I should speak only of a few of his personal qualities. As a young man what at first struck me most forcibly was that there seemed an absence from his life of recreation. He had no taste for hunting, fishing, or either outdoor or indoor sports of any kind. He went rarely to the theatre; he had no small vices or amusements; he never played cards or used tobacco and took no interest in any of the pastimes or playthings to which men of his class usually turn for recreation. His life was absolutely devoted to his family, his professional work, his books, and the society of his friends. The whole of his tremendous energy was turned in these directions, and in them he found his pleasure and recreation. His devotion to his wife and only daughter, when living, and to their memories after their death, was refined and beautiful, and his high ideal of the domestic relations was one of his most striking qualities. His conduct of life and habits

of thought and speech were as pure as crystal. He was as modest as a woman. His loyalty to and activity for his friends was intense, and while it was inevitable that a man of his temperament should have enemies, it will be found that they were chiefly made in the causes of his friends, an injury to whom he often remembered long after the friend himself had forgotten or forgiven. His private papers have disclosed what was never published by him, that he has in years past given a respectable fortune to objects of charity and friends in need.

He always retained a strong liking for and loyalty to those of his own nationality, and the possession of Irish blood was no mean advantage to any one seeking his aid. He was fond of books and had the social instinct developed to a high degree. He liked people and enjoyed being with them, especially if he was entertaining them.

The qualities of which I speak are necessarily the possession of one who is capable of writing such a beautiful, sincere, and touching tribute as Judge Wilson presented to this Court on the occasion of the death of his lifelong friend and companion.

It is difficult to believe that a man who took a leading part in the constitutional convention of 1857 and who was Chief Justice of this Court in 1864 was not only active but effective in the practice of his profession until some few weeks ago. It is ten years since he presented to this Court his parting tribute to his oldest and best friend. He was then seventy-four years of age. His beloved wife and daughter had gone before and now his friend as well. That address breathes the thought of one who finds himself alone and sees the shadows deepening around him. It was the speech of a man who felt that life had nothing more to hold for him, and yet for ten long years afterwards, with sadness in his heart but with all his old dauntless and cheerful courage, he lived his life as he had always lived it. And what a wonderful old man he was! What courage, what industry, what a fighting spirit he possessed, and yet what gentle modesty and purity of heart and mind! It has been a great privilege to know him, and it is a great privilege to have this opportunity to speak from the heart what as between men often remains unspoken.

Hon. Charles C. Willson, then addressed the Court and said:

51

I have known Judge Wilson fifty-odd years since 1856. I shall speak of him plainly, as he would have me do it.

Hon. Thomas Wilson was the second Chief Justice of this Court. He succeeded Honorable Lafayette Emmett, January 10, 1865, and presided a few days over four and a half years. He was a practical man of affairs, keen to discern and sure to disregard adulation and flattery. Had he arranged the presentation of our memorial, he would have admonished us in the language of Othello: "Speak of me as I am; nothing extenuate, nor set down aught in malice." Hence the plain directness of what I intend to say in support of the motion of our chairman.

Hon. Thomas Wilson was born May 16, 1827, Tyrone county, northern Ireland. He came with his parents in 1838 to Venango county, western Pennsylvania. There he spent his youth, a farmer's son on the banks of the Allegheny. At Meadville, in the adjoining county in 1852 he graduated from a Methodist Episcopal school, Allegheny College, and in February 1855, was admitted to the Pennsylvania bar. Three months later he came to Winona, Minnesota, and entered into partnership with M. Wheeler Sargeant from Franklin county, northern Vermont. Sargeant was a land surveyor as well as lawyer and came to Minnesota in 1854 in the employ of William Ashley Jones, who had a contract with the Secretary of the Interior to survey public lands in the vicinity of Winona.

In 1856 William Windom, a young lawyer from Knox county in central Ohio, was admitted to the firm, and its name became Sargeant, Windom & Wilson. The United States land office for the sale of public lands in southern Minnesota north of Township 104 was located at Winona, and the law practice of the firm was largely in controversies between settlers before the register and receiver of this land office. The business of the firm was not wholly professional. They ventured into speculation in lands and town lots and were caught in the financial revulsion of 1857. Wilson early foresaw the probable extent of the disaster. He dissolved the partnership, paid his third of the liabilities, got release from the residue, and remained solvent. The others were more confident and less fortunate.

At the election of delegates to the constitutional convention, which convened July 15, 1857, Thomas Wilson was elected on the Republican ticket from Winona county. Ex-Governor of the territory Willis A. Gorman was elected on the Democratic ticket from Ramsey county. Each party claimed to have elected a majority of the members of the convention. Each party organized a convention, and both were anxious to have the territory admitted as a state. A conference was agreed upon, to which each party sent five of its members. Wilson was one on the Republican side and Gorman on the Democratic. Wilson said in the conference there were some men there in whom he had no confidence, personally or politically. Gorman asked if he applied that remark to him, and Wilson said he did. Whereupon Gorman struck him violently with his cane, breaking it over his head. Others interfered, and the parties were separated. The Democrats excused Gorman by saying Wilson was highly provocative and too loquacious. But the Republicans claimed the incident to be a local repetition of the then recent attack in Congress of Brooks upon Senator Sumner and signified their approval of Wilson by nominating him for Judge of the Third Judicial District, the district then embracing the five southeastern counties. His Irish birth attracted his countrymen, who were mostly Democrats, and he was elected, although the three Democratic nominees for the Supreme Court had majorities in the district and were elected.

Judge Wilson presided in the district for six years with general satisfaction. Some of us, the younger practitioners, if beaten, thought the elderly lawyers won from age and condescension and not on the merits, and we sometimes appealed to this court with success. During those six years twenty-five appeals from decisions in that district were taken. Fifteen of them were reversed. But this is no decisive test of the ability of a judge. Honorable William Mitchell, while on the same district bench, was, on appeal, often reversed, but the fame he subsequently acquired while a member of this Court is known wherever the Minnesota Reports are studied.

In 1864 the two Associate Justices of this Court resigned, and the Governor appointed District Judges Wilson and McMillan in their stead. In November of that year Justice Wilson was the candidate for Chief Justice on the Republican ticket and was elected. His judicial opinions written while on this bench appear in Volumes 9 to 14 inclusive, of the Reports. On July 14, 1869, he resigned this high office, and Honorable James Gilfillan was appointed in his stead.

It was surmised at the time, in the profession, that the Chief Justice became ambitious of a more active political career, thought that the isolated and exacting duties of a judicial station were unsuited to his temperament, that he was better equipped for legislative or executive office, and that he acted on such conviction.

He resumed the practice of law at Winona and obtained throughout the state great celebrity as an able lawyer and an artful advocate. He won many important cases. An example of his untiring persistence and his sagacity is seen in the Reports of the case of the City of Winona against Horace Thompson and Minnesota Railway Construction Company, reported at different stages in 24 Minn. 199, 25 Minn. 328, 27 Minn. 415, 29 Minn. 68, and 93 U.S. 612. By this litigation he relieved the city of Winona from the payment of its bonds for one hundred thousand dollars, issued in aid of the construction of a railroad with truss bridge at that point across the Mississippi river.

In 1872 Judge Wilson, becoming estranged from the Republican party on account of its reconstruction measures and its protective tariff legislation, joined the movement for the election of Horace Greeley as President and thereafter affiliated politically with the Democrats.

In November 1882 he was elected on the Democratic ticket from the Winona District to the state senate and served one term. In November 1886 he was elected by the same party to the federal congress and served two years. In 1890 he was the Democratic nominee for Governor but was defeated by Honorable William R. Merriam by the small plurality of 2,267 votes. Meantime the immigration of Norsemen was unprecedented, and practically they all joined without further inquiry the party of Lincoln that had abolished slavery. Judge Wilson found that for political success he should have suppressed his convictions on federal policy and remained a Republican. His integrity forbade him such betrayal of his convictions.

He removed to St. Paul in 1892 and became the chief counsel of the Chicago, St. Paul, Minneapolis & Omaha Railway Company. He served it in that capacity to its entire satisfaction to the time of his death.

He was a moral, upright, and honest man. He had a vigorous constitution and by exercise and a plain diet he enjoyed robust health throughout his long life. The younger men of the profession can discern, if they will, in the story of his life the wisdom of refusing office. Join the party of your choice, take part in shaping its policy, and advocate its principles before the people, but beware its offices and honors. Uninterrupted devotion to your profession will, in nearly every instance, bring greater rewards and a happier life.

Richard L. Kennedy, Esq., then addressed the Court as follows:

While concurring fully in all that has been said and passing over without further comment Judge Wilson's remarkably successful professional and political career, I desire to emphasize his private life—honorable and without a flaw—that he was an ideally devoted husband and father and a royal friend. What I have said as to his private life can be attested by all those here today.

Of his family life, I know little personally, as I became intimately acquainted with him after the death of his immediate family. I have been informed of it, however, by those who knew him intimately during that entire period, and their testimony is unanimous—without a dissenting voice.

That he was a royal friend I can attest, and all who knew him best and enjoyed his friendship will join with me in paying him this tribute.

Underlying it all was a deep and keen sense of honor and justice, which was the keynote of his character.

Chief Justice Start then said:

It was my privilege to know Judge Wilson for more than forty-six years, and I can bear witness to the justice of your eloquent memorial. He was a masterful man, of pure life and high ideals. He leaves behind him the memory of a great lawyer, an able and just judge, and a good man. It is therefore fitting that your memorial should be entered in the record of the Court, and that the Court adjourn as a tribute to his memory. [110 Minn. xvii]

Samuel J. R. McMillan

1826–1897
Associate Justice, 1864–1874; Chief Justice, 1874–1875

On the afternoon of Thursday, November 15, 1897, in the Supreme Court room at the state capital, Hon. George Brooks Young, as chairman of a committee of the Bar of the state, presented to the Supreme Court, then in session, the following memorial of Chief Justice McMillan and moved that it be entered upon the records of the court:

The members of the Bar of the State respectfully offer to the Court this memorial of their respect and affection for the Honorable Samuel J. R. McMillan, who for many years filled the offices of Associate Justice and Chief Justice of the Court with an integrity, learning, and ability that were never brought into question and with a kindly courtesy that has endeared his memory to all who knew him.

As a District Judge, as Associate Chief Justice of this Court, and as a Senator of the United States for twelve years, he illustrated in those various stations all the virtues of a just judge, of a wise and patriotic statesman, and of a sincere and consistent Christian. In his death our profession has lost a most distinguished member; and the community in which he lived and our State that he served so long and so well, one of their most eminent and upright and beloved citizens.

In our own deep sorrow for the death of our beloved friend and brother, we tender to his family our sincere condolence in their great bereavement.

Judge Young then addressed the court as follows:

It is now nearly twenty-three years since Chief Justice McMillan presided in this court. It is more than ten years since he retired from public life. Of the present members of the Bar, many—perhaps most—never argued before him in this court. With them his judicial reputation rests on his reported opinions

and on the report of the elder members of the profession. Even to them he needs no eulogy, and the memorial in which they have joined and which it is my high privilege to present to the court, expresses the respect and affection in which Judge McMillan was held by all the members of the Bar. But as one of those who practiced before him, who was for a brief time his associate in his judicial duties, and who was honored with his friendship, I desire to add a few words touching his life and character as they appeared to those who knew him best.

Samuel James Renwick McMillan came of Scottish ancestry and was born in Brownsville, Pennsylvania, February 22, 1826. He received a liberal education and was graduated from Western University of Pennsylvania in 1846. Having studied law, he was admitted to practice in 1849. He removed to the then territory of Minnesota in 1852, settling at Stillwater. Upon the admission of Minnesota as a state, he was chosen Judge of the District Court of the First Judicial District. In that office, which he held till 1864, he gained an enviable reputation. I have been told by those whose practice in our courts covered that now remote period (among others by the late Gordon E. Cole, than whose opinion on this point none could be higher) that the state never had his superior as a district judge. In 1864, on the resignation of Judges Atwater and Flandrau from the bench of this court, he was one of the two associate justices appointed to succeed them. The appointment met with universal approval, and in 1864 and again in 1871, he was elected to the same office. In April 1874, on the resignation of Chief Justice Ripley, he was appointed Chief Justice of this Court, and again the choice of the Governor was approved by the people, and in

November 1874 he was chosen Chief Justice for the constitutional term. At the next session of the Legislature he was elected a Senator from Minnesota in the Congress of the United States and in March 1875 resigned the office of Chief Justice. In 1881 he was again elected Senator, and [he] continued such until March 1887. For many years he was a trustee of the State Reform School. From March 1887 until the illness that resulted in his death, he was engaged in the practice of the law in this city.

The opinions of Judge McMillan in this court begin in Volume 9 and end in Volume 21 of the Minnesota Reports. They are characterized by ample learning, a clear comprehension of the questions involved, a firm grasp of legal principles, a terse and lucid expression. They usually go to the heart of the matter, to the real merits of the case, unless the presentation of it made this impossible. There is no parade of learning or acuteness, no attempt to appear wiser than his predecessors, no yielding to the temptation to decide questions not really involved—to decide too much. But there is no weakness, no paltering, no attempt to evade questions that called for decision. They are replete with that judicial wisdom that is better than mere legal learning or dialectic skill. They exhibit him as the fearless, wise, clear-sighted, prudent and careful judge.

As a senator of the United States he exhibited the same high qualities that characterized him in the judicial office. With strong political convictions and local attachments, his patriotism and statesmanship were yet broad enough to embrace the whole country and all its citizens. He was not and never aimed to be a party leader. He early won and always retained the respect and confidence of his fellow senators without regard to party; he was entrusted with the chairmanship of important committees and the charge of important legislation and proved himself a wise, judicious, and faithful senator.

It was my own great good fortune to enjoy a friendship and intimacy with Judge McMillan that, beginning in an official association early in 1874, continued until his death. No one could know him well without recognizing that his was a character of the highest type. The man was more than the jurist or the statesman. He was free from all self-seeking. While not careless of the approval of his fellow men, it was the approval that follows worthy actions, not that which is sought after, that he valued. His disposition was amiable, modest, and retiring. He had a kindliness of manner as gracious as it was sincere, a humility as genuine as unobtrusive, a smile that was a benediction, and a heart open as day to melting charity.

Yet he would be much mistaken who should have inferred from this amiability of disposition that Judge McMillan was a man of weak character or timid spirit. He had the unflinching courage, the unbending and uncompromising devotion to duty of those heroic Scottish Covenantors whose blood flowed in his veins and whose faith he had inherited. Over his grave as over that of John Knox might it be said: "There lies one that never feared the face of man. To him the judgments of men were as nothing in view of the eternal and immutable decrees on which, as he believed, the fate of all mankind depends. Except for their outward austerity, their uncouthness and their extravagances, he was a Puritan such as Macaulay depicts them in his famous essay on Milton. Had his lot been cast in the seventeenth instead of the nineteenth century, he might well have been among those

> Who sat with Bibles open around the Council board
> And answered a King's missive with a stern—
>   "Thus saith the Lord."

And he would, I believe, have sealed his faith with his blood as fearlessly as any in the roll of martyrs commemorated by the historic tablet in the old Greyfriars Churchyard in Edinburgh—a roll that ends with a name that he himself bore—James Renwick.

And with their rock-ribbed strength of character, he had a sweetness that was all his own. Himself living as ever in his Great Taskmaster's eye, no man was less disposed than he to sit in judgment on the frailty or the failings of others.

In placing and maintaining such a man in the highest offices for nearly thirty years, our state, while it honored him, honored itself yet more. His life was a daily teaching of every public and private virtue. He has left to the profession and the public a shining example of great merit crowned by the unsolicited bestowal of great civic rewards; and to his family and his intimates, the blessed memory of the just, and in their deep affliction, the solace of those celestial hopes that spring from the grave of the upright man.

Hon. Thomas Wilson then addressed the court:

It was my good fortune to become acquainted with Judge McMillan when we were both young men. Our acquaintance soon ripened into intimate, confidential friendship that lasted unclouded until his death. That friendship has been one of the great pleasures of my life, for he was a true friend and no ordinary man.

He came to Minnesota while it was a territory, and he practiced until he took his place on the bench, when the state was admitted into the Union. The business of the lawyer at that time was neither abundant nor important. After his first election he remained continuously on the bench of either the District or the Supreme Court until he was elected to the United States Senate in 1875. After leaving the Senate he never was very actively engaged in practice.

I shall not say aught of him beyond the plain, simple truth. If he hears what we say to-day, that would please him best. There have been and are in our profession many who would outrank him, either as a jurist or as an advocate. But he was an able lawyer. In natural ability, learning, and sound judgment, he deservedly stood very high. He was, if I may be permitted the expression, healthy—without isms, or hobbies, or any deforming idiosyncrasies. As a judge he was not the equal of some of the great jurists of our country—few attain to their stature—but he was in every respect far above mediocrity. He was not only an able, learned, and sagacious lawyer, but he had in a notable degree those other attributes and qualities that are equally essential to a good judge. Every party before him had a courteous, attentive, patient hearing. No matter how trifling the sum involved, he never consented to a decision without careful investigation and consideration of every question of fact that could affect the result. Every case, to him, was important. While his sympathies were always with the poor, the needy, and the defenseless, he was too good and too just a judge to be a respecter of persons, well knowing that justice, irrespective of class or condition, is the only safeguard of the rights and liberties of the citi-

zen. He had a feeling of contempt for either the parasite or the demagogue, and for all those "miserable aims that end in self." I verily believe—and no one had a better opportunity to observe than I—that on the bench the question never occurred to him whether any act or decision of his would please or displease any person or class or how it might affect himself. To my mind man is not endowed with a nobler attribute than courage. The Romans not inappropriately styled it virtue. That virtue Judge McMillan possessed in a marked degree. While he was gentle, mild-mannered, and devoid of demagogism, he was absolutely fearless in the performance of his duties. He did no act to be seen of men. Whatever he deemed it his duty to do, he did unostentatiously but unhesitatingly and fearlessly. He was always willing to be shown his error and took pleasure in admitting and correcting it, which is a degree of magnanimity that no essentially little mind possesses.

He was a Republican without qualification or mental reservation, accepting the most extreme doctrines of the party, but he was not in any sense a politician. He did not know how, nor had he any inclination, to resort even to those arts and methods that are allowable to a man who seeks popular favor. His success in obtaining judicial preferment was due solely to his admitted fitness and his high character. Until the session of the legislature at which he was chosen United States Senator was convened, I do not remember that he was spoken of as a candidate, and I think I know that he had neither hope nor thought of his election until it appeared probable that neither of the candidates who were actively seeking the place could be elected. He owed his election at that time to two influences—the confidence of the members of the legislature in his integrity and the confidence of the politicians that he did not understand, and even if he did would not resort to, the methods and practices that are often found to be necessary for political success and that, therefore, he would be the more easily displaced. As the sequel showed, both judged correctly, for he left the Senate with a well-earned reputation of having been a conscientious, industrious, and able senator and without any knowledge of practical politics.

He was in no sense a man of the world or a money-getter. He was in all his doings conscientious, single-minded, and artless, and as pure as a girl in thought, word, and act. With his friends and intimate acquaintances he was a genial, frank, jovial companion. A Presbyterian from his youth up, he accepted the creed and doctrine of that church and, with an unfaltering faith such as in these times of agnosticism is very rare, he every day modestly and unassumingly did that which was right as God gave him to see the right.

I never knew a man of whom it could be said more truthfully that he lived up to the admonition of those beautiful lines of *Thanatopsis*:

> So live, that when thy summons comes to join
> The innumerable caravan which moves
> To that mysterious realm, where each shall take
> His chamber in the silent halls of death,
> Thou go not, like the quarry-slave at night,
> Scourged to his dungeon, but, sustained and soothed
> By an unfaltering trust, approach thy grave
> Like one who wraps the drapery of his couch
> About him, and lies down to pleasant dreams.

The influence of our departed brother is not inurned with his body, for "example acquires authority when it speaks from the grave." Until the last record is made up, none can tell how many have been made better and braver and truer men by his example.

Godfrey Siegenthaler, Esq., then addressed the court as follows:

In the death of our lamented friend and brother, Judge McMillan, one of the highest, noblest, purest, most useful, and at the same time most unpretentious careers has been closed. That the praise I have bestowed and shall bestow upon him here may not seem at random or unadvised, I will state that mine has been the honor and privilege to know him as a friend for more than thirty-two years, and that during this period I have had ample opportunity to form a fair basis for my estimate of his life and character.

To have seen him in his daily walk of life was to respect him. To have known him more or less intimately was to love him. To have observed with what fidelity, integrity, and signal ability he discharged the duties of high official stations was to admire him. And to have heard him while Supreme Court Judge,

Chief Justice, United States Senator or Lawyer, in the House of God, offer up to the Almighty a simple fervent prayer of thanks for blessings received and for the welfare of mankind was to arouse in the infidel as well as the Christian a feeling of reverence, not only for him individually but also for the religion of which he was generally admitted to have been a devout, consistent, and exemplary follower.

To show what was thought of his exemplary Christian conduct, even among the irreligious, I will relate an incident that came to my notice. While he was yet an Associate Justice of the Supreme Court in the later sixties, I happened one day to meet several non-Christians engaged in discussing the doings of a certain church member who had not lived up to his religious professions. One of them, after having denounced this man as a hypocrite and a disgrace to his church, said: "But there's Judge McMillan. If every church member were like him, I'd like to become one myself. He is an honor, to any church." To this compliment the rest of the party assented.

Like all mortals, he was sometimes criticized; but the critics soon discovered that while they had been looking at the matter in question in the light of the moon, he had gazed at and acted upon it in the light of the sun.

To those who, like myself, were admitted to the bar of the Supreme Court while he was one of its able and honored justices, to young practitioners at the bar and to young men generally with whom he came in contact, he was especially endeared because of the wise counsel and kindly encouragement that he had given them and the continuous interest he took in their welfare. Indeed one of the principal reasons for his great and surprising popularity during his long official career was his kindly and sympathetic treatment of all persons, high or low, rich or poor, whom he met, so that when they left him, it was with the conviction that he was their friend.

Doubtless you have all seen and admired last summer at our beautiful Como Park the majestic yet humble Victoria Regina, its sturdy stem, its large circular leaves, and a blossom—a lovely blossom—resting upon the water as if, in sheer modesty, it sought to hide itself beneath the surface. This gem of the floral creation is, in some respects, symbolical of the life of our departed brother. In its harmonious structure, we behold his moral grandeur and Christian meekness; in, its sturdy stem, his tried ability; in the huge circular leaves, his great and general usefulness; in the all-permeating sap, his integrity; and in the blossom, his rare and exemplary piety. In the poetic language (slightly altered by me) of an old English author, I say of our departed brother: He was a judge—

> A man so learned,
> So full of equity, so noble, so notable;
> In the process of his life so innocent;
> In the manage of his office so incorrupt;
> In the passages of state so wise; in
> Affection of his country so religious.
> In all his services to the state so
> Fortunate and exploring, as envy
> Itself cannot accuse, or malice vitiate.

He is gone to his long home! But, as the waters of the mighty Mississippi, flowing by this city toward the Gulf of Mexico, are recalled by the voice of nature to bedew, to besprinkle, and to nourish the famished soil, so memory will bring back to us the kindly features of our lamented friend to influence our hearts for higher and nobler aims and for simple, blameless lives.

Hon. Henry J. Horn then addressed the court as follows:

My acquaintance with the late Judge and Senator McMillan began in 1855—the time of my first residence in Minnesota. I was intimate with him down to the time of his death.

I unreservedly concur in the memorial and expressions of the bar as to his worth and ability as a lawyer, judge, and senator, and in the approbation and esteem entertained for him by the citizens of the State of Minnesota.

I found him in 1855 a hard-working, conscientious, and indefatigable member of our profession. He soon acquired a position at the bar that won him judicial honors, first as Judge of the District Court and at last as Chief Justice of the Supreme Court—the highest judicial position in this state—leaving his judicial office only to accept the exalted position tendered to him, without solicitation, of United States Senator.

His long official career has ever been characterized by an honorable, able, exacting, and successful discharge of his public duties, without blemish or even suspicion. He was a modest and unpretending man throughout, though always firm and decided in the performance of duty. In his elevation to high judicial and civic positions he never abated the observance of those duties, private or public, that he owed as a citizen, or as a friend, neighbor, or Christian.

His career begins prior to the commencement of our statehood, and he belongs to that class whose characters, acts, and examples are intimately connected with the upbuilding of the state and have become part of its history.

The Bar of Minnesota is also privileged to claim such men as Judge McMillan as examples of what a true lawyer should be and the honor that may await him in the end.

While we, his professional brethren, deplore his loss and sympathize with his family and friends in their sad bereavement, it is a source of satisfaction that his illustrious name and character have conferred signal honor on our profession.

Associate Justice Collins then said:

I deem it a privilege to join in the tributes of love and respect paid on this occasion to the memory of one who for many years held high judicial position in this state, first as a District Judge, then as an Associate Justice, and finally as Chief Justice of the Supreme Court. and who later and for two terms of six years each filled the responsible position of United States Senator. It is well known that for a long time in our early history Judge McMillan was a very prominent and distinguished citizen holding these high judicial and political positions, which he filled with great credit to himself and to the perfect satisfaction of the people who honored him and to whose service he gave the best years of his life. So zealous was he in the proper discharge of his official duties that he paid little or no attention to private business, and while others of his profession availed themselves of the many opportunities in the early days to accumulate wealth, he lived and died in very moderate circumstances. I first knew him in the spring of 1862 when he, as Judge of the First District, held court at

Hastings. My acquaintance was limited, and I am not qualified to speak of his career in that position. I can only say that he had the reputation of being an exceedingly careful and painstaking officer. His work while sitting as a member of this court is found in 13 volumes of our reports and fairly illustrates the character and ability of the man. Every decision tells of his loyalty to the work in hand, of his determination to be thorough in his investigation, and of his fidelity to well settled principles of our jurisprudence.

As a member of the legislature of the 1881 session, I had the pleasure of voting for him when he was re-elected to the Senate. It was a place that was never so satisfactory to him as a position on the bench. While we cannot say that he was a leader at Washington, all know that he was held in great esteem by his associates and occupied an enviable place in their councils. Judge McMillan was an excellent example of noble manhood. He was unassuming upon all occasions and perhaps too much so for his own welfare. He was upright in every sense of the word. His faithfulness in public life was never questioned, and as a private citizen he was most loving and lovable. His career was not one to attract widespread attention, but it commends itself to us as a striking example of what may be accomplished by a man of dignified modesty and true worth. His was the life of a Christian gentleman, and when the hand of death, after nearly forty years of active life in this state, was laid upon his worn-out body, not one man within our borders could say aught against him.

Associate Justice Mitchell then said:

Having been intimately acquainted with Judge McMillan for nearly thirty-five years, I not only entertained the highest respect and admiration for him as a man and a citizen but had also formed a very warm attachment for him as a personal friend. I should therefore be derelict in the performance of duty if I should permit this occasion to pass without paying tribute to his memory.

I am gratified, both as a member of this court and as his friend, to hear such high and evidently heartfelt commendations of his noble character from those who knew him best, in all of which I heartily and fully join.

In emphasizing the nobility of his character we may perhaps seem to have partially lost sight of its strength. There was nothing weak in Judge McMillan's character. Modest in the estimate of his own ability and charitable toward the opinions of others, he was never obtrusive in asserting himself; but he was a man of decided and positive convictions, and he had the courage to assert them when duty required; and he always lived up to them. Unless a man displays an inordinate degree of egotism, the world is very apt to accept his own estimate of himself as correct. If Judge McMillan had been dogmatic and aggressive in the assertion of his views, people generally might have placed a higher estimate on his talents. Only those who knew him well were in position fully and correctly to appreciate his ability and strength of character. By his death this city and state have lost one of their best and most eminent citizens, whose memory will always be honored and revered by all who knew him.

Chief Justice Start then said:

Your Memorial happily expresses the sentiments of the court with reference to the life, character, and public services of Chief Justice McMillan. As Judge, Chief Justice, and Senator in the Congress of the United States, he rendered distinguished services that entitle him to grateful remembrance by the whole people of the state. He quietly discharged the duties and responsibilities of private and public life with rare ability, fidelity, courage, and manly vigor. He was a just, gentle, sincere, wise man, "Who reverenced his conscience as his king."

It is proper as a tribute to his memory that your memorial is spread upon the records of the court for the day and that the court now adjourn. So ordered.
[67 Minn xxvii]

John M. Berry

1827–1887
Associate Justice, 1865–1887

The Honorable John McDonough Berry, senior associate justice of the supreme court of Minnesota, died at his home in Minneapolis, on the eighth day of November 1887, in the sixty-first year of his age, and the twenty-third year of continuous service on the bench of the court, where he sat for the last time on June 15, 1887.

Judge Berry was born at Pittsfield, in Merrimac county, New Hampshire, on the eighteenth of September 1827. He was prepared for college at Phillips (Andover) Academy, was graduated from Yale College in 1847, was admitted to the bar in July 1850, and began the practice of law at Alton, Belknap county, where he remained for two years. In the year 1853, after a two years' sojourn at Janesville, Wisconsin, he became a citizen of this state, making his home at Faribault. In 1879, he removed to Minneapolis, where he resided until his death.

He was a member of the territorial legislature in 1856–7, chairman of the judiciary committee of the house of representatives, chairman of the same committee of the state senate in 1863 and 1864, and a member of the board of regents of the state university in 1860 and 1861. He was elected an associate justice of the supreme court in 1864 and qualified and took his seat on the tenth day of January 1865 and was continued in office by successive re-elections until his death. His first reported opinion is in the case of *Bidwell v. Madison*, 10 Minn. 1, (13,) and the last in the case of *Wyvell v. Jones*, 37 Minn. 68, filed June 8, 1887.

On the seventeenth day of December 1887, Hon. S. J. R. McMillan, as chairman of a committee of the bar of the state, presented to the supreme court, then in session, the following memorial resolution and moved that it be entered in the records of the court:

Since the opening of the present term of the su-

preme court, the earthly career of Hon. John M. Berry, the senior associate justice of the court, has terminated. As members of the bar of Minnesota, we desire to express our deep sorrow on account of his death and testify of our respect and veneration for his memory.

In the early part of his professional career, he was called to the bench, and for nearly twenty-three years he held the high and responsible position that was made vacant by his death.

By his natural endowments and intellectual discipline and attainments, he was peculiarly fitted for judicial life. His learning and ability were quickened in their exercise by a strong sense of justice and an ardent love for the equity of the law. Free from prejudice and undue intellectual bias, he sought only for the truth in his conscientious discharge of his official duties.

In his long judicial career he has indelibly impressed upon the jurisprudence of the state his own wisdom and ability and the purity and uprightness of his own character.

Honorable, generous, and kind, he was loved and respected by all who knew him. In his death our state has lost one of its ablest judges, our profession one of its brightest ornaments, the community a useful and upright citizen, and his family a devoted husband and father.

Removed from earth in the midst of his labors and usefulness, we mourn his loss, and extend our sincere sympathy to his family in their sad bereavement.

We respectfully request the court to direct that this expression of our respect for our departed friend be entered upon its record, with such other proceedings as may be had in connection therewith, and that a copy thereof be transmitted to his family.

Judge McMillan then addressed the court as follows:

I met Judge Berry on his first visit to Minnesota

in 1853. He soon thereafter took up his residence in the southern part of the territory, which was then attracting the attention of the country and soon filled up with an intelligent and thrifty population. He afterwards changed his residence to Faribault, where he continued to reside until his removal to the city of Minneapolis. During the early period of his residence in the territory I knew him only as a professional brother, esteemed in the community and giving assurance of early distinction and success.

Called by his fellow-citizens to represent them in the legislature at a period in our history when we were laying the foundations of our political institutions, he took a prominent position in the body of which he was a member, and among other measures of public importance accomplished by him, he was influential in obtaining legislation that preserved and resulted in augmenting the resources of the state university, of which he was afterwards a regent and in which he retained a deep interest throughout his life. It was not, however, until he entered upon his judicial office that I became intimately acquainted with him. For the first ten years and more of his judicial life I had the honor of being associated with him in his judicial duties, and I count this intimate association with him and his friendship, which continued till his death, among the richest treasures of my life.

If there is any place or relation in secular life that reveals the mental and moral characteristics of a man to his associates or to himself, it is the consultation room of an appellate court, and here our beloved friend appeared to the most advantage. He was thorough and diligent in his investigations and calm and free from excitement in his deliberations. No prejudice or pride of opinion clouded his mind, perverted his judgment, or prevented his reception of the truth. His understanding was comprehensive and clear; his judgment was sound and accurate. With a sacred regard for individual rights, without respect of persons, he sought the right and justice of the matters submitted to him. His intellectual taste was cultivated and refined, and his reading varied and extensive. He was an intelligent observer of men and things, and his knowledge of affairs was extensive and practical. In his judgment of others he was charitable and kind. Honorable and upright in his conduct, generous and broad in his sympa-

thies, unselfish and sincere in his feelings, he was true and faithful in his friendships. His tastes were simple, his manners unaffected; he was approachable by all.

In his family he was tender, devoted, and affectionate.

His labors are over; his life work is done. In the fruit of his labors he has left to the state and to the profession a rich and enduring legacy. We will honor his name, cherish his memory, and commend his example to those who shall fill our places in the profession we love.

Hon. Isaac Atwater then presented to the court the following memorial resolution:

The bar of Minneapolis, assembled for the purpose, adopt this as their memorial to the worth, the integrity, the purity, and the learning which were embodied in the character of Judge John M. Berry, late an associate justice of the supreme court of Minnesota.

His continuous service in that exalted position for a period covering nearly a quarter of a century gave him an opportunity such as few men may enjoy for exhibiting both his native talents and his stores of learning, while at the same time it tested his ability to exercise without despotism the great powers with which a republic clothes its judiciary. How well he improved the opportunity and endured the ordeal is attested by the large place he held in the affections and esteem of the people of this state. In their exchange of opinions, he has for years been an example of high excellence as a jurist, a scholar, and a citizen. Knowing him as we have, not only as the judge but as our townsman and our friend, it is our pleasant privilege on this occasion to join in these encomiums. His affability of demeanor and his solicitous respect for the rights and feelings of his fellows bespoke a warm, true heart and endeared him to us as a neighbor.

The wealth of judicial learning with which his opinions as a judge were enriched will long in the future as it has in the past awaken the emulation of other ardent students of the law. His sterling independence and integrity, his well-balanced intellect, and his robust common sense were his guides through many judicial mazes and prompted him continually in the practical application of his professional knowledge to the myriad phases of the new cases presented to the bench. The young state of Minnesota needed such advisers and guides in the formative period of her polity and jurisprudence, and she was fortunate in securing the services, among others, of a Berry.

His opinions crowd the pages of twenty-six volumes of the reports of decisions of her court of last resort, and they largely illustrate the rapid development of all the material, industrial, commercial, and political interests of the commonwealth in her earliest years.

While mourning his loss to the state, we shall, as his townsmen, point proudly to his monument, one more enduring than marble shaft or granite tomb—one reared by himself and fixed forever in the very structure of the state—the monument of his invaluable contributions to our jurisprudence.

Hon. Gordon E. Cole then addressed the Court as follows:

In the rush and whirl of this busy world of ours, the removal of any man, no matter how commanding his intellect, how correct his morals, or conspicuous his station, creates but a ripple upon the current, and the tide of human life sweeps onward with no perceptible change in its flow. But sometimes a person disappears whose absence creates an aching void, which seems to leave that segment of the world in which he lived and moved cold and desolate, a less desirable residence for friends and family. Such a loss, it appears to me, the bench he adorned, the bar that esteemed him, the family that adored him, the friends who loved him, have sustained in the death of Judge Berry.

For thirty years on the bench and in the forum, I have known our lamented friend as intimately as it often falls to the lot of one man to know another. The most conspicuous trait of his character, which his intimate friends knew and prized, was a fund of genial humor whose unceasing flow made his companionship more delightful than that of most men. There was a flash and sparkle of wit that in the intervals of dry discussion of legal problems constantly diffused its radiance. He was a true and loyal friend and a charming companion. As a Christian gentleman, while scorning all sham and cant, his belief in the fundamental facts on which Christianity rests was as fixed and positive as that of any man I ever knew, while the quiet and unobtrusive benevolence that has so often lent a needed assistance to those

of his friends and acquaintances less fortunate than himself will never be forgotten by the recipients of his aid.

His official life almost spans the arch that circles our history as a state. He may be almost said to have rocked the cradle of the infant commonwealth and to have done more than any other man in shaping her rising destinies. Whatever of material prosperity has followed from the selection of a north and south line as the western boundary of the new state that was erected out of the old territory of Minnesota is largely due to his pen and voice.

As a lawyer and judge, Judge Berry was not what might be called a book or case lawyer. A fine classical and legal education had made him a good scholar and a good lawyer. His range of general reading was extensive, and his knowledge of law accurate. But he was more fond of reasoning from those general principles that he had acquired by a youth of hard study than of an appeal to the musty precedents of the law books, although his habits of industry did not permit him to neglect these. An authority to carry with it his judgment must have been sustained by logical reason and commended itself to his sense of equity. A precedent, as such, had no charms and no terrors for him. He had little reverence for the authorities merely because they were such.

He was a man of thought rather than of action. For the fierce conflicts and rough jostling of frontier practice, he had little taste. His mind was that of a judge, rather than of an advocate. Thoroughly honest in all his thoughts and actions and possessed of a moral courage that, while it never led him outside of the line of his duty to espouse or advocate untried or doubtful experiments yet in that line never failed him in the discharge of those duties that fell within his appropriate sphere of action. A restless reformer he could never have been. His innate modesty ever shrunk from notoriety. The Socratic mode of inquiry, by which while apparently seeking for information he detected and exposed the fallacies that underlie much crude and illy considered thought, was with him a favorite weapon.

This gentle and kindly friend, this genial humorist, has gone, and going has left a sweet memory behind him.

Like the vase in which roses have once been distilled,
You may break, you may shatter the vase if you will,
But the scent of the roses will hang round it still.

His body is gone; the vase is broken that contained these delightful qualities; but the sweet savor of his wit, the memory of the kind friend and cheerful companion, of the good judge and citizen, will linger in this room once made so cheerful by his presence, so long as his surviving associates on the bench and at the bar shall continue to carry on the work that he has resigned.

Hon. Charles E. Flandrau then addressed the court as follows:

I came to assist at the obsequies of Judge Berry as a listener, to hear the strong points of his character pictured by the members of the bar and this court, not intending to add anything myself, but on reflection I think it not altogether inappropriate that I should say a few words.

Judge Berry and myself were contemporaries in our arrival in the territory of Minnesota. He located in one part of the territory and I in another, distant from each other, and we have never been inhabitants of the same locality in the thirty-five years that have passed since our arrival; consequently, my intercourse with Judge Berry was more official than social; but it has been sufficiently intimate to impress me with a profound respect for his many excellent qualities as a judge and a man. He possessed the gravity of demeanor that is demanded by the proprieties of the bench, and at the same time that seriousness of deportment was ever ready to relax and yield to the influence of good fellowship for which the western bar is celebrated; he possessed a line sense of humor and was a genial companion. Judge Berry was a man of more learning than is usually found among western lawyers. He was devoted to his profession and preferred the honors that are its incidents to its emoluments. Our almost perfect state law library, in which the bar takes such just pride, is much indebted to his learned and judicious selection. He was one of the most conscientious judges it has ever been my experience to practise before. The decisions of all courts will be subjected to criticism by those whose interests they affect adversely, but I never heard during all the long period of Judge Berry's administration a suggestion from any source that he had not been actuated solely by a desire to arrive at the just and legal result in every decision in which he participated.

I might enlarge upon the good qualities of our deceased judge and friend, but it would be only a repetition of what has been said in the several memorials that have been presented by the bar associations. No eulogy could be pronounced upon Judge Berry in which I would not heartily concur.

In the infancy of our history I occupied a position upon the supreme bench of the territory and state. That time might well be designated as the crude and disorderly period of the administration of the law. We were compelled from the necessity of the case to make the law rather than to interpret and construe it. Under the territory we were without the guiding light of a constitution, save the organic act; and in the earlier days of the state, with the heterogeneous character of our people and our bar, our labors were largely experimental and original in their character. Judge Berry was called to the bench just about the time when the administration of justice was assuming its normal status, and his well-trained mind found a splendid field for its exertion in moulding the jurisprudence of a new empire.

It was a very serious question in the constitutional convention of the state whether the judges should be elected or appointed for life or during good behavior, and the dominant opinion was in favor of the life tenure. I was in accord with the majority, but having a very extensive acquaintance with the bar of the territory—in fact, knowing nearly every member of it—I feared that there did not exist at that early day sufficient material to fill all the judicial offices with credit and satisfaction as a permanency, and this view obtained. So we adopted the elective system, and it is a very satisfactory reflection that the people have with very rare exceptions shown great wisdom in their selection of our judges; and whenever a judge has proved himself worthy of the choice, they have re-elected him term after term, practically inaugurating the life tenure. Judge Berry was a conspicuous example of this determination of the people to retain their worthy representatives on the bench.

There is a moral in such a life as that of our beloved

and lamented judge, and those who follow in his footsteps will do well to emulate his noble example.

Chief Justice Gilfillan, in behalf of the court, responded as follows to the addresses of the bar:

On behalf of the court, I thank you for your graceful and just tributes to the memory of our deceased associate.

Mr. Justice Berry was the second of the members of this court who have died in service. A little more than six years ago, Mr. Justice Cornell, then one of the judges of the court, died. Now, Judge Berry, who had long been one of his associates in judicial station and labors, has also gone while in the exercise of his duties upon this bench. He had been on the bench nearly twenty-three years, more than twice as long as any other judge of the court, except one.

It was a long term of faithful, laborious service. Twenty-six volumes of reported decisions are witnesses to the fidelity, industry, and ability with which he discharged the duties of his office. His influence in moulding the jurisprudence of the state, in some measure crude and unformed when he came upon the bench, has by far exceeded that of any other judge, and it will continue for many years to come.

The judge who for a considerable time occupies a place in the court of last resort in a comparatively new community makes his impress upon the future of the state and society more than almost any other man. True, it is usually done quietly, without display, and almost imperceptibly, as the dew falls or the trees grow. His decisions concern men in all their daily lives and business and establish their code of business morality. He marks out the path in which those who come after him in the judicial office or in the profession of the law must follow.

It was fortunate for the people and the state that Judge Berry came upon the bench when he did and remained on it so long as he did and that he possessed so largely the qualities that so peculiarly fitted him for the duties of the office. Patient, judicial, impartial, clear-sighted, his was the mind to adopt and establish safe, wise, and conservative rules. He was always careful and painstaking in the examination of cases before him, conscientiously devoting to their consideration great labor and research and giving to them a logical mind well stored with legal learning.

But what need that I speak of these things to you? They are well known to you all. No one can now or hereafter occupy worthily a place at the bar in this state, or in the future fit himself in it for the profession of the law, without having these qualities of Judge Berry as a magistrate brought daily to his attention, without making part of his necessary learning the decisions announced and put in form by him.

He had other qualities, fully known only to those who were so fortunate as to be in some degree intimate with him and that endeared him to them. He was too modest to bring his personal traits much to the notice of any but his personal friends. He always shunned, almost dreaded, anything like ostentation and notoriety. His tastes and habits were almost quaintly simple. He had no ambition as that word is commonly understood. He cared nothing for but rather avoided preferment. When offers of such that would have tempted most men were made to him, he not only declined them but felt so little interest in such proffered honors that he rarely alluded to them even among his most intimate friends. But he had a nobler ambition—that to fulfill his whole duty to the utmost of his ability.

He knew himself more thoroughly and accurately than most men know themselves—knew where his strength lay and what was the bent and capability of his mind. His proper place was on the bench, and he knew it; and no temptation, however brilliant and dazzling, could ever for a moment cause him to waver in that knowledge. So, when on one occasion there was offered him a place in another sphere, a place that many court and few would decline but which he knew he was not so well fitted for as for the bench, he declined it without hesitation,

He was a diligent and careful student, not only of the books pertaining to his profession but of those of the best kind belonging to general literature. To his familiarity with law books the state and the profession are indebted for the selection and arrangement of the excellent law library in this building. He gave to it a great deal of time and labor, and it twice grew to be almost perfect for its size, under his superintending care.

Not only in his judicial duties but in various branches of knowledge, he was a thinker, original in his modes and lines of thought. Though fond of books, especially those of a rare kind, no author that he read could affect the independence of his reasoning and judgment on the matters treated of.

You, gentlemen, know how courteous and respectful he always was in his personal and official intercourse with all. In the closer intercourse with us, his associates on the bench, he was uniform in his kindness and good nature. Constant association and frequent discussion upon differences of opinion are apt to reveal, at times, infirmities of temper, if there be any. During twelve years of such association, meeting him daily for the greater part of the time, nothing so far as apparent to me ever ruffled the evenness

and gentleness of his temper; nothing ever occurred, however various the opinions or earnest the discussions on them might be, to leave even a momentary bitterness behind. We all remember, with pleasure touched with sadness, his cheerful daily greeting, his pleasant smile, and harmless jest; and we recall how true and steadfast and sympathizing a friend he was, ever ready to counsel and assist.

And now that his life has closed, it can be said of him with more truth than of most men, that his was a useful, well-spent life, a life devoted to the laborious, conscientious discharge of his duties to his fellow man. What higher praise can be said of a man than that he has faithfully done his duty? [37 Minn. xix]

James Gilfillan

1829–1894
Chief Justice, 1869–1870, 1875–1894

Memorial services, held January 7th, 1895, commencing at 11 o'clock A.M., in the Supreme Court at the State capitol in honor of the late Chief Justice, Hon. James Gilfillan.

Present: Chief Justice Start, Associate Justices Mitchell, Collins, Buck, and Canty.

[Speaker unknown]:

The bar of Minnesota, as an appropriate testimonial of its appreciation of the character of the late James Gilfillan, respectfully request that the deliberations of this Court over which he so long presided as its Chief Justice yield to a brief tribute to his memory.

On the 16th day of December 1894, James Gilfillan, in the midst of his official duties and before the powers of his mind had been enfeebled by wasting age, was removed by an all-wise Providence from the ranks of the living.

That the deceased was a great jurist, the voice of the bar of this country and numerous volumes of the reported decisions of this court bear ample witness. How he adorned his high office by wealth of legal learning, marked powers of analysis, great breadth of mental grasp, quickness of apprehension, unfailing courage, probity, and industry, none know so well as those who during the last twenty years have most frequently appeared before him. All who knew him in the private walks of life testify to the purity of his thoughts, the warmth of his affections, and the simplicity of his manners.

With what wisdom he wrought and how deep was his influence in shaping the jurisprudence of this State must indeed be left to the final judgment of the future but tested by the opinions of his cotemporaries [*sic*], he has by such labor reared an enduring monument to his fame. His own words, fitly spoken on another solemn occasion over the bier of one he loved, are most appropriate now:

"The judge, who, for a considerable time, occupies a place in a court of last resort in a comparatively new country, makes his impress upon the future of the State and society more than almost any other man. True, it is usually done quietly, without display, and almost imperceptibly, as the dew falls or the trees grow. His decisions concern men in all their daily lives and business, and establish their code of business morality. He marks out the path in which those who come after him in the judicial office, or in the profession of the law, must follow."

A veil, impenetrable to mortal vision, has been drawn between him and us. The State has thereby lost one of its most illustrious citizens; the bench, a shining ornament; the bar, its most conspicuous member; a family, a devoted husband and father.

We therefore respectfully request that this memorial, although but feebly expressive of our regard for the memory of the deceased, be entered at length upon the records of the Court, with such other proceedings as may be had in connection therewith, and that a copy thereof be transmitted to the afflicted family.

Address of Hon. Henry W. Childs, Attorney General:

A great brain and heart have been stilled by the mystic touch that we call death and know no more. A bright light that has long illumined our professional pathway and directed the course of the jurisprudence of this State has been extinguished forever. James Gilfillan, who but yesterday presided over the deliberations of this Court, a tribunal that he strove with all his great powers to elevate in the estimation of the bench and bar of this country, will hereafter live only in the hearts of those who knew him, and in that noble work that he has left behind him for the guidance and instruction of this and future generations.

The day is most appropriate for this proceeding. It was today, in the ordinary course of official events, that he was to have relinquished his exalted station among you to resume his place in those ranks that twenty years ago he reluctantly and at great personal sacrifice abandoned in obedience to the call of duty. The ermine that fell upon his shoulders then, now descends unsullied upon the shoulders of his successor.

He was a great judge. Many of the decisions of this Court written by him bear unmistakable evidence of his masterful abilities. They will be received everywhere as authoritative expressions of the law. They will, moreover, serve as notable examples of judicial writing. Conciseness of expression was his characteristic. Years of careful self-discipline and exhaustive research had brought to him a profound and unfailing knowledge of the law. His comprehensive mind grasped instantly what the ordinary mind attains by slow and laborious process. His decisions are models in their paucity of citations. In expounding the law, in applying its principles to a given case, he found slight occasion to fortify his position by reference to authorities. So quick was his perception of the truth, so accurate his power of analysis, that his deductions were rarely at fault. He felt safe upon his ground not because it had the endorsement of some other court or judge but because he knew by those infallible tests never absent from a powerful and analytic mind that he was right. In vain will his writings be searched for expressions penned for mere effect. Words with him were vehicles of thought and never the trappings of display. Not always faultless either in his choice of language or the structure of his sentences, he has, however, rarely failed to dress his thoughts in diction so clear as to leave no doubt as to his meaning.

No man can worthily occupy a seat upon a judicial bench who is not endowed with great fortitude of mind. It is the duty of a court to declare the law. Who has ever yet long presided in a court of justice without hearing the voice of that tempter whose presence is always a profanation of that sacred temple? It comes rarely in the form of a bribe, but in the more familiar guise of fear, or passion, or prejudice, or ambition—

infirmities from which human flesh can never wholly free itself. Few judges, be it said to the great praise of the deceased, have allowed such considerations to influence them less than he. Where weak men have fallen by the wayside, he has maintained the straightforward course, counseled only by that inward monitor that rarely leads astray. Through good report and through ill report, whether the popular clamor was for or against him, whether the fortune of friend or foe was in the balance, that brave and sincere man and just judge was moved neither to the right nor to the left in the discharge of manifest duty. He removed not the landmarks.

What higher praise of a judge than this?

Gradually and imperceptibly the true character of the judge may become masked by an austerity of bearing that wounds and repels. This was to some extent true of the deceased. The generous-hearted sympathetic man had become more or less obscured by the formal judge, schooled to listen while withholding that subtle chord of sympathy that is the life and soul of speech. And thus it has sometimes happened that counsel who saw only the judge upon the bench and knew nothing of the lovable nature of the man, closed his address to the Court with a belief, deep-rooted and pernicious, that his cause had been prejudged, his argument unappreciated, and himself ill-used. This was more especially true of young men to whom the attentive ear and appreciative kindle of the eye are requisite to any degree of success in argument. But time, association, and truer insight rarely failed to efface the error. A word exchanged in the private chamber, in the library, at the home, or on the street, was a beam of sunshine that melted away the ill-timed frost.

But why these words? The ear of the venerable Justice will not heed them, and the lips of all who participate in this memorial proceeding will, in a few years at best, be as silent as his own.

> Can storied urn, or animated bust,
> Back to its mansion call the fleeting breath?
> Can honor's voice provoke the silent dust,
> Or flattery soothe the dull, cold ear of death?

We speak to-day not to the dead but to the living. We raise our voices in testimony of the virtues of a great and good man that they may serve to inspire others to emulate him. To the bar of this State, both of to-day and the future generations, we present the life of the late Chief Justice as illustrating the value of industry and integrity in the pursuit of a noble profession.

Address of Hon. Isaac Atwater:

I doubt not but that every member of the bar in this room, if permitted, would be glad to pay his tribute of honor, love, and regard to the memory of the lamented Chief Justice James Gilfillan. I can trespass but for a few moments upon your patience to give expression to the feelings to which this occasion gives rise. But, from my own acquaintance and I may say somewhat intimate relations with the deceased, I would not willingly keep entirely silent upon this occasion.

It is thirty-seven years since I first made the acquaintance of the deceased, upon his appearance before the first Supreme Court of this State in the argument of his cases. Even now, his argument in the first case presented is hardly less vivid than it was at the time. The names of the parties to the case and the decision have passed from my memory, but his clear and concise statement of facts, the application of legal principles thereto, the logical deductions drawn therefrom, his broad grasp of equitable principles, left an abiding impression on my mind of a lawyer of rare legal acumen and ability. Indeed, I am reminded even now, of a remark made by a prominent member of the Hennepin County bar a few days since, upon an occasion such as that upon which we have assembled, of the prediction I then made in regard to the deceased that, if he lived, he would stand front in the profession in this State; and even then we had men eminent at the bar such as Hollinshead, and Rice, and Ames, and Brisbin, and Bigelow, and Chatfield, and others I could name, with all of whom he stood easily the peer.

It would take too long to enumerate the eminent qualifications that the deceased enjoyed for the bench that he so long honored—his fearlessness in expressing his honest convictions whenever demanded, even at the sacrifice of personal interest; his broad grasp of equity; and his entire impartiality between suitors, whether persons, corporations, or political parties—you know them all; I need not enumerate them. Indeed, in the presence of those thirty-nine volumes in the adjoining chamber, which form his imperishable

record and monument, any eulogy that we could pronounce here would seem tame and commonplace.

It has been my fortune in over forty years of experience at the bar to have appeared professionally before the twenty judges, if I remember the names correctly, including the Territorial, who went upon that bench; and I may say without disparagement to any among them, he was *facile princeps*.

But what has been said relates to only one side of his character. Eminent lawyers are not always great men. His broad sympathies were never dwarfed by his devotion to his profession and his judicial duties. He recognized the claims of humanity and Christianity to his services and his time so far as possible. The church, to which he belonged and that he loved, honored him, and I may say equally herself, by conferring upon him the highest positions accorded to a layman. For years he was a member of the standing committee, a trustee of the diocese, a delegate to her general councils, and to each and all of these he devoted time so far as he possibly could from the labors of his judicial duties. No man has found a warmer recognition in the church that he so well served.

And in these three relations of which I have spoken, the honest lawyer, the incorruptible judge, the sincere Christian, it seems to me all others are comprised.

I know not what impressions may have been formed upon others; they depend upon the point of view at which one looks at his character, the intimacy of acquaintance, and its length of continuance. If faults are to be found—as indeed they must be in everything human—they are so insignificant as not to obscure nor even dim the luster of his greatness. The State that he adopted is the richer for his learning and genius; the community in which he lived has been uplifted by the purity of his life and the savor of his good deeds, and posterity blessed in the ages to come by the rich inheritance that he has left. His life has been a daily benediction upon all that came within its influence. Fortunate and thrice happy he who can leave so noble a record and an example so worthy to be followed.

Address of Hon. Chas. E. Flandrau:

The prominent position that has been assigned to me in these memorial proceedings arises no doubt from the fact that I occupied a seat upon this bench when the first session of this Court convened in the year 1858. It may be a fact worth noticing that every judge of the Court who sat at its first session is still alive and well and one at least of them in active practice, although thirty-seven years have passed since that interesting event took place.

I think the love of a man for the State of his adoption becomes much stronger than that which he entertains for the State of his nativity. He generally emigrates at the period of early manhood from a State, the institutions of which are practically matured and have become and will probably remain so without his ability to influence them. He comes to a community the governmental characteristics of which are, like the commonwealth, in their infancy. His active participation in their formation and growth engenders profound interest and deep sympathy; as they develop they become part of himself, and his pride or sorrow largely depends upon their success or failure.

We all recognize that the judicial arm of the State is the protector of our liberties, the guardian of our property, and the conservator of our happiness.

The temporary aberrations of the legislative branch, growing out of the ill-directed passions of the people, may be regretted but do not affect the confidence of the citizen in the stability and excellence of republican government, while the fantastic eccentricities of the executive that are sometimes indulged in only excite the good-natured derision of thinking people, as long as they feel assured of the purity, wisdom, and courage of the courts.

If your Honors please, my heart swells with patriotic pride when I can stand in this conspicuous place and proclaim without a shadow of reservation that never since the organization of this our own Supreme Court has it, or any member of it, been charged or even suspected of entertaining in the slightest degree any attribute that would detract from the full and deserved possession of the most exalted title that can be worn by man—*a just judge*. Happy is the State that can say so much; no record can surpass it. The glories of successful war are superb; the triumphs of literature and inventive genius are rich possessions, but the certainty of a pure and just judiciary is a jewel surpassing in value the riches of the world and approaching those of our promised heaven.

The highest encomium that I can pass upon our deceased Chief Justice is to say that his long presidency of this Court has done as much, if not more, than that of any other man to create and perpetuate all its admirable traits that I have alluded to. No one can add a word to the well-deserved tribute to his life and career that has been presented by the Honorable, the Attorney General.

Address of Hon. S. J. R. McMillan:

Among the elements entering into the early settlement of Minnesota, one of the strongest and most favorable was the influence and power of the lawyers who gave tone and character to the bar of the State. They were men in the vigor of manhood, well equipped and disciplined for their professional labors—men of broad and vigorous intellects, diligent and faithful in their duties, and loyal to the high principles and honorable traditions of our profession. Among such men at the bar of St. Paul and as one of them, James Gilfillan, upon coming here to live, took his place and throughout his professional career was regarded as one of the ablest lawyers of the State.

In 1869, upon the resignation of Hon. Thomas Wilson, Chief Justice of the Supreme Court of the State, Mr. Gilfillan was appointed to fill the vacancy and held the office under this appointment for a short time. Subsequently and on the 5th of March 1875, he was again appointed to the office of Chief Justice, that he held until his death.

It was my privilege to be associated with Chief Justice Gilfillan during the time he held his office under the first appointment I have adverted to. His professional life was the basis and the prophesy of his judicial career. His legal knowledge was extensive and profound; his judicial views were broad, comprehensive, and clear; his judgment was sound and wise. He was conscientious in all his duties, impartial and upright in his consideration and determination of all matters submitted to him, and the strength of his convictions were equaled only by the courage with which they were declared. He was an able, upright Judge. What higher tribute can be paid to his memory?

By his ability and integrity through his long judicial career, he has rendered high and noble service to the

State, in his faithful and efficient labors, in extending and establishing a system of jurisprudence of which every citizen of this State may well be proud. In the midst of his work he has been called from earth. He laid aside unsullied his judicial robe and in its stead has put on the spotless robe of the righteousness of the Christ whom he loved and served in his life.

Address of Hon. Greenleaf Clark:

I should not be satisfied to let this occasion pass without a word of personal tribute to the memory of James Gilfillan, nor do I fear that my love and respect for the man will carry me beyond the limit of just encomium.

We have to contemplate a marked and vigorous personality: marked and vigorous both in mental and moral qualities. I cannot hope in the short time I feel at liberty to consume to cover the ground of an analysis of his mind and character. It would require a commemorative oration. I can only allude to a few salient features that have most impressed me.

If I were called upon to designate the most prominent characteristic of his mind, I should say it was analytic power. He had a gift, the result both of natural endowment and development, to a degree that is possessed by but few men, of seeing through the obscurations and false issues to the very pith and substance of the matter, not by an intuitional jump but by a deliberate though rapid analysis.

Most important legal determinations turn upon one or two, scarcely ever more, leading legal principles correctly applied. Judge Gilfillan excelled in the readiness with which, brushing away the extraneous matter, he grasped strong hold of the principle involved and applied it. Nor was this incisive, logical process at the expense of breadth or strength. No jurist of his time brought to the consideration of grave constitutional questions or others involving weighty consequences, broader or more far-reaching views. Not as ready as some men to exert his powers, if he erred it was more likely to be in comparatively trifling cases involving no important principles upon which his powers were scarcely got to operate in their best estate.

If I were called upon to designate the prominent trait of his character, I should answer self-abnegation. This showed itself in his splendid moral courage. No man ever sat on any bench who was more fearless in the discharge of what he deemed his duty than James Gilfillan. No consideration of what popular prejudices might be antagonized, or current theories having some dissemination overthrown, or animosities against him personally aroused, as the effect of a decision ever had the slightest lodgment in his mind, or effect perceived or unperceived on his action. If he satisfied his own mind and conscience, that was enough for him, and it was all. In this respect he was the stuff of which martyrs are made.

It showed itself further, in the direct, simple method of his work. In his written opinions he goes straight to the work. He had literary ability of a high order, and he wrote strong, vigorous English. He had the analytic power to define and set out a legal principle in the abstract so as to make it circulate through the whole realm of jurisprudence clothed in his language. But there never was apparently the slightest effort for any such effect. He seemed to do nothing for his own fame, to all appearances was indifferent to it. And it may be partly due to this that personal contact with the mats never failed to produce in one who had that privilege a higher appreciation of his strength of mind and character. He showed it in simple, unostentatious ways.

Take him for all in all; I have no hesitation in saying that Chief Justice Gilfillan was competent for and would have adorned a position upon any bench administering English law.

I will not attempt to speak of him as a soldier but leave that to those who are more competent.

As a man he was single-minded and true; it was yea, yea, and nay, nay. Deception had no place in his make-up. Policy had no more. As a companion he was delightful. The first crust of acquaintance being broken through, he was one of the most genial of men. He had a keen sense of humor and quite a fund of anecdote collected from his extensive general reading, and he was quite happy when he could have a chat with his friends, letting the conversation drift and take its own course.

A marked man has fallen, one who has done honor to his State and to his race, one of the chiefs among the powerful men of his time. He now rests from his labors, but his memory will live in the record of his work and in the hearts of those that loved him.

Address of Hon. Geo. B. Young:

After the high tribute and just presentation of the characteristics of our great Chief Justice in the memorial that has been read, there is very little if anything that can be added by me.

It was my good fortune, however, during many years, to be in a sense the "organ" of the Court, in reporting its decisions—including, of course, those of the Chief Justice. In performing those duties, it became necessary for me to make a more exact and thorough study of the cases in which they were delivered than would ordinarily fall to the lot of one simply consulting the reports. As a result, I had early impressed upon my mind the very marked ability that characterized Judge Gilfillan in at once grasping the real point, the real issue, the real merits of a case, disregarding and brushing aside all extraneous matter whether of law or of fact.

Another characteristic I noticed was in the expression of his judgment; in many instances it seemed ragged, uncared for, unadorned; yet the legal principles and their application to the case in hand were expressed with singular felicity.

Of the many decisions by which he made his mark upon the jurisprudence of this State and country, one stands forth preeminent, his decision in the case of the State Railroad bonds. It has always seemed to me that that decision touched the high-water mark of judicial opinion in this generation. I think it will bear comparison with the best constitutional opinion of any court in the land, save possibly the greatest opinion of Chief Justice Marshall.

In Chief Justice Gilfillan we had a judge who would rank with Judge Gibson and the greatest jurists who have adorned the bench in other States of the Union.

Address of Hon. Chas. E. Vanderburgh:

The Governor of the State, in his proclamation closing the public offices of the Capitol on the day of his funeral, characterizes the late Chief Justice as a most able, fearless, upright, and impartial judge.

That tribute implies a great deal, but it is eminently just and well merited, and it is precisely the tribute that every honest man who knew him spontaneously accords to him. There were not many abler jurists in his generation and certainly none more fearless and upright.

He was eminently qualified for the position of Chief Justice, his perception of correct legal principles was unusually clear and accurate. His strong analytical mind readily grasped the leading points in a case, and he surpassed any man I ever knew in his ability to separate and state them concisely and clearly. This made him a model chief in the consultation room. The late Justice Berry, whose public services will not soon be forgotten and whose memory will long be revered, used often to speak of the remarkable power of mental concentration possessed by Chief Justice Gilfillan and the facility with which he was able to dispose of the most difficult cases and decide them well.

Absolutely truthful and thoroughly honest and independent, he was no respecter of persons. He would turn neither to the right nor to the left to secure personal favor, and doubtless his manner was often misunderstood by those who did not know him well. Yet he was one of the kindest of men and a most faithful and devoted friend.

He was not only a strong man but a just and good man, a man with a conscience, and of strong convictions of right and duty. His character was grounded on sound morals and religious principles—fundamental qualities of a good judge, which cannot safely be undervalued.

The Chief Justice commanded the respect and confidence of his associates on the bench in a remarkable degree. Upon the separation of the members of the Court as formerly constituted a year ago, he remarked with much satisfaction and evident feeling that during all the previous years that the Court as then constituted had served together and even extending back through his whole term of service, there had hardly been an incident to disturb the harmony of feeling and pleasant intercourse among the members of the Court in which he had so long presided.

During that time his contemporaries on the bench in other States have been Cooley and Campbell of Michigan, Dixon, Ryan and Cole of Wisconsin, Dillon of Iowa, and Brewer of Kansas, and it is safe to say, without disparagement to them, that if we consider the full measure of his abilities and judicial qualifications, he stands the peer of any of them.

Address of General John B. Sanborn:

In the fall of our illustrious Chief Justice, example and emphasis is given to the poetic conception that

Death loves a shining mark, a signal blow,
A blow which, while it executes, alarms,
And startles thousands with a single fall.

It was but yesterday that our departed friend was walking on the high places of the earth in "The excellency of dignity and the excellency of power;" his voice was the voice of magistracy and dominion, a sovereign voice, potent and controlling in all the litigations and controversies of fifteen hundred thousand men. Today all is changed; the voice is silent, power and dominion have departed, and nothing visible remains except what is seen in the light and hues of immortality. On such occasions and more than on any others, we turn to immortality as the only solution of the problems of human life, the only teacher that deciphers man and explains the mysteries involved in his life and death. With firmness, faithfulness and zeal, our departed friend met and unraveled all the knotty problems of his own life, with patience and undying faith in the great future. Born a Scotchman, educated an American, he possessed the firmness, decision of character, clearness of mental vision, and strong reasoning powers of the former and the activity, zeal, and patriotism of the latter. At the bar he at once became conspicuous for his learning, sound judgment, and careful practice, never failing to reach a determination of his case on the real merits of the controversy.

His public spirit and patriotism were unbounded. Personal interest and personal security were without power to restrain him, and fatigue, hardships, danger, and death were without power to deter him in the least from the fullest discharge of all his duties as a citizen of our State and country. Although enjoying the sweets of quiet civil life and the practice of his chosen profession far more than the great majority of men, he at once abandoned all and cheerfully took his place in the ranks with those who were ready to sacrifice life, health, property, all that men hold dear, for the preservation of the institutions of his country and the liberty of all men. In the military service of the United States, which he voluntarily entered on the 6th day of August, 1862, a service always most trying to those of sound judgment and independent thought and action, he was governed by one motto and one principle—obedience even unto death of all the lawful orders of his superiors, whether personally entertaining for such superiors respect or contempt. Success in this branch of the public service could not fail to attend him acting upon such motives and under such a motto. His military service was one of the most arduous and trying character and of such a nature as could not in the very nature of things bring fame and renown. It is but the slightest impression that is made upon the mind by the statement that the deceased, with the rank of captain, marched on foot at the head of his company from the Mississippi to the Missouri river through Northern Minnesota and Dakota in the summer of 1863. Our minds are so constituted that they do not grasp from such a statement the wearisome march for ninety or more consecutive days in burning suns across alkali deserts and plains, with the air filled with dust and the tongue swollen for want of pure water, or the difference between sleeping in comfortable beds in quiet homes and resting upon the ground in cold and storms, disturbed constantly by savage and wily foes. Language cannot portray the hardships, sufferings, and exposures endured by officers and men on such a campaign, and only those who have participated in them can form any just appreciation of such a public service. The public interest required this service in 1863, and it was rendered by our departed friend with the determination and vigor that characterized all his acts.

Afterwards, at the head of his regiment, on the bloody field of Tupelo, on July 14, 1864, he stood with his command as a rock unmoved amid the varying fortunes of that hardly contested field. After the battles of the summer and autumn of 1864, he was assigned to the important, hazardous, annoying, and inglorious service of guarding and protecting the line of communication to the armies at and south of Nashville, where the least failure at any point might result in the greatest possible disaster to the government and force the withdrawal of troops and the abandonment of the country from Atlanta to points far north of Nashville. This is that kind of military service that oftentimes covers an officer with disgrace, but even when well performed, never is known to bring to him any glory.

This fatiguing, trying, hazardous military service made serious inroads upon his physical powers and undoubtedly shortened his days on earth. So great had been the strain and wear that, in the weakness and delirium of his last sickness, although the long period of thirty years had intervened, the exciting, trying scenes of the war seemed again to pass in review before his mind. The tried and trusted veterans of his command, with faces scarred and ranks thinned by battle and disease, again appeared in line waiting his command to hold their positions or move against the foe. He again seemed to see the flag of his country full high advanced over bleeding and prostrate enemies and again shared in the excitement of glorious victory.

On account of the character of the military service he was required to perform, it may be that his larger fame will be best preserved and will most securely rest on the great service he has rendered the State in the judicial department and as Chief Justice of this Court. Through the long period of twenty years during which the state has passed from infancy to manhood, the great questions that rise from rapid development have come before the Court and have been considered and decided upon sound principles of law and with due regard to precedent. He always recognized and acted upon the fundamental truth that the primary object of every judicial system is to establish justice and that the only lawyer and only judge who can gain preeminence is he who can so apply remedies and principles as to secure justice in the highest degree. Judged by this standard, the illustrious Judge will always stand preeminent. His views upon all the great questions that have come before this Court for twenty years are expressed in a body of case law that will run through forty volumes of the Minnesota Reports and constitute an enduring monument to his memory and, at the same time, remain a light and guide to future generations.

> So when a great man dies,
> For years beyond our ken,
> The light he leaves behind him, lies
> Upon the paths of men.

Address of Hon. Wm. J. Hahn:

It is eminently fitting, when death invades the ranks of our profession and removes one of its honorable and honored members, to pause for a moment, give public voice to our sense of loss, and register a brief memorial of his worth and public services. We have met for that purpose to-day. Our ranks have again been broken. A noble, modest, pure man, an upright, faithful, distinguished citizen, an eminent, conscientious, leading member of our bar, a great, fearless, spotless judge, has fallen. No eulogy that any of us may be able to pronounce and no memorial that we may enter on the rolls of this Court can add one jot or tittle to the well-earned fame that he himself has achieved and left on record here. It is with no such hope, it is with no such purpose, that we ask this minute to be made. It is for the living and not for the dead; it is for us, his comrades at the bar who still remain, we ask this to be done, that thus we may say to those who come after us, we knew, we appreciated, we honored this, our brother.

I have not the ability, neither was my association with Judge Gilfillan intimate enough, to warrant my attempting an analysis of his character. That is more ably done by others than I could hope to do. But I esteem it a privilege to be permitted to lay my poor though willing tribute on his tomb. I knew him well enough to say with all my heart that he was "a true and brave and downright honest man," who held faithfulness and sincerity as first principles; that he was a citizen who valued duty more than success and who esteemed an upright and irreproachable character more highly than distinction; that he was a pure, just, wise, and fearless judge who, by his great gifts and noble character, adorned the judicial office, added luster to our profession, and materially advanced the cause of good government and of right living.

I would name as one of the distinguishing and most commendable characteristics of Judge Gilfillan his fearless independence. I think he showed in his entire career that he was a firm believer in the truth of Ben Jonson's epigram that "He that departs with his own honesty for vulgar praise doth it too dearly buy." He cannot and will not be charged with truckling in any way to popular influences or excitements. Fearlessness of opinion deliberately formed is a *sine qua non* for a judicial position. Judge Gilfillan possessed this in a more than usual degree. He was by nature, by temperament, by character, exalted above popular influences and therefore was enabled to serenely administer the noble science of the law. It is such an administration that has heretofore been and will continue to be the sheet anchor of the republic. The judiciary of this country, state, and nation has been, is, and must continue to be, if our noble heritage is to be handed down to future generations unimpaired, the great balance wheel in the machinery of our government as it must be in the government of every free people who desire to preserve and maintain their freedom. It is and must continue to be the compass that steadily, unerringly, constantly points toward the great polar star, so that when storms rage and darkness overshadows us and danger surrounds us, we may confidently look to it to guide and direct us. It is the great dyke whose staunch timbers and solid masonry must protect us if we are to be protected from the storms of passion and the waves of faction that are sure to arise and roll. To maintain this position, to exert this influence, there is no qualification more necessary to be possessed by the men who occupy these exalted positions than this fearless independence. The importance of this trait in the judicial character cannot be, in my judgment, overestimated. Without it, no man, however great he be either by natural gifts or individual acquirements, can ever attain the ideal conception of the judicial office or discharge the duties of such a position in a way to command the lasting respect of bar and people.

As was well said by a distinguished member of our profession in concluding a brief review of the life of one of the most eminent men who ever graced the bench of the Supreme Court of the United States (Chief Justice Taney): "Ours is a profession whose labors and talents are expended for the most part upon the controversies of individuals and about transitory affairs. And yet it is of all professions the one most important to good government and to just living. In our favored land, with its great natural advantages and its freedom from arbitrary government, where individual rights are protected even against the government itself by fundamental laws, the administration of the law is that exercise of government which is at once the most frequent and most important. To it we must look for relief from injustice, for the preservation of personal rights, and for the protection of property. We may differ about political questions, about the nature of government, about public policy; but for ourselves and our daily lives, what we most need, what is of the highest importance to each one of us, is a pure, just, wise, and fearless administration of the law."

Address of Hon. Moses E. Clapp:

The fact that we are prone to eulogize the dead has been regarded as one of the weaknesses of human nature. This is a mistake. It is but one of the many evidences of the wonderful power of the mind to adopt itself to conditions. When bowed in grief for the dead, we naturally turn to a contemplation of their virtues, that in so doing we may at least somewhat dull the keen edge of our sorrow. We do this not so much to extol the dead as to lessen our own grief. This is the mainspring from which flows, among the immediate associates of the dead, the recollection and appreciation of their virtues, carrying out into the world beyond only the recollection of good deeds and exalted character; thus it is that the evil is forgotten and the good remembered.

Fortunate the living if, beyond the mere office of eulogy, they can discover in the life and character of the departed those qualities that enlist respect and admiration and thus, in a measure, divert the mind from grief. Such is our lot to-day. To do right is but simply duty. We ask ourselves sometimes why we should extol the mere performance of a plain duty. The fact is that in our willingness to praise and crown with honor the name and memory of one who has been conspicuous for his conscientious discharge of his duty, we may not perhaps recognize man's proneness to do wrong, but it is at least a recognition of man's frailty in the light of the temptations that beset him. It is one of those many forces, little thought of in themselves, yet all powerful as factors in shaping and molding thought and action.

Those who knew our late Chief Justice recognized in him a man of such sterling qualities that while they mourn his loss they can find consolation in paying a tribute to his memory as deserved as it is voluntary, a free-will offering from the heart, freely paid to one who is powerless alike to punish or reward. The law is sought, declared, and administered by a profession in touch with the world around them; their lives and associations, social and professional, are interwoven with those of all about them; they lay no exclusive claim to the virtues, nor are they free from the vices incident to human nature, except so far as their character may be molded by their pursuit.

This is not the time or place to speak at length of our profession or to defend it from the attack of those who hate the law and our profession because they stand the sole unsurmountable barriers to oppression upon the one hand and disorder upon the other; nor from the aspersions of the thoughtless, who overlook the fact that human law must be declared and administered through the agency of fallible men and cannot overlook their occasional mistakes. Suffice it to say that in the law society finds its only safeguard and protection; the order-loving are its votaries, the bench and bar the ministering priesthood; at its shrine every true friend of human rights must worship.

While at times complaints—oft-times just complaints—of our ministrations may be made, yet it is the one universal faith, as perfect in its aims and objects as man's instinctive longing for the right can be, as imperfect in its administration as man's fallible nature falls short of perfection.

While our late Chief Justice was esteemed as a citizen and soldier, yet he will be remembered chiefly as a lawyer and a judge, an honorable member of this profession, wherein, above all others, responsibility finds a parallel only in its attendant duty, and I know of no higher tribute to pay him than to say that as a lawyer he was as learned as he was honorable, as a judge deaf alike to clamor and applauses—as fearless as he was just.

Address of Hon. John M. Gilman:

I can, of course, add nothing in commemoration of our dear Chief Justice to what has already been said; but in view of my long acquaintance it perhaps is not out of place for me to join with others in moving the adoption of the memorial that has been read.

I came to St. Paul to live the same year as did Mr. Gilfillan—1857. We soon became acquainted, and from that hour to the day of his death we were most intimate and cordial friends.

Mr. Gilfillan came with a mind well stored with a knowledge of the law in all its departments and ramifications. He at once took a leading position at the bar. His abilities were widely recognized, not only by the bench but by the bar, from the start.

Mr. Gilfillan was distinguished more for strength, breadth, grasp, and force of intellect than for brilliancy, yet he was a very strong man at the bar. His candor,

his sincerity, his purity, which shone in his very countenance, his power of analysis, his clearness of statement, his logical reasoning, made him a formidable antagonist before the jury as well as before the court.

He continued in the practice of his profession and was in the full and successful tide of it when the civil war broke out. When volunteers were called to go forth in defense of the Union, Mr. Gilfillan locked the door of his office, shouldered his musket, and went into the military service of his country. He served until the close of the war, when he returned home in the fall of 1865, I believe. Receiving his discharge, he again unlocked the door of his office, brushed away the dust that had accumulated upon his books, resumed the practice of his profession, and again took the same position at the bar that he held when he entered the service of his country.

The bar, as I well recollect, had marked him as eminently fitted for the bench long before he was called to that position, and, in fact, he was exercising the functions of a judge long before he was called to the bench. In those days we had here, in the first place, but one District Judge; afterwards we had a Court of Common Pleas, but those judges could not do all the business that was brought before them. As a result, most of those cases, which are denominated court cases, were tried by referees, and Mr. Gilfillan was, I may say, a standing referee in all cases where he was not an attorney. Such was the confidence that the bar had in him that no one objected to his acting as referee. I have tried many cases before him, and he evinced the same qualities as a referee that he did as a judge—dispassionate, cool, calm, courteous, kind, clear-headed. He decided many cases, and I do not recollect a single instance where his decision as a referee was reversed.

Continuing in practice up to the time that there was an opening, he was called to the bench, as we all know. Of his career on the bench no encomium is needed from me. There is his record. I may say, however, of the position Mr. Chief Justice Gilfillan will hold in the estimation of the bar of this State, he will be spoken of as is Chief Justice Parsons of Massachusetts by the bar of that State, and Chief Justice Gibson of Pennsylvania by the bar of that State—"The great Chief Justice."

Now, may it please your Honors, he has gone from us, and when we go into that court room where he sat for so many years and miss his manly figure from the seat he so long occupied, we cannot but feel oppressed with a feeling of sadness, especially so when we reflect that we are never to see him occupy that seat again. All we can do is to spread upon the records this memorial, that the future bar of this State may refer back and have before it some evidence of the estimation in which Chief Justice Gilfillan was held by his contemporaries. I therefore join in moving its adoption.

Associate Justice Thomas Canty said:

I shall delay the proceedings but a few minutes. As one of the members of the bar who was called to the bench, I will just say a few words, as I have been both before and behind "the scenes" a little.

When I was practicing, I felt—as a good many others of the younger members of the bar and some of the older ones felt—that he was just a little contrary sometimes and a little brusque and curt in his rulings. Sometimes he would "sit down" on me in a way that I did not like.

But I must say that since I became more intimately associated with him, I formed a different opinion of his character. I found him, on closer association, to be a man of great simplicity of character, absolutely unaffected and unprejudiced.

I found him to be a man of very strong character, of great will power, clear-headed, logical, and very analytical. In fact, he paid no attention to subterfuges at all; he simply struck for the central principle and rested at that.

Generally, in his conferences, I found him to be a man that was easily approached, easily got along with. He and I have had a good many controversies in the short time I have been on the bench, but it never created the least ill feeling; the warmer we got over it, the better friends we were before we got through.

I found him to be a very companionable man, and I began to think a great deal of him.

Associate Justice Daniel Buck said:

On the 16th day of December, 1894, there died in this city James Gilfillan, the Chief Justice of our State.

His chilled form lies pulseless and still, and over his grave have been said the sad words: "Earth to earth, ashes to ashes, dust to dust." There is a vacant chair here; and at his home a grief-stricken household, for the old arm chair has ceased its rocking and a loved one gone over to the other side. He died, not in the season of beautiful flowers, gleaming grain, and ripening fruit, but with the judicial harness still upon him, he passed away as the dying year was singing its last requiem. "The wheels of weary life stood still," for "God's finger touched him and he died."

When the pall of death falls upon our fellow man, we draw nearer together and keep faith with the usages of the past, while we respect and mourn for one who sleeps beneath the fresh earth and the changeless stars. Over every threshold death sweeps with a resistless force, and there is a vacant chair in nearly every household. We know not the mysteries of this coming and going, this living and dying. We do not know the hour when life's struggles shall be over and the heart cease its beatings, although—

> We know when moons shall wane,
> And summer birds shall cross the sea—
> But who shall tell us when to look for death?

And it is well that we pay a tribute to the honored dead. Then the shadows of selfishness are stilled, and in the presence of death we forget the jealousies that sometimes mar our better manhood. With the sting of death and the victory of the grave come the white robes of charity and the balanced scales of a truer justice, and to-day we do well to honor the memory of our great Chief Justice.

It is a great honor to be the Chief Justice of a great State; but it is a greater honor to be fully worthy of it. Chief Justice Gilfillan won that honor and deserved it, for he won it through merit. He pandered to no partisan spirit; he climbed no mountain peak in search of the tricks of the demagogue; he floated upon no popular wave to win judicial honors. He knew what it was to labor and toil upon the farm in boyhood days. There, amid the fragrance of the clover blossoms, the perfume of a thousand flowers, and the development of physical strength, is the best starting point for the battles of after life. The victories of manhood are frequently the result of the struggles of boyhood. With the maturity of his years came the industry and love of labor that marked his early life.

Fearless in the cause of right, he would not turn aside to avoid an enemy nor bend to grant unjust favors to a friend. He wrote no opinions to obtain notoriety; he made no decisions at the dictation of wealth or political influence. He could defy the storm because his knees were strong as the "unwedgable and gnarled oak." He would rather go down with colors flying than be silent when justice was endangered.

The judiciary travels no flowery pathway. Selfish greed, partisan malice, and criminal violence may hurl their poisoned darts into the judicial forum, but the burning torture must be borne with unflinching silence. Criminals and sometimes, unfortunately, criminal lawyers, would pull down the pillars in the temple of justice that they may revel in the ruins their power has wrought. When liberty is confused with chaos and unbridled license with righteousness; when violence would nullify the law and strike down the constitution—then we need a Gilfillan among our judiciary, stern and brave but able and just, to proclaim the ban of his disapproval even though threats and thorns beset his judicial path.

It was not great learning and great intellect, merely, that made him our noble Chief Justice but because with these elements of character he never flinched from duty nor bowed to unjust popular clamor. At Thermopylae, he would have been one of the Spartan heroes; at Balaklava, he would have charged with the six hundred; and he would have died at the stake or suffered martyrdom on the cross rather than yield his convictions of human right. Although born where rise the Grampian Hills and Ben Nevis, in the land of John Knox, Walter Scott, and Robert Burns, yet he loved this great American Union, and in its hours of peril he stood ready to offer up his life in behalf of its starry banner. He had a patriot's love because he knew a patriot's duty.

There are no mists hanging over his life or grave, of clients wronged or public trusts betrayed. There is no hoarded wealth, in home or bank, purchased at the price of dishonor and violated faith. His life's sun, burnished with golden hues, has gone to its western setting to rise, perchance, upon some fairer shore. Silently he sleeps upon the banks of that majestic river whose waters come and go; and if over his grave there shall be no monumental stone, yet in your library there will be the enduring monument of his fidelity and his intellectual greatness.

People of Minnesota, keep fresh and green the memory of your Chief Justice—Gilfillan—for

Thy stalwart son deserves a Roman's fame,
 For Cato was not more supremely just;
Augustus was not greater in the state,
 Nor Brutus truer to the public trust.

Associate Justice William Mitchell said:

Having during the past fourteen years been brought into very intimate relations, personal and official, with our late Chief Justice, I feel that I owe it to myself on this occasion, even at the risk of repetition, to pay my humble tribute to his memory.

One of the chief inducements to my acceptance of a place on this bench was the rare combination of talents possessed by the three judges then composing this Court. There was Justice Cornell with his remarkably clear, acute intellect, Justice Berry with his sound judgment and great fund of practical common sense, and Chief Justice Gilfillan with his great mental vigor and remarkable power of analysis. A better combination of talent to constitute a safe and able court is not often found on the same bench at the same time. The peculiar talents of each seemed to be the complement of those of the others. All three fell in the harness at the very height of their intellectual powers—first Cornell, then Berry, and last Gilfillan.

If I were to name what I considered the most marked moral and mental qualities in the character of the late Chief Justice, I would say moral courage and the power of accurate analysis. His single aim was to decide a cause rightly according to legal principles, and this he did to the best of his ability, regardless of the effect of the decision upon himself or of adverse popular criticism. I never knew a man more impervious to outside pressure than he in the discharge of his official duties. In the consideration of a cause, he knew neither class nor condition among litigants or counsel. This was not the result of mere indifference to public opinion but of fearless independence and of a profound sense of duty. He never talked about his duty—I never heard him mention it once—but I never knew a man who was actuated by a higher sense of it than he, and he always performed it as he understood it, regardless of consequences. You will not find in all his opinions a single utterance designed to catch the popular ear or to trim to the passing popular breeze.

As has been already remarked to-day, he possessed an unusual power of analysis. Many cases are obscured by immaterial issues and inconsequential argument. These his vigorous mental grasp and great power of analysis enabled him to strip off and brush aside with celerity and thus reduce the case down to the real questions upon which its determination depended. And, having done this, his acute and extensive knowledge of legal principles enabled him to decide the case with the clearness and conciseness that always characterized his style. His opinions were usually noted for their brevity. He did not consider it any part of the duty of a judge to write essays on the law, and he never stepped aside to deliver lectures on either law or morals. Above anything like pedantry or affectation of learning, master of his subject and of the English language, he did not waste pages to express an idea. Having made up his mind as to the principles upon which the decision of a cause turned, he said neither more nor less than was necessary to the decision and to state the grounds upon which it rested. His written language was a transcript of his mind. It was accurate because he accurately understood the principles he discussed. It was readily understood because he understood, himself. His clear, pure, terse English is decidedly refreshing amidst so much diffuse rhetoric in this day of type-writers and stenographers. And yet with all his powers, I never knew a more modest man in his estimate of himself. He never thought of display and seemed unconscious that he had the power to make any.

While he was too great to be the slavish follower of mere "case" law, and while he well understood that the law was not a code of cast-iron rules but a system of principles capable of application to new conditions, yet he was a firm believer in strict adherence to established legal principles. He looked upon novelties of decision in derogation of those principles as "the plague of the commonwealth," and with Lord Camden he believed that "the discretion of the judge is the law of tyrants." Hence, he believed it better to apply established legal

principles inflexibly, even if it seemed to work harshly in the particular case, than for the Court to bend them or depart from them to meet a "hard" case.

All of my colleagues will join me in testifying that in the consultation room he was a most helpful counselor and adviser. His discussion of a case never digressed into immaterial side issues. He never indulged in mere elusive legal platitudes but went directly to the pith and core of the case. Everything he said was helpful and suggestive, and if we did not always agree with his views on a question, we often found it easier to overrule him than to answer him.

From my mere general acquaintance with Chief Justice Gilfillan before coming on the bench, I had the impression that he was somewhat cold and reserved in disposition and blunt and even brusque in manner, which might prevent the forming of warm personal friendships, although his ability and integrity would command the highest respect. But I soon found out my mistake. While never demonstrative, no man ever possessed a warmer heart or was more capable of forming sincere and close personal friendships, and I can truly say that I became attached to him by as warm a personal friendship as to any man with whom I have ever been associated on the bench.

His apparent bluntness or even brusqueness was a mere unconscious mannerism and was never intentional. And I think the bar will bear me witness that, even in the exhibition of any such bluntness of manner, he was, as in all other things, strictly impartial. He was as liable to display it towards the oldest and ablest members of the bar as he was to the youngest or most obscure. The only difference was that the former generally understood and overlooked it, while the latter did not always do so.

The State has lost an able and upright Judge. We, the surviving members of the Court, have lost a most helpful associate, and I, certainly, have lost a most valued personal friend.

Chief Justice Charles M. Start said:

The Court receives with grateful appreciation your just and merited tribute to the worth and work of Mr. Chief Justice Gilfillan.

The special work to which he gave long and laborious years of useful service was the molding of the jurisprudence of our young State. To this work he brought natural abilities of a high order, the ripe experience of a learned lawyer, a keen sense of justice, an extraordinary command of the resources of reason, perfect integrity, and great moral courage.

His judicial opinions in this Court are the rich fruit of that work. They are the landmarks in our jurisprudence and disclose a lawyer like penetration to the very heart of the matter in hand and a clearness of statement that leaves no uncertainty as to the point involved and decided, while his conclusions follow naturally from the underlying reasons and principles upon which the science of jurisprudence is based.

These opinions are a monument to his fame as a jurist. That fame will widen as the years advance. He administered justice without fear or favor, giving to the weak and the strong, to individuals and corporations, their legal rights. His life was pure and his reputation stainless; neither was ever tarnished by an unmanly or dishonest act. Few men have left behind them stronger claims to public respect and esteem and none a more undoubted title to the grateful remembrance of the whole people of the State.

It is fitting, then, that your memorial should be recorded in the records of the Court for the day, there to remain a lasting testimonial to the virtues and public services of an honest man and a great judge. It is so ordered. [59 Minn. 539]

Christopher G. Ripley

1822–1881
Chief Justice, 1870–1874

The Hon. Christopher Gore Ripley was born September 6, 1822, in Waltham, Massachusetts, where his father, Rev. Samuel Ripley, was the settled Unitarian minister. His mother, who is said to have been one of the most remarkable women of the century in her intellectual attainments, was the daughter of Capt. Gamaliel Bradford of Boston. The future chief justice was prepared for college by his parents and graduated from Harvard College in 1841. He spent one year at the Harvard Law School and then entered the office of Franklin Dexter, Esq., of Boston, a celebrated lawyer of that day. In 1855 he came to the then territory of Minnesota, settling first at Brownsville but removing to Chatfield in 1856, where he practiced his profession.

In 1869 he was elected Chief Justice of this court for the constitutional term beginning in January 1870, but in April 1874 he was compelled by failing health to resign. The remainder of his life was spent at Concord, Massachusetts, where in the "Old Manse" he died October 15, 1881.

The opinions of Judge Ripley begin in Volume 15 and end in Volume 20 of the Minnesota Reports.

On Wednesday morning, November 30, 1881, in behalf of the bar of Fillmore county, the Attorney General, Hon. William J. Hahn, presented to the Supreme Court the following report of proceedings had in the District Court of that county with reference to the death of Chief Justice Ripley:

At the general November Term of court begun and holden at the court house in the Village of Preston, County of Fillmore, State of Minnesota, on the 9th day of November, A.D. 1881, Hon. John Q. Farmer, district judge, presiding.

At the opening of the court H. R. Wells, Esq., sug-

gested the decease of Hon. Christopher G. Ripley, late Chief Justice of this state, and that such action be taken as will show the high esteem in which the deceased was held by the court and the members of this bar. Whereupon, the court appointed H. R. Wells, N. P. Colburn and J. R. Jones, a committee to draft appropriate resolutions of respect. After fitting remarks by the members of the bar and court, the committee reported as follows:

Whereas, the Honorable Christopher Gore Ripley, an honored member of our bar from 1856 until he was called to the responsibilities of Chief Justice of this state, in 1870, departed this life at his residence in Concord, Massachusetts, on the 15th day of October 1881, as a tribute of our respect for his memory and in appreciation of his worth, we present the following:

First. That from long and intimate association with the deceased we bear sincere and earnest testimony to his fidelity to every trust. He was a genial associate and a true friend, obedient to every requirement of society, cheerfully acceding to its calls and anticipating its demands. He loved truth and hated oppression. As an attorney he endeavored to protect the weak and to promote justice. As a judge he illustrated the qualities of mind and heart essential to and exalting his high office.

Second. Sharing his confidence and regard, his friendship has endowed us with pleasant memories, but his loss fills our hearts with sorrow.

Third. That these proceedings be engrossed and made a part of the records of this court.

That authenticated copies thereof be forwarded to the Attorney General of this state, to be by him brought to the attention of the Honorable Supreme Court, also to the widow and family of the deceased at her residence in Concord.

H. R. Wells,
N. P. Colburn,
J. R. Jones,
Committee

Thereupon in behalf of this court Associate Justice Berry responded as follows:

The proceedings of the bar of Fillmore county that have just been presented as a tribute to the memory of Chief Justice Ripley are the more significant because they are the testimony to his learning and worth of those whose opportunities for knowing him were of the best—the testimony of his professional brethren among whom he was engaged in the practice of the law for more than fifteen years and among whom he resided during the four years of his judicial service. They doubtless express not only the sentiments of the bar but the general regard and esteem in which he was held by the entire community in which he dwelt, as a learned and skillful lawyer, a wise counselor, and an honorable, courteous and upright man.

Coming into southeastern Minnesota in the infancy of its settlement, he was brought by professional and other business relations in contact with a large proportion of the early settlers, so that there was hardly a man among them of any, even local, prominence who did not know him.

In a new settlement, into which every man comes almost as a stranger, there is, as many of us can bear witness from personal observation, a prevailing feeling of mutual dependence and a sense of obligation for kind offices that, to a considerable extent, disappear as the country grows older and people are more able to depend upon themselves. But for the years during which it lasts, this feeling of dependence brings men very closely together and affords them unusual opportunities for forming estimates of character and ability that are seldom mistaken, and the resulting likes and dislikes are ordinarily well-founded and lasting. This is well exemplified in the case of Judge Ripley. No man in that part of the state made more, warmer, or firmer friends, especially among the early settlers, than he did by his cheerful readiness to do a public service or a private kindness and by his entire reliability in every matter of business or duty.

My own personal acquaintance with Judge Ripley substantially began when he became a member of this court. After that time we were brought together almost constantly during the terms of court and at the meetings held in vacation for consultation. He was a most delightful companion not only on account of the extent, variety, and accuracy of his information, his knowledge of men and affairs, his large fund of anecdote, his fresh, genial, and abounding wit and humor, but equally on account of his unfailing courtesy, his unaffected modesty, and his genuine kindness of heart.

He was well descended, and his advantages in youth and early manhood were uncommonly great. His father was a Unitarian minister of high repute in the days of Channing, and his mother the most learned woman of her time. He was born and reared at a period of great intellectual activity in New England, when questions of high import, theological, literary, and scientific, were familiarly discussed at the fireside. A critical observer and an incessant and thoughtful reader, he failed not to profit by his opportunities.

As one marked result, his familiar and unstudied conversation, aided by a ready and retentive memory, was instructive and entertaining to a degree that those whose privilege it was to enjoy it can never forget.

As a judge he was animated with the highest sense of the sacredness of the judicial function and with an ardent desire so to administer the law as to do equal justice between man and man. He brought to the discharge of his official duties much learning and all the application by study and thought of which he was capable. No man ever questioned the purity of his intentions or his unspotted integrity of purpose. To his associates upon the bench he ever manifested, both in public and private, the same unassuming modesty and considerate kindness and courtesy that always characterized his relations to the bar.

I speak for my brother McMillan, as well as myself, in saying that we look back upon our association with Judge Ripley upon the bench of this court with the most gratifying recollections.

To this inadequate tribute to the memory of a good man it only remains for me to add that, after his impaired health compelled him to resign his judicial office, he returned to Concord, Massachusetts. There he died on the 15th day of October last, at the age of 59, among the friends of his youth, having received during a long and patiently endured illness of seven years the devoted care of his most estimable wife, of his surviving sisters, and of other near and affectionate relatives. [67 Minn. xxiii]

George B. Young

1840–1906
Associate Justice, 1874–1875

On the afternoon of April 3, 1907, in the court room at the State Capitol, Hon. Daniel Fish, in behalf of the Minnesota State Bar Association, addressed the Supreme Court, then in session, and said:

The thirteenth day of October next will be the fiftieth anniversary of the election whereby the people of Minnesota Territory adopted a constitution preparatory to admission into the Union. On the same day they chose from their number three eminent citizens to constitute the first supreme court of the new commonwealth. Today, near the close of a half century of statehood, the bar of that court presents, for incorporation in its records, a brief commemorative notice of one of those pioneer justices, the last to pass from earth of a distinguished triumvirate. But three and a half years have elapsed since a like service was performed for the first of them, Judge Flandrau, when an eloquent tribute to his memory was read at this bar from the pen of the last survivor whose death we now deplore. In the meantime Lafayette Emmett, the first chief justice, departed this life, and he, with Justices Clark and Buck of later times and Judge Nelson, the first occupant of our federal bench, have all been commemorated here. And now George B. Young, once a member of this court and but yesterday the peerless leader of our bar, has passed away. Of the six former chief justices but one survives, Thomas Wilson, still in full practice. Of fourteen associate justices (not counting Judge Wilson who served in both capacities) but four remain and they of the more recent. All the territorial justices are gone and nearly all of the earlier practitioners.

Fifty years are but few in the life of a state, yet already the age of tradition is upon us; the story of our bench and bar begins to take on the soft haze of antiquity.

Hon. William E. Hale, in behalf of the Minnesota State Bar Association, then addressed the court and presented the following:

George Brooks Young was born July 25, 1840, in the city of Boston, Massachusetts. Both of his parents were descendants from early settlers in the Plymouth and Massachusetts Bay colonies and represented families of consequence in the annals of New England. His father was a Unitarian, clergyman, and an overseer of Harvard College.

Judge Young was graduated from Harvard in 1860, and in the fall of the same year as a law student he entered the law office of Henry A. Scudder in Boston, where he remained for about a year, when he entered the Harvard Law School, from which he was graduated two years later with the degree A.M. In 1864 he went to New York City and for some time engaged in post-graduate study in the office of William Curtiss Noyes, and in November of that year he was admitted to the bar. He then entered the office of David Dudley Field and for a time occupied the position of managing clerk. After leaving that office he engaged in an independent practice in the East until his removal to the West.

In 1870 he came to Minneapolis and was admitted to the bar in this state and continued in the practice of law until 1874, when he was appointed by Governor Davis an associate justice of this court, to fill the vacancy occurring through the resignation of Chief Justice Ripley. His term of office expired in 1875, and he then moved to St. Paul, where he remained in active practice until the time of his death. He became associated with Stanford Newel under the firm name of Young & Newel, and in 1883 entered into a partnership with William H. Lightner under the name of Young & Lightner, which continued until his death.

From 1875 to 1892 he was the reporter of this court and compiled twenty-seven volumes of the court's reports, volumes 21 to 47 inclusive. For a number of years he lectured in the law department of the University of Minnesota on the subject of "Conflict of Laws."

The first case of great importance in which he was engaged was the proceeding by which the St. Paul, Minneapolis & Manitoba Railway Company first acquired its railroad; in this case he was the chief counsel, representing the railway company and others specially interested. His work attracted a great deal of attention and at once brought him to the front as one of the foremost lawyers at this bar; and from that time until his death, his services were constantly sought for by those interested in large and important enterprises.

He was one of the counsel for the Northern Securities Company in all the merger litigation, prepared the main brief, and made an argument in the case both in the circuit court and on appeal in the supreme court. For many years he represented the Great Northern Railway Company and its interests in much important litigation.

He was indeed a great lawyer, and his reputation was not confined to his own state, but he was well known among other great lawyers, railroad capitalists and officials, and men engaged and interested in large enterprises throughout the Eastern and Western states.

He was a ripe scholar and a profound thinker. His reading covered a wide range both in the law and general literature, so that his mind was stored with valuable knowledge systematically arranged and classified, to be used when need required with great force and effect upon any question of law presented to him for consideration. His study of the history of the law had been particularly confined to noting and analyzing its changes and growth as it adapted itself to advancing civilization. He took a connected view of the past and the present—the old and the new—never confused or losing his way but traveling in his orbit symmetrically, with no meteoric flashes, onward, until he reached that point in his planetary system attained only by a few of his profession.

His love of his books and his chosen profession so occupied his time and attention that the circle of his personal acquaintance was not large, but those who had

the good fortune to come within it will remember his charming conversation and his kind and genial ways. Great men have but few real friends, and his case was no exception; but to these friends he bound himself with bands of steel to be severed only at death.

In the death of Judge Young the state and the bar have met with a loss that cannot be supplied, and we ask this court to have spread upon its records this brief expression of our regard for his memory.

W.E. Hale

C. W. Bunn

C. E. Otis

Charles W. Bunn, Esq., then said:

Judge Young was a man of books, scholarship, culture. While he was also a man of friendships and human sympathies, his prevailing passion, as I esteem Judge Young, was for knowledge and learning. Combined with this passion was a wonderful memory. He had a memory equal to that of any whom we have ever known and an infinite capacity for labor. No task was too great for Judge Young to undertake. The result of this was that at his ripe age he was full of learning. He had accumulated a wonderful knowledge of the law. He not only knew the principles and the principal cases of the law, but his mind was full of collateral learning. A man could not fail to be a man of great ability when such qualities are combined as they were in Judge Young with a logical and remarkably lucid and clear mind.

His habits of work were such that I think without exception he wrote out all of his papers, including his elaborate briefs, with his own lead pencil. I never saw a piece of dictation come from Judge Young with respect to anything of any consequence.

All this contributed to make Judge Young a man of commanding ability, a most formidable antagonist. Associated as I was with Judge Young in some litigation and against him in other, I can testify that the briefs of no man gave more food for thought to his adversary than the briefs of Judge Young. He was a fine example to hold up to young men, an example of what may be achieved—and his was a great success, a great eminence—without one of the arts of the politician and without one of the graces of oratory.

Wade Hampton Yardley, Esq., then said:

I esteem it an honor to join in this last tribute to the memory of George B. Young.

For more than twenty years though much his junior, I was privileged to enjoy his intimate acquaintance and learned to know his character as a man and his ability and attainments in the profession that he so adorned. And like all who knew him best, I early acquired and ever held for him a deep affection and profound respect. He was sincere, unaffected, without sham or pretence. His wide reading and wonderful memory, his genial humor and a most winning manner, made conversation with him delightful, and I look back upon the many hours spent at his charming home with mingled feelings of keen pleasure and of sadness that they can never be again.

As a lawyer Judge Young was an inspiration. With knowledge and wisdom he combined a remarkable power of concentration. His energy and application were untiring, and he carried into his cases an enthusiasm that was infectious. I rejoiced in his victories and sorrowed in his defeats as though they were my own. It has been said that genius consists in the capacity for taking infinite pains. By this standard he was truly a genius. He was always prepared. He conducted much important litigation, in all of which he demonstrated his eminent fitness. In success he was modest, in defeat philosophically resigned.

He was a great lawyer, an honorable kindly gentleman, and a friend whose memory I shall ever cherish with affection and with pride.

Henry Burleigh Wenzell, Esq., then said:

Twenty-four years ago an oral examination of candidates for admission to the bar was held in the presence of this court. In accordance with the practice then, the court made its order, on the first day of the term, fixing the time of examination and naming the members of the bar who were to conduct it. Of the three examiners appointed at that term one was Judge Young. Of the three candidates admitted, one was the speaker.

He was not only one of my examiners, but it was due to his friendly word in my behalf ten years later that the opportunity came to me to take charge of the work of arranging and completing the compilation of our laws since known as General Statutes, 1894. And

after he had ceased to be the reporter of your decisions, I think it was in large measure due to his opinion of my fitness for the work that led Your Honor and the justices then sitting on this court to appoint me to the position he had so long filled.

There are diverse opinions as to the proper method of reporting. Actual experience may give to the reporter a point of view that is not always shared by members of the profession unacquainted with the details of the work. In cases of doubt, I have always found Judge Young's volumes models to follow. If at times changes have been introduced, the change has been due to the search after a form that would make it possible for busy lawyers to use the volumes most conveniently.

At the time of my arrival in Minnesota there was a rapid growth in the population of our capital city. Many college-bred young attorneys were arriving from other sections of the country. We found a small group of very able lawyer leaders of the Ramsey County Bar. Among these leaders none stood higher, especially in court cases, than Judge Young. He was regarded by us as a model of the able, thoroughly trained, and high-minded lawyer. Being a native of the same state, a graduate of the same college and of the same law school, it was natural we should soon meet. From the acquaintance thus formed sprang in time a friendship that steadily grew warmer until his death.

In the earlier years of our practice we younger attorneys stood somewhat in awe of his reputation as a master in the profession. But whenever an especially knotty question in our practice arose and we ventured to ask advice, we found that he manifested a kindly interest in our problems, gave us his undivided attention, and placed at our disposal freely all his mental keenness and his wide experience. Early in our practice my partner and myself had occasion to bring a suit that involved points of unusual difficulty. The amount involved was far less than that in the cases to which Judge Young gave his personal attention. Yet he came to our aid, and on the trial his handling of the case showed he had made himself familiar with the smallest detail. And so powerful was his summing up of the evidence that men gathered in the court room to listen to him. The case was won and by him, yet his fee was as modest as that of a novice at the bar.

But my real relation to Judge Young was not so much professional as personal.

To strangers he was reserved in manner, but those whom he admitted to his friendship forgot that fact. To his friends it was a delight to meet him. Even a casual meeting lighted up his face, seemed to kindle in him the fire of friendship and diffuse warmth and good cheer. He was a man singularly averse to any verbal expression of feeling. But whenever any person in whom he was interested could benefit by his word or act he was tireless in his effort to help him. No one who reads his appreciative memorial of Chief Justice McMillan in Volume 67 of our Reports can doubt that he possessed great warmth of feeling.

But it was in his home that one learned to know Judge Young best. Given to hospitality, his house was always open to friends and acquaintances, and his welcome was always cordial. Fond of books, he was able to gather them in fine editions. In spite of a busy professional career he read much. And he read widely. He was exceptionally well informed on many subjects. He cared little for the new but enjoyed thoroughly that which was well-seasoned and classic. Nor was his reading limited to our mother tongue. And it seemed as if he never forgot anything he had read. His memory rarely failed him for a word even in quoting some ephemeral rhyme of his college days. His talk was delightful. It took a wide range. It might be a vivid account of some lawsuit of the past, a keen comment on current events, or critical comment on some book. Only a little while before his death he brought out a Year Book he had been reading and read to me extracts from it to show that human nature in the fourteenth century was the same as it is in the twentieth.

In recalling his home life, one cannot forget his wife. A leader in charitable and social activities, she was his inseparable companion and support until her death. And that event hastened his end.

Our profession has lost a most conspicuous member, whose reputation was not limited to our own state or to the Northwest, and his friends have lost one whose place cannot be filled.

Associate Justice Jaggard [in behalf of the court] then said:

You have paid a just tribute to a great lawyer. The records of this court fully evidence his versatility, his learning, and his intellectual pre-eminence. As a member of this court, he delivered its opinion in twenty-four cases marked by lucidity of style, painstaking research, and progressive certainty of reason. In connection with the history of this court it is interesting to note that this is less than one-third of the average number of cases written by each member of the court at present within the same time.

Of Judge Young's decisions, *Keffe v. Milwaukee & St. Paul Railway Company,* 21 Minn. 207, decided on January 11, 1875, was given prominence by Judge Cooley's book on Torts (see page 356). A considerable part of the opinion was quoted with approval by Mr. Justice Harlan in *Union Pacific Railway Company v. McDonald,* 153 U. S. 262, 14 Sup. Ct. 619, 624. It remains the most meritorious of the so-called Turntable cases. While there has been much controversy on the subject and considerable conflict of opinion, the doctrine therein laid down that reasonable care must have reference to the natural instincts of children remains unshaken. The case of *Paine v. Sherwood,* 21 Minn. 225, finally established in this state the rule for damages in case of breach of contract laid down in Hadley against Baxendale. While not the first case on the subject by this court, it has become the leading one and has been frequently cited in other jurisdictions with approval. In *Ames v. Lake Superior & Mississippi Railroad Company,* 21 Minn. 241, Judge Young was of the opinion that an act amending a territorial charter so as to constitute a charter under the name of the Lake Superior & Mississippi Railroad Company was unconstitutional. Of its own motion the court added a memorandum suggesting an application for further hearing. Upon re-argument the court held that the act was constitutional. The case was probably the most conspicuous one decided while he was on the bench. Mr. Richard L. Ashhurst and Mr. John C. Bullitt of Philadelphia appeared as counsel.

Largely as a labor of love he served as official reporter from the twenty-first volume of the reports to the forty-seventh volume, that is, from 1875 to January 1892. He established the standard of good reporting in the West. His work has become at once the model and the despair of his professional brethren engaged in the same important labor.

The work of Judge Young in preparation of the General Statutes of 1878 was great; its merits corresponded. As an illustration of the microscopical care with which he labored, it is interesting to note that he included in that compilation the section of the laws of 1877 which required that, before the right to redeem from tax certificates could be eliminated, the so-called Williston notice must have been given. It was supposed by the Bar that chapter 1 of the Laws of 1878 impliedly repealed that requirement. Judge Young, however, inserted the section as a part of the General Statutes of 1878. The matter came before the Supreme Court; it held that the requirement of the notice had not been repealed by implication. See *Merrill v. Deering,* 32 Minn. 480.

His mental operations were judicial by nature. His argument was invariably enlightened and unprejudiced. His comprehensive vision saw all sides of a controversy fully and fairly. Even as an advocate intense in conviction and indignant at wrong, he relied solely upon the temperate presentation of legitimate considerations. He stood in eloquent antithesis to the lay conception of the small lawyer. Astuteness he had in a large degree, but of sharpness he had none. His dexterity in handling facts was sometimes startling, but their distortion was as impossible to him as their misrepresentation. Of the art of drilling a witness, he was as guileless as a child. He knew no cunning; absolute honesty was the basis of his shrewdness: "Perfect candor was his sword and shield." His scorn of technical subterfuge was too instinctive to be called lofty. With emphasis he pointed out to his scholars that not in a score of years had a case been reversed in an English appellate court on mere error in evidence or practice.

His great ability, learning, and industry were at the disposal of his clients, but never was his conscience controlled to subserve any interest for which he was however ardent a protagonist. This was entirely unconscious. Cant was precluded by the inherent logic of his mind. None the less he ridiculed the logic of the schoolmen. Even the study of John Stuart Mill he used to condemn as futile. He often said to me, "You can no more learn from logic how to think than you can

learn from grammar how to talk." His general distrust of metaphysics was characteristic of a mind eminently practical alike in both analysis and synthesis.

He was, I believe, the most erudite man at the bar of this state in its history. His knowledge was wisdom, his learning a philosopher's and not a pedant's. One was at a loss which to admire most—the variety, the readiness, or the aptness of his quotations from ancients and moderns. His memory was photographic, his perception instantaneous, his observation exact. However extensive the details of law or fact presented, his powers of reflection were employed without the subtraction because of any effort of reproduction.

A genial spirit illuminated all his labor, and he worked night and day with a swiftness excelled only by his precision. He was happy in his work, pleased with some quaint turn of expression, delighted by the discovery of unexpected confirmation by authority or of unanticipated and favorable evidence. The brilliancy of his mental processes depended upon hard practical good sense. A keen and ever alert sense of humor saved him from too fine distinctions and from following close reasoning into any absurdity. The soundness of his judgment has been demonstrated time and time again by the prescience with which he foresaw and foretold what the famous men of commerce had failed to anticipate.

The world knew little of his emotional life. Unobtrusive, undemonstrative, and self-contained he always was. The flower of the kindness of his nature grew in retirement. He came to the easy, generous, and open hospitality of the West from the formal conventionalities of a more highly crystallized civilization. The impression made on him was deep. He retained the refinement of the environment of his birth and added to it the cordiality and breezy optimism of his adopted home. His social life, based upon the worship of qualities not of accidents, was simple, full of charm, and singularly generous. Its elevating influence was widely extended. He loyally followed his early friends in this state through subsequent fortune and misfortune. He did not waste his affection by undertaking to spread it over an impossibly large number of people. Whom he loved, he loved well. His inner feelings were occasionally revealed to the public, as when he said at the memorial exercises of his dead friend James B. Beals, "He wore the white flower of a blameless life."

Judge Young's hand was ever extended to help and guide aright the younger men in the profession. I gratefully bear testimony to his tact as spontaneous as his sympathy was gracious and to a friendly, and to me almost paternal, thoughtfulness as uniform as it was inspiring. He was to those who saw him oftenest, and he remains, an ideal of intellectual disinterest-

edness and an examplar of the highest conceptions of professional ethics. It seemed natural that the end should have come to him while he was at his work: "Like a peaceful river with green and shaded banks, he flowed without a murmur into the waveless sea where life is rest."

Accordingly, with a deep appreciation of the fitness of your testimonials, it is ordered that they be inscribed upon the records of this court. [99 Minn. xxii]

F. R. E. Cornell

1821–1881
Associate Justice, 1875–1881

The Honorable Francis R. E. Cornell, an associate justice of the supreme court of Minnesota, died at his home in Minneapolis, on the twenty-third day of May 1881.

Judge Cornell was born at Coventry, in Chenango county, New York, on the seventeenth of November 1821. He was graduated from Union College in 1842, was admitted to the bar in the supreme court at Albany in 1846, and began the practice of law at Addison, Steuben county, where he remained until 1854. He was a member of the state senate of New York for 1852 and 1853. In the year 1854 he became a citizen of Minnesota, making his home at Minneapolis, where he resided until his death. He was a member of the state legislature in the years 1861, 1862, and 1865, and attorney-general for six years, from January 10, 1868, to January 9, 1874. In November 1874, he was elected associate justice of the supreme court, and qualified, and took his seat on the eleventh day of January, 1875.

On the tenth day of June, 1881, at a fully attended meeting of the bar of the state, a memorial resolution was adopted, and Hon. Gordon E. Cole, chairman of the meeting, was instructed to present the memorial to the supreme court.

On the same day Mr. Cole presented to the supreme court then in session the memorial of the bar and moved that it be entered in the records of the court:

We, the members of the bar of the state of Minnesota, deem it appropriate that we should place upon record an expression of our sense of the great loss to our state, and its Judiciary, and to our profession, caused by the death of Hon. Francis R. E. Cornell, one of the justices of the supreme court of our state, which occurred on the twenty-third day of May last.

More than twenty-five years of his vigorous manhood were passed among us in the constant and successful practice of our profession. Endowed with quickness of perception and clearness of judgment to a degree rarely united in the same person with his thorough training and close application, he excelled in all branches of the profession and stood foremost at the bar of the state, his career being marked no less by eminent ability and strict integrity than by that uniform kindness and courtesy toward his brethren, which won for him the especial regard of the younger members of the bar, to whom he was the model of professional excellence.

His fitness for the highest professional honors was recognized by his brethren at the bar and by the people of the state. After discharging the duties of attorney general for repeated terms with signal ability, he was elevated to the bench of the supreme court, and [he] has left a judicial record without blemish and above criticism [that] will remain an imperishable testimony to his learning and ability after his fame at the bar shall have faded in the shadows of tradition. Deeply deploring our loss, which has taken from our state one of its most gifted and estimable citizens, from the bench one of the ablest of justices, and from our profession a brother loved and revered by us all, we can contemplate with satisfaction his useful and blameless life and rejoice that so much of him is left to us in the records of the state and of the supreme court; and we respectfully ask that this court permit this brief expression of our regard for the memory of our honored brother to be entered upon its records.

Mr. Cole then addressed the court as follows:

In presenting this memorial it will perhaps be expected that I accompany it with some comments upon the life and character of Judge Cornell. I might perhaps have made careful preparation and culled some flowers of rhetoric to strew upon his grave, but I cannot do it; I leave that for those who knew him less and loved him less. I must speak from the heart and rely upon the inspiration of the moment.

Nearly a quarter of a century ago I came to this city, a mere boy, to assume the discharge of the duties of the office of attorney general, without acquaintance or friends; and the first acquaintance and friend I made was Judge Cornell. The acquaintance thus begun ripened into an intimacy and friendship that I cherished as I never cherished another friendship, and that ceased only with his life.

My opportunities for forming a correct estimate of his character and talents I believe to have been unusual, meeting him at the bar, first as prosecuting officer while he was engaged in the defence, afterwards when he had become attorney general and prosecutor and I was employed for the defence. In later years I had the good fortune to be associated with him in a very important civil case in the federal courts until, at the close of the litigation in the trial court, he was removed from the case by his appointment to the supreme bench. In the subsequent progress of the cause in the supreme court of the United States, he was succeeded by a gentleman who then stood and still stands at the head of the bar of the country, with a reputation and fame only circumscribed by the territorial boundaries of the nation. The opportunity of measuring Judge Cornell's powers by contrast with those of the highest, I believe I did not abuse. I do not think that my judgment was swayed by personal friendship. At any rate it was deliberately formed and has been since carefully reviewed, and I then thought and still think that, in every attribute that contributes to form the character of a great lawyer, Judge Cornell was the peer of his successor and that a reversal of opportunities would have produced a corresponding reversal of station, fame, and reputation,

The salient feature of Judge Cornell's character as a lawyer was the unerring certainty with which his mind glided from premise to conclusion. I have often had occasion to note and to admire the rapidity with which, with almost the precision of intuition, he would arrive at the correct solution of a difficult legal problem then first submitted to his attention,

the comprehensive glance with which he would instantly sweep the entire subject and take it in with all its qualifications and limitations. While his high character and standing in the state made him the constant recipient of civil honors and in the politics of the state as well as at the bar his position was always conspicuous, yet a marked characteristic of the man was his innate modesty. In self-conceit he seemed absolutely wanting, and yet no man that I ever knew had a more constant and abiding confidence in himself.

No man who has ever embellished and adorned the bench or official position in this state was ever more conspicuously distinguished for the perfect purity of his public and private character than our lamented friend.

He was not a mere lawyer; he was not a man of the cloister and the office. In all the great enterprises [that] have made the beautiful and flourishing city of Minneapolis what it is, he bore a prominent part. In the politics of the state he was a leader, and although for a quarter of a century participating in the always earnest and often bitter contests that politics engender, and often a candidate and elected to political office, yet at those periods when the character of no man is secure from the envenomed shafts of political enemies if there is a flaw in his armor through which the spear of an opponent can pierce, nor ever during the quarter of a century during which he has lived and moved, always a prominent figure among us, has the breath of scandal ever so much as essayed to reach him. His character and reputation have remained untarnished by a whisper of suspicion.

The uniform urbanity of his manner, the innate kindliness and gentleness of his character, endeared him to all, and especially to the young neophyte embarrassed in the intricacies of his first case before the most august tribunal of the state, and then essaying his first flight in the atmosphere of jurisprudence, his gentle manners and attentive ear carried the same ease as to the older barrister with assured reputation, flushed with the triumphs of hundreds of forensic successes.

He has gone from among us and has left the judicial ermine not only spotless as when he assumed it but has left to his family the priceless legacy of an unsullied private character as a citizen and a man. The bar of this state, with uniform accord, will endorse me when I say that in him were blended, with a harmony that the faultless hand of nature seldom achieves, the attributes that make the character of a great judge: profound legal learning combined with the keenest accumen [*sic*] in its application, purity of public and private life, and the suavity of manners that marks the gentleman, producing a magnificent self-poise and a beauty of character that is rarely permitted by the frailties of our common humanity.

Hon. Isaac Atwater then addressed the court:

Having had occasion recently, at a meeting of the Hennepin County Bar Association, to render my tribute to the memory of the late Judge Cornell, I shall trespass but a few moments on your time today; and the more especially inasmuch as I observe that most of those present have long known the judge professionally and can render a more eloquent tribute to his eminent ability than I could hope to do. It seems peculiarly fitting that one who has so long been a distinguished member of the bar and bench of the state and who has also adorned other important offices in the gift of the people should not be permitted to pass away without some public recognition on our part of his merits. It is due, not less to the living than the dead, that this should be done.

Young as we are as a state, the profession is not yet so affluent in distinguished names that we can afford to forget the well-earned fame of any one. And shut out as we are by the nature of our profession from what are usually considered the highest prizes of life, there is the more reason that we should jealously guard the reputation fairly earned by any one of our number in the strict practice of his profession. The law is a jealous mistress and excludes her votaries from the rewards obtained by our merchant princes and railroad magnates. But such as she has are better worth effort to the true lawyer than all others, and it should be ours to see that, when once earned, they lose none of their value to the living.

But on this occasion, standing as we might say almost in the shadow of death, I find my mind dwelling on the qualities of the deceased that distinguished him as a man, a neighbor and friend, rather than on his eminent abilities as a lawyer. It was my privilege

to know him somewhat intimately for more than twenty-five years. And I do not overstate when I say that, for a high, delicate sense of honor, unswerving integrity, and a conscientious desire to discharge with scrupulous fidelity every trust committed to him, I have never known him surpassed.

But there was more than this. He was ever ready to assist his neighbors, and especially the younger members of the profession, with his valuable counsel and pecuniary means, so far as he was able. And I was forcibly struck, at the meeting of the association to which I have referred, at the number of young lawyers who bore feeling and earnest testimony to this trait in his character. Herein he has left an example that I am sure we should all do well to heed and follow. We are too apt to become so wholly absorbed in the study and practice of our profession that we often forget our duties to the younger members thereof— forget those kindnesses and amenities that perhaps cost little but are of more value to the recipients than we are wont to think. It may not happen to any of us to attain [the] eminence in the profession that was the rare fortune of our deceased friend to reach, for that was largely due to natural gifts that few possess. But in the practice of those moral virtues that adorned his life and the full development of which is largely a matter of cultivation, we may reasonably hope to approach more nearly the degree of excellence that he attained. And at the last supreme hour, if I mistake not, success in such an effort will give, in the retrospect, more satisfaction than the highest professional honors due to intellectual effort alone. For we must not forget that—

Only the actions of the just
Smell sweet and blossom in the dust.

Hon. William Lochren then addressed the court as follows:

It is difficult in the brief time that can be taken at such a meeting to say anything at all commensurate with what is fitting or to what is felt by every one respecting the loss of such a man as Judge Cornell.

I was with him at the bar of our county since my coming to Minnesota twenty-five years ago, have been frequently associated with him and oftener opposed to him in the trial of causes, and came to know him intimately. In my judgment he was the ablest lawyer who has ever practised at that bar and second to none in the state. He excelled in every branch of the profession—equally as a counsellor, as a pleader, in the examination of witnesses, as an advocate before juries, and in the argument of questions of law to courts. It is seldom that one man possesses such varied ability, and whenever it occurs in our profession, it cannot fail to place the possessor in the foremost rank.

He loved his profession, and its work, and never permitted anything to divert or withdraw him from it. Trained to it from youth, he was familiar with the underlying principles of jurisprudence, and with his natural powers of perception and accurate judgment he seemed to reach correct conclusions with the rapidity of intuition. But he never relied too much upon his natural powers, and [he] was familiar with leading authors and decisions to which he could refer with readiness whenever necessary to enforce his arguments.

A noted characteristic was his unfailing courtesy and consideration for others, especially his brethren at the bar. He was always ready to assist and encourage young men starting in the profession, and many such will gratefully remember his acts of professional kindness and friendly assistance.

Although his practice was large, he seemed to work more for love of his profession than for gain and was proverbially careless about securing compensation for his labor. Without being a politician in the ordinary sense of that term, he took a lively interest in everything affecting the material prosperity of the state and of the city in which he lived, and on such matters his counsel was always sought and his influence great.

Reaching at last the goal of a laudable professional ambition—a seat upon the bench of this honored court—I shall not speak of how well he performed the duties of that high station. That is too well known and recent to call for more than reference. Had he lived beyond his term of office, nearly closed at the time of his death, he would have been chosen without opposition to continue in the place for which all felt he was so well fitted. But the judicial honors by him worn so worthily have been laid down with his life.

His labors are ended, and our brief testimony to his worth closes the record.

Honorable R. R. Nelson, Judge of the United States District Court for Minnesota, then addressed the court as follows:

I desire as a member of the legal profession, a native of the same state, to add my tribute of respect to the memory of the deceased. I was not intimately acquainted with Justice Cornell. Others, his coworkers and associates in the profession who learned by social intimacy to appreciate the man, have dwelt upon his excellent qualities of head and heart. My estimation of Judge Cornell is derived from a careful examination of his opinions, emanating from him in the discharge of public duties, and I can justly say no counsellor or judge was influenced by purer motives or surrounded by a higher moral atmosphere. His opinions show thorough education as well as cultivated literary taste. He was learned in the law, which he administered wisely, and thus won confidence and esteem.

The example of such a life should not be lost to the community, and the resolutions presented express the unanimous opinion of the legal profession.

Gen. John B. Sanborn then addressed the court:

It was my purpose to do honor to the memory of the illustrious dead by sympathy, silence, and considerate attention to the words of eulogy uttered by others possibly more intimately acquainted with him as a neighbor, friend, or relative than myself. But the sentiments already expressed bring so vividly to my mind the scenes and friends of the past, the important and great services rendered by the deceased, his faithfulness in all positions, and under all circumstances his wonderful mental acuteness and great legal attainments, that I cannot refrain from uttering a few words of tribute to his memory on this sad occasion.

More than twenty-five years have passed away since I first met him at the bar of Hennepin county, and such was the impression made upon me at the time of his mental power and legal knowledge that within a year, when called upon to defend in that county a most critical case of murder prosecuted by the late James R. Lawrence, whose vigor and legal capacity all the old members of the bar will well remember—I mean the case of the United States against Moon—I called Judge Cornell to my assistance. The impressions previously made by his management and argument of the civil case were deepened and strengthened by his skill and conduct of this criminal cause. He demonstrated, beyond controversy, that he was the possessor of one of the most clear, incisive, and accurate legal minds. The slightest shades of difference in the facts and the legal principles governing a case were as distinct and clear to him as the widest difference is to many of our profession. With his aid in that case the accused was discharged, although the homicide was admitted and was without excuse and the alleged criminal was of sound mind upon all matters not connected with the person killed.

The conclusions then reached by me respecting the great powers and attainments of our departed friend have been retained to the day of his death. It has been my fortune often—almost every year since that time—to meet him at the bar, in political conventions, in the legislature, where we represented constituencies who considered that they had interests that were adverse; and in all positions and at all times he has shown himself a wise counsellor, a high-toned honorable man, a faithful and far-seeing legislator, an able lawyer who respected and adorned his profession; and even without his legal attainments he would have been a good judge. For, although a good judge may be a bad man, a good man cannot be a bad judge. And this vacancy made by the death of the learned and upright judge will be hard to fill.

Be it ours to cherish his memory and emulate his example.

Hon. M. J. Severance then addressed the court:

The vacant seat on your bench has convoked this assembly today. Its late revered occupant has crossed the ocean that has no refluent wave, his earthly duties all performed.

We are not here today to tender to any the cold and formal courtesies always due to the great catastrophe of death, but we are here in the interest of the living and those who are yet to live, to pay a just and merited tribute to the life and character of one who on the forge of life wrought out an honorable and enduring fame. We do not yield this tribute for the benefit of the dead but to excite and awaken the emulation of the living, who, hearing the applause we bestow on noble action, may take the only pathway that can justify the highest hopes of mankind.

As a lawyer, our friend possessed those natural endowments that could but give him preeminence in the forensic arena, and as a judge on the bench, those same endowments lifted him far above the common plane. A quick perception and a power of analysis that never lent its ear to the sophistries of ingenious debate ever enabled him to test the soundness of any proposition presented to his mind and to bring method out of the chaos of conflicting opinions. Add to these natural endowments an inherent love of justice and an unswerving integrity born with him and in him, and you behold Judge Cornell as a lawyer and as a judge.

Splendid original gifts and high intellectual endowments lavishly bestowed invoke human admiration and give to their possessor the stately tread of a giant. But it is not on these that we bestow our highest encomiums today, though they rounded out the majesty of our friend's career. We instinctively turn to the social department of his life, generous with sensitive emotion, unobtrusive but ever radiating the vernal warmth of love and kindness. Exacting in nothing, he acknowledged the mutual obligations of his race and yielded that deference to others that forbids personal tyranny and smothers that effusive self-assertion which so often breeds hatred and contempt. No cloud of egotism ever drew its shade across his generous mind to mildew its opening flowers. He cultivated the finer emotions of the heart, for he knew that they were the headlight that ought to gleam along the pathway of intellectual action in every walk of his earthly duty. And when his life went out, another ray of light and warmth vanished from the earth forever.

Judge Cornell was a brother in the great brotherhood of man and ever held out his hand to the weary as he ascended the hillsides of life. He never looked back with contempt on those who had just entered with uncertain step on the long pathway over which he had passed, but he pointed to the summit illumined with hope and then with kindly counsel wooed them along.

As a man, a lawyer, or judge, he never embraced the shallow fallacy of personal triumph in order to prod the feelings of others, but in every condition of life, its highest amenities furnished the rule of his action. In the spirit of love and equality he fashioned his character with all the graces of moral symmetry so that whatever blemishes it had were easily hidden under the mantle of human infirmity. His domestic life, so full of sunshine, is sacred to others. I will not unroll its once bright panorama, now moist with pearly tears, the offerings of love to love. If his death left broken hearts, let them heal again under the benign radiance of a life's sunset, golden with personal honor. Judge Cornell loved his home, and every night the neighboring waterfall of Saint Anthony throbbed its soft music through the trembling lattice of his window and lulled him to earthly sleep. Now let it forever murmur the requiem of his dreamless slumber.

Other remarks were made by Messrs. Eugene M. Wilson, William M. McCluer and John M. Shaw, at the conclusion of which Chief Justice Gilfillan, on behalf of the court, responded as follows to the addresses of the bar:

The memorial that has been read will be entered in the minutes. It is peculiarly fit that it should be of record in the court of which Mr. Justice Cornell was a member for the last six years of his life and in the performance of his duties in which he spent his last strength. He had in the highest degree every claim to appropriate memorials.

His career and character as a man, as a citizen, as a shaper and leader of public opinion, as a legislator, as a member of the legal profession, and finally as a judge in the court of last resort in the state, were such as call for marked public recognition now that he is gone. Of his public services to the state at large and to the more immediate community in which he lived, the press has made honorable mention. His personal friends, those who got to know his inner life and character, have in their private discourse, as you have done, recalled and borne their testimony to his virtues as a man, virtues [that] made him dear to all who had the good fortune to be on terms of intimacy with him. It is for us, at this time and place, more especially to dwell upon and pay our tribute to his memory as a member of our profession and as connected with it by his judicial station and services. Most of us, the oldest of us at any rate, knew him for many years. His position at the bar from the first was such that no one could be a member of the bar in the state without knowing him either personally or by reputation. At a very early day, at the time when the bar here may be said to have been in its infancy, when as a political community Minnesota was about passing from the guardianship of the general government to the free condition of a self-governing state, he was already among the foremost in the profession. Who would for the next quarter of a century lead in its labors, contests, and honors was then to a great extent uncertain. But he had taken his place. Whosesoever future standing might seem doubtful, his was not. He was then an acknowledged leader; his ability, learning, eloquence, and force of character, already recognized, made it evident that whoever else might fall behind, he would so long as he remained in the practice of the profession stand in its front rank, the equal of the highest. From that time the bar steadily increased in numbers, in strength, in learning, in influence and importance. Through all its growth his relative position in it remained the same until he took his place upon the bench.

The mental qualities and characteristics that enabled him to maintain so high a position at the bar eminently fitted him for the bench. The character of his mind indeed was more judicial than forensic. Its more appropriate field of action was the bench rather than the bar. To assure a lawyer the highest success as an advocate, his mind must be capable in a large degree of taking a partisan view of a cause, of adopting as its own the feelings and prejudices of the client, and of seeing and judging of the cause through the medium of such feelings and prejudices. A mind of that stamp is apt to see but one side of the case, though to make its possessor a great advocate it must see all of that side at once and as by the full light of the noonday sun. One with such a mind, especially if that be its controlling characteristic, rarely if ever makes a great judge. Erskine, by far the greatest advocate who has spoken in the English language, was a striking instance of this. Those who, while he was at the bar, knew Judge Cornell not intimately, who saw his sanguine, nervous temperament, the zeal with which he engaged in the trial of a cause, his instantaneous perception of the rules and principles of law governing it, and the intense force and clearness, and fervid, energetic eloquence with which he set forth and urged upon the courts those rules and principles, might be led to suppose that his was that stamp of mind. But to suppose that would have been a grave mistake. His more intimate acquaintances knew then, his career on this bench has demonstrated since, that his success at the bar was owing to other and larger intellectual attributes than the peculiar characteristic I have ascribed to the advocate. From the time of his transfer to the bench it became apparent to all that his intellect was notably liberal and comprehensive and singularly impartial, calmly and dispassionately taking in the whole of a case and judging it only upon those considerations that lead to a correct result. His learning in the law was great; his quickness to apprehend the true issues in a cause and the right solution of them was marvelous—more so than I ever knew in any other man; and at the same time his judgment was cautious and profound, his habit of investigation patient and conscientious. In his mental operations were united two characteristics not often found together—quick, intuitive perception and careful, patient reasoning. To these was added a clear, unfailing natural sense of justice, of moral right and wrong, on the rules of which the rules and principles of law are mainly based. These mental traits, with an intimate knowledge of human nature and a generous but discriminating charity towards its failings, united in him the elements that go to make the great magistrate. In respect to the harmonious combination of these conditions, it will be long before his place on the bench will be wholly filled. To the bar and to the judiciary his loss is well nigh irreparable.

I should fail of doing justice to his memory, and to his associates' appreciation of his memory, if I omitted to mention as you have mentioned his uniform courtesy of manner and the amiability and gentleness of his disposition and temper, an amiability and gentleness joined with the highest degree of manly energy. These were very marked in his intercourse with his brother lawyers and the courts while at the bar. They were more conspicuous to us, his associates on the bench, brought as we were into most intimate relations with him. Two of us were with him on the bench for more than six years. During that time our intercourse with him and knowledge of him and of his traits, both of mind and heart, were necessarily very close and intimate. In the hearing of causes, in the subsequent investigation of and consultations upon them and the preparation and comparison of decisions and opinions, we were together day by day. Frequent conflicts of opinion have necessarily arisen, followed by earnest discussions sometimes leaving irreconcilable differences as to how causes should be decided. But in no instance that I can recall during all that time did he ever let fall any discourteous, unkind, or irritating expression to either of his associates; nor did any difference of opinion or anything occurring in the discussions ever for a moment interrupt the unvarying kindly relations between him and them. In this his forbearance was the more remarkable because for the latter part of the time the disease of which he died was upon him, causing him often severe suffering, at all times harassing anxiety. That under such trying conditions he should at all times preserve even temper and exercise towards others perfect courtesy and consideration marks strongly the character of the man.

Gentlemen, I have endeavored briefly, I know with imperfect success, to express what his survivors on the bench think and feel in regard to our departed associate. Your eloquent and appropriate memorial shall be entered in the records of the court, there to remain as a testimony so long as those records shall be preserved. [27 Minn. xv]

Daniel A. Dickinson

1839–1902
Associate Justice, 1881–1893

On the afternoon of June 20, 1902, in the court room at the state capitol, Mr. W. R. Begg, secretary of the State Bar Association, addressed the supreme court then in session, as follows:

The bar of the state of Minnesota has recently lost by the death of Hon. Daniel A. Dickinson, of Duluth, one of its most distinguished and illustrious members. The state has lost a patriot of unsullied purity and spotless integrity. The State Bar Association, which I am here to represent, has thought fit that there be recorded in this high tribunal some proper and permanent memorial in recognition of the ability and the virtue of our departed brother. To that end a memorial has been prepared by the president of this association, which I will read, and I ask to have it entered upon the records of the court:

The members of the bar, deeply mourning the loss of their universally beloved brother Daniel Ashley Dickinson, respectfully present for preservation among the records of this court, of which for twelve years he was a distinguished member, a brief memorial of his many virtues.

For a third of a century Judge Dickinson devoted his undivided energies to the administration of justice in our own state, spending fifteen of these years at the bar and seventeen upon the bench. To this service he brought a character of singular purity and probity, a cultivated but peculiarly practical mind, a sound legal judgment, scorn for every form of wrong, candor and patience unsurpassed, and industry unstinted.

In all the relationships of life, public and private, the ease and accuracy with which he appreciated the attendant obligations and amenities were equalled only by the alacrity with which he performed them and by the constancy with which he imposed upon himself higher standards of conduct than he exacted

from others. It is rarely indeed that we are permitted to contemplate a character so altogether pleasing from so many different points of view. Upon the law, upon our profession, upon the judiciary, and upon mankind he reflected honor; and it is but justice that we and those who follow us should honor him.

Hon. M. J. Severance then addressed the court as follows:

Again I must speak in eulogy of the dead. Pleasure, veiled by sadness, is the inspiration of the sacred duty I cannot shun, for I stand in the afterglow of a life that will linger with me as long as memory lasts. When the great orb of day sinks in the dark waves of night, it is not only a recollection of its noonday splendor that entrances the mind, but more it is the afterglow that lingers behind and bathes the forest and the vales with its cerulean light. So when a useful and lovable life comes to its setting, it is in the radiance it leaves behind that we recall its living splendor. An ended life that does not leave this trail of light behind is a life lived worse than in vain. The dying do not carry the influence of their character into eternity, but they leave it on this side of the river, either to encourage or discourage the living. Fortunate indeed was Judge Dickinson in leaving behind him the iridescent effulgence of a perfect, virtuous, and symmetrical life. As I extol the virtues of the deceased, I shall invoke no mantle of charity to cover and hide his faults, for he was as perfect as it was ever given to man to be.

I should not dare thus to speak before this august court without reserve were I not fully aware that one member of this court, at least, from long association with the deceased, must know that I am paying no tribute to rhetoric and that I am not beguiled into fulsome praise by that generous judgment the living are always prone to pass upon the dead. Sometimes there stands beside high endowments towering passion that topples over and wrecks the brightest virtues; but in him of whom I speak, his moral and mental attributes were mingled in such equal poise that virtue always controlled his action. "He was one of those who always placed his ear down by his heart, listened, and then followed its chidings."

For years I was associated with Judge Dickinson in the practice of the law. Time and time again afterwards I appeared before him as he presided in the District Court, and here again when he adorned this bench, a place he ought never to have left until he went to the tomb; and I knew him better than I know myself. A lofty sense of duty always over-shadowed him and controlled his every action, often impelling him beyond his physical strength. Constitutionally frail, yet he never shunned a duty or refused a burden.

At the end of his collegiate course, warned that his vigor must be reinforced, he went before the mast as a common sailor and for more than a year he rode the billows of the sea, quaffing the ocean breezes that renewed his lease of health and life; after this, on foot and alone he traveled through the principal European countries, visiting all places of renown and alone musing over their history. In our Civil War he acted well his part, and when it was ended he found his reward in the new household of the Republic. In his whole career he never trembled at anything but his own infirmity, fearing that through it his duty might elude him.

In his practice as a lawyer, chaste in thought and chaste in speech, he never sacrificed the dignity of his character to angry debate, and he never prostituted the forensic arena to snarling contention, for he could shiver a lance with any foe and still maintain the poise of a gentleman. At the end of any trial in which he was ever engaged, he left the court room with the respect of all, no matter what the result might be, for never in his life did he hurl a poisoned arrow. To what height would such an example, if universally imitated, raise the dignity of our profession that so often suffers from abuse and flippant raillery. He was peculiarly fitted for a judge—with an acute and analytical mind, always subservient to the highest demands of justice, and passionless as a dove; nothing could disturb the balance of his judgment. When a young lawyer stumbled before him, he did not permit him to fall but put out his generous hand and saved him from chagrin and placed him at his ease. All who knew Judge Dickinson will always remember the sweet placidity of his temper and the graceful ease of his demeanor in every walk of life. If, dying, he left a single enemy behind, I do not know it; and it is not because he was an overlooked cipher in life but because he illustrated all the humanities that exalt human character.

One of the proudest of all the Roman emperors returning to his palace from the Coliseum, where he had been confounded at the spectacle of a fragile girl down in the deep arena with folded arms serenely smiling on a crouching tiger, wrote to the great Tertullian and said: "What is this Christianity the Roman maidens have? Tell me, Tertullian, I wish to know." Tertullian, who knew if ever anybody did, for he lived when the azure morn of Christianity still sparkled with the dew of Jesus' breath, replied: "Christianity is the innocency of life, nothing more and nothing less, and its creed is—do unto others as you would have others do unto you." By this creed Judge Dickinson fashioned his life, and on it he rested his hopes in death.

Then, as I review the life and character of Judge Dickinson when the long shades of evening are falling upon my own, when ambition and envy are dead in my bosom, I find that in civic life he left no duty unperformed, that in social life he knew no creed but the Brotherhood of Man, that in his professional life he always wore the robe of a chivalrous gentleman, and when he left this bench he laid aside the unstained ermine of an upright, just, and able judge. Then the universal verdict must be that the name of Judge Dickinson must forever stand high among the illustrious names that have adorned the bench and bar of Minnesota.

I cannot, I will not, enter his home where love's altar is still bedewed with weeping, but I leave its broken hearts to heal in the mellow radiance he left behind him.

Hon. Greenleaf Clark then addressed the court:

It is permitted us on this occasion to contemplate an honorable and useful career. We may speak without reserve, for it is closed and the record is made up. It cannot now be marred by any misadventure.

Daniel Ashley Dickinson was born at Hartford, Vermont, October 28, 1839. Having lost both his parents in childhood, he was reared and educated under the guardianship of his grandfather at Mendon, Vermont. He graduated at Dartmouth College in 1860 and at once entered upon the study of law in the office of Smith M. Weed at Plattsburg, N.Y. He entered the naval service of the United States as assistant paymaster May 15, 1863, and resigned this position January 28, 1865. He then returned to Plattsburg, and having been admitted to the New York bar, practiced his profession there in association with Mr. Weed until 1868, when he removed to Mankato, in this state, where he resided and continued the practice of law until January 1875, when having been elected Judge of the Sixth Judicial District, he entered upon the discharge of the duties of that office, which he held until June 3, 1881, when he was appointed by the governor Associate Justice of this court to fill the vacancy caused by the death of Justice Cornell, which position he held in virtue of two successive elections until October 1893. After his retirement from the bench he resumed the practice of law at Duluth as a member of the prominent law firm of Billson, Congdon & Dickinson, which relationship continued until his death on February 12, 1902, at the age of sixty-two years.

It appears that he was for nearly nineteen years engaged in the discharge of judicial duties. In estimating the value of the elements that contributed to make up Judge Dickinson's character as a jurist, I should give especial prominence to the characteristic of mental composure. He was endowed by nature with a sound mind that was cultivated and strengthened by education, study, and experience, and he had its operations under full control. His understanding was not obscured nor his reasoning powers perverted by passion or emotion, or the weight of responsibility, or the difficulty of the matter, or its delicate or perplexing nature. This sedateness was a potent factor in the development of a steady and reliable character, for "he that is slow to anger is better than the mighty, and he that ruleth his spirit than he that taketh a city." With such mental equipment and in such mental attitude, he heard, considered, and investigated with painstaking, persevering, and conscientious industry the matters that came before him, anxious only for the light and the right; and as a consequence he must have done, and he did do, good work.

His service on the district bench was in public view, and the people of his district had opportunity to observe the fair, impartial, and dignified manner in which his duties were discharged and to feel the influence of his kind, serene, and genial spirit. He attached the people to him and secured their confidence and respect in, I think, an unusual degree. Work on this bench is in seclusion. It is communicated to the world by its announced and published results, and its value is largely estimated and determined by the opinions of the bar, but the reputation Judge Dickinson had acquired on the district bench was not impaired by the new and severer test.

As a lawyer, the qualities of which I have spoken made him a safe adviser and fitted him for good work. He brought to the bar, after his retirement from the bench, the maturity of his powers, and his work was important and successful. His whole life was filled up with useful work; he was faithful to every trust; no blemish rests upon his career, and he lies in an honored grave.

Hon. W. J. Hahn then addressed the court as follows:

It is difficult to estimate the far-reaching influence for good of a manly life, however circumscribed and obscure the orbit of its existence. Who, then, will pretend to measure the helpfulness and elevating power of such a life, whose circuit embraced so large and prominent a space as did that of our departed friend? Personality, consciously and unconsciously, exerts a more potent force upon individuals and upon the community than almost anything else. In the contemplation, therefore, of the lives of the just, the pure in heart, the gentle in spirit, the noble in aim, we not only do ourselves honor but serve a duty to the living in honoring the dead. We have met today to perform that duty. A just man, whose purity at heart, gentleness of spirit, nobleness of aim are recognized and acknowledged by all who were brought within the immediate sphere of his daily life, has gone to his reward. Daniel A. Dickinson will no longer by his genial presence and manly bearing serve as an ocular example to his brethren at the bar or to the community in which he lived. But his spotless life, the high sense of duty that ever actuated him, his honorable career at the bar and on the bench, will stimulate and elevate in an ever-increasing circle both bar and people.

But our departed brother has not only left his impress for good as a man and as a citizen but in a larger and more obvious degree has stamped his personality upon the public administration of the affairs of this great and growing state. When we remember what Judge Dillon has so truthfully suggested, "That the strength of the nation largely depends upon its laws and the manner in which they are administered," we cannot fail to grasp the importance and sacredness of the judicial office. "What we most need," said Chief Justice Taney, "what is of the highest importance to each one of us is a pure, just, wise, and fearless administration of the law. If this be true, what more honorable legacy can a lawyer leave than the record of nineteen years devoted to a conscientious performance of this high prerogative? It was during Judge Dickinson's occupancy of a seat upon this bench that this court attained its high position among the able courts of last resort in this country. To his calm, judicial temperament, his studious attention to the arguments at the bar, his upright character, his wise and conscientious consideration of the points involved, and to his fearless pursuit of the conclusion that his judgment dictated, no small part of that deserved reputation is due. A more attentive listener never sat upon this bench. A more courteous gentleman never held the scales of justice in equipoise. A judge actuated by a higher sense of duty never took part in the administration of this department of the government. May we not justly apply to him the words he so fitly spoke in this court on the occasion of the memorial services in memory of Justice Mitchell? He then said: "The result of the years of his patient, tireless, earnest, honest work here are wrought into, and constitute an important part of, the grand structure of the law of this state and country, a temple of justice wherein dwelleth righteousness." What higher eulogy than this need any lawyer covet? What more desirable sentiment can he hope may be engraved upon his tomb? What monument more enduring can he expect to leave?

It is not what we have but what we are, not what places we filled but how we filled the place we occupied, not how our talents compared with another but how we used the talents we had that will at the great assize determine the question of the success or failure of our existence. Tested by this formula, the life and work of Judge Dickinson will receive the plaudit, "Well done, good and faithful servant."

Hon W. B. Douglas then addressed the court:

In affirming all that has been said on this occasion, it is a distinctive privilege to me, as one of the younger generation of lawyers who knew Judge Dickinson but slightly, to pay humble tribute to his work and to his memory. My best acquaintance with him comes from the respect paid by others and from his recorded work. The opinions of the court expressed by him always impressed me as being clear, terse, just, forceful and logical; and if deductions can be drawn therefrom as to his general characteristics, they are if anything that he leaned to the generous and charitable side. He was a man of high ideals and has gone to the reward that is due to the most honorable of the members of our profession.

Hon. W. W. Billson then addressed the court:

It is the good fortune of a good judge of a court of last resort that his fame does not rest upon the shifting sands of popular tradition. In the judicial opinions that he commits to writing, his moral and intellectual stature are chiseled by his own hands in materials more enduring than marble and with an unconscious fidelity that puts the sculptor and the biographer to shame. It is therefore doubtless true that we can say nothing here to-day that will materially exalt or depress the ultimate estimate of our valued friend. As for myself I am persuaded that Judge Dickinson's opinions are and always will be read with admiration and profit by those interested in solving the questions with which they deal. I believe he has won for himself that splendid immortality that awaits all those judges of last resort who are able to state the rules of the law luminously, to apply them with sound discrimination, and by rational and moral interpretations to subdue and adapt them to the ends of justice.

My intimate acquaintance with Judge Dickinson covered only the closing decade of his life. During that period, however, I have been a very interested and indeed a charmed observer of his modes of thought and action.

I concur enthusiastically in what I believe to be the feeling of all whose privilege it was to know him well that, upon what in the broadest sense may be termed the moral side of his nature, he was remarkably constituted. The flaw that, more sadly perhaps than any other mars the moral order of this world of ours, is the rift that in the average man so obstinately opens between his perception of duty and his performance of it. Who can estimate the regeneration that would ensue if the chasm between "I ought" and "I will" could be closed up, so that action would never lag behind insight and so that to see a duty and to do it would be one and the same thing? The peculiarity about Judge Dickinson was that in him the closing up of this troublesome gap seemed to have been practically accomplished. Toward an act or a forbearance no matter how distasteful that seemed to him to be suggested by considerations of fitness or propriety, he moved as the needle does to the pole; no effort seemed to be put forth; he simply gravitated toward it by what seemed a law of his nature. The pleasure of life that is so commonly derived from the gratification of some form of ambition, he extracted from a simple sense of duty performed. His life was nothing short of an inspiration to all who came in contact with it.

Associate Justice Collins said:

It is an honor and a fitting custom that there should be entered upon the minutes of this court a memorial of one who has occupied a place as one of its judges. By so doing, we preserve the memory of those who, during their lives, were called upon to discharge the highest judicial duties in this, the court of last resort in the state. As one of his associates for nearly six years I follow the commendable custom and pay tribute to the high character and great worth of Daniel Ashley Dickinson, an associate justice of this court for upwards of twelve years. Like so many who have reached high public office in our country, he was the builder of his own fortune, rising from the ranks to the highest position attainable in the legal profession of our state.

With the high character of his work on this bench members of the bar of this state are well acquainted.

His written opinions are contained in Volumes 28 to 54, inclusive, of the Minnesota Reports. His peculiar qualifications for judicial duties were strongly marked and always noticeable. He was never effusive, always straightforward, was particularly free from bias or prejudice of any kind and singularly modest. He possessed a mind that grasped the full details of a case, seeing with great clearness all the legal rules and the principles involved and reaching a logical conclusion thereon with accuracy and facility. His strong natural sense of justice led him to patiently hear and weigh the arguments made and to be susceptible to the moral aspects of every cause. By following these instincts that taught him to uphold what was right and to condemn what was wrong, aided by his great legal learning and unbiased mental attitude, his conclusions were in accordance with vital and basic principles. In every relation of life he was most honorable and conscientious and in his domestic relations peculiarly devoted and unselfish.

As the sole survivor of the four gentlemen who were associated with him in the performance of the work of this bench from November 1887 to October 1893, I can bear witness to the unfailing courtesy and constant amiability of his manner and temper, qualities that robbed of all irritation those inevitable differences of opinion that must arise when causes are to be decided. His resignation of the judicial office caused to all who knew him a feeling of deep loss, and his absence was sincerely regretted by those with whom he had been so closely associated for many years.

Of his untimely demise after a long period of sickness we heard with deep sorrow, and the tribute to his worth by means of this memorial is the testimony of his brethren of the legal profession to the value of his work and services. Few men there are who perform their full duty as citizens or in the public service with greater zeal, integrity, and honor than did he who has passed away and to whose memory we are this day paying an affectionate and deserved tribute.

Chief Justice Start then said:

Justice Dickinson was not self-centered or self-asserting but a modest, unassuming, lovable man of positive convictions, decided ability, pure character, and lofty ideals. He was a judge who had a high appreciation of the exalted character of the judicial function and brought to the discharge of his judicial duties ripe learning and an earnest desire to do equal justice to all men without fear or favor. The court gratefully receives your memorial, for it is a just and true estimate of his character and public services that we heartily endorse. It is but just that the memorial and the responses thereto should be entered upon the records of the court as a tribute to the memory of a patriotic citizen, an eminent judge, and a good man. So ordered. [86 Minn. xxv]

Greenleaf Clark

1835–1904
Associate Justice, 1881–1882

On the afternoon of May 26, 1905, in the court room at the State Capitol, Hon. Edward C. Stringer, in behalf of the Minnesota State Bar Association, addressed the Supreme Court, then in session, and said:

The Angel of Death has, with unwonted frequency, invaded the ranks of our profession during the past year and has chosen many shining lights. Not the last, but among the last of these, is Greenleaf Clark, a former member of this court [who died December 7, 1904], and one who was respected, honored and loved by every one whose good fortune it was to be within the circle of his acquaintance. The bar of the state desires to perpetuate his memory and to record a memorial in the records of this court appreciative of the sterling qualities of mind and heart that this jurist possessed, and in compliance with the request of the court and the appointment of its committee that memorial will now be presented.

Hon. H. W. Childs said:

The bar of this state, as a testimonial of its profound regard for the integrity, learning, and ability displayed in the life of the late Greenleaf Clark, respectfully present for preservation in the records of the court, this memorial:

Greenleaf Clark was born at Plaistow, New Hampshire, August 23, 1835, of the marriage of Nathaniel and Betsy Clark. His American ancestry of nearly two hundred years was promise of the man. It was thoroughly New England and reflected the best of New England traditions. His paternal grandfather was a soldier of the Revolution on the patriot side and was wounded in one of its engagements. He prepared for college at Atkinson Academy, New Hampshire, entered Dartmouth College in 1851, and was graduated therefrom with the degree of A.B. in June 1855.

For a few months immediately following his graduation, he was a law student in the office of Hatch & Webster at Portsmouth, New Hampshire, after which he entered the Harvard Law School, from which he was graduated in 1857, with the degree of LL.B. He was admitted the same year to the Suffolk Bar. In the fall of the following year he removed to St. Paul, Minnesota, where he continued to reside until the close of life.

His labors in the new field began when in the same year he became a clerk in the law office of Michael E. Ames. This clerical service was of short duration, for within a few months he had entered into a law partnership with Mr. Ames and ex-Judge Moses Sherburne under the name of Ames, Sherburne & Clark. This firm continued until its dissolution in 1860. He then associated himself with Samuel R. Bond, as the law firm of Bond & Clark, which was terminated in 1862 by the senior member's removal to Washington, D.C. For about three years thereafter, the subject of this memorial was engaged in an individual law practice and until 1865, when he entered into partnership with Horace R. Bigelow. The firm of Bigelow & Clark was enlarged in 1870 by the accession of Charles E. Flandrau, who was already distinguished at the bar and in the public service of the state. The firm of Bigelow, Flandrau & Clark continued until in March 1881, when the junior member retired therefrom to accept an appointment as a member of this court.

A lifelong Democrat, his elevation to the bench by Governor Pillsbury, a Republican, not only evidences the praiseworthy efforts of the latter to advance the cause of a nonpartisan judiciary, but it testifies moreover to the high place that the appointee had reached in public esteem both as a lawyer and a citizen. The commendable action of Governor

Pillsbury was, however, of little avail as the convention of his party that met in the same year failed to endorse it, and accordingly the appointee's judicial office terminated January 13, 1882. Brief as was the judicial tenure, it was of sufficient length to demonstrate the eminent fitness of the incumbent for the office. It embraced a period in which many important causes were adjudged, among which is the case of *State v. Young*, which will long remain conspicuous in the judicial history of the state. The opinions written by Judge Clark are, with the exception of three, contained in Volume 28 of the official reports of this court. They display throughout careful statement of the facts involved and admirable clearness and simplicity in the application of legal principles. Nowhere is there discovered any attempt at striking phrase or exhibition of personal feeling. Few as are his opinions, they constitute a body of excellent judicial writing that cannot fail to excite the admiration of the thoughtful student.

Upon his retirement from the bench, Judge Clark at once resumed the practice of the law, and during the four years immediately following he remained alone in professional work. The only law firm with which he was ever subsequently identified was that of Clark, Eller & How, formed in 1885 by the association with himself of Homer C. Eller and Jared How, the junior member being his nephew. His retirement from this firm, January 1, 1888, necessitated by impaired health, marks the close of his active pursuit of the legal profession.

The professional career of Judge Clark covered a wide field of practice. Two of the firms with which he was associated prior to his elevation to the bench had been extensively employed in the legal work incident to the organization and development of certain companies now component parts of the present great railway system known as the Chicago, Milwaukee and St. Paul Railway Company. After his retirement from the bench, he was frequently retained "in matters connected with the organization and construction of extensions and proprietary lines and properties, the preparation of trust deeds and securities connected with the financing of various companies, the preparation of leases and trackage, traffic and other contracts connected with their operation and their relation to other companies, and the purchase and consolidation of other properties."

The qualifications that gained him distinction at the bar made him a useful citizen in other fields.

He served the state as a regent of the University of Minnesota continuously from the date of his first appointment in 1879 until the close of life and was president of the Board of Regents during the last three years and more of that time, he having been appointed December 10, 1901, to fill the vacancy in the office of president caused by the death of Hon. John S. Pillsbury.

For many years he took an active interest in the welfare of the Minnesota Historical Society, was long a member of its council, and elected to the presidency thereof in 1904 to fill the vacancy caused by the death of Hon. John B. Sanborn, a position that he continued to occupy until death. Dartmouth College conferred upon him in 1904 the degree of LL.D.

In all his relations in life, Judge Clark was calm and judicious and faithful to the highest and purest conceptions of duty. Great as were his attainments as a lawyer, he reached a higher station in the calm beauty of his everyday life.

Now that the able lawyer and noble man is gone from us, it is fitting that we who walked with him and are witness of his wealth of character leave for the inspiration of coming generations our testimonial to his virtues.

Hon. Henry W. Childs then said:

I move the adoption of the Memorial and in support of the motion desire to contribute a few remarks.

The time of this court is rarely employed to better purpose than when it gives ear to testimonials from the bar in recognition of the character and attainments of those who have shared in the determination of its judgments and closed the period of their lives.

The professional career of Judge Greenleaf Clark, first and last, may be compassed in the remark that he was a calm, diligent, faithful, clear-sighted, thoroughly read lawyer who commanded the respect of courts and the confidence of clients. His sterling manhood was never impaired by professional strife nor obscured by professional achievements. Who ever questioned his integrity at the bar? When was not his spoken word as good as the written stipulation? What court ever heard a false note in his speech? On what occasion did he lay aside the grace of the courteous gentleman, save when, perhaps, insolence or the tricks of the shyster had to be exposed and rebuked? There was righteous wrath in him, as in all noble men, and if occasion ever required, he must have displayed it. I cannot conceive a situation in his professional career, whether at the trial or in the office, when he would not have recoiled from the temptation to either employ a false witness or counsel a dishonest advantage.

I have read with some care the opinions of this court that he wrote. From first to last they discover the utmost simplicity of style. He had learned the strength of the simple words of our English speech, and they are plentiful throughout his judicial writings. No lawyer can read his pages and doubt his masterful grasp of legal principles or the keenness of his vision in searching out the real issue in the cause or the soundness of his judgment in the application of the appropriate rules of law. His thought is never turgid or lost in that interminable verbiage that at once betrays uncertain grasp and painful labor. Great thoughts are ever garbed in plain words; truth shines of its own lustre; and he had learned those lessons before the ermine had touched his shoulders. His retirement from the bench was a great mistake. There were few men then at the bar who were able to take up and bear with equal strength the burden that he laid down.

Judge Clark had acquired a complete mastery over himself. He was remarkably self-poised, rarely, if ever, displaying the agitation of mental weakness. His speech was always clean. No word ever dropped from his lips that was stained with any coloring of vice or that jarred the most sensitive ear. But there was never a parade of his virtues. They had the naturalness of the fragrance of a flower. He wore them in a face brightened at times with a smile of unmixed sweetness—a face that, once seen, left a pleasant memory in the thought, the face of one at peace with himself and the world.

He was eminently a man of peace. His very presence rebuked contention. Strife retired at his coming. This characteristic discovered the grace of a noble soul endowed with a knowledge untaught in the schools that angry strife is hurtful and that the problems of this life are best solved in the calm atmosphere of dispassionate discussion. Why express the obvious truth that one so endowed was possessed of qualities that must needs have made him a valuable member of this court? I do so that I may present on so fitting an occasion the brief yet expressive testimonial of the late Justice Mitchell, who was his associate here and whose words were never idly spoken. He once said in reminiscent mood that Judge Clark exercised a marked influence over his associates in tempering discussion in the deliberations of the court. Such was his influence always and everywhere in the various relations in which he came in contact with his fellowmen. Truth had in him one of its most faithful champions.

The deference always shown him by those who knew him best argues strongly the power of his influence and the worth of his opinions. Such men move mountains not by brilliant flashes of genius, too often erratic, nor by sudden exhibitions of unbridled power, too often the expression of ill-timed zeal, but by a calm, steady, and intelligent pressure that rarely fails to win its way.

He was a gentleman in the best sense of the word. He was every day the same. No cares were so pressing, no trials so severe, no infirmity of body so distressing that he forgot, as most men sometimes do, the obligations of a gentleman. He had no stilted and conventional phrase with which to greet either a cherished friend or a passing acquaintance. His handshake was something to be remembered. He took you by the hand and drew you to him. Who will ever forget his smile that ever felt its warmth? Few conversed like him. His was a low, sweet voice that went straight to the heart. You had not to be told, for you knew, that you were in the presence of one of the choicest of men—a veritable God's nobleman. So he impressed me in those all too few but priceless moments that tied my life to his.

He was a cultured man. In early life he had received the benefit of a liberal education, enlarged and corrected by the studious habits of after years. Not only had he taken a full academic course at his Alma Mater but he had fitted himself for professional work at the greatest of American law schools. Dartmouth and Harvard had helped him greatly. Not only so, but his whole subsequent life was passed in the best society of his adopted state and in intimate association with the strongest and best-trained lawyers who have practiced in our courts. A student by nature, thus trained by the schools, improved by years of thoughtful reading, broadened and strengthened by professional association, he was fitted as few men are to speak the wise word or lead discussion or direct and enliven conversation on any occasion in which he participated.

His mind was not a miser's box filled with unused treasure. He gave of his wealth of thought wisely. The author of "The Simple Life" expresses in few words a great truth. "All the strength of the world," he says, "and all its beauty, all true joy, everything that consoles, that feeds hope, or throws a ray of light along our dark paths, everything that makes us see across our poor lives a splendid goal or a boundless future, come to us from people of simplicity, those who have made another object of their desires than the passing satisfaction of selfishness and vanity and have understood that the art of living is to know how to give one's life."

This art he had learned. I dare not say fully, for so great a measure of virtue is the portion of the faultless only. And who are they? Where shall we seek them? He gave his life in generous counsel to those who were wise enough to seek it. He gave it in the calm beauty of his daily walk that shed a wholesome radiance upon the society in which he moved. He gave it in the discharge of his duties as a regent of the State University, which grew greatly during the incumbency of his office. He gave it in his relations with the State Historical Society and the St. Paul Public Library, with both of which he was long and closely identified and whose value to the moral and intellectual life he was too wise to undervalue. He gave it finally in those multiform associations that long years gather and cluster about strong and useful characters.

His last public appearance was when, a few weeks before his death, he presided at the meeting of the Minnesota Historical Society appointed to memorialize his life-long friend, the late John B. Sanborn. He signalized that occasion by a brief but noble tribute in which the sentiments of an admiring friend were clothed in beautiful diction, thus demonstrating that the ravages of disease had not yet weakened the powers of his mind.

Vainly have my lips sought to pay the tribute that my heart would offer to the memory of a friend. I loved him because he sought me out and drew me to him and held me fast by the most sacred bond that can be found in life's treasure-house.

Dr. William S. Pattee, Dean of the College of Law of the University of Minnesota, then said:

Whether Athens should bestow a crown upon Demosthenes was the question that gave us the two greatest orations of antiquity. Aeschines reminded the Athenians that "the character of a city was determined by the character of the men it crowned." For, he went on to say, "If you take one whose life has no high purpose, one who mocks at morals, and crown him in the theatre, every boy who sees it is corrupted." And the opposite of this is equally true. For if we crown the man of high aims, of upright conduct, and of noble character, the lives of the young and old alike are made better. By recounting the virtues of Judge Clark, by recalling his fidelity to every trust, his conscientious discharge of every duty at the bar, upon the bench, in social life, by recalling his admiration for the noble and his contempt for the mean, the bench and the bar are themselves made better. In honoring Judge Clark, if recounting his virtues is to honor him, we honor ourselves. It requires something of character and goodness to appreciate character and goodness in others. The bench and the bar of Minnesota appreciate this great lawyer and genuine man. One of the best gifts Providence ever bestows upon a state is a man of that life and character that challenges the admiration and compels the respect of his fellow citizens. Such a gift was bestowed upon Minnesota in her early days in the person of our departed friend. He reflected honor upon the bar, the bench was dignified by his presence upon it, and the average quality of our citizenship is higher because he was a citizen among us.

Upon an occasion like this we naturally consider the character and deeds of him whose memory we cherish, and there is but one way for us to learn what the character of any person is, and that is by the revelations he has made of himself. This is a universal law. We know something of that Eternal Energy that has posited this universe in space by the revelations it has made of Itself. We find life revealed in the universe, hence the Revealer must have had life. We find intelligence revealed in the universe, hence the Revealer must have had intelligence. We find personality revealed in the creature, hence we are compelled to conclude that the Creator Himself was personal. And just so we learn what our friends and fellowmen are by the revelations that they make of themselves in human life. In other words, we know what our friend was by what he did. We know he was thoughtful by the thoughts he expressed; we know he was kind by the expressions of kindness that he uttered and the deeds of kindness that he performed; we know he was wise in counsel by the soundness and results of his expressed judgments; we know he was learned in the law by the disclosures he made of his legal knowledge; we know he was an impartial and a faithful judge by the impartiality and fidelity that he revealed in his judgments; we know he was a successful and a great lawyer by his achievements at the bar; we know he was a true friend by his uniform and unmistakable words and deeds of friendship; and we know he was a refined and courteous gentleman and worthy of the most studious emulation by the purity of his words and the dignity and urbanity of his manners. Eminent at the bar, honored as a judge whose term of service was unfortunately too short, and recognized as a true and noble man, he has left a name behind him that will ever reflect honor upon this North Star State, whose adopted son he was and of whom she may ever be proud.

While associated with him to some extent in professional life, I knew him best as a regent of the University, in which institution he is held in universal esteem and honor. As a regent in the spring of 1888 he was active in the establishment and organization of the College of Law. He was present at the meeting of the executive committee the first time I had the honor of meeting the regents with reference to the organization of the Department of Jurisprudence. From that day until his death he was a true and pronounced friend of the department and a most highly esteemed friend and counsellor of the Faculty of Law. Not once in nearly seventeen years did I ever go to him in vain

for assistance or advice. Anxious to learn its needs, jealous of its efficiency and reputation, ambitious for its usefulness to the bench and bar of the state, patient in listening to all suggestions for its growth and improvement, helpful in his criticism and equally so in his practical provisions for its financial assistance, he was a tower of strength to the management of the department and an appreciative listener and loyal supporter of all our efforts looking to the improvement, enlargement, and efficiency of the school.

At the first session of the legislature after the school's organization in 1888, Judge Clark prepared a bill providing for annual and permanent aid to the law library. This bill was the result of his forethought, written out in detail by his own hand, passed by legislature as prepared by him, and has ever since been operative in bringing most valuable books and documents into the library of the department. He also urged an appropriation for a law building that was generously provided by the state, and when the time came for locating the new building Judge Clark was chairman of the committee for selecting a site; and in connection with this occurred an incident illustrative of his decision of mind. While walking through the oak grove he proceeded to one of the most attractive spots on the campus, as it then existed. When he asked the committee why that spot was not the proper one, it was suggested by another that the building better not be placed there because it would necessitate cutting down so many of those large and venerable oaks; but looking around over the campus and assuming a thoughtful air, he said, "Gentlemen, this College of Law is to be one of the most important departments of the University; it deserves a good location," and holding a stick in his hand he stepped to a certain spot, and thrusting the stick into the ground he continued, "The southeasterly corner of the building shall be right there, not one foot to the right or the left, but just there; this campus is not a place for raising trees chiefly, but a place on which to put buildings." The committee all acquiesced in the Judge's decision. Judge Clark was chairman of the committee of the regents who considered all matters pertaining to the College of Law, and we are all indebted to him for the thought and careful consideration he gave to every item of business that came before him for action. Prompt, intelligent, and thoughtful attention was given to every matter submitted to him; and the element of his character that in all these years most deeply impressed me and awakened in my heart the most lasting gratitude and a feeling of undying friendship was his thorough and sympathetic appreciation of every effort made by us for the establishment of such a Department of Jurisprudence as his ideal required. The Judge held his profession in high esteem. His professional ideals were high. His educational ideals were equally so; but at the same time a man of the world and of affairs, he appreciated the difficulties encountered in making the real conform to the ideal.

In recounting thus the details of a great man's life, it may seem at first as though they are trifles and belittle rather than exalt his importance to the world; but such is in no sense the fact. All great things in this universe are composed of elements atomic in their proportions. The universe itself consists of spheres of comparative insignificance when compared with the universal whole, and each sphere in its turn is composed of microscopic elements. All greatness is made up of an aggregation of things in themselves small. And so a great and brilliant career at the bar like that of our friend, when analyzed, is found to be composed of small duties, so-called, faithfully performed. It is the manner of their performance, the spirit of fidelity that is breathed into them, the conscience that is put into every action, however unimportant apparently, that welds the whole aggregation of life's actions together and gives to the whole life a form at once attractive and beautiful. Such was the manner in which the noble character of our departed friend was made. Fidelity in all the details of his professional, judicial, and social life was his distinguishing characteristic. And we may easily imagine that in rendering his final account to his Great Judge it was said to him as to the servant with five talents who had made other five, "Well done, thou good and faithful servant; thou hast been faithful over a few things; I will make thee ruler over many things, enter thou into the joy of thy Lord."

Hon. Samuel R. Thayer then said:

I hesitate to occupy a moment even of the time that I feel properly belongs to those members of the bar who were more intimately associated with Judge Clark than myself. My knowledge of Judge Clark covers a period of thirty and more years, but it was not until he had relinquished his more important duties that I was brought into such a relationship with him that I was able to form a definite judgment of the motives and purposes that governed his conduct throughout the varied activities of his life.

That sturdiness of character that has been referred to both here and elsewhere as a distinguishing attribute of his nature I think was largely due to his New England training, perhaps more especially to his New England Congregational parentage and to the influence of the wooden church and the wooden schoolhouse, all of which influences bred in him those habits of industry, economy, and method that resulted in accumulations that he dealt out in no stinted charities.

He was a civilian, a lawyer, and a jurist, eminent in every department of usefulness that engaged his attention. His conception of his legal duties in the early formative period of the state led him outside the narrow range of his professional life into the more important work of laying the foundations of those institutions that ultimately became the glory of the commonwealth. Hence his continuous activity in upholding and enlarging the sphere of our State University—which, I think, after all, was his chief pride.

There was something about his career that reminds one continually of what has been aptly termed the quality of high citizenship—the disposition to subordinate self and selfish ends to the public good—of which his life furnishes very many ample illustrations.

I think his mind was essentially judicial. His voice was frequently heard in this temple of justice, not only as an advocate but as an expounder of the law, and his judicial experience was such as to justify the hope and belief that had the will of the people given him greater opportunities he would have made very many valuable contributions to our legal lore and doubtless augmented his own fame.

It is no small compliment to the memory of Judge Clark to say that he was a worthy associate of the late Horace Bigelow—a name illustrious in our legal annals—and I think it will be generally conceded that the firm of Bigelow & Clark and, later, the firm of Bigelow, Flandrau & Clark were governed by as high professional ideals as those of any legal firm in this or any other state in the Union and that Mr. Clark contributed his due share to their professional preeminence.

He was not eloquent in speech, but he possessed the more enduring eloquence of a virtuous and noble life, and though "the places which once knew him know him no more," the world will remember him as a man who made the best use of the gifts that God had bestowed upon him.

Harris Richardson, Esq., then said:

More than twenty years ago Judge Clark honored the people of this state by serving as a member of this court. While here he gave to them daily the benefits of his great industry and ability. The early training that Dartmouth College gave him, the later training that his leadership at the bar of this state gave him, the business training that his active life among men gave him, fitted him for the work. When we examine the opinions that he rendered here we find them clear, logical, forceful, business-like. They are beyond criticism. They bristle with precedents, yet are they also alive with the personality of the just judge.

We are met here today to assist in perpetuating the facts as to his ability, his scholarship, his manhood. When he left this court he was in his prime; when he left us—so recently—his age was ripe. We must all draw the same conclusion as to his ability, his learning, his success in life. He occupied so prominent a position from early manhood to old age that there can be no difference of opinion.

To the older members of the bar, to the younger members, to those of us who by chance now occupy the middle path, he must ever serve as a model. We are not here to mourn him; we are here to honor him. By recounting the facts of his life, by hearing its story, we can gain great profit. May it make us all more manly, more just, more helpful one to another.

Former Chief Justice Thomas Wilson then said:

I did not come here intending to say anything—I very seldom speak on such occasions. I will now say but a few words.

From the time Mr. Clark came to Minnesota un-

til his death I knew him well, though we were never intimate as they who know what real intimacy is understand by that expression. We looked at many problems from different standpoints; on some we were very far apart. I often met him at the bar, sometimes with him, oftener opposed to him. As actions at times speak louder than words, I wish to refer to one incident showing my estimate of him as a man of integrity.

A good many years ago a suit was brought by the city in which I lived against a corporation whose stockholders and officers were very prominent men in the financial world. It was alleged in that suit that the defendant had illegally obtained and misappropriated the bonds of the plaintiff. The law firm of Bigelow, Flandrau & Clark represented the defendant, I the plaintiff. After the litigation in its different ramifications had been carried to both the Supreme Court of the United States and of the state, the plaintiff obtained a judgment in the state court for the full amount of its claim, which on appeal was affirmed in the Supreme Court. The defendant thereupon moved the latter court for a re-argument of the case, alleging that a material fact not set up or at issue in the pleadings had, without objection, been litigated and established by the evidence in the court below. The granting of that motion would probably have been decisive of the case in favor of the defendant, and in support of the motion numerous affidavits were offered. The feeling engendered was much more than commensurate to the amount involved, which was then considered large, about two hundred thousand dollars. Each of the attorneys for the defendant was present in court and had been present at every step in the litigation. After offering some affidavits in opposition to the motion, I said to the court (I believe I remember nearly the very words used, for I never felt more personal interest in a suit), "In addition to these affidavits, I wish to offer another item of evidence. There is present a gentleman who was present at every step taken, who heard every word of evidence offered or received in the suit— Mr. Clark, one of the attorneys of the defendant—and I now consent that he state, without being sworn, whether any such question was suggested in the court below or any such evidence offered."

It goes without saying that had I not been perfectly certain that neither personal interest nor personal feeling could influence him to in the least swerve from the truth, no such offer would have been made. He spoke not, of course well knowing the consequence—the defeat of the motion and of his client.

Chief Justice Start then said:

The court receives with great appreciation your memorial. It is a just estimate of the character and services of a true man, a great lawyer, and a public-spirited citizen.

Justice Clark was a man of interesting personality, of rugged manly sense, unquestioned integrity, and great intellectual force. His opinions in this court show that he possessed a practical and accurate sense of justice and a comprehensive grasp of legal principles, with the rare gift of illustrating and applying them.

The court concurs without reservation in all that has been here said in his praise and as a tribute to his memory directs that your memorial and addresses be entered in the record of the court of today and that the court now adjourn. [95 Minn. xxi]

William Mitchell

1832–1900
Associate Justice, 1881–1900

On the afternoon of October 2, 1900, in the chamber of the house of representatives at the state capitol, Hon. James A. Tawney presented to the supreme court, then in session, in behalf of the Winona and State Bar Associations the following memorial of Associate Justice Mitchell, who died August 21, 1900, and moved that the same be spread upon the records of the court:

William Mitchell, who for forty-three years was a member of the Minnesota Bar, for seven years was judge of the Third judicial district, and for nineteen years was an Associate Justice of this court, having been called away by death, the members of the Winona and state Bar respectfully submit the following, as a testimonial of their esteem and affection for him while living and as a tribute to his memory now that he is gone.

We honored him for his noble and dignified character; we loved him for his fraternal spirit. In all the relations and duties of life he aimed at what was true and pure and good. His large intellectual gifts and liberal culture gave him prominence and power. His fine social qualities, uniform courtesy, and kindness won the favor of all who knew him. His spotless integrity and conscientious fidelity in the discharge of duty won their confidence. It falls to the lot of few men to be as universally respected as was Judge Mitchell.

That he was a great lawyer and a great jurist, great in legal learning and great in those qualities of mind and character essential to judicial eminence, is the uniform testimony of the Bar of the state. In his large and invaluable contribution to the judicial literature of the state and nation, he has shed undying lustre upon the Bar and the courts with which he was directly related. In losing him Minnesota has lost one of her brightest or-

naments—one of her most distinguished and valuable citizens.

We ask, therefore, that this brief memorial be preserved in the records of this court, together with such other proceedings as may occur in connection therewith.

Hon. James A. Tawney then addressed the court as follows:

Having presented this Memorial I should rather leave undone that which I am about to do, were it not for the solemn debt that the living owe to the dead. Not because I do not take pleasure in acknowledging my personal debt to the distinguished dead we honor to-day, not because I do not dwell with joy upon his extraordinary virtues, nor is it because I feel that any words of mine will exaggerate the beauty of his life and the beneficence of his influence. Not for any or all of these causes do I hesitate to speak but because he was my personal friend in that sense which makes it difficult to speak. Excepting my father, there is no living man to whom I owe so much as to Judge Mitchell.

This tender, loving husband, father, and friend lived close to the hearts of all who knew him well and were every one for whom he did some noble service to speak the thoughts that arise in his heart. Judge Mitchell's name would live to-day in a symphony of grateful eulogy. In the hearts of all who knew him best he will always be remembered the soul of gentility, of nobility, and manliness. He was justly esteemed as a judge, a citizen, and a man. He had strong, pure affections that bound him to his country and to his friends like bands of steel. He

> Best seem'd the thing he was, and join'd
> Each office of the social hour
> To noble manners, as the flower
> And native growth of noble mind.

. . . And thus he bore without abuse,
The grand old name of gentleman.

The story of the life of William Mitchell is a simple tale of struggle and progress. He grew in purity and power of personality as he grew in influence and usefulness in the commonwealth. Born in Canada in 1832, he was graduated from Jefferson College at Cannonsburg, Pennsylvania, in 1853; he taught two years in Morgantown Academy of West Virginia; he was admitted to the Morgantown bar in 1857. Soon thereafter he moved to Winona, Minnesota, and entered upon a successful practice and, upon a long career of public usefulness, suddenly terminated at its zenith by the touch of death. He was elected to the second legislature of Minnesota for 1859 and 1860; he was elected county attorney for Winona county and served for one term; he also filled various other municipal offices with great credit and was elected judge of the Third judicial district of the state in 1874 and re-elected in 1880. He was appointed to the supreme judiciary of the state by Governor Pillsbury in 1881 and for nineteen years was one of the central figures of this important tribunal. When the people of the state departed from the policy of a nonpartisan judiciary instituted by Governor Pillsbury, Judge Mitchell's place, in January 1900, was filled by another, and the state lost one of its brightest minds.

From the foothills of obscurity he rose among the mountain peaks of fame. Exquisite and yet tremendous, he moved unobtrusively among men, seeking everywhere with singleness of purpose that noble realm, where across the ages the friends of justice and of God hold silent converse with each other and their Great Original. His parents were born and educated in a land where the heather grows over the granite, and no nobler union of sturdy principles and gracious manner ever sprang from a Scottish home

Many men have sought by tongue and pen to express their deep sorrow at his irreparable loss and their profound sense of his great worth, but no one whose words I have heard or read has noted one of the most beautiful traits of his exquisite personality—the Christian gentleness and becoming modesty of his manner.

Judge Mitchell was a lawyer of profound scholarship. It would be difficult to portray his great legal and literary attainments, his swerving loyalty to the principles he loved, or the justice with which he applied those principles to human life; but it would require volumes of narrative to convey any impression that would approximate the truth of the affability of his bearing, the kindliness of his manner, and the charity of his life. It is not necessary in this presence that I should dwell upon the great legal learning or upon the fine literary ability with which he expressed his opinions and graced the literature of this court. Of all this and more, you are profoundly assured while others whose knowledge and ability peculiarly qualify them will speak. No judge ever strove more faithfully to apply the principles of truth and justice to the common contests of human life, and but few have succeeded as he did. He was a great analyzer of complex practical situations. No general saw with more unerring insight the critical moment in battle than he saw the central question at issue, whether of law or fact, in any legal controversy to which his attention was called. His thought flew to the essence of the matter like an arrow to its mark, and his heart ever turned toward justice like a planet toward its sun. He loved the problems of equity and justice as the poet loves beauty, as the philosopher loves truth, and coupling with this passion, as he did, keen powers of analysis and a sense of logical consistency, it is not difficult to understand the peculiar judicial cast of his mind.

To this passion for justice between man and man is traceable his patience and disinterestedness as well as his almost unerring insight. No lawyer ever argued a case before him without feeling that Judge Mitchell listened attentively to the end. Love suffereth long and is kind, said the Great Teacher. There can be no doubt that the patience exhibited continually by great jurists, by great scientists, and great practical heroes everywhere is the immediate fruit of some disinterested passion or another. An intense interest in some impersonal thought-relation or equally impersonal ideal sustains human effort and renders men oblivious to circumstances that annoy those of less devotion.

Judge Mitchell was a man of sound legal judgment. Men always judge soundly of that toward which they turn with intense disinterested passion. Ambition— "that last infirmity of noble minds"—undoubtedly stimulated but never debased him. He devoted much time and effort to tasks that could never bring him individually any adequate return.

My first acquaintance with him was in 1877 as a teacher of a Bible class in one of the Sunday schools of Winona. As a teacher, a lawyer, or a judge he always took a deep interest in young men and assisted not only me but more than one youth with whom he came in contact in this way in the attainment of an education; but no sense of personal obligation was ever occasioned either by the fact or the manner in which his aid was thus bestowed. He served as president of infant enterprises in the city of Winona when they were too feeble to give him strength in return. He visited the sick, cared for the weak and helpless, and always displayed in all personal relations a thoughtfulness and charity rarely found in those who hold justice so dear.

It is not possible for human eyes to see what lies beyond the grave, but this we know: That he experiences to-day the consequences, whatever they may be, of having lived justly, loved mercy, and walked humbly with his God.

As I close a sense of my personal loss comes over me and fills me with regret. I know of no sincerer compliment that the living pay the dead than their sorrow, and as for Judge Mitchell, with all my heart I wish he were living still. There was, there is, no simpler, gentler, manlier man.

Hon. Thomas Wilson then addressed the court:

Judge Mitchell's father was a farmer. While he and his family lived comfortably and well, they lived plainly, for that comported with their tastes and views of propriety; and besides, they had but a limited amount of this world's goods. William was therefore early taught frugality and plain living, and he never forgot the example and lesson.

As was usual at that time with that class of people—his parents were both natives of Scotland and Presbyterians—the clergyman was a good scholar, and he aided William to lay the foundation of his education, especially in the languages. William afterwards pursued his studies in Jefferson College, Pennsylvania. When he graduated he at once commenced the study of the law with the Honorable Edgar Wilson, a prominent lawyer of Morgantown, Virginia,

and while studying law he taught some advanced classes in an academy in the same town.

Having finished his law studies, early in 1857 he removed to Winona, where he continued to reside until he removed to this city about eight years ago. Almost immediately on his coming to Winona, I had the good fortune to become intimately acquainted with him, and thereafter until his death, unless one or the other was absent from home, a week rarely passed in which we did not spend more or less time together. Our intimacy was never for a moment interrupted, and happily between our families there was also the closest friendship. While I was on the bench he practiced before me, both in the district court and in this court. After I left the bench we very frequently met at the bar as opposing counsel, and all the while he was on the bench I practiced before him. I therefore can speak knowingly of him as a man, as a lawyer, as a judge, and as a citizen.

Nature endowed him with much more than ordinary ability. He had a good literary education, was a thoroughly educated lawyer, and beyond that had wide general information. He was constantly seeking knowledge. Unlike most people, he did not take a vacation for physical rest; on the contrary, except when he was fishing he kept going from place to place to learn what he could about the country, its inhabitants, resources, and institutions. He was a keen and accurate observer and had a very retentive memory. He loved nature in all her forms and aspects. His love of trees shrubs and plants, especially flowers, was almost a passion. While he lived in Winona, in addition to such as he could find at home, he was accustomed to get from other states and to import rare plants, bulbs, and seeds, the cultivation and growth of which he greatly enjoyed.

He was pure and simple-hearted as a girl. While he lived comfortably and surrounded himself and his family with whatever might in any way add to their comfort, enjoyment, or improvement, he always lived modestly. He intensely disliked ostentation or unseemly display of wealth, learning, or superiority of any kind and hated all forms of guile or duplicity. He did nothing to be seen of men. Considering that he was not a wealthy man, he was a liberal giver, especially to those who were in need; but in his giving he let not his left hand know what his right hand did.

He sincerely sympathized with and prized the classes who earn their bread by the sweat of their brow. Nothing aroused his ire more than an attempt to oppress or wrong them, or excited his contempt more than a word or act intended to belittle them. By his life he showed his belief in that sacred fundamental truth that the greatest good of the greatest number is the proper foundation of morals, legislation, and political action. While he recognized the fact that the best interests of society and of every class require, and that it is the duty of the state to see to it, that there be rendered to Caesar the things that are Caesar's—that the person and property of every citizen, irrespective of his wealth or rank, be sacredly protected at all hazards—he never forgot that the protection of the poor, the weak, and the defenseless is the first duty of the state.

As a father he was fond, tender, and kind but showed his feelings by acts rather than by words. He was a true friend and a most interesting and attractive companion. He had a fine vein of humor, an almost inexhaustible fund of anecdote and information, and an abnegation of self that was at times embarrassing to his associates, for it required constant watchfulness—sometimes emphatic protest—to prevent him from giving them the preference in everything and the best of everything.

He was not a member of any church, but he attended and contributed to the church of his fathers, and he had no toleration for any one who spoke disrespectfully of religion.

I here venture to refer to what may be considered a weakness, for his reputation does not require that aught should be hidden; it needs no eulogy but the truth. He was not an optimist or a very hopeful man; he did not dream of or hope for any great social or political reformations. He was not a bold or masterful man. In great crises he would not have been a leader. He did not willingly meet—on the contrary, if he reasonably could, he avoided—a conflict. When wronged, even by falsehood or treachery, he was prone to forgive and forget, or when that was not possible to hold his peace rather than expose or denounce the malefactor. For some such (as it seemed to me) weaknesses, I sometimes chided him, for between us there was no

enforced ceremony. In our intercourse we were accustomed to speak with a freedom that would have been inadmissible had either entertained the least doubt of the unfailing friendship of the other. In these respects it is probable that I, not he, was wrong. If these were not, I never discerned in his character a fault or weakness. A more upright man, a better citizen and neighbor, a more kind master, or a more genuine and lovable friend, I never knew. There was no base alloy in his nature. His hands were clean, his heart was pure; he had not lifted up his soul to vanity nor sworn deceitfully. It need hardly be said that his neighbors and acquaintances loved and honored him. He had no foes but such as good men must expect.

He never liked the ordinary practice of the law. He was not an orator or a master of those arts that make men notably successful advocates or trial lawyers. He was very strong at the bar, but the foundation of his strength was his superiority as a lawyer and his confessedly high character. I hardly know whether he merited more praise as a judge on the circuit or on this bench. I think—and I believe those whom I see before me who used to practice before him on the circuit will agree—that he was almost perfect as a *nisi prius* judge.

The judicial bench is holy ground. "Honesty," as applied to a judge, means more than when used in the ordinary transactions of men. To be an honest and good judge, a man must be devoid of pride of opinion, regardless of either popular commendation or condemnation—uninfluenced by the desire to be consistent—must, for the time, forget all enmities and friendships, and also himself, which is above the reach of the ordinary man. David Dudley Field, in one of his addresses, did not exaggerate when he said: "To have the power of forgetting, for the time, self, friends, interests, relationship, and to think of doing right toward another, a stranger, an enemy perhaps, is to have that which man can share only with the angels and with Him who is above men and angels." Measured by even this high standard, Judge Mitchell was not found wanting. As a judge he seemed to be absolutely without pride of opinion—to be oblivious of everything but the demands of justice. He was not only willing but anxious to discern and correct any mistake—if mistake there was—in any judgment or opinion that he had rendered. It was a pleasure to listen to his trial of a case without a jury or his charge to a jury. He listened patiently, and he so clearly and with such manifest fairness stated the real issues—eliminating all that were irrelevant—that no jury of ordinary intelligence could misapprehend the questions that they were to try; nor could any attorney or party feel that he had not been justly treated.

It is hardly necessary in this presence to speak of him as a member of this court. Every citizen, and especially every lawyer and judge who is jealous for the reputation and honor of the state and its courts, must be proud of the fact that his opinions have been so often quoted and commended by the ablest jurists throughout the country as models of learning and ability. That he was appreciated at home is shown by the fact that for more than a quarter of a century he was kept continuously on the judicial bench—having been twice elected in a judicial district, and three times in the state, and once appointed by a Republican governor, both the district and state having a large majority against him politically—and by the fact that at the Republican nominating convention preceding the last general election, over three hundred of the delegates voted for his nomination, notwithstanding the most strenuous efforts of the politicians who, considering the judgeship a mere political asset, insisted that no one not belonging to the party should be considered.

His standing abroad is shown by the following excerpt from a letter of Professor Thayer—eminent not only as a professor in the Harvard Law School but also as an attorney and legal author—written to a friend of his in this state two years ago when it became known that an effort would be made to defeat Judge Mitchell's nomination and election. Prof. Thayer wrote:

> I am astonished to hear that there is doubt of the re-election of Judge Mitchell to your supreme court. I wish the people of Minnesota knew the estimate that is put upon him in other parts of the country, and there could be no doubt about it then. I never saw him and have no personal acquaintance with him. I know him only as a judge whose opinions, like those of all the judges in the country, reach me through the excellent law reports published in your state. In the course of my work at the Harvard Law School I have long had to search carefully through these reports for cases relating to my special subjects. In that way I have long recognized Judge Mitchell as one of the best judges in this country and have come to know also the opinion held of him by lawyers competent to pass an opinion on such a question. There is no occasion for making an exception of the supreme court of the United States. On no court in the country to-day is there a judge who would not find his peer in Judge Mitchell . . .
>
> Pray do not allow your state to lose the services of such a man. To keep him on the bench is a service not merely to Minnesota but to the whole country and to the law. Your state it is that is now on trial before the country. The question is: Can Minnesota appreciate such a man? Is it worthy to have him? I am not going to believe that a state that can command the services of one of the few judges in the country that stand out among their fellows as pre-eminent, that give it distinction, will refuse to accept these services. You lawyers of Minnesota must not let party politics work any such result.

In a recent edition of one of our ablest law books, the authors, referring to a question on which the highest courts of the country were irreconcilable, say: "The best statement of this rule, and the reasons for it, is in *Morse v. Minneapolis, etc. R. Co.*, 30 Minn. 465. The rule has been repeatedly enforced in New York, although never with a statement of reasons approaching to the clearness of Judge Mitchell's opinion in the Minnesota case," Shearman and Redfield, Negligence (5th Ed.) § 60c note 3 (Reporter).

I might multiply such references, but it is unnecessary. His opinions are his best monument.

He was in every sense a model citizen of a republic. At a time when wealth, acquired suddenly and sometimes by questionable means, is flaunted in the face of honest men by its vulgar possessors—when that which is so often heralded as liberality or charity is merely a sounding brass or tinkling cymbal, an effort to advertise or glorify the donor when honest worth is so often superseded by self-asserting ignorance, what an object lesson and inspiration such a life is to those who unselfishly aim to serve their state and benefit their race! What a contrast it is with the life of those whose sordid aims all end with self! What a reproof to the demagogue who seeks promotion by disingenuous appeals to ignorance, passion, and prejudice! Who can measure or foretell its influence on those who follow after for example, acquires authority when it speaks from the grave.

Our friend was not quite sixty-eight years old. Though some live and work longer, it is still as a rule true that the days of our years are three score years and ten. Most men, perhaps all, before they reach that limit have some premonition that the afternoon of life is nearly gone. Lowell, on his sixty-eighth birthday, thus beautifully expresses this truth:

> As life runs on, the road grows strange
> With faces new, and near the end
> The mile-stones into head-stones change.
> 'Neath every one a friend.

Not a few of Judge Mitchell's early friends had taken their departure within the last two or three years. He not infrequently spoke of this to me. He was not unmindful of the fact that as to him the sun would soon set. His life work—the work for which he was so peculiarly fitted—was done. For the last few months his physical strength was waning; the hills were beginning to get rugged and steep, the light to wane, and the shadows to deepen and lengthen. The last walk I took with him he spoke of his failing strength. Though he was surrounded and cared for by a lovely, loving, and loved family, he saw that they were following him with anxious, almost tearful eyes, and he was not the man to delude himself with the hope that their anxiety or fears would grow less or his strength greater. Under such circumstances, what could an old man do but die? And death came as he hoped it might at the last come to him—suddenly.

While his going away took out of my life much of the little sunshine that is left, I would not be so weak and selfish as to call him back if I could. Having been absent from the state, I did not see him for nearly two months before his death, and the first news of his illness was a telephone message that he was dying, followed in a few minutes by another that he was dead.

> Some tears fell down my cheeks, and then I smiled
> As those smile who have no face in the world
> To smile back on them. I had lost a friend.

I condole with his family and friends but at the same time congratulate them. I know that the loss of his presence and companionship cannot be expressed by any words, but when the keenness of the pang is past, with what pride and pleasure will they remember the beauty and simple grandeur of his life. What a heritage for his children!

Hon. Daniel A. Dickinson then addressed the court as follows:

Before this court of supreme jurisdiction, of which for nearly nineteen years William Mitchell was a member, appears to-day with one mind and heart an unusual assemblage of the bar of the state to offer a tribute of esteem and love and to express our appreciation of his eminent virtues and his great service to the commonwealth. This is fittingly done in the formal memorial that has been presented to your Honors that it may be inscribed in the enduring records of this court. The language of that memorial and that which is spoken here to-day is not a merely customary, conventional expression of just appreciation of the character and services of a jurist distinguished in his time for eminent ability, learning, mental vigor, and the highest qualifications for the office that he filled so long. While he was thus justly esteemed throughout our own state and wherever beyond our borders the common law prevails and the decisions of this court are consulted, the large circle of those who had intimately known William Mitchell in social life, in the law-making branch of our government, at the bar, on the bench of our court of general jurisdiction, and of this highest tribunal of the state, and especially those who were closely associated with him in the labors and familiar intercourse of daily life, acquired for him a personal attachment that has rendered his death an individual bereavement. And so we are here to express not merely eulogium of the dead but a widely felt personal sorrow for his death.

Few men, and probably none, have rendered greater or more enduring and beneficent service to the state. Few, either here or elsewhere, have been in all respects better qualified by natural endowments mental and moral, and by education, experience, and habit of life, for the discharge of the duties of the high office to which he was called in the prime of his manhood and to which he devoted with constant, strenuous, forceful study, thought, and action about one-half of the period of his life labors. Passing over his distinguished service in the years that preceded his coming into this court, that which he rendered here for almost nineteen years is beyond our power fully to measure or estimate. He never sought display, and the results of his work are not a mere monument, a structure of no practical or beneficent use, save as a memorial of what he achieved. The results of the years of his patient, tireless, earnest, honest work here are wrought into, and constitute an important part of, the grand structure of the law of this state and country, a temple of justice wherein dwelleth righteousness. And while we cannot measure and define the extent of what he thus contributed to the benefit of his own time and of future ages, we know that few here or elsewhere have wrought better or contributed more to make that structure what it is today. He, far more than most jurists, by daily patient research among the often confused and even contradictory declarations of the expounders of the law, brought forth as pearls from ocean's obscure depths the clear legal principles that should control human action. No well-sounding legal proposition, though familiar and current as true coin, was accepted by him without test, whether expressed in the decisions of this or other courts or in argument at this bar, if wanting in the true ring of reason and right. We can all recall how often he challenged some widely current declaration of the law and after painstaking examination demonstrated its fallacy. And such demonstrations, expressed in the decisions of this court, have been time and again accepted in other courts as true statements of the law. No labor was too great if he could thereby discover the truth and do justice.

It is fitting on this occasion that I, who was associated with Judge Mitchell for more than twelve years in this court, should testify as I now do, not only in behalf of myself but of three of his associates no longer living, Gilfillan, Berry, Vanderburgh—for I know they would desire such acknowledgment to be made if they could speak here to-day—the great assistance that we all derived from his wise counsel in the deliberations of this court.

The executive appointment of Judge Mitchell to this court, his repeated re-election by the people without party division, and the unanimous sentiment of the bar attest the general sense of his fitness for the highest judicial office. Though he could not but be conscious of the esteem in which he was held, he was absolutely without affectation, ignoble pride, egotism, or apparent sense of the general estimate of his worth. He was quick to acknowledge, and if possible to correct, his own mistakes—for all judges and all courts do make mistakes. (If it were not so we should not find in the reports of every jurisdiction tables of overruled cases.) His sense of justice and right was a strong, even a so dominant quality of his mind that he sought every way of escape from such application of fixed legal principles as might result in hardship or wrong in the individual case. He was affable, courteous, genial, sincere, and manly always, everywhere and toward all. In characters as strong and positive as Judge Mitchell's there is often manifest some quality of mind or heart falling below the standard of real excellence—some defect that, on an occasion like this, we would cover with a mantle of charity. But neither your Honors, nor we of the bar who have known Judge Mitchell most intimately during all the years past, can recall anything detracting from the general symmetry and beauty of his life and character, anything wanting in purity, strength, breadth, nobility of purpose and action, or in any of the qualities that justly earned for him the highest esteem of all who knew him and a high place for all time among the eminent jurists of this country.

Hon. Thomas Canty then spoke as follows:

Judge Mitchell was a bright jurist of quick perception, great capacity for work, and a wonderful facility and felicity of expression. His opinions will always stand as amongst the best written in the English language.

He was a simple, modest, learned gentleman, with a heart full of the milk of human kindness. He was a great lover of justice, but he also loved to temper justice with mercy. Neither long years on the bench nor the rush of business nor the vast labors thrown upon him ever stifled in the least his sympathy for the wronged; and whenever a case arose in which through the ignorance of the party, the blundering of his attorney, or the misconception of the court below, injustice was done to the poor and unfortunate and there seemed to be no way by which the supreme court under the law and its rules of practice could remedy the wrong, Judge Mitchell always worked and worried and strove to find a way. While he was constantly engaged in the work of bringing criminals to justice, he was too kind-hearted to prosecute those who wronged him and violated his confidence.

Judge Mitchell was a man singularly free from prejudice, bias, and bigotry, and it always pained him to discover that any judge in his judicial duties was influenced by anything of the kind. He had no pride of opinion. If he came to the conclusion that a decision in which he had participated was wrong, he was always ready to overrule it or grant a re-argument.

He was a scholarly man of wide reading and possessed a large fund of general information. He was well versed in the ways of society and was always welcomed by its votaries, but he cared nothing for the ordinary whirl of society; there was too much sham and subterfuge in it to suit him. He always liked to meet his friends and was a genial and companionable man.

Judge Mitchell had done much to give this court a standing with the bench and bar of this country and England; and his opinions, running through more than 50 volumes of the Minnesota Reports, will stand as a monument to his memory long after all the granite monuments now in the world have crumbled to dust and drifted away.

Hon. Charles E. Flandrau then addressed the court as follows:

It being my desire that the testimony of the oldest practitioner of the law in the state and a member of the first supreme court of the state to the excellencies of the late Judge Mitchell should go on record in these memorial proceedings, I have prepared a brief but none the less heartfelt tribute, which with the permission of your Honors I will present.

It is with reluctance that I attempt to say anything on this occasion, because of my inability to rise to the deserved heights of eulogy demanded by the subject under consideration and because the speakers who have preceded me have exhausted the language of panegyric in presenting the virtues of our deceased friend. I cannot add to his universally acknowledged reputation as a man, a lawyer, and a judge. In each and every relation that he bore to his fellowmen in

life, he was as near perfect as it falls to the lot of man to be. I feel that to have been chosen from the members of the bar of the state as one to portray his characteristics for perpetuation in the record of this court is more honor to me than anything I can add to his fame, much as I loved and esteemed him.

Judge Mitchell passed a large portion of his life on the bench, actively engaged in administering the law among his fellowmen, in adjusting their many and complicated differences and misunderstandings. I have known him intimately from his first elevation to the bench to his retirement only a short time ago, and I cannot recall a single instance in which his judgments have not been approved by those best fitted to decide as model expositions of the law, clothed in scholarly, lucid, and eloquent diction.

To be a good and just judge, a man must be endowed with many, if not with all, the virtues of mind and disposition. He must have good practical sense, experience, and understanding, a clear and quick perception of facts, with the power of logical arrangement and application of them to the matter in hand, aided and guided by a thorough knowledge of the law in point. He must be absolutely impartial and free from prejudice. He must be patient to listen and to learn. He must be courageous and firm without obstinacy but tempered with mercy. His life conduct must be so exemplary as to preclude the possibility of wrong doing or wrong thinking. Judge Mitchell possessed all these attributes in an eminent degree. In his death Minnesota mourns the loss of one of her most beloved and distinguished citizens.

Hon. William J. Hahn then addressed the court:

We can do ourselves no greater honor as men than to pause and approvingly contemplate the pure, conscientious, patriotic, high-minded character of a departed friend. We can, as lawyers, offer no better evidence of our appreciation of the highest and best aspirations of our profession than by giving public voice to our sense of loss when death invades the ranks of our profession and removes one of its honorable and justly honored members. We can, as a part of one of the great subdivisions of our governmental machinery, perform few more commendable and helpful duties than registering in the archives of the court a brief memorial of the worth and public services of some great, fearless, spotless judge who has gone to his reward. We are here at this time to thus honor ourselves, to proffer testimony, to discharge that obligation.

In this rushing, grasping, sordid age of materialism in which we live, it is refreshing and inspiring to contemplate the life and character of one whose gaze was fixed on higher things than the mere acquirement of wealth and honor, whose ears were open to more harmonious sounds and nobler strains than the din and turmoil of selfish achievements, whose voice was heard in gentler tones and sweeter accents than the fierce cry of personal victory, whose heart throbbed with warmer impulses and more embracing motives than earthly gain or kindred ties, whose soul yearned for higher achievement and more enduring fame than mere success or passing applause, whose life was actuated by manlier ambition and truer purpose than social distinction or personal renown.

It is such a life and character we are here to reflect upon. Gentle, kind, modest, considerate, sympathetic, helpful, and yet strong, firm for the right, persistent in duty, unyielding in principle in every fiber of his being, in every emotion of his heart, in every impulse of his soul, a shining example of God's exalted handiwork, a noble man.

As a lawyer few men have added as great luster to the bar of this state either by marked ability, fearless performance of professional duty, keen and quick perception of controlling principles, high-minded and courteous demeanor, honorable and fair conduct toward court, jury, and opposing counsel, as did Judge Mitchell. Cogent, vigorous, terse, clear, effective, obliging, polite, honest, he was my beau ideal of a lawyer. No court ever listened to him without being enlightened. No jury was ever addressed by him without being thereby helped in the performance of its duty. No opposing counsel ever met him in the heat and stress of a legal contest, without carrying away with him a truer view of the proper and possible amenity that should characterize the conduct of the profession.

He was not content to devote his faculties to the mere accretion of wealth or to the selfish pursuit of his own interests and the interests of his individual clientage, important and sacred as they were. He also felt it to be his duty as a lawyer to exercise a salutary sway in the fashioning and moulding of our jurisprudence and laws and to exert a healthy and conservative influence on the community in which he lived, through the clients whom he advised, the juries whom he addressed, and the citizens with whom he mingled. He took a broad view of what, as a member of the legal profession, was due from him to the state. He acted upon the theory that as a citizen his obligations were commensurate with his opportunities, and these by reason of his training, learning, and ability were greater than those of any other class of citizens. To the discharge of these obligations, the embracing of these opportunities, he devoted his faculties with the same conscientious estimate of his calling as in the performance of his more immediate professional service. It was because of this and of his sweet, blameless character that his death was regarded by the citizens of Winona, where he lived so long, as a personal loss.

> Only the actions of the just,
> Smell sweet and blossom in their dust.

But it is as a judge that William Mitchell will be longest and most universally remembered and revered. It was in that exalted and sacred place, in the full gaze of his brethren at the bar and the community at large, that all the elements of his high character, all the solidity and brilliancy of his natural gifts and individual acquirements, all the clearness and keenness of his logical mind found full opportunity for their display and exercise.

With a vast business experience, an extensive and varied practice at the bar, a profound knowledge of the science of the law, and a mind peculiarly fitted to apply such knowledge to the varied and ever changing circumstances and conditions of a highly progressive people coupled with a kindly considerate disposition and naturally fair and honest operation of mental processes that he possessed in a remarkable degree, he was especially fitted for the discharge of the weighty responsibilities devolving upon a man occupying a position on the bench.

I knew him intimately. I was honored by his

friendship. For twenty-six years it was my privilege, from time to time, to stand before him as an advocate either in the district or supreme court. No man, in my judgment, has occupied a judicial position in this state, in state or federal court, who possessed the qualities of an ideal jurist in any greater degree than Judge Mitchell. I never knew a man so utterly devoid of pride of opinion as he. I never appeared before a judge more eminently fair, more clear headed, with a more discerning and discriminating judgment, with a vaster fund of common sense, with a surer intuition of what the law ought to be, more genial and affable than he. In my opinion there is no mental quality, moral requirement, or dispositional tendency that can be named or required in the ideal judge that was not found in his make-up. I think it may be truly said that he was regarded by the bar as being one of the ablest and clearest-headed judges who ever sat upon this bench, and with equal truth that but few men in this state are or were so generally esteemed by laymen or lawyers and but few who had or have the unbounded confidence and esteem of our citizens as he.

How often have each one of us, in arguing some case in this court, had a query propounded by him in that kindly way of his that showed beyond preadventure that he had clearly grasped the real and controlling point in the case. A question not to embarrass but to help, asked not to display his own discernment but to aid in the solution, submitted not as indicating his own unalterable view but with the evident desire to overcome and remove if possible what at the time occurred to him as an objection. And in endeavoring to answer such question I think I am warranted in saying that counsel invariably felt that what he had to say was addressed to a mind as free from bias or preconceived notions and as open to conviction and conversion as if the same had proceeded from some other source. And when he put upon paper the ultimate conclusion of this court in cases assigned to him, there never was any doubt in the mind of any lawyer as to what the court had determined, or any lingering suspicion that any material fact in the case had been suppressed or warped, or any position of counsel misunderstood or evaded to meet the exigencies of the decision. Clear, luminous, forceful, judicial was the tone, matter, and manner of his

opinions. In them and by them he has erected for himself a monument "more enduring than brass and more lasting than the Egyptian Pyramids."

Quietly, peaceably, and largely unrecognized, he conscientiously and well performed his public duties. Loved as a man, admired as a lawyer, revered as a judge, he has in the very height of his well-won praise been gathered to his fathers.

God's finger touched him and he slept.

For us who remain his life will be a benediction, his character an exaltation, his example an inspiration.

Hon. M. B. Webber then addressed the court:

I certainly cannot hope to add anything to the eloquent words already uttered in commemoration of the life of William Mitchell; and except for the sense of duty that impels me, I should have preferred to remain a respectful and silent listener in this hour of eulogy. The accidents and vicissitudes of life, which play so controlling a part in the career of each of us, led me to an acquaintance with Judge Mitchell while I was yet preparing for the bar, and his condescending kindness and consideration of me challenged my admiration and won my esteem, and I shall ever revere his memory. Under him I was admitted to the bar and began my practice at Winona while he was yet judge of the Third judicial district, and although the interim was brief before his elevation to this bench, it was ample for me to learn his worth as a citizen, a man, a friend, and a judge. Like the rocks, the trees, and the fields where we roamed as children, our first efforts, victories, and defeats in our profession are indelibly stamped upon our memories, and I shall ever remember the patient forbearance and kindly offices of Judge Mitchell, his counsel and encouragement in my first feeble efforts at the bar, and his words of consolation in defeat when defeat was hard to bear.

There is a passage in one of Lucian's Dialogues where Jupiter complains to Cupid that he had never been beloved; and Cupid advises him to lay aside his aegis and his thunderbolts and to place a garland on his head and to walk with a soft step and assume an obsequious deportment. Jupiter replies that he is unable to "resign his dignity; then Cupid tells him he must leave off desiring to be loved. It was one of Justice Mitchell's traits of character that endeared him to all that he was always approachable, and while he never doffed dignity to don vulgar familiarity, he was the same to all men at all times. Liberal in his views, unobtrusive in his convictions, plain, unostentatious, he came near to the common people who never questioned when he had spoken. His best eulogy is indeed the speech of his neighbors. From the humble abode of the laborer as well as from the more pretentious mansion of the banker or merchant prince come alike expressions of admiration for his life and sincere regret at his sudden demise.

I would avoid the tendency on occasions like this to fulsome Praise, for nothing would be more distasteful to the deceased could he hear, yet—"Praising what is lost makes the remembrance dear." Justice Mitchell was fortunate in his reputation. A man's character is builded by himself; it cannot be created nor destroyed by another: "But reputations are the sport of circumstances, or the prey of malice, often beyond the control of the possessor and as often fictitious and unjust." But the deceased in a marked degree enjoyed a reputation that was unsullied as his character. Hence his sudden death, stricken down with his faculties still unimpaired, came as a sudden shock and irreparable loss to the community where he so long lived. After all, perhaps to him thus taken in the very zenith of his fame, it were better than a lingering death: "For whether in mid-sea, or, among the breakers of the farther share, a wreck at last must mark the end of each and all." No words of ours here to-day can build for Justice Mitchell a monument one-half as lasting as he has constructed for himself in the records of this tribunal, which will be read and quoted when eulogy shall have been forgotten.

Occasions like this are accustomed to impress me with much emptiness; the words of eulogy here uttered to-day come late to him of whom they are spoken and can console but little those who mourn his sudden demise; and perhaps all of value that in them lies is whatever of inspiration to better things is found in his modest, plain, simple, rugged, and stainless life. Memorial exercises would be not only an idle ceremony but a mockery if they were merely to afford an opportunity for public expression of sorrow for the dead and extolment of their virtues. Commemorating thus publicly the distinguishing qualities, whether of character or intellect or both combined, furnishes an incentive to emulation by the living, making better citizens, better men and women. They at least tend to contribute to the fashioning of a higher order of society and stimulating in youth ambitions to loftier purposes and the achievement of higher ideals.

The life of Justice Mitchell may well furnish an example, and he will long live in memory.

> The dead are like the stars by day,
> Withdrawn from mortal eye,
> But not extinct, they hold their way
> In glory through the sky.

Hon. William H. Yale then addressed the court:

William Mitchell and myself came to Minnesota in the early spring of 1857, and we lived as neighbors and friends for more than forty years. For several years and until he was called to the bench, we were partners in the practice of the law, both of us having been admitted to practice in the year 1857, while Minnesota was a territory. I think, therefore, that it is not egotism on my part if I claim that, by reason of my greater opportunities during the forty-three years since April 1857, I came more thoroughly to know and understand Judge Mitchell in all of his various relations to the bar and to the people than perhaps any member of this court.

While all members of the bar practicing before this, the highest judicial tribunal in the state, had the greatest respect for Judge Mitchell as an able, impartial, and conscientious jurist, the members of the bar of the Third judicial district, where he lived and practiced as an attorney for the first seventeen years of his residence in Minnesota, are more competent to speak of his character and many excellencies as a practicing attorney and counsellor.

Judge Mitchell never attempted to be an orator, but every district judge before whom he appeared had the utmost confidence in his sterling integrity, his keen powers of analysis, and the eminent fairness with which he treated all questions of fact or law. His courteous and generous treatment of opposing counsel and his pleasing manner of questioning witnesses, not only those on his own side but the witnesses opposed as well, won for him the confidence and good will of all the people in his district. In his arguments and addresses to juries he never attempted by any specious sophistry to mislead or deceive, never attempted any flowery flights of eloquence, but simply stated the facts as given by the witnesses on the trial with fair and temperate comment as to his ideas of the merits of the case, in such a forcible and unpretentious manner that it was very difficult for counsel opposed to eradicate the strong impressions he had made on the minds of those jurymen.

While [he was] district judge, his courteous and kindly treatment of the members of the bar who appeared before him, especially the younger members, made them his friends and helped to smooth over the rough places in their practice of law.

In the city of Winona, where Judge Mitchell had spent more than forty years of his life, the people of all classes not only respected him for his many sterling qualities, but they had learned to love him. He had enshrined himself in their hearts. And I do not think I state it too strongly when I say that they not only respect but cherish his memory more than that of any other man who ever lived in that county.

As a citizen, Judge Mitchell never pandered to the prejudices and weaknesses of the people but ever stood firm for the right. In all matters pertaining to the welfare and upbuilding of the city where he made his home, he gave of his time and energies toward the accomplishing of what he believed would be for the best interests of his fellow townsmen and neighbors, freely and lavishly but not ostentatiously. In the legislature of 1859 and 1860, he was one of the representatives from the county of Winona. In that legislative body he was known by his colleagues, and especially by those who were on the house judiciary committee, to be not only a hard and untiring but a judicious worker. The state was then in its infancy, the inhabitants a heterogeneous people scattered over a large extent of territory. They had come from the eastern, middle, and northern states with a fair sprinkling from nearly every nation in Europe. The future prosperity of the state was largely dependent upon the kind of laws with which we started. To assimilate the views of the New Englander with the views of the southern and western members was no

easy task, but it was accomplished. And the bulk of our city, town, and county regulations framed at that session of the legislature is the law under which we now live. The few members of that legislative body who are still living will freely testify that William Mitchell, then a young man, was one of the most tireless, indefatigable, and successful workers of that lawmaking body.

Fifty years ago but a mere handful of white people had ever lived within our borders. To-day a population of nearly two millions causes Minnesota to stand in the front rank of that glorious galaxy of states that make up this great American republic. I think sometimes that we forget the lasting obligations we are under to those early settlers of Minnesota who fashioned our laws and marked out the policy of our state on such broad and lasting foundations. To few, if any, among the pioneers of Minnesota is greater credit due than to our deceased brother, Judge William Mitchell.

As lawyer, as jurist, as citizen, in all and in every capacity he was called upon to act, he performed life's duties fearlessly, conscientiously, and wisely and during all his mature years led a blameless life and maintained a pure and incorruptible character.

This court and the members of this bar all feel that we have sustained an almost irreparable loss, but we have this consolation that we can join with the people of the whole state in pointing with pride to the stainless and unsullied reputation that Judge Mitchell has left behind him as a legacy to the people of the state of Minnesota.

Associate Justice Collins then said:

The appointment of Judge Mitchell to the position of associate justice in 1881 brought to a tribunal that had from the beginning been extremely fortunate in its membership, a man who, probably above all others whose names had been mentioned, was regarded as the best equipped for the place, and his work here for more than eighteen years fully justifies me in asserting that this estimate of his ability and fitness was amply and fully warranted.

The first opinion written by him as associate justice was in the case of *Fenno v. Chapin*, filed April 28, 1881, and published in 27 Minnesota at page 519, and his last opinion was written in *State ex rel. Zaske v. Matter,* and was filed December. 15, 1899, reported in 78 Minnesota at page 377.

He enjoyed, while district judge, the distinction of being called by the governor to sit in 1877 as a member of this court and of writing an opinion at that time in an important case, *State v. Young,* 23 Minnesota 531. But one other judge of the district court, the Honorable Samuel Lord long since deceased, has been so honored. In the almost nineteen years of service, Judge Mitchell wrote, as has been stated, over 1,500 opinions—more than any of his predecessors or colleagues have written and many more than have been prepared by any of the justices of the supreme court of the United States, although several have served a greater number of years than did Judge Mitchell.

It was his fortune to be a member of this court when the business before it had grown to be extremely burdensome. He saw the calendar increase from 108 cases at the April term in 1881 to 358 at the October term in 1895, an increase in fourteen years of 250 cases a term. During the period of time referred to, I find that the paper books and briefs, as bound and filed in the State Library, constitute 809 volumes averaging 800 pages to a volume. The amount of labor performed by Judge Mitchell in the examination of these files is not easily comprehended even from these figures, but no member of this court ever gave more thorough study to the printed record in each case than did he.

Socially Judge Mitchell was extremely attractive. His early education was liberal, and in his mature years he broadened it by a persistent reading habit, continuing to the day he was stricken down. There were few subjects worthy of consideration in which he had not taken interest, and upon all the topics that from time to time were brought to the surface of the swiftly-moving current of daily events he promptly and thoroughly advised himself and became familiar. While not averse to society, he never mingled in it freely or with entire satisfaction to himself. He much preferred his books, the presence of a few intimate friends, and above all association with the members of his own family. He was a great lover of nature and never happier than when he was taking a few days' recreation in the woods, within easy reach of an inviting body of water. I never knew Judge Mitchell as a practicing attorney and for that reason cannot speak of him in that capacity from personal knowledge. Others have done that, and their words of praise come from the lips of those who met him at the bar and in the sharp contests that we find there, contests in which the true nature and character of all men of our profession are brought out and developed and their worth and merit exhibited to their fellow men, who as a rule measure and determine honestly and fairly. With his clear legal mind, his ability to seize upon the pivotal points, his capacity for professional work, his conciseness of statement, which in itself was always a powerful argument upon the merits of a case, and above all his fairness in any controversy, he must have been an adversary to be feared as well as honored in any legal battle.

I was associated with him in the work of this court from November 1887 to the end of 1899, a little more than twelve years. I do no injustice when I say that not one of his predecessors or colleagues surpassed him in learning or ability, and not one has been or will be held in greater esteem by the people of this state or by the professional men who have been brought in close relation and almost daily contact with the members of this court. His patience and courtesy as an official were proverbial, and it was rarely that his equanimity became at all disturbed. He despised unfair practices, and pretenders and frauds sometimes found this out in a way well calculated to be remembered and perhaps to remedy and reform. His acute legal perceptive qualities and his clean-cut logical reasoning are to be found all through the opinions prepared by his hand and now adorning the pages of the 52 volumes of reports in which they are perpetuated, time-enduring evidences of the professional skill and ability of a man who, in my opinion, as a justice of this court has had no superior among the many distinguished men who have occupied like positions in the courts of the northwestern states.

Of the close relations that existed between our friend and his colleagues I need say but little. They were always of the most satisfactory character. No one could be intimately associated with Judge Mitchell and not be impressed with his commanding ability, his simple unaffected ways, and his perfect character. No one could serve with him on the bench without appreciating his genial qualities, his general information, his capacity for work, his natural vigor of mind, and the ease and promptitude with which his mental faculties were exercised. His conclusions upon the legal propositions involved in a case were never hastily reached, nor from mere cursory, incomplete examination. They were almost invariably correct and, in consultation, maintained with vigor and effectiveness but never with any air of consciousness of his own superb mental attainments or with pride of opinion. Unaffected, genial, anxious to be of assistance, and always surpassingly helpful, a more companionable associate in the labor of this court could not be imagined.

The messenger of death came very suddenly, but it found him ready, for his whole life had been one of preparation for that which lies beyond. His friends should be thankful that to one whose deportment as he went in and out among men had been so tranquil and whose life work had been so patiently and perfectly performed, there came not days of lingering painful disease but a peaceful passing to the eternal sleep.

And now to the memory of a man whose days were filled with honor and usefulness and whose life abounded with right thought and good deeds, we must say the last words of reverence and affection. Not many men of our personal acquaintance have performed their parts in life more modestly or worthily, and not many have gone hence of whom their fellow travelers upon earth could wish to speak in more eulogistic words, and few have gone from among us to whom we could have been more reluctant to say the final farewell.

Chief Justice Start then said:

Your memorial is a just and merited tribute to the learning and worth of Justice Mitchell and aptly expresses our own estimate of his character and public services. He was a great lawyer and a great judge, but he was more—he was a great man. His life was an open book with no sealed or impure pages. He was a modest man. His sail was never bigger than his boat. His manner was direct, simple, and unaffected. He was a man of the best abilities and of the weightiest character. His mental grasp was clear and incisive,

his impulses honorable, his aims lofty, and his love of justice and truth supreme. To those who did not know him intimately he may have seemed untender, but in fact he was a man full of "the gentilest humanities" as loving and as tender as a woman. He, however, seldom expressed his regard for others in words, but he did so by his gentle, unobtrusive, and kindly services to them. Like Cordelia, he could not heave his heart into his mouth, for his love was richer than his tongue. He never prated of duty and conscience, but he was absolutely loyal to both and fearlessly did that which he believed to be right regardless of consequences to himself. He achieved success without elation and accepted defeat with equanimity. His simplicity of character, his practical and sturdy common sense, his profound knowledge, his genial humor, and his tactful kindness made him a delightful companion and a most valued friend.

I first met Judge Mitchell thirty-five years ago, and for a quarter of a century we were intimate friends. The longer I knew him the greater was my respect and friendship for him. I shall ever cherish his memory with reverent affection.

The period of his judicial career was twenty-six years approximately, seven years as district judge and nineteen years as a justice of this court. He discharged the duties of judge of the Third Judicial district with promptness, great ability, rare discretion, absolute fairness, and to the entire satisfaction of the people and bar of his district. His high character, great abilities as a jurist, and the magnitude and value of his services to the state have been extolled by you with generous appreciation but without exaggeration. My associates and myself sincerely and gratefully concur in all that has been here said in commendation of him and his judicial work, which has enriched American jurisprudence.

It is proper that your memorial should be recorded in the records of the court, there to remain a perpetual testimonial to the virtue and work of a public-spirited citizen, a just and fearless judge, and a good man, William Mitchell. It is so ordered, and that the court now adjourn as a further tribute of respect to his memory. [79 Minn. xxi]

Charles E. Vanderburgh

1829–1898
Associate Justice, 1882–1894

On the afternoon of Monday, January 9, 1899, in the supreme court room at the state capitol, Hon. Henry W. Childs in the unavoidable absence of Hon. Moses E. Clapp, president of the State Bar Association, presented to the supreme court, then in session, the following memorial of Associate Justice Vanderburgh and moved that the same be spread upon the records of the court:

The members of the bar of the state deem it appropriate that we should present to the court an expression of our sorrow and sense of loss to the profession and to the community, occasioned by the death of the Honorable Charles E. Vanderburgh, for many years one of the justices of this court, which occurred at his home in the city of Minneapolis on the third day of March 1898.

After a service of more than twenty years upon the bench of the Fourth Judicial District, Judge Vanderburgh was in the year 1881 elected an Associate Justice of this Court and continued to serve in that capacity with great acceptability until the beginning of the year 1894. It will thus be seen that more than thirty years of his vigorous manhood were passed in the judicial office, the latter twelve of which were in this court. This long continuance in the public service, by repeated re-elections, fully attests how well his fitness for these high professional honors was recognized by his brethren at the bar and by the people at large.

Judge Vanderburgh brought to his high office a wealth of legal earning and genuine love for the service that made him a most able and acceptable jurist. Endowed with a keen sense of honor and of right, he was ever alert to see that substantial justice should prevail. Brushing aside, therefore, technicalities and false issues, he would seek to grasp the real merits of the case. Fidelity to duty and strict integrity

were his marked characteristics no less than his uniform kindness and courtesy to all; he therefore commanded the love and confidence of all. He was a devoted Christian, a sincere friend, a true man.

Deeply deploring our loss, which has taken from our profession a brother loved and revered by us all, we contemplate with satisfaction his useful and blameless life and respectfully ask that the court permit this brief expression of our regard for the memory of our honored brother to be entered upon its record.

Hon. John B. Gilfillan then addressed the court as follows:

Our profession has again been invaded, and one of distinguished standing at the bar and on the bench has been removed from among us. Reverence for his high character and exemplary life has brought us together to-day to pay suitable tribute to his memory. To me, presumably because of my early and long-continued acquaintance and friendship with our brother, has been assigned the honor of adding a few words to the testimonial already presented by the bar.

Charles E. Vanderburgh was born in Saratoga County, New York, in 1829, was fitted for college at Cortland Academy in Homer, and graduated from Yale in 1852. Soon after taking his degree, he commenced the study of law in the office of Henry E. Mygatt, a lawyer of great prominence and ability, and was admitted to the bar in 1855. In the springtime of the following year he came to Minnesota and located in the then sparsely settled village of Minneapolis, which was from that time his home. Very soon after coming to the territory he formed a partnership with the late Justice Cornell that continued until his elevation to the bench in 1859. In the fall of the latter year he was elected Judge of the Fourth Judicial District and successively re-elected in 1866, 1873, and 1880, and while still serving in that capacity was, in the fall of 1881, elected Associate Justice of this court and re-elected in 1886 and served until the beginning of the year 1894. He then resumed the practice of law. It will thus be seen that nearly the whole of the active life of Judge Vanderburgh was passed upon the bench.

When first he commenced his judicial office his district embraced a wide circuit, including the counties of Hennepin, Carver, Wright, Meeker, Stearns, Mille Lacs, Benton, Morrison, Crow Wing, Cass, Itasca, Todd, and Pembina, covering an area of nearly one-half the state and stretching from Fort Snelling to the British boundary and from the Red River of the North nearly to the Great Lakes. This area was of course rapidly curtailed as the newer portions became more populated and new counties and new districts were created and boundaries readjusted.

My personal acquaintance with Judge Vanderburgh commenced while he was still at the bar and while my own law studies were being pursued in a neighboring office to that of Cornell & Vanderburgh. Even at that early period he had acquired an enviable reputation for skill, accuracy, and neatness in the drafting of pleadings and other papers and in the careful preparation of cases for trial. From the time of my coming to the bar in the year 1860, it was my lot to see much of Judge Vanderburgh, both as an observer and practitioner in his court, at home, and on the circuit, and I came to know him well. The memory of those days is a pleasant one, and it is a gratification now to speak of his sterling qualities as a man and as one fitly chosen for the administering of law and justice. He brought to his high office a thorough scholarship in the law, a love of right, and a studious and painstaking habit that inspired and impelled him to a true and just solution of all matters coming before him for adjudication. What is the right of this matter was ever his guiding thought. He was kind and considerate to all, whether counsel or litigant, court officer or plain citizen, and yet his love of truth and justice was so strong that anything that savored of deception or unfairness was sure to kindle his righteous indignation and meet his merited rebuke. No one with good cause ever feared to come into his court. If mistakes were made, as must need be at times, the right of

review was fully and fairly preserved in the record. His love of substantial justice, regardless of technicalities, made him a close student of the principles of equity, and long before his elevation to this court he had won fair fame as a jurist in equity cases. In this court practitioners well remember how carefully and closely he followed the arguments of counsel and with what painstaking care he elaborated his opinions. His value in the consultation room can better be attested by you, his associates.

But his labors were not confined to the bench or the bar, nor circumscribed by any six-day limit, for the seventh seemed the busiest of all. His life was full of good works, for he was ever active in the interests of literature, of education, the church, the mission, the Sabbath school, charity, in fact in everything that makes for good in a young and developing community. As a citizen he was the peer of any man. Whether considered as a man, a citizen, or a jurist, the mainsprings of his life and character seemed to be steadfast fidelity to duty, sincere convictions of what he believed to be right, and fearlessness and courage in expressing those convictions. These qualities surely distinguished his whole life work. The words of Judge Vanderburgh upon an occasion similar to this are so eminently fitting to himself that I may be permitted to quote them here:

"Absolutely truthful and thoroughly honest and independent, he was no respecter of persons. He would turn neither to the right nor to the left to secure personal favor, and doubtless his manner was often misunderstood by those who did not know him well. Yet he was one of the kindest of men and a most faithful and devoted friend. He was not only a strong man but a just and good man, a man with a conscience and of strong convictions of right and duty. His character was grounded on sound morals and religious principles—fundamental qualities of a good judge, which cannot safely be undervalued." (See 59 Minn. 548 [Reporter].)

These words of Judge Vanderburgh were a sober tribute to real worth, and that is what we would give to him to-day.

The people of this commonwealth owe much, very much, to a long life of public service like that of our honored friend and to the lives of others, who have preceded him from this tribunal to a higher service, whose memory will ever be revered by those of us who knew them here. How much he and they have done for us and for the future in establishing a safe and exalted system of jurisprudence is beyond our powers to estimate. Judge Vanderburgh has passed on to receive his reward. "It is appointed unto men once to die." He approached the end with an unfaltering trust. He had lived in active usefulness almost the allotted span of three score years and ten. He was spared the torture of racking pain or the slow inroads of wasting disease. The call came to him while in the rigor of life physically and mentally; the final trial was short and he rested from his labors. In all this there is much to console, and the example of his life work remains with us as a benediction inspiring us to emulate his virtues, holding in reverent honor the profession that was his and is ours. The veil that separates this life from that to which he has gone is impenetrable to the natural eye, but to the eye of faith and hope there opens a field of view that goes far to reconcile us to the death of the just who, having borne the last supreme trial of mortality, have been admitted to the life of the mysterious future.

Hon. A. H. Young then addressed the court:

In the strife and contentions of active life, we are quite as prone to criticize as to praise those who are called to public service, and hence it is no idle form, when one faithful to the public trust closes his account and submits for review the record of a long life, that those who are left behind shall for a brief time turn aside from business engagements and take note of those qualities of character and that service, which have contributed to the betterment of the world.

The record of the life of Judge Vanderburgh will bear the closest scrutiny and will elicit naught but words of commendation and approval, for he was a noble man and a just judge. In laying down the work of a lifetime in large part spent upon the bench, he has left to the world and to posterity the record of a service not excelled in fairness or ability. In him were found the qualities of Christian manhood. He has left the impress of his life upon the community in which he lived, and it will be to our profit as well as our pleasure that we gather up in our memory those

qualities of "that life which in their abiding influence upon the world will never lose their power."

I first became acquainted with Judge Vanderburgh nearly thirty-three years ago. He had then been upon the bench of the Fourth Judicial District of this state more than six years. He was elected to the office of District Judge at a time when the practice in the state was quite unsettled and crude and needed for adjustment wise and patient administration. The newly elected judge was but a young man, barely thirty years of age, but though comparatively young in practice as well as in years, he was able to bring to the work to which he was called qualities of mind and a legal preparation that eminently fitted him for the position. He was first of all a noble man, the prime element in judicial fitness. No man ever esteemed more highly than did he, integrity, truth, and virtue. All these qualities he possessed in good measure. He had a thorough classical education, was well read in the law, and possessed in general a judicial mind.

When I first knew Judge Vanderburgh, though still a comparatively young man, he was mature in all that contributed to make him an able judge. After six years of practice before him at the bar, I was called to be his associate in the work and from thence came to know more of his personal worth and the controlling principles of his private and public life. He had then been upon the bench more than twelve years and was in term of service the senior judge upon the district bench in the state. His long experience, his acquaintance with the practice, and his mature judgment gave him a high place in the esteem of the bar as a judicial officer.

The memory of ten years of association with this distinguished and able jurist is very dear to me. Our limited accommodations for the transaction of business brought us very near together and in some respects inconveniently so, and our relations were from necessity both close and intimate. The district was large in extent, and that feature of the service that brought him into contact with the common people was to him peculiarly agreeable. Without any patronizing on his part or letting down of official dignity, he was able to meet these people, to take an interest in those things that interested them, and so win their esteem and regard. The experience of those twenty-two years during which Judge Vanderburgh served upon the bench of the Fourth Judicial District of the state can never be repeated and can only be recalled and understood by those who in service helped to make the history of those years. The bar of the district, as of the entire state, was composed in large part of young men of fair legal ability, ambitious for success, vigorous and active in the practice of their profession. No small measure of responsibility rested upon the judiciary to give such direction to this element of power as to secure the best ultimate results. In this respect Judge Vanderburgh, by a conscientious discharge of his official duties and by his personal influence, did his full part.

He was especially popular with the younger members of the bar. In 1882 he was called to serve upon the Supreme bench, and John M. Shaw, Esq., was appointed his successor in office. And he too had, from my first arrival in the state, been my near and dear friend. And these two men, universally beloved and respected, within a few weeks of each other were called to another service, the character of which we do not know, but we feel confident that it is one every way worthy their character and fitness. For thirty-four years, the best half of a long and useful life, did Judge Vanderburgh serve the people of this state as judicial officer.

But his service in that behalf is ended. We speak of him as dead. But he is not dead. He lives as truly in the hearts and affections of the people, in the influence of his private life, and in the record and value of his judicial service, as he did when he walked with us the streets of the city and sought in his daily life and in the administration of the law to exalt justice and bless the world. Those who knew him most intimately will remember Judge Vanderburgh as a friend and neighbor. We shall recall more frequently his exalted Christian character and his kindly spirit, his devotion to the service of the Master. But those not so intimately associated with him in his daily life will remember him as a just and impartial judge, the record of whose work will remain for all time as a part of the judicial history of the state.

Hon. William E. Hale then addressed the court:

Richard Grant White, in his essay upon Shakespeare's *Hamlet*, has said, "That a man may have kindliness, and grace, and accomplishment, high thoughts and good impulses, and even a will that can stand firmly up against attack (as it were, leaning against opposition), and yet if he have not strong, urgent, exclusive desire which compels him . . . to seek one single object; if indeed he be not ballasted with principle and impelled by purpose, he will be blown about by every flaw of fortune and be sucked down into the quicksand of irresolution."

It has also been said that no man ever became a truly great lawyer or a great judge who was not thoroughly honest, that his star might for a while shine with brilliancy but sooner or later it would go out in darkness and leave its light in ashes.

Judge Vanderburgh came into the race of life well equipped for success. He graduated, as has been said, at one of the first universities of this country and studied law under Mr. Mygatt of New York, an able lawyer and a very honorable man, and I have often heard him speak of the good influence exerted over him by this association. Coming west, he associated himself with another great lawyer, and I have sometimes thought, and without any reflection upon any other member of the bar, the greatest lawyer in the northwest—F. R. E. Cornell. Not only was he a great lawyer, but he was in every sense a manly man, and the association with him was certainly of great advantage. With these advantages, with a strong, active intellect, with high thoughts and good impulses, with the law as his single purpose in life and always well ballasted with principle, he entered upon the more honorable and responsible duties of administering the law as judge of the District Court of the Fourth Judicial District.

At that time and for a long time afterwards, his territory included the greater part of the northwestern part of this state. There were then no railroads, and the mode of getting about the country, in all kinds of weather, was by conveyances stages and wagons and oftentimes with his own horse and buggy. The means for administering justice were decidedly crude. For a long time, hardly a county except Hennepin could boast of a court house, and he was often obliged to hold his court in some public hall or in the dining room of some hotel. But wherever he held court and under whatever discouraging circumstances, he administered justice always alike and equally to all. It mattered not with him who was engaged in the trial of the case, whether upon the one side was his friend and a leading lawyer at the bar and upon the other a young and inexperienced lawyer, the friendship and the ability of the one were never permitted to override the case or to prevent justice being done. His court was the people's court, in which they had the utmost confidence, firmly believing that under his administration all litigants, no matter whether rich or poor or what their position in life might be, would have an equal and fair chance.

He did much to create in the minds of the masses of the people the greatest respect for law and its administration. In those early days when the history of the state was being formed, titles to land being settled, and new laws made that needed interpretation and application, the people needed just such a man to preside in their courts. Although he was not aggressive, and rather retiring in disposition and manner, yet he nevertheless had great courage and never was known to shrink from performing a responsible duty; and no matter what the circumstances might be to influence his mind and action, he was never known to swerve a hair's breadth from what he conscientiously believed to be his duty. This made him the great, strong equity judge that he was.

He was constantly progressing and kept abreast of the age in which he lived, so that as the litigation increased not only in amount but in importance, he was always found to be equal to the occasion. No man was ever loved or respected more by the masses of the people than was Judge Vanderburgh. He came to the Supreme Court of the state ripe in experience and full of knowledge. He had grown up with the state, was familiar with its laws and knew the necessities and circumstances of their creation and hence was well prepared to adopt and apply them in cases in this court. Because of his love for justice, he was one of the strongest equity lawyers that ever sat upon this bench. His death was a great loss to the people of this state, but his life and its beneficial influence upon the people will always remain.

Men build monuments out of the most lasting and enduring materials to perpetuate the names of great men, great deeds, and great events, but time and the elements of nature soon crumble them into dust, and the wind picks it up and scatters it over the face of the earth. But it is not so with character. That lives on and on forever. It becomes a part of the elements entering into the evolution of the human race, always rising higher and higher.

Judge Vanderburgh, at the time of his death, was in the full possession of all his intellectual powers, and when he wrapped the mantle of his couch about him and laid down to pleasant dreams, it might well have been said that he was at that period of his intellectual growth all that he could possibly be, that his powers at that period of his existence could not have been more unfolded than they were, that he was conscious of an inward energy that had its root and ground in a qualification that had always been permanent and progressive.

Hon. Daniel A. Dickinson then addressed the court as follows:

For more than a third of a century—a period exceeding a whole generation, as we count the ages of our race—Judge Vanderburgh was an honored justice in the court of general jurisdiction of this state and in this court of last resort. It is fitting that upon the death of one who had so long and so honorably served the state in the exercise of the most exalted governmental duties there should be entered in the records of these tribunals an expression of the esteem in which he was held by his contemporaries, who knew not merely the magistrate but the man.

The setting apart by your Honors of this day as one for the commemoration of the deceased jurist and this responsive assemblage of the bar of the state, constitute in themselves, though we were silent, a tribute of respect and just appreciation that spoken words can but inadequately express. No man's life or character can be reproduced in speech. It is lived, not recited. The life is the substance; what may be said of it is at best but an imperfect shadow or picture.

In the records of this court and published to the world there stands the enduring memorial that Judge Vanderburgh himself fashioned in the faithful and honorable discharge of the duties of his judicial office. But to other generations, and even to those now living who did not enjoy an intimate acquaintance with him, these judicial utterances cannot bring to mind the personal qualities that linger in our memories and import to his words a color, life, and character that must be wanting to strangers. What others may contemplate in the decisions rendered by him will be as a lifeless statue, however faultless. We have known the living man, and we associate with the preserved record of his life-work the admirable qualities that belong to him as a man.

The ability and learning that he possessed in a high degree are manifest in his opinions, published in the reports of this court. Of uniform excellence, they show his worthiness to exercise the high vocation to which he was many times recalled by the approving voice of the people of that district of the state where he spent his life and afterwards by the citizens of the whole state. They bear the stamp not merely of legal learning and sound judicial discretion but of the study, thought, and care that he was impelled to bestow from a professional sense of duty and a just appreciation of the responsibility resting upon one who sits in judgment to determine the sacred rights of his fellow men. The fidelity and painstaking care with which he discharged judicial duties may be likened to that which a sculptor bestows in chiseling the face and form of a statue, anxious always that no fault or flaw should be revealed in the finished work.

His strong, keen sense of natural justice led him to delight in the study and application of the principles of equity jurisprudence, and it was in this field of the broad domain of law that his learning and wise judgment were most conspicuous.

But not alone do the opinions of this court that bear his name measure or indicate the extent of his labor and influence in its adjudications. As one of his associates on this bench I desire to acknowledge the wise counsel and helpful assistance rendered by him to us who sat with him here. How far his learning, counsel, judgment, may have influenced or shaped the decisions of the court, it is impossible to express or even to estimate; but it may be said that they largely contributed, and lent an immeasurable influence, to the determination of all the thousands of causes adjudicated here during the twelve years of his service on this bench.

His private life and character, as well as that which was public and official, were stainless and far above reproach. During twelve years of intimate and almost daily association with him, I never heard him express a word or thought unworthy of a judge or of a gentleman. Integrity, purity, piety belonged to him as really and as constantly as did his form, his features, his voice. Self-denying, he was beneficent without ostentation. In brief, the motive inspiring all his life was duty—duty to God and to his fellow men. He rendered unto Caesar the things that are Caesar's, and unto God the things that are God's.

Hon. John B. Sanborn then addressed the court:

An occasion like the present more than any other fills us with reminiscences of the past, and brings before the mind at a single glance the events in the life and the habits of thought and character of the deceased.

More than forty years have passed since he first appeared at the bar of an adjoining county and entered upon the practice of his chosen profession. It required but a short acquaintance to become impressed with some of his leading characteristics; that he was by nature, as well as by education, a man of perfect integrity, of high purposes and aims, and possessed of a clear analytical mind and devoted to the pursuits of his profession, while recognizing at the same time the great obligations resting upon him as a citizen of his adopted state and of the United States, and with a high and clear sense of his duties to the church, to the schools, and to all the institutions of his country. As a practitioner at the bar he was a lawyer who sought little if any advantage from the technical points of practice and ordinarily stood upon the merits of the cases that he brought before courts and juries with clearness and force. He became a successful attorney, far beyond the average, and gained the attention and respect of the bar to such an extent at a very early day that he was, as the result of a sentiment almost unanimous, selected as the District Judge of the Fourth Judicial District, at that time extending over nearly all the northern portion of the state. Over this large and rapidly developing district composed of many counties and courts, he tried all cases for a great number of years. The cases tried grew out of large lumber traffic, great commercial interests, rapid railroad development, pre-emption and homestead settlements, and all those other interests that occupy the population on a rapidly developing frontier.

All these duties were so performed and all his numerous cases were so decided that animosities were avoided, universal satisfaction was maintained, and his reputation as a jurist was constantly advanced till at last the attention of the whole state was drawn to it and to his character and attainments, and he was wisely selected to the high position of an Associate Justice of this court. In this last exalted position the respect and confidence that he had gained while presiding on the district bench was more than maintained; it was increased and strengthened during every year that he served on this bench; and in the arduous services performed by him during the long period of more than thirty years devoted to the determination of controversies in the exercise of the judicial powers of the state, it is not known that he ever made an enemy or sent a suitor away from his court with the feeling that he had been deprived of his natural or legal rights to an extent not warranted by the constitution and the laws. This is a record of which any jurist should be proud and indicates not only a well-balanced mind but great study and research and a preparation almost perfect for the discharge of judicial duties so various and so grave, and entitles the deceased even under the maxim of *de mortuis nil nisi bonum* to the highest need of praise.

During an acquaintance of more than forty years, at times intimate, he impressed me as having some very peculiar traits. He seemed to be possessed of a sunny, mirthful disposition. Others may have seen him in a grave or morose mood. I never did. He was always cheerful, mirthful, and buoyant. In all business transactions he was perfectly upright, in society and in his church the most generous and faithful and one of the most sincere of worshippers. He dealt justly, loved mercy, and walked humbly, and thus fulfilled all the requirements of the most perfect man.

It is a habit of the mind on an occasion like the present to reflect somewhat upon the vast changes that have taken place in the society in which he lived during the period of the life of the deceased. He entered upon his duties on the bench when there was not a mile of railroad in Minnesota, when the popula-

tion of the state was less than two hundred thousand, when there was no such mechanical power as electricity and no such light known, and was called upon to apply and construe the abstract principles of law to the great variety of questions growing out of the use of these marvelous powers in the daily occupations of men, and he aided as much as any man in establishing those just principles of law and equity that secure the same rights to the humblest subject that are secured to the greatest monopoly and most powerful money king. This is the true glory of the law and the highest achievement of the bench, and for this our deceased friend is entitled certainly to his share of glory and to grateful remembrance. Peace to his ashes.

Associate Justice Mitchell then said:

My acquaintance with Judge Vanderburgh began over forty years ago, but as we resided in different parts of the state, our intimate personal association with each other only commenced when he took a seat on this bench seventeen years ago.

Our almost daily intercourse for the twelve years during which we were associate members of this court necessarily resulted in our very intimate acquaintance. On my part it resulted in a very warm personal friendship for Judge Vanderburgh—a feeling that I have reason to believe was reciprocated on his part. It is not my purpose to indulge on this occasion in an overdrawn eulogy of the deceased. I know that nothing would be more distasteful to himself if he were present with us to-day. Neither shall I enter upon any extended consideration of his talents as a judge and jurist. The results of his labors as a member of this court are recorded in twenty-eight volumes of our reports and are familiar to the bar of the state and speak for themselves.

It is more particularly to the memory of Judge Vanderburgh as a man and a friend that I wish at this time to pay my humble tribute of respect. As indicative of his character as a man I may, however, say that I never knew any one who was more conscientious in the performance of his judicial duties. He was peculiarly cautious and careful to see to it that, if possible, no mistake should be made in the decision of any case, however small or unimportant. As indicating the natural bent of his mind I might state that he took especial pleasure in the study and application of what are usually termed equitable, as distinguished from legal, doctrines and principles, as being more nearly consonant with the principles of natural justice and less hampered by technical and inflexible rules. He was remarkably familiar with the chancery reports of New York, which probably constitute the most valuable body of equity law in this country, especially the decisions rendered by Chancellor Kent.

Judge Vanderburgh was a man of unsullied purity, not only of action but also of thought and speech. Nothing was more distasteful to him than anything bordering on the coarse or impure.

He was always on the side of every cause that he thought would elevate the intellectual, moral, or religious condition of the world. Without becoming what is sometimes called a "hobbyist," he always gave his support to every charitable, educational, and religious movement that he thought was calculated to benefit his fellow men. The extent or amount of his benefactions in these directions will never be fully known because they were always bestowed quietly and unostentatiously.

He was a profoundly religious man, adhering strictly to those standards of faith and practice that obtained more generally in the past than at present, especially in the observance of Sunday, and yet he was a man of the broadest catholicity of spirit. He never obtruded his religious views upon others but conceded to every one the same liberty of individual opinion and action that he claimed for himself.

Chief Justice Start then said:

Your memorial expresses our own estimate of the life, character, and services of Judge Vanderburgh. His life was pure, his character sturdy, his perception of justice keen. He was an honest man, a generous and public-spirited citizen, an able and fair-minded judge, who honorably and faithfully served the state for a generation. [71 Minn. xxi]

Loren W. Collins

1838–1912
Associate Justice, 1887–1904

On the afternoon of October 22, 1912, in the court room at the State Capitol, Hon. Ell Torrance addressed the Supreme Court, then in session, and said:

On behalf of the Minnesota Bar Association and upon motion of the Attorney General, the committee appointed by this Court to prepare and present to the Court a memorial of the life and public service of the Honorable Loren W. Collins, late Associate Justice of this Court, who departed this life September 27, 1912, in the discharge of its duty has prepared a memorial that will now be read by Mr. Farnham, secretary of our committee.

Charles W. Farnham, Esq., then read the following memorial:

The Honorable Loren Warren Collins, once Associate Justice of this Court, died at Minneapolis on the twenty-seventh day of September last.

He was born at Lowell, Massachusetts, August 7, 1838, of old New England stock. His ancestors served in the French and Indian War of 1760, King William's War, the defense of Fort Edward and of Black Point. They also held many positions of trust and responsibility in civil life, one of whom was the last Colonial Governor of New Hampshire.

At the age of sixteen Judge Collins came to the then territory of Minnesota with his father, who located on some unsurveyed land at Eden Prairie, Hennepin county. His education up to that time had been meager, being such as was afforded by the public schools of Chicopee and Palmer, manufacturing towns in Massachusetts, where his father, a mill operator, resided.

In the fall of 1858 he taught a four-months term of school near Cannon Falls, for which he received a school district order for $60; and in 1859, with this as his sole asset, he commenced the study of the law at Hastings with the firm of Smith, Smith & Crosby. In January 1862, the firm dissolved, and he remained with Judge Crosby until August following, when he entered the army and was at once promoted to Second Lieutenant of Company F, Seventh Minnesota Volunteer Infantry. While reading law he had some experience in trying cases before justices of the peace, but that was all. His army service was a meritorious one. For eighteen months he defended his adopted state against the depredations of the Indians, the ancient foes of his ancestors. He participated in the Sibley campaign, which terminated in the Battle of Wood Lake, in which the Indians were routed and five hundred white women and children released from captivity.

In the winter of 1864 his regiment was ordered south, and until the close of the war he was actively engaged in operations against the Confederate forces. He participated in the decisive battle of Nashville and was breveted Captain for gallant and meritorious services. He was honorably discharged from the service August 16, 1865, and spent the following six months in Alabama as a treasury-agent.

In May 1866, he commenced the practice of the law at St. Cloud and continued such practice until April 1883, when he was appointed to succeed Judge McKelvey of the District Court. During this period of seventeen years he acquired distinction as a lawyer and man of affairs. For four years he was associated with Colonel Charles D. Kerr in the practice of the law, and for a somewhat shorter period with Theodore Bruener, Esq. In 1876, 1877, 1878, and 1880 he was Mayor of the city of St. Cloud, and for eight years was County Attorney of Stearns county. From 1881 to 1883 he was a member of the State legislature.

November 16, 1887, while serving as Judge of the Seventh Judicial District, he was appointed an Associate Justice of this court, to fill the vacancy caused by the death of Justice Berry. The following year he was elected to succeed himself, and again in 1894 and again in 1900. April 1, 1904, he resigned to become a candidate for Governor of the state. In his unmerited defeat, the state of Minnesota sustained a loss from which she has not yet recovered.

At the age of sixty-six he resumed the practice of the law in Minneapolis and met with a success quite unusual for one so advanced in years and who had been out of active practice for so long a period of time. At the time of his death he was a member of the firm of Collins & Eaton.

While he was a member of this court, he wrote over fifteen hundred opinions. They are models in style and composition, and no one, in reading them, would question his scholarly attainments or surmise that his early education had been fragmentary. He had the manners of a scholar and in his conversation and writings disclosed a self-culture that was the full equivalent of a liberal education.

He was a man of sterling integrity, of great moral courage and unblemished honor. He had a profound sense of duty that with his natural vigor of mind enabled him to accomplish much. The history of Minnesota from territorial days down to the present time cannot be properly written without a recital of the civil, military, and judicial service of Judge Collins. He was a man of strong personality, uniformly courteous and agreeable, and commanded the respect, confidence, esteem, and friendship of all who knew him. Of him it can be truly said that he combined in rare degree the virtues, qualities, and excellences of jurist, statesman, soldier, and citizen.

> Ell Torrance
> Knute Nelson
> Theo Bruener
> J. N. Searles
> Lyndon A. Smith
> Charles W. Farnham
> M. B. Webber
> Wallace B. Douglas
> C. L. Lewis,
>   Committee

Hon. Ell Torrance then addressed the court and said:

The records of this court contain many cherished memorials, and today another is added to the lengthening roll of honor. These memorials are the incense that envelops the shrine of justice. They are tributes that the living pay to those

> Whose actions, like the just,
> Smell sweet and blossom in the dust,

and their chief value consists in the inspiration to better things that follows the contemplation of the lives and services of those distinguished for excellence of character, efficiency of service, and nobility of soul.

Minnesota, since her birth, has been fortunate in the character of her judges and especially so as to those who have constituted the court of final resort. In the history of American jurisprudence the opinions of this court will, I am sure, share immortality no less illuminating and instructive than that of the courts of other commonwealths, and the moral qualities and high ideals of her judges will lend strength and beauty to the written page.

Invaluable as the work of this court has been in interpreting and applying right rules of conduct to human affairs and in safeguarding life, liberty, and the pursuit of happiness, I firmly believe that the character of the eminent men, who from time to time have composed the Court, has exerted upon society a beneficial influence as helpful and enduring as the product of its official labors.

A just, wise, and fearless administration of the law is possible only when those who administer the law are men of wisdom, courage, and uprightness, and to the memory of one whose life and public services measured up to the highest standard that can be applied to conduct and duty, we today out of grateful hearts pay a sincere and affectionate tribute.

For more than half a century Judge Collins stamped his personality upon the affairs of this great state, and it is a pleasure and a privilege on this occasion to speak his just praise.

He was a learned, clear-headed, right-minded, honorable, and just judge. He met all the requirements of his great office. His services as a member of this Court were contemporary with those of some of the greatest jurists of the state. For years he was a co-laborer with Chief Justice Gilfillan and Justices Mitchell, Dickinson, and Vanderburgh. He had great capacity for work and was a man of extraordinary industry. Patient, tireless, painstaking, he could not rest content with a single duty unperformed. He had an attentive mind and a retentive memory. He grasped with readiness the facts in a case, even to the minutest detail, and with ease arranged them in orderly sequence so that, with the law clearly in mind, he could speedily reach a right conclusion.

But I will not longer dwell upon his services as a member of this court. They are monumental and constitute a part of the permanent wealth of the state, and among the illustrious names that have adorned the bench and bar of Minnesota, none will shine with a clearer or steadier radiance than that of Judge Collins.

For a few moments I now ask the indulgence of the court while I speak of him as a man, for he was more than a great administrator of the law. He was a lovable man, a good citizen, a true patriot, a devoted husband, an affectionate father, and a sincere friend. He was a many-sided man, but at all times and everywhere he was sincere, steadfast, and dependable. He was a courteous, well-bred gentleman, and although at ease in the abodes of the rich, he was not a stranger in the homes of the poor. He was a popular man in the best sense of the term. His friends were legion. I have often walked with him on the crowded streets of my home city, feeling that I was almost among strangers, while Judge Collins would again and again be greeted in the most cordial manner by those who knew him. I have traveled with him on long journeys, rarely seeing anyone that I knew, while he would meet and greet friends at every turn.

He had a sane and wholesome mind, always hopeful, optimistic, and of two evils he rejected both. He believed in his fellow men, and his fellow men believed in him. He looked upon the bright side of life, and the windows of his soul opened toward the south and to the sunshine. He did not, as many do, regard the age in which he lived as a sordid one. While recognizing the evils in society and the importance of their correction, he believed that the world was growing better every day and that belief helped to make the world better.

His attachments were strong and applied to places as well as to persons. While his duties made it necessary for him to be absent from St. Cloud much of the time and finally to change his residence to another city, his real home remained at St. Cloud until the day of his death. For it was there that he had achieved his early successes in life. It was there that his children were born and where the hearth burned brightly with a sanctifying warmth. It was there that the wife of his affection and his dearly beloved daughter fell asleep and at whose graves sorrow carved deep lines of grace and beauty upon his soul. It was there that many of his compatriots of the Great War resided, and strong as were the inducements for him to transfer his membership in the Grand Army of the Republic to another Post, he would not desert his old comrades in their declining years, and one of the most touching and pathetic incidents connected with his funeral was the tender tribute paid by the venerable survivors of his Post as they gathered about his casket and covered it with flag and flowers.

True friendship is the staff and comfort of our earthly pilgrimage, and the severing of the silver cord that binds friend to friend gives lasting pain. Nevertheless, there is more of joy than of sorrow on occasions like this. When the summer is ended, the bountiful harvest is gathered with gratitude and song into the barns, and the ripe fruit is plucked with gladness from the overladen branches. If it were not so, then would the remembrance of the blossoming trees and the waving fields of grain bring pain rather than pleasure, for without fruitage all ends in disappointment and sorrow. But the contemplation of the useful life of our friend brings to our hearts comfort and satisfaction, and we are thankful that he rests from his labors and is at peace in the abodes of the blest.

Hon. Wallace B. Douglas then addressed the Court:

While shocked at the sudden going from our midst of Justice Collins, it still affords me pleasure to bear testimony to the fact that my thought harmonizes with the expression of his most intimate friend, Judge Torrance, who has spoken here today. It was my very great good fortune to know Judge Collins intimately while judge of our District Court in the old Seventh Judicial District, and I recall the first impression gained after his appointment, namely that he was always alert and quick to decide, and as our acquaintance deepened, I was impressed by his sound judgment and the hearty good fellowship in his make-up that was always dominant. We learned later that he was an accurate lawyer, and he gained in full measure the regard and confidence of the bar upon his circuit. It was my good fortune to be associated with him still later in many ways during the longest period of his usefulness, while he was Associate Justice of this court, and it occurs to me at this moment that naught has been said by his most intimate friend except that which we can all testify to with reference to his many-sidedness, his judicial ability, and to his accuracy as a lawyer, and it affords me very great pleasure to say that, during the many years of our acquaintance and friendship, I always found him to be a man of the highest integrity, great courage, and one of the most useful officers who ever served in this state.

Hon. Marshall B. Webber then addressed the Court and said:

It had not been my expectation to say anything, personally, in memory of justice Collins, except what is uttered in the memorial, and I do so only through insistence on the part of members of the committee. I am very glad to bear testimony to the many lovable characteristics of Justice Collins. These occasions always appeal to me as somewhat hollow. What we say in commemoration of those that have gone on cannot be heard by them, and the thought often comes to me of the expression of another that "A single rose to the living is more than sumptuous wreaths to the dead." Of course, all the virtue there is in these memorial exercises is in commemoration of those characteristics of the dead that are worthy of exemplification on the part of the living.

I remember Justice Collins as a very lovable and approachable man, a man, who upon all occasions, whether upon the bench in his official capacity or upon the street or in any social gathering, was always a lovable acquaintance and valued friend.

I have thought, at times, that there was seemingly an impenetrable wall between the bench and the bar, but with Justice Collins I believe no lawyer ever felt that he was not at any time welcome or that he could not

approach him as an acquaintance on terms of intimacy, and with that intimacy between the bench and bar, judge and lawyer both become stronger and better.

I cheerfully bear my testimony to the lovable characteristics of this dead Justice. I shall ever revere the memory of Justice Collins.

Charles W. Farnham, Esq., then addressed the Court and said:

From Mr. Bruener, of St. Cloud, a member of our committee, comes this communication:

Owing to my inability, on account of illness, to be present at the memorial exercises in honor of the late Justice, Loren W. Collins, I have requested the secretary of your committee to present this my tribute of respect, of love and admiration, for the life and character of the deceased jurist.

I regard it as a great privilege and my utmost good fortune to have made the acquaintance of that good and noble man, Judge Collins, soon after my arrival in the North Star state in 1879, and to have become associated with him in the practice of law in the summer of that year in the city of St. Cloud. Having at that time just graduated from the University of Michigan with but a meager working knowledge of the law, Captain Collins, as he was then addressed by everybody, was ever ready and willing to be interrupted in his work to answer questions and to extend a helping and sympathetic hand. He was indeed a father to me in these early days of my career. But not to me alone did his kindly and sympathetic soul go forth, but to everyone needing assistance. No young man ever applied to Captain Collins for assistance, advice, or comfort in vain.

Courteous and cheerful at all times, casting sunshine wherever he went, Judge Collins was loved and admired by everybody. The fact that he was elected County Attorney for three consecutive terms and once for the legislature in a county where the great majority of the voters affiliated with a different political party than his is evidence of the great esteem in which he was held by the people.

It was, therefore, not surprising that with his untiring energy, a well-educated mind, and his admirable traits of character, he rose rapidly in his profession, was chosen District Judge of the Seventh Judicial District, and while still a young man was elevated to the high and responsible position of Associate Justice of the Supreme Court, which he filled so excellently for so many years. In his death the state has lost one of its best, most beloved, and most distinguished citizens. Long will his memory live in the hearts and minds of all who knew him, and long will his services to his country be gratefully remembered by those who justly appreciate them.

Hon. J. N. Searles then addressed the Court and said:

My first recollection of the late Judge Collins dates back to the time he became a citizen of Hastings, in the state, in the year 1858, I think. I remember his being in the law office of the late Judge Seagrave Smith and his partners for the purpose of qualifying himself for the legal profession. Under the tuition of Judge Smith he had the leadership of one of the many solid legal intellects who have graced the bench of this state, one who had graduated from a Connecticut law office at a time when lawyers were confined in their studies chiefly to the leading text books. Then it was difficult to find what we now speak of as a "case lawyer." In those days we took delight in consulting the text books for the principles of law. It was chiefly a day of Kent, Greenleaf, and leading works on Equity and the other main branches of the law that constituted the lawyer's library. It has been a matter of common knowledge that lawyers of that age were among the most successful members of the bench and bar in this country. Judge Collins had that very desirable training.

When the war broke out, circumstances led him in one direction and me in the other. My next acquaintance with him was of a casual character, when I found him practicing law at St. Cloud. Afterwards I had the pleasure of meeting him in the legislature in the session of 1881, where he took a leading and active part in the House as one of its members. I remember the activity and zeal that was displayed by him in the adjustment of the old Minnesota Railroad bonds. They had been a subject of constant discussion ever since the organization of the state. With the aid of this Court that controversy was adjusted. He was largely instrumental in bringing about that result.

Judge Collins' intellect as a lawyer was exceedingly alert. He had the faculty of taking the proper focus of legal propositions. He could hold off a state of facts at the right distance and get a correct photographic outline of its legal qualities. He was always ready to justify his opinion by reference to the fundamental principles that he had absorbed from his early reading, and he possessed, in addition to that, the quality of a good mixer among men. He had, far beyond most of us, the quality of extending his acquaintance with men with whom he associated. He was thereby less subject to the criticism that has been made of the legal profession, especially in these later years, that they are so conservative that they do not keep abreast of the movement of the masses of people, that their studies lead them to look backward instead of forward, that they are looking for precedent on which to base their action and, consequently, their eyes are turned rather to what has been than to what is or should be. Judge Collins was comparatively free from such criticism, largely owing to his extended acquaintance with all classes of men. The seventeen years that he served on this bench as one of the members of this Court, were seventeen of the most eventful years of the legal life of this state, and during the entire period he acquitted himself with honor and credit not only to himself but to the people who placed him there. The fifty or more volumes of this Court that contain the results of his labors on this bench are, and ever will remain, a memorial to the industry, integrity, and courage of Judge Collins. And those are the fundamental elements of good citizenship.

Lew K. Eaton, Esq., then addressed the Court and said:

In all that has been said I concur and deeply cherish this opportunity of saying something of the affection and admiration that I bore for Judge Collins and of the reverence I bear for his memory.

I believe that it is perhaps more difficult for me to express my regard for him than for any person present outside of his immediate family. My association with him was wholly confined to the later years of his life, and I can only speak of his more active period from the records of this court, where for all time is preserved the remarkable of his mind. I do not believe that in the records of any are found the principles of justice, however profound, laid down more directly, more clearly, or more purely than in the opinions written by Judge Collins,

My knowledge of his character, mind, and disposition comes from intimate, personal, and daily contact as a business associate. It is difficult to say which of his many admirable qualities seemed to predominate, but during our association what seemed to me more remarkable than anything else in these late days of new theories and ultra-modern economics was his admirable sanity.

Though past threescore and ten, his mind was that of ripened manhood. Whatever public question was being discussed, in a few sentences he would go to the root of the subject, discard its nonessentials, and give his opinion clearly and concisely, and one might always be sure that that opinion was the reasonable and sane opinion. He could not abide the sycophant, the demagogue, nor any of those "miserable aims that end in self." He stood for humanity. He had many charities and gave freely in a material way, and what was vastly more important, he gave his sound healthy-minded advice.

Wherever he was known he was respected and admired, and I believe that admiration was caused by his rugged honesty, which stood four square to all the world.

His love for his comrades in arms and his enthusiasm for their well being showed itself by some act each day. He gave unstintedly to these objects, both of his purse and of his life. No journey was too long, no work too hard for him to undertake, if it concerned the Grand Army. Since January 1911, his health had not been of the best, but in spite of the fact that he had full knowledge of his condition, he did not in any wise diminish this labor of love, nor did it in any wise diminish his interest in affairs, his nimble wit, or kindly humor. He was always courteous, always kindly to every person, whatever be his or her circumstances.

I find it very difficult indeed to speak of our relationship. It taught me that he was an ideally devoted father and a firm friend. Our relations were more than those of professional associates, for with the same feeling with which I would have consulted my own father I repeatedly asked and took his counsel and ad-

vice in the every-day affairs of life, and that counsel and that advice were always good.

In him the state has lost one of her first citizens, the bench and bar have lost one who should be an example to all members, his sons have lost a devoted father, and I have lost my guide, counselor, and friend.

It is therefore trebly difficult for me to express my affection and admiration. From his own lips and from the records of this Court, from the history of this state and the testimony of those who knew him well, I have learned of his life; from daily association I learned to know his mind and character; from all of this, it seems to me that when I say that Judge Collins was of the finest type of the American and the lawyer, the jurist and the citizen, one who was a true friend whose memory I shall ever revere, I have only spoken the truth.

Chief Justice Start then responded for the Court:

It is difficult for me to speak of Judge Collins without seeming exaggeration, for he was one of my most intimate and cherished friends. I knew him personally for some thirty years; but it was not until 1895, when I became a member of this Court, that I came to know him intimately and to appreciate his great ability and sterling character. We were associated in the work of this court for more than nine years, and our official relations resulted in a close and devoted friendship, which grew stronger as the years advanced.

His was a lovable and interesting personality, and he made friends readily and retained them by his worth and cheerful readiness to help them. He was a devoted father, and his care for his motherless boys was touching. He was to them a loving father, mother, comrade, and friend, their inspiration and example. His mental grasp was clear and incisive, his impulses honorable, and his manner simple and unaffected. He was a man of manly common sense, of unquestioned integrity, and of great intellectual force.

He was, as was his nature, always courteous to his associates on the bench and deferential to their views. He was, however, a man of independent judgment, reaching his conclusions with care to which he adhered unless, upon a full discussion in the consultation room, he became satisfied that they were not legally right and just.

He was a keen and accurate observer of men and things that with his knowledge of the history and traditions of the state, its public men, laws, and institutions, together with his great ability industry and legal learning, made him a practical, able, and just judge. The state in his death has lost one of its best and most eminent citizens, whose life was clear and clean and full of useful work and unobtrusive kindness.

The Court receives with grateful appreciation your memorial, which is a just and merited tribute to a loyal friend, a public-spirited citizen, a brave soldier, an able and just judge, and a man of unblemished honor. [119 Minn. xix]

Daniel Buck

1829–1905
Associate Justice, 1894–1899

On the afternoon of October 3, 1905, at the court room in the State Capitol, Charles W. Farnham, Esq., Secretary of the Minnesota State Bar Association, in its behalf addressed the Supreme Court, then in session, as follows:

At the instance of the Bar Association of the State of Minnesota a committee was designated to prepare and present to this court a Memorial expressive of its estimate of the character, life, and public services of Honorable Daniel Buck, late Associate Justice of this court, who died at the city of Mankato on the 21st day of May, 1905, at the age of seventy-[five] years. In discharge of the duty imposed upon such committee, it respectfully presents the following memorial:

Judge Daniel Buck was born at Boonville in the State of New York, on the 28th day of September 1829, and after receiving an academic education in his native state, he removed to Mankato in this state where he located on the 18th day of May 1857 and there practiced his profession as counselor and attorney at law, with the exception of the time he was a member of this court, up to the time of the sickness that ended in his death.

The people of his county soon recognized in his ability and integrity his fitness to serve and represent them in many official positions. He held the office of County Attorney for Blue Earth County for the term of four years and discharged his duties in such office with singular ability and fidelity. In 1866 he was a member of our House of Representatives, and in 1881 he was a member of the Senate. Whilst a member of the House of Representatives he procured the passage of the law that established the Normal School at Mankato, and in his whole legislative career he devoted his energies to the advancement of education and the enactment of such laws as would safeguard the highest interests of his state. As a member of our Court of Impeachment that sat in 1881, he took a prominent part, and in an argument showing deep research and unusual mental acumen, he made clear the law of the case, which frustrated every attempt to apologize for judicial impurity.

In 1892 he was elected an associate Justice of this court for a term of six years commencing on the first day of January 1894, but this position he resigned a few months before the expiration of his term by reason of the mortal sickness of his wife.

Judge Buck held many other positions of trust and in none of them did he disappoint the suffrages of the people or betray their confidence. He never shirked any of the obligations of civic duty, and he was always distinguished as a champion of the rights of the people.

As a lawyer Judge Buck was intensely loyal to his client and seemed to make his client's case his own, and if his client fell, he fell with him. His sturdy intellect in action accompanied by his physical vigor and his known integrity and sincerity of purpose made him a formidable antagonist in the forensic arena.

As a Judge of this court, Daniel Buck easily won distinction for his invariable devotion to the principles of justice, all of which he portrayed with marked ability. His written opinions among the records of this court show with what vigor he assailed every attempt to evade or prostitute justice in the conduct of human affairs. He met every fraudulent purpose with a withering rebuke and tore away every subterfuge under which dishonesty could hide. That he adopted the highest ideals of justice and applied them to his conduct as a member of this court no colleague of his will deny. He appealed to conscience from which all salutary law is derived and made it the monitor of his duty.

The Bar of Minnesota, recognizing and remembering his nobility of character and the estimable services he performed as a citizen, lawyer, and judge, respectfully asks that this memorial be admitted to the records of this court as their tribute to the memory of Judge Daniel Buck.

> A. O. Eberhart
> A. E. Clark
> W. A. Funk
> M. J. Severance

Hon. M. J. Severance then addressed the Court:

I can add nothing to the substance of the memorial, but I may speak more particularly of the characteristics of Judge Daniel Buck as I observed them during my long acquaintance with him.

I preceded him by a year in the State of Minnesota, but I soon knew of his advent here, for at once he took a prominent position in the politics of the times and at the Bar. Very soon after his arrival here it was my fortune to shiver a lance with him in the forensic arena, and I soon learned that one in contest with him must not leave his shield hanging in his tent.

In some respects Judge Buck was peculiar. In his habits and tastes he was as stern and austere as Miles Standish. He had no familiar circle outside of his household and the Penates were the gods he continually adored. He shunned all places of popular amusement and shut his ears to the chimes of social abandon—hence he was never an idol with those who spiced their lives with laudable pleasure mingled with duty. His office and home bounded his aspirations and seemed to satisfy his heart. This isolation bereft him of much of that sympathy born of social communion.

If genius did not flash its gems upon his mind, and if he did not have that witchery of tongue that could beguile when it could not persuade, yet his stately presence and physical energy, all in harmony with the heavy laboring of his mind, gave him a distinguished prestige at the Bar.

It is an unwritten historical fact that my fear of Judge Buck as a prosecuting attorney gave to the defendant the closing argument in criminal trials.

If he was sometimes clumsy and awkward in speech, yet he always dexterously played with the idioms of the common people, and this with his personal presence was argument and eloquence with them. In some of his judicial opinions the expression of his thoughts is in choice and admirable phrase. Whether or not his thoughts in expression were slovenly or carefully clad depended upon the duty he had to perform.

As a parent his devotion was simply sublime and if an angry bolt of nature fell upon one of his household, as more than once it did, it left in his heart an unhealing wound and cast a shadow upon his life that time would never remove, for he imbibed no philosophy from that lesson that teaches us that the living by hundreds of billions are outnumbered by the dead.

As a citizen he should be numbered with those who would apply the rule of morals that adorns private life to the conduct of government in all of its departments. In political life he was the uncompromising enemy of any system that would curtail the inalienable rights of the people or substitute for the broadest liberty the rule of the few over the many. Others might take their stand with the Thirty Tyrants of Athens, but he would take his with the fierce Democracy of Rome.

As a lawyer he never prostituted his profession by conduct his dignity would not commend.

As a judge, I am sure he was emancipated by his very position from that ambition for personal triumph that often beguiles the lawyer into forbidden paths, that he was oblivious to persons and political traditions and animated by the sole desire to hold justice securely on its throne. If his mind did not volunteer ready-made legal conclusions, yet down deep in his sturdy intellect there were hidden gems of correct legal analysis only awaiting the demands of labor and thought. Such a mind is as apt to arrive at a safe legal conclusion as one absolved from labor by some generous gift of genius or intuitive perception.

If I should say that Judge Buck had no faults, I should only exalt and crown human infirmity. Some great minds that have explored deeply into man and his nature have said that many of our venial but glaring faults are born of resplendent virtue; if this is so, how easy it is for a generous mind to forget and forgive.

My heart will not permit me to follow Judge Buck through the last year of his life and up to the portals of the tomb. I cannot do it without reproducing the story of Promethean torture and suspending the rock of Tantalus over one condemned longer to live.

I have spoken briefly, but I have endeavored to speak truly of Judge Buck. I believe that he always desired to be right and to do equal justice to his fellow men. Of this I am certain, that he left no example behind him that will encourage immorality, injustice, or wrong. When this can be truthfully said of any man there is no fear that a recollection of his virtues will ever perish from the earth.

At the conclusion of this address Chief Justice Start made the following response:

The court is in entire sympathy with the sentiments of your memorial and unreservedly concurs in the eloquent and appropriate tributes you have paid to the memory of a good man and a fearless judge. I was associated with Justice Buck in the work of the court for some five years, and my affection and respect for him as a friend and as a judge increased with each succeeding year.

During that time he was sorely afflicted by physical ills and subjected to great mental anxiety by reason of the mortal illness of his wife, to whom he was devoted. This necessarily embarrassed him in the discharge of his judicial duties, but he accepted his misfortunes with equanimity, bravely faced the situation, and discharged the duties of his high office with fidelity and upon the whole to the satisfaction of the people and bar of the state. Many of his opinions are valuable contributions to the jurisprudence of the state, especially those relating to constitutional questions and to questions involving personal rights.

He was a man of unique and intense personality; of commanding figure, broad of brow and shoulders, he looked the ideal judge. He was of sturdy spirit and temper, which made him a chivalrous and loyal friend and a stern and consistent enemy. He loved whatever was right, just, and true, and hated all that was wrong, unjust, and false. With perfect candor, it may be said of him what he spoke of another on a similar occasion: "Fearless in the cause of right he would not turn aside to avoid an enemy, nor bend to grant an unjust favor to a friend. He wrote no opinions to obtain notoriety; he made no decisions at the dictation of wealth or political influence. He would rather go down with the colors flying than be silent when justice was endangered."

The court receives your memorial with grateful appreciation and directs that it be entered in the records of the court for the day, as a deserved tribute to a public-spirited citizen and a just judge, and that the court now adjourn as a further mark of respect to his memory. So ordered. [95 Minn xxxvii]

Thomas Canty

1854–Unknown
Associate Justice, 1894–1899

No silver spoon was involved in the birth of Thomas Canty, who served on the Minnesota Supreme Court from 1894 through 1899. To the contrary, the long list of his many achievements demonstrates that His Honor was self-made all the way.

Born in London on April 24, 1854, the future Minnesota justice came to America when but two years of age. His father was a laborer who settled first at Detroit, Michigan, moved to Lodi, Wisconsin, then on to Clayton County, Iowa, and finally to a farm he purchased near Monona, Iowa. There he died when Thomas, his eldest son, was 20 years of age, leaving a widow and seven children.

Thomas Canty attended school regularly until he was nine years old and was an apt pupil. After that he was able to attend school for only a few months each winter. An ambitious lad, he pursued his studies with diligence and success.

When Canty was but 13 years of age, a dispute arose with regard to the rent his father should pay for the farm he occupied, and it was agreed that the farm should be surveyed. Young Thomas Canty found an error in the surveyor's figures, caused the error to be corrected, saved his father $60, and avoided an expensive and potentially disastrous lawsuit. The experience appears to have pointed him toward the law. Despite his mother's wish that he become a blacksmith or learn some other trade, Thomas Canty determined early he would become a lawyer.

But first he had to earn something of a living. In 1872, he took a 16-hour-a-day job as a mule driver in a Carbondale, Illinois, coalmine. In this way he earned money enough to take him to Texas. There he taught school for four years, in the meantime applying himself diligently to his studies; although

unable to take a college course, Canty thus acquired substantially the same advancement that college training would have provided. In the meantime, his physical strength was exhausted and his father died; so he went back to the Iowa farm to regain his health and help his mother take care of the family. He remained on the farm two years, devoting all his spare time to the study of law.

Owing to crop failures, family debt had accumulated; the future lawyer and judge assumed that debt and ultimately resolved it.

In the spring of 1880 Thomas Canty went to Grand Forks, Dakota, to practice law, and on October 1 of that year, he moved to Minneapolis, joining the law office of Seagrave Smith. Canty was admitted to the Minnesota bar the following February.

After a series of victories in several civil cases, Canty won distinction and popular applause at the time of the Minneapolis streetcar strike in 1889, when his successful resistance to workhouse sentencing by the municipal court of men who, he believed, were in no way connected to the strike. He took the men under sentence out of jail on writs of habeas corpus, carried their cases to the district court, argued them before Judge Smith, and secured his clients' release.

Thomas Canty was a Republican on state and national issues, but he was largely independent on local matters. In the fall of 1890, Canty was nominated by the Democratic Party for judge of the district court in Hennepin County. He was elected and held that office for three years.

On July 14, 1892, the People's Party of Minnesota nominated him for associate justice of the Supreme Court; the Democratic Party nominated Canty for that position on August 3 the same year. Canty won the election and began the discharge of his duties on January 1, 1894.

Canty's six-year term on the Minnesota Supreme Court yielded 575 opinions and 58 dissents. He had the distinction of writing the opinion for the last capital punishment case, *State v. Hayward,* 62 Minn. 474, 65 N.W. 63 (1895), to reach that court. The court affirmed, Hayward was executed, and capital punishment was not abolished in Minnesota until 1911. Following Justice Canty's defeat after only one term, in the 1899 election, little was recorded of his life. But this proud, Protestant, Irish American stands as one who rose from abject poverty to become a respected jurist on the Minnesota Supreme Court.

—James S. Simonson

Charles M. Start

1839–1919
Chief Justice, 1895–1913

On the morning of April 30, 1920, in the court room at the State Capitol, Chief Justice Brown presiding, the following memorial of former Chief Justice Start was presented to the court and read by Chester L. Caldwell, Esq.:

Charles Monroe Start, Chief Justice of the Supreme Court of the state of Minnesota from January 1895 until January 1913, died at his home in St. Paul, December 19, 1919.

Judge Start was born at Bakersfield, Vermont, October 4, 1839. He was of New England ancestry and throughout his entire life exemplified the best qualities of that people, for he was simple in taste, frugal and temperate in his habits of life, and while stern and unyielding in his sense of right and wrong, his predominating characteristic was a sense of justice and an inflexible determination to deal justly with all those with whom he came in contact.

To be just in the determination of individual rights is much more difficult than to be honest. The ordinary man is honest and naturally well disposed, but he is often saturated with prejudices and is a victim of environment, and in attempting to adjudicate upon individual rights he is hampered by the mental bias he has acquired from his associations and habits of life.

He who can overcome these human tendencies and look upon each individual as a being endowed by his Creator with rights equal before the law to those of every other citizen and fearlessly protect those rights, has reached the pinnacle of juridical integrity without regard to the concrete correctness of any particular decision that he may render.

If this test be applied to Judge Start, it will show him to have been one of the really great men of his generation.

His early life was that of the ordinary Vermont farmer's son, helping his parents to secure a scanty sustenance from a rocky soil. Later, when he entered Barre Academy, his vacations were spent in earning sufficient to keep him at school, and when he entered the office of his preceptor in the law, Judge William C. Wilson of Vermont, he earned his board in Judge Wilson's family by the performance of those chores that were considered a necessary part of a Vermont boy's education. This period of apprenticeship was not without its romance, for he subsequently married his preceptor's daughter, Miss Clara A. Wilson, who continued throughout his long life to be his devoted helpmeet.

No higher tribute could be paid to the character of this lady than was expressed in the chivalrous attitude that Judge Start always maintained towards women.

It was typical of him that he should enlist as a private in the Union Army, which he did in 1863 as a member of Company I of the Tenth Vermont Volunteers, and as was naturally to be expected, his character and talent earned him a commission the following month. Shortly afterward he was compelled to resign because of disability, and next we find him in Minnesota in 1863 entering upon the practice of law at Rochester.

In the state of his adoption, his integrity, ability, and devotion to duty have always been recognized by his fellow citizens. Thus he was prosecuting attorney for Olmsted county for eight years; attorney general of Minnesota from January 1, 1880 until March 12, 1881; judge of the Third judicial district from 1881 until 1895; and Chief Justice of the state from 1895 until he voluntarily retired in January 1913. His opinions appear in sixty-one of our reports: Volumes 60 to

120 inclusive; they are models of clearness, showing close application and deep research, and indicate a simple and direct honesty and devotion to the fundamental principles of our system of government rather than any desire to individualize himself or to secure a reputation by the expression of sensational views.

The high regard in which he was held by the bar of the Third judicial district is shown by the fact that when he presided, three jury trials in civil cases were the exception.

Judge Start believed in human progress and was alert to sustain legitimate progressive legislation, but he believed that such legislation should be a matter of gradual development, realizing as he did the danger of sudden revolutionary changes.

A memorandum in his own hand-writing, found amongst his papers after his death, illustrates his attitude:

> A reform movement ought not be sent straight to the mark, like a cannon ball, without regard to the wreck and ruin which may follow. It should be strenuous, but fair; persistent, but deliberate; it should be based upon justice and controlled by reason, for no permanent reform can, or ought to be, secured in any other way.

Only those who knew him intimately knew how kind and sympathetic were his mind and heart. In his opinions he avoided, as far as possible, harsh statements and advised against any unnecessary reflections on counsel practicing before the court. "Perhaps," he said upon one occasion, "some statement which we make while smarting under the discourtesy of a practitioner may in future years cause grief or embarrassment to some innocent child."

His attitude upon public questions was always that of the sincere and patriotic American; after the Spanish War he delivered an address at Rochester before Custer Post G.A.R., in which he said:

> Since the victory of Manila, we have suggestions from influential sources, that we must permanently hold the Philippine Islands, and enter upon a career of colonization and imperialism, and become a potent factor in the political factors of the world.
>
> This is to be deprecated. Let us remember that when we entered upon this war, the national honor was pledged that it was not for the purpose of conquest, nor the acquisition of more territory, and that it will be an act of national perfidy not to keep that pledge. Also that our nation is a union of sovereign and equal states, with no place for dependent colonies.

Every quality of good citizenship so necessary to America at this time of unrest was possessed by judge Start. He was devoted heart and soul to the American system of government; he was invincible in honesty, devoted to the public services, an uncompromising champion of individual liberty. He realized that law is necessarily a progressive science but had reverence for, and held fast to, all that was good in the past. He respected authority but hated arbitrary power and had so developed and trained the natural impulses of his character that he was an ideal officer of justice.

Burt W. Eaton, Chairman
Thomas D. O'Brien
David F. Simpson
L. L. Collins
Harold J. Richardson
Victor Stearns
Chester L. Caldwell,
    Committee

Bunn W. Willson, Esq., then addressed the court and read the following eulogy, prepared by his father, Honorable Charles C. Willson:

Honorable Charles Monroe Start was born October 4, 1839, at Bakersfield, Vermont. His father, Simeon Gould Start and his mother, Mary Sophia (Barnes) Start, were also natives of that state. His father was a farmer by occupation and was justice of the peace in his township for twenty-five years. From his farm and the assistance of his children he made a humble livelihood. His son Charles worked as a farm laborer summers and taught country school winters and in that manner obtained the necessary means to defray his expenses in securing an education.

In July 1862, he enlisted as a private in Company I of Tenth Vermont Infantry. In the following August he was commissioned first lieutenant and went with his regiment to Virginia, but in December of that year he resigned from the service on a surgeon's certificate of physical disability. The next summer, 1863, he came to Rochester, Minnesota, and entered my law office as a student to learn the Minnesota practice. He had previously studied law in the office of Honorable William C. Wilson at Bakersfield, Vermont. On August 10, 1865, he married Miss Clara A. Wilson, a daughter of the judge in whose office he had read Blackstone.

In the spring of 1864 he was elected city attorney of Rochester, Minnesota, and held that office several years. In November 1871, he was elected county attorney of Olmsted county, Minnesota, and held that office eight years. In November 1879, he was elected attorney general of this state. In March 1881, Judge William Mitchell of the Third judicial district of this state was appointed one of the justices of the Supreme Court, and Governor Pillsbury appointed Mr. Start judge of the district court in the place of Judge Mitchell. Judge Start held that office by successive elections until January 7, 1895. In the preceding November he was elected Chief Justice of this state and held that office by successive elections until January 6, 1913.

Justice Start was slightly under medium height but of quick and vigorous action and of untiring industry. He had unusual self-control and never permitted himself to indulge in disparaging remarks concerning anyone. His self-control in this regard and his unfailing cordiality kept him in office nearly all the first fifty years of his residence in this state. As judge of the district court he was well esteemed and had the confidence and good opinion of everyone. He was upright and impartial between high and low, rich and poor, frugal in expense, and entirely void of ostentation.

The story of Justice Start's life should stimulate the youth of the county to imitate his rugged, untiring industry and his unswerving purpose to acquire an education and a position of usefulness and honor. Proud and grateful should every youth of our county be that he is a citizen and member of this republic where the humblest can attain any position of trust and honor that he is capable. The obligations of this citizenship are paramount to every other duty. To the member of the legal profession they especially appeal.

Justice Start's purity of life and devotion to duty exhibited the great benefits and concurrent obligations that membership in the American republic imposes. If we look around among the prosperous and success-ful men of our acquaintance we find that nearly all came up from humble and obscure origin. From such origin Chief Justice Start rose to the highest judicial honor in the gift of his fellow countrymen.

In Continental Europe, feudalism more or less modified still obtains. The eldest son in succession from a remote conquering ancestor holds, by entail, title to land and exacts rent and military service from his tenants. The land is not taxed or assessed directly in any way. Rent, income taxes, licenses, and tariffs on imports are the chief sources of revenue. Many of the uneducated children of these servile tenants find their way to America and are prone here to regard with aversion anyone having wealth or position, as their fathers regarded the landowners of their native country.

To stem this disloyal tendency of some of the newcomers, Justice Start's voice and example were never wanting. He was ever ready to uphold and honor the Stars and Stripes, the emblem of his country. In youth he marched under arms beneath its folds and in mature manhood he invested his earnings in his country's securities and gave his voice in its loyal support. In what other country could his successive honors have been acquired? It is to be regretted that there are here a few ungrateful sons born to such great opportunities who give their voice and effort, plausible and insidious, to that socialism that would overthrow this republic and bring ruin, riot, and misfortune in the place of present prosperity and happiness. If such a man there be in the legal profession, let him repent and take Chief Justice Start for his example or unrepentant be disbarred. He is unworthy to speak in this honorable court. Let him go down

> To the vile dust from whence he sprung,
> Unwept, unhooked, and unsung.

Honorable Thomas S. Buckham then addressed the court and said:

I hardly know upon what ground a man who has been so long divorced from all connection with the courts of the state as I have should be entitled on such an occasion as this to take part in the program of the day. My only excuse for being here at all is the fact of my long acquaintance, my somewhat intimate acquaintance, with the late Chief Justice Start, and the suggestion of the present Chief Justice of this court that he considered it to be appropriate for me to say something on this occasion, a suggestion coming from such a source being to a member of the bar in the nature of a command.

I was very much pleased with the memorial presented by the committee. I knew Mr. Start pretty well during his whole lifetime. I knew something of his ancestry and of his parents and of the men among whom he spent his early years, men who best represent the original settlers of New England, men who have no superiors the whole world over. He might well feel proud of his origin and his ancestry, and the committee did well to speak of him as a representative of the time-honored original New England Vermont stock.

I will not go except very briefly into any statement of the acquaintance that I had with Judge Start. I knew him when he first came to the state. I was the judge of a neighboring district, living at Faribault. I met him often, met him quite intimately, held court for him a number of times when he was cleaning up his work as a lawyer to take his seat on the bench. I never met him as a practicing lawyer in the trial of a cause, but he did try one or two cases before me just before his own appointment; the only remembrance that I carry of those cases was the extreme zeal and urgency with which he pleaded the cause of his clients. He was matched at that time against one of the leading lawyers of the state, the late Gordon E. Cole of Rice county, and I watched his trial of the cases with a good deal of interest on account of his Vermont origin.

I am not going to eulogize Judge Start as a lawyer and a judge. The memorial that was presented here states exactly what I should say if I could say it as well as that does. He was an able judge, he was an upright and honest judge, he was a very modest and unassuming citizen, a warm, cordial friend, one of those men whom it is a delight to remember. The mere fact that he was elected and re-elected in his own district and afterwards to the supreme bench of this state at a time when the selection of judges was left almost entirely to the action of the bar, when no man could presume to stand for an election who was not the choice of the bar and no man could expect to be elected who was opposed by the bar, is sufficient proof that he was held in high esteem by the lawyers of the state and that he deserved the honors that were put upon him.

I think one of the most entertaining and one of the most instructive exercises on the part of a practicing lawyer who knows anything personally about the judge who writes an opinion is to trace back that opinion and the course of reasoning that it employs to what he knows of the character and habits, mental and moral, of that judge; or if he does not know the judge, to build up a picture of him by the reading of his written opinions. That is the way the judge lives in the memory of the bar, through the opinions in which he was the spokesman of the court, when personal memory of him wholly or partially fades away. I doubt not most of the lawyers here have forgotten the earlier judges of this court. They live in their memories only by tradition, Judge Emmett, Judge Flandrau, Judge Atwater, the first court before whom I had the honor to appear; and Judge Berry, Judge Wilson, and Judge McMillan, the last judges whom I ever addressed before today. But though we have lost memory of them personally we trace them in their reports.

Now I think that the opinions of Judge Start, which of course were in substance the opinions of the other judges of the court and which I have read and carefully studied for they often criticized the views that I had presented as a district judge, show just two characteristics on the part of Judge Start that have been so strongly dwelt upon in the memorial presented here and in the remarks of Mr. Willson, namely, his unbending love of justice and his view of the duty of a supreme court judge in passing upon a case brought before him on appeal. And this is the impression that I always had of the man from his opinions apart from my knowledge of him and of his own statements. He never troubled himself with anything but the exact particular points that he was called upon to decide. He did not discuss the length and breadth and height and depth of the principles involved in the case itself. It was sufficient for him to decide the controversy in hand and decide it rightly. He did not consider it necessary to solve any future problems. He was content to let those questions take care of themselves when the time came. There was very much water to pass under the bridge before that time arrived. Possibly the bridge itself might be carried away, and it might be necessary to find some other method of crossing the stream; but the present duty was to decide the instant case. He considered his duty done ordinarily with a case when he either directed that the successful litigant should proceed to put his judgment into execution or that he must go back and begin over again and try his case anew. I don't mean to intimate for a moment that he could not exhaustively consider legal questions. I could refer to cases in our reports in which he has shown his ability to do that, but his object always was, and so he said, to see that the case he was examining, whether he would write the opinion or not, was so decided that absolute justice so far as it is possible for human beings to do it should be rendered the parties.

He was a man who in his every action showed a strong, genuine sympathy with what has come to be called the average man, the man, who without attempting or thinking that he could if he did so attempt to unravel the mysteries of the divine economy of the universe, wrestles manfully but blindly all his life with those great problems that Job and his friends so ineffectually discussed, who struggles through a lifetime unable to understand why so often the bad man flourishes like the green bay tree while the "good man's share in life was gall and bitterness of soul" but yet who keeps on with the struggle, does his duty as he best sees it to his community, to his country, to those of his own household, and finally passes on to that world, if it may be called a world, where he will doubtless be enlightened further—that is the man that Judge Start always spoke of with respect and feeling, and I was glad that the memorial which will be the record of this court, or part of it, of his life should make a strong point of that feature of his character.

I knew Judge Start quite well. I knew his family somewhat before he came to this state. They lived in the same county in Vermont where I resided as a boy. They were well known in that community and highly respected. When we both moved to this state and I came to know him personally, I admired him and had a strong personal loss outside of his loss as an honored citizen. After he came to St. Paul to live I did not

see so much of him as I had in former years, but it had been a great pleasure even in this imperfect way to testify as a lawyer, as a neighboring judge, and as a personal friend to my opinion of his ability, his character, his learning, and his sterling integrity.

Honorable Frank B. Kellogg presented the following tribute to the memory of his former associate at the Rochester bar:

I am honored by your kind invitation to pay my humble tribute to the life and character of the late Chief Justice. It was my good fortune to know Judge Start intimately for 45 years. When I went to Rochester from the farm in 1875 to study law, he was one of the first men whose acquaintance I made, and from that time until his death, he was to me as to many others a kind friend and a wise and able counselor, and I know of no one who needs encouragement, advice, and assistance more than the young lawyer.

Judge Start was of English descent. He came from that virile, self-reliant New England stock. He was born and reared in Vermont, educated in the schools and colleges of Vermont, and started his profession in the Green Mountain state. He enlisted in the army as a private in the great Rebellion that threatened the destruction of the Union, was promoted to lieutenant, and after serving about six months, was compelled to relinquish his commission because, of ill health. He came to Minnesota in October 1863 and settled at Rochester. He was one of those vigorous, forward-looking, able young men who came in the early days to the Great West—a land of surpassing richness and unequaled opportunity—there to lay the foundation of his future career. The next half century that followed in the development of this country and the world were the most important ever recorded in history. Never was there such progress and advancement in science, art, invention, increase of wealth, production, and commerce as during this period. He took his place among the able, progressive men of his day. At the bar, as city attorney of Rochester, county attorney of Olmsted county, attorney general of his state, judge of the district court, and Chief Justice of this supreme tribunal, he met the expectations of friends and the public. He was a thoroughly educated and profound lawyer, a patriotic, liberty-loving citizen, and a just judge. He had the attributes necessary to success—untiring energy, fixedness of purpose, and devotion to duty. His most pronounced characteristics were patriotism, a thorough understanding of the duties of citizenship, and of the principles upon which rest the foundation of representative democracy. He was liberal in his political views, the champion of the weak and unfortunate, with an unshakeable confidence in the wisdom of democratic institutions and in the destiny of his country. And yet he thoroughly believed in the conservative forces of law and those constitutional principles of the Bill of Rights, so essential to human liberty and happiness and the perpetuation of our institutions. He realized the importance of the purity and stability of the courts; that the lawyer is a great, conservative force in political life; that his study of the science of government, his respect for law and precedent make him so.

De Tocqueville once said that "when the American people is intoxicated by passion or carried away by impetuosity of its ideas, it is checked and stopped by the almost invisible influence of its legal counsellors." [Democracy in America C. XVI]

And yet the lawyer is not a reactionary. He has been a leader in all great movements for the development and advancement of representative government. He lends stability to these evolutionary forces, which sometimes stir people to unwise innovations. There never was a time in the history of the world when there was more need of these conservative forces of society than at present if we are to preserve the principles of representative democracy. Of all governments that the wisdom of the ages has devised, ours is more nearly fitted to preserve liberty, encourage individual enterprise, and promote the highest development of civilization. Our Constitution was not the inspired conception of a few men, but the evolutionary work of centuries of experience and struggles for self-government. It was bought by human sacrifice and sanctified by the blood of martyrs. Those great principles of our Constitution that constitute the foundation of human liberty and progressive nationalism cannot be lightly discarded. Freedom of speech, of religious belief, protection to the person, the right to pursue one's own vocation, to enjoy the fruits of individual energy and enterprise, permanency, and stability of law, protection against

the tyranny of government or the tyranny of the mob, integrity of the courts, and all the other constitutional rights are priceless heritages of a free people. There are today, in this land, as in other countries, revolutionary and disturbing forces at work, great organizations, largely of foreigners, teaching their doctrines of destruction and revolution—the Communists, Socialists, I.W.W., the Bolshevists, and others. These organizations and their propaganda must be uprooted and destroyed, the people must be educated in sound principles of government, the world must return to the pathways of peace and industry, or our twentieth century civilization will disappear as the Roman civilization disappeared over fifteen centuries ago.

While Judge Start's sympathies were with the great mass of the toiling millions of his countrymen, while he was quick to lend his influence to aid in those reforms necessary to human happiness, no man whom I ever knew had a more profound understanding of those conservative principles of government necessary to society than he. He was charitable to the weak and unfortunate but strong and merciless in his prosecution of evil. Laws, in his judgment, were made for the benefit of society and to be obeyed. He did not believe that the principles of our constitutional form of government, with the guarantees of the Bill of Rights, were mere matters of expediency to be cast aside in the changing tides of public opinion, and he looked with apprehension upon the wide-spread propaganda teaching the people of this country doctrines so foreign to our institutions. He believed that those principles were better safeguards to human liberty and happiness than the speculative philosophy and untried theories of agitators and political opportunists.

It is unnecessary for me to say that he had the greatest veneration for the judicial office. Political honors were often within his grasp, but he never swerved from his purpose to devote his life to the administration of the law. No one realized more than he that law is the embodiment of the highest ideals of civilization. It has governed the relations of men in the most primitive and savage state and in the modern and highest developed society. Before history recorded and left to succeeding generations the deeds of men, law was the governing power and controlling influence of communities and nations. With the growth of government, the uplifting of physical and social conditions, law has been keeping pace with the march of progress. Its invisible forces dominate and control nations, man in all his relations in society, the tremendous transactions of modern economic life, and the minutest details of our social and industrial fabric. It is all-pervading and ever-present. Without it there is no government, no social order, no home. Its administration is the highest and noblest duty of man to his fellows. Its purity and stability are necessary to the peace, happiness, and prosperity of peoples. Its corruption is the destruction of the state and of the nation. For more than a quarter of a century, Judge Start, realizing these principles, labored to make them vital forces of society and government.

His career was long and honorable. With learning and ability, with patience and a belief in our institutions, he helped to write the judicial history of the state, and he left it as a legacy to his country. His last days were troubled by the great conflict that cast its shadow over the world, but through it all, he believed in the destiny of his country and that this government and all its institutions would be preserved for the benefit of the countless generations to come. It is fitting that we honor his memory and exalt the judicial office that they may both be perpetuated.

Honorable Lorin Cray then addressed the court:

I feel quite incompetent to speak of the virtues of our brother lawyer, Charles M. Start, late Chief Justice of this court.

As a man, a lawyer, and a judge, he has attracted public attention in this and other states for many years, very generally commended, very seldom otherwise.

After years engaged in the successful practice of the law, in March 1881, he assumed the duties of judge of the district court of the Third judicial district of this state, where he served with marked ability until January 1895, when he was raised to the exalted position of Chief Justice of this court, which position he held with honor to both this court and to himself, until a short time before his death

It was my good fortune to make the acquaintance of Judge Start as early as 1886, and in all sincerity I can say that I have highly prized that acquaintance-

ship and the friendship that resulted from it, which grew stronger and more intimate as time passed by.

There is to the practitioner a comfort and satisfaction that cannot be easily expressed in knowing when approaching a forum that if he have law and natural justice on his side he is going to prevail, and in knowing that although he may err in law or in its application his cause will be given all due consideration and that his views, if candidly expressed, will be duly weighed. All this he could confidently expect from our deceased brother.

Judge Start, as a jurist, seemed by mere intuition to be able to grasp the salient points in a case, to solve intricate legal problems, to brush away technicalities, and take in the entire subject and determine how and where natural justice required that the law should be construed and applied.

Supremely honest in his convictions, courageous to a fault, his decisions, eminently satisfactory to one seeking after justice, must have been eminently satisfactory to himself as well and to have met with the approval of his own conscience, which was a controlling factor in all of his acts and which is the highest reward due to any man.

When he left us, he left a spotless record and an unsullied name, both as a jurist and a citizen. His taking away was a great and distinct loss to the law-loving people of our state. His life was an inspiration to all members of the bar who knew him well, and all they whose mentor he was are the better because of having known him.

When a boy living in the country, I wrote to an able and quite noted lawyer in this state, asking the privilege of studying law in his office; my inquiry elicited no response. This lawyer was not Charles M. Start. Not he, who was always considerate of the young, kindly of heart, and courteous to a fault.

He loved his profession, and when in health his greatest pleasure was found in work at his desk and among his books. The profession profited and the bench was more highly honored because of this.

He has passed from his labors to the other shore, and memories of his true worth close the book.

Honorable Christopher D. O'Brien then addressed the court and said:

According to the traditions of the bar, this court assembles today to inscribe upon its records in enduring form our recognition of a useful and well spent life—a life that was beneficial to this commonwealth and to our entire republic, the life of a citizen who while among us and during all of his years well and fully performed all of his duties to God and to his fellowmen.

It is well for us to contemplate such lives as these. It is well that they should be described by those who are living witnesses to their existence. It is well that such history should be preserved in the enduring records of this court for the benefit of generations yet to come.

The services of Justice Start to his country and fellow citizens began with his early manhood when he gave them to the Union cause in our Civil War. Upon its termination, he gave them to the people of this state through our profession, as county attorney, attorney general, district judge, and Chief Justice of this court. For more than forty years he gave his fellow citizens his services in these public positions, and in each of them all of his duties were fully, efficiently, and honestly performed with no thought of self-advancement, with no ambition other than the complete performance of the duties that arose and with a full appreciation of his responsibility to his Creator and his follow citizens.

I know of no profession save that of the ministry that exacts more industry, fidelity, and self-sacrifice from its members than does that of the law, and in that profession there is no position more exacting than that of a judge—for a judge must surrender to the proper performance of his duties a large share of those associations and personal activities that form most of the comforts and attractions of life. He can have no intimate associations among the members of the bar because that might create scandal. He cannot associate closely with the officers or managers of large corporate interests for a like reason, and socially he must be reserved and dignified to an unusual degree. It follows that the occupants of the bench are largely men who have selected that walk in life because of their desire and ambition to be useful to the community and to devote themselves to the welfare of their fellow citizens rather than to their own.

To pass upon the multitude of questions affecting the lives, liberties, properties, and social conditions of their fellow citizens; to disentangle the intricate convolutions and entanglements of human life; to look through and behind the mass of misrepresentation, intentional or unintentional, that envelope all litigation; to see through them only the light of truth; to recognize and distinguish the "ignis fatuus" of self interest, passion, cupidity, malice, and falsehood that may be present in any cause from the truth; to resolve the varying and contradictory representations of the litigants; to determine the effect of such representations upon the manifold human interests that cause their presentation; and, at the last, to resolve these controversies by the sole light of truth, reason, and justice, present to the human mind one of the greatest problems that it can contemplate. Verily, the judge must bring to the performance of his high and complex duties, the best capacity, the best training, and the best skill of which the human mind is capable, and this must be again controlled and reinforced by a spirit of justice, truth, charity and mercy, to entitle the conclusions of the court to the respect and obedience that just decisions deserve.

Not only are the mental difficulties almost beyond description, but if possible a judge must bring to the performance of his duties such physical equipment as will enable him to give to those duties his full mental capacity. And when it is reflected that hour by hour, day by day, month by month, and year by year, the entire mental capacity of a Judge must be given to the determination of causes that, though presenting all of the difficulties that have been hinted at, absolutely vary from each other so that one instance is not an aid to the determination of the other cause, the duties of a judge and of a court become almost beyond the capacity of the human language to adequately describe.

It is, however, a great satisfaction to know that our citizens do recognize in the capable judge the qualities that enable him to fulfill the duties of his office. And though popular election is charged with many faults, insufficiencies, and mistakes, our experience is in this state at least that the popular instinct rarely goes wrong and that when the proper man has been found to accept the duties of such high office, whether in the district courts or in this court, the performance of those duties by him has been recognized by the electorate by constant and continual re-election during the time he may desire it. This is true as to a large majority of the members of our judiciary. It is particularly true in the case of Justice Start, who was continued in his high office of Chief Justice up to and until the time when he felt the right to retire from the performance of his duties for the brief interval of rest and reflection that was allowed to him.

It is easy to indulge in high-toned sentiments. It is easy to couple together oratorical superlatives and cast them lightly upon the grave of a man who has passed away. But a good, faithful, and efficient man deserves more than that. He deserves the grave, studied, and sincere expression of approval of those of his fellow citizens who know what has been and how well it has been done. It is the work and the history of such a man that we commemorate today.

Of course we have among us or have had among us men of great brilliancy. I sometimes doubt if they are the most useful. A meteor comes from obscurity, casts its brilliant light around its pathway, and descends into darkness. It challenges our admiration but not any permanent recollection. For my own part, I prefer the more lasting rays of those useful planets who, while not so brilliant, are steadier and more effective, whose light continues to illuminate the rugged pathways of human experience even when they have gone to the most distant extremity of their orbit.

The beneficial effects of the services of Judge Start as Chief Justice of Minnesota did not cease with his death. In the just and wise opinions formulated by him in this court, we find the proper methods as well as the proper directions for the administration among the citizens of this community of proper and equitable rules, as well for the conduct of the citizens in their dealing with each other as for the settlement of their varying contentions and disputes, and this court and other courts of like character will continue, as long as the republic endures, to reap the benefit of his judgment and opinions. To the practitioner, they will point the way to a serviceable, orderly, and effectual performance of the duties of his profession. To the judges who succeed him they will show with what a just, equitable, and clear mental apprehension he determined the causes brought before him. And so his services and influence will continue, particularly in this court, and with the bar of Minnesota for many, many years still to come.

Like Chief Justice Marshall and Chancellor Kent his determination of the vexed questions of human affairs in all phases of life will remain to be found for the benefit of our profession and our citizenship at large. That all of his duties were well and completely fulfilled, those of his profession who knew him in his lifetime know full well. That his life was a high, virtuous, useful, and beneficial life to his fellow citizens we stand here today to testify of our own knowledge and without fear of contradiction. That he is today in the receipt of the greatest reward that the soul of man is capable of receiving we sincerely believe. And that he is now in the greatest of courts in the presence of the greatest of judges an eternal witness to the administration of those great laws that are perfect in their justice, as well as in their mercy, we confidently believe. And so, his life work done and so well done, he rests in that eternal peace and happiness that "passeth all understanding."

Honorable William E. Hale then addressed the court and said:

I first became acquainted with Chief Justice Start in the years of 1880 and 1881 when he was attorney general of this state and I was prosecuting attorney of Hennepin county. During this time I saw him occasionally in consultation about cases pending in this court that I had tried and that he was to argue. I also tried some cases before him while he was judge of the district court in Olmsted county. But I became better acquainted with him after he came to this court. I rarely came to the Capitol that I did not drop in at his chambers and have a few moments of friendly conversation—not about law and cases but about men and things in general. I formerly lived in Wabasha county and knew many of the people in southern Minnesota whom he knew, and he liked to talk about them and the early days of Minnesota. There are others, of course, who knew him much more intimately than I did and who can bear testimony to his great worth as a man and a friend, but from my somewhat limited acquaintance with him covering a period of more than forty years, I can truthfully say that he was my friend.

He was true to his principles and to his friends, never unfaithful to the former or forgetting the latter. In devotion to what he considered right, he was as inflexible as steel. As Chief Justice of this court, he gave the best part of his life to the state he so much loved. He came here in the fullness of his manhood, well equipped for the responsible duties that he had assumed. He came to this state from New England, bringing with him many of the characteristics of the early settlers of the birthplace of our American civilization, among them industry, honesty, and economy.

He was quite set in his ways and at times seemed blunt in the expression of his opinions. But to those who knew him best, this was never offensive, for they knew that beneath the outside appearance there was an honest mind and a great, warm, sympathetic heart—as tender as that of a woman.

He was in no sense a politician, nor was he known as a mixer among men, and he resigned his office some years ago rather than engage in a political contest for re-election.

The key to his success in life was his singleness of purpose, his close application, and determination to make out of himself all that could be made. He was never blown about by the flaws of fortune or cast down into the quicksands of irresolution.

In his opinions there is entire absence of technicalities. He never indulged in fine-spun theories. He was broad-minded, taking comprehensive views of the law and facts. His appeal was to an innate sense of justice, to reason and intelligence, and he did it in plain and familiar phrases. He never attempted a display of his learning or attempted to write a thesis on the law of the case in support of a proposition; he was generally content to cite a few of the leading cases instead of all the cases on the subject, taken from some encyclopedia. And these opinions will be his monument so long as the records of the court are preserved.

He believed in self-government—a government of laws—and he believed in their enforcement as necessary for the safety and happiness of the people. The law never leads civilization but always follows in its wake. Its purpose is to regulate and control the relations of men with each other and their relations to the state, and to produce if need be justice out of injustice. The nation today seems to stand almost upon the verge of a new and remarkable destiny—for good or bad we cannot tell, and there never was a time in its history when it was in greater need than at the present time of able, conscientious, and fearless men to fashion, interpret, and enforce the laws. We are a government of laws, and unless they can be enforced to protect all alike in their lives, liberties, and property, anarchy and barbarism will follow and the government and civilization will come to an end.

And now as we look backward over the long and useful period of the life of our friend and call to mind the many whom we and he knew but who have gone with him out into the unknown, we are reminded of the lines written by Lowell on his sixty-eighth birthday:

> As life runs on, the road grows strange
> With faces new, and near the end
> The milestones into headstones change,
> 'Neath every one a friend.

Honorable Albert Schaller then addressed the court and said:

It would be repetition to say again what has been so well and truly said of the life, the character, and the heroic virtues of the man in whose honor we are here assembled. It is truly meet and just that the great tribunal, over which he so ably presided for so many years, should specially assemble in his honor, and join in the tributes paid to his memory.

Repetition is perhaps the highest praise. We read that the choirs of angels are continually repeating in praise of their Creator the words: "Holy, Holy, Holy," "Hosanna in the Highest." So it will not be deemed unfitting that we, following so venerable a precedent, laud again and again the great qualities that distinguished the former Chief Justice.

We knew his upright character, his stern integrity, his loving kindness. We knew the loyal American, the good citizen, the kind father, the learned, honest and upright judge, and withal the faithful Christian gentleman.

Perhaps the most prominent trait in the character of the late Chief Justice was his Christian sincerity. His faith was childlike, his trust in God was absolute, his devotion to duty was profound. The virtues that we so highly honor today were the outgrowth and fruition of his faith, his trust, and his devotion.

But of what avail are praise from human lips or marble monuments or eloquent testimonials when we have passed the portals of death, if they are not justified by a life filled with good deeds, those messengers from earth that penetrate to the very throne of God?

Charles M. Start at his mother's knee learned to honor God and obey His commandments. This teaching dominated all of his actions; to it he held fast to the hour of his death.

His sincere faith, his simple Christian trust, and his devotion to duty for duty's sake sustained him throughout a long and useful life and finally led him into the very presence of God—the eternal, kind, and loving Father of us all, who knows our frailties and forgives them and who rewards our good deeds with the eternal joys of the Beatific Vision.

Honorable W. B. Douglas then addressed the court and said:

It was my good fortune to know Judge Start well. Our association covered a period nearly a quarter of a century, most of the time in that relation which an active member of the bar bears to the Chief Justice of our highest court. Five of those years we were associates upon the State Board of Pardons for a short time as members of this court. Naturally a strong friendship developed between us, and it deepened at his fireside after he laid away the ermine he had worn with such conspicuous courage and devotion to the public service.

His was a rare mind and his temperament naturally judicial. True it is that in separating the wheat from the chaff he was sometimes misunderstood by the bar, but let us not forget that "The truest steel the readiest spark discloses."

The clear, incisive opinions written by him and preserved as a part of the published records of this court are his best monument. They show us a man of wide vision and constructive mind, still one whose energy and studious habits clearly proved that he knew and respected the precedents. However, he was fearless in extending, developing, and applying settled principles in such a manner [as] to deal justly, humanly, and charitably with constantly changing conditions.

To me, this strong desire ever present with Judge Start to deal kindly with and excuse many weaknesses in human nature as far as settled rules and sound policy permitted, contributed much to placing him as a man and public officer among our greatest and most deserving. Perhaps this characteristic was better understood by the few who were privileged to serve with him upon the board of pardons. While Judge Start hated crime and could not tolerate or excuse certain acts, still the folded records in many cases, if opened, would bear striking testimony to this trait in his character.

Mentally he was a rugged man and tenaciously stood for high ideals. Coming as he did from old Vermont, I have often wondered what effect that rugged environment had in his development. Certain it is, however, that he shared many of the characteristics of his distinguished predecessor, Chief Justice Gilfillan, who (as we know) was born under like surroundings at Bannockburn, and each brought to the then far Northwest many of the sterling qualities of the people with whom they were early associated.

Honorable L. L. Brown then addressed the court:

When I came to the Third judicial district as a law student, Judge Start was on the bench. There he continued until promoted to the Chief Justiceship, where he so long conscientiously dedicated his full strength to the service of the state. The office was an honor to him as it is to any man, but he in turn reflected honor upon the office. He was the servant of his obligation to duty and at all times, without stint or reservation, delivered the full wealth of his power to the fulfillment of his obligation. This is not simply an extravagant eulogy, which Judge Start of all men did not approve on such occasions as this. It is a plain statement of what the people of the whole state know, but the people of the Third judicial district knew Judge Start best, and we wish to place upon the record of this occasion, where we are come not to praise but to truly and solemnly record a genuine estimate of the public services of one who has passed beyond the range of praise or blame, the testimony of those people and their estimate of Judge Start as a jurist and citizen that it may be known of those who come after. Their estimate [is] not one only now expressed but one fully formed and unanimously vouched for as neighbors long before he came to this bench and while he worked among them. That estimate is an historical fact. Politically the Third district was opposed to Judge Start. By the statute his term was fixed at six years; by a higher law decreed by the people of that district as one man, it was made for life. This is the value long ago placed upon the character and services of Judge Start by his neighbors who knew him well and over whose court he so long presided. This might be said of other men, but when this simple fact has been recorded, we have done enough. It proves more than many words of eulogy. It is a complete and fitting memorial, and no more need be said—but a word yet.

I was examined and admitted in Judge Start's court and there commenced practice very poorly prepared. And, as courage consists in equality to the problem before one accordingly distraught by misgivings and doubt as well as want of bread, the problem of my obtaining any footing at the bar was a serious one. My fate was as has been that of other beginners in the hands of the court. What is in a man will come out, will shine through the judge. It is possible being a great judge, but it is not possible to be a great judge without being a great man, and Judge Start was a great judge. That I would here be short of my duty to Judge Start's memory is my justification for this personal allusion, when I say that the man shining through gave to me, as it did to others, the encouragement that has saved the day for many a young practitioner. All of the discipline that Judge Start administered to me in after years was drowned in his earlier kindness and consideration, and he did not go to his reward without knowing what I record here. A wonderful human-heartedness, broad, clear, and just, with simplicity and uprightness, characterized the man.

All in all, the Chief Justice, although conservative, was always in touch as judge and citizen with that occult thing, the spirit of the times, and his work on this bench is and will remain a solid major factor in the jurisprudence of this state as moulded by its judges. All men seem to think that humanity and its institutions may change, recede, and deteriorate. By that token we ought to believe that advancement and improvement toward greater enlightenment and justice

is possible, and I am one of those, as was the Chief Justice, who do so believe. That is faith in humanity that we must have and that we call sanity.

Cardinal Newman paints the canvas in these words:

> To consider the world in its length and breadth, its various history, the many races of man, their starts, their fortunes, their mutual alienation, their conflicts; and then their ways, habits, governments, forms of worship; their enterprises, their aimless courses, their random achievements and acquirements, the impotent conclusion of long-standing facts, the tokens so faint and broken of a superintending design, the blind evolution of what turn out to be great powers or truths, the progress of things, as if from unreasoning elements, not towards final causes, the greatness and littleness of man, his far-reaching aims, his short duration, the curtain hung over his futurity, the disappointments of life, the defeat of good, the success of evil, physical pain, mental anguish, the prevalence and intensity of sin, the pervading idolatries, the corruptions, the dreary hopeless irreligion, that condition of the whole race, so fearfully yet exactly described in the Apostle's words, "having no hope and without God in the world"—all this is a vision to dizzy and appal, and inflicts upon the mind the sense of a profound mystery, which is absolutely beyond human solution.
>
> [Apologia pro Vita Sua. Part VII]

If we broaden this canvas to include the passing tragedy that has shattered the world and the epidemic of unmoral materialism following in its wake, this is a serious picture but not appalling. Though the hopes of some are at zero, the mystery is not beyond human solution, and that solution can come and will come as the timely fruit of the hard labor of those rugged men and women of the type and character of him whose memory we recall to-day.

William D. Mitchell, Esq., then addressed the court and said:

The work that our judges have to do upon the courts of the states and of the nation may be properly grouped under two heads.

At times they have to consider controversies of great public interest involving governmental questions of importance, the decision of which, sometimes temporarily but often permanently, determines in some degree the direction of governmental activity and affects the character and powers of the government under which our people live.

On the other hand, by far the larger part of their work is in the ordinary administration of justice between private citizens, having to do with matters of a purely personal and private nature.

Although epochal decisions of great public questions may seem overshadowing in importance, it is, after all, the daily administration of justice among the people, the ordinary affairs of every day life that is of vital interest to the greatest number, and it is the manner in which that work is done that creates in their minds either satisfaction or discontent with our judicial system.

In looking back over the work performed by Chief Justice Start during his eighteen years upon this bench, it seems to me that among all his accomplishments the outstanding feature of his judicial career is the splendid manner in which he did the very work of which I speak: the daily administration of justice in disputes between all kinds and classes of people arising in the ordinary affairs of every day life.

He believed that to the average suitor, justice was denied unless speedy and without delay, and with that in mind as presiding justice of this court, he endeavored, notwithstanding the great volume of litigation before it, to promptly dispose of its business.

Earnestly and conscientiously he strove during all those years to produce results that appealed to his sense of right justice and to make all litigants, of whatever station in life, feel that their causes had received painstaking attention.

He sometimes chafed under the restraint of the rules of law, the application of which in particular cases seemed to produce results that did not accord with his conscience and, within the limits of the judicial power, endeavored to mitigate their harshness in practical application.

How well he performed his duties is evidenced by the fact that from the time he assumed the office of Chief Justice of this court until he voluntarily laid it aside eighteen years later, he continuously enjoyed the universal respect and confidence of the people of

this commonwealth. His work added to the dignity of this court and brought luster to his name. He was, in every true sense, a guardian of the rights and liberties of the whole people, and for his long and faithful service to this state he deserves the grateful remembrance of his fellow citizens.

Honorable George W. Peterson then addressed the court and said:

There is splendid representation here on behalf of the senior bar and the judges. I would like to pay my respects and the homage of those similarly situated in behalf of the relatively junior bar. Even so, it is almost 25 years since I came to the bar of this court. The court has wholly changed except one. I think there should be a reference in this memorial to the letter of Judge Start of October 29, 1918. It was addressed to the bar. It was written of the court. I read from it as follows:

> As the years have gone the Minnesota Supreme Court has become more and more a humanitarian, equitable, nontechnical, and business-dispatching court. It is, indeed, such a court. The humblest has his personal and property rights protected. Laborer, mechanic, farmer, business man—all are alike before it. There are no favorites. It has been the effort of the court to make law and justice approach and co-ordinate without impairing the law. The symmetry of the rule has been made to yield to practical justice. All this has not come about without some struggle. It is the work of no one man. A procession of men have helped.
>
> A court is very much a composite of the men who form it. A good judge ought to be vigorous, keen-sighted, forward-looking, industrious, and of exact legal learning. He should be fair-minded, conscientious, patient, forebearing, and withal he must not have lost the common touch that puts him in appreciative contact with average humanity and its aspirations and its problems. He must not truckle to class, nor fear public clamor, nor yield to public nor private threat. He must be independently square. If he is unwilling to lose judicial life rather than break with the truth, he is unfit to have it.

It is not unfair to any man to say that no other man could have written so fine a letter, and even then Death plucked him by the cloak to come with him.

In *Leavitt v. City of Morris,* 105 Minn. 170, 117 N.W. 393, Judge Start showed a broad and comprehensive constitutional sympathy. In *Railway Company v. City of Minneapolis,* 115 Minn. 473, 133 N.W. 174, in a dissenting opinion, he showed great independence, courage, and a fine appreciation of constitutional limitations. In *Gilfillan v. Schmidt,* 64 Minn. 29, 66 N. W. 126, he dissented from the doctrine of *Sheehan v. Flynn,* 59 Minn. 436, 61 N.W. 462, but in *Oftelie v. Town of Hammond,* 78 Minn. 275, 80 N.W. 1123, he consistently adopted that doctrine and wrote the opinion of the court.

He said of a distinguished member of this bar, "He was never false to any man or cause." Could those words be more fittingly said of anyone than of Judge Start? He was never false to any man or cause. He wore the white rose of a stainless life and gracefully bore that grand old name of gentleman. He loved his work, his chambers, and his books. These lines of Kipling, taken from "When Earth's Last Picture is Painted," are appropriate:

> And only the Master shall praise us, and only the
>   Master shall blame;
> And no one shall work for money, and no one shall
>   work for fame,
> But each for the joy of the working and each,
>   in his separate star,
> Shall draw the Thing as he sees it for the
>   God of Things as They Are!

Harold J. Richardson, Esq., then addressed the court:

On this occasion I cannot attempt to speak in words of eulogy but to my affection and love for a life-long friend. Judge Start was an heroic ideal of my boyhood. He was then judge of the Third judicial district. He was the first citizen of his beloved city of Rochester, first in patriotic and civic affairs, first in the affections of the people.

Yet he took time to be one with the school boys who met him in the street and who used, on frequent occasions, to visit his court room. He was a neighbor, one of my father's closest friends, and today there comes to me words that my father used to say of him in those years: "Judge Start is one of God's noblemen."

The last years of Judge Start's life were among his bravest and best. He had finished his great work as Chief Justice of this court. Yet with the wisdom that ruled his life, he renewed his practice of the law and so kept in contact with the world's work. It was a privilege to associate with him and to enjoy his friendship, to witness his devotion to the law and his wisdom and skill in the practice of it during those years. It was an inspiration when the war came on to observe the depth of his love for his country and to see the glow of his fiery and courageous patriotism.

And now this Valiant-for-Truth, having fought his fight, has passed over. He has left his sword in the opinions he has written, to be wielded by those who shall succeed him in the Pilgrimage.

The memory of his wisdom and his skill, his faith, and his devotion, will linger as a legacy in the hearts of all who knew him. Let it be said of all his life as was said those earlier days in Rochester: "Judge Start was one of God's noblemen."

Honorable Thomas D. O'Brien then addressed the court and said:

Mr. Burt W. Baton, chairman of the committee on memorial, is in a hospital at Rochester and unable to be present. Judge Callahan of Rochester and Mr. Webber of Winona are unavoidably detained by their professional engagements and asked that their names be included among those who desire to pay their tribute. I now move that the memorial and the addresses that have been presented be made a part of the permanent records of this court.

Chief Justice Brown then said:

Former Associate Justice David F. Simpson expected to be present today to pay his last tribute to the memory of Judge Start but is unavoidably absent, and this may be noted as a part of the proceedings of the day. Associate Justice Quinn had prepared his tribute also to the memory of Judge Start, but he is unable to be present and his remarks will be spread upon the records of the proceedings of the day.

Judge Lees [for the court] then said:

If Judge Start could speak, he would protest against praise of himself or his work despite the fact that eulogy of the dead is the common thing. It would be his wish that whatever was said of him should be temperate in expression and should not overdraw his virtues, and I shall attempt to be mindful of what he would wish.

My acquaintance with him began in 1887, when he had already been judge of the district court of the Third judicial district for over six years. I was a practitioner before him from that time until he became Chief Justice and met him frequently both in and out of court. The admiration of him that was then formed continued to the end of his life and prompts me to pay a tribute to his memory.

His natural temperament was fervent. He had been a vigorous advocate when at the bar. He was the contemporary of Thomas Wilson, William Mitchell, Charles C. Willson, W. C. Williston, Thomas S. Buckham, and other lawyers of Southern Minnesota of perhaps equal ability. They all agreed that in the trial of an action he was a dangerous antagonist, skilful in the examination of witnesses, eloquent and forceful in argument, and sure in his knowledge of the facts and the law of his case. He made his client's cause his own and championed it with the utmost earnestness and zeal but always fairly, for he abhorred everything that savored of fraud or sharp practice. So marked was this trait that when as a trial judge he detected anything indicating trickery or deceit, he would flame with indignation, and thereafter the party whom he believed to be guilty of it stood little chance of getting a favorable decision. His conclusions as to the rights of the parties were apt to be unconsciously communicated to the jury by his demeanor. As a consequence, verdicts were usually in accordance with his idea of what they should be. His findings in cases tried without a jury were generally followed by a memorandum summing up the evidence and stating the law he deemed applicable. An attorney once said to him that in following this practice he furnished a ready-made brief for the prevailing party in case of an appeal. He retorted that such was not this purpose, that he wrote only to point out to the defeated litigant and his attorney why the case was lost. He was prompt in the dispatch of business and looked with disfavor on the tendency of many attorneys to put off the trial of their cases. To the younger members of the bar, he was invariably helpful and considerate; with the older ones, who sometimes ventured to presume on their standing and experience, he was firm and decisive, so that few attempted to take any undue liberties a second time. He came to be regarded as one of the ablest trial judges in the state, and

this reputation had much to do with his advancement to the position of Chief Justice of this court. It is interesting to note that when he came here, his brother, Henry R. Start, was one of the judges of the Supreme Court of Vermont, having been elected in 1890 and holding office until his death in December 1905.

Judge Start became a member of this court when its business had reached the high water mark. The April calendar for 1895 had 340 cases upon it; 98 were continued to the October term and the remainder disposed of. The calendar for October contained 357 cases, and all but 37 were disposed of. With but five judges on the bench, this meant working at white heat for all of them. He was convinced that justice delayed is apt to be justice denied and that, so far as possible, all cases on the calendar should be disposed of during the term. He believed that a long drawn out opinion is not helpful to the bench or bar, and that it is unnecessary to write a legal essay in deciding a case involving no novel application of legal principles.

No man ever sat here who was more concerned that cases should be correctly decided. He often remarked that this is a court of last resort and that errors in its judgments are subject to review only in the few instances in which a question arising under the Federal Constitution is presented. He was solicitous that no fact or principle of law that might have a bearing upon the decision should be overlooked. He did not spare himself the labor of examining and considering the records and briefs in every case before the court. He was a tireless worker, wholly absorbed in his work. Being asked by a friend how he had spent the summer vacation, he replied: "Principally in reading our decisions since last October and annotating the statutes and reports." His annotations of his set of Minnesota Reports are a marvel of industry.

He respected himself and his position but was wholly free from pride of office. By habit, as well as by instinct, he was strongly democratic. At bottom he was a Puritan—not in a religions sense but in that his code of morality was strict. He was not inclined to condone an offense or excuse an offender by putting the responsibility on heredity or environment. He believed that a man should answer personally for his conduct, and he consistently acted on his belief. Those who did not know him well thought they saw in him asperities of temper and manner. In truth, he was a warm-hearted man, deeply attached to his friends and with impulses that were invariably kindly. He enjoyed the visits of members of the bar who dropped into his chambers for a chat. Such visits were less frequent than he wished them to be because most of us feared we might be trespassing on his time, known to be greatly occupied.

Judged by the standards of today, he was a conservative. He did not look with favor upon experiments in government, believing that the original lines laid down in the Constitution should be followed in the development of the state. He respected property rights, stating more than once that the small property holder was concerned even more than the man of wealth in having secured to him and his children the fruits of his industry and self denial.

Endowed by nature with an alert and vigorous mind and of a strong and resolute character, he impressed his convictions upon others to a marked degree. Of unfailing probity and with a deep sense of duty to which he was always true, he justly gained the respect and confidence of the public. He was an important figure in Minnesota. His death marks the passing of an earlier generation of lawyers who have had the principal part in giving to the state the system of laws by which it is governed.

Associate Justice Quinn's tribute is as follows:

It was the sturdy manhood of Chief Justice Start that appealed most to me. There was in him no fawning or yielding of self-respect. His chart of life was: "To thine own self be true." He lived always on the heights, he "walked on the mountain range" and never descended to the plains where lesser men falter. The nobility of his character permitted homage to none save to his God and the eternal truth. While such abounding self-respect may at times lend to man an apparent austerity, yet it constitutes the chief source of power, leadership, and greatness among men.

Such a man was Judge Start. It was his rugged, unflinching manliness, manifested in his every act, that attracted the profound respect of all classes and endeared him so closely to his associates of the bench and bar. It was this that in early life led him to the duties of a soldier where all manly qualities are so fittingly employed.

It was this trait of his character that caused him to so despise everything like cant, hypocrisy, and subterfuge. Show and pomp were entirely foreign to his nature. Neither could he tolerate the slightest taint of fraud or deceit. His decisions abound with unmeasured condemnation of everything approaching dishonesty or double dealing.

Believing in himself, he believed in humanity. He spent his life administering justice with the single aim to make it approximate as nearly as possible the justice of the infallible Ruler of the Universe. He believed in the teaching that "the law was made for man and not man for the law." He studied deeply the ever growing complexity of our modern life and strove to adapt the law to humanity's needs as they arose. His legal attainments were of the highest order, his knowledge of precedents profound, but they were always subordinated to his idea of service to man. Precedents were to him but guides blazing the way; he never permitted them to thwart what he believed to be the purpose of the law—that is, the protection of those who were entitled to protection. His life after quitting this bench was devoted to generous ministrations to obtain what he believed to be justice to all men.

I have said that such a man was likely to be judged as cold and austere, but to those whose privilege it was to come within the circle of the friends of Charles M. Start was given to know the wealth of his personal feeling for his fellows. His nature was singularly desirous of comradeship; he craved the society and companionship of men. But he was drawn to them never by their wealth or prominence but solely by their honor and manliness, which qualities he discerned with almost unerring intuition. During the "overtime" allowed him at the close of his life, it was his never failing delight to gather with his friends and satisfy his longing for human fellowship. Those whose privilege it was to join in this circle were often amazed at his sparkling wit, quiet humor, and rich fund of anecdote. His gentleness, however, never permitted him to say for the sake of humor a word that might wound the feelings of any man; rather would he choose such incidents as made himself the object of the witticism. Justly was he ever allowed to do most of the entertaining, and his good sense, originality, freedom from personalities and purity of thought and language made these occasions a delight never to be forgotten.

It is a singular truth that men often characterize themselves in characterizing others. I think our departed friend did this when he so aptly said of his long loved friend and associate Judge Severance: "He was gentle and genuine, tender and true. His genial humor, his sympathetic kindness, his perfect integrity, his chivalrous manliness, and his pure life endeared him to his friends and associates and made him one of the best-loved of men and judges." [102 Minn. XXXII]

Chief Justice Brown then said:

Intimate personal as well as official relations with Judge Start for twelve years of his term of service as Chief Justice, constant and almost daily association with him during that time, qualify me to bear witness to the truth of the Memorial and of the deserved tribute paid to his memory by those who have addressed the court. Nothing can be added to what has been so well and eloquently presented. One of the conspicuous characteristics of Judge Start in his judicial work was a strong inclination to turn all fair doubts in controversies submitted to him for decision in favor of human as distinguished from strict property rights. Yet in no case would he violate settled rules or principles of law to reach result of that kind. He was honest to himself, upright in the performance of his duties, and his conscience led him along the path of rectitude in the discharge of all his obligations, official as well non-official.

May the example of his pure life, his high character, his faithful devotion to duty, be an inspiration to those who in future are to follow in his footsteps as trusted judicial servants of the state.

The Memorial will be spread upon the records of the court there to remain a perpetual testimony of an exemplary life, a faithful public servant. [144 Minn. xxi]

Calvin L. Brown

1854–1923
Associate Justice, 1899–1913, Chief Justice 1913–1923

At the opening of court on Tuesday, January 8, 1924, in the court room at the State Capitol, Chief Justice Wilson presiding, Hon. Thomas D. O'Brien, a former Associate Justice, addressed the Court and said:

Shortly after the death of the late Mr. Chief Justice Brown, a committee, selected from the State Bar Association of Minnesota, was honored with the request that it prepare a memorial of him and present it to your Honors at a proper time and place, for inscription upon the permanent records of this Court.

It is proper that I should announce, so that this fact may also be of record, that in nearly, if not all, of the Judicial Districts in Minnesota, today has been set apart for some suitable action by the Bench and Bar of each District, in which the veneration accorded to the memory of the late Chief Justice may be expressed. The executive officers of the State, as well as many of the Judges of the District and Probate Courts, are present to grace this occasion, so that over the entire domain included within the jurisdiction of this high tribunal, the life and character of Mr. Chief Justice Brown is receiving the universal tribute of love and respect to which it is so well entitled.

Chester L. Caldwell, Secretary of the State Bar Association then read the following:

Calvin Luther Brown, Associate Justice of the Supreme Court of the State of Minnesota from 1899 to [1913] and Chief Justice from then until his death, was born at Goshen New Hampshire, April 26, 1854, and died at his home in Minneapolis, Minnesota, September 24, 1923.

Like his close friend and predecessor, Mr. Chief Justice Start, he possessed the heritage of New England ancestry. His great-grandfather, William Brown, was a solider of the Revolution; his grandfather, Luther Brown, took part in the war of 1812, and his father, John Harrison Brown, for many years a District Judge in this State, was in the Commissary Department of the Union Army during the Civil War, stationed at Madison, Wisconsin, with the rank of Captain.

When the late Chief Justice was but one year old his parents settled at Shakopee, in this State. Minnesota was then a territory, so that during the subsequent sixty-seven years of his life he witnessed and took part in the development of the State to its present position.

As a boy in Shakopee he saw the trembling fugitives from the Sioux massacre of 1862; he experienced the thrill of horror that swept over the nation at the assassination of Lincoln; he saw the survivors of the Minnesota regiments return to their homes after the suppression of the rebellion; he knew when the first mile of railway was constructed in Minnesota and when the Indians ceased to come with their Red River carts to barter with the fur traders; and then, when the St. Paul and Pacific Railway pierced the "Big Woods" and emerged upon the prairie, he joined in the movement that filled the western lands of Minnesota with happy homes and prosperous citizens.

In 1870 the family removed to Willmar, Kandiyohi County, Minnesota, and there, on September 1, 1878, the late Chief Justice married Miss Annette Marlow, who bore him five children, one, Olive, dying in infancy, and four who survived him—Alice A., now the wife of Dr. B. J. Branton of Willmar; Edna M., and Margaret E., residents of Minneapolis; and Montreville J. Brown, attorney at law of St. Paul.

Mrs. Brown, an ideal mother and helpmeet, died at Minneapolis, October 13, 1919.

After some ventures into other fields, usually to be expected of a restless and ambitious young man in a frontier state, Calvin L. Brown seriously took up the study of law and was admitted to the Bar of Minnesota, February 22, 1870. He first practiced in Willmar, in partnership with his brother, Horace W. Brown, and in 1878 removed to Morris, Stevens County, where he served as County Attorney from 1883 until his appointment by Gov. McGill on March 10, 1887, as District Judge of the Sixteenth Judicial District.

Presiding for eleven years as District Judge, he earned the approbation and love of all with whom he came in contact, with the result that in 1898 he was elected Associate Judge of the Supreme Court for the term commencing January 1, 1900. Before the beginning of his term Mr. Justice Buck resigned, and Gov. Lind, on November 20th, 1899, appointed the newly elected Justice to fill the vacancy. In 1913, when Mr. Chief Justice Start refused to accept a re-election, Justice Brown was elected Chief Justice and continued to serve in that position until his death.

The real life work of the Chief Justice began with his elevation to the Supreme Court, and his legal attainments, his clear vision and common sense, and his gentle heart and intellectual honesty may be gathered from the opinions written by him, beginning with *Skone vs. Barnard,* 78 Minn., 200. Since then he delivered the opinion of the Court in cases that cover the whole field of law and show him to have been a profound lawyer as well as a practical man of affairs.

The dignity, poise, and patience with which he presided in the Supreme Court as its Chief Justice and the unfailing courtesy that he extended to counsel appearing in that tribunal won him the universal esteem of the members of the bar in addition to their admiration for him as a jurist.

The Chief Justice was essentially an original thinker, and in the performance of his judicial duties he first endeavored to arrive at what he felt should be the law and justice of the case under consideration. Following this, he studied precedents to test the correctness of his judgment, and when he found sufficient authority to support his own conclusions, he immediately and in longhand wrote his opinion, the first draft of which was generally so clear and simple as to need little or no revision.

Although occupying the highest judicial position in the State, he never lost his simplicity or kindness of heart, and although pre-eminently of a domestic disposition, he mingled freely with other men in a spirit of fraternity and was Grand Master of the Grand Lodge of Masons of Minnesota during the years 1894 and 1895.

His sympathetic and broad Christian charity came into full play in connection with the performance of the duties imposed upon the Chief Justice as a member of the Board of Pardons. No shrinking waif, unhappy parent, or distracted wife failed of a sympathetic hearing from him, and even when he could give no assurance of mercy, his sympathetic bearing and kindly counsel brought solace to the class upon whom the punishment for crime often bears the heaviest.

His is the story of a real American, and although to some the maxim noblesse oblige may present the picture of an armored knight of the old regime, to the American, saturated with traditions of his country, it brings a vision of a sturdy, self-reliant, and self-supporting man who reveres God, believes in the sanctity of the home, recognizes the dignity of labor and equality of all men before the law, of one who appreciates a government of laws and not of men and who classifies humanity not by wealth, religion, or race but by conduct and attainments.

And so this man who endured the privations of the frontier remained unsullied by its rudeness. With only the scant aid of inadequate educational institutions, he mastered the intricacies of the great legal profession. Called to high positions, he remained a kindly, simple gentleman, unspoiled by the temptations of place and power. He thought upon the things that are good and true and beautiful, and we do not so much sorrow at his death as rejoice in the fact that we knew him and loved him and that his name will always stand high on the Honor Roll of Minnesota.

Thomas D. O'Brien, Chairman
David F. Simpson
G. E. Qvale
S. A. Flaherty
L. L. Collins
John D. Sullivan
C. A. Severance
W. D. Bailey

L. L. Brown
I. A. Caswell
Chester L. Caldwell

Hon. Stephen A. Flaherty, Judge of the District Court for the Sixteenth Judicial District, then said:

It is indeed an appreciated privilege to have the opportunity of participating in these exercises held in honor of my highly esteemed friend, the late Chief Justice Brown. Our acquaintance commenced nearly forty-three years since, and intimate, friendly relations existed between us from that time until the termination of his life. While occasions of this character have their proprieties, which should not be disregarded, and it is realized that usually whatever one speaks of himself is too much, some reference to my early associations with him may be permitted and entitled to indulgent consideration.

When we first met, in 1881 at Morris, he had been admitted to the bar six years and three years before that had taken up his residence and opened an office there for the practice of his profession. I had but a year previously begun the study of law and was admitted to practice in 1882, in what was then the due and usual course. We were then comparatively young men, of nearly the same age, he being my senior by about a year. He was at that time a careful student of the law and an able, successful lawyer with a rapidly increasing practice and a constantly widening circle of favorable acquaintances. My own attempt to undertake the trial of a case was very much delayed by the fear of having him as an opponent, and only unavoidable necessity at last overruled this timidity—my partner having deliberately contrived to abandon me to my fate. The Sixteenth Judicial District of this State was organized in 1887, and his appointment as its first judge was cordially approved and endorsed by the people of that district. While he occupied that position, my practice enabled me to observe and note his work on the bench, and it was quite usual for us to ride circuit together with horse teams. Until his election as an Associate Justice of this Court and the removal of his family from Morris, year after year we took outings and spent our vacations together in fishing expeditions and otherwise. It may not be amiss to add that we were next-door neighbors for a long time and that our families were always on the most intimate and friendly terms.

These things are recalled here only for the purpose of indicating that for a long, interesting, and important period in the life of the late Chief Justice, my opportunities for knowing and understanding him were ample and extremely favorable. And it may as well be said now that no person of my acquaintance ever stood less in need of that charitable saying that nothing save good should be spoken of the dead.

He was a man to whom nature had been very generous. In person he was tall, erect, well formed and strong, active and graceful in his movements, and he had an attractive and expressive countenance, bespeaking friendliness and the kindly, humane sentiments. His mental gifts were of a very high order, although because of his plain, quiet, and unassuming manner, this might easily escape the notice of an ordinary, casual observer. His mind was clear, comprehensive and acute, and so well-balanced and poised were his mental faculties that it would be difficult to determine which predominated. His memory was retentive and ready and enabled him to recall with ease and at will almost everything that had come to his attention in his reading or experience. His sense of honesty was inborn, innate, and part of his very being and not at all in kind or quality like that so-called honesty that results from a careful calculation of policies and consequences. And crowning all, he had that combination of virtues and qualities called character. Nothing could tempt him to court applause or angle for compliments. He avoided and shunned all this, for his modesty was such that the most deserved praise would not be welcome and probably would disconcert and embarrass him. In his association with people as he passed through life, he was cordial and affable but not effusive, and he possessed, to a surprising degree, the capacity for making and retaining the most devoted friends. It may be owing to this trait of character that, although he was frequently a candidate for public positions and apparently did not greatly exert himself to promote his success, he never suffered defeat. So easy it all appeared and so much a matter of course were his successive promotions in public life, and at convenient stages, too, that it might have seemed as if "his conscious destiny made way."

163

As District Judge he made an admirable record and gave abundant proof of the great natural ability and attainments that were thereafter more conspicuously exhibited in a higher and ampler sphere of activity. He was careful, diligent, and prompt in the disposition of all work and business that required his attention. While presiding on the trial of actions it is but little to say that he was impartial, fair-minded, and just. He paid the utmost degree of attention to the evidence, and on arguments of counsel upon questions of law he followed them closely, seldom interrupting, and scarcely ever assuming to anticipate the result of a line of reasoning. He was notable for his patience, which was imperturbable, even under conditions when some manifestation of displeasure or restlessness might well be expected and excused. He never showed the least inclination to take the management of a case on trial out of the hands of counsel or to do or say anything that would give the slightest intimation in advance toward which side his judgment might lean or his sympathies be enlisted. His instructions to juries were concise and were invariably written out with rapidity while counsel were summing up.

When he took his seat on the bench of this Court, he brought to the performance of his important and onerous duties all the advantages of previous experience in a subordinate position, together with all that deep, continued, and extensive study of the law could furnish to a vigorous mind still growing and capable of further development. He looked upon the functions of a court of justice and the administration of the law, almost, if not wholly, in the light of a sacred office and consecrated his life and all his energy to the work here with the zeal and ardor of one who was confident that he had found his true calling. It may not be true, but to me it has always seemed that a position on the bench of this Court requires and calls for many renunciations, as well as for the most arduous, exacting mental labor. While Chief Justice Brown was not by habit or temperament disposed to put forth great and spasmodic efforts on occasions to be followed by periods of needed relaxation, his ability was better ordered and enabled him to support prolonged and sustained effort. It is not for me to discuss his work here, but it cannot be questioned that he labored faithfully and greatly to the end of his

days in accordance with his lofty conceptions of the duty of his position. It may be observed that the mere bulk alone that must have passed through his hands was prodigious, as shown by the reported decisions. The volumes containing his opinions when fully published will be found to be nearly half of the official reports of this state. No claim is made, of course, that bulk or mass affords any true measure of the extent, importance, or almost infinite variety of the matters embraced. At this point one might be tempted to dwell on his opinions, written in judicial tone and temper and bearing the impress of a powerful mind, keen and discriminating. However, I withhold comment and will conclude this imperfect and altogether inadequate tribute by saying that The Honorable Calvin L. Brown, by reason of his fine character as a man and his long and distinguished judicial career, has left a name and a memory ever to be cherished by friends and acquaintances and has maintained and advanced the standing and honor of this Court.

Hon. John Lind, former Governor of Minnesota, then addressed the Court and said:

The usage of the bar of this state to meet as we meet today to give expression to our memories, our esteem, and our affection for the life and character of a departed member of our profession is a custom that we should never permit to be commonplace or perfunctory. The man whose memory we meet to honor was not only a member of our profession but a great judge of this Court—the head of the judicial department of our beloved state—during the most active and fruitful years of his life.

In this instance, therefore, it is more than a usage. We all feel at this moment as though we were looking into a new-made grave, digged to receive the mortal remains of a man whom we all respected and loved. My acquaintance with Judge Brown covered a period of nearly thirty years. Whether or not he was born in this state I do not know, but he must have spent the years of his youth as well as his manhood with us, for I remember that his father was the District Judge of one of our judicial districts when I was a mere boy. I also remember that I tried one of my early cases before him, I think in 1877, at Beaver Falls, then the county seat of Renville County. Gorham Powers, later judge of that district (another great and good man in the early history of our state), was my opponent. Judge Powers was my senior both in years and experience, and I remember with gratitude to this day how the elder Judge Brown with suggestion and kindliness but without bias, encouraged me to present my case in good form. I mention this only to emphasize my conviction that the similar traits that we so often observed in his eminent son were inborn and in no sense simulated or prompted by political ambition. In District Court I do not recall that I appeared before Judge Calvin Brown but once, but my impression of him then, and the estimate in which he was held by the bar in his district, convinced me that he was a worthy successor of his father. Later, when I was in office in this city, a vacancy occurred in this Court. It did not take me long to determine that Judge Brown was the best fitted available man to fill that position, and I accordingly appointed him. One of the considerations that actuated me in making the appointment was the fact that Judge Brown, while not a farmer's son, had spent part of the active years of his life in the midst of a farming community and was in touch by observation and contact with that independence and spirit of true democracy that we are likely to find better developed in an intelligent town meeting community than anywhere else.

After I left St. Paul, I became engaged in active practice and had cases in this court from time to time. For some reason that I can neither explain nor justify, I felt sensitive about calling on the Judge personally at his room; it is only in the last two or three years that I have done so, and when I did, we had most interesting conversations about the profession and about affairs in the state generally. I may be pardoned for mentioning one of the topics we discussed at our last meeting. I made the remark that in the 150 volumes of our Minnesota Reports then available, virtually the whole realm of human relationship and activities had been covered, in principle at least, and I hoped that the Court would take some steps to indicate to the bar the desirability of confining their citations to our own reports as much as possible. He said he did not know how that could be done very well, but that he hoped that both he and his colleagues would hereafter confine themselves to quoting our own cases

and those of the Supreme Court of the United States when necessary, as much as possible. We both agreed that less hunting for "authorities" and more studious work and reflection would give us better lawyers and better decisions. This was the last conversation I had with him.

He was a great citizen as well as a great lawyer. I shall not stop to review his work. It is of record and known to us all. I realize, as every member of this Court should and must, that if it is to retain the respect and confidence of our citizenship that it has had in the past and now enjoys, then this Court as the guardian of our institutions and our bill of rights is one of the political divisions of our government, and in respect of questions of that character that come before it, it must apply the principles embodied in our constitution in the light of conditions as they are today and not to be hampered or misled by specious arguments that those principles when once applied to economic and social conditions have become static, settled, and defined, and must in all future time be applied today as they were when invoked and applied to the conditions of centuries ago. Principles do not change, but they must be applied to human affairs in the light of the conditions as they are. That our late Chief Justice on the whole saw his responsibility and his duty in this regard is apparent from his many opinions bearing on questions involving constitutional government.

In the departure of Calvin Brown, the State of Minnesota lost a great man, a great citizen, and a great and good judge. May the spirit that guided him and Gilfillan and Start guide us and guide his future successors.

Attorney General Clifford L. Hilton then addressed the Court and said:

The legal attainments and the judicial career of Chief Justice Brown have been justly commended in the memorial and the previous addresses. From an intimate acquaintance of many years, it is of Calvin Luther Brown, the man, the citizen, and the public official, I would speak.

Of sterling New England stock, to a marked degree he possessed a stable, unflinching respect for rectitude of conduct and yet with entire absence of puritanical censure for its lack in others. His standards were for his own guidance, not for use in criticism of his fellows.

He made ample provision for the education, care, and comfort of his family. This primary duty to those of his own household did not, however, cause him to forget the needs of others. In an unostentatious way he was ever doing kindly, generous deeds that carried blessing and benediction to many. These acts of charity and kindness were never heralded abroad, and only after his death did many of them come to light. His family life was beautiful. The reverence and respect of his children were deserved. His home was an ideal one, and his happiest hours were in the family circle. Yet his kindliness of disposition and love of his fellowmen, his interest in all human affairs, made him a most gracious and enjoyable companion.

In later years he was "the first citizen of the state," an appellation often given to the one holding the high position that he so honorably filled. All through his life, in private walk as well as in public office, his regard for the duties of a citizen was grounded deeply in the fundamentals. The obligations of a citizen were as sacred to him as were those guiding him in official life. Loyalty to his country and devotion in its service were as natural to him as the breath of life. In this man were properly blended all the elements of a sturdy, God-fearing, loyal American citizen.

Justice Brown's service on the Supreme Court as an Associate and as Chief Justice extended over a period of twenty-four years and is a lasting memorial of his ability and concentration. His written opinions will more and more, as time passes, magnify his reputation as a jurist.

Before closing I desire to refer to another official position held by him that displayed an element in his character not so well known to the public. Under our constitution the pardon board is composed of the Governor, the Chief Justice, and the Attorney General. For more than five years it was my privilege to serve with Judge Brown on that board. Opportunity was thus afforded me of seeing and knowing him as but few did. The duties imposed upon the board of pardons are arduous and trying, calling for the exercise of good judgment, the tempering of justice with mercy as occasion requires, and with all the utmost restraint, lest one allow sympathy and sentimentality to sway and control action. Many a time the circumstances and heart-rendering appeals of suffering relatives make the denying of clemency most difficult. To one of Judge Brown's kindly nature such a denial was a truly heroic act when duty required it. Never to my own knowledge was he unduly swayed by sentiment, sympathy, influence, or anything other than his high sense of duty.

He has served his day and generation well. His fellow citizens and associates honor his memory. His life and work furnish an inspiring example worthy to be followed.

Hon. Ell Torr[a]nce then said:

It is not within my power to convey to the members of this Court any information not already possessed by you regarding the character and judicial attainments of the late Chief Justice Brown.

He was your associate and co-laborer; your relations with him were intimate; you knew him better, perhaps, than anyone who may on this occasion address you. Your opportunities for estimating his ability as a jurist were many and exceptional. The memorial submitted by your committee and now awaiting the action of the Court is illuminating, comprehensive, and just.

My tribute, therefore, will be personal and brief—personal because of our mutual friendship and brief because virtue is its own interpreter.

Many years ago I visited the home of my childhood for the last time. On the morning of my departure I partook of a simple breakfast with my aged father and mother. A single candle lighted the table. Few words were spoken, and the silence was oppressive. Finally my father said:

"My son, I have no advice to give you, but I have a wish that I hope may be exemplified in your life. My wish is that you possess of all things the grace of humility. Clothed with that grace, your life will be simplified and without offense to others. The possession of that grace will exempt you from envy and jealousy and perhaps save you the mortification of being requested to occupy a lower seat."

In my opinion, Chief Justice Brown exemplified that grace in its completeness. All kindred virtues flourished in its train—kindness, friendliness, gentleness, simplicity, and modesty marked his daily life.

His life was destitute of display and pomp and parade. He was without pretense and was genuinely good.

We can contemplate with professional pride his judicial learning, his industry and fidelity in the discharge of the duties of his exalted office. We can contemplate with satisfaction the enduring record he has left in the decisions of this Court. But best of all, his moral qualities crowned the labors of his brain and mind with that spiritual inspiration and power that leavens society and gives strength to free institutions.

His patriotism was of the finest texture, woven out of the best traditions and teachings of the founders of the Republic. With an undivided heart, Judge Brown truly loved and faithfully served his country. At the last annual meeting of the Minnesota Commandery of the Military Order of the Loyal Legion of the United States, he was chosen its Commander, a worthy successor to former Chief Justice Gilfillan and Justice Collins of this Court. He was the first one without a military record to hold that office, the honor coming to him through the services rendered by his father, Captain John H. Brown, in the war for the preservation of the American Union.

The few surviving officers of the Loyal Legion entertained for Judge Brown the highest respect and admiration, and they looked forward to a happy year with their beloved Commander. But alas! another vacant chair.

We who knew and shared the friendship of Calvin Luther Brown will always think of him, not like a distant lighthouse casting brilliant rays across the storm-tossed sea of life, but as a friend with a lamp, walking by our side and by precept and example disclosing step by step the path of safety and right living.

Hon. Albert Schaller, a former Associate Justice, then addressed the Court and said:

It is meet and just that the representatives of the Bench and Bar of this state assemble here at this time to do honor to the memory of one who sat on the Supreme Bench of this state for so many years.

During more than a quarter century, he gave to the Jurisprudence of this state a high purpose, a firm courage, an exalted devotion to the principles of the law, a keen and judicial mind, deep learning, and a great love of justice.

His judicial opinions show a clarity of vision, a profound knowledge of the law and of human nature and its foibles, a sympathy with human weakness, and withal a respect for the dignity of man, and a charity and kindness that were the outstanding human traits of this truly great judge.

Other great justices have interpreted the law and administered justice. Others have contributed to the growth of the principles of the law. Many others have spent their time and devoted the powers of great intellects, learning, and wisdom in the exhaustive work of the bench, but none had in greater measure the lovable, human qualities of the late Chief Justice.

He was always kindly and human, easily approachable, and always helpful. His personality invited confidence and affection—little children loved him and trusted him as an older brother. They gave and received love for love and trust for trust.

His charity for his fellow man was as universal as all humanity, and his desire to be helpful was as broad. He did not distinguish between conditions in life, except perhaps that he might deal more patiently with the ignorant and the unfortunate.

No one ever asked him for help in vain. He gave from his pecuniary resources as freely as he gave from the treasures of his vast experience or his tender heart.

He was uncompromising in the performance of his duty, but he did what he had to do in such a way that the hand that dealt the blow also salved the wound. Never a sting was left by anything he said or wrote. He shot no poisoned arrow to rankle and fester in the wound.

He was a man of simple tastes, simple and direct in word and deed. He despised sham, ostentation, and parade. In Court and in conference he presided with urbanity and dignity. His conclusions were arrived at after a thorough examination and were supported by clear and logical reasoning based on apposite authorities.

In all his associations with other members of the Court his attitude was frank and open, kindly and helpful. He had no overweening pride of opinion, treated his associates with the greatest respect and friendliness. He was essentially a modest man.

The personnel of the Court over which he presided was harmonious, kindly, and considerate. Differences of opinion occasionally arose and questions were freely debated, but the discussions were invariably conducted with a view single to arriving at a correct decision. The kindly spirit of the great-hearted Chief Justice pervaded the Court and its officers, whether in chambers, on the Bench, or in the consultation room.

Every human being adds in some measure to the total sum of good or evil in the progress of humanity. The good must necessarily overcome and survive the evil. It must do so because of its very nature.

He who contributes to the advancement of the race by his learning, his wisdom, his science, or his character is accomplishing lasting good. His name is written among the great ones of the earth. He takes his place in history and is remembered by mankind. But the name of him who, in addition to such great achievement, loves and helps his fellow man, the name of him to whom the poor, the neglected, and the obscure, created in the image and likeness of the Creator, are as brethren and who treats them as such stands out more brightly on the tablets of the Recording Angel.

We assemble here today to honor the memory of a great citizen, a learned and just and upright judge, a kindly human soul whose services have placed him high on the honor roll of this great commonwealth.

But even more do we sincerely mourn the loss of the great-hearted, considerate, charitable, tolerant, and lovable man whom his friends knew in life as Calvin L. Brown.

In the words spoken by him on the occasion of the death of his illustrious predecessor on the Bench: "May the example of his pure life, his high character, his faithful devotion to duty, be an inspiration to those who in future are to follow in his footsteps as trusted judicial servants of the state."

Hon. Lorin Cray, former Judge of the Sixth Judicial District, then said:

'Mid the responsibilities and duties of this care-burdened life of ours it is well that we for a moment pause to do homage to the memory of one who has passed beyond the tasks cast upon us by its problems and perplexities.

Chief Justice Calvin L. Brown was a man whom it was a pleasure to know. It was as well a pleasure to stand before him in forensic contest. Always mild in manner and courteous to all was he.

When at critical times we have felt that we were standing on slippery places and that we could not find firm foundation on which to place our feet, he was always ready and willing to bear with us and afford opportunity to gather and make ready for another assault on the works of our adversary, so that if fall we must, our fall might be on easier fields.

Honored by all of us in life, greatly missed from among us in death, we can illy afford to spare such a one as he from among us.

In these days when we are nervously moving along all lines at such a furious pace and incline to be forgetful of man's duty to man, we must guard with jealous care the vulnerable places in Bench and Bar, and to such as he we may well look for a guiding star.

Outside of his official duties he worked painstakingly to tiring about such simplification of the practice in Court as to make more easy, more speedy, and more economical the disposition of cases, all in earnest effort to secure the administration of justice swift and sure to all, rich and poor alike.

He had scant patience with that distorted sentimentalism that would unreasonably shield the wrongdoer and let the law-abiding one care for himself.

Just and righteous in both public and private life, when the chair midway between your chairs was made vacant, we may well feel assured that he heard that welcome call, "Come unto Me."

Hon. J. L. Washburn then said:

It is not fitting to seek for superlative phrases in which to eulogize adequately the life and character of our honored and loved late Chief Justice. His was a simple unostentatious life, free from all semblance of vainglory.

He administered his high offices of trial judge, Associate Justice, and Chief Justice, covering a period of more than twenty-five years with singleness of purpose, without fear or partiality and with distinguished ability.

He always sought to administer justice according to law and not in violation. He recognized that the rights and contentions of parties must be related to the law, even though sometimes it might appear that a controversy would be more fairly concluded between the individual contenders by forgetting the law. That has sometimes been done at the expense of making a poor or uncertain rule of conduct for future contestants.

It is not proper for me to cite volumes and pages, but the recorded decisions of Justice Brown in this Court, though they may have been dissenting ones, destined thereafter to become the unanimous opinion of this Court, conclusively establish his independence, his fearlessness, and the subjection of self and all thought of personal advantages in the one object of arriving at a just and righteous judgment under the law.

Justice Brown came to Duluth when he was a Judge of the District Court to assist our over-worked judges, and I had the good fortune to appear before him. I think this was my first acquaintance with him. I have been here often when he was an Associate Justice, but in recent years I have seldom appeared personally in this Court.

I know of no judge who more than he always presided in the same simple, dignified manner without any suggestion of antagonism, always willing to listen to argument and to consider patiently the issues and the authorities, moved only to arrive at a just decision. If others have had a different experience, I have not known of it.

In private he was friendly, and he associated with members of the Bar on a basis of freedom and equality without embarrassment to them or to himself.

He was well versed in public affairs, and his judgment was sound and discriminating in matters affecting the nation, the state, and the people. It is devoutly hoped that the influence of such men in this nation, and especially in this state, shall not wane. It is devoutly to be hoped that each generation will produce enough of such men to preserve the foundation principles of our government and guide it in the true way of progress without departing therefrom—enough of such men to protect our scheme of government, which the people wisely established for themselves, from destruction by those who have no sympathy with it and perhaps no use for any government, and to cause those who have wandered off or have been led astray by selfish politicians into byways, to turn around and reach again the main traveled road of representative government, wherein alone perpetuity and progress are to be attained, liberty enjoyed, and the protection of individual rights assured.

We had hoped that Chief Justice Brown could have been spared to us for another decade, but we can still be thankful that there are others to take his place and, stimulated by his example, carry forward the work of his high office.

The more we dwell upon the merits of those who have gone, the more we emulate their virtues and seek to avoid their mistakes, if they made them, the better fit the living will be to serve wisely in their own day and generation.

We honored Chief Justice Brown in life. We trusted him and he did not betray the trust. Let us cherish his memory and assure to him the permanent place of honor in the annals of this state to which his life, his character, and his distinguished service entitle him.

Hon. F. H. Peterson, former State Senator from the Forty-ninth Senatorial District, then said:

I met Judge Brown at the term of Court held at Breckenridge almost immediately after his advancement to the Bench and practiced before him in Wilkin and neighboring counties until his appointment to the Supreme Court, since then from time to time in this Court.

It did not take long for the lawyers who appeared before him up in the Sixteenth District to learn the character of the new judge and to appreciate the just but kind-hearted and helpful man who had come to preside over their Court. The esteem in which he was held as a District Judge grew as the years went by, and he was called to the performance of a higher duty in this Court.

As I recall my long acquaintance with him I can easily note the characteristics that have specially impressed his personality upon me.

One of these was the absolute confidence that he inspired in lawyers practicing before him in his fairness, impartiality, and ability to analyze testimony and apply to it the appropriate principles of law, so that whether the case was for the jury of the Court or upon review in the Appellate Court, we felt very certain that he would grasp the facts and without fear or favor apply to them the law, and so far as lay in his power, would reach a just conclusion. This feeling was common to all who knew him.

In troublesome problems that sometimes came before the legislature—when new and untried ventures were placed on the statute books that we knew would be contested in the courts—members always felt that in Judge Brown we had a judge who not only knew the law and would bring to the construction of the particular act his great skill as a jurist but that he would look at it as a patriot, with a wide outlook upon life and with a mind animated by a sincere desire for the uplift and betterment of all the people.

He was a great lover of justice. To him the important thing about a lawsuit was that it should be decided right and that exact justice, so far as possible, should be given the litigants, and when technical rules of construction interfered with this main purpose they met with slight favor at his hands. You will search his opinions in vain for traces of narrowness, bigotry, or partiality.

Always it was the larger and finer view of life and the application of the broad principles of justice and equity that moved him.

His varied experience in life, the environment in which he grew to manhood, and his association with the plain country folk in the pioneer day gave him a rare insight into life and character and enabled him to draw just conclusions where many men might have been misled and hesitated or gone wrong entirely.

Judge Brown was the soul of courtesy and kindness. He decided after hearing and deliberation. He listened to the merest tyro at the Bar explain his views of the law with as much patience and courtesy as he did the most erudite scholar argue a new and untried proposition.

He started out with the presumption that litigants and counsel were sincere in their contentions and yielded respect to all arguments presented in good faith, but he had no time for the shyster or trickster and, when occasion warranted, was unsparing in his denunciation of sharp practice.

He recognized the fact that he held an exalted position as the head of the highest Court of a great state, and he actually was the embodiment of the simple dignity of his high office, but his official position never turned his head; his dignity was wholly without ostentation, and he was easily approached, cordial and affable to all.

His many excellent qualities made him a very useful citizen and a much-loved friend.

That part of him which is human has ended at the narrow door of the grave. His memory, however, will be living and fragrant as long as the generation with which he labored shall survive. His wisdom, his great common sense, and ability as a jurist shall abide permanently of record shaping human conduct and guiding business dealings between man and man so long as the state shall endure and wherever the opinions of this Court are read and cited.

Extravagant and fullsome eulogy as applied to Judge Brown is as much out of place as it would be distasteful to him.

Enough for me to say that this plain, sincere man, rising out of the common walks of life, saw before him the road to great service for the state and his fellow men. He laid hold upon the opportunity and calmly and steadfastly trod the road that opened before him. With vigorous hands he seized upon the opportunities for work that came within his reach. He gave his whole strength and the highest light he could summon to the accomplishment of this work.

Tired out with his toils, he fell asleep with his hands still full of unaccomplished tasks and while the sun of his day appeared to be still high in the heavens.

It remains for us who are left, each in his separate sphere, "to carry on" so that the state shall not suffer loss and the great onward sweep of humanity shall not be hindered.

Associate Justice Holt [on behalf of the court] then said:

The uncertainty of life was brought home to us with startling effect when early Monday morning, September 24 last, the sad message was received of the passing during the night of our beloved Chief Justice. Not one of his family and, in all probability not even he, suspected the approach of the Grim Reaper. Every member of the Court vividly recalled his customary visit of a few minutes in their chambers the Saturday previous then apparently in full physical and mental vigor, eagerly planning for the future. But often was he heard to express the wish thus quickly to pass when his time came.

Judge Brown became an Associate Justice of this Court November 30, 1899, after having been a District Judge for twelve and one-half years. His judicial services thus covered a period of more than thirty-six years. His opinions will be found in nearly eighty volumes of the Minnesota Reports. This will exceed by about one-fourth the work in which any other judge participated. His period of service on this bench extended more than a year beyond that of Judge Berry, the next in duration.

His long judicial experience aided by a retentive memory gave him a firm grasp of the law, as announced in the decisions of this Court. He also followed current events with great interest, enjoyed travel and meeting people, was a keen observer, and well versed in the political history of the state and nation. This, added to a natural broadmindedness, served to develop a marked trait in Judge Brown's opinions and his method in consultation, namely discerning and laying hold of the dominant points of the controversy, ignoring or brushing aside trivial matters whether of law or fact. He did not favor placing a decision upon closely drawn distinctions. Chief Justice Start often used to turn to Judge Brown when a complicated or doubtful legal problem came up with the remark: "How does it strike your good New England common sense?" The answer as a rule was so convincingly stated as to win ready assent. Whether speaking for the majority or expressing a dissent, his opinions disclosed a mind always alive to the great truth that courts exist for the purpose of administering justice and that legal principles and procedure are but means to an end. He weighed well the practical results to follow from a decision. Local self-government as exemplified in the town meeting, wherever granted by the law, appealed strongly to him. At the same time he was ever mindful of the Court's responsibility in protecting the rights and liberties of the individual as guaranteed by the Constitution. His opinions are direct, clear, and forceful, written in a style that does not suggest that he had only the meager schooling afforded the children of the early pioneers in this state.

Others have already recounted the valuable public labors and private virtues of Judge Brown. Able men and distinguished men and jurists have preceded him as Chief Justices, but it is safe to say that not one of them attained a higher place in the esteem and affection of his associates or of the members of the bar. His uniform good nature, his fair, courteous, and considerate treatment of everyone he met, was every day in evidence. Kind, plain and unassuming though he was, a quiet dignity always characterized his presence whether on or off the bench, so that no one was tempted to impose upon his good nature. A mere hint from him sufficed to direct an argument into proper channels.

His public work was not wholly confined to that of a judge. The leaders, irrespective of party, in both houses of the legislature had great confidence in him and through them he secured the enactment of laws to simplify practice and prevent delays in litigation.

Chief Justice Brown will long be remembered not only as an able and upright judge and a helpful and considerate associate but also as a noble and gracious man, a model citizen, and, above all, as one tender, true, and beloved in his home.

Associate Justice Quinn [also on behalf of the court] then said:

It is not in eulogy that I would speak of our friend who has been called away. Rather would I speak in gratitude and love. Intellectual force, power of leadership, [and] attainment of high place excite admiration and stir eulogy, but to touch and to hold the chords of loving remembrance and gratitude, nobler qualities are required. Intelligence may be selfish, leadership unscrupulous, ambition ruthless, but to reach into the hearts of men and "grapple them to the soul with hooks of steel," true love and the great spirit of helpful service must be given. These finer gifts were Calvin L. Brown's to a pre-eminent degree. True, his native ability was of the highest order, his power of leadership unsurpassed, his attainment of place the most exalted in our commonwealth, but to such a character as his, ability was but an instrument for greater service; power of leadership, a gracious gift leading men to better work; position, an enlarged opportunity to be just and kind.

Faithful service was the outstanding characteristic of his life. In him, a helping hand was natural and spontaneous. We who were associated with him in daily life can see him as he passed from one to another, offering the kindly word of encouragement, the anxiously sought word or phrase, the lucid statement of the law, the citation directly in point. Never was his assistance proffered in a spirit of obtrusion, never with an air of superiority, never for the purpose of self-exaltation. He sought no credit for himself; neither did he tolerate any display of deference or homage form anyone. His help was offered solely that right might be done. Harmonious in his own life and thought, he earnestly sought consistency in the work of the Court. That the Jurisprudence of Minnesota might become more coherent, he made full use of

> All his reasoning powers divine
> To penetrate, resolve, combine.

With all his constant desire to help, his aid was never given to an unworthy cause. In what he believed to be right he was as unyielding as granite. Friends could not influence him; foes could not daunt him. Always open to new ideas and to reason, he formed his conclusions with deliberation. To them, when formed, he was as true as a magnet. He never compromised with wrong. He chose the right and none could swerve him from it. Full well he knew that life was a battle. It left its deep scars upon him. Fair, manly, unflinching, he fought a good fight. He left us at a time when perhaps more than at any other in its history the Court needed his wise counsel, his serene and patient leadership, his inspiring aid.

Except from those closest and dearest to him, the warmth of his nature did not receive full appreciation. His kindly heart was partially hidden by the stern lines of a face that betokened his inflexible will, his towering integrity, and the purity of his character. It was in his home, by his own fireside, that his kindly nature shone the brightest. Most dearly he prized the hour that he could spend in close companionship with those who blessed "the little group" that he so tenderly called his own. Truly may it be said that through all his toil and stress, his home was to him "as an hiding place from the wind, and a covert from the tempest; as rivers of water in a dry place, as the shadow of a great rock in a weary land." There peace was found and harmony prevailed. There he fell asleep, as he would have wished, in the quiet hours of the night, in the very heart of his home. In the last analysis, the measure of a man's worth is the love he leaves in the hearts of his fellow men. By this standard, we find no words to tell of this friend who made life beautiful for us. It is because of our great love for Calvin Luther Brown that we stand bereft today.

> Gently Death came to him and bent to him asleep;
> His spirit passed, and, lo, his lovers weep,
> But not for him, for him the unafraid—
> In tears, we ask, 'Who'll lead the great crusade?'

Chief Justice Wilson then said:

We have met today in honor of one whose career, character, and ability well deserve these just tributes that have been paid him. He was a grand man; his obvious simplicity and directness of character gave him a universal friendship. The state has lost an able jurist and a leading citizen. We do but a sacred duty in these memorial services in recording our esteem, admiration, and gratitude for the great service that Chief Justice Brown has given to the state.

He was a just man; and he may justly be called a great and good man. [155 Minn. xxix]

Charles L. Lewis

1851–1936
Associate Justice, 1900–1912

In the afternoon of November 25, 1936, at two o'clock, the court being assembled at the court room in the State Capitol, Chief Justice John P. Devaney called upon Michael J. Doherty, president of the Minnesota State Bar Association.

Mr. Doherty then said:

The bar of Minnesota asks leave at this time to join with the court in honoring the memory of three men who have passed from this life since this court last convened for a similar purpose. Each of these three men was during his lifetime a leader of the bar of this state and a distinguished member of this court. The Honorable Charles L. Lewis died February 11, 1936 . . . The bar is represented by Mr. Frank Crassweller, Mr. Hugh J. McClearn, Mr. A. L. Agatin, and Mr. John B. Richards, who will present a memorial of the Honorable Charles L. Lewis . . .

Mr. Frank Crassweller then said:

Mr. McClearn, the chairman of this committee, unfortunately is unable to be here, and he has asked me to represent him and to present this memorial:

Charles Lundy Lewis was born in March, 1851, on a farm five miles from Ottawa, in LaSalle County, Illinois. His parents were Samuel R. and Anna Harley Lewis, who were natives of Pennsylvania. Samuel R. Lewis was of Quaker descent and emigrated to Illinois with his father, Jehu Lewis, in 1833 when Samuel R. was 15 years old. Before emigrating, Jehu Lewis kept a "station" on the "Underground Railroad" on the Baltimore Pike in Washington County, Pennsylvania. Both Jehu and Samuel R. Lewis kept "stations" on the so-called "Underground R. R." in Illinois. Samuel R. Lewis was a friend of Abraham Lincoln. He was one of the founders of the Republican Party. He attended the convention that nominated Lincoln in 1860. Samuel R. Lewis was County Treasurer of LaSalle County, Illinois, for four years and State Senator for four years.

Charles Lundy Lewis was named Charles Lundy for Charles Lundy, a brother of the celebrated Abolitionist Benjamin Lundy, who lived and died in LaSalle County, Illinois.

Charles Lundy Lewis attended a district school situated on his father's farm until he was 16 years old, when he entered the Ottawa high school. After graduation from Ottawa high school, he entered Oberlin College, from which institution he graduated in 1876. He spent two years in a law office in Chicago. In 1879 he opened a law office in Fergus Falls, Minnesota. While there he served as prosecuting attorney. He was a delegate to the convention that nominated Benjamin Harrison in 1888. He moved to Duluth in April 1891, and on March 14, 1893, he was appointed judge of the district court by Governor Knute Nelson and moved to Duluth. Some years later he resigned from the bench and became a partner of J. L. Washburn of Duluth.

In 1898 he was elected a justice of this court and took his seat on the bench January 1, 1900. He was reelected in 1906. Judge Lewis retired as a justice of this court January 1, 1912.

About a year after Judge Lewis left the bench he went to Duluth, where he was ill. From there he went to Wisconsin to be near his son, Charles L. Lewis Jr., and remained there until some time in 1915, when he went to California for his health. He stayed in California until the early part of 1916, when he left for Kingman, Arizona, to establish a business and home, as his health had improved. He was admitted to the bar in Arizona and practiced law there until 1922. During the latter part of

1922 he returned to Los Angeles and formed a law partnership with Don Lehman, formerly of Minneapolis, and this co-partnership continued until his death. He was admitted to practice law in California in January 1923, and died there February 11, 1936. Because of ill health, Judge Lewis was not active in the practice of law the last three years of his life.

Don Lehman, his law partner, says of Judge Lewis: "During my association with him I found him very honest, reliable, and kindly, always considerate of the rights of others, and always ready to do the fair thing. Until a very few days before his passing his mind was very clear, and he had a very comprehensive grasp of all matters."

One of the outstanding happenings in his later years was a celebration of his fifty-fifth wedding anniversary with Mrs. Lewis in May 1935. At this celebration there were three couples who had been married 55 years, all of whom had been students at Oberlin College, Oberlin, Ohio, all living in Los Angeles at the time of the celebration. This being such an unusual occasion, one of the radio broadcasting stations of Los Angeles arranged a special party at which each of the six celebrants made short radio talks.

Judge Lewis passed away February 11, 1936, and his body was cremated and placed in an urn at Forest Lawn Memorial Park, Glendale, California. He is survived by his widow, Janet D. Lewis, now residing at 149 North Gramercy Place, Los Angeles, California; Laurel Lewis Buckle, a daughter, residing at 2254 Arthur Street, N. E., Minneapolis, Minnesota; William Murray Lewis, a son, residing at 38 Lafayette Avenue, Haddonfield, New Jersey; Charles L. Lewis, a son, residing at 125 South Oxford Street, St. Paul, Minnesota; and Margaret Lewis Fees, a daughter, residing at 538 Harps Street, San Fernando, California.

> Hugh J. McClearn
> A. L. Agatin
> Frank Crassweller
> John B. Richards

Mr. Crassweller then said:

I regret that there are not more from Duluth who could say something in reference to Judge Lewis. From the time that he became a member of this court he was very little in Duluth, and in 36 years many things are forgotten. His law partners, J. L. Washburn and W. D. Bailey, are both dead.

My recollection of Judge Lewis is of a kindly, courteous man of high ideals, unpretentious but dignified, of great integrity, and of good courage. It came to be his duty during the time he was on this bench to make a decision affecting the city of Duluth and the iron ore district of the North, and he made that decision and wrote the opinion knowing that it would arouse strong feeling and antagonism in that northern country. He made his decision as he believed it should be, and he stood by it. I take it as a high grade of courage when a man will do his duty knowing that his position will be misunderstood, his motives misconstrued, and his decision derided and bitterly resented by those who had theretofore been his strongest friends.

Judge Lewis was a good lawyer, a good judge, a good citizen, and well upheld the high traditions of this court.

Associate Justice Clifford L. Hilton [for the court]:

Charles L. Lewis became a member of the Fergus Falls bar in 1880. At that time I was a young student in the Fergus Falls high school. As a boy and young man, I became well acquainted with him. I knew the high esteem in which he was held not only by the members of the local bar but also by the citizenry of Fergus Falls and Otter Tail County. Although of a reserved nature, he had a pleasing personality. His reputation was that of a studious, careful, and capable lawyer. He was not a brilliant orator but as an advocate was convincing. I heard it frequently said by those who knew him best that his preparation for the trial of a case was always thorough and left nothing to chance.

He served as county attorney of Otter Tail County for four years. His manner of conducting a prosecution was fair. Although [he was] very successful in securing convictions, there was never an attempt to obtain them by other than proper methods. He moved to Duluth in 1891 to continue the practice of law. In 1893 he was appointed judge of the district court in St. Louis County by the then governor, Knute Nelson. The attorneys who there practiced before him held him in the highest regard.

In the fall of 1899 he was elected associate justice of this court, which office he held for 12 years. The first opinion written by Justice Lewis appears in the last five pages of volume 78 of the Minnesota Reports. The case, a criminal one, was tried before Judge David Simpson of Hennepin County, afterward a justice of this court. For the state in that case appeared Wallace B. Douglas, then attorney general, who later also became a supreme court justice.

Justice Lewis brought to the discharge of his duties in this court the same sterling qualities and ability that had made him outstanding in the private practice of law and in his work on the district bench. It fell to his lot to write the opinions in many important cases. He expressed his views with remarkable clearness. His contribution to the opinion law of this state made a most favorable impression both within and without its borders.

His friends were many and devoted. His learning and ability were exceptional. His consecrated faithfulness to duty earned for him wholehearted regard and affection. [198 Minn xxvi]

John A. Lovely

1843–1908
Associate Justice, 1900–1905

On the afternoon of April 7, 1908, in the court room at the State Capitol, Charles W. Farnham, Esq., Secretary of the Minnesota State Bar Association, in behalf of the committee of that Association appointed to draft a memorial of Hon. John A. Lovely, late an Associate Justice of the Court who died at Albert Lea, Minnesota, on January 28, 1908, addressed the Supreme Court, then in session, and read the following memorial:

John A. Lovely was born in Burlington, Vermont, November 18, 1843, and came West in 1863, was admitted to the bar at Milwaukee in 1864, practiced law in Watertown, Wisconsin, until 1867, when he moved to Albert Lea, Minnesota, where he engaged in the practice of his chosen profession and where he resided at the time of his death.

At the general election in 1898 he was elected to the Supreme Bench of this state and served as Associate Justice from January 1900 until October [1905], when he voluntarily resigned to resume the practice of law and was engaged in active practice when he was stricken by the illness that resulted in his untimely death.

He became a resident of this state early in its history and during his long residence and useful life occupied many high positions of trust and honor, with distinction and credit to himself and strict fidelity to all concerned. He was an intellectual and highly gifted man, an eminent lawyer and jurist, forceful and aggressive at the bar, calm and deliberate on the bench, persistent and insistent in his contentions, yet above all an unyielding respecter of truth and a lover of justice, and his elevation to the Supreme Bench was a fitting tribute to his character and attainments.

His official professional and private life was marked by such courageousness of action, fearless-

ness in the expression and defense of his convictions, and loyalty to friends and the cause that he expounded, as won the love of his friends and the admiration of those whom he opposed. Such a man necessarily exerts a strong influence upon his surroundings, and always the life of such a man is a useful one. The death of such a man cannot but bring great loss to his state and the community in which he lived and great sorrow to his associates as well as to near friends and the members of his family.

In every position in which he served, whether by appointment or chosen thereto by the people, he fully met all requirements. He never disappointed his friends nor betrayed the confidence reposed in him. His integrity and sincerity of purpose no one ever questioned. He enjoyed the unbounded confidence of all who knew him.

While loyal and devoted in his personal friendships, he never allowed them in matters of importance to override his judgment and sense of duty. When confronted by difficult problems, his strong common sense and intuition to deal justly and his quick sense of justice always enabled him to correctly solve them. His example in public and private life was beneficial and helpful to all who knew or came in contact with him. In his untimely death this state lost one of its most honorable, useful, and best beloved citizens. It is therefore fitting that we pay tribute to his memory and place in the minutes of the proceedings of this court an enduring record of the high esteem in which he was held.

We respectfully submit the foregoing brief and imperfect statement of the life and virtues of our deceased brother and friend as an expression of the high esteem in which we held him in life, the regret we felt at his death, and the honor in which we hold his memory, and ask that the same be spread upon the records of this court.

Lafayette French
John D. O'Brien
Henry A. Morgan
Howard H. Dunn
Frank E. Putnam,
Committee

Hon. Lafayette French then addressed the court and said:

When these proceedings are at an end, the record of our deceased brother is closed. I wish before that record is closed to pay a brief tribute to my friend.

We met for the first time nearly thirty-six years ago at the first judicial convention held to nominate a candidate for judge of the Tenth Judicial District. We were delegates from our respective counties. Our brother had been in practice in Wisconsin and this state five or six years. I had just started in my practice. He was at that time a young lawyer of great promise. He had high ideals of his profession. With him the practice of law was a profession, not a trade. He possessed a fine form, a strong, well-modulated voice, a rich vocabulary. He had heard Ryan and Carpenter and had become inspired by the latter and courted the graces of the orator. He was fond of books; he read much, and his marvelous memory enabled him to remember what he read that was worth retaining. It was said of William Pinckney that he never read a fine sentence from any author without committing it to memory. When a young man, this could be truthfully said of our friend. His fund of anecdotes, general information, and keen wit lent a peculiar charm to his conversation. There was scarcely a subject on which he conversed that he could not illustrate or adorn by a quotation from the poets or the classics. He fully realized as Mr. Wirt once said, "that a mere bookworm is a miserable driveller, and a mere genius a thing of gossamer fit only for the winds to sport with." He was not a book-worm, nor did he rely upon his genius. He read much, both in his profession and general literature. He had the habit of not only reading but thinking and observing. One possessed of such varied gifts, with sound judgment, long experience in his profession, coupled with a strong sense of justice, could

not fail to be other than a great judge. A great judge should have his sense of equity and justice attuned to the living humanity of today. To this rule our brother tried to adhere.

I have been told by the young lawyers that they were inspired while he was on the bench by his sympathetic courtesy. But his temperament was rather forensic than judicial. His fearless and aggressive personality had full scope in the trial of causes. It was there that he showed to the greatest advantage.

For a quarter of a century I have been associated with him or on the opposite side in the trial of many important cases, and I now repeat what I have often said when he was living, that in my judgment he was one of the strongest and best *nisi prius* lawyers in the state. When he believed that his client had suffered some great wrong through fraud perpetrated upon him or wrongful oppression, he arose to his greatest height and displayed the consummate ability of the advocate.

The spirit of commercialism never appealed to him. He preferred to commune with the great authors rather than converse with Captains of Industry. Nothing was more abhorrent to him than to witness the spirit of greed and commercialism take hold upon the members of his profession like creeping paralysis. He lived and toiled for his family, the success of his clients, and to gain an entrance into the front ranks of his profession but was absolutely indifferent to retainers and fees.

He had his faults, but he would not have been human without them. He did not wear his heart upon his sleeve. He occasionally excited enmity, but it was not necessarily to his discredit. He attracted troops of friends who are bound to him by hooks of steel. If at times a sturdy fighter, yet toward those whom he respected and loved he possessed the affections of a brother. He possessed a religious nature, but he judged religion by its duties rather than by its dogmas, and he was the most tolerant of men in matters of conscience. A devoted husband, a kind father, a good citizen—kind and sympathetic to the poor and needy—he leaves behind him not only the members of his own family but a host of friends to mourn his loss.

I was associated with him and his partner in the last case he ever tried. He possessed an intense interest in its results. His whole being was aroused because he believed that a young life had been needlessly and thoughtlessly crushed out. During the trial of this case I noticed that he was not what he had been, and "that the glow which in his spirit dwelt was fluttering fast and low." A few days afterwards I went to Albert Lea to attend an adjourned term of court. I met him in the corridor of the hotel in the early morning waiting for me. He seemed to have a premonition of what was to befall him. He informed me that he was going that day to St. Paul to be examined by an eminent physician of that city. At the noon recess, as I entered the hotel, he came up to me and affectionately put his arm around me and said, "I want you to take lunch with me at my table. Harry (referring to his partner) will be with us also, and it may be the last time we will lunch together." His words were prophetic. It was the last time we dined together. Within a few weeks after he left us his great intellect went into an eclipse, which finally terminated in his death. While at the table I tried to divert his attention from himself, but he seemed to be conscious that the end was near. During the conversation he quoted from Swinburne:

> That no life lives forever;
> That dead men rise up never;
> That even the weariest river,
> Winds somewhere safe to sea.

Let us hope that our friend and brother has at last found rest in the love of our Heavenly Father.

John D. O'Brien, Esq., then addressed the court and said:

I had intended to say nothing further than was writ down by my duty in making the report and memorial that has been presented to your Honors, but it has been thought fitting because of my personal relations to Judge Lovely that I should say a word.

It is so difficult on such an occasion to say the right thing, difficult to express a feeling instead of an idea—and feeling must be predominant at this time.

Judge Lovely always reminded me of the best traditions of Rufus Choate. There was something about him—the swarthy complexion, the flaming eye, the impassioned utterance, his fondness for the arena in the trial of jury cases, his success in the management

of jury cases—that always reminded me of what I have read of Rufus Choate; and there was with it all that further characteristic, a mordant wit that he brought into effective play in the trial of his cases.

How can we better eulogize Judge Lovely than by saying that he was a worthy lawyer? That meed of praise nobody can deny him. Does that not sum up everything that can be said to a man's honor? Does it not fulfil the highest eulogy that any of us could expect to have spoken over our grave?—a "worthy lawyer" engaged all his life in the administration of justice. Justice is a divine attribute. In the administration of justice man is in a certain measure, at any rate, attempting to approach the divine ideal, and to say that a man was a worthy lawyer, that he was a priest in the temple of justice honestly and fairly engaged in the administration of justice is the highest eulogy that can be paid to any human being.

It is one of the ironies of life that in literature, tradition, and public sentiment, the lawyer has been pictured as greedy, self-seeking, avaricious, cunning, indulging in selfish subtleties for his own purpose. Anybody who has a slight acquaintance with the profession must know that the contrary is the case, that the very heart of the profession consists in its unselfishness, its devotion to ideals, its giving of himself for the service of others, and that there is no occupation in the world that touches humanity at so many different points as the profession of the law, that it is applied sociology, that there is no relation of life where the lawyer's view of the science of life does not become important. When a lawyer performs functions of this sort in society, he must be an idealist, and such a man was Judge Lovely.

As has been intimated by Mr. French in the address to which we have just listened, Judge Lovely was not what in the parlance of the day is called a business lawyer. He was a business lawyer in the sense that every lawyer must be a business lawyer, because it is with the business of life, as I have said, that the lawyer has to do, but in the modern sense of commercialism Judge Lovely was not a business lawyer. His was not the character, his was not the disposition that could be made a mere panderer in the train of wealth or power. He was a business lawyer to the extent only that in this larger sense he took the business of mankind, the affairs of men and women and of society, and whatever was best in the ideals of men into his scheme of thought and action.

But the thing I think that, perhaps more than anything else, attracted people to Judge Lovely was his humanity. We were made to feel at once that he was one of ourselves. He was not removed into an atmosphere of cold, impersonal intellectuality. His emotions we recognized as being ours. His strong likes and dislikes made him very human, and we loved him, and so he came nearer to men's hearts perhaps than he did to their intellects. When we come to die we shall be pleased if we can realize that in our lives we came near to men's hearts, and that after all is the attainment we should seek in life—to try to get nearer the hearts of men, nearer their emotions, nearer their best instincts. Judge Lovely was a highly attuned man; he could not take things indifferently; everything affected him one way or the other and affected him deeply. He was fond of men's approval and loved to think that his actions merited the approbation of his fellowmen; he was much cast down by criticism. The same impulses that led him to hope and wish for approval led him to shrink from criticism, and in both his intense nature made him very often magnify the situation, which was not always to his peace of mind.

I honored him in life; I regret him in death. He died at an untimely age. He was at an age when his powers should have been at their very highest, but for many years before Judge Lovely died I often thought that he had not a long period of life before him. He seemed like a man who was burning himself out by the very intensity of his feelings and emotions, often upon matters more sluggish men would consider of slight importance; the very tenseness with which he pulled the cord of life I felt sure would result in its being snapped before the normal period was reached. He died when he had reached the very pinnacle of his profession. It is idle to moralize over these things, and I shall not attempt it but lay my humble tribute of admiration and grief before the court in memory of my friend.

Hon. Henry A. Morgan then addressed the court and said:

I apprehend that it is perhaps more difficult for me to express my reverance and high regard for Judge Lovely than any person present and perhaps than any person outside of his immediate family. I desire to say a word at this time simply to pay tribute to a man whom I always admired.

I entered his office twenty-eight years ago, when Judge Lovely and my late brother, D. F. Morgan, constituted what was then considered one of the strong law firms of Minnesota. I learned to know him, and he said to his dying day that I was one of the few men that he had been associated with for any great length of time that he never had any friction with. In many ways the Judge was a man moved by strong impulses. He had as big a heart as ever grew in the human body.

We never had a word during all of our twenty-eight years of association, simply because we knew each other, we respected each other, and acted together and acted for the interest of the clients and interest of the public. That seems to me to be the highest aim that an attorney can gain—to be honest, to be truthful, and to be fair, and he always had that. He could look straight through an individual, determine almost intuitively or instinctively whether a man was deceiving him or wanted to deceive somebody else.

He was a man that didn't look for a retainer, didn't say you have got to lay down so much money here or so much money there. He sympathized with the unfortunate and oftentimes to his financial loss.

He was not a politician; he didn't have the faculty of making his way in politics. I don't think that his greatest achievements were on the bench. I think that he made his mark always as a trial lawyer. He was an upright judge, an intelligent judge, and hard worker; but it was harder for him to work on the bench, to write his opinions, than to try cases. The writing of opinions to be printed in the books and laid down as the law is one thing; to try a case and try it according to the facts and according to the interests of justice is another thing. As a trial lawyer I don't believe that he has had a peer in this state in many years. During the twenty-five or thirty years that I have known him, I admired him as a man. He was always honest, truthful, and had no patience with any person who undertook or attempted to dodge a fair question or dodge the truth.

He was stricken at a time when he was in the last case he tried. I have a very strong recollection of having tried on the opposite side the next to the last case that he tried. He had others associated with him in that case, but he summed up the case magnificently, and it is idle to say that he got a verdict. When he had finished his argument in that case he was practically stricken, in my judgment. It wasn't a case that called forth any great amount of energy; it was fought and tried as earnest suits are tried, but he was very much exhausted. Later on, and within a few days after that, he was stricken as your Honors well know and never recovered his ability to transact business. I met him a number of times. I did visit him quite often immediately after he had the shock, but it became more painful each time, and I prefer and always have preferred to remember my friends as I knew them at their best, so I didn't see him very often in the later days of his illness.

I only speak now for the purpose of expressing the sincere regret that I have, the pain that I feel in the loss of our brother, Judge Lovely. Having gotten the greater share of my legal training from him and knowing all of his moods and temper, of course there is nobody that can more truthfully, conscientiously, and earnestly pay tribute to him than I can; and my sentiments are expressed in the resolutions that were adopted by our local bar association, of which he has been a member during all of the time he has lived in Albert Lea. In closing I want to say that memorial embodies my sincere, honest, conscientious feeling, and disposition.

In behalf of the Court Associate Justice Brown then said:

The court is in full accord with the sentiments expressed in your memorial and with the eloquent tribute paid the life and character of Judge Lovely.

It may be truthfully said of Judge Lovely that he was a lawyer of eminent ability with few, if any, superiors in the art of conducting litigation either before court or jury. His keen penetrating observation, comprehensive and quick conception, thorough knowledge of human nature, and complete command of the language prepared him in a degree approaching perfection for those scenes of intellectual and fo-

rensic exertion in which the greater part of his life was spent. His natural genius always accompanied and never failed him in an emergency. As a practitioner he was direct and honest, aggressive and fearless, tactful, prompt in meeting unexpected situations with which the lawyer is often confronted, bold and insistent in the presentation of his client's cause, and feared an encounter with none of his brethren at the bar. He abhorred shams and sophistries, believed with Lord Brougham that law is "the staff of honesty and the shield of innocence," and the guiding star of his life work was truth, almighty and everlasting. One of the prominent features of his character was his earnest sympathy for persons in distress. His whole life was embellished by commendable yet unostentatious acts of benevolence and kindness. This characteristic naturally made him averse to espousing the cause of the rich and powerful; though he entertained toward them no ill will, his kindly sympathetic nature made it to him an odious task to employ the powers of his eloquence against the defenseless and oppressed. His long record at the bar finds him with few exceptions on the side of those to whom his kindness of heart never permitted a deaf ear. Yet he did not regard himself as a mere agent of his client, whether rich or poor, to gain a verdict or favorable decision at all hazards, but with a knowledge of what was due to himself and to his honorable profession, his efforts were tempered by considerations affecting his character as a man and lawyer and also by considerations affecting the orderly administration of justice along the lines of truth and equality before the law. It may well be said of him, as he spoke when a member of this court, of the late Senator Davis, "He may not have been upon the right side of every cause he advocated, but he developed in his advocacy of every cause transparent candor, acknowledged respect for correct principles, and enforced his views in behalf of his contentions upon the plane of exalted sentiment, with genuine love for truth and sturdy hate of wrong."

He served as a member of this court with distinguished ability. In the discharge of his duties he was calm, deliberate, thorough, and his opinions, found in volumes 79 to 96 of our reports, furnish abundant testimony of his character and worth as a judge and jurist. He brought with him here no previous judicial experience but was endowed by nature with a sound discriminating mind, possessed a wide knowledge of the fundamental rules and principles of law, which together with his long experience at the bar enabled him readily to adapt himself to his new surroundings. He believed that justice is the foundation of liberty. Not that liberty or freedom of action which justifies the doing of those things our inclinations may prompt but that liberty which permits the doing of those things the law, enacted for all, sanctions and approves. And he always insisted, and on broad grounds, that it was best preserved and protected by an administration of the law on the basis of truth and substantial justice, wholly divorced from technicalities, or what the late Justice Mitchell would term lawyer's quibbles.

His elevation to this bench was a fitting tribute to his character and attainments, his retirement therefrom, not for unfitness or unfaithfulness to duty, an occasion of sincere regret to all his friends: "Your memorial will be spread upon the records of the court for today, there to remain in testimony of his high character as a citizen, lawyer and jurist." [103 Minn. xvii]

Wallace B. Douglas

1852–1930

Associate Justice, 1904–1905

On the morning of February 7, 1931, the court being assembled at the state capitol, Chief Justice Samuel B. Wilson called upon Morris B. Mitchell, vice president of the Minnesota State Bar Association.

Mr. Mitchell then said:

On December 9, 1930, Honorable Wallace Barton Douglas, formerly associate justice of this court, departed this life at Ferndale, Washington. The Minnesota State Bar Association, in appreciation of the distinguished public career of Judge Douglas, has appointed a committee to prepare a memorial to his life and public service and to present the same to the court, with the request that it be made part of the permanent records of the court. With Your Honors' permission, Senator F. H. Peterson of Moorhead, a member of the committee, will read the memorial.

Senator Peterson then said:

In the absence of Honorable Carroll A. Nye, one of the judges of the seventh judicial district . . . I have been asked to read the following tribute prepared by the committee of which he is chairman:

Wallace Barton Douglas was born on a farm near Leyden, New York, September 21, 1852. His parents were Asahel M. and Alma E. (Miller) Douglas. The former was of Scotch and the latter of Holland descent. The father was descended from the Clan Douglas in Scotland, his direct ancestors Sir William Douglas and wife, who was a Miss Ringstead, having migrated from Scotland to New England in 1640. One at least of their descendants served in the Continental Army in the Revolutionary War. Another scion of the family was the well known Stephen A. Douglas of Illinois.

There were three children in the Asahel Douglas family: Cordelia, who died in childhood, Wallace Barton, and his twin brother, William A., who died several years ago. The family removed from New York to Momence, Illinois, in 1866. The father died three years later; the mother lived for many years thereafter.

Wallace was educated in the common schools of New York and Illinois. As a youth he worked as assistant agent of the railroad company at Momence, then spent one year in study at Cazenovia Seminary in New York. Returning to his home he obtained employment for another year at the local bank, and with the money so earned he entered the law department of the University of Michigan and was graduated there from in 1875 with the LL.B. degree. He was admitted to the bar and began to practice law in Chicago the same year.

In 1883 he removed to Minnesota and settled at Moorhead, where he continued the practice of his profession. He served there as city attorney of Moorhead, member of the board of education, and county attorney of Clay county. He was elected to the house of representatives of Minnesota and served in the legislatures of 1895 and 1897. He was elected to the office of attorney general of Minnesota in the fall of 1898 and was re-elected in 1900 and 1902. He resigned this position March 31, 1904, and on the same day was appointed associate justice of the supreme court by Governor Van Sant and served in that capacity until January 1, 1905. He then retired to private life and practiced his profession in St. Paul as the head of the firm of Douglas, Kennedy & Kennedy.

He died December 9, 1930, at his farm at Ferndale, Washington, where he had gone to recuperate his health. His body rests in the cemetery at Moorhead, the scene of his early struggles and victories.

Judge Douglas was married May 19, 1881, to Miss Ella M. Smith of Illinois, and of the children born to them two are still surviving—Harold B. Douglas, who is engaged in dairy farming near Seattle, Washington, and Lila L. (Douglas) Tousley of Colorado, Texas.

The public career of Wallace Barton Douglas was a distinguished one. In speaking of him nothing need be suppressed or withheld. His life is an open book, clear, upright, and free from the breath of scandal. His honor and integrity have always remained unquestioned. He was fearless and devoted to the duties of his position. There came before him in his capacity as attorney general many important questions of public policy, and in dealing with them he did not shrink from taking the stand that he concluded was for the best interests of the state although he knew that he thereby might incur the determined opposition of a large and powerful group of people who would be interested in forcing him into retirement. No question of policy or personal popularity ever caused him to make a compromise with what he considered an evil to the state.

As a lawyer he reached the goal of his ambition when he became a member of this court. His long and varied experience at the bar and in public life, his mental equipment, his broad knowledge of the law, and his preeminent love of justice and fair play marked out his course for a long and useful career in this court; but that opportunity for useful service was prevented by the shifting sands of political upheaval, and he was retired at the end of the year.

The work done by him however in that period was of a high order. The opinions written by him are models of judicial literature—terse, clear, comprehensive, and full of promise of what the author might do in the future.

His private practice covered a large field. Business men and those needing legal assistance hastened to avail themselves of the services of this man, and he maintained until his death the high standards of practice with which he had begun his work. He was fair and just with his clients, the public, and the courts, whose respect and confidence he held in large measure. He was a tower of strength for those whom he represented.

Judge Douglas was a Master Mason, and his religious views were in accord with the doctrines of the Unitarian Church.

His family and home life were beautiful. He was simple in his tastes and habits, sociable and friendly by nature, blessed with a life companion of rare charm and character and with children who responded freely to their parents' thoughts and desires, and this rendered his home life almost ideal.

Judge Douglas was an ardent lover of nature and of the great out-of-doors. He served for 20 years as a member of the state forestry board, and it was largely through his personal efforts that the beauty spot known as Itasca State Park escaped the woodman's axe and was set apart and preserved for this and future generations. One of the principal buildings in that park has been named Douglas Lodge in his honor. He was one of the first and strongest advocates of laws to protect the wild life of the state and assisted in drafting the first statute for its protection.

Edward Florance of Humboldt, Minnesota, a comrade of the woods and streams, wrote his tribute to this phase of our friend's life, in which I am sure we all can join:

His spirit roams the woods today
Where tall pines moan for the heart that's still;
With oak and alder and birches gray,
He sleeps tonight on a wind swept hill.

Itasca, could thy wooded hills
And waters read the human heart
And lend thy tongue to one that thrills
To this, that was of him a part,

I'd voice the charm of thing he knew
And put such meaning in each word
That when its message spoke to you
You'd think it was his voice you heard.

But though imperfect to express
His worth to me; his gifts to you;
I know he'll thank me none the less
For any verse that I can do.

And now I thank thee, noble friend,
That I can miss thee unto tears
And bless the memories that bend
To comradeship of other years.
[Unpublished]

Carroll A. Nye, Chairman
F. H. Peterson
Thomas D. O'Brien
James D. Shearer
Henry N. Benson
Frank E. McAllister
Asa G. Briggs
John P. Kennedy
George W. Peterson

The following tribute, prepared by Honorable Thomas D. O'Brien, was read by McNeil V. Seymour, Esq.:

Wallace B. Douglas was a man who served the public well in many important positions and at the same time retained the simplicity and gentleness of a sincere and kindly disposition. As attorney general of the state he conducted the very important litigation arising in connection with the organization of the Northern Securities Company and met in opposition some of the leading lawyers of the United States. Naturally, litigation of that magnitude took on many different aspects, but ultimately the fundamental position taken by the attorney general of Minnesota was sustained. As associate justice of this court, he wrote many able and important opinions, which were characterized by clearness and brevity.

He loved nature and delighted in the beauty of the forests and lakes of this state. Douglas Lodge on Lake Itasca, filled with historical associations, will long remain a monument to his appreciation of one of Minnesota's beauty spots.

Justice Douglas was an unusually able lawyer, whose high integrity and honest manliness fitted him to adorn the bar. When he left the bench in 1905 he at once secured with his associates a lucrative and credible practice and continued until his death to be an honored citizen of the city of St. Paul, where his talents, coupled with his unassuming kindliness and good will to all the members of his profession, gave him their respect and affection.

Honorable James D. Shearer then said:

It is fitting and proper that the passing of one who has filled two such important positions in the state as attorney general and supreme court justice should move his associated and friends to pause in the day's work of this busy life to pay tribute to his life and services. It is not to be expected that anyone in this world so impresses himself and his personality and characteristics upon others that even his intimate daily associates can justly and completely evaluate his life and services after he is gone. This is because we are all many-sided, and while glimpses of all these sides of our nature may occasionally be seen by intimates, some of them are never revealed to anyone outside of his own immediate family, for there are few who wear their hearts on their sleeves.

So on occasions like this, one cannot hope to do more than present some small part of that kaleidoscopic thing that we call life and character.

I was not one of Judge Douglas' intimate personal friends; therefore my impressions of him must be given as to certain natural qualities of mind and heart, leaving to others those more public, outward, and acquired qualities manifested in his public career.

Wallace B. Douglas was of Scotch ancestry. He had strongly the racial characteristics of that lineage, some of which are industry, frugality, common sense, a mind of his own, and a strong sense of duty.

I had occasions to meet Judge Douglas chiefly while he was attorney general and during legislative sessions. He was reticent and reserved on those occasions—I had to do most of the talking. He was a good listener. One felt during the interview that the interests of the state were being well looked after. Sometimes he had a peculiar way of looking you intently in the eye, while his eyes seemed to grow smaller and smaller. That to me was his signal that he did not agree.

Some might think that Wallace B. Douglas was not what we know as brilliant. How few are. And how much more useful in the world are those who are not. Brilliance is largely for show and is neither for strength nor permanence. Iron, steel, and copper are more important and useful than diamonds.

I asked a lawyer friend who practiced law with Mr. Douglas for years before his public career what was his outstanding characteristic. He answered, "Independence."

It would have been much easier to concur than to dissent, as he did, in the case of *State ex rel. Frank A. Day v. Peter E. Hanson*, 93 Minn. 178, where the question involved was the right and duty of the secretary of state to place on the election ballot after the name of Calvin L. Brown, as a candidate for associate justice of the supreme court, the party designations "Republican–Democrat"—since he had been renominated for that office by both parties. The majority opinion by Special Judge Brill of St. Paul, concurred in by Special Judge Brooks of Minneapolis (Judges Brown, Lovely, and Lewis all being candidates and not sitting), granted the writ, but Justice Douglas was joined by Special Judge Cant of Duluth in a dissenting opinion. Notwithstanding an associate on the bench would have been greatly benefited by the granting of the writ and the question was not one of substantive law but merely construction of a transitory statute, he followed the gleam. This was an evidence of independence of thought, where independence might have cost him the friendship of associates on the bench or at least have been embarrassing.

During his short period of service on the supreme bench Judge Douglas wrote the decisions in 51 cases. It may have been entirely without significance that, of these 51 decisions he wrote, 12 were reversals, and during the nine months that he served he wrote six dissenting opinions. Independence requires courage. And it requires less courage to go with the crowd than to follow one's own conscience or convictions. One cannot hope to be right all the time in this world, but it must be true that one is doing his best when he does not compromise with his convictions. And the record tends to show that Judge Douglas was a man of strong convictions and was not afraid to stand alone.

There are few prosecuting officers, even in this age of enlightened jurisprudence, who can and do, from the beginning to the end of a criminal trial, maintain a just poise between their duty to protect the innocent and their duty to punish the guilty—to be dispassionate and compassionate at the same time. Yet we are told by county attorneys that Attorney General Douglas, assisting them in such cases, seemed always able to maintain that attitude.

A former official of the supreme court who saw much of him officially and in a friendly way had this to say: "I think Justice Douglas' most noticeable characteristics were his kindliness and consideration for others. He was always a student and somewhat reserved—almost shy at times, and while for the most part his attitude and demeanor were serious and earnest, he had a sly vein of humor and knew the value of a smile."

On page 77 of vol. 94, Minnesota Reports, Justice Douglas had, in writing the opinion of the court, reversed the lower court's decision and granted a new trial. Upon reargument he said: "A re-examination of this case upon reargument convinces us that the court misapprehended the force and effect of the instruction that was the basis of reversal in the decision heretofore filed." It takes a deal of courage to make so frank an avowal.

The pearl of great price in the Anglo Saxon system of government is justice between men. If that be accomplished, then is our system secure.

How fortunate as a people are we when our judges endeavor to dispense that even-handed justice enjoined by Holy Writ: "Hear the causes between your brethren, and judge righteously between every man and his brother, and the stranger that is with him." [Deuteronomy, 1.16]

Attorney General Henry N. Benson then said:

I deem it a great privilege to have had the personal acquaintance of the late Judge Wallace B. Douglas over a long period of time. I knew him first as a practitioner at the bar and later and more intimately as attorney general of this state and as an associate justice of this court.

He was elected attorney general in 1898 and assumed office in January following. He was re-elected attorney general in 1900 and in 1902 and served in that office until the 31st day of March 1904, on which date he was appointed an associate justice of this court by the then governor, the Honorable Samuel R. Van Sant.

Mr. Douglas was a successful lawyer in the best sense of those words. He enjoyed and merited the confidence and the respect of the courts before which he practiced as well as the members of the bar with whom he practiced. His home was at Moorhead, Minnesota. My acquaintance with him prior to his becoming attorney general was not intimate, but his close associates in the practice of law speak in the highest terms of his personal and professional qualities. After he assumed the office of attorney general I had occasion to confer with him in reference to legal matters in which the people of my section of the state were interested as well as on matters that concerned individual clients. I found him at all times a most friendly, helpful, able, and honest public officer. He was broad-minded, alert, and candid. He was anxious to find the truth and to act in accordance therewith. He brought to the office of attorney general a trained capacity and seasoned experience for the duties of that important office. His long and varied experiences as a practitioner afforded him not merely a helpful background for the solution of legal problems that arose in the conduct of the office of attorney general but also for that which is almost equally important, a full appreciation and understanding of the executive duties that are required in the administration of that office and in the discharge of the manifold duties [which] were many and often extremely difficult. He approached them with a calm, open, and judicial mind. He invited discussion and information upon difficult questions; but having reached a conclusion therein, he was firm and unafraid in his position. He discharged his duties as attorney general with an eye single only to the faithful service of the people of the state. He had a very keen appreciation of the responsibilities of his office. A great many requests for official opinions came to him, and he gave them the most serious consideration. These opinions disclose the breadth and clearness of his legal perception. They speak with unusual commendable clearness. The fact that he discharged his duties well is probably best evidenced by the fact that the people of the state twice re-elected him to that important office.

As attorney general he conducted many and important cases for the state of Minnesota. A considerable number of these cases were of the greatest importance, and the prosecution of the same discloses the personal and professional qualities of Mr. Douglas in a very marked degree.

It might be of interest to call attention to several of these cases, but this is not the occasion; neither will the time permit of an extended discussion of any of them. One of these cases, however, assumed special importance and was of such state-wide and national interest and importance that it may not be amiss to mention the same.

The case in question was a suit brought by the state of Minnesota in the Supreme Court of the United States to restrain the consolidation of two great systems of railway through the Northern Securities Company, which consolidation was deemed to be inimical to the best interests of the people of the state. He was also associate counsel with the attorney general of the state of Washington in a suit brought by that state for a similar purpose. While these cases were pending, a suit was brought by the United States against these companies for a similar purpose, and the litigation was in effect consolidated and finally brought to a successful conclusion by decision of the United States Supreme Court in the case of *Northern Securities Company v. United States,* reported in 193 U.S. Reports 197.

In these and the many other cases that he conducted in behalf of the state he evidenced high personal and professional endowment, sincerity, and steadfastness of purpose. After serving more than five years as attorney general he retired to accept the appointment as associate justice of this court.

He assumed the office of associate justice of this court on April 1, 1904, to succeed Justice Loren W. Collins, who had resigned to become a candidate for governor of the state. Mr. Douglas was succeeded in the office of associate justice by the late Edwin A. Jaggard, who was nominated and elected to that office in the fall of 1904. Since his retirement from this court and almost up to the time of his death, Justice Douglas was engaged in the active practice of law at the city of St. Paul.

I knew him personally during his long experience at the bar, while he was attorney general and an associate justice of this court, and since his retirement from the bench; and during all of that time he was held in the highest esteem by all who knew him for his splendid personal and outstanding professional qualities. His service in these important places and at the bar was actuated by the purest motives, and he exemplified at all times the highest ideals of the legal profession. The elements were so mixed in him that of him it might truthfully be said that he was a lawyer, a jurist, a loyal friend, and a Christian gentleman. His conduct in both private and public life was spotless and above reproach. In the passing of Mr.

Douglas the legal profession had lost an outstanding lawyer and the state one of its valued citizens. I feel that we honor ourselves in presenting to this court this tribute to his memory.

Frank E. McAllister, Esq. then said:

I appear before Your Honors today as a lawyer and as a plain man who loves his friend to pay my tribute of esteem and affection to a former member of this court, the Honorable Wallace B. Douglas, who lately passed away.

I spent the period of my novitiate with Judge Douglas and was associated with him for many years thereafter. It was my good fortune to enjoy his sage counsel and guidance for many years, those years so trying to a young lawyer and to his associates. It was my privilege to know him intimately and to see his fine, noble qualities at first hand. To his inexhaustible patience, his ripe experience, his profound knowledge of the law, and his kindly encouragement I owe whatever legal skill or experience I have ever acquired. He was my pattern and my mentor.

No one knowing Judge Douglas but was struck with his great qualities, his quick analytical perception, his strong logical powers, his tenacious memory, his unflagging devotion to the highest principles and ideals of his beloved profession, his indefatigable zeal, his leonine courage, and above all his kindliness. He often said, with Lincoln: "I have never willingly planted a thorn in any man's breast."

He was one of the most modest of men, devoid of affectation and hypocrisy; he would be the first to decry the use of superlatives or of fulsome praise in his behalf. And so I speak these few words only as truth and justice to his memory, which I revere and honor.

His cheery and sunny temper and flashing humor gave a quaint touch of philosophy to all of his life and acts. In a hard-fought case he would often ease the tension and lighten the strain with a witty anecdote or timely story. He despised sharp practices, trickery, and selfish greed. He was not a loud or noisy lawyer. His court manner was so kind, so winning, and so fair that he was a master cross-examiner who disarmed witnesses and then quietly destroyed their false testimony. His deep, penetrating mind instantly detected fraud, sham, and lying, and he quickly and mercilessly exposed them

in court. His fortitude was admirable. Never a rich man, he bore the "whips and scorns of time" [*Hamlet,* Act III, Sc. 1] with calm and resignation. He loved people and was a brilliant conversationalist. His versatility was astounding; no subject was alien to him.

He never supported an unworthy cause. He would never compromise with principle. He adorned both bench and bar and excelled as both jurist and as advocate. He lent dignity to judicial robes. His decisions in 92, 93, and 94 Minnesota Reports bear eloquent witness to his industry, his deep knowledge of the law, and his mastery of clear statement of it and the ease, accuracy, and comprehensiveness of his grasp of complicated facts. These qualities ever remained with him, and as an advocate he still retained his judicial mien and was detached and dispassionate in his analyses of cases.

His love for justice was the great and abiding passion of his life. In following it he exemplified the fighting heart of the crusader. Yet his life was like his works—simple, sincere, direct.

He loved nature. His hunting trips especially gave him keenest delight. He would recount the searching fire of questions leveled at him on such trips by guides and rough woodsmen, miles in the forests and the interior, upon their nearest and dearest law subject, that of self-defense and his analyses of their involved hypothetical cases, the while extolling their own common-sense solutions. His duties as chairman of the state forestry board carried him to all the forests and ranges of the state, and he rendered yeoman service to the cause of forestry. He was an authority on wildlife, and Itasca Park was the fruition of his dream.

His greatest fight was probably his celebrated attack upon the merger of three great railroads, which merger was planned by the Northern Securities Company and its officers. He was then attorney general of Minnesota. For years he relentlessly waged this battle through to the highest United States courts, performing prodigies of labor personally, later to see the case completed by the federal department of justice and the merger dissolved by a divided United States Supreme Court. Arrayed against him were the wealth, power, and influence of the then Titans of industry. He never wavered in his objectives, and he prevailed.

His record is an enviable one. His viewpoint was always sympathetic, liberal, and broad, and his humanity above all controlled his judgments. His life and achievements well merit this solemn and reverent tribute by this court. When he wrote to me shortly before his death that if anything should happen to him he desired that I should appear and say a few words before this court, I little suspected that his words were prophetic. His end came before I was able to answer his letter. During the last years of his life he sometimes spoke of "feeling tired." Yet he could not bring himself to the idea of retirement until a short time before his death. He did not outlive his professional life long.

In an age of crass materialism his words upon law practice come to me like the voice of another era: "Never turn away a deserving client. Some will be rich and prosperous and will pay well. Others, poorer in goods, may not be able to pay at all. Some, such as the widow and the orphan, can pay you only with their tears and their prayers. These will be the richest of your fees."

His political idealism was upon the same high plane. He often said, with Brutus:

> By heaven, I had rather coin my heart
> And drop my blood for drachmas, than to wring
> From the hard hands of peasants their vile trash
> By any indirection.
> [*Julius Caesar*, Act IV, Sc. 3]

In a nature so gentle, kind, benevolent, and forgiving there was no place for malice or vengeance. He never complained over defeat or betrayal. He spoke of men to praise them, or he spoke not at all.

Our profession has lost a worthy and illustrious member who consecrated himself to the loftiest ideals of truth and justice. Yet his life and deeds live forever in the hearts of those who knew and loved him. His voyage is closed and done, and the objects are won. He left the world better for his having lived. We who remain are poorer for the loss. We mourn the passing of a fine, noble, lovable gentleman whose life was an inspiration to young men, challenging them to "come-up higher."

> After life's fitful fever he sleeps well.
> . . . nothing can touch him further.
> [*Macbeth*, Act, III, Sc. 2]

This court honors itself in honoring such a man. In closing I will quote a poem he loved and often read:

> Under the wide and starry sky,
> Dig the grave and let me lie.
> Glad did I live and gladly die,
>   And I laid me down with a will.

> This be the verse you grave for me:
> *Here he lies where he longed to be;*
> *Home is the sailor, home from sea,*
>   *And the hunter home from the hill.*
> [Robert Louis Stevenson, *Requiem*]

Asa G. Briggs, Esq. then said:

I join in the other tributes to Judge Wallace Barton Douglas given here today and wish to add a brief statement of some of his personal characteristics as I saw them.

I first met Judge Douglas, shortly after he came to St. Paul, as attorney general of the state of Minnesota. We soon came to know each other intimately through membership in a club organized for discussion of questions of the time. This acquaintance grew more intimate, so intimate that I had good opportunity to know his opinions and his character.

During the 30 years of our acquaintance I never heard him utter a mean word or knew that he had done an unworthy thing. His voice was ever raised and his acts were performed in support of what he understood to be right and to confound that which he believed to be wrong. He was a mild-mannered, soft-spoken, sympathetic, kindly, sincere, intellectual man; bluster and boasts were not in him. He was courageous and firm in support of his understanding and convictions.

He was a sportsman; he looked forward with great anticipation to an annual big game hunt in the north woods. He took great pleasure in those hunts and in relating to friends his interesting experiences in connection with them.

He was an intense lover and defender of his country and of his government. He feared for their future welfare. He believed that our people and our nation are seriously menaced because of general disregard of law and order, not in respect to one law or a few laws but because of general disrespect and disregard of all laws. He felt that great newspapers and great men were justifying and advocating disobedience of some laws, thereby leading unreasoning men, who do not distinguish between the gravity of different crimes, to believe that they had the support of what they thought to be a higher class in committing these crimes.

He also knew that the people of our nation are divided into two classes, each of which believes uncompromisingly that its opinions are right and that the opinions of the others are wrong. He knew this difference had been widening and growing more and more bitter and acrimonious for 140 years. He could not see the way out of the serious dilemma in which he believed we are involved. He looked forward hopefully, however, to a time when an unexpected happening would clear the situation and avoid disaster. The situation disturbed him.

This is but an example of the tendency of his mind and his conclusions.

Judge Douglas has gone; his seat at the club is vacant; his voice in discussions will not be heard again; his handshake and a few minutes' friendly talk whenever and wherever he was met will be missed. But the compensations of having known him and associated with him have been many and pleasant.

Our loss is great.

Honorable John P. Kennedy then said:

Mr. Douglas began the practice of law in the city of Chicago. He was very successful there, but close application to professional duties undermined his health. He was advised to change his residence to the western prairies. In 1883 he reluctantly closed his office and came to Moorhead, where his health was restored and further success and distinction awarded him.

As an illustration of the lasting impression that he made, it might be mentioned that some of the clients whom he counseled in Chicago more than 40 years before still sought his services in St. Paul until the end of his career. Also his former clients in the vicinity of Moorhead frequently came to him in St. Paul.

On January 30, 1931, the House of Representatives of Minnesota adopted a resolution of condolence upon his death in which his career was summarized as follows:

The people of Minnesota called him to many positions of great importance, all of which he filled with singular ability and distinction . . .

In his intercourse with his fellowmen he was always kind and friendly and tolerant of the opinions of others. He loved Minnesota and its institutions and contributed liberally of his genius and learning for their advancement. His personal charm and kind friendship will long be cherished by those who enjoyed the pleasure of his acquaintance.

[Journal of the House, p. 5, Friday, January 30, 1931]

He was also highly appreciated by the executive department, which frequently requested his advice. Three governors appointed him to important positions in the state service. He enjoyed the esteem and confidence of his successors in the legal department of the state. He always cherished the kindness and friendship of those who ministered in the courts.

On the 9th day of December 1930, at Ferndale, Washington, in the fullness of years, with his faculties unimpaired, he answered the final summons. With Masonic rites he was consigned to the tomb in the city of Moorhead, where he received the sorrowing tribute of a great concourse of people. As we trace his footsteps we marvel that so much could have been accomplished in a single lifetime.

As these accomplishments are reviewed we believe they will receive the approving acclaim, "Well done, thou good and faithful servant." [Matthew, 25.21]

Honorable George W. Peterson then said:

I esteem it a compliment that Judge Douglas in his declining days expressed a desire that I participate in this memorial. I was hardly aware of such an intimacy. All have friends, but to a few only are intrusted the closest things.

Most worthy lawyers and judges are above mere praise, and simple declaration of a good and useful life held to right standards of preparation, work, and purpose is all sufficient. Such a spirit characterizes this memorial and rightly reflects Judge Douglas.

Speak of me as I am; nothing extenuate,
Nor set down aught in malice
    [*Othello*, Act V, Sc. 2]

is the index of what Judge Douglas would wish in his memorial.

Courtesy always animated his expression. The

stream of his life flowed quietly but deeply. He was simple, sincere, and honest. He restrained any feelings in dignified statement. He welcomed the humblest suitor, was easy of manner, and his presence always provoked respect.

One's background and trial of life and the discipline of life is about the same for all of us, and one's perspective spiritually, intellectually, and judicially are the true countenance of a man, and Judge Douglas had these things in nicely balanced measure. He was a good judge and ever wore the white mantle of this morning's freshly fallen snow. He never shaped his works and ways that "thrift may follow fawning." [*Hamlet*, Act III, Sc. 2]

Judge Douglas, in the fortune of politics, failed to receive the nomination to succeed himself in the Republican convention of 1904. Believing he was entitled to the nomination, I cast my vote in the convention for Judge Douglas. He was defeated by Judge Jaggard, whose popularity was unusual and who had great strength because of his affiliations as a professor of law at the University. Mere defeat is not serious, for one may always rise on stepping stones of his defeated self to better things.

To this court he added the qualities of sympathetic consideration, fine ethics, a right sense of public service, respect for authority, and a good appraisal of our people and the state.

And he could truly say: "I have done the state some service, and they know't." [*Othello*, Act V, Sc. 2]

It properly appears in the remarks of others that Judge Douglas loved trees. It is true it is "only God can make a tree." [Joyce Kilmer, *Trees*] I presently recall the following figure as appropriate. It was said of Lincoln by Edwin Markham:

> And when he fell . . . he went down
> As when a lordly cedar, green with boughs,
> Goes down with a great shout upon the hills,
> And leaves a lonesome place against the sky.
> [Edwin Markham, *Lincoln, the Man of the People*]

James M. Witherow, Esq. then said:

I studied law in Judge Douglas' office and was associated with him in practice for nearly three years—1895 to 1898. Few had a better opportunity for observation of his character and habits than I, and few knew him more intimately.

He exemplified many of the higher and better qualities of both the lawyer and the gentleman. He was kind; he was faithful and honorable to his clients; he was fearless, indifferent to criticism and abuse when he was convinced that he was right. He was hardworking, with a very keen sense of both justice and equity. In the 30 years that I have known him intimately I never knew him to resort to dishonest strategy or chicanery. He was a splendid legal strategist. I have never known a better director of the trial of the lawsuit than he was.

Judge Douglas was a highly moral rather than religious man. He had a sincere appreciation of the province of a Divine Being but disliked exuberant vocalization of platitudes as an expression of religious convictions.

He had remarkable control of his temper and emotions. Never once, even under many annoying, irritating circumstances, did I see him exhibit temper or profanity.

In the "fun side of his life," as he called it, he dearly enjoyed a good horse, a good dog, and a good gun. He loved horse racing and hunting as an exhibition of scientific breeding and physical development, but never once could he be induced to gamble a penny in betting, drinking, or any of the other undesirable practices usually connected with that line of sport. In all his desire for the open and for hunting, no one could persuade him to violate even the spirit of the game laws by hunting out of season or bagging more than the required number.

As a legislator he did a great many things by which the state as a whole has benefited. He helped to arrange the finances on a sound business basis. He was the author and draftsman of the greater portion of our drainage laws, our game and conservation laws. Our laws against monopolies and trusts are also his workmanship. He drafted a distance railroad tariff law for agricultural products that eventually became embodied in the so-called Cashman Law. Always friendly and gentlemanly, he was subservient to no one, constantly maintaining his independence of thought and action both as an individual and as an official.

In his passing this court has lost one of its counselors who always observed the highest ethical standards of the bench in a clear and vigorous exposition of the principles of law and justice as he understood them, with utmost fidelity to the bench in recognition of the canons of his profession not to mislead the court to its prejudice, and at the same time present[ed] the interests of his client with the utmost fidelity and fearlessness—believing all this in the ultimate triumph of right through the maintenance of the highest ideals of both the bench and the bar.

We shall miss him in his kindly sympathies and cheerful example as a friend, and in his high ideals and splendid, fearless qualities as an advocate and counselor.

For these reasons I deem it fitting that this tribute should be entered on the records of the court of which he was a splendid member and example.

Justice Royal A. Stone [for the court] then said:

By a lifetime of professional and public service, most of it spent in Minnesota, Judge Douglas well earned the tribute you pay him this day. You do not overrate his character when you say, concerning him, that "nothing need be suppressed or withheld." He was fearless and devoted to the duties put upon him by any position either of a public or private nature. Truly he was a living epistle, the reading of which by all men need never to have been feared by its author.

Before becoming an associate justice of this court he had, as you well point out, a distinguished career of public service. As usual, public recognition of professional merit followed as the natural consequence and reward of an efficient, thoroughgoing, and always high-minded service to private clients. In his professional activities, both in and out of public office, he exemplified the highest ideals of the American bar. However absorbed in private practice, he never forgot that both as citizen and lawyer it was his duty always by precept and example to support the constitutions and other laws of the land. The Minnesota bar probably has never had within its ranks a more devoted champion of the ideals and objectives of American constitutionalism than Judge Douglas.

His professional accomplishments, great when he became attorney general, were of course enlarged and embellished by his years of strenuous service in that office. His experience there rounded out and so completed, his professional equipment that when he became a member of the supreme court he brought with him unusual qualifications for the place.

If anybody is disposed to question that the unfortunate feature of his service on this bench was its brevity, let him spend even a short time in a studious examination of the opinions of Judge Douglas. He will be struck first by the admirable manner in which they achieve comprehensiveness of consideration with brevity of treatment. He did not resort to that elaboration either of facts or law which so easily becomes tedious supererogation. But on the other hand he did not scant either the facts or law of a case. There was always the most careful consideration not only of the result but also of the manner in which it was reached. He was careful not only to cite the authority but also to assign the reason for the rule announced.

One needs read but a few of his opinions in order to come to the conclusion that in each case the writer had a very clear notion not only of what he was deciding but why. Complying with the traditional rule of the court he of course prepared his own syllabi. They are models of brevity and yet comprehensive indicia of the bases of decision. That is a result frequently difficult of achievement, but so far as possible Judge Douglas did it in each case. To an unusual degree the headnotes of his decisions are accurate and complete digests of the opinion.

There was in him a quiet courage of conviction that, though always tempered by a due and courteous regard for the opinions of others, never permitted him to submit quietly to a result that he considered seriously in error. Deferential in disagreement as in all else, he yet stated his dissenting views fearlessly and clearly, setting forth his reasons in such fashion as to show that he had given the opposing opinion full consideration—both as to fact and law. Not for anyone or any price would he prevaricate with either his own conscience or his own judgment.

The opinions of Judge Douglas have now stood the test of a quarter century's use by the bench and bar. The resulting appraisal of them is such that the all too early termination of his judicial service is now recognized as a distinct loss to the state.

You do well to stress the distinguished line from which he came. If America is great, she owes it largely to the strength and high character of the many and diverse racial sources from which she has drawn her citizens. In Judge Douglas was a typical combination of the best that some of the first families of Scotland and Holland could give. Against such a background of distinguished heredity was a life much affected by near frontier conditions in our own Red River Valley. Their broadening and humanizing influence surely had a fine exemplification in the kindliness of Judge Douglas, a trait always dominant and manifesting itself constantly in his daily walk and conversation. As friend and lawyer, as citizen and public official, and particularly as judge, he endeared himself to all who knew him and made the state and its people debtor to him forever.

To an unusual degree was the life of Wallace Barton Douglas one of duty performed, one of noble example by force of its own intrinsic value a potent factor in building higher and better the fabric of the social, economic, and legal integrity of a state still new. His private life and public services were such as to richly entitle them to the memorial and permanent record you are making on this occasion. The supreme court of Minnesota joins therein and records with you our deep affection for the man and our high personal and professional estimate of the life and services of a departed colleague.

Chief Justice Wilson then said:

My personal recollection of Mr. Justice Douglas is that he was conspicuous for his genteel kindness and consideration of others.

The memorials that have now been presented to the court will be published in our reports. [182 Minn. xxix]

Edwin A. Jaggard

1859–1911
Associate Justice, 1905–1911

On the afternoon of April 4, 1911, in the court room at the State Capitol, James D. Shearer, Esq., president of the Minnesota State Bar Association and chairman of a committee to draft a memorial of Associate Justice Jaggard, addressed the Supreme Court, then in session, and read the following:

Edwin Ames Jaggard was born June 21, 1859, at Altoona, Pennsylvania, and was the son of Clement and Anna Jane (Wright) Jaggard. In 1879 he was graduated from Dickinson College, Carlisle, Pennsylvania. Three years later he secured his degree of Bachelor of Laws from the University of Pennsylvania. He came to Minnesota in 1882 and engaged in active legal practice in the city of St. Paul. In 1898 he was elected a Judge of the District Court of Ramsey county and served one term on that bench. While a district judge in 1904, he was elected an Associate Justice of this Court and was re-elected at the general election held in November 1910, remaining a member of this Court until his death. In 1887 he was chosen to succeed the late Senator Cushman K. Davis as lecturer in the St. Paul Medical College on medical jurisprudence. This college was subsequently merged with the medical department of the University, and he became a member of the faculty of the law department of that institution. He remained an honored and deeply beloved member of this faculty until his death.

He was the author of *Jaggard on Torts*, a recognized authority throughout the country. In recent years he published *Jaggard on Taxation in Minnesota and the Dakotas* and *Jaggard on Taxation in Iowa*. He mastered the intricacies of this technical subject. He was also the author of articles on Malicious Prosecution and false Imprisonment and the Historical

Anomalies in the Law of Libel and Slander.

He was married in 1890 to Anna May Averill, the daughter of General and Mrs. John T. Averill, pioneer residents of Minnesota.

Few judges have been so close to the people. They knew him and loved him as a man. His presence was always a cheer. He was sympathetic and responsive to every human appeal. Endowed with the spirit of unfailing kindness, he was the personification of generosity. He had a genius for companionship. Friendliness was his birthright. A spirit of infinite patience and forbearance tempered his relations with others. He always tried to build—not destroy. He spread the mantle of charity over human failings and shortcomings. Barely has a man so completely entered into the life of this state. He was a welcome guest at every public gathering. In his addresses, he was both humorous and humanly philosophical. He was ardently fond of outdoor sports. His nature craved the outdoor life. This trait in a judge appealed to the hearts of the people. It broadened his vision and gave him a far-reaching perspective.

He was a scholarly author of wide research, an able judge of the closest application. He had a brilliant mind that intuitively turned toward investigation. His method of reasoning was scientific, and his opinions were the result of unflagging industry, whose goal was the complete mastery of every subject.

He had a fatherly interest in the younger members of the bar of this state. Their love and affection for him was wholly responsive.

His character was notably shown in the enjoyment that he had in the companionship of his wife and in his love for children. In his death, the State has lost one of its best beloved and most distinguished citizens, this Court an able Judge.

We move that this brief expression of our sincere regard be spread upon the records of this Court.

>James D. Shearer
>Charles W. Farnham
>Alf. E. Boyesen
>Thomas S. Wood
>John D. Sullivan
>Henry B. Wenzell
>Hugh T. Halbert,
>>Committee

William H. Lightner, Esq., then addressed the Court and said:

In seconding the motion in support of this memorial that pays so generous and well-deserved tribute to the memory of the late Mr. Justice Jaggard, it is hardly necessary to add a word.

It was my good fortune to have known intimately Mr. Justice Jaggard for nearly thirty years. When he made St. Paul his home, he spent some time in the office of the legal firm of which I was a member. As bachelors, we lived together. The friendship commenced upon his coming to Minnesota continued uninterrupted until his death.

He loved the sunshine and the cheerful side of life. He loved his fellow men; he was ever ready to aid them in their troubles, to encourage them in their successes, which he enjoyed with them. He was particularly fortunate in being free from any disposition to criticise the actions of others. Enthusiastic by nature, he applied himself to his legal studies with fervor, he devoted himself assiduously to the interest of his clients and with love for the companionship of men; as he advanced in his profession he made countless friends. Fired by a praiseworthy ambition to succeed in his chosen profession, with a well-educated mind, with a natural fondness for the study of the law, and with enthusiasm supported by untiring energy, it is not surprising that in a comparatively short time he built up a good practice, was chosen District Judge, and while still a young man was elevated by a pronounced vote of the people to the high position that he occupied at the time of his death.

He brought to this bench a disposition to labor to maintain and, if possible, to improve the high standing of the court. He applied himself closely to the arguments and studiously and patiently examined into the law. His opinions in this Court, many of which relate to most important questions, not only evince great learning and ability but also exhibit patient, thorough, and painstaking investigation of authorities and discussion of legal questions. They show forth a broad and developing mind. Mr. Justice Jaggard had but served his apprenticeship upon this bench. Cut down in the prime of his life, it may be confidently asserted that the State has suffered a great loss in being deprived of the great benefits that it would have derived from his ripened mind and his devotion to legal studies.

Howard T. Abbott, Esq., then addressed the Court, and said:

It is indeed fitting and proper that at such a time as this we pause from our labors and daily tasks and gather together, the Bench and the Bar, to pay a last tribute to a just Judge and a sincere friend. I shall not touch upon the legal or judicial ability and qualifications of Judge Jaggard in the few words that I shall say. While I have the greatest admiration for him as a lawyer and a judge, I knew him so much better as a true gentleman and as a sincere friend and companion, that my thoughts more quickly turned, upon hearing of his sudden end, to my own personal loss because of the friendship and association that had existed between us than they did to the loss that the Court and Bar and the State had sustained. Of late years we had come to know each other well. He had been my personal guest upon numerous visits to Duluth and was such last summer upon one of the outings that he was known so much to enjoy, and our plans were tentatively arranged for a similar but longer outing this coming summer. I have had in the last few years the extreme privilege of a very close personal association with him. I have often been favored with his innermost principles and ideals, and I knew him in his deeper personality and thoughts perhaps as well, or better, than many of his older friends. My intimate acquaintance with him was not of such long standing, covering possibly only a period of the last eight or ten years, but that friendship had developed and enlarged greatly as those few years passed, and when his sudden end came and the news thereof reached me, the loss was that of something that was very near and dear to me. The bar of the northern part of the state knew him well and were deeply grieved; they were his friends and he was theirs, and each felt that he had sustained an irreparable loss in his sudden demise.

Judge Jaggard had the inherent qualities to make the thorough gentleman that he was. He had many talents committed to him and consequently more work and engagements to attend to socially, as well as professionally, than one much less endowed. He had accomplishments and refinement of parts by birth, labor, and education. He had the help of parentage, association, environment, and friendships; he had honor and authority; he had many useful talents entrusted to him, and he did not hide them away or squander them for selfish purposes but used them in his daily life, in his work, and in the service of his friends. Often has he, to my knowledge, directed and advised in more than the ordinary ways those who needed it and encouraged many by his wisdom, and particularly was this true and applicable to the younger generation of attorneys. It was his gift to be hospitable, kind, and helpful to all and ever ready to meet friends and strangers with bountiful courtesies. It seemed his joy to cultivate his mind with knowledge, with all worthy accomplishments befitting his condition and qualifying him for honorable thought and action in all walks of life, so that in very much and in all ways he excelled no less in real inward worth than in his genteel exterior appearance. He possessed to a marked extent the two essential qualities characteristic of the true gentleman—courtesy and courage. It is a truism to say that, with these and other resources that he had, his conversation was at all times rich and instructive in no ordinary degree, that it was as pleasing as it was wise, and had all the charms of familiarity with all the treasures of knowledge. No man could be more social in spirit, more democratic in his demeanor with friends or strangers, or more kind or indulgent towards those who approached him. He was much loved by all the youth who came in contact with him, and I speak from personal knowledge when I say that his fondness and affection for children was immeasurable. Fond of conversation he was, and readily and

quietly discoursed upon what was presented by those around him and often astonished them by the treasures that he drew from the mine that they had, unconsciously perhaps, opened up. In conversation he seemed to have no choice or predilection for any one subject rather than another but allowed his mind to be opened at any letter that his friends might choose to turn up and selected from his inexhaustible supply what might be best adapted to the taste of those about him. This was true whether the subject was that of law, medicine, mathematics, music, or the arts.

We will always recall the pleasant and genial smile so symbolical of the humor within and the temperate jocularity that gave infinite zest and effect to what he had to say. By those who knew him best, who enjoyed his society apart from the daily duties, who enjoyed his friendship and his comradeship, it is these qualities and courtesies that will be ever before us.

I had no intimation of his ailment until last summer, when I noticed in the trout streams and on the forest trails his exhaustion and fatigue. I remarked upon it to him once or twice, but he made as little of it as possible and always passed it off as of no consequence. It was, however, apparent to me that he was not in his usual health, and while I was aware of the last trip that he had taken and for what cause, I had no anticipation of its sudden and serious termination. It is hard to have his kind so suddenly removed from earthly activities; the State needs such character and citizenship as his and will need it more and more; his friends will miss his kindly intercourse, but his genial personality and the many fond memories we have of him no time can forget nor distance wear away but will remain with us forever.

Hon. Oscar Hallam then addressed the Court:

We are here to-day to pay a tribute to the memory of a friend and perhaps to draw some lessons from an active and useful life that is closed. There are those who say that such occasions as these are not worth while; and if there were nothing in life to be desired but meat and drink, then this were true; but it is upon such things as these that character is builded and the thoughts of men rise to higher things. There are those, too, who say that we might better spend our time in an endeavor to cheer the living rather than to praise the dead; but after all, I know of no loftier motive to right living than the consciousness that if men live aright their lives will be held in fragrant remembrance after they are dead.

Judge Jaggard will be remembered for many things. He filled official position creditably and well. He will be remembered for that. He instructed young men in the principles of law, and he will be remembered for that. He wrote useful books, and he will be remembered for that. But more than all these, he will be remembered for certain traits of heart and character. Some man in Baltimore said shortly after his death that Judge Jaggard's greatest work was not *Jaggard on Torts* or *Jaggard on Taxation*, nor any other of his numerous intellectual achievements, but Jaggard on Humanity. He knew many people, and he loved to meet them. He had many friends, and he loved to associate with them. He knew how to help people, and he loved to extend his assistance where it would afford help.

Judge Jaggard was a man of singular individuality. His mode of life, his manner of thought and work, his forms of expression, were singularly his own. I remember well the first time I ever heard him speak. It is now nearly twenty years ago. There were other talented men who spoke on that occasion. Of them I simply remember the fact that they spoke. Of him I remember the theme, the treatment of it, and many of the things that he said. I heard him speak many times afterward, and somehow, I knew not just why, I seemed to carry away more of what he said than I had expected I would. He possessed the singular faculty of impressing his thoughts and words in such manner that they would be remembered.

His written decisions were characteristic of the man. Open a volume of the Minnesota Reports to one of his opinions, start to read it in the middle or where you will, and it is likely that before you have read a page you will strike some expression that will make you say: "That sounds like Judge Jaggard." His writings bear the stamp of the writer's own individuality more than anything I have ever read.

When the news of his death came, I was sitting with a regent of the University and with a graduate of its college of law. With one accord they at once stated: There was one of the best beloved teachers that the university has ever had. The men of those classes clung to him, and his memory is entwined in their lives. He had and he exercised an influence beyond that of the mere position in life that he held, beyond that of his intellectual attainments or his intellectual achievements; it was the influence of a lovable character.

His last days among us furnish a beautiful example of Christian fortitude. We who knew him well and met him often did not know that he was suffering pain, and yet we know now that he was.

His life, his character, his example, and his influence were such that we may truly say the world is measurably better that this man has lived.

Hon. Julius Haycraft then addressed the Court:

It is my privilege to have known Judge Jaggard. It is my privilege to have claimed him as a friend, not exactly an intimate friendship such as is caused by daily association yet intimate in the sense of men separated by some distance. It is my privilege to have been one of the young attorneys in this state in whom he manifested a fatherly interest. It is now my privilege to stand before this tribunal, before his associates and his successor, in the presence of the Bar of this state, and participate in his memorial exercises. I join with the authors of his memorial and with the gentlemen who have spoken in their estimate of Judge Jaggard as a jurist, as a scholar, an author, and an orator. Without detracting in the slightest degree from his worth in these accomplishments, yet I shall direct my remarks more particularly and specifically to Judge Jaggard, the man. While his claim to fame as a jurist, as a scholar and author, is pre-eminently of an enduring nature and high degree, still it occurs to me that his greatest claim to fame and to fond remembrances in the hearts of the people is based upon his acts as a man. For he was a man in all the term "man" implies, in all for which it stands. I can pay him no higher tribute, I can accord him no loftier panegyric, than to say of him in this sense he was a man broadminded, large-hearted, charitable, kind, considerate, and lovable, traits that spell greatness in its truest sense. He was such a man as to whom unacquainted children would intuitively go to have him mend their toys or act as arbiter of their disputes, and children are the best judges of human character.

Shortly before last Christmas, he said to a friend in this building that he was happy because he had all his presents arranged for. He was asked how many he remembered with Christmas presents; he replied about three hundred. I offer the statement that no one in this state remembered so many friends with presents on the anniversary of our Saviour's birth. Fishing companions, country hosts on outing trips, neglected children, lawyers, statesmen, employees, and associates—all came within the compass of his great and generous heart.

Judge Jaggard was pre-eminently a child of nature. He loved the brooks and rills, the lakes, the hills, the fields and meadows. He loved to hunt and fish, and, as he was wont to state it, "watch the pussy willows grow." His companions upon these jaunts invariably became his lifelong friends. It is told me that a native fisherman in this state who was careless about the exercise of his franchise, after a fishing expedition one summer with Judge Jaggard, appeared at the polling place at the next election and to the surprise of all called for a ballot. In the booth he was assisted in marking. He said, "Where is Judge Jaggard's name? The name was indicated. He said, "Cross his name and fold the ballot; I do not care to vote for anybody else." It is these traits and these characteristics that warrant any tribute and any honor we may choose to accord our late lamented brother as a man. Give me a man like that who is charitable to all, who is king to his neighbors, loves his friends, forgives his enemies, is true to his family, cherishes his wife, adores his children, worships his God, and I'll pay him tribute though he never held an office.

Judge Jaggard is dead, but his memory lives, lives as lives the name of Mitchell, the name of Flandrau, the name of Davis and other distinguished characters of our profession in this state. And for months and years and decades to come will live the name, the illustrious name, Edwin A. Jaggard.

James Paige, Esq., then addressed the Court, and said:

Edwin A. Jaggard was a lecturer in the College of Law of University for nineteen years and during that time wrote the two well known treatises on Torts and Taxation.

Such in mere outline is the history of the work of Judge Jaggard as a teacher of law. It is a privilege to speak of those attributes of mind and that attractive personality that made him such a charming and successful teacher. As a student of law he approached it from its philosophical and analytical side, and the resolving of questions back to their elementary principles was his delight. He loved to trace the law's growth, its tendency, and sometimes to utter a prophetic word. He had a vivid and bright imagination, enabling him to make truths living and real to the student's mind. To these mental gifts was added that graciousness of manner and charming personality with its broad human sympathy that brought a smile from the class as he entered the room and made his lectures full of humor and incident. To one in the corridor, rippling laughter over the transom might suggest an entertainment, but within the lecture room, stories, touches of satire, and pungent criticism were being used to fasten difficult points in the student's mind. This was Judged Jaggard's method of keeping the attention of the student—by the force of his personality—using his charm as an individual to compel attention upon matters difficult of comprehension or possibly dreary and tiresome. He thought it worth while to put himself into his lectures, and it was worth while. His inextinguishable youth made him a young man among young men and established a comradeship, drawing students in clusters around him before and after his lectures. The work of his lectureship he regarded as serious, though his lectures were thus embellished with literary allusions and were brilliant with humor and satire. He never treated his work with indifference and always arranged it on the bench and at the bar so as to meet his obligations to the bar of the state as a legal educator. His scholarship, his brilliancy, and his genial and loving personality insure him a living memory in the mind of alumni and faculty.

Charles W. Farnham, Esq., Secretary of the Minnesota State Bar Association, then addressed the Court, and said:

Mr. Kay Todd, of the Ramsey County Bar, having been called from the city, has asked me to present his tribute, the testimonial of a protégé, pupil, and friend.

With a sense of the deepest personal bereavement, I bear this testimony of my admiration and love for Edwin A. Jaggard. It was my great privilege to come under the influence of this wonderful man at a period when impressions are vivid and lasting and the heart is warmed with the springs of youth. That acquaintance so formed continued for more than a dozen years, growing more intimate with the years. It was as a student in the University Law School that this friendship began.

As a lecturer, Judge Jaggard peculiarly impressed and held the students, both by the charming and interesting manner of the presentation of his subjects and by a certain broad, human sympathy that immediately placed every man in his classes on a plane of equality with their lecturer and cemented a feeling of fraternity and comradeship that put every man upon his honor and drew from him the best that was in him both as student and man. Every one whose privilege it has been to be a student in any of Judge Jaggard's classes has immediately become his warm personal friend and admirer, his follower in future years.

Instances can be multiplied without number of the material assistance extended by Judge Jaggard to ambitious and deserving young men in their efforts as students and later in the more serious pursuits of life. No such young man ever applied for counsel that was not graciously and freely given or for assistance that was not extended with a generous hand. He was invariably tolerant, broad, and sympathetic, and his fine heart qualities won their devotion, his mental attainments and abilities as a jurist their admiration.

For fifteen years or more, students of Judge Jaggard in the Law School of the University of Minnesota have gone forth in the various avenues of life and have assumed positions at the bar and on the bench and in other pursuits; and time and again these men who have passed out from that influence have returned to the ever ready, cheerful adviser and comforter to renew the happy fellowship of their student years.

When in the fullness of time, Judge Jaggard was called from the bar to the bench, he became as judge what he had been as a law lecturer—the friend of the young man. By those means so well known to the Judge, with suggestions and advice he constantly assisted the struggling young practitioner before him. No young man ever came into Judge Jaggard's court, especially when opposed by a seasoned, expert practitioner, without feeling that, in so far as it lay within the proper power of the Court to do so, in the presentation of his matter it should be upon equality with his more expert opponent. He had the same indescribably charming manner in the court room as in the lecture room, and without loss of dignity, it at once created the atmosphere of human kinship and tolerance that so distinguished him at all times and under all circumstances. These attributes were not alone discernible by those who had the privilege of being thrown into close contact with him as students or members of his own profession but extended in an all-embracing degree to laymen as well. This beautiful side of Judge Jaggard's character was accentuated by the fact that as a Justice of this high Court and a recognized international authority on several subjects of his chosen science, he remained as simple, unaffected, and sincere in his manners, tastes, and habits as in the early days of his own struggling professional career. His students were still his "boys," even though they occupied judicial or other eminent positions and as such were greeted, treated, and loved by him. Other men may have had as wide a fame in their profession or inspired the love of their own circle of friends, but few ever had a wider, deeper, or more genuine affection in the hearts of so many men in the legal profession as had Judge Jaggard, and when the news of his unexpected and untimely death flashed to his home state, there has rarely been more genuine or more intense sorrow experienced by so many men of all walks in life.

It has fallen to the lot of few men to so influence those upon whose shoulders, in time, must fall the more serious responsibilities of the commonwealth.

In the death of this eminent scholar and jurist, the State has lost a valued servant, but he has left a rich heritage, not only by reason of his labors on the bench but in the full influence of his life, especially as a guide and coworker, a helper, and an inspiration to the younger members of the bar not only as an instructor in the law but as a preceptor and as a brother in the lessons and struggles of life.

Hon. John W. Willis then addressed the Court:

I am sure that no dissent from the eulogium that has been pronounced upon Edwin Ames Jaggard will ever be heard. The expressions of the memorial are just and could not well be more than adequate because of the dignity, the importance, and the amplitude of the subject to which they are addressed. Fortunate as was the State of Minnesota in acquiring Jaggard as a citizen, commensurate is the sadness of the bereavement that the state and its citizenship now experience.

When the district Court honored me with the position as examiner in law and a young gentleman who had recently come from the state of Pennsylvania presented himself before that board for admission to the bar, the members of the examining board knew nothing except that his name was Jaggard and that he handed us a certificate of graduation from Dickinson College and from the law department of the great University of Pennsylvania. But no sooner had the questioning begun than the excellence of his training, the scholarship that he possessed, and the philosophical insight that he had obtained regarding the principles of jurisprudence became manifest, and, not to dwell too long upon this subject, it is one of those pleasant recollections that echo through the halls of memory to recall that Justice Jaggard and I always joked with each other when we met over the fact that he could read the Latin of his certificates and translate it into good English, a test that no other applicant for admission to the bar was ever able to undergo with success.

I wish to emphasize only one characteristic of Judge Jaggard that perhaps has not been dwelt upon sufficiently. We hear much to-day of the responsibility of the scholar and of the desirability of having the scholar in politics and having the attention of the scholar directed to the control and influence of public affairs. If we have ever had an example of the scholar in politics and the scholar in public affairs, such is the example of the lamented jurist towards whom our words of commemoration are this day directed. He was a scholar who did not treasure selfishly in his own heart and brain the learning of past ages and the learning of modern times, but he placed it all at the disposal of his fellow citizens in a generous effort to help in every walk of life with the lessons drawn from the experience of the past and from the wisdom stored in the great libraries that the human race has accumulated. He was a glorious character in social life, an ornament to the Bar, a memorably successful jurist in the concluding years of his useful life, and all the recollections that can be gathered from the common people, from the members of our profession, and from the world at large will constitute an amaranthine wreath that will forever hang revered in the halls of Minnesota's memory.

Associate Justice Bunn [for the court] then said:

Gentlemen, the Court is in full accord with your memorial and with the merited tributes to the late Justice Jaggard. I knew Justice Jaggard well. I knew him when we were both at the bar; I knew him as a lawyer trying cases before me after I went upon the district bench. We were closely associated on that bench for six years, and I have watched his work since he left that bench to adorn this with the peculiar interest that the trial judge has in the decisions of the higher court. I also knew Jaggard the fisherman and Jaggard the man.

As a lawyer he was learned in the law: a careful pleader, a close reasoner, a powerful advocate. As district judge, his record made during the six years that he held that position was such that he was called by the people of the state to the highest sphere of usefulness, the bench of the Appellate Court.

He served as an associate justice of this court a little over six years. His work here is preserved in Volumes 94 to 114. He wrote opinions in approximately four hundred cases, many of them important. His opinions bear conducive evidence of great research and are uniformly scholarly and illuminating. He had a great command of language and a wonderful facility in expressing his thoughts and generally exhausted the law in each case. Indeed, many of his opinions are elaborate treatises. He loved to find the source of a legal principle and follow it down through its various branches even as he loved to follow a trout stream, not missing any prominent brook or rivulet along the way. To quote Charles Lamb: "He was a brother of the angler, and just such a free, hearty, honest companion as Mr. Isaac Walton would have chosen to go fishing with." He delighted in the waters, fields, and woods. He really loved nature. He who knew Judge Jaggard around the camp fire after a strenuous day with the trout or bass knew him at his best. He was delightful. Indeed, personally he was a lovable character and always a charming companion.

He was a remarkable public speaker and a writer of great ability. His works on legal subjects will live.

But it is Jaggard the man that is most missed. He had more friends than most men, and they loved him. He was always courteous and thoughtful of others. He was kind and charitable. The guides on the river and trail, the janitors in the capitol, the servants in his club and in his home, are losers by his death. He was essentially a cheerful man, a true optimist. He loved life, and got much out of it. It is characteristic of the man that while suffering from the incurable disease that caused his death and knowing that his life might end at any time, he not only did not complain, but his greeting was as cheery, his smile as infectious, his company as enjoyable as ever. His associates and intimate friends never knew of his condition. This was heroism, and, to me, wonderful. He was, if not happy himself, still the cause of happiness in others. The world can ill spare such a man.

Chief Justice Start then said:

To live in hearts is never to die. Mr. Justice Jaggard lives in the loving remembrance of the Bench and Bar and people of Minnesota, and it is fitting that your eloquent and just memorial should be entered of record, with the addresses in support of it, and, as a further tribute to his memory, that the Court now adjourn. [113 Minn. xix]

Charles B. Elliott

1861–1935
Associate Justice, 1905–1909

In the afternoon of November 25, 1936, at two o'clock, the court being assembled at the court room in the State Capitol, Chief Justice John P. Devaney called upon Michael J. Doherty, president of the Minnesota State Bar Association.

Mr. Doherty then said:

The bar of Minnesota asks leave at this time to join with the court in honoring the memory of three men who have passed from this life since this court last convened for a similar purpose. Each of these three men was during his lifetime a leader of the bar of this state and a distinguished member of this court . . . The Honorable Charles B, Elliott died September 18, 1935 . . . The bar is represented by . . . Mr. James D. Shearer, Mr. Fred B. Snyder, and Mr. Willard R. Cray, who will present a memorial of the Honorable Charles B. Elliott . . .

Mr. James D. Shearer then presented the following:

Charles Burke Elliott was born on a small farm in Morgan County, Ohio, on January 6, 1861. His father, a gentle Quaker, was a man of limited education who had married Angeline Kinsey, the daughter of a neighboring farmer and a descendant of a celebrated Pennsylvania family of lawyers, one of whom was the first chief justice of that state.

Before he was 15 years old, young Elliott had mastered all that the country school teachers of the community could teach him. For a few years he alternately taught school and worked on his father's farm, saving his money to pay for additional schooling at nearby Marietta Academy and College. He attended that institution for a year or more and then accompanied his family when they removed to Iowa. In the fall of 1879 he entered the law school of the University of Iowa and was graduated in June 1881. Not yet being of age, he could not be admitted to the bar, and for a period of six months he worked as a clerk in the office of a law firm in Muscatine. Shortly after being admitted in Iowa he removed to Aberdeen, South Dakota, and was engaged as legal representative of a land company. In 1884 he removed to Minneapolis, and in the spring of the same year he was married in Muscatine to Edith Winslow, daughter of Charles C. Winslow, who had come to Iowa from Maine before the Civil War.

Judge Elliott's early years in Minneapolis were filled with desperately hard work in his struggle to become established as a lawyer. His diaries for the years between 1884 and 1890 are interesting records of his grim determination to succeed in spite of discouragements. He worked at a terrific rate during the day, and work or study into the night was the usual thing. In 1887 he earned his first academic distinction, being granted by the University of Minnesota the first degree of Doctor of Philosophy ever conferred by that institution. His excellent doctoral thesis, "The United States and the Northeastern Fisheries," published by the University of Minnesota, brought him immediately to the attention of scores of distinguished public men in this country and in Europe. The paper remains today an outstanding disquisition on the subject. During the period from 1890 to 1899 he was professor of Corporation and International Law in the University of Minnesota.

In 1890 Judge Elliott was appointed by Governor Merriam to the municipal bench of Minneapolis. He was then only 29 years old but quickly demonstrated his fitness for the position, and on January 4, 1894, he was advanced to a place on the district bench, being appointed by Governor Knute Nelson. He remained there until October 3, 1905, when he was appointed to the supreme bench by Governor Johnson. The Republican State Convention of the same year nominated him as candidate for justice of the supreme court, to which he was elected without serious opposition. His decisions while a member of the supreme court mark him as a jurist of unusual learning, great industry, sound judgment, and superior understanding of humanity.

Judge Elliott, always the scholar and analyst, was deeply interested in history and international law. His grasp of international affairs early became recognized through his addresses and contributions to legal and historical publications. It was doubtless in recognition of these unusual qualifications that President Taft, himself a great lawyer and jurist, in 1909 appointed Judge Elliott Associate Justice of the Supreme Court of the Philippine Islands. Two years later he was asked to accept the portfolio of Secretary of Commerce and Police in the Philippine Commission, it being understood that this appointment was made in order that the Commission might embrace an outstanding lawyer who was in sympathy with the President's legal policies as to the government of the Philippines. Following the success of the Democratic party in the election of 1912, the entire Philippine Commission was replaced, and Judge Elliott resumed the practice of law in Minneapolis.

Almost equally well as a jurist, Judge Elliott was known to the legal profession as an author and publicist. He wrote with great industry and exactitude a number of well known legal works, his principal books being those on the Law of Private Corporations, the Law of Municipal Corporations, the Law of Insurance, and an early work on Minnesota Practice and Procedure, which was supplemented and supplanted by his more recent work. In addition to these, he found time to compose a two-volume history of the Government of the Philippine Islands, a work that gave evidence of his capacity as a historical scholar and that received wide praise.

Seldom has a lawyer and jurist in the years of a busy professional life found time to perform so many varied and outstanding services to society. In 1911 Judge Elliott was designated to represent the Government of the Philippine Islands at the coronation ceremonies held in Hong Kong for King George V of England. He attended as head of an imposing group of officers and officials, among them General John J. Pershing. While in the Philippines he lectured on constitutional law at the University at Manila, and in 1911 he was president of the Philippine Industrial Exposition. During the Spanish-American War he was adjutant general of the state of Minnesota.

Judge Elliott served for a year as president of the American Branch of the International Law Association. In August 1921, he attended the meeting of the International Law Association at The Hague and was the sole American delegate to deliver an address at that meeting. In the Palace of Peace he delivered his address upon "The Relation of the Monroe Doctrine to American International Action" before a large congress of distinguished lawyers from all parts of the world and was entertained at luncheon by Her Majesty the Queen of Holland. Before returning to America he had the pleasure of being invited to visit the late Rudyard Kipling at his home at Burwash, where few Americans have been welcomed.

Judge Elliott was not one who "wore his heart upon his sleeve," but he was unostentatiously a religious man, believing that religion is the basis of civil society. He was a life-long member of the Episcopal Church, having been confirmed at Trinity Church in Minneapolis in 1884 and later attended St. Mark's Church. He was a member of the various bar associations, a member of the Minneapolis Club, a Shriner, a Knight Templar, an Odd Fellow, and a life member of the Minnesota Historical Society, as well as a member of numerous other societies and associations of a legal, historical, and scientific nature. His fraternities were Alpha Sigma Phi, of which he was Grand Senior President, Phi Beta Kappa, and Delta Chi. He held the following degrees: LL.B., University of Iowa, 1881; Ph.D., University of Minnesota, 1887; LL.D., University of Iowa, 1895; and LL.D., Marietta College, 1904.

Judge Elliott was always more concerned with correcting wrongs and with matters intellectual and of wide interest than he was with personal material gain. He enjoyed the personal acquaintance and esteem of many leading lawyers, jurists, and others of high station in various parts of the world. To those who enjoyed his close association and companionship he was ever a source of pleasure and of intellectual benefit. His fairness and kindliness matched his attainments in learning and his activities for good. Personally he was a man of great dignity, fine manners, kind and cordial, not lacking in humor, always serenely calm, always gentlemanly. His magnificent library, accumulated through years of discriminating selection, indicated his studious habits and elevation of thought. During the last ten years of his life he spent considerable time at his spacious country place on Long Lake, near Brainerd. In his family life he was eminently happy and contented until the death of his wife on the fiftieth anniversary of their union in marriage, May 13, 1934. After the death of his helpmate he evidenced a marked decline in health and passed away September 18, 1935. Surviving him are four sons and one daughter.

> Willard R. Cray
> Fred B. Snyder
> James D. Shearer

Chief Justice Devaney then said:

Your memorial is a just and merited contribution to the learning and worth of Justice Elliott and expresses our own estimate of his sterling character and valued public service.

Justice Elliott came to this court shortly after the Spanish-American War. As a people we had achieved world-wide recognition for our industry and commerce. We had taken our place as a world power. Since then, in the span of one generation, we have seen a veritable social revolution occur. From a rural people and from a rural civilization we have emerged in one generation, with our urban population trebled and with a mechanized rural life. Overnight the thousand-year old rural and economic order and manner of living were supplanted by mass production and mass distribution. This has brought serious economic dislocations and vast social changes. In the midst of the confusion of a rapidly changing world, Justice Elliott came to this bench. His influence on the court and on the part that this court had in the social and economic changes of his time was great.

He was a superb artist and an accomplished scholar and jurist. Beyond his place as scholar and jurist, he will also be long remembered as a teacher and author. Prior to his appointment to this court, he served with distinction as a professor of corporation and international law at the University of Minnesota. He resigned from this court to accept the office of Associate Justice of the Supreme Court of the Philippine Islands. His interest was world-wide, his intellectual curiosity was great. He was not content to remain associate justice of this court but moved on to a wider field of usefulness and activity and to the work of a pioneer jurist in the Philippine Islands.

As a teacher of law, as a lecturer, his fame was not confined to the state of Minnesota or to this country but was international in scope. His connection with the World Court and its activities, his appearance before the World Court, marked him as one of the most distinguished jurists that this state has ever produced. I doubt if any member who ever sat on this court has reached a higher level as a lawyer and a jurist than was reached by Justice Elliott in his appearance before the World Court, where he was recognized as a jurist and scholar whom the whole world must note.

His books are many. He has written able texts on taxation and corporation law and on the law of insurance. His text on Minnesota practice was an outstanding work and has been one of the most useful books ever placed in the hands of the lawyers of this state.

It is fitting that a man of his sterling character and great ability should be honored here today. His services have been of outstanding value to this court and to the state. The honors he won have reflected credit and distinction on this court and on the bar generally. It is proper that your memorial should be placed in the records of this court, there to remain a perpetual memorial to the work of this public-spirited citizen. Jurist, scholar, teacher, Justice Charles Elliott will not soon be forgotten. [198 Minn. xxvi]

Thomas D. O'Brien

1859–1935
Associate Justice, 1909–1911

In the afternoon of November 25, 1936, at two o'clock, the court being assembled at the court room in the State Capitol, Chief Justice John P. Devaney called upon Michael J. Doherty, president of the Minnesota State Bar Association.

Mr. Doherty then said:

The bar of Minnesota asks leave at this time to join with the court in honoring the memory of three men who have passed from this life since this court last convened for a similar purpose. Each of these three men was during his lifetime a leader of the bar of this state and a distinguished member of this court . . . The Honorable Thomas D. O'Brien died September 3, 1935 . . . The bar is represented by . . . Mr. Charles Donnelly, the Honorable Frederick N. Dickson, Mr. James D. Shearer, and the Honorable Pierce Butler, who will present a memorial on behalf of the Honorable Thomas D. O'Brien. Although the last mentioned of this group [Butler] has for some years occupied a high judicial position, he is still, I think it is safe to say, in spirit, a member of the bar of Minnesota.

Mr. Charles Donnelly then said:

As a member of the committee consisting of Mr. Justice Butler, Judge Frederick N. Dickson, and myself, I desire to submit this memorial:

Thomas Dillon O'Brien died at his home in this city on September 3, 1935, in his seventy-seventh year. He was an associate justice of this court from September 1, 1909, until January 1, 1911. Except for his short service on this bench and a service of two years as insurance commissioner of this state, he was throughout this long period a practicing lawyer, devoting himself unsparingly to the interests of his clients.

He was a member of a remarkable family. His father, Dillon O'Brien, and his mother were natives of Ireland, highly educated, and living the carefree life of people who have leisure and means to enjoy it, until the depression that descended upon Ireland in the Forties swept away their possessions and left no choice but to emigrate and begin life anew in some other land. They came to America and settled at LaPointe on Madeline Island, Wisconsin, near the head of Lake Superior, where the father became a teacher in a mission school. Here Thomas was born on February 14, 1859. In 1863 the family moved to Minneapolis, and two years later to St. Paul, Minnesota; and for the remaining 71 years of his life Thomas was a resident of this state and, except for a short period during his boyhood, a resident of this city,

In 1877 or 1878 he entered the office of Young & Newell as a student and clerk. Later, and at the time of his admission to the bar in 1880, he was clerk of the municipal court, where he remained for a year. In 1885 he was appointed assistant city attorney. A partnership formed with his brother John D. O'Brien continued until 1888, when he entered into a partnership with his brother C. D. O'Brien. In 1891 he was elected county attorney of Ramsey County and served one term. He disliked the role of prosecutor, felt that he was not by temperament fitted for it, and declined reelection.

In 1905 Governor John A. Johnson appointed him insurance commissioner. This position he held until 1907, when he resigned to enter private practice and organized the firm of O'Brien & Stone. On September 1, 1909, he was appointed by Governor Johnson a justice of this court, to fill out a term that ended January 1, 1911, when he returned to private practice, organizing the firm of O'Brien, Young & Stone, later O'Brien, Horn & Stringer. In 1917 he became the first president of the St. Paul Association. He was one of the founders of the St. Paul College of Law, lectured there for many years, and until his death was a member of its board of trustees. When the St. Thomas College of Law was organized, he became its dean and so remained during the period of its existence.

His service as a member of this court was too short to enable him to achieve fully the high place in the ranks of the judiciary that, with a more extended service, his abilities would undoubtedly have won for him. He was a member of the court for but 16 months, and during this period he wrote the opinions in about 100 cases, appearing in Volumes 109–113 of the Reports. Strong, clear, direct, firm, and easily understandable, his opinions exhibit the ease and mastery with which long training and earnest thought and study enabled him to move over the whole field of jurisprudence; and they are informed throughout with the love of justice and the determination to do right that, during his whole life, were so characteristic of the man.

It was as an advocate, however, that he won the high place that he held in his profession; and it is as a great advocate and a great citizen that he will be remembered by those who knew him. His sense of civic duty was high, and it was a matter of wonder to his friends and associates how, in his busy career as a lawyer, he found so much time to devote to the public service. His death marked a great loss to the profession and to the state; and it is eminently fitting that a tribute to his memory should be placed on the records of the court on which he served.

Pierce Butler
Frederick N. Dickson
Charles Donnelly

Mr. Charles Donnelly then said:

In presenting this memorial to a man who had achieved such distinction in his profession and who, throughout a long life, was ready at all times to respond unselfishly to any call made upon him to render public service, I feel that I ought to say a word about my own relations to him and what his friendship meant to me.

There are doubtless many of the older members of the bar of the state who knew Judge O'Brien longer and better than I knew him, for my acquaintance with him began only about 25 years ago, and at that time he had already been a practitioner at the bar of the state for nearly 30 years. When I first met him he was immersed in the work and study involved in the Minnesota Rate Cases; and, as it happened that at that particular juncture I was myself pretty much occupied with that branch of the law, we had a common intellectual interest, and in this our friendship originated. I saw a good deal of him thereafter in the trial and argument of cases and came to share the admiration in which he was universally held for his gifts as an advocate. He was a most formidable antagonist, and few who encountered the rapier-like thrust of his wit or sarcasm cared to provoke it a second time. But it was not an embittered wit. He did not like to feel that he had left a wound. Indeed I have sometimes thought that he suffered more than his opponent from the blows he gave, for of all the strong, forceful, rugged men whom I have ever known he was, I believe, the most gentle-hearted.

It was a matter of regret to those of us who knew and admired Judge O'Brien that he did not have the opportunity in a more extended service on this bench to exhibit the qualities that we believe would have placed his name high among those of the eminent men who have occupied places on it. It is sometimes said that exceptional gifts of advocacy such as he possessed are not compatible with that calm and serenity that are supposed to go with or form a part of the judicial temperament. Names will readily occur to the minds of all of us that completely refute that notion. Judge O'Brien was undoubtedly a strong and resolute champion, or even partisan, of any cause that he had taken up or that had enlisted his sympathies. But his sense of justice was also strong; he was fully capable of taking the detached view that is a necessary preliminary to judicial action; and in the work he did in the short period of his service here we have an earnest of what he might have done.

Yet though the brevity of his judicial career was a disappointment to his friends, and may have been a disappointment to him, no one can look back over that long life that, beginning on a little island at the head of Lake Superior almost with the beginning of the history of our state, came to a close only a year ago in the city that he loved, without realizing not only that this life was lived from first to last with a strong unity of purpose but that that purpose was always high. In whatever field his activities were cast, he never slurred his work, nor did his interest in it ever slacken or flag. To the task in hand, whatever it was, he gave the best that was in him. His interests were keen to the end, his sympathies were quick and warm to the end; and in taking our farewell of him the lines of Milton may, I think, in very truth be applied to him:

> Nothing is here for tears, nothing to wail
> Or knock the breast, no weakness, no contempt,
> Dispraise or blame; nothing but well and fair,
> And what may quiet us in death so noble.

The Honorable Frederick N. Dickson then said:

Judge O'Brien was a very good friend of mine for many years, and it is as a friend that I would like to submit this memorial.

Thought is deeper than speech and feeling deeper than thought, and it is extremely difficult, in fact impossible, to set down in words a satisfactory tribute to the memory of such a man and such a friend as Judge O'Brien.

The scion of a distinguished, cultured, and at one time opulent family, he yet enjoyed the advantage of passing his youth in the straightened circumstances common to the pioneers of a new country and thus was brought in touch with the common people and learned to know and appreciate their problems and their methods and means of getting happiness and enjoyment out of life as well as overcoming their obstacles and disappointments.

For nearly 50 years I knew Judge O'Brien quite intimately, was associated with him from time to time in some legal matters as well as in a social way, and many times have enjoyed the benefit of his wise and kindly advice.

Judge O'Brien lived in a remarkable era. The span of his life measures an era of the most stupendous progress in civilization the world has ever known. Born in 1859 at LaPointe on Madeline Island at the head of Lake Superior, a far-flung outpost on the extreme frontier of western civilization, he witnessed and experienced the transformation of Minnesota and the Northwest states from a wilderness into the splendid commonwealths of today. He witnessed and experienced the progress from the dim illumination of candlelight to the brilliant electrical lighting systems that now banish darkness and turn night into day; from transportation through rivers and forests and prairie trails by canoe, oxcart, and horse to transportation by railroad, the automobile, and the airplane. From a time when news was sparsely and slowly disseminated by the weekly newspaper and by word of mouth from one to another, he lived to see general news of all kinds hourly disseminated to a great nation and the world at large by means of the telephone and the radio from a time when the national election could not be known generally for weeks and months to a time when such result is known to the whole nation and the world on the evening of election day. He saw the crude entertainment of pioneer days supplanted by the marvel of the talking pictures. He witnessed the marvelous and almost miraculous development of medical and surgical science and the very extensive development and amelioration of the law of the land through judicial decision and statutory enactment by the representatives of a free people, extending to the humbler and laboring classes protection of their property and human rights.

Of all of these marvelous changes and developments Judge O'Brien was not only a witness but was himself a part, especially in the development and improvement of our laws and in the liberalizing of our political philosophy. Living in such an era, with his cultured family background, his wide experience in human affairs, his innate intelligence and broad human sympathy, and his youthful experience and observations of the struggles and problems of the humbler classes, he could hardly avoid developing into the splendid character he was and rendering to society the humane and beneficial services he performed.

For two years Judge O'Brien was county attorney of Ramsey County. At the end of his term he refused again to stand for the office because he felt that he did not possess the stern qualities of a successful prosecutor. While he abhorred crime and the motives that inspired it, his sympathy with the innocent who necessarily suffer from the wrongs of those upon whom they depend made that phase of official duty most distressing, and he felt that he lacked the implacable and uncompromising attitude so necessary to a successful prosecutor.

Judge O'Brien was born and bred in the Roman Catholic faith and remained throughout his life a staunch and consistent member of that church. He was, however, less intrigued with its ritualism than impressed and motivated by its fundamental Christian doctrine. He was a devout Christian, believing absolutely and unquestioningly in the fundamental principles of Christianity. He believed in the existence of a personal God who rules and orders the universe, who has a kindly personal interest in humanity, and to whom humanity owes a personal allegiance, who has equipped humanity with a capacity to know right from wrong and with a knowledge of its duty to choose the right in preference to wrong. And he believed in that other wonderful doctrine of the immortality of the soul and a life beyond the grave for which this life is but a training and probation, a philosophy of life that in all ages has produced the finest results in human character. His religion was not a mere philosophy but rather a very practical rule of conduct, and in all his ways he sought earnestly to conform his life to the ethical teachings of Jesus.

Judge O'Brien's keen wit and delightful sense of humor, his wide and varied fund of human knowledge, and his broad and liberal outlook upon and appraisal of the problems of humanity made him a most delightfully entertaining and instructive companion, and his generous, sympathetic, and lovable nature made him a wonderful friend. While he will be remembered as a great lawyer and a sound judge, a loyal and capable public servant who in his official and public capacities rendered valuable and lasting service to his state and country, he will, I believe, be best and most lovingly remembered by those who were fortunate enough to have enjoyed intimate social relations with him, as a delightful companion, a wise, kindly, helpful, and beneficent friend, and a genuine Christian gentleman.

Mr. James D. Shearer then said:

Judge Thomas Dillon O'Brien, known to his intimates as Tom O'Brien, was a very unusual man.

He was large physically, mentally, morally; a kindly man, temperate in speech but convincing; dignified but not unbending; quietly humorous among friends or to clarify a business proposition.

He recognized that beneath a rough exterior there was often a warm heart and a discerning mind.

He had great poise in bearing and manner, was a good friend.

His going has left a void in the bar of this state.

In closing I would pay him the tribute that Hamlet paid to his father, the deceased king:

> He was a man, take him for all in all,
> I shall not look upon his like again.

Chief Justice Devaney then said:

The tribute of the Honorable Pierce Butler of the United States Supreme Court in memory of Judge Thomas D. O'Brien will be read by Mr. M. J. Doherty.

Mr. Doherty then read as follows:

Official work makes it impossible for me to attend the session at which will be presented the memorial to Honorable Thomas D, O'Brien. We were friends since first associated in professional work nearly 50 years ago. I ask that I may express and leave upon the records of the court a word concerning him.

He was indeed a fortunate man. Among the things that developed and sustained him were: A fine physique and vigorous mind, just pride in an honorable lineage, steadfast adherence to the religion of his ancestors, sound instruction by a father distinguished among the men of his day for culture and character and wise guidance by a mother eager to uphold all that makes for right living, strength in professional standards reinforced by counsel and example of leaders of the bar with whom he worked during the period of preparation and his first years in the practice, persistent purpose to be worthy of his high calling, encouragement grounded upon the strong attachment ever existing between him and his brothers and sisters, and above all the constant support of a loved and loving wife and of their children.

He was ever ready to help all belonging to his great family. His friends were legion, and willingly he served them. He was liberal in thought and wanted to know and was keen to help to attain that which best will serve the people, the State, and the Nation. He believed in our form of government and that, consistently with the Constitution, there may be accomplished all desirable changes. He was a good lawyer: as counselor, diligent, sensible and frank; in negotiations to settle controversies out of court, alert and effective; in the conduct of litigation, a skillful strategist and powerful advocate. By conscientious preparation and faithful presentation of his clients' causes according to the truth, he merited and attained high standing in the community and before the courts. He was a good judge. In every case he was careful to ascertain the controlling facts rightly to apply the law and plainly to state the reasons for the judgment of the court.

He was an admirable man and will be affectionately remembered by all who knew him. Long may the record of his successful life serve to encourage and guide.

Pierce Butler

Chief Justice Devaney then said:

Justice Royal A. Stone, who was to speak for the court in memory of Judge O'Brien, is unable because of illness to be here at this time, and he has asked me to read this tribute:

It is so much our habit in matters of necrology, when the subject in his lifetime was an object of our respect and affection, to indulge in exaggeration that tributes such as we are now rendering are seldom taken by the thoughtful at their face value.

There is another reason why any tribute of mine to Thomas D. O'Brien should be taken with some allowances. For the 16 years from 1907 to 1923, except for the period from September 1, 1909, to January 2, 1911, during which he was a member of this court, we were partners. From 1906 to 1907, inclusive, while he was insurance commissioner and I assistant attorney general, we were in almost daily collaboration. We both resigned in the autumn of 1907 and organized the firm of O'Brien & Stone, which, with the usual changes due to the kaleidoscopic nature of human life and its affairs, has continued to the present time.

After such an association, with a spontaneous beginning and ever increasing admiration and confidence on my part for my friend, my partner, and my elder brother in the law, it is not to be expected that anyone can acquit me of a disposition toward overstatement on this occasion.

Notwithstanding, it is my fixed purpose to indulge so far as in me lies in fair statement, without effort to add another hue to the complete spectrum that Thomas D. O'Brien made for his own life.

More than any of you, probably, I know how well merited are the things that have been said at the bar. I know especially how much Judge O'Brien would appreciate, sincerely and deeply, the making here of a proper and fair record in his memory. I know also that no opposition would be greater than his own to the utterance here of praise of him that he did not deserve.

Entirely aside from his professional life, he was a most unusual man. There was a largeness, a symmetry, and a balance about his mental and spiritual makeup that were fittingly symbolized by his large, splendidly developed, and always well-carried physique. His outward appearance of poise, courage, and forward-looking was a true reflection of the inner man. In all that, he enjoyed a rich heritage from the very finest quality of cultured Irish ancestry. He had the good fortune to be able to carry on that tradition in his own family life.

On the professional side, while I have known many lawyers better versed in the case and book learning of our profession, I have known none with a better instinctive understanding of the verities of the law and their proper application to the duties and controversies of life. He was frank in expressing his dislike for the mounting volume of law books and for the increasing vogue of the case lawyer. Against their technique, he wanted liberty to invoke and apply to the ever changing situations presented by human evolution those principles that would work out what to him seemed justice. And with what seemed in any case to be justice to Thomas D. O'Brien, it was always difficult to express reasoned disagreement.

If I were to select from his numerous public services those that to me seemed the most important,

I would first choose one that at the time was somewhat of a political secret. When the late John A. Johnson first became governor of the state in 1905, he knew that his attorney general would be of an opposite political faith. Wanting close at hand a counselor of his own party and his own choice whom he could trust, Governor Johnson chose Mr. O'Brien as his insurance commissioner. The first important advice that the governor sought and obtained from him was to the general effect that the Republican attorney general, Edward T. Young, was the constitutional head of the legal department of the state and that it was the governor's duty to seek, and if possible to be guided by, his advice. Governor Johnson followed that counsel and found that in Mr. Young he had a legal adviser of the highest professional capacity, whose judgments in the affairs of his office and the state would be influenced not at all by partisan considerations. Ever afterwards Governor Johnson gave Judge O'Brien credit for having at that important juncture started his administration on the right track and for having kept him, the governor, from making a serious mistake.

Later on, while he was insurance commissioner, Judge O'Brien became the chairman appointed by President Theodore Roosevelt of the committee of insurance commissioners that did so much in collaboration with the activities of Charles Evans Hughes and his committee to put the old-line life insurance business of the country on a sound basis. The old and vicious tontine system was uprooted and destroyed, and in important particulars, in respect to the assurance of important rights to the assured, policies were standardized all over the nation.

Again in 1907, when labor disputes on the Iron Ranges of Minnesota threatened the disorganization of an important industry in a large portion of the state, Governor Johnson sent Judge O'Brien as a conciliator and mediator to the scene of the trouble. He took such steps that chaotic conditions immediately became orderly, and industrial peace was established where industrial strife had been imminent. For his work there, that keen and accurate appraiser of men, Charles B. Cheney, then and now on the editorial staff of the *Minneapolis Journal,* characterized Judge O'Brien as the Taft of Minnesota, and the name Taft was then at the zenith of its significance in American affairs.

To an extent I have never known in any other man or woman, Judge O'Brien had the capacity for deciding justly, notwithstanding the personal interests of himself or his clients. He could appraise fairly and justly the views of opponents. He was never afraid to point out where they were right even when exposing an error of his own. If at times he leaned over backward, as the saying is, in that respect, it was one of those weaknesses nearly always found with such greatness as was his.

His greatest delight was in aiding law students and young lawyers. He was never too busy or too weary to take time off from his own work to counsel them in theirs. He was generous to a fault—altogether more free at times in extending financial aid, sometimes to deserving needy and sometimes to mere impostors, than was just to himself. That was but one manifestation of his habit of resolving doubt against his own interests. One magnificent result was that he never intentionally wronged anyone.

Instinctively, as well as by training, he was one of those automatically just men concerning whom it was said so long ago: "The path of the just is as the shining light that shineth more and more unto the perfect day."

If in our profession, if in our affairs of government and business, lawyers and businessmen and politicians would follow the path from which the life of Thomas D. O'Brien never consciously strayed, we would be on the way to "the perfect day." [198 Minn xxvi]

David F. Simpson

1860–1925
Associate Justice, 1911–1912

On the afternoon of April 15, 1926, in the court room at the state capitol, Howard T. Abbott, Esq., as president of and in behalf of the State Bar Association, addressed the court:

We meet today to express our admiration, respect, and love for the late David F. Simpson, a most exemplary citizen, an able lawyer, and an upright judge, who passed away but a short time ago. It seems regrettable indeed that such expressions of loyalty, admiration, and affection as will follow are seldom conveyed in time to those whom we honor and respect so much. If it were so it would tend greatly to increase the happiness, joy, and contentment of the recipient, but unfortunately such does not seem to be the scheme of life.

The State of Minnesota Bar Association, through its appointed committee, desires to present a memorial of Judge Simpson. Mr. James D. Shearer of Minneapolis is the chairman of that committee, and I will ask him to read such memorial.

Hon. James D. Shearer then read the following:

David Ferguson Simpson was born on June 13, 1860. His parents, William Simpson and Catharine Goodsir, were born in Scotland. Mr. Simpson's father came of seafaring people. His mother's people were manufacturers and farmers, and both had the advantage of a liberal education. William Simpson and Catharine Goodsir met in Glasgow and were married in 1850. They purchased a farm near Waupun, Wisconsin, where David, the youngest of five children, was born.

His parents were honest, sturdy, industrious, and ambitious people who lived their quiet life on their farm happy and contented, always useful leading citizens of their locality. David's early education was obtained as many another's, in the little district school a

mile away, which had but one teacher and twenty to forty pupils ranging in age from five to twenty years. After that, he attended school at Waupun, walking two miles each way every day and working hard nights, mornings, and vacations on the farm, as all farmers' sons have to do. When fifteen years of age, he entered Ripon College where he spent three years in preparation for college. In the fall of 1878 he entered the University of Wisconsin and received his Bachelor's degree in 1882. In that day, debating was made a special feature of University work and a place on one of the debating teams was considered a great honor. This he won and was given the place of honor and of offering rebuttal.

He was a leader in college activities and served in various capacities as an officer of his class and was, especially during the last two years of his course, conspicuous in the social life of the University, where he was a leader as he was always and everywhere. At graduation he received the Lewis prize for the best commencement oration. Although not himself an athlete, he took great interest in college athletics and when he came to Minneapolis and became a member of the Caledonian Club, later its president, he was always a judge at that Scotch Society's annual games. He was awarded Phi Beta Kappa soon after graduation. After receiving his degree of A.B., Mr. Simpson was retained by the University authorities for a half year as assistant professor of English. In 1882, he entered the law department of the University of Wisconsin, but after something over a year, he entered Columbia University Law School and received from that institution the degree of LL.B. in 1884. Wisconsin University also conferred upon him that degree the same year.

David F. Simpson came to Minneapolis a few weeks after receiving his law degree with exactly ten dollars in his pocket. He entered the law office of J. H. Giddings, and like many another, he built the fire in the morning and kept the office swept and dusted and helped Mr. Giddings in payment for his office rent and incidentally took over small business that Mr. Giddings did not want. Perhaps no young man ever came to Minneapolis who was better equipped by inheritance and education for the practice of the profession of the law. In height more than six feet, broad shouldered, and of commanding presence, strong, self-assertive features, and a deep resonant voice, a genial personality, but of gentle and modest demeanor, the young attorney soon won the admiration, respect, and confidence of the bench and bar. He rose rapidly in his profession and in 1891, when Robert D. Russell was City Attorney of Minneapolis but in frail health, he selected David F. Simpson for his assistant, stating to the Council at the time that his first assistant must be able to try the City's most important cases.

Mr. Simpson was City Attorney from 1893 to 1897, and during that period two very important cases were successfully concluded, one reducing the price of gas and the other compelling the granting of transfers by the Street Railway Company. In the fall of 1896, Mr. Simpson was elected a Judge of the District Court of Hennepin County and was twice thereafter re-elected to that office, resigning from the District bench upon his election in 1910 to the Supreme Court. He only remained a year on the Supreme bench, from January 1, 1911, to January 1, 1912, when he resigned to form the firm of Lancaster, Simpson & Purdy, which became the present firm of Lancaster, Simpson, Junell & Dorsey upon the retirement of Judge Purdy.

Judge Simpson was married on January 14, 1886, to Miss Josephine Sarles. They were college sweethearts, she having graduated in a later class at Madison University.

When finishing his term as City Attorney, friends advised him to enter the practice as being more lucrative than public service, but he only said that he desired to give his best service to the public and that a lucrative practice could wait. From 1912 until his death, October 11, 1925, he was engaged in active practice of his profession and was one of the outstanding leaders of the Bar. During that time he was engaged in much important litigation, and clients who could entrust their interests to him always felt that their interests were in the most trustworthy and capable hands.

Judge Simpson was endowed with a strong mentality and to this he added deep culture. He had drunk deeply at the "pierian spring." His mental processes were keen and very unerring. He had a fine grasp of legal principles and could usually tell what the law was by his sense of justice and his instinctive feeling of what the law ought to be in a given case. He had the Anglo Saxon passion for justice, and when on the District bench his decisions were rarely reversed. He did his legal work easily, aided by good judgment and a large fund of common sense.

He presided in Court with dignity and courtesy to all but was quick to sense and detect shams, acts, and purposes not in keeping with a Court of Justice.

Judge Simpson was gifted with a keen sense of humor and often smiled at some humorous phase of evidence or situations in the trial before him. When on the bench he had that great judicial quality of being a good listener and that perhaps rarer quality as a counsellor in the practice of not wholly agreeing with a client at the start. To him, facing the facts in an endeavor to reach the very truth of a matter was more important than securing a client. He was courageous for the right and intellectually honest. He hated intellectual dishonesty above all things. A former member of the Hennepin County District Court, now gone, while Judge Simpson sat with him there, told the writer this: "In our full bench discussions, no matter what or who was involved, Simpson could always be depended upon to 'toe the mark'." This from an intimate associate is high praise. Judge Simpson's legal opinions were clear, and analytical, and always rang true to the principles governing the matter in hand. He had received from inheritance, and the precepts and example of honest parentage, the advice given by that other father to his son: "This above all to thine ownself be true, and it must follow as the night the day, thou canst not then be false to any man."

If an intimate of Judge Simpson were asked to name his predominant equalities of heart, I think he would say unflinching integrity, loyalty to friends and associates, and a fine democratic spirit that led him to admire character and merit irrespective of position.

These traits made him friends in every walk of life. No one was too humble to have his friendship, and the man on the street respected and believed in him. It was in the home that Judge Simpson showed at his best. About the time he was first elected to the bench, he purchased land at Lake Minnetonka and built a home, where for thirty summers with his family he lived an idyllic life surrounded by his woods and flowers and near to nature's heart. There in vacations and out of Court he toiled in the garden, cared for the trees and shrubbery on the place, fished, and rested. There he loved to meet his friends, and the spacious home often resounded with mirth and stories, music, and laughter. There his garden had but one rival in his heart, his granddaughters, with whom he loved to romp and play. His wit, his humorous sallies, and good stories as well as his sober observations on all subjects made him always and everywhere a welcome guest.

For several years he belonged to a private gridiron club, where prominent citizens were wont to meet once a year for the purpose of mutual abuse, and he greatly enjoyed these intellectual encounters.

The out-of-doors in any form was always a source of joy to Judge Simpson. He rarely missed taking an annual hunting trip, not for the pleasure or lust of killing but to enjoy the beauty and uplift of forest, hill, and stream and of nature in all her moods. He once said that the best hunting trip he ever had was for ten days in the forest for deer, during which time he never saw a deer. It was while driving his automobile on the way to his favorite duck pass last fall that the accident occurred which finally resulted in his death on October 11, 1925. He was in the best of health at the time of the injury, and even he supposed that it was trivial. He was patient and optimistic to the very last, smilingly assuring visitors that he had no pain and was getting on fine. Truly, "In the midst of life we are in death."

Judge Simpson, without ostentation, was a religious man. He could scarcely be otherwise, with his forbears. He was for many years a member of the First Unitarian Church of this city, but in later years he attended Plymouth Congregational Church.

Perhaps no man fully realizes how much his life and career have been influenced by wife and mother. We believe it was Ruskin who said: "The buckling on of the Knight's armor by his lady's hand was not a mere caprice of romantic fashion. It is the type of an eternal truth that the soul's armor is never well set to the heart unless a woman's hand has braced it, and it is only when she braces it loosely that the honor of manhood fails."

We mourn today the passing of a strong lawyer, an able and upright judge, an outstanding citizen, and a genial and loyal friend.

> James D. Shearer, Chairman
> Frank Crassweller
> W. E. Rowe
> Oscar Hallam
> George W. Buffington
> John O. P. Wheelwright
> Albert Schaller
> Frank E. Putnam
> C. O. Baldwin
> Ambrose Tighe
> Chester L. Caldwell,
> Memorial Committee

Hon. James D. Shearer then said:

If the Court please, the Committee has received from Hon. Tracy Bangs and his brother, of Grand Forks, North Dakota, warm personal friends of Judge Simpson, a letter containing their tribute, and regretting their inability to be present on this occasion, with the Court's permission, I will read the letter:

Dear Mr. Shearer:

We profoundly regret our inability to be present at the memorial program for the late David F. Simpson, to there join in a just tribute to the memory of a distinguished citizen and lawyer, a valued friend.

Judge Simpson was not only a distinguished citizen and lawyer, but he was a great, strong, broadminded, big-hearted man, with whom an acquaintance meant a friendship.

He, by years of honest, earnest service, built his character, wrote his own history, and so fixed his reputation that the record will always remain a guide for those who would build well.

He has left us—no more will we hear the music of his voice, no more will we feel the warm clasp of his friendly hands, no more will we enjoy his pleasant smile.

He has gone from this world, but the memory of his high ideals, of his splendid personal and professional life, continues an influence for good, He has "slipped his moorings and sailed away, o'er the ebbing tide of the unknown sea.'"

> He has 'Peacefully furled his sail,
> In moorings sheltered from storm or gale
> And greeted the friends who have sailed before
> O'er the unknown sea to the unseen shore.

We who are left to travel a little longer the shadowy paths of this darkened world cannot bring him back by sorrow and tears, but we will not say Goodbye—no—only Good night.

> Sincerely,
> Tracy R. Bangs
> George A. Bangs

James E. Dorsey, Esq., then said:

Some of us knew Judge Simpson only in his years of maturity. He has left us not privileged to enjoy a longer friendship, a clear picture that will last. His human qualities were joined most amiably with his legal abilities. This union made an admirable and likeable personality, the flavor of which can but poorly be given by words.

His good legal sense and his mastery of his special branches of the law are well known. With these attributes was an utter absence of any pride of opinion. The humblest or the jauntiest clerk in his office always found ready to discuss, on a basis of equality, any legal proposition in hand. No office matter of his was too serious to escape the whimsical turn of phrase or apt allusion that frequently aided in reaching a decision. A junior, flushed with court victory or disspirited by a jury's waywardness, could always find in Judge Simpson a ready listener with sincere words or approval or sage counsel of consolation. A temperament based on ability and a desire to do more than his share, aided by self-effacing generosity and a tranquility difficult to upset, made him an ideal head of his office. When engaged in a matter that engrossed him, his powers of concentration were enormous. He would become oblivious to the passage of the hours, the encroachment of darkness, and even to the insistence of the telephone. This single-mindedness bore

its fruit. The Courts listened to him, brother lawyers sought his advice, clients returned for further services. When his office duties did not press, he could play whole-heartedly. His garden, fishing and hunting, his friends, were all fresh joys to him. His heart remained young. To us who served under him, his memory will be an inspiration ever sweet.

Former Associate Justice Hallam then said:

Others have spoken of the ability and achievements of Judge Simpson as a lawyer, as a public official, as a Judge. I join with them in their tribute, but I feel still more the impulse to pay my tribute to David F. Simpson as a friend. Not merely as a friend of mine but as a friend of men.

I remember well the first time I saw David F. Simpson. I was taking my examinations for entrance into the University of Wisconsin. He had graduated a few months before with the highest honors both in oratory and debate and had just been chosen by the Board of Regents to fill the chair of the full professor in Rhetoric and Oratory who was absent for a year on leave. Simpson, of commanding presence and impressive personality yet so easily approachable, inspired in me the greatest admiration.

It was my privilege to become a member of the college fraternity to which he belonged. We always esteemed as an honor his presence at our gatherings, and yet it seemed to him such a matter of course, and he mingled so naturally with us that his distinguished presence never made us ill at ease. Through all the years of his life he continued his intimate relation with these young men and also with those connected by present or by past association with the University from which he had graduated.

It was not my privilege to sit with him as a member of this Court, but for several years we occupied coordinate positions on the District Court of the state. During this time we had frequent conference and association, and I enjoyed his uniform kindliness and courtesy that pays such big dividends in the happiness and satisfaction to himself and others.

These things are but examples of the uniform course of his life. He loved the society of his fellow men. He prized friendship not as a means but as an end. In his busy life he always had thought for the things that would help a friend, and he always had time for the things that a friend can do. He was frank and square and true. No voice was ever raised to disparage his fidelity or sincerity. He scattered smiles and words of cheer. I like to remember him as one who would live in a house by the side of the road and be a friend to man.

John O. P. Wheelwright, Esq., then said:

I first met Judge Simpson either in 1884 or 1885. From that time until the day of his death we were warm and intimate friends. I know that he would dislike anything that savored of fulsome eulogy and for that reason shall give expression only to a few of his characteristics and attainments as I saw them. In my judgment he was one of the ablest trial Judges Minnesota has ever had. Learned in the law, presiding in his Court with patience, poise, and self-possession, knowing men and being able to penetrate the motives by which they were controlled in all matters coming before him for his determination, he had the happy faculty of almost invariably reaching a sound and righteous conclusion. Had he remained on the Supreme Court, I am confident that he would have developed into a great Appellate Judge.

After his resignation from the Supreme Court we were associated together in some important litigation. He was the wisest man in conference I have ever met. With unerring instinct he always placed his finger on the salient features of the case. He abhorred sham and hypocrisy. For the demagogue he had no use. He was a good citizen and loyal to our institutions. He was possessed of great personal charm and was universally courteous to all with whom he came in contact. A great leader in the profession has fallen, and it will be difficult to fill his place.

Asa G. Briggs, Esq., then said:

What we think and what we say here today in tribute to our dear departed friend David Ferguson Simpson will not add to the merits that he achieved during his lifetime, but the contemplation and review of his life, his good deeds, and his good qualities will enrich and make us better and more capable to do our parts in life.

We regard the loss of a dear friend as a privation,

yet it often proves a guide pointing to higher and better things and calling to greater effort.

My memory goes back forty-five years to the first general meeting of the students of the University of Wisconsin that our freshman class attended. The students had met on the campus to consider what seemed to them to be a serious and important question affecting their rights. After a number of volunteers had spoken with varying force and effect, someone called "Simpson." Many voices joined in the call. Attention was centered on a tall slender boy with a strong, kindly, friendly face as he rose from the crowd, straightened himself, threw back his shoulders as was his habit when about to speak, and began to talk in a sincere, deliberate, forceful manner. He commanded respectful attention. At the close of his talk the student gathering was satisfied and prepared to act, and to act in accordance with his views. Every freshman present knew from that time that the senior boy Simpson was the student leader of the University of Wisconsin. Upperclassmen had learned it before.

It was my pleasure and my profit to know Judge Simpson well from that day until the time of his death. As a member of his Literary Society and his College Fraternity and as a student in his class and under his training when he was an instructor in the faculty of the University, I observed and felt and knew his worth. I saw his Literary Society confer upon him the greatest honor within its power to bestow. I saw the entire student body of the University do him such homage as is given in the spirit of hero worship. I saw him receive the highest honors the University bestowed for oratory. I saw him receive the commendation of the faculty.

He was admired and loved as a fraternity brother; his cheerful smiling face and jolly good nature were welcome everywhere. His successes created no envy, no ill will, for he was entitled to them; he earned them. He bore his honors so well and with such humility and poise that his fellows were pleased that it was he who had received them.

Justice Simpson's career in the University of Wisconsin gave promise of what his future life would be. An even temper, strong reasoning power, good common sense practically applied, were always at his command. They were most formidable qualities.

As Judge, he one time listened patiently to two long

technical arguments that seemed quite necessary to the attorneys on both sides. But when the case was submitted, by the application of his good common sense Judge Simpson in a few minutes swept aside the questions argued, went to the substance of the controversy, and disposed of it to the satisfaction of both parties upon a basis neither side had previously considered.

He was prudent; he acted only when fully advised, hence he acted accurately and justly. His most pleasing personality added to his great strength. He was big-hearted and strong; he was kind and friendly; he was gentle and loving; he was without pretense or display.

Foremost and above all else it must be written: Justice Simpson loved all mankind, and all mankind loved him.

Hon. George H. Sullivan then said:

It is a privilege to be here today to take part in this memorial to Judge David Simpson. As already related in these proceedings, he had a wide and varied experience at the bar, on the bench, and in the general practice of his profession. He had a wealth of learning, a clear logical mind, remarkable ability, and great forensic power. Nature fashioned him in a mould of greatness in physique, character, intellect, and heart.

It was during the last three years of his life that I was most intimately acquainted with him. He was then at the zenith of his physical strength and intellectual power and at the height of his professional career. As a young man he had been city attorney of the City of Minneapolis, later he was Judge of the District Court of Hennepin County, and then became an Associate Justice of the Supreme Court of the State of Minnesota. He had retired from the bench and had resumed private practice in the City of Minneapolis. He was at the head of a great law firm; he had the responsible management of the extensive and important business of that firm and was consulted and retained by many of the great and important business interests of that city and throughout the state. He personally conducted a great deal of important litigation. During this period I was associated with him as counsel in an important proceeding that, in its various phases, occupied the attention of one of our state commissions for several years and involved actions in the District Court, Supreme Court, and Federal Courts, so that for

several years before his death I was in more or less constant and close association with him and came to know him intimately and [was] able to gauge his capacity as a lawyer and to know his value as a friend.

I have often heard lawyers prominent at the bar say of Judge Simpson, "he is a great lawyer," and in all candor and sincerity that was and is my opinion. He was a profound student of the law. He understood all its great fundamental principles, was ready and sure in his application of the law to the facts and circumstances of the given case. He had a clear and comprehensive mind, sound and accurate judgment. His mental horizon compassed all the factors of a problem so that when he had resolved upon a course of action, all possible difficulties, obstacles, and alternatives had been duly considered, and his decisions rarely required revision. He had wonderful practical judgment ripened and informed by long experience. He was therefore invaluable in counsel, and his advice [was] widely sought and confidently relied upon. He was an expert in all the intricate and delicate work of a law office, familiar with all the legal detail of the organization and management of great business enterprises. His wide experience had made him familiar with questions of practice, jurisdiction, extraordinary remedies, and unusual legal proceedings. He was a master of the technique of the legal profession. He was skillful in the examination and cross-examination of witnesses, master of the strategy of a trial, alert to every possible move of his opponent, quick to seize upon every point to the advantage of his cause, logical, forceful and convincing in argument, honest, sincere, and helpful to the court, always fair, frank, and square. He had the confidence of every tribunal before which he appeared. He was a great trial lawyer.

He was sound, able, and brilliant in every branch of the profession. It was a great pleasure to listen to his exposition of legal doctrine and its application to the matter in issue, and this was especially true of any legal question that had not yet been thoroughly and finally settled by decisions of the courts of last resort. He used the historical method beginning with the earliest decisions in point of time, clearly showing their application to the question involved, going forward with irresistible logic, arriving at a conclusion amounting almost to a mathematical demonstration.

Because of his complete mastery of the subject and the illustrations he so well knew how to use, under his skillful treatment a dry legal theme became a subject of absorbing interest. He had the faculty of summing up in a few crisp sentences the essence of a lengthy legal decision. In the annals of the legal profession of this state David Simpson will be written down as one of the great lawyers of his time.

Judge Simpson never indicated by anything in his manner that he was conscious of any superior intellectual attainment or ability. He was simple, unassuming, unaffected, even modest in manner. He was genial, gentle, kind, courteous, and considerate in all his relations with other members of the bar whether adversaries or associates.

He was richly endowed by nature with that rare and delightful combination of qualities of mind and heart that drew men to him and compelled their affection. He was a charming and delightful companion, and those who were closely associated with him could not help but love him. He had the sincere affection and admiration of a host of friends.

Just at the hour when the Judge had arrived at the period of his greatest usefulness, when he was in the full vigor of physical strength and intellectual power, time having dealt so gently with him as to leave no trace of its passing, when he walked serene and secure the heights of professional fame surrounded by loving associates and devoted friends proud of his attainments, suddenly with but a moment's warning, the final summons came and he passed on.

The Bar of the State of Minnesota has lost a great leader. A host of friends keenly regret and sincerely mourn his loss.

Hon. James H. Hall then said:

Judge David F. Simpson is one of the outstanding influences of my life, and I deem it a privilege to take part in these exercises held here in his honor.

I fortunately became associated with Mr. Simpson in a very important case some years ago and during my early practice before the bar. His power to grasp quickly legal questions, his clear and concise way of stating facts and the principles of law applicable thereto, his courtesy and kindly treatment of counsel and witnesses, his perfect poise and control during the trial, made a profound impression upon me, and he has been and is my ideal lawyer.

I never had the privilege of appearing before him while he was on the bench, but I am proud to be able to say that I have been associated with him in the practice of law and was numbered as one of his friends.

I never knew him to exhibit a small trait or a weak sentiment, but on all occasions [he] displayed the most noble characteristic of ideal manhood, and my life has been enriched because he was my friend.

Nature endowed him with a splendid physique, a sunny face, and a cheerful disposition. His outstretched hand greeted all alike. He was kind, always loyal to his friends, and generous to his enemies. In his professional life, Mr. Simpson exhibited in a marked degree those traits of character that guarantee success at the bar, that bring to their possessor the confidence of clientage, inspire esteem and affectionate regard in the hearts of associates, and add luster to the noble profession of the law.

As we review the kind, genial companionship of our departed friend, recalling his kindly disposition and smiling countenance with which he always met us, we reverence his memory for himself alone.

> Green be the turf above thee,
> Friend of my better days,
> None knew thee but to love thee,
> None named thee but to praise.

Hon. Horace D. Dickinson, presiding judge of the district court for the Fourth Judicial District, then said:

"One Sunday morning, in the far-off town of Basel," says an unknown author, "I sat in my window listening to the melody of the bells. All the bells were chiming, and one mellow, deep-toned tolling-bell, swinging alone in its tall bell tower, gave the master tone to the clamoring strife of sound. How their jangling voices wrangled in the air, striving for the right of way. Yet, in spite of it all, through the midst of it all, undisturbed by multitudinous discords, even bringing them all into concord, came unfailingly to the ear the steady swing and sway of that calm, mellow boom that seemed to soothe the ruffled air and from its own abundance lend grace and meaning to all that aerial disquietude, which else it had not had."

I would not desire to appear on this occasion to

indulge in extravagant or exaggerated phrase or metaphor. It is to be expected, perhaps, and forgiven that memorial addresses are apt to be more highly laudatory than otherwise, especially where the individual whom we attempt to honor was a man of so extraordinary and outstanding a character as the one in whose memory we assemble today in this distinguished forum where his talents shone both upon and before this Bench.

Yet may we not liken the master mind and soul of David F. Simpson, whose calm voice has been so often heard in these halls, rising in its quietening, harmonizing influence above the tumult of discordant controversy to the great bell in its tall tower, soothing the ruffled air, as it were, with the grace of its mellow resonance and power?

I cannot hope by general or generous phrase to either adorn or enrich these eloquent contributions that have been dedicated to the character and memory of Judge Simpson. I prefer rather to speak briefly from a more personal standpoint.

I cannot but recall the consternation and shock that the announcement of his death brought not only to his own home community but the entire state. To myself it came with not only shock and dismay but with a poignancy of sincere grief that for the time being amounted almost to melancholy.

I had not seen him for a long time. Hearing of his accident, which though serious enough was not regarded as threatening life itself, I had resolved, as it were, in atonement for past neglect to visit him in the hospital. As the days went by he was reported to be much improved, sufficiently indeed to make it possible for him to indulge in some dictation of work from his bed. And then all unexpectedly, the end came and my call had not been made.

How often it happens that we delay the call of friendship and duty until it is too late. "Around the corner—and a vanished friend."

My love for Judge Simpson was grounded on years of personal contact tried out on many a field of action in our professional life. Call it love, admiration, respect, esteem, or what you will, it was of the lasting kind. It was a kind that outroughs all weathers and outrides all storms. It goes back to days prior to the time when as junior judge, in company with Justice

Holt, I came to the District Bench of the Fourth District, over which Judge Simpson then presided.

For many years we were colleagues, and I always found him kind, considerate, generous, sympathetic—an ever-present help in time of trouble; in many a difficulty I learned to lean upon him. A bond of friendship—almost boyish in its attachment on my part—grew up between us that no divorcement of time or circumstance could weaken or estrange. My thoughts and recollections of him today and forever more will be always of the tenderest and sweetest nature.

Dying, Horace Greeley exclaimed: "Fame is a vapor. Popularity an accident. Riches take wings. Those who cheer today will curse tomorrow. Only one thing endures: character."

And it is my privilege in this august presence today, in great sincerity and affection that will abide, to add my testimony to the high character of Judge Simpson and the grandeur of his splendid spirit.

At his death I was attracted by the appropriateness of an editorial appearing in one of our papers:

> Nature cast Judge David F. Simpson in generous mould. Symbolically as well as literally he was a big man. He was big as to stature, big as to heart, big as to mind. Not often do we find an individual whose character was so perfectly mirrored in his appearance. To see him once was to remember him always—a fine giant of a man with a presence that, contradictorily enough, seemed no less judicial than jovial . . . He was richly human at all times and needed only to be seen to be liked . . .
>
> To the very end there was a touch of the boy in his composition, a heartiness of manner, and a zest of life such as were not easy to associate either with one of his profession or his years.

The most cherished days of my judicial life were those when Brooks and Brown and Simpson and Holt and John Day Smith were my associates on the Bench—all men of towering individuality.

In those days there was a fellowship of the Bench and a communion of spirit that, since the judges have doubled in number, is no longer experienced, and that close comradeship was due in a large measure to the radiant personality of Judge Simpson—a radiance and spirit of youthfulness that even so staid and steady a soul as Judge Holt could not successfully subdue.

So long as memory lasts will the name of Judge Simpson be cherished in the hearts of all who knew him.

Associate Justice Holt then said:

I was an interested observer of Judge Simpson's whole professional career, he having come to Minneapolis to practice law two years after I did. Young lawyers naturally take a hand in civic affairs. Judge Simpson had more than ordinary aptitude in that direction. His sound judgment and agreeable personality soon attracted the attention of the leaders of the political party with which he affiliated. So, when the gentlemanly Robert D. Russell became City Attorney, young Simpson was selected as his first assistant; and by the time Mr. Russell was promoted to the district bench, the assistant had so favorably impressed the City Council that he readily became city attorney, serving as such until elected a district judge.

As a judge he singularly distinguished himself during his fourteen years of service. His commanding stature, dignified bearing, and calm disposition inspired respect and avoided many of the disagreeable scenes that are so prone to disturb the trial of closely contested cases resulting in ill-considered rulings and unjust results. During six years it was my good fortune to be an associate of Judge Simpson on the district bench. In my judgment he was an ideal *nisi prius* judge, so recognized by the bar. Among the eminent, congenial, and helpful men who then adorned that bench, he stands out as one whose calm and wise counsel was always cheerfully extended to those of us of less experience when met by perplexing legal problems. This means much when it is recalled that such men as Judges Frank C. Brooks, Fred V. Brown and Wilbur F. Booth were also on that bench, each one also equally ready and capable effectively to help an associate. To my mind the outstanding compensation that comes to a man from the drudgery of judicial work is the influence, aid, and counsel derived from close contact and associations with the men of outstanding ability and integrity who have occupied and do now occupy the bench both in the district court and in the supreme court of this state.

But as highly as I valued Judge Simpson as a lawyer and a judge when serving as an associate with him, I afterwards came to esteem his capabilities as a jurist still more, not only from the work he did as a member of this court but especially on account of the assistance his briefs and arguments were to us in his subsequent practice. The lucrative and congenial partnership offered by his friend, the highly efficient lawyer Judge Lancaster, and his former assistant Judge Purdy, was too attractive; and he resigned after serving only one year upon this bench. His opinions rendered during that short period sufficiently demonstrate the high class of judicial work he did and was capable of doing on an appellate bench; and I know that his associates, only one of whom is now living, Judge Lewis, valued very highly his judgment and ability as a jurist. I also know that I voice not alone my personal conviction but the conviction of my associates, those now here as well as those who have passed beyond, in asserting that no attorney who has appeared before this bar the last fourteen years has uniformly been more helpful to this court in the presentation of a case than Judge Simpson. He had the faculty of stating the salient facts of a case frankly, clearly, and tersely and singling out the controlling legal propositions with convincing force. He never pressed small points nor apparently sought to take advantage of pure technicalities. From the character of his work as an advocate, the inference was irresistible that his clients had in him a safe and valuable counselor in not only legal controversies but also in the practical and common sense way of avoiding or settling disputes.

This court had in Judge Simpson a steadfast and sympathetic friend. From experience he knew what the task is, and that with our best efforts it cannot be performed to the entire satisfaction of either the bar or the public. Hence, even in defeat, his friendly attitude towards the court never changed. It therefore is but natural that we greatly regret his sudden passing at the height of his physical and mental powers, and we join with the bar in paying a deserved tribute to his abilities as a lawyer and in expressing our love and esteem for him as a man and friend. [165 Minn. xxviii]

George L. Bunn

1865–1918
Associate Justice 1911–1918

On the afternoon of Friday, January 10, 1919, in the court room at the State Capitol, Chief Justice Brown presiding, the following memorial of Associate Justice George L. Bunn was presented to the court and read by Chester L. Caldwell, Esq.:

George Lincoln Bunn was born at Sparta, Monroe County, Wisconsin, June 25, 1865, and was the son of Romanzo and Sarah (Purdy) Bunn. He inherited the judicial traits that marked his career as a Judge in both the District and Supreme Courts of Minnesota. His father, Romanzo Bunn, was a Judge of the Circuit Court of Wisconsin from 1868 to 1877, when he was appointed Judge of the United States Circuit Court for the Western District of Wisconsin, which position he held until his death. George L. Bunn died October 9, 1918. He received his early education in the public schools of his native town and when sixteen years old entered the preparatory department of the University of Wisconsin. Two years later he entered the University, graduating from the Academic Course and received his degree of A.B. in 1885, in which year he moved to La Crosse and studied law in the office of J. W. Losey, Esq. In 1886 he returned to Madison and entered the law office of S. U. Pinney, at the same time attending the law school of Wisconsin University, from which he was graduated in 1888 with the degree of L.L.B. He came to St. Paul in the fall of 1888 and practiced law from 1888 to 1897, when he was appointed Judge of the District Court of Ramsey County by Governor Clough to fill the vacancy caused by the death of Judge Kerr. He continued to occupy the position of District Judge from 1897 to 1911, when he was appointed to the Supreme Bench by Governor Eberhart. He was married to Ella Spaulding of Madison, Wisconsin, August 9, 1890, who died in 1891, and married Fanny Losey of La Crosse, Wisconsin, October 2, 1908, who survives him.

Judge Bunn was a man in the highest sense of the word. Of a naturally judicial temperament, a keen analytical mind, and with an unswerving sense of justice, he was most admirably equipped to discharge the high duties of the office that he has so ably filled for many years. Modest and retiring in his life and habits, he was slow to impose or intrude his opinions and beliefs upon others, but when they were invoked they were thoughtfully and conscientiously given and tenaciously defended against all attacks save only those of pure reason. Quiet and retiring in his private as in his public life, his circle of intimate friends was not large, but those who were privileged to be included in that circle found him invariably genial, unselfish, and lovable. His interests were broad and varied and his fine mind was tempered and kept wholesome and pure by contact and association with nature, both in the wilderness and in the garden. His unswerving courage, patience, and gentleness in the fight with the terrible disease that fastened upon him more than two years before his death were nothing less than magnificent. He was a devoted husband, a staunch friend, an able jurist, and an honest man, and the State itself has in his death suffered irreparable loss.

Morton Barrows, Chairman
Pierce Butler
David F. Simpson
J. L. Washburn
M. L. Countryman
L. L. Brown
Chester L. Caldwell,
Committee

M. L. Countryman, Esq., then addressed the court:

Upon the recent occasion of presenting to this court a memorial of the late Justice Philip E. Brown, Mr. Justice Bunn, responding on behalf of the court, paid a tribute to Justice Brown every word of which is strikingly appropriate to his own character. As he said of his associate, 128 Minn. xxxiii, so we can say of him: Minnesota has before mourned great judges, but I doubt very much if she ever had greater cause. The elements were so mixed in him that it is no disparagement of either living or dead to say that George L. Bunn was one of the greatest judges that Minnesota ever had. He was a man with a passion to do right and a wonderful capacity for seeing the right. He possessed a keen and sane wholesome mind, thoroughly equipped. He was a tremendous and tireless worker. He met every question squarely. He never dodged. He was no temporizer or compromiser. Himself a man of broad and human views, he had little sympathy with technicality and none at all with anything that approached dishonesty. No case was ever presented to this court that failed to receive the most painstaking scrutiny on his part, and it mattered not how small the amount involved was. He never wrote an opinion without exhausting the law on the subject in his researches. He was absolutely fearless. He never courted popularity with the people or with the bar. He never thought for one moment of the possible effect upon his own future of an unpopular decision. He nevertheless stood exceedingly high in public esteem.

I feel very deeply the personal loss in the death of Judge Bunn. We were intimate friends and companions with the rod and gun for nearly thirty years. He was a loyal friend, a lovable companion, and a big-hearted man.

Charles W. Farmham, Esq., then said:

I hadn't intended to say one word, but may I, as a member of this Bar and as one who in the phrase of the memorial was privileged to be a friend of Judge Bunn, bespeak for him happiness in Paradise—a lover of little children and flowers and gardens, and of games and sports, and yet a very great judge.

Honorable David F. Simpson, formerly Associate Justice of the court, then addressed the court and said:

May it please the court, I did not expect to say anything. My feeling that I would not say anything came not from any lack of intense appreciation of the great worth of Justice Bunn nor from lack of the wish to pay him tribute but rather from the belief that I would be unable to express in words my regard for him. The reports of this court and other courts will always preserve a tribute to the unusual power and ability of Justice Bunn, and yet I feel that full knowledge of his power and qualifications as a Judge comes to one not from reading his finished product but from an understanding of the methods by which he produced that result. This understanding came to those associated with him in work. Justice Bunn's ability was individual, unusual. He approached a legal question peculiarly free from any prejudice or leaning; his mind naturally followed a direct and logical course, and deep in his very being was a full and absolute regard for the broadest and most fundamental principles of justice. From this character and disposition and mental trait or power came Justice Bunn's unusual quality as a jurist. To me it always seemed that in the law he possessed the power that a woodsman has in the forest. Without resort to instruments for guidance or continual looking for the blazed trail, he was able, by some power within himself, to follow a line of legal principle to its logical termination. It has sometime been said that "orators think in sounding phrases." By applying a similar suggestion to Justice Bunn, we might fairly say that he thought in legal principles. His mind seemed to follow naturally and normally lines of established legal principles. Law is simply applied ethics. It develops from an application of the fundamental rules of right and wrong, and the appreciation of those fundamental rules and the ability to apply them Justice Bunn had in a marked degree.

Not only as a jurist was Justice Bunn unusual but as a friend as well. He never went far afield in seeking associations with other men. He never, by any marked demonstration, evidenced his friendship when he came in contact with men, and yet his kindly interested warm regard for his friends was unmistakable. You felt certain of his great enduring friendship even though you might be entirely unable to tell by what sign or by what word he had indicated that he regarded you as a friend.

My close association with Justice Bunn will always remain with me, an inspiration in my work, a delightful memory of a satisfying friendship.

Chief Justice Brown then said:

Mr. Morton Barrows of St. Paul and Mr. L. L. Brown of Winona, personal friends and acquaintances of Justice Bunn for many years, are unable to be present today, and they have expressed their regrets at their inability to be here and offer their words of praise and commendation on the life and character of Judge Bunn.

Associate Justice Hallam [for the court] then said:

It is one of the natural promptings of men living to pay their tribute of respect to the dead. Some say this is not worth while. If we were to spend this time in mere flattery it would not be worth while, for such words do no honor to the dead and bring no profit to the living. But a man who has lived a life of honor and usefulness leaves behind him much of which it is worth while to speak with truth, and in recalling the memory of these things we do fitting honor to the dead and impress an example for those who still live.

It was my privilege to know Justice Bunn for thirty-six years. When I first knew him, he was, at 17, just entering on his second year in college. He graduated before the age of twenty. I knew him as a fellow student, as a fellow practitioner at the bar, as an associate upon the district court, and as an associate member of this court.

When he was still a young lawyer, those who knew him best thought the best field for him was in a judicial career. He became a judge at thirty-one and continued to be a judge for nearly twenty-two years, and it was in this line of activity that he spent the better part of his active life, achieved his greatest usefulness, and gained his greatest distinction.

As a boy he learned his lessons more easily than most boys, but he learned them well. As a judge he wrote opinions and decided cases more easily than most judges, but he always did his work well. He never left any task half done or shabbily done, and he never avoided any task that fell to his lot. To the very day of his death, in spite of the handicap of failing health, he kept up his full share of his work upon the bench.

The opinions he wrote as a member of this court are contained in some thirty volumes of the Minnesota Reports. Able and exhaustive, they rank among the best in the books. But his contribution to the law is not measured by his written opinions alone. At the conference table, around which all cases are decided, his influence was strong, for he was quick to analyze, so clear of judgment, so forceful in speech, that his opinion on every pending question was always regarded by his associates with the most careful consideration.

In the later months of his life he was obliged, in conference, to express his views in writing, but this seemed to detract but little from the weight of his words. He would always in a few words go to the very heart of the case.

To him the work of a judge was wholly impersonal. He forgot parties and attorneys in his search for the justice of the cause. No person, no motive, could swerve his judgment save as it could show him wherein lay the right. Quiddities and technicalities never appealed to him. His aim was to mete out justice and he went straight to that end.

He loved to teach law students the law, and they loved to hear him. He impressed them with his own dignity and character. He impressed upon them the need of forever allying law and justice and made clear the great trust that would be reposed upon them when they became members of the profession of law. He was fond of his students, followed their career with kindly interest, and always rejoiced in their success.

He did not cultivate many intimate friendships, yet he was fond of friendship. and those who knew him best were his warmest friends. He did not like to speak ill of men, yet he despised the practices that are petty and mean.

He liked the lighter side of life and the diversions of life. He liked best those of the outdoor sort, was fond of hunting and fishing and of the things that brought him close to nature. In his later years he was never so happy as when he lived among the flowers he so patiently cared for.

He was brave in the misfortune that befell him. For the last two years of his life he must have been continually conscious that his life was gradually slipping away, but he never made complaint. He accepted his lot with true grace and fortitude. He typified the truth of the lines that "the man worth while is the man who can smile when everything goes wrong." As a jurist he enriched the law. He helped to make it better serve its true purpose. He made the law clearer to judges, to lawyers, and to students of the law. Able, honorable, courageous, sympathetic, true to the best ideals, surely the world is better that he has lived.

Chief Justice Brown then said:

The court is in full accord with the sentiments expressed in the memorial, and in all that has been said concerning the character and ability of the late Justice Bunn. The memorial will be entered in the record of the court there to remain as a perpetual testimonial of a great jurist and a just and upright judge. [141 Minn. xix]

Philip E. Brown

1856–1915
Associate Justice, 1912–1915

On the afternoon of April 6, 1915, in the Court Room at the State Capitol, Hon. Charles M. Start, formerly Chief Justice of the Supreme Court, addressed the Court, then in session, and said:

Your committee to prepare a memorial of Justice Philip E. Brown has discharged the duty, and the Secretary of the Minnesota State Bar Association and of the committee, Mr. Caldwell, will now read it with your permission.

Chester L. Caldwell, Esq., then read the following memorial:

Philip E. Brown was born on the nineteenth day of June 1856, in the town of Shullsburg, Lafayette County, Wisconsin, and was the son of George O. and Sarah (Robson) Brown. He died February 6, 1915.

He was graduated from the University of Wisconsin and received his degree of Bachelor of Law from the Albany College of Law in 1881. The following year he began the practice of law at Luverne, Minnesota. In 1891 he was appointed judge of the Thirteenth Judicial District. He was elected to that office in 1892 and re-elected in 1898 and 1904, which position he filled with marked ability until his election as Associate Justice of this court in November. He assumed the duties of that office in January 1912 and remained a member of this court until his death.

He married Ellen Ford in 1882, who survives him.

Judge Brown was a plain man, retiring, unassuming, and never sought public attention or applause. He was learned in the law, honest, and conscientious both as a lawyer and a jurist. No man ever was more industrious or painstaking in his work. He never slighted any task. His days were spent in arduous and conscientious labor in the performance of his duties. He was possessed of strong common sense, a natural love for justice, always courteous and considerate, a patient and candid listener, firm and fearless in the discharge of his duties, both as a lawyer and a judge. He was a pronounced aid to both the Bench and Bar, and his death is an irreparable loss to both.

His character in private life was as unsullied as was his public life.

While records of court endure, they will be a memorial to industry, ability, integrity, and sense of justice.

Our deepest sympathy is with his family and friends—their loss is our loss.

We move that this brief expression of our sincere regard be spread upon the records of this court.

> Charles M. Start, Chairman
> John G. Williams
> Lorin Cray
> David F. Simpson
> Alexander L. Jaynes
> J. H. Town
> Chester L. Caldwell,
> Committee

Hon. Charles M. Start then addressed the Court:

I desire briefly to express my appreciation of the work and worth of Mr. Justice Brown and to add a word of personal tribute to memory.

Our acquaintance began while he was judge of the Thirteenth Judicial District, and the longer I knew him the greater was my esteem and affection for him. For some years it was a part of my duties in connection with my associates on this bench to make a critical study of his rulings and decisions in the district court that were brought to this court for review. The Justices of the Supreme Court have a good opportunity when studying appeal records to determine the ability and character of a district judge. If he is able, fearless, fair, and true, controlled by no motive except a sincere purpose to do justice without fear or favor, giving to all their legal rights as he understands them, the record will show it. If he be the reverse of this, a trimmer, shaping his rulings and decisions to win popular applause or to avoid a reversal, the record will also show it. The truth is that, under our system of reporting trials in the district court, an appeal record is to an appellate judge a mirror unerringly reflecting the mental and moral characteristics of the trial judge. Minnesota has been and is exceptionally fortunate in the character of her district judges, and it would be invidious to say that Justice Brown was the ablest and best of them all. But my deliberate opinion, based upon the appeal records of this court and my personal knowledge, is that Minnesota has never had a better or fairer judge than Philip E. Brown. His opinions in this court show judicial ability of a high order, laborious and conscientious work, and a firm grasp of the pivotal facts and controlling principles of the case in hand. They also show that he was possessed of a keen sense of justice that no quibbling of counsel could obscure. His knowledge of constitutional law is shown in the opinion of the court written by him in the case of *State ex rel. v. City of Mankato*, 117 Minn. 458. The question in that case was the constitutionality of the commission form of government. The opinion is a masterly one and entitles Justice Brown to rank with the great Justices of this court who have passed not away but on to a higher and better life. In his judicial work he was dominated by a sense of duty that would not permit him to spare himself although suffering from physical ill, for he was responsive to every call of duty and resolute in his devotion to right. He was an unassuming, heart-true, lovable man, of positive convictions, great ability, pure character, and high ideals. He was a loyal and loving husband and father, a sincere friend tender and true, and a brave chivalrous gentleman, worthy of Brutus' eulogy:

> His life was gentle; and the elements
> So mix'd in him that Nature might stand up
> And say to all the world: "This was a man."

Hon. J. L. Washburn then addressed the Court:

In the mighty conflict now pending in the very heart of the advanced civilization of the world, the intellect, the learning, and the inventive genius of educated man are all brought into full activity to the end that the greatest number of men may be destroyed in the shortest time possible.

Brave men, good citizens, of the best blood of the warring nations have been destroyed by the million in a few months and their places in the serried ranks of the combatants filled by others of the same character, who carry forward the contest of battle and the work of carnage with equal courage and ferocity.

Men are scored only by numbers *en masse*, and they share in common and without identification the shallow burial trenches of the heroic dead.

The individual is ignored only as he is a part of a great fighting machine. Losses are counted by numbers, and if only a few hundred or few thousand are slain, it is given out that the losses were slight. Only the effectiveness and fortunes of aggregations receive interested attention from the recorders and readers of the conflicts upon hundreds of miles of battle lines.

Nevertheless the fact remains that the power, the value, the effectiveness, and morale of the contending armies all depend upon the mettle of the individuals. The men who fight and die side by side in such conflicts have known the worth of one another.

It is our province in the peaceful struggle of life to know even more thoroughly one another individually, to measure one another's worth, to bear an individual part in the upward striving for social development, and to mark with sorrow the calling of an individual comrade.

It may not be possible for surviving soldiers or commanders to pause in the conflict to give extended attention to the dead and too often but little care to the wounded, but we may pause in our work, however strenuous it may be, to consider the life and character of those to whom the final summons has come and to do deserved honor to their memory.

It is both fitting and beneficial that we should do so. It is fitting that a good citizen should be remembered and honored, and it beneficial to the living to recount the virtues of the noble dead.

When Philip E. Brown was touched by the wand of Death, he was occupying a place in the first rank of distinguished citizens of this commonwealth.

He was endowed with a mind of power and discrimination. A liberal preparation followed by his years of careful, conscientious application gave him in his maturity superior strength as a lawyer and jurist.

Judge Brown was born in Lafayette County in Southern Wisconsin, June 19, 1856. He was educated at the University of Wisconsin, and graduated from the Albany, New York, Law School. He began the practice of law at Darlington, the county seat of his native county but after two years settled in Luverne, Minnesota, where he practiced from 1882 to 1891 and where he continued to reside until his death. In 1891 he became judge of the Thirteenth Judicial District of this state and continued in that position until the close of 1910, having that year been elected to the bench of this Court of which he was an honored and most efficient member until his death.

It is to be noticed that Judge Brown's career has run along a definite line. He was not diverted from giving his undivided efforts to the pursuit of the law as practitioner and as a jurist. There was that confidence in the accuracy of his judgment and justice of his conclusions that only such a course and such habits can inspire.

I met him for the first time in the early eighties. I think he had not long been at Luverne. I had heard of him, for that he was a lawyer who knew how to work and who was an adversary to be feared soon became known.

We first met at an encampment of the old Second Regiment of the Minnesota National Guard, and I deem it an honor to myself to say that I believe we always thereafter felt that we were friends, although after my removal to Duluth we lived in extreme opposite parts in the State and did not often meet. I was glad to see him elevated to this bench, for he was fit.

My brethren of the Northern part of the State and especially the members of the Bar Association of the Eleventh Judicial District, whose guest he was on several occasions, acquired a great fondness for him and a high appreciation of his judicial abilities and his personal character.

It is as their representative that I assume to occupy any time or place in these memorial exercises.

At the risk of repetition of what others may say, I recount that a discriminating sense of justice, a keen judgment of the law, modesty of assertion, unlimited courage, a genial and generous disposition and chivalrous spirit, a high sense of personal honor, and an elevated standard of duty as a citizen, all crowned with habits of industry and sobriety, were the dominant characteristics and virtues of distinguished citizen.

The tug at the sleeve that such a life makes tends to stimulate his companions who still abide to emulate his virtues and when the summons comes to them to courageously cross the threshold into the unknown, but let us hope not unknowable, sequence of human life and human effort.

Hon. Royal A. Stone then addressed the Court:

The inadequacy of words on this occasion is as painful as it is obvious. Our hearts are full, but because the content is grief for a departed friend, brother, leader, we cannot lighten the burden.

But that is not our purpose here. We are met at the bar of this Court to bear witness as to the life and character, and more especially the judicial life and character, of one who was an Associate of your Honors upon this Bench.

For many years prior to his coming to this Court, he was a judge of the Thirteenth Judicial District. As district judge and as Associate Justice of this Court, he made for himself an enviable reputation. He became unusually well known personally to the Bar of Minnesota.

His place among us has been vacated by Death, and as is always the case, we are thereby for the first time brought to an adequate appreciation of his great merits as a man, his true value as a citizen, and his splended service as a judge.

> We are to say what we take the law to be. If we do not speak our real opinion, we prevaricate with God and our own consciences.

These words of Lord Mansfield furnish a most fitting text for any dissertation on the life of Philip E. Brown, and especially his work as a jurist, as an expounder of the law.

> We are to say what we take the law to be.

How simple, how direct, how courageous a statement is that of the duty of a judge!

And how simply, how directly, how courageously did Philip E. Brown perform that duty.

"To say what we take the law to be"—and to that task Judge Brown applied a persevering diligence, a profound learning, a ripe experience, and a balanced judgment.

"If we do not speak our real opinion, we prevaricate with God and our own consciences."

There we have, in the language of a judge of a bygone century, motif of the judicial work, aye, of the very life of him, in tender memory, in loving respect for whom we are now gathered at the bar of the Court from which so recently the hand of Death has snatched him.

The fearless and confident expression of his "*real opinion*" was Judge Brown's most outstanding trait.

Careful in judgment, seeking all proper aids, applying carefully the most rigid tests, he had an unusually accurate process of reasoning.

Not opinionated, he yet had that confidence in his own conclusions which such mental processes ought to beget in their fortunate possessor.

The frankness and confidence with which he expressed his deliberate judgment was equalled only by the open-mindedness with which he listened to and weighed the contrary view and the readiness with which he would detect, acknowledge, and remedy his own error, if any.

And when finally his conclusion was reached—his "real opinion"—it was expressed without fear, expressed confidently because without fear of "prevarication with God" or "his own conscience."

What a horror he had of such prevarication—of intellectual dishonesty!

If all that can be said of a deceased lawyer, especially if he be a judge, is that he was morally honest, better far that his brethren not attempt to memorialize such relatively scant virtue.

But if in addition to moral rectitude there is an uncompromising upstanding and outstanding intellectual cleanness and honesty, we have a man indeed.

Judge Brown was as much an exemplar of intellectual as of moral honesty.

Quibbles, indirections, uncertainties, evasions, were all abhorrent to him, whether they pertained to considerations of ethics or of logic.

Justice was ever his goal, to be right his constant aim.

These are days of progressivism. So have been all days since creation. So will be all days to the end of time. It must be so or the philosophy of civilization and the tenets of Christianity are alike untenable.

Human conduct is ruled by law. Therefore, as humanity is constantly progressive, so must law be constantly progressive. Static or retrograde law cannot achieve justice.

How accurate, how broad, how human, was Judge Brown's conception of this truth.

If ever there was a sanely progressive expounder of the law, it was Judge Brown. With wonderful clarity of vision he discriminated between precedents. He properly and courageously discarded those, and only those, that had been rendered *passe* because the changes wrought by time had deprived them of all propriety, if not of all possibility, of application to modern conditions.

Appreciating to the full the undying and unchanging attributes of truth, of justice in the abstract, he yet realized that justice in the "myriad of single instances," the controversies that arise between man and man, must be found and expressed not in the records and rules of a dead past but in the ideals and terms of contemporaneous humanity.

As district judge, as Associate Judge of this Court, his life was preeminently one of service to his community and the state.

His "community" the Thirteenth Judicial District, there where he had his home, where his "daily walk and conversation" were known of all, is the place to find the best record of Judge Brown's great qualities of mind and heart and soul. It is in the high opinion, the great and affectionate regard of lawyer and layman, of those who have known him longest and best.

Some years ago, it was my good fortune to attend a banquet tendered to Judge Brown at Windom (or was it Worthington?) by the Bar of the Thirteenth District. The occasion was Judge Brown's return to active service after a considerable absence, which had been enforced by his ill health. Never has there been a more genuine expression of good will, of confidence, of admiration, aye of affection, for a public man.

Our modern citizenry is ready enough to proclaim

its admiration for a political servant for the time being in its good favor. It is very slow to give expression to any appreciation of the work of a judge, however long continued and distinguished his services may have been.

But on that occasion the Bar of the Thirteenth District broke down the usual reserve and spoke what was in their minds as to their regard for judge Brown. So sincere, so affectionate was their greeting, so genuine their pleasure at having him back on the Bench and in his accustomed place, that it seemed to be a large family festival held to celebrate the return after a long absence of the *paterfamilias*.

It was an occasion unique in the experience of the judiciary of this State and showed in an unusually convincing manner the high regard in which Judge Brown was held by his professional "home folks," and their opinion in such matters is always the best.

The illness that at that time had temporarily removed him from his judicial labors never entirely left him. He was urged to retire, but even though he might have saved himself by leaving the Bench, he refused to do so.

He kept on, and finally his life was a forfeit to his work, a sacrifice on the altar of his duty as a citizen and a judge of this great Commonwealth.

His loyalty to his ideals of judicial duty kept him at his labors long after physical affliction justified and his own circumstances permitted his retirement. The ills of the flesh availed not against his courageous soul. But they finally overwhelmed his body, and struck him down at the post from whence they could not drive him.

Thus ended a mortal career in which there was realized a high ideal of service.

Truly this life was a living "epistle . . . known and read of all men." In his life, but still more in his untimely death, there is that which should inspire all, especially the members of his profession, to that life of unselfish service by which only its highest purposes can be achieved, its greatest privileges enjoyed, and its richest awards attained.

Hon. Alexander L. Jaynes then addressed the Court and said:

It is with a strong sense of my own inability but with a feeling of obligation that I rise here to add a few words to what has already been said about Justice Brown.

I knew Judge Brown probably as well as any man. To me he was not only a friend but almost a father and all that word means with its kindly love and sympathy. When I was a boy he played with me; in my college days he did much to direct my course and inspire my energy. Later in the practice of law in his court in a kindly manner he corrected my errors and endeavored to inspire in me a sense of the nobility and dignity of our profession. I say this, for mine was the common experience of all young men who began the practice of law before him. He inspired all of us to do the things that were right. We knew that his mind quickly detected the false and arrived unerringly at the truth. To him we always went for advice whatever our difficulties—love, law, or politics. It was as freely given as it was freely sought. He knew and understood young men. He loved young men. He was always young. Our ambitious dreams he could make his own—our faults overlook—our virtues encourage. He conferred upon us all the same consideration and interest that he would have given to a son. All of us who grew up in the Thirteenth Judicial District loved him and he loved us; nothing more can we say. Why then at this moment when for the last time we give public expression to our common loss should our hearts be sad, but rather in the language of one of England's great poets we say:

> Enough of sorrow, wreck and blight;
> Think rather of those moments bright;
> When to the consciousness of right
>   his course was true;
> When wisdom prospered in his sight
>   and virtue grew.

Harrison L. Schmitt, Esq., President of the Minnesota State Bar Association, then addressed the Court:

We are here today to commemorate and perpetuate upon the permanent records of this court the name and fame of a brother lawyer who was at the time of his death an honored member of this the court in the state and who, through his uniform kindness, his great ability, and sterling honesty, had become very dear to us all.

I cannot add to what has already been said by members of the Bar of Minnesota in honor of Justice Brown. I want to endorse every word from the bottom of my heart. No human mind can frame or human voice express any sentiment that Justice Brown did not deserve. However, in behalf of the Minnesota State Bar Association, of which Justice Brown was a valued and active member, I feel it my duty to call the attention of the members of our Association and members of the Bar of Minnesota in general to a few things.

For years every lawyer here present, in fact every lawyer in the state, having knowledge of the enormous amount of work members of this court have been compelled to do in order that unjust delays in the meting-out of justice might be avoided, has known that no human being could continue to do that work for any considerable length of time without ruining his health and paving the way to an early grave.

For years, and notably during the 1914 campaign, this association endeavored to bring home to the voters of the state knowledge of the fact that our Supreme Court Judges were being shamefully overworked and that it was imperative to increase the membership of the Court to secure relief.

But as usual, the voters of the state, on account of lack of knowledge of the facts and general indifference, said "No, the Court is keeping up the work, why add to the expense of the taxpayers by increasing the number of judges?" Members of the Bar generally have not done their duty as citizens in that they have not used diligence in informing their friends upon this important matter.

The result is that Justice Brown is but another victim who has been sacrificed upon the altar of public duty, and we lawyers must bear the stigma of having contributed to this our irreparable loss. Justice Brown was always under all circumstances while holding public office a public servant in the truest sense. So deep rooted was his sense of public duty that rather than permit the work of the Court to fall behind he labored beyond all human endurance.

We have been and are requiring our Supreme Court Justices and Commissioners to hear three appeals a day, five days every week, almost the year round, in order that the lawyers and litigants of this state and of many other states might not be denied speedy justice.

Justice Brown assumed this burden cheerfully and went to his grave with a smile on his face and nothing but love in his heart for his fellows.

In view of all this, is it not our solemn duty to see to it that these conditions are speedily changed? We can and must do it. We must do our utmost in this regard if we would purge ourselves of blame for future conditions. Justice Brown does not need our praise. His name and fame will continue to shine as a beacon light showing us and our followers the way to glory and success. If his untimely death shall wake us up and shall show us our responsibility to such an extent that there will be no cause for blaming ourselves in the future for such conditions, we may at least feel that our sins of the past have been condoned.

Let us therefore take the lesson home to our hearts, and remembering that our departed brother labored unceasingly in the public service and thereby crowned his career with everlasting pillars of honor, try to profit by his example.

Associate Justice Bunn responded on behalf of the Court:

You do well to commemorate the life and services of Philip E. Brown. Minnesota has before mourned great judges, but I doubt very much if she ever had greater cause. The elements were so mixed in him that it is no disparagement of either living or dead to say that Philip E. Brown was one of the greatest judges that Minnesota ever had. He was a man with a passion to be right and wonderful capacity for seeing the right. He possessed a keen and sane, wholesome mind, thoroughly equipped. He was a tremendous and tireless worker. He met every question squarely. He never dodged. He was no temporizer or compromiser. Himself a man of broad and human views, he had little sympathy with technicality and none at all with anything that approached dishonesty. No case was ever presented to this court that failed to receive the most painstaking scrutiny on his part, and it mattered not how small the amount involved was. He never wrote an opinion without exhausting the law on the subject in his researches. He was absolutely fearless, never courted popularity with the people or with the Bar. Never thinking for one moment of the possible effect on his own future of an unpopular decision, he nevertheless stood exceedingly high in public esteem. I feel the personal loss deeply. We were very close to each other during the last few years. He was a loyal friend, a lovable companion, and a big-hearted man.

Chief Justice Brown also responded on behalf of the Court and said:

The memorial presented is a fitting tribute to the character and worth of a just and upright judge. It may be truthfully said that no member of any court ever entered upon his judicial duties with a firmer or more determined purpose, faithfully to discharge every duty imposed upon him, even to minute details, than the late Justice Philip E. Brown; no member of any court ever devoted himself more laboriously and earnestly in the examination of every cause presented for decision, and the labor and research disclosed by the opinions written by him furnish an illustration of the time and attention given to other causes. He neglected no duty, was faithful to every trust, and pre-eminently qualified for judicial work. He was not in robust health during his term of service, yet he labored continuously from early morn until late at night, striving to master the records and briefs before the Court and uniformly come to a clear understanding of every cause presented. By his constant application he obstructed the healing qualities of nature and undermined his strength, gradually weakening his vital forces until the end of life's journey came without warning. He was a martyr to his fidelity.

Your memorial will be entered in the records of the court, there to remain in perpetual remembrance of a member of this court of whom it may well be said, "Well done, thou good and faithful servant." [128 Minn. xxi]

229

Andrew D. Holt

1855–1948
Associate Justice, 1912–1942

In the afternoon of June 4, 1948, at two o'clock, the Court being assembled in the courtroom in the State Capitol, Chief Justice Charles Loring said:

The Court recognizes the president of the Minnesota State Bar Association, Mr. Horace Van Valkenburg.

Mr. Van Valkenburg then said:

The Bar of this state, through the Minnesota State Bar Association, has requested this Court to set a time at which it would receive and accept memorials in behalf of Mr. Justice Andrew Holt and Commissioner Myron D. Taylor, two very distinguished judges formerly of this Court.

The Bar Association wishes to express to the Court its appreciation of the fact that the Court has been willing to convene this afternoon after its regular term has ended and during the summer months. That this Court has been willing to convene out of term for the purpose of receiving these memorials is a token expression of its respect for these two former members of this Court.

The Bar is honored in being permitted to present for preservation among the records of this Court these memorials . . . Mr. Justice Andrew Holt died this year. He served on this Court from 1912 to 1942, a period that exceeds the entire professional career of many of us in this room. Memorials to Mr. Justice Holt will be presented by Mr. Sigurd Ueland of Minneapolis and by Judge Henry M. Gallagher of Waseca, who was Chief Justice of this Court during a portion of the time of Judge Holt's tenure.

Mr. Ueland then said:

On the eleventh day of last February occurred the death of one of the most remarkable men in the his-

tory of Minnesota. Andrew Holt then was 92 years of age. The salient facts of his life are familiar to most of us, and their recital on this occasion should be brief.

He was born of parents of Swedish immigrant stock on May 20, 1855, on a small farm in Carver county. His early home was a log cabin, in the best American tradition. He was brought up in the Lutheran Church and remained throughout his life a deeply religious man. His heredity and early life as a pioneer farm boy gave him that physical strength and inclination and capacity for hard work that were so notably witnessed by his long and industrious life. He earned his way through St. Ansgar's Academy (now Gustavus Adolphus College) and the University of Minnesota. At the University, which now boasts some 26,000 students, he graduated in a class of 17 and received his Bachelor of Arts degree in 1880.

He was undecided as to his calling; it was a student's dilemma between the ministry and the law. The advice of John Lind, later to be governor of the state, saved him for the legal profession. There were no law schools in Minnesota in those days, and he followed the usual practice of reading law in a law office, at first in Chaska and later in Glencoe. After a few months of such study, he was admitted to the bar in 1881.

For the next 13 years he was engaged in the general practice of law, as a junior member of the firm of Ueland, Shores and Holt, in the city of Minneapolis, where he continued to reside until his death. In 1894 he was appointed judge of the Municipal Court, and from that time forward his work was that of a trial or appellate judge. In 1904 he was elevated to the District Court, in 1911 to this the Supreme Court of this state. He was several times reelected to the position of Associate Justice of this Court and finally retired in 1942 at the age of 87, having been continuously engaged at the law for 61 years and as a judge for 48. Even then he did not cease to labor but was appointed Commissioner by the judges of the Court and for several years continued to write opinions for the Court but did not vote.

While on the Supreme Court, Judge Holt maintained a routine of living that has become almost an epic. He took the Nicollet avenue streetcar near his home in Washburn Park, Minneapolis, at 5:57 A.M. on every working day and arrived at his office in the Capitol at seven o'clock. At the end of the working day he returned home on the same conveyance. While on the streetcar he read records and briefs. His industry, by the standards of the present day, was prodigious.

His reported opinions are the fruit of that industry. They are clear and to the point, intellectually honest in their treatment of prior decisions, simple, unbiased, and restrained. He was not one of those judges who feel a call to remake the common law, amend the statutes, and revise the Constitution. Yet he recognized that the law is neither rigid nor inflexible but rather subject to gradual evolution so as to keep step with those imperceptible changes that are continually occurring in the living conditions and customs of mankind. For example, in the litigation involving various zoning statutes he exercised a decisive influence in upholding the constitutionality of these laws. He wrote: "It is time that courts recognize the aesthetic as a factor in life." That does not sound startling today, but it was strong judicial medicine in 1920. His opinions that expound and clarify the laws of Minnesota will prove an enduring contribution of great value to the bench, the bar, and the people of the state.

Any lawyer who in his younger days appeared before the Supreme Court while Judge Holt was a member will retain an indelible impression of his personality. He was tall, straight and spare. His blue eyes, attentive gaze, fresh complexion, white mustache, and pointed beard, the perennial white bow tie, a friendly smile all combined to give the young advocate a feeling of confidence on an occasion when that feeling was much needed. Notwithstanding his great age, one felt that his face was beautiful, illuminated as it seemed by an inner light. No judge ever won a more unanimous love and respect from the lawyers admitted to practice before him.

He was a disciple not only of Blackstone but of Isaac Walton as well. He found his recreation from the law books amid the beauties of nature on our lakes and streams, where he angled for the small-mouthed bass and other denizens of the deep. His other interests included a love for good music and a keen interest in Swedish literature and culture.

He was not a lively man in social affairs and, in recent years at least, rarely left his fireside in the evening. He loved his home, and the domestic side of his life appears to have been not less happy than his professional career. He survived his wife and was in turn survived by his two children. One, a son, Dr. John E. Holt, is a successful physician in St. Paul. The other, a daughter, Miss Agnes E. Holt, is the principal of West High School in Minneapolis.

Throughout his long life Judge Holt enjoyed the good health that his temperate habits so well deserved, and he retained to the end a mind and memory of which many younger men are denied. He derived those great hopeful dispositions. Take it all in all, his life seems to have been as rich in achievement and tranquility as ever falls to the lot of man.

Such is my impression of our friend, whom I may truly call the gentlest and best of all the men that I have ever known.

The Honorable Henry M. Gallagher then presented the following memorial:

It is wholly fitting that the deliberations of this Court be interrupted for the purpose of paying tribute to one who served as a member of this honorable body for almost 35 years, during 30 of which he was an Associate Justice and the balance a Commissioner.

Judge Holt was appointed to the Court on December 21, 1911, by the late Governor Eberhart, to fill a vacancy caused by the resignation of Justice David F. Simpson, who served only one year of a six-year term. Judge Holt was then almost 57 years old, a few years short of the age men in many occupations are now expected to retire. Nevertheless, at the time of his retirement Judge Holt had served as a member of the Court longer than any other man since statehood, and, we may add, no one has ever served more faithfully or more honorably.

During his service Justice Holt wrote the opinion of the Court in 1,687 cases. He also wrote 114 dissents and a few concurring opinions. When he concurred specially or dissented, he did so in very few words.

The first of Judge Holt's opinions is reported in Volume 116, Minnesota Reports, and the last in Volume 213. He served with six chief justices and 22 associate justices during his terms on the Court, and his incumbency in office extended throughout the terms of eight governors. It is said that at the time if Judge Holt's appointment he was the first native Minnesotan to serve on the Court.

Judge Holt could well be called a "perfect judge." He possessed all the necessary characteristics of a jurist. He had a judicial mind and a judicial temperament. He possessed a high degree of patience and tolerance and, above all, a kindly heart and a sympathetic nature. He did not rely upon brilliance or snap judgment but persisted in plowing every furrow of the law as a farmer would his field, and the rewards reaped therefrom are reflected in the richness of his opinions, all of which were written in longhand and transcribed after careful study and consideration.

Every man who ever served as an associate with Judge Holt will vouch for his helpfulness to the other members of the Court. He was a stickler for precedent but would listen with patience to the viewpoints of others and would always present his view in a calm but persuasive manner. Criticism of the work of other justices or judges was not in his makeup. In short, he was the idol of the Court.

Layman and lawyer alike respected and loved Judge Holt. They respected him for his staunchness of character, his philosophy of life, and his proficiency in his profession. They loved him for his mild-mannered courtesy, unprejudiced point of view, and his understanding sympathy.

While not a politician in any sense of the word, Judge Holt was one of the best vote getters of his time. He was first elected in the year following his appointment and reelected in 1918, 1924, 1930, 1936, and 1942, each time by increasingly larger majorities. It is doubtful whether in all his years in public life Judge Holt ever asked anyone to vote for him,

and it is likewise certain that he never accused anyone of voting against him.

The people of Minnesota are justly proud of Judge Holt. He was often honored by his associates and his friends, particularly in the later years of his life. He always "stole the show" at any gathering at which he appeared, regardless of whether he or someone else was being honored. He always accepted tribute with humility and honor with modesty. He never really appreciated his greatness.

The stability of our past and the foundation of our future are due in no small way to the work and the efforts of this Grand Old Man, who served his state so long and so faithfully. May his memory linger as long as the books in which his opinions appear retain their pages.

Judge Henry M Gallagher then said:

With the permission of the Court I would like to add a few personal remarks.

I began the practice of law the year Judge Holt was appointed to this bench. In the years that followed I had occasion to appear before the Court about as often as the average country lawyer. There was something about him that always offered encouragement to lawyers appearing before the Court, particularly young lawyers.

He administered the oath the day I was appointed Chief Justice.

After my appointment was announced, former Chief Justice Wilson called to see me. His only advice was, "Lean on Judge Holt." My predecessor, former Chief Devaney, gave me the same advice, and I always followed it.

I suppose that in an ordinary lifetime every man has some brickbats thrown at him, and he receives some compliments. The highest compliment I ever received was a silent one. It came from Judge Holt. On the day I terminated my services as a member of the Court I met Judge Holt in the corridor. He stopped and clasped my hand. The tears were trickling down his cheeks. He didn't say anything, and I couldn't. I merely patted him on the shoulder, and he went his way and I went mine. By the time I reached my chambers there were a few tears trickling down my cheeks too. I shall never forget that parting.

I presume that Judge Holt parted company in the same manner with every man who left the Court during his incumbency, but that didn't in any respect lessen my appreciation of the way he parted company with me. I accepted the compliment in the same spirit as if I were the only one to whom it had ever been afforded.

Chief Justice Loring then said:

Judge Wilson, you were Chief Justice for ten years while Judge Holt was a member of this Court. Would you care to say something?

The Honorable Samuel B. Wilson then said:

For a period of ten years while I was the Chief Justice, Andrew Holt, as the senior Associate Justice, sat at my right hand.

No man ever had a more loyal co-worker than I. Rare compassion graced his spirit.

He was a common man with common attributes dedicated to the judiciary. From his experience in early life he built a foundation that served well in his long judicial career. He was a humble man. There was greatness in his simplicity. His heart could hold no malice. For him, there was no middle ground for the solution of morals of right or wrong.

Mr. Justice Holt was a patient man, always maintaining a calm, cautious, and dignified attitude. He held to the traditions in the sphere of his work. He was not a phrasemaker. He was always moved by his sense of justice. He was a valuable member of the Court. In some respects he was a timid man, but his timidity never swerved him from his line of duty as he saw it. He kept his rendezvous with justice.

While he was on the Court there was nothing so bad that he could not better it by simply being present. His presence always sweetened all of his surroundings with his goodness. I have sat in his presence and observed his ability to remain silent when and where one could not speak favorably. What a great bounty and blessing it is to hold such a royal gift! It is really a great virtue to know how to be silent even though you are right. I believe Mr. Justice Holt followed my philosophy: Never laugh when you win; then you don't have to cry when you lose.

The association of men on an appellate court gives one an intuitive understanding. You sense a partner-ship. You experience a brotherly feeling. Each cheerfully gives help, and each gladly receives help. They, *ex necessitate*, are bound together in a realization of a common destiny.

We honor Mr. Justice Holt for his mental strength and admire him for his humanity. His loyalty to duty reflected both his ancestry and his heritage.

To live is to strive and to venture and to win or lose. Man can't live easy and small. He is full of things meant to be used or given away or maybe destroyed. The more he spends, the more comes back. That is all he is, something to be used, scorched by the sun, warped by the wind, to have his fingers smashed and his body bent, to fall down and get up, to hunt and find. All a man has at the end of life is a set of memories. Things done well and things done poorly. The great sin is to end up with nothing done. Mr. Justice Holt lived and served. He accomplished much.

He never shirked. His head was high. It never drooped. It carried the spirit of a clear conscience and a definite aim.

Because of his charming personality and ten years of delightful association, I shall cherish the memory of the Honorable Andrew Holt.

Chief Justice Loring then said:

These proceedings in which Bench and Bar participate in memory of departed judges afford us an opportunity to record the respect, the esteem, and the affection with which in their lifetimes we regarded our professional brethren. It is wise that we pause in the course of our active work to conduct such ceremonies. It emphasizes in our minds the fact that all that is of real value that a judge can acquire is a fair name and the respect that we have for lives well spent in service in the cause of impartial justice. When a lawyer accepts a call to the Bench, he must reconcile himself to serving without hope or prospect of other reward.

Those of us who served for years with Mr. Justice Holt were greatly impressed with his ability, his application to work, his quiet and patient attention to the arguments of counsel, and his systematic method of disposing of business. Among his intimates, he occasionally displayed a keen sense of humor.

His 31 years of service on this Court covered the period of its heaviest burden in number of cases decided per annum. In spite of his advancing years, he did his full share of the work, even when this Court was rendering opinions in over 500 cases a year—more than twice the work per judge considered to be a year's work in the Circuit Courts of Appeals. The constant abuse of his eyes impaired his vision to a point that finally forced his retirement when his mental faculties were still at their full vigor. It was a privilege to practice before him, both when he was on the District Bench and during his service here, and more especially to serve with him on this Bench—a still greater privilege to know him as a friend . . .

By their devotion to the cause of justice, the judges whose memories we honor today have added their names to the illustrious list of distinguished: men who have devoted their lives to the service of the state. [226 Minn. xxviii]

Oscar Hallam

1865–1945
Associate Justice, 1913–1923

On the morning of January 11, 1946, at ten o'clock, the Court being assembled in the courtroom in the State Capitol, Chief Justice Charles Loring said:

The Court is convened here today for the presentation of memorials to Mr. Justice I. M. Olsen and Mr. Justice Oscar Hallam. This session is at the request of the State Bar Association, and now the Court will recognize the president of that association, Mr. Donald D. Harries.

Mr. Harries then said:

This Court and the Bar of the State have lost from our ranks two of the foremost exemplars of the ideals of our profession. We are met today to do honor to their memory.

The record of their services to the State is of course their best memorial, and it is not easy for us afterward to review that service in the light of the circumstances and events that give it lasting vitality. As Winston Churchill has put it: "History, with its flickering lamp, stumbles along the trail of the past, trying to reconstruct its scenes, to revive its echoes, and kindle with pale gleams the passion of former days. What is the worth of all this?"

And he answers: "The only guide to a man is his conscience; the only shield to his memory is the rectitude and sincerity of his actions. It is very imprudent to walk through life without this shield, because we are so often mocked by the failure of our hopes and the upsetting of our calculations; but with this shield, however the fates may play, we march always in the ranks of honor."

In their practice at the Bar and in their judgments rendered from the bench of this Court, Mr. Justice Olsen and Mr. Justice Hallam bore this shield. The Bar of the State of Minnesota is therefore proud to move the Court to receive the tributes that we have

prepared to their memory . . . The chairman of the Committee of the Bar appointed to present the memorial to the late Justice Oscar Hallam is Mr. William H. Oppenheimer of St. Paul.

Mr. Oppenheimer then presented the following:

Oscar Hallam was born on a farm October 19, 1865, near Linden, Wisconsin, the son of Joseph and Mary Hallam. In 1892, he married Edith Lott, who died about three years ago. He died at St. Paul, September 23, 1945, leaving surviving his daughter, Cornelia Hallam Miller, three grandchildren, Mrs. Ernest Andberg, Mrs. Robert Lewis, and Stanley F. Miller Jr., and three great-grandchildren, Ernest White Andberg, Cornelia Andberg, and Polly Lewis.

Oscar Hallam attended the University of Wisconsin, where he was awarded the degree of Bachelor of Arts in 1887 and that of Bachelor of Laws in 1889. Shortly after he graduated, he came to St. Paul and engaged in the practice of the law.

To the public generally, he leaves a record of civic patriotism and public achievement; to the Bar of the State, he leaves a record of unfailing devotion to the ideals of our profession.

He served as District Judge of the Second Judicial District from 1905 to 1912, when he was elected Associate Justice of this Court, a position he occupied for ten years, returning to the active practice of law in St. Paul in 1924. During this latter year, he was a candidate at the primary election for the office of United States Senator.

Despite the demands upon his time occasioned by legal work of high importance, he somehow found time to take an active interest in civic and public affairs. Always interested in the law and the interests of the profession, he served as a member of the faculty of the St. Paul College of Law from 1901 to 1945. He was Dean of the college from 1919 to 1941 and President of the college thereafter until his death in 1945. He was also at various times Vice Chairman of the Section on Legal Education and Chairman of the Section on Criminal Law of the American Bar Association. In 1926, he served as Chairman of the Minnesota Crime Commission. During his term of office as such Chairman, the Commission, largely through his efforts, originated the State Department of Criminal Apprehension and established the full-time Board of Parole, measures that have added materially in the apprehension of criminals and in the administration of the parole system. He also served as President of the Ramsey County Bar Association, was Chairman of the Board of Governors of the Twin City Unit of the Shriners Hospital for Crippled Children, and Chairman of the 4-Minute Men of Minnesota during World War I.

He also served as President for many years of, and was very active in organizing and stimulating interest in, the Navy League of Minnesota. He was Vice-President and later a Director of the St. Paul Council of Camp Fire Girls, retaining until his death an active interest in the work of that organization.

He was a member of the Congregational Church, of the American, Minnesota State, and Ramsey County Bar Associations, of Phi Delta Theta, Phi Beta Kappa, and Delta Theta Phi fraternities, as well as of the Kiwanis Club, Town and Country Club, and St. Paul Athletic Club. From 1933 until the date of his death, he was chief counsel of the Minneapolis-St. Paul Sanitary District, which constructed and manages the sixteen-million-dollar Twin City Sewage Disposal System.

Oscar Hallam brought to the District Bench the knowledge acquired in a long and active practice of the law. He brought to this Court the experience of a trial lawyer and trial judge. He brought to the Bench qualities that assured an even-handed dispensation of justice, a full knowledge of the law, practical common sense, and sound judgment. First and foremost in his mind at all times was a consciousness of that responsibility that rests upon one who undertakes to decide between his fellow men, an active desire to be fair and just, never to let pride of opinion or prejudice

sway him from the path of justice to his fellow men. He welcomed the assistance of, and was always courteous to and patient with, counsel. His work on the Bench disclosed a keen, analytical mind, a profound knowledge of the law, of its place and function in meeting changing social and economic conditions.

As a judge he maintained that high record of justice, integrity, industry, and ability that has and does characterize the trial and appellate bench of this State—a record that constitutes one of the State's most highly prized and valued assets.

Oscar Hallam was not only a distinguished lawyer and jurist but was also a public-spirited citizen. The community in which he lived is better because of his life as a lawyer, judge, and citizen. His fellow members of the Bar will recall him as a good lawyer, a sound judge, a useful citizen, and a courteous gentleman. No greater tribute can be paid any man.

William H. Oppenheimer, Chairman
Bruce W. Sanborn
Richard A. Golling

Mr. Harries then said:

Your Honors, both Mr. Justice Olsen and Mr. Justice Hallam, before ascending to the bench of this Court, were judges of the district courts of the State of Minnesota. The District Court Judges Association is a constituent member of the State Bar Association and is represented here by Judge Albert H. Enersen and Judge Albin S. Pearson, who wish to be heard on behalf of their association.

Judge Albin S. Pearson, of the Second Judicial District, then presented the following memorial to Justice Oscar Hallam on behalf of the District Court Judges Association:

Judge Moriarty, as president of the District Court Judges Association, has designated two Ramsey county judges, Judge Rensch and myself, to appear on this occasion. We, therefore, on behalf of the Association, now express our concurrence in the memorial that has been so well presented by Mr. Oppenheimer.

Commissioner Andrew Holt [in behalf of the court] then said:

As to Judge Oscar Hallam, no one except Myron D.

Taylor and myself is now alive who worked with him in the Supreme Court. He was a keen, able judge. He had had the advantage of education, both academic and law, in Madison, Wisconsin, and he had served several years as a district court judge in Ramsey county, and he came well qualified to this Court when elected in 1912. He undoubtedly could have served well in that capacity as long as he lived or his health permitted, but he had political ambitions. That ambition failed, but that did not sour him. He took up the practice of law as unruffled as before, and I wish to say that in all his work on this Bench he was uniformly kind and courteous to his associates but always had a firm conviction of the correctness of his own conclusions in the study of the cases.

I think the memorial of Mr. Oppenheimer fully corresponds with the opinion of the Court, and we assent and concur in that memorial.

Chief Justice Loring then said:

These proceedings in which Bench and Bar participate in memory of departed judges afford us an opportunity to record the respect, the esteem, and the affection with which in their lifetimes we regarded our professional brethren. It is wise that we pause in the course of our active work to conduct such ceremonies. It emphasizes in our minds the fact that all that is of real value that a judge can leave behind is a fair name and a good reputation—the respect that we have for lives well spent in service to the State and to the profession. When a lawyer accepts a call to the Bench, he must reconcile himself to serving without hope or prospect of other reward.

Mr. Justice Hallam I knew only as I practiced before him during his entire tenure on this Court. He was especially considerate to the younger men of the Bar, and we respected him as the able lawyer and good judge that he was, and we regretted that he felt that he should leave this bench for other fields.

The justices whose memories we honor today have added their names to the illustrious list of distinguished men who devoted a large share of their lives to the service of this State by their devotion to the cause of justice. [220 Minn. xxix]

Homer B. Dibell

1864–1934
Commissioner, 1913–1918; Associate Justice, 1918–1934

On the morning of October 18, 1934, at ten o'clock, the court being assembled at the court room in the State Capitol, Chief Justice John P. Devaney called upon Rollo F. Hunt, president of the Minnesota State Bar Association.

Mr. Hunt then said:

The Minnesota State Bar Association has arranged, with your permission, to present memorials for two distinguished members of our association and of this court, Homer B. Dibell, who died February 17, 1934, and Albert Schaller, who passed from this life March 31 of this year. Both of these men were distinguished in learning and in public service; and, more than that, they personified the ideals of our profession. It is our privilege at this time to pay tribute to their memory. A committee has been designated to arrange a program to be presented at this time, and I will ask the court to recognize the Honorable Oscar Hallam, chairman of that committee, who will advise the court of the speakers who will deliver the memorial addresses.

Honorable Oscar Hallam then said:

I will present the memorial of the State Bar Association for the Honorable Homer B. Dibell:

Homer Bliss Dibell was born on a farm in Fillmore county, Minnesota, January 17, 1864, the son of Elihu Dibell and Elizabeth Ann Bliss Dibell. He was the youngest of three brothers, one of whom, Edwin J. Dibell of Wolcott, Indiana, survives him. The family moved to Illinois in 1865 and in 1875 to Wolcott, Indiana. Justice Dibell attended the local schools and for a number of years taught country school in Indiana. He entered Indiana University and graduated in 1889. He received the recognition of merit in scholarship by election to Phi Beta Kappa. As a senior he

won a $300 prize for an essay on the tariff against competitors in universities throughout the United States.

After graduation he studied law for a time in law offices in Logansport, Indiana. In 1890 he graduated from Northwestern University Law School. As a law student he was one of four who divided the highest prize.

In 1890 he went to Duluth, and in October of that year he was admitted to the bar of Minnesota. He was a law clerk in the office of McGindley & Cotton from 1890 to 1891, a member of the firm of Cotton & Dibell from 1891 to 1893, a member of the firm of Cotton, Dibell & Reynolds from 1893 to 1895, and of the firm of Dibell & Reynolds from 1895 to 1899. He was elected judge of the district court in 1898, taking his seat in January 1899, and was re-elected in 1904 and 1910. On April 1, 1913, he was appointed by the supreme court to fill one of the two newly created offices of supreme court commissioner. In 1918, upon the death of Justice George L. Bunn, he was appointed an associate justice of the supreme court, to which office he was elected in 1920 and re-elected in 1926 and 1932.

During his service on the supreme court he lectured at the St. Paul College of Law and the Law School of the University of Minnesota. In various summer sessions during this time he also lectured at the law schools of Yale, Michigan, and Northwestern universities. In 1927 the honorary degree of Doctor of Laws was conferred upon him by Northwestern University.

For a number of years, beginning in 1927, he served at various times under appointment by President Coolidge, President Hoover, and President Roosevelt on arbitration boards and boards of mediation in labor disputes between various railways and their employees. During his last illness he received an appointment from President Roosevelt to serve on a mediation board in connection with a labor dispute between the Denver and Rio Grande Railway and its employees. His illness and death prevented his acceptance of this appointment. He died February 17, 1934. Justice Dibell's record in these numerous labor controversies was so fair that he won the confidence and respect of both sides. His picture in a recent edition of *Labor* carried the caption "Square Shooter."

President William Lowe Bryan of Indiana State University said of him: "Justice Dibell of the supreme court of Minnesota was one of the most brilliant students at Indiana and one of the most able jurists in the United States. He is one of the men of Indiana who has walked stride for stride with the strongest men of the nation. To me his loss brings profound personal grief."

Those of us who knew Justice Dibell best loved him most. He had a breadth and vigor of mind but withal a human touch. He had the education of a scholar, but his was a native culture. He did not seek glamour, but the plaudits of his admirers followed him. He did not seek the crowd, but no man kept in closer touch with the stream of human thought or the trend of human activities. He mastered books, but there was more than this that made him a great judge. A judge must have a mind that grasps. He had that. A judge must have decision of character. He had that. A judge must be fearless. He had that quality. A judge must have a human sense of justice. He had that. A judge must have the patience that hears. He had that. A judge must have the quality of mercy that tempers. He had that. He carried the dignity of his position yet with the grace that accorded courtesy and recognition to all. He knew the problems of the workers about him, of the artisans he met about the capitol, of those who served his table, of those who scrubbed the floors, and his words cheered them. Gifted with a keen sense of humor, he was genial in companionship. He was molded and regulated by the highest standards of honor. He will fill a large niche in the state's hall of fame.

> Oscar Hallam
> Bruce W. Sanborn
> Charles W. Briggs

Judge Hallam then read the following tribute from Judge Henry J. Grannis, who was unable to be present:

I regret more than I can express my inability to accept your thoughtful invitation to be present at the memorial services for the late Supreme Court Justices Dibell and Schaller to be held Thursday of next week.

Having become acquainted with the late Justice Dibell soon after he came to Duluth to practice law in the early 'Nineties, it has been my privilege to enjoy his friendship throughout the intervening years and to note his progress in his chosen profession, first as a painstaking, courteous, and successful practitioner at the bar, then as judge of the district court of the eleventh judicial district, then as supreme court commissioner, and finally as justice of the supreme court.

In all these capacities Homer B. Dibell was always the same friendly, unassuming, and sincere individual. As a district judge he was noted for his legal learning, his fairness to litigants and attorneys, and his broad human sympathy.

His enduring monument is embodied, as I fancy he himself would have wished, in the reported decisions that he wrote as the expression of the court with such clearness of statement and embellishment of legal learning. These decisions and others in which he joined with his associates in working out did not affect the immediate matter in hand only but will serve as beacon lights to guide the bench and bar so long as free institutions and constitutional government shall endure in Minnesota.

In what seemed the untimely passing of Justice Dibell, the bench and bar suffered the loss of a truly great lawyer and judge, and the people of the state were deprived of a sympathetic and understanding friend.

I did not have an intimate acquaintance with the late Justice Schaller. His service on the supreme court was comparatively short, but I know that he gained and deserved the reputation of being a well qualified lawyer and judge and was recognized as a real gentleman and true friend.

Judge Hallam then said:

I have also a tribute from a distinguished citizen, the greatest law commentator of our generation, Dr. John H. Wigmore, whom we ordinarily know as Dean Wigmore. Dean Wigmore's tribute is as follows:

Judge Dibell's career was long known and admired by me. I first took an interest in it because he was an alumnus of Northwestern University Law School, though he had graduated before I came to the school. Afterwards I studied and followed with great respect his opinions as commissioner and judge of the supreme court of Minnesota. His opinions not only showed that sound learning of law that we expect always to find in our supreme judges, they had also qualities of their own that gave them individuality—a conciseness, a directness, an economy of expression such as is seldom found. His unfailing devotion to his task, his solitary industry in preparing his opinions, are known to all. His stern disinterestedness, his persevering detachment from the usual distractions of everyday humanity, were unique. But a quiet and shrewd sense of humor was always apparent in his personal relations and tempered agreeably his severe social modesty. The supreme court of Minnesota, which can show an eminent roster of jurists, has no name more worthy of honor as typifying the impartial and competent judge who merits the entire confidence of the profession and of the community at large.

Honorable John B. Sanborn then said:

To me Homer B. Dibell was a great deal more than a justice of this court. He was a very old and a very dear friend. I will not flatter myself by thinking that I merited his confidence and affection, but it has been a great satisfaction to know that I had them.

He had every quality to make him what he was—a great judge—humility, modesty, selflessness, intelligence, industry, honor, courage, freedom from prejudice, a keen sense of humor, a sympathetic understanding of human nature, utter frankness, and an instinctive and unerring sense of justice.

He was the most unselfish person I have ever known. For himself he wanted none of the things that most men crave—neither wealth, nor power, nor fame, nor even public recognition of the services that he had rendered. Whenever he could help a friend without that friend knowing from whom the help came, or whenever he could do a kindly act and have the doing of it attributed to someone else, he was delighted. While asking nothing for himself, he wanted his friends to have everything that they wished for and gloried in their successes.

If he were here today he would, partly in jest and partly in earnest, charge us with a breach of trust for taking any note of his departure. When his time came he wanted to step quietly out into the shadows, leaving behind him no grief, no trouble for others, and no memorials. He accepted life simply and naturally and accepted death in the same way. When he became ill and knew that he had but a few days to live, he never thought of himself, and his only worries were for those whose future might in some way be adversely affected by his going. After he had done all that he could do to assure their future, he entered upon his last great adventure as simply as he had entered upon any of the adventures of his lifetime. He asked for no rewards in this world and expected none in the next. To him his work was its own reward. Few will ever know the extent or the importance of the services that he rendered both as a judge and as a teacher of the law. That devotion which most men during an entire lifetime lavish upon their families he gave to his work on the bench and in the law schools.

This court, to which he devoted so many years of his life, is not a group of individuals, but an institution that has its roots deep in the soil of the past. Its character and reputation are not a composite of the character and reputation of its justices but have been built up through the years by the great men, living and dead, who have served it both on the bench and at the bar. Perhaps the greatest tribute that can be paid to one of our profession whether he be a lawyer or a judge is that he has added something to the dignity, the standing, the reputation, or the usefulness of the courts that he has been called upon to serve. This court is a better court because Homer B. Dibell was a member of it. He has gone, but his fine spirit and character have become a part of the institution that he served so well.

Mr. H. G. Gearhart then said:

It is a great privilege to be permitted to address this court as we members of the bar of Minnesota meet with it to do honor to the memory of our dear friend, the late Justice Homer B. Dibell.

His career has been outlined in the memorial presented by the bar association, and it is in many respects similar to that of an astonishing number of our leading jurists—a boy with less than the usual material advantages, a good mind with a determination to make the best possible use of it, an honor student in college, a successful lawyer during his years of practice, a good and respected judge of a trial court, and finally an honored member of the highest court in our state. Such a career is one that any one of us might point out to his son as an example of the success and honors that can be attained by serious study and persistent application to one's chosen life work.

I will say little of his legal ability and his work as a justice of this court. You members of the court who worked with him doubtless know, better than his warmest friends, his great legal ability and untiring labors in accomplishing what he felt to be his duty as a justice of this court.

Those members of the bar who lacked a personal, intimate acquaintance with him gained a knowledge of his ability through the decisions of the court as written by him. Therefore, what I may say of him will necessarily be of a somewhat personal nature.

As a judge of the eleventh judicial district he won and kept the warmest admiration of all of us who practiced before him. He was a natural teacher or instructor, and during the period when he was with us as a district judge, many were the young lawyers whom he assisted by a quiet suggestion as to the presentation of evidence or some similar item, with the idea that not only did he wish to aid the young lawyer but that a case might be so presented that justice could be accomplished.

While ranking high among its members during the existence of this court, for a number of years past he had in his mind an inclination to give up his honorable position here and devote the remaining years of his life to teaching law. I think he felt an unusual ability to impart to law students something from his store of legal knowledge, for he frequently remarked to me that almost any good lawyer would, with experience, make a good judge, but that few lawyers were capable of instructing untrained minds in the application of legal principles.

We in the northeastern part of the state ever looked upon Justice Dibell as our judge. We took pride in him and read decisions written by him with exceptional interest. His home was in our city of Duluth, and he was one of us. Upon his frequent visits to Duluth after his elevation to the supreme bench, most of his time was spent in and about our courthouse, where he had previously sat as district judge, visiting with everyone from the janitor to the sitting district judges. Word that he was in Duluth would take many of the lawyers from their work and to the courthouse for the sake of a chat with him.

The dignity of his office never burdened him in the least, nor did it in the least embarrass his friends. Though from force of habit we usually called him "Judge," in our minds he was always "Homer," a friend among friends. Yet I have never heard a suggestion that such friendship influenced his work in the slightest degree, for he was always a "just judge."

His greatest pleasure he found in his work. He did not indulge and never had indulged in the pleasures that appeal to the average man; the great out-of-doors life, a reasonable amount of which in my judgment is necessary to the well-being of each one of us, was to him a closed book. In this I think he missed much, and it may well have been that his close application to his work, without any of what you and I call recreation, was to a considerable extent responsible for his untimely death. However, he lived the life which most appealed to him, a life as to which none can offer a word of criticism, and departed from us respected and honored by all and loved by his intimates.

Mr. Hugh J. McClearn then said:

It may with candor and sincerity be said of Judge Dibell that he feared praise, not blame. He was a very sensitive man. He shunned publicity. He was a disciple of the doctrine of plain living and high thinking. His whole philosophy of life may, I believe, be summed up in the famous line from Micah: "And what doth the Lord require of thee but to do justly, and to love mercy, and to walk humbly with thy God." I have on several occasions in private heard him quote the last stanza from Bryant's *Thanatopsis*. I think it was one of his favorite poems. Thinking of the Judge suggests the hope that some day someone competent to deal adequately with the subject will bring vividly to the attention of the bench and bar, as well as the general public, the great influence our district judges exert on the lives and work of the lawyers of their districts, especially the young lawyers. It is a subject, I am convinced, worthy of great treatment.

I tried my first case before Judge Dibell 30 years ago. I have never forgotten the experience. Afterwards I tried many cases before him as a trial judge. Looking back over the years, I can testify from experience that he possessed the great virtue called patience. Many have acclaimed him a great judge. So he was. To me, however, and to many others who came to the bar while he was on the district bench, he was more than a great judge. He was a great man.

It is true, as has been said, that he possessed a fine mind; he also had a big heart. His sympathies were very broad. To many in trouble and to the young lawyer just beginning his practice, he was more than a judge; he was a friend.

The experienced judge is necessarily a serious-minded man. By the world at large, no doubt, Judge Dibell was so regarded. He was, however, a many-sided man. The general public saw only the serious side. His friends knew there were other sides to his nature. The Judge had a number of cronies among the older members of the bar. It was always a delight for the younger lawyers of the eleventh district to see and hear these in friendly rivalry and combat with him. The Judge had a sense of humor. He enjoyed a good story. He could appreciate a joke. Moreover, he could laugh when the joke was on him. To me, these are unmistakable signs of greatness.

After the Judge came to this court, I and many others who commenced their practice before him never came to the Twin Cities without making an effort to see him. A visit with him did us good. He always appeared glad to see us. We were his boys. He was still interested in us. We were interested in him. He was very human. He was interested in people. He never lost the common touch. Always he would inquire about old friends and acquaintances. Conversation with him was a pleasure. You never felt any disparity in talking with him. His manner always put you at your ease. His attitude was friendly.

It would be a mistake to believe that the Judge was interested only in the law. Everything human seemed to interest him. He was widely read outside the law. Aside from his kindliness, the things that impressed all of us who knew him well were his keen sense of justice, his alert mind, his untiring industry, his enormous capacity for work. That he worked to a purpose is attested by his opinions, which find a permanent record in our reports.

No outline of the work and influence of Judge Dibell would be complete without mention of his work at the University Law School and the St. Paul College of Law. While teaching at those institutions, he touched the lives of many young men destined to be lawyers. Those who knew him will not doubt that he influenced them in the right direction. He was an influence for good in many directions.

In his passing the state has lost an able judge, an outstanding character, a fine influence. I have lost a friend.

Justice Andrew Holt then said:

So far no two persons have had the privilege of working side by side as members of this court for 20 years except Judge Dibell and me. Not only that, but during the entire period there was an intimate friendship and affection between us, never interrupted for a moment no matter how widely our views differed in respect to some particular problem for decision. Judge Dibell had also the distinction of being one of the two men selected by the court as members thereof. It is needless to say that the court looked solely to the qualification of the men selected for the work. Not only the opinions of Judge Dibell and Judge Taylor, the two commissioners first selected, but the opinions also of the subsequently selected commissioners vindicate the wisdom of the court's choice. My participation in the selection of Judge Dibell for membership in this court is one of the very few acts in my life that I look back to with complete satisfaction. Judge Dibell and I occupied adjoining chambers for 15 years, and scarcely a working day passed that we did not consult and advise with each other concerning cases in hand. Notwithstanding such opportunity to know and appreciate Judge Dibell, I am embarrassed in the attempt to pay him a just tribute because of his oft expressed objection to the tributes usually paid the dead. I shall therefore let a few bare facts speak.

Judge Dibell remained single. He had no recreations of any sort. He pursued no hobby. He devoted his entire time to work and study with this exception, that he seemed to enjoy meeting and talking with people in his chambers or elsewhere; but even so he appeared to be in the pursuit of knowledge, for by skillful questions he extracted information from a visitor without the latter often realizing that any had been given.

Judge Dibell was mentally well endowed. He was an honor graduate of a university. He kept in touch with current events of state and nation. He had a keen and analytical mind. His judgment was sound and free from bias. He despised sham and pretense. When to these traits are added a consuming desire to discharge every duty imposed to the utmost perfection attainable, the result of his work must accord him a place in the front rank of able judges and teachers. In the opinion of his associates and friends, he permitted this consuming desire to drive him beyond human endurance. Nearly every morning, holidays and Sundays not excepted, found him at six o'clock in the capitol at work in his chambers or in the law library, and he frequently returned after supper to labor way into the night. Knowing that he was subject to recurring spells of severe headaches, his friends sought to prevail on him to take his work less strenuously and to seek some rest or relief. But our efforts went for naught. He persisted in attending the sessions of the court when it was apparent to everyone that he was suffering intensely.

Judge Dibell's desire to serve was not confined alone to the work of the court. During the 20 years he was a member thereof he taught or lectured in the University of Minnesota Law School and in the St. Paul College of Law, and sometimes he spent his summer vacations lecturing at noted law schools. From the many hundreds of lawyers who have been his pupils comes the most ample testimony of the excellency and thoroughness of his teaching. It is generally not known, nor did he seek to make it known, that for these years of teaching he accepted no compensation. In addition to the work already spoken of, he several times served for weeks on national arbitration boards in labor disputes between railroads and their employees. His ability, fairness, and patience in hearing and judging controversies had come to the notice of both the president of the United States,

who made the appointment, and to the employers and employees, who were satisfied with the appointment. For the services so rendered he likewise refused remuneration except for his travel expenses.

From the facts stated one would know that the opinions prepared by him would bear intrinsic evidence of their worth. They appear in 70 volumes of our reports, beginning with volume 121, and are models of terse and lucid statement of both the facts involved and the applicable law. They reveal a painstaking effort to make them exact and concise. Lawyers will find little opportunity to claim that any legal pronouncement in his opinions is *obiter dictum*. Few men on this bench have been better grounded in legal knowledge than Judge Dibell, but you will look in vain for any attempt to display learning in his opinions no matter how exhaustively it was found necessary to treat the question for decision.

In the tributes here today paid to Judge Dibell as a man, as a judge, as a teacher, and as a friend, this court joins. But I cannot refrain from quoting and applying to Judge Dibell this eloquent tribute composed by him and published in the *Legislative Manual for 1929*, to the memory of Judge Lees, esteemed and loved by all, who was selected as commissioner to succeed Judge Dibell when appointed a justice. It reads:

> He enjoyed his work on the bench. His years there were happy years. His opinions were incisive. He coined no words and was no phrase-maker. He thought his case to a clear conclusion and stated the result in language not to be misunderstood. He was in the first rank of Minnesota jurists. He was a friend and helper of young men. He lectured at the University of Minnesota Law School and at the St. Paul College of Law. His students were appreciative listeners. They were then and afterwards his friends and he theirs. He was beloved of his associates on the bench, was enjoyably companionable, and was devoted to the cooperative work of the court. Judge Lees is a memory. This is our appreciation of him; this is our tribute.

Even so is our appreciation of Judge Dibell and our tribute to his memory. [192 Minn. xxix]

Myron D. Taylor

1855–1946
Commissioner, 1913–1930

In the afternoon of June 4, 1948, at two o'clock, the Court being assembled in the courtroom in the State Capitol, Chief Justice Charles Loring said:

The Court recognizes the president of the Minnesota State Bar Association, Horace Van Valkenburg.

Mr. Van Valkenburg then said:

The Bar of this state, through the Minnesota State Bar Association, has requested this Court to set a time at which it would receive and accept memorials in behalf of Mr. Justice Andrew Holt and Commissioner Myron D. Taylor, two very distinguished judges formerly of this Court.

The Bar Association wishes to express to the Court its appreciation of the fact that the Court has been willing to convene this afternoon after its regular term has ended and during the summer months. That this Court has been willing to convene out of term for the purpose of receiving these memorials is a token expression of its respect for these two former members of this Court.

The Bar is honored in being permitted to present for preservation among the records of this Court these memorials. Judge Taylor died April 24, 1946. He served upon this Court from 1913 to 1930. Judge Samuel B. Wilson of Mankato, who during that period was Chief Justice of this Court, will present a formal memorial for him. Mr. James J. Quigley of St. Cloud will likewise present a memorial in the name of Judge Taylor . . .

The Honorable Samuel B. Wilson then presented the following memorial:

While I knew Judge Taylor before he came to the Supreme Court, I speak of him largely from my personal contact with him and of the work he did here.

Myron D. Taylor was born in Byron, Maine, on December 30, 1855, son of Morvalden A. and Sarah J. Bernard Taylor. He was less than three years old when his parents brought him to Minnesota in 1858. They resided in Albion in Wright county. In 1862 the family moved to Melrose. He received the education the district schools afforded, later attending the University of Minnesota where he graduated in 1878. This class, upon graduation, placed in front of the old administration building a stone with marker that is still there. For two years he served as principal of the school at Henderson and during that time studied law in the office of S. and O. Kipp, there being at that time no law school in Minnesota. On March 9, 1881, he was admitted to the bar and located at St. Cloud.

During his practice in St. Cloud he had as partners Oscar Taylor, D. T. Calhoun, and James E. Jenks. He was city attorney for 12 years. He was the father of the best part of the city charter and most of the city ordinances of that period. He was appointed register of the United States land office in 1888 and held that office until 1913.

Judge Taylor was elected District Judge in the Seventh Judicial District in 1906 and was so serving when he was appointed Supreme Court Commissioner on April 1, 1913. Judge Taylor's opinions rendered in the Supreme Court are found in Minnesota Reports, Volumes 121 to 181 inclusive, he having served in this Court substantially 17 years.

Upon retiring from the Supreme Court on August 1, 1930, Judge Taylor and his family moved to Berkeley, California, taking up their residence at 145 Alvarado Road. He lived there until his death on April 24, 1946, he then being 90 years of age. His death followed a stroke. The funeral was held in Berkeley and burial in Mountain View Cemetery at Oakland, California.

Surviving Judge Taylor were his wife, now deceased, and two daughters, Miss Zama Taylor and Mrs. Dexter Richards of Berkeley. There are three grandchildren and three great grandchildren.

Judge Taylor was a considerate gentleman. His courtly conduct was admirable. He was a profound man. Judge Taylor must be accepted as a conservative judge. He never shrank from a judge's duty or prerogative. He was a writer of marked force and originality. He was a very deep thinker. He thought faster than he spoke, and at times it seemed difficult for him to orally express his ideas as they came to his mind—when he finally expressed an idea it was correctly expressed as he saw it and in excellent English. Back of his quiet way he had a keen sense of humor and enjoyed reminiscence. He was a good storyteller.

Judge Taylor was a member of the Masonic fraternity and had become a Knight Templar therein. He was a member of Osman Temple of the Shrine of St. Paul in St. Paul. He was a charter member and founder of the Chi Psi fraternity. He was a member of the Minnesota State Historical Society, a member of the Men's University Club at Berkeley, the American Forestry Association, and a member of the Save-the-Redwoods League. He was a member of the American Bar and the Minnesota State Bar Associations.

In Judge Taylor we find one with level and stable views of life and government, devoted to law and constitutional authority. He had an unusual judicial mind. He was one of Minnesota's great judges. He was remarkable for his power of exposition. He wrote out of the fullness of his heart. He had the great strength of a penetrating mind. Nothing discouraged him. Nothing disturbed him. Nothing daunted his cold courage. In his juridical service he had an outstanding memory. Indeed, with him, memory never slept.

In the *History of Stearns County*, Attorney James E. Jenks, a former partner of Judge Taylor, once said this: "He has a wonderful power of concentration and when he sets himself to a task, he can digest and assimilate more law than any man I have ever known. He has also an exceptionally retentive memory. I have seen him turn to a whole series of cases bearing upon a given point, running through a number of volumes of Minnesota Reports, without looking once at either a digest or an index."

Judge Taylor's opinions were constructive and always strong for the future. With him, passion or bias never prevailed over reason. He was strong in his superb intellect. He went directly to the heart of the subject matter. He was always a torch of warmth and encouragement. In the midst of discussion he was calm in temperament, moderate in language, but fearless in expressing his legal views. His lucid reasoning removed the confusion that less penetrating minds would have created in reaching the same conclusion. Violence of public opinion meant nothing to him when in conflict with his ideas as to the law. His burly strength was never reduced to trembling weakness. He was a great credit to the court. He performed his duty with rare zeal and devotion. He viewed the law as the undoer of wrongs and injustices. He considered the court as a refuge for the wronged. He, however, was never tigerish in his assaults on wrong and injustice. He was close to the "spirit of the people." He gloried in maintaining the stability of the court. He hewed to the line with a razor-edge declaration, yet he never showed bitterness. His common sense and loyalty to purpose were as true as a surveyor's level. To him, though kind, tolerant, and indulgent, sympathy never whispered compromise with justice.

Judge Taylor apparently followed the philosophy "that the force of idealism is wasted when it does not recognize the reality of things."

He was a New Englander, and the courage of a New Englander is the courage of conscience. While others doubted, he resolved; while others hesitated, he pressed forward. He was a man of action in rough weather.

Myron D. Taylor is dead, but his work in this Court will not perish with him. He was not an egotistical man. He was a modest man; but he did know his own talents. Yea, I am sure he knew that he carried heavier guns than most men.

Mr. Quigley then said:

The Bar of Stearns County and all the lawyers of the Seventh Judicial District enthusiastically join in this tribute to the memory of Judge Myron D. Taylor.

For a great many years Judge Taylor was a practicing lawyer and occupant of public office while a resident of the city of St. Cloud; and following that period, while a member of the Supreme Court, he continued to regard St. Cloud and Stearns county as his home.

Probably no lawyer in the history of the county of Stearns or the Seventh Judicial District had a finer legal mind than Judge Taylor, and no lawyer attained higher regard by his brother lawyers than he did.

Judge Taylor was a quiet, unassuming, and studious type of individual. He had no false conceptions of his own greatness or importance. He was content to live much closer to his books than to individuals and had a constant occupation of acquiring knowledge.

With those who knew him well, Judge Taylor was a delightful conversationalist, and his dry humor brought him very close to a limited circle of friends. With these close friends, while comparatively a young man, Judge Taylor did much hunting and fishing and was a great lover of the outdoors and all the living things of nature. He was a lifelong Republican and a member of the Republican State Central Committee during the [18]80s.

Judge Taylor during his many years of practice made no claim of being, or any attempt to be, an outstanding trial lawyer. His extremely modest and reticent nature, his extremely quiet demeanor, and his natural tendency to avoid publicity were inconsistent with triumphs in the courtroom as a practicing attorney; but his ability to reason soundly and to understand the law far beyond any usual degree secured for him the reputation of being a particularly sound and outstanding lawyer.

Judge Taylor reached his high point of usefulness when he became a judge, and both on the district bench and as a member of the Supreme Court, his particular brilliance of mind and unusual legal ability were shown constantly in the work of the courts with which he was connected.

Judge Taylor lived a long and useful life. He died with a record of service to his community and to his fellowmen. He exemplified the ruggedness, the determination, and the principles of good government of those who pioneered and developed this great Northwest. The life and the accomplishments of Judge Taylor will always remain an inspiration to every young lawyer who believes that the practice of law is a sacred trust and who is determined that human rights shall be protected through courts dedicated to the principles of justice and equality. [226 Minn. xxviii]

Albert Schaller

1856–1934
Associate Justice, 1915–1917

On the morning of October 18, 1934, at ten o'clock, the court being assembled at the court room in the State Capitol, Chief Justice John P. Devaney called upon Rollo F. Hunt, president of the Minnesota State Bar Association.

Mr. Hunt then said:

The Minnesota State Bar Association has arranged, with your permission, to present memorials for two distinguished members of our association and of this court, Homer B. Dibell, who died February 17, 1934, and Albert Schaller, who passed from this life March 31 of this year. Both of these men were distinguished in learning and in public service, and more than that, they personified the ideals of our profession. It is our privilege at this time to pay tribute to their memory. A committee has been designated to arrange a program to be presented at this time . . .

Mr. Bruce W. Sanborn then said:

On behalf of the committee of the Minnesota State Bar Association I desire to present the following tribute to Justice Albert Schaller:

The members of the bar of the supreme court of Minnesota deeply lament the death of the late Albert Schaller, at one time a justice of this court, and record their appreciation of his learning, ability, and high character, the affectionate regard with which they cherish his memory, and the great loss to the bar and to the state occasioned by his death.

This court has been called upon to perform many important duties, but none more sharply commended by the proprieties than that which we are attempting here today.

A former member of this court is dead, one whose talents and exalted purpose placed him in the

front rank of the profession that he adorned. In attempting to portray his career and to mention the qualities of mind and heart that set Judge Schaller apart and made him individual, that constituted what we call his personality, we find what a poor vehicle language is.

Albert Schaller was born in Chicago, Illinois, May 20, 1856. When but a few months old he was brought by his parents to Hastings, Minnesota, which place from that time forward, for a period of 77 years, he called his home. He graduated at St. Vincent's College at Cape Girardeau, Missouri. He spent two years of study in France and then attended the Washington University Law School at St. Louis, Missouri, from which school he graduated with honors in 1879. In that year he was admitted to the practice of law in Minnesota. Judge Schaller's first public office was that of county attorney of Dakota county, which position he held for ten years, from 1880 until 1890. He was legal adviser to the city of Hastings from 1891 until 1897; he was city attorney of South St. Paul from 1895 until 1899; he was state senator from Dakota county from 1895 to 1915, associate justice of the supreme court of Minnesota by appointment of Governor Winfield S. Hammond from March 1915 until January 1917. Thereafter he practiced law in St. Paul and Hastings until his death on March 31, 1934.

In 1881 he married Kate E. Meloy of Hastings, and she and two daughters, Mrs. Wilbur B. Joyce of Duluth and Mrs. Cecil Shiell of Tarrytown, New York, survive him. Judge Schaller's tender love for his family, his delight in their presence, his constant watchfulness for their welfare, were dominant and lovable characteristics of his private life.

Judge Schaller was endowed with a strong intellect, with a sound judgment and an impartial, considerate temper. His mind was stored with an accurate knowledge of the law, an intimate acquaintance with general literature, a refined taste, and a canny insight into the purposes evidenced by the acts and sayings of men. The human side of the man was especially delightful. In hours of relaxation he sparkled like a jewel. Genial and joyful himself, his flashes of wit, his mirth-provoking stories, which seemed to flow from an inexhaustible source, amused and charmed his companions.

Such is the naked canvas on which the needle of time has wrought the picture of the lawyer learned and careful, the legislator experienced and thoughtful, the judge able and unafraid, the citizen discharging each duty of citizenship, the friend who was indeed a friend.

We deplore the death of the distinguished lawyer and citizen, of a lovable man, of a fine friend, and bow to the Will of Divine Providence.

> Oscar Hallam
> Bruce W. Sanborn
> Charles W. Briggs

Mr. Sanborn then said:

I desire also to read a tribute to Justice Schaller from Judge Julius E. Haycraft of Fairmont. Judge Haycraft's tribute is as follows:

I enjoyed a friendship with Judge Schaller over a long period. We served together in the state senate for three sessions, and it was there that I knew him best.

There is arduous labor in the senate. There one learns to know his Colleagues intimately and well. He learns their characteristics, their integrity, their ability, and their worth. In that body there are dramatic and tense situations—situations that lead to anger and strife, hot words and utterances that afterward one would like to retract or expunge. I never, however, knew Albert Schaller to "lose his head" or to become indiscreet. With a smile, a witticism, a humorous anecdote, he has broken the tenseness of many a dangerous moment.

He was the very embodiment of good humor. He was a lovable character.

I join in all and indorse all that is said of him in the memorial as an associate justice of this court. But I knew him best as a legislator by service with him in

the sessions of 1911, 1912, and 1913. He was conscientious, fair, and able. What greater tribute can one be paid?

His love for his family was beautiful. The almost tragic, unlooked for, untimely deaths in the family were enough to ruin the disposition and change the life of another. Not so with Judge Schaller. He lived on, possessed of the same characteristics.

Judge Schaller, or Senator, as I like to call him, was all-Minnesotan and all-American. He was born in the United States and came, as a babe in arms, not to the state but to the territory of Minnesota. He came to Hastings on the nation's birthday, July 4, 1856. There he lived substantially his entire life, and there he died early in this year.

I mourn his passing but am proud to add my humble tribute to my old friend in these memorial exercises.

Honorable Thomas D. O'Brien then said:

In appraising the life and accomplishments of a friend and companion, we should content ourselves with dwelling upon those individual characteristics that, when found in the mass of humanity, make for order, happy homes, and decent living.

Albert Schaller belonged to that great army of Americans, the children of the first generation of the sturdy and intelligent people who about the middle of the last century came to this country to enjoy the opportunities for betterment and happiness it afforded. It was a strong group. Brave and self-reliant, thrifty, and industrious, its members faced the trials and the hardships of the frontier with a serene confidence in themselves and transmitted to their children the virtues they themselves possessed.

With no other inheritance than this, Judge Schaller throughout his long life was true to every duty imposed upon him. As a member of the bar, as county attorney, as state senator, and as associate justice of this court, he was recognized as a capable and honest public official.

Predominant characteristics of his were cheerfulness and good humor; for though like most of us he encountered the vicissitudes of life, he never allowed himself to be cast down, never indulged in self-pity, nor was his kindliness or courage ever affected.

He was a sincere Christian and, with the aid of his

estimable wife, established a truly Christian and happy home, which he maintained by his own industry and efforts.

He faced life bravely and met its obligations without faltering. He loved to be of service to his friends and rejoiced in their success.

And thus he lived a full and useful life, playing his part manfully and adding to the happiness of those who came within the sphere of his influence.

We who knew him and enjoyed the privilege of his friendship, rather than mourn because he has found reward and rest from a long and useful life, should rejoice in the good example his life afforded and the happiness we derived from our association with him.

Honorable Manley L. Fosseen then said:

It is a great privilege and honor to join with other tributes to Judge Albert Schaller, and I desire to add a very brief review of the many characteristics that belonged peculiarly to Judge Schaller, particularly as a legislator, having served in the house of representatives for four years while he was a senator and eight years as a fellow senator. I am not going to speak of him as a judge for the reason that his decisions are the best evidence of his worth and value as a member of this court. It was not my good fortune to know him as a neighbor or as a fellow practitioner, but it was my great privilege to know him intimately as a legislator.

Senator Schaller, as I wish to call him, was the most kindly and lovable legislator that it was my privilege of meeting during my legislative experience. As a younger member I naturally, especially during the beginning of my legislative work, listened and watched the older members at their work, and it was not long before it became perfectly clear to me that Senator Schaller was an outstanding member of the senate. What he said and did had a powerful influence over the members in the senate, and his great work became so effective and valuable that fellow senators soon forgot that Senator Schaller belonged to the minority party. He rose above party lines, and as his work progressed both in the senate and the committees, particularly in the judiciary committee, no one ever regarded him in any other light than that of an able, fearless, honest, and dependable senator . . . he belonged to no party.

His every action and utterance was exercised for the best interests of the state. He never questioned from what source a proposed law emanated; the question was always foremost in his mind: What benefit, if any, will the people receive should the bill become a law? He knew of no class distinction, always believing that all men were created equal in the right to exercise full liberty so long as the exercise of such liberties did not interfere with the rights of others. He dearly loved to be able to add a word here and another there in a proposed law in order to make the law more understandable and give greater and better effect to the bill so that the people of Minnesota would benefit thereby. He was always ready to give attentive hearing to those who sought information regarding pending bills or to those who desired to be heard on such bills; and I remember, on several occasions when his presence was urgently needed in the senate or the judiciary committee, he would give the persons seeking such information ample time before responding to such call. I can well remember that on more than one occasion, particularly before the judiciary committee, he often became an ardent advocate of some proposed law that some outsider was interested in. The judiciary committee usually concluded that he was right and agreed accordingly.

Patience was another splendid quality of Senator Schaller, and we all loved him because of his patience and also for his dependability and rugged honesty—never afraid to work for and advocate a cause he believed in, even though he was practically alone in the advocacy thereof. He never sought popularity, never asked favors, but always demanded fair play.

The last time that I had the pleasure of meeting Senator Schaller was shortly before he passed away. He came over to Minneapolis to see me about a probate matter. Naturally, I addressed him as Judge, and his quick reply was: "Call me Senator, as we know each other best by that title." Naturally, we drifted back to our senate experiences, the many struggles, the differences of opinion. We discussed the old members, both living and dead, and from such conversation I am firmly of the opinion that if Senator Schaller could live his life over and could choose between one road leading to wealth and fame and the other that of rendering humble assistance, comfort, and courage to all mankind and be a friend to man by the side of the road, he would choose the latter. Such was the life of Judge Schaller.

Mr. Otto Kueffner then said:

In memory of my lifelong friend, Albert Schaller.

He was born on May 20, 1856, in Chicago, Illinois, son of Jean Michael and Barbara (Klein) Schaller. His parents were Alsatians who had emigrated to this country, and when he was six weeks old his parents took him to Hastings, Minnesota, where he lived, highly respected and dearly beloved by all who knew him, until March 31, 1934. His long funeral cortège gave due proof of what his fellow citizens, laymen as well as professional men, thought of him. All the judges of the supreme court and many judges of the district court followed his hearse, and we all agreed that we buried a good man, a friend, a lawyer, and a Christian gentleman.

He attended public schools at Hastings and then St. Vincent's College at Cape Girardeau, Missouri, then studied two years in France and two years at St. Louis Law School, which gave him his LL.B. on June 12, 1879. He and I were classmates and graduated together. Then he returned to Hastings, Minnesota, to practice law . . . was elected county attorney for Dakota county the following November, and reelected until 1891. He was also city attorney for Hastings and South St. Paul. He was also a delegate to the Democratic National Convention in 1896, which nominated William Jennings Bryan, and was delegated to represent his fellowmen at numerous other conventions.

He was married in Hastings on May 24, 1881, to Miss Katherine E. Meloy, of Dutch-Irish lineage. Five children blessed their union. Rose Marie and Marion are still living, and so is his grandson, Albert Louis Schaller, and his granddaughter, Jane; but his dearly beloved son Karl and daughter Josephine died when the flu epidemic swept over this country. Josephine was the very image of her father and like him in all his ways, and when her brother was stricken with the flu she nursed him and contracted the same disease and died a few days before he did. Rose Marie, now Mrs. Wilbur Joyce of Duluth, is a graduate of the University of Minnesota and while attending there was appointed by Governor John A. Johnson to

christen our Man of War *The Minnesota* at Newport News.

In religion Judge Schaller was a devout member of the Roman Catholic Church. He lost his father in the early part of his life and like most great men had a special reverence and affection for his beloved mother.

Albert Schaller was tall and athletic, an excellent swimmer, good swordsman, an expert with the foils. He also spoke French and German. He also was a good actor, and he and his sisters and brother gave Hastings many a treat in amateur performances. His keen and intellectual face and beautiful brown eyes were able to portray any emotion the play might call for. He was a true friend and companion and a most congenial gentleman, fond of indulging in interesting conversations spiced by his keen wit and humor and apt illustrations. He enjoyed a good smoke but tasted no liquor. He was keen in upholding the legal ethics even at his own loss. After his term on the supreme court bench expired he returned to his private practice in St. Paul and, upon meeting an old friend of his who did not know that Albert was off the bench and who asked him to recommend to him a good lawyer, he modestly did so without disclosing that he himself was in active practice again.

As county attorney he was efficient from the start and during his first term convicted all the accused who did not plead guilty, so that the board of county commissioners passed a commendatory resolution on account of it. As city attorney he was equally successful. In politics he was a Democrat and an influential member of the senate. Although at that time the Democrats were in a woeful minority, he helped to pass many measures looking to the development of the state and utilization of its vast resources; but while a member of the senate, I am sorry to relate, he had a great disappointment. He told me that it was the ambition of his life to pass a law making it "a gross misdemeanor for any man to work between meals," and although his fellow senators agreed with him in principle, they failed to have the courage of their convictions and did not vote for the law; so, after trying to pass it for 20 years, he gave up in despair and refused a renomination, but the Democratic Governor Hammond came to the rescue and consoled him by appointing him in March 1915 to the highest honor in the state of Minnesota, a judge of this supreme court, and the record of Albert Schaller as a lawyer and a judge confers distinction upon the Minnesota bar, of which he was an illustrious member for 55 years. He dispensed justice with an even hand, and his comprehensive legal knowledge, his wide experience in the courts, and the patient care with which he ascertained all the facts of each case that came before him gave his decisions a soundness and exhaustiveness to which no member of the bar could take an exception.

I, myself, have known Albert Schaller for 57 years. We were very intimate friends, law schoolmates, and kept offices together for a good many years; yet I have never been able to say to him: "Albert, you have done wrong," and I repeat it now: he never did wrong.

May he enjoy during all eternity his due reward for his clean life, his kindness of heart, his unselfishness, and his many good deeds to his fellow-men. Amen.

Justice Andrew Holt then said:

Judge Albert Schaller came to this court after a long experience as a lawyer and legislator. He was appointed in February 1915 to fill the vacancy created by the death of Justice Philip E. Brown. Judge Schaller had always taken a leading part in the political party of his choice, which unfortunately for him happened to be numerically small when he came up for election, and he was defeated. So his services on the bench did not last quite two years. But that notwithstanding, we soon came to know him as an upstanding man and an upright and conscientious judge whose chief concern was that the decisions of the court should be right and just. He was a cheerful companion and an agreeable co-worker. He never overestimated his own ability or legal attainments. He worked hard and was very appreciative of the assistance his associates could give. His wide experience as a lawyer and long connection with public and private business had broadened his vision and matured his judgment so that he was very helpful in the practical solution of many problems confronting the court. To his state and nation Judge Schaller was the exemplary citizen, always ready to discharge any duty required. To this court he was not only the esteemed and beloved associate while here but also the loyal friend and supporter ever after. To his wife and children he was always the devoted husband and the affectionate father.

This court joins in the tribute today paid his memory. [192 Minn. xxix]

James H. Quinn

1857–1930
Associate Justice, 1917–1928

On the morning of March 22, 1930, the court being assembled at the court room in the state capitol, Chief Justice Wilson called upon Honorable John E. Palmer.

Mr. Palmer then said:

This hour has been graciously and appropriately set apart by Your Honors for proceedings commemorative of the life, the character, and the public service of former Associate Justice James H. Quinn, who five weeks ago today passed from this life. Shortly thereafter the State Bar Association, through its president, the Honorable S. D. Catherwood, appointed a committee of its members to prepare and present to this court a memorial statement, that with Your Honors' kind permission might be made a part of the permanent records of the court. As chairman of that committee I have the honor to state that its work has been done; and on behalf of the bar of the state we respectfully submit, and I will read, the following memorial:

James H. Quinn was born June 23, 1857, on a frontier farm near Kilbourn, Columbia county, Wisconsin. He died at St. Paul, February 15, 1930, living nearly to the close of his seventy-third year. Of this span of life more than half was spent in faithful service to Minnesota. He was for 8 years county attorney of Faribault county, 20 years judge of the seventeenth judicial district, and 11 years associate justice of the supreme court, his continuous public service covering 40 years save one.

His parentage was Irish and English. Rugged self-reliance marked the stock. His father, Andrew Quinn, came alone to America at the age of 15, and without aid of acquaintance or relative made his way to independence on the borders of civilization. His mother's family (Mountford) came from near London and was

of the substantial farming class that settled Marquette county, Wisconsin. It is sufficient eulogy of these parents to say that they were hardy, industrious, God-fearing, and honest; that amid the hardships of being twice pioneers they had a family of 11 children. Three died early. Eight were reared to lives of usefulness and honor.

James was the third of this family. Early in 1863 they journeyed to Minnesota by covered wagon, settling on a farm in southeastern Blue Earth county. The privations and horrors of the frontier were theirs in full measure. Eight neighbors were murdered by Indians. The sight of mutilated forms of men, women, and children lowered into their graves, the great blizzards taking their heavy toll of life, and the awful scourge of locusts were experiences that left deep impressions upon his young mind. But the frontier had its charm. Blue Earth county, always accounted one of the most beautiful in the state, was in those times a veritable fairyland of forest and prairie and lake and stream, abounding in wild life, fruits, and flowers. From this early environment came a lifelong love of the open, of flowers and every natural beauty.

His education was acquired in characteristic fashion. Toil on the farm in summer, wood-chopping, hunting, and trapping in winter, left scant time for even the primitive school in the little log schoolhouse; and after acquiring the rudiments he set out from home, a tall, raw-boned, roughly clad youth of 16, possessed of nothing save resolute purpose and definite aim. We find him laboring on an Iowa farm for a start, next at Poynette, Wisconsin, for three years making his way unaided through the village schools, returning to Minnesota and working his way through high school at Mapleton, then taking up the study of law in the office of William N. Plymat. In 1882 he married Sarah M. Annis, a teacher whose family had come from Vermont and settled near Mapleton. Judge Quinn often recounted how greatly she aided and encouraged him in his educational struggles.

In 1884 Judge Martin J. Severance appointed a commission consisting of J. L. Washburn, Lorin Cray, and William Plymat to examine applicants for admission to the bar in Blue Earth county. The young student creditably passed and began practice at Minnesota Lake. Two years later he moved to Wells and with Frank E. Putnam formed the firm of Quinn & Putnam. An office was also established at Blue Earth, of which Mr. Putnam took charge. Commencing with the election of 1888, Mr. Quinn was five times elected county attorney, and March 19, 1897, while serving his fifth term, he was appointed by Governor Clough judge of the new seventeenth district, serving by successive elections until that of 1916 called him to a seat on this court. He was re-elected in 1922, but ill-health forced his retirement January 1, 1928. He had moved to Fairmont in 1899, and that city remained his legal residence.

The opinions of this court written by him in 39 Reports, 135 to 173, are the best memorial of his industry, clearness of statement, knowledge of legal principles, and that excellence which is best described as sound common sense. His greatest strength as a lawyer and judge lay in his comprehensive grasp of the facts of every case, however difficult or involved. Nature endowed him with a strong and orderly mind, and he had a positive genius for holding clearly in memory every detail of any personal experience or any experience narrated by others. He used to remark that he "never got lost in the forest or the swamp," and this peculiar power was always manifest in his mental processes. His instructions to juries were models of clear and lucid statement of the facts, followed by a statement of the applicable law in a few simple sentences. In person he was tall and of broad and heavy build; his mental structure was likewise massive and powerful, and he possessed the physical and moral courage to make the fullest use of both. It may be aptly said of him, as it was of his beloved and lifelong friend Judge Severance, "God made him in a large mould." He was methodical and rapid in his work, though painstaking and thorough, and was able

to dispatch a large amount of business with apparent ease. Though not pretentious or harsh, he was emphatically the court when on the bench. To the young or inexperienced practitioner he was most considerate, aiding by kindly suggestion and without partisanship to the full presentation of the case.

A good example of his style is his statement of the scope and purpose of the federal employers liability act in *McLain v. Chicago Great Western Railroad Company*, 140 Minn. 35, 39, that part of the opinion being quoted in full by Chief Justice Taft in *Chesapeake & Ohio Railway Company v. Stapleton*, 279 U.S. 587, 595. That he was also capable of elevated and beautiful thoughts and appropriate language wherewith to clothe them is shown by his tributes to Chief Justices Start and Brown in 144 and 155 Minnesota Reports. Of the former he said: "It was the sturdy manhood of Chief Justice Start that appealed most to me. There was in him no fawning, or yielding of self-respect." [144 Minn. li]

And of Chief Justice Brown he said: "Faithful service was the outstanding characteristic of his life . . . Fair, manly, unflinching, he fought a good fight," 155 Minn. xlvii, xlviii. No more fitting words can be found by which to characterize Judge Quinn himself. Unconsciously, in speaking of these two noble friends, he gave to us the chart by which he shaped and guided his own life.

Judge and Mrs. Quinn were blessed with three children: Roswell James, an attorney; Donald Annis, a mechanic, both of Longview, Washington; and Cecelia, now Mrs. Bingham, of Auburn, New York. After his own family circle, to which he was tenderly devoted, was broken, he found solace in the homes of his children, and the grandchildren in each were to him an unfailing source of pride and delight. His love for all young people was deep and genuine; and mindful of the steep and rugged path up which he had climbed, he extended a strong and helping hand to all of them, even those brought before him as offenders against the law.

Mrs. Quinn, in the truest sense a helpmeet, mother, and homemaker, died in 1919. A few years later, through bank failures, Judge Quinn's earthly fortune was swept away. During the last two years continuous and almost indescribable physical suffering came upon him. He bore all with the calm fortitude taught by the frontier; the iron lines of his strong countenance deepened, but no word of complaint or bitterness came from his lips. The final summons came at break of day, and fearlessly as he had lived he died, in the abiding faith that it was for him the dawn of the eternal morning. Truly, he was "a type of the true elder race" and deserves from the state he loved and served its farewell tribute—Well done, good and faithful servant, enter into thy rest and thine exceeding reward.

> John E. Palmer, Chairman
> Frank E. Putnam
> Julius E. Haycraft
> John W. Hopp
> J. L. Washburn
> Frederick N. Dickson

Honorable Frederick N. Dickson then addressed the court and read the following tribute prepared by Honorable John W. Hopp, who was unable to be present because of illness:

I deem it an honored privilege to be permitted to take part in these memorial exercises.

The right to be remembered and honored after death belongs to all who serve a righteous cause. The life work of Judge Quinn was that of a seeker after the truth to the end that justice should obtain between man and man. Truth was the pole star controlling and guiding him in all his judicial acts. He never compromised a wrong or supported an unworthy cause. As a member of the judiciary he fought a good fight, he kept its faith, and [he] wore the judicial ermine with dignity to the institution and with honor to himself. His stations in life were but tributes to his worth. A just and upright judge has gone to his reward. His friends and associates will long cherish and revere his memory.

It is not as a member of the judiciary that I desire to speak of him but rather as a plain, honest, and faithful friend. Judge Quinn was intensely human. He loved his fellow man. Of him it cannot be said: "Laugh and the world laughs with you, weep and you weep alone," but rather may it be said that your joys were his joys, your sorrows were his sorrows. He would enter the "valley of the shadow" with you, speaking words of consolation and encouragement.

Judge Quinn was a lover of the beautiful, whether that beauty was manifested in the handiwork of the Creator, the chisel of the sculptor, the brush of the artist, or in "pictures, robes and gems of thought," the promptings of a master mind. Sitting one day in my office after a hard day's work on the district bench, he picked up 93 Minnesota Reports and said: "John, I want to read you something that I have read time and again." He then read with all the feeling at his command Judge Severance's wonderful eulogy on the life and character of that great man the late Judge R. R. Nelson; and as he read that part wherein reference is made to "the ivy that entwined," his voice faltered and I noticed a tear in his eye—also in mine.

His helping and friendly hand was always extended to the perplexed and sorrowful. It was a character such as possessed by Judge Quinn that prompted and inspired the poet to pen:

> When a man ain't got a cent, and he's feeling
> kind o' blue,
> An' the clouds hang dark an' heavy, an' won't let
> the sunshine through,
> It's a great thing, oh my brethren, for a feller
> just to lay
> His hand upon your shoulder in a friendly sort
> o' way.
>
> It makes a man feel curious; it makes the tear drops
> start,
> An' you feel a sort o' flutter in the region
> of the heart;
> You can't look up and meet his eyes—
> you don't know what to say
> When his hand is on your shoulder in
> a friendly sort o' way.
>
> Oh, the world's a curious compound, with its honey
> and its gall,
> With its cares and bitter crosses, but a good world
> after all;
> An' a good God must have made it—leastwise,
> that is what I say,
> When a hand is on my shoulder in a friendly
> sort o' way.

Honorable Julius E. Haycraft then said:

I knew Judge Quinn for more than a quarter of a century. For a number of years we lived as neighbors in the same town. I served as a pallbearer at Mrs. Quinn's funeral and in like capacity at the Judge's funeral. I tried many cases in the district court over which he presided. I argued appeals to this court after he became an associate justice. Later appeals were taken from orders made by me as district judge of his old district. I saw him take the oath as an associate justice in this building in January 1917. I was with him on Saturday, December 30, 1916, when he left the court room and court chambers at Fairmont and locked the door for the last time—left never to return until he lay in state, still in death, before the bench where he had so long presided.

These experiences and this friendship established an intimacy and an opportunity to know his character and his ability.

I agree with the praise accorded him as an associate justice of this court. I would not minimize nor mitigate it. However, he was typically and peculiarly a district court judge. No one was ever in doubt as to who was in control when Judge Quinn presided. He made the court function as though it were made of steel. He had courage and backbone. He was one of the few trial judges who could take a case by its four corners and present the facts in plain, understandable language. His instructions dissipated the confusion and unraveled the snarls of the case and made it easy for the jury to decide disputed and controlling facts.

Judge Quinn was a strong character. He rose above humble surroundings. He overcame difficulties and handicaps. He succeeded by blunt force, energy, and perseverance. May his name ever be an inspiration to all who begin in humble circumstances. May his life and his success be an encouragement to every American boy who has to fight life's battles alone.

Honorable Frank E. Putnam, who was unable to be present because of illness, submitted the following tribute:

James H. Quinn was born in Wisconsin in June 1857. His father was North Ireland Irish and his mother English. He was one of a large family. In 1863 the family moved to Verona township, Blue Earth county, and shortly moved to Medo township in the same county. He grew up under all the privations of pioneer days, living in a dugout, then a log house, and finally a more substantial dwelling.

His education was in the red schoolhouse of his boyhood days; later in a grade school and high school in Wisconsin—meager as compared with the educational advantages of today.

He studied law in the old-fashioned way in the county law office of William N. Plymat at Mapleton, Minnesota, and was admitted to the bar in 1884. His law practice began in Minnesota Lake in Faribault county, where he lived until he moved to Wells in the same county in 1886. His whole professional life as a lawyer was in Faribault county, Minnesota.

He was married to Sarah M. Annis before his admission to the bar. Three children were born to them, all of whom are living. Mrs. Quinn died in 1919.

He was county attorney of Faribault county a little over eight years. He was a very competent county attorney and faithfully served the public in that capacity. During his term of office as county attorney he prosecuted four murder cases and many other major criminal cases.

In March 1897, the seventeenth judicial district was organized, and he was appointed judge thereof. He continuously held that position until January 1, 1917. At the 1916 election he was chosen associate justice of the supreme court and entered upon the discharge of his duties of that office January 1, 1917, and held that office until January 1, 1928, when he voluntarily retired because of failing health. He finished his professional career in life on the supreme bench with honor to the bench and to the court.

The major part of his professional life was in public service, and that service was rendered with a wholesome regard for the best interests of society. In all his public relations his guiding star was the administration of justice without fear or favor. In his judicial labors he was deaf to public clamor. He fully realized that compliance with such clamor was not true administration of justice. Often public outcry is against the innocent, not the guilty.

His experiences of life enabled him clearly to understand and share the viewpoint of the common man and to give it due regard. In the court room he was at all times in command and insisted on due decorum in court. Levity and clamor instantly ceased. He bent the knee to no man nor to any group of men. Poor and rich were alike when they entered the door of his court room. In his mind courts were founded to administer equal justice to all. In criminal cases his administration of justice was always tempered with mercy where the exercise of mercy was proper.

He was to an extraordinary degree possessed of good sense and an unerring judgment in getting at the roots of a lawsuit. He had a peculiar instinct in separating the material facts from the immaterial ones. He acted only on the material facts. He was a master in stating the respective claims of the plaintiff and the defendant in his charge to a jury, and his separation of facts from the law was clear and clean-cut.

These characteristics, combined with his character and integrity, made him a great judge. He enjoyed the confidence of the citizens of his district and of the state.

He carried with him to the supreme court all these habits and characteristics. He took no second place in the court. His presence honored that court. There the administration of justice under the rules of law was his sole aim.

Reduced to its lowest terms, he was an honest, upright, and learned judge, and the administration of justice was bettered by his presence on the bench.

Figures of speech and words cannot express the loss that has come to the bench, the state, by his death.

Honorable John E. Palmer then said:

He to whose character and services we today pay our tributes of love and respect would sternly deny and rebuke the statement that he is entitled to rank as one of the greatest of Minnesota judges, lawyers, and citizens. He would rejoice if it could be said with truth that he met and discharged the duties of life with such fidelity that he is entitled to a place among the good judges, the good lawyers, the good citizens of Minnesota. That can be said with absolute truth and without any qualification; and I wish to bear that testimony from an intimate personal friendship and association with Judge Quinn for a third of a century,

In these days it seems quite the fashion to discourage our best young men from entering upon the legal profession. To counteract such mis-teaching we point to the career of Judge Quinn as a great lesson in encouragement. From the most humble beginnings, with most meager educational opportunities, with no financial assistance, and without the business environment of wealth or population, he rose step by step to what is worthily esteemed the pinnacle of our profession. What did it? Unconquerable will to succeed and entire consecration of his life to the highest ideals of our profession. If what is done here today accomplishes no more than to impress this teaching upon the younger members of the profession and upon those who contemplate entering upon it, our labors are not in vain. Our friend who has passed on did not believe that success in the legal profession is to be measured in material possessions. He profoundly believed in the saying: "There is a true glory and a true honor, the glory of duty done, the honor of the integrity of principle." That glory and that honor he achieved.

The committee now respectfully moves that the memorial and responses thereto be made part of the records of the court.

Judge Myron D. Taylor [for the court] then said:

Recognizing Judge Quinn as an able, upright, and conscientious judge, the people of this state kept him in continuous service for nearly 31 years—20 years as a judge of the district court and 11 years as a justice of this court. Plain and unassuming, he would dislike that anything be said of him that savored of fulsome eulogy. He performed his duties at all times with a steadfast purpose to secure to all litigants the personal and property rights to which they were justly entitled under the law. Technicalities that stood in the way of a just result received scant consideration. Quick to detect fraud, trickery and overreaching, he was quick to remedy the wrong so far as lay in his power. He was courageous in maintaining his convictions and stood for what he believed to be right, whether popular or unpopular. An exemplary citizen, a loyal friend, an upright and conscientious judge, he earned and retained the respect and confidence of the public, of the bar, and of his associates.

In his later years he suffered much from illness and physical disability. For a long period he was unable to walk without the aid of a crutch and a cane. He bore his afflictions uncomplainingly. He always had a smile and a cordial greeting for everyone. His physical disabilities lessened in no degree the zeal and fidelity with which he performed his duties to the public. Although physically weak he was mentally strong and, until he retired, continued to devote all the powers of a well-trained mind to the correct solution of the perplexing problems before the court.

Of a cheerful, genial, and companionable disposition and always considerate of others, his unaffected spirit of good fellowship attracted to him those in all walks of life with whom he came in contact and made them his friends. His life history has been sketched in the memorial presented by the bar and in the remarks of those who knew him from early days. It is an enviable record. It shows that the respect and esteem in which he was held by friends, neighbors, and associates was fully merited. Nothing we can say can add to it. We cherish the memory of his friendship and of his unvarying courtesy and kindliness and join with the members of the bar in paying a deserved tribute to those sterling qualities of mind and heart that won the good will of all and endeared him to his intimate friends and associates.

Chief Justice Wilson then said:

These memorials will be filed with the clerk and printed in our reports [179 Minn. xxxi.]

Edward Lees

1865–1928
Commissioner, 1918–1927

On the morning of May 18, 1928, the court being assembled at the state capitol, Chief Justice Wilson called upon Frederick H. Stinchfield, Esq., president of the State Bar Association.

Mr. Stinchfield then said:

The supreme attributes of deity are wisdom, knowledge, the power of reasoning. Wherever we find in man to a degree above the ordinary wisdom and knowledge, we should express our gratitude and appreciation. We sometimes in men see an approach to perfection with reference to the divine qualities called honesty and sincerity, but in this quality of wisdom it seldom can be claimed that human beings even approximate deity.

We are here today in memory of Edward Lees, a former member of this Court. We may honor him for his sincerity, for his humanity and for his kindness, but above all things we should honor him for his wisdom. I cannot, Your Honors, speak of his kindness or his sincerity or his humanity. I am unable to detail these qualities because I was not fortunate enough to have that personal association with him that alone is essential to enable one to know about them; but I do praise his wisdom, because the evidence of that I have read in his decisions. In regretting his having left this world, we regret chiefly that the too small total of our collective wisdom has been lessened by his death.

This court has permitted the Minnesota State Bar Association the privilege of presenting a memorial to Judge Lees. The chairman of the committee who has the matter in charge for the association and who will, with your gracious permission, direct this service, is former Justice O'Brien.

Chester L. Caldwell, Esq., secretary of the state bar association, then said:

The committee chosen to prepare a memorial to be presented to the court at this time respectfully offers the following in remembrance of Edward Lees:

Judge Edward Lees, who honorably and ably served the State of Minnesota as one of the Commissioners of this Court for nearly ten years, was of Scotch ancestry. He was also of a family of lawyers; both his father and his grandfather engaged in the practice of law and held public positions of importance in their respective communities.

Judge Lees was named after his grandfather, Edward Lees, who came to America from Scotland in 1848, bringing with him his son Robert, who was the father of Judge Lees. In 1855 the family settled in Buffalo County, Wisconsin, where the grandfather served as District Attorney and as Representative in the State Legislature. Robert Lees, the father of Judge Lees, served in the Civil War between the States and was a member of Wisconsin's famous "Iron Brigade." Robert Lees, at the close of the war, was Superintendent of Schools in Buffalo County, Wisconsin; following that he served in both Houses of the Wisconsin Legislature and was County Judge of Buffalo County, Wisconsin, from 1881 to 1908.

Judge Edward Lees, the subject of this Memorial, was born in Buffalo County, Wisconsin, in 1865. He was educated in the public school and at the State University of Wisconsin, was graduated from its law department in 1886, and was admitted to practice law both in Wisconsin and in Minnesota. From the time of his admission to the Bar until the year 1918, he practiced his profession in Winona, Minnesota, when he was appointed Commissioner of the Supreme Court and continued in such office until shortly before his death, which occurred at St. Paul on the 25th day of

March 1928. For a period of more than twenty years before his appointment to the Supreme Court, he was associated in the general practice of law with Marshall B. Webber, under the firm name of Webber & Lees.

Judge Lees was endowed with intelligence of a high order. He had inherited a mind predisposed to that clear and logical thinking so necessary to the success of a lawyer and of a judge; he possessed in a marked degree the ability to grasp the essential facts of a situation and consider them in their right proportions. His ability as a lawyer was recognized early in his professional work, and at the time he was chosen as Commissioner of the Supreme Court he was rightly known as one of the ablest lawyers in Minnesota.

Judge Lees, however, was not only a distinguished lawyer and an able, courageous, and upright judge. He was a good neighbor, a congenial, loyal friend, a believer in the rights of the common man. He was filled with patience, kindness, and good nature. He heard and heeded the simple story of the deserving poor. He advised and counseled the unfortunate widow with the same patience and fidelity with which he counseled and advised the manager of a powerful corporation. In Winona, where he was best known, it was often said that he would always help anyone to secure his rights without regard to whether compensation would follow or not. He himself often remarked that he would rather have a man's friendship than his money. In a newspaper editorial written of him shortly after his death, it was truly said that Judge Lees was devoted to "those who have a hard time getting along when they are doing their best."

As a member of the Supreme Court, Judge Lees stood deservedly high. His opinions are sound, logical, and noteworthy in that they show a comprehensive grasp of the facts involved and a direct and careful application of the law thereto, thus indicating that he made an exhaustive study of the evidence and a thorough analysis of the authorities and legal principles involved.

Following are a few of the cases where the opinions written by Judge Lees are characteristic of his thorough, painstaking work:

- *State ex rel. Inter-State Iron Co. et al. vs. Armson et al*. 166 Minn. 230.

- *In re Application of Morton Denison Hull for Vacation of Town Plat of Hibbing*, 163 Minn. 439.
- *Bothwell et al. vs. Buckbee Mears Co*. 166. Minn. 285.
- *Johnson vs. Sampson et al*. 167 Minn. 203.

Judge Lees left surviving him his wife, Mrs. Katharine E. Lees; two daughters, Mrs. Sidney H. Henderson and Mrs. James Selvage. His mother, Mrs. Robert Lees, and a sister, Miss Mary Lees, live at Alma, Wisconsin; two sisters, Mrs. Norman Fetter at St. Paul and Mrs. Robert Gesell at Ann Arbor, Michigan. A brother, Mr. Andrew Lees, is a practicing attorney of La Crosse, Wisconsin.

Words are inadequate to express the loss to the community and the state occasioned by this man's death. He had not reached the height of his usefulness as a member of this Court; he was taken away from us while there was much work left to be done; yet he had done more and better work than most men do.

Respectfully submitted,

Thomas D. O'Brien, Chairman
George W. Granger
John W. Murdock
J. L. Washburn
L. L. Brown
M. B. Webber
A. J. Rockne
George W. Buffington
Kenneth G. Brill
Francis B. Tiffany
W. B. Anderson
Chester L. Caldwell
S. D. Catherwood

Hon. M. B. Webber then said:

If I were to follow my personal preference on this occasion, I would remain silent, content with the memorial that has been presented by the committee of which I am a member. Tributes of respect and memorial eulogies to the dead always impress me as filled with much emptiness. He of whom we here speak hears not, and the only excuse for extolling the virtues of the departed is a questionable consolation to family and friends, and to hold up to the living an example of a useful life that may urge the young of our profession to a better and loftier manner of living—this latter has some virtue. Judge Lees' family and friends knew his sterling qualities and are in need of no eulogy. Modern education has many advocates of the object lesson theory, and not only the young but the old are quickened by this method. In the life of Edward Lees, all we who knew him find much to commend and the young lawyer a model he can safely follow.

Edward Lees came from a rugged Scotch ancestry, loved and confided in by all. He was born in the year 1865 in the little village of Fountain City, in the State of Wisconsin, whose rugged hills border the Father of Waters, its beautiful valleys, fields, and farms, where honest industry and economy left little time or place for the vices and frivolities that taint and corrupt. His family subsequently moved to the village of Alma, Wisconsin, where he was graduated from the high school, and in 1886 graduated from the law department of the University of the State of Wisconsin, and came to Winona, Minnesota, in 1887, and there engaged in the practice of his profession, where his industry and manly, courteous bearing soon commanded attention.

In the fall of 1895 he and I formed a partnership for the practice of law, which continued until his elevation to this Bench in 1918. This long period of intimacy gave opportunity for judgment of his ability and character. He was a man to whom one could turn for counsel, sympathy, and encouragement, and one of the very few whose presence was fraught with conviction in the accuracy of his judgment. Urbane, courteous, and affable to all; a keen sense of right and justice—not always in accord with the law as written. No one ever doubted his honor or questioned his sincerity. He made friends never to lose them. Like every lawyer in practice, he now and then lost his case, but he never lost a client. He was wedded to his profession; the law with him was a profession, its ultimatum, justice; and he never stooped to commercialize it. His high talents, extensive reading, learning, and logic merited that compensation [which] his modesty denied him. In our long association the only difference or controversy that ever arose between us was the value of the services performed. It was a trite expression of his that he would rather retain the friendship of a client than have his money. He was as orderly and fastidious in

his work as he was in his person. He was devoted to his family, and his daughters were the apple of his eye; and that he lived to see them both happily married was a consummation that gave him great consolation.

In the intimacy of professional intercourse with Judge Lees, in the office, at trial, on the bench, and in social functions where lawyers get together unbridled by the restraint of formality, at all times and in all places his presence gave color to the occasion; or as said by Wordsworth, "I have felt a presence that disturbs with the joy of elevated thoughts." [Wordsworth, *Tintern Abbey*; Reporter]

He was not profoundly religious in that sense that he was committed to any particular creed or dogma, but he respected the faith of all others and lived an upright life; and for such there is no need for a reward in another world. He lived a clean and wholesome life uninfluenced by any dangling bait to such living—that hung out from another world. We are prone to philosophize and stand aghast when our associates in the fullness of life fall by the wayside and to ask why when we have in mind many others who could be better spared to answer the call. Judge Lees had not reached the age that lessens the enjoyment of life and at the same time increases the desire of living, but his lingering infirmities and suffering caused him to welcome death. His untimely taking off in the vigor of his unusual mentality is regretted by all who knew him best; but his life, his fidelity to every trust, his service to the state and the locality where he so long lived, furnish a model and incentive to the junior members of the profession and constitute a sufficient memorial.

Senator W. B. Anderson then said:

Edward Lees and I began the practice of the law at about the same time in the city of Winona, and during the more than 40 years that have since passed I was privileged to enjoy his friendship. The great admiration of and affectionate regard for him that I formed in the early years of our practice at the bar continued until the end of his life, and I feel honored in being permitted on this occasion briefly to pay a loving tribute to his memory.

A rich inheritance of the finest qualities of mind and heart came to Judge Lees from his forbears. Liberally educated and possessing the capacity and desire for deep study, he came to the bar splendidly equipped to become the fine and high type of lawyer, the able and just judge, the true and charming gentleman that he was.

In his great oration on Mr. Justice Story, Daniel Webster said, "Justice, Sir, is the great interest of man on Earth" [*Works of Daniel Webster* (8 ed.) 1854, p. 300; Reporter], and I am sure Judge Lees was in agreement with this sentiment, for in my judgment his predominating characteristic was a keen sense of justice and a rigid determination to act in accordance therewith in all his private and professional activities.

His pure life, high character, and devotion to the highest ideals in his practice as a lawyer and in his judicial work as a member of this Court will always serve as an example and inspiration to those who are to follow him in the profession he so greatly adorned and for the advancement of which he gave unsparingly of his time and talents.

Let us cherish his memory in the affectionate recesses of our hearts, be ever grateful for the service he rendered the Bench, the Bar, and his adopted state, and dare to believe with the poet Longfellow:

> There is no Death! What seems so is transition;
> This life of mortal breath
> Is but a suburb of the life Elysian,
> Whose portal we call Death.

Hon. J. L. Washburn then said:

I come from my northern home not to speak but to testify by my presence here my affectionate memory of Edward Lees during his lifetime. I shall occupy but a moment of the time allotted to me on this occasion. The first time I ever appeared in this Court, well and adequately scared, I faced Justices Gilfillan, Berry, Mitchell, Clark, and Dickinson. Those are great names. There have been many changes in the personnel of this Court membership, and there were able judges before; but I believe that the place of Edward Lees is in the front rank of the best and the ablest who have adorned the Bench.

Hon. George W. Granger then said:

While my acquaintance with Judge Lees dated back to the beginning of my practice nearly 38 years ago, my close personal friendship with him did not really commence until about 1915 and then slowly grew and ripened until I considered him one of my closest personal friends; and the extent of my remarks will be in no way indicative of the value I placed upon that friendship. It is a memory I will always cherish. As a lawyer, Judge Lees came into court thoroughly prepared on the law of the case and with correct knowledge of that to which his witnesses would testify, and he proceeded to bring that out without unnecessary details or waste of time. I think I can say without fear of contradiction that he came into court to try his cases better prepared than any lawyer in the Third Judicial District. He had a great capacity for making and retaining friends; and his friends at Winona, where he was better known, were legion. He was honest. That was an outstanding trait. He was honest with himself, and he was honest with his clients, and he was honest with the court; and I want to speak of one incident in the early beginning of our friendship that indicates that more thoroughly than anything I can say. At the time of Judge Snow's death there were three cases he had tried but that were undecided. Counsel agreed to submit the cases to me on transcript. One afternoon after court had adjourned Judge Lees came to me and handed me a transcript and said: "This is the transcript of the 'King' case. I thought you would like to read it before we argue it, but I will tell you here, I am treading on mighty thin ice." However, I decided the case in his favor, after which this court affirmed me. He was that way all his life. He never tried to cover up anything. A few days ago I ran across a few lines by Jerome B. Bell, that are expressive of his character.

> Mystery
>
> What is this mystery that men call death?
> My friend before me lies; in all save breath
> He seems the same as yesterday. His face
> So life to life, so calm, bears not a trace
> Of that great change that all of us so dread.
> I gaze on him and say: He is not dead,
> But sleeps; and soon he will arise and take
> Me by the hand. I know he will awake
> And smile on me as he did yesterday;
> And he will have some gentle word to say,
> Some kindly deed to do; for loving thought
> Was warp and woof of which his life was wrought.
> He is not dead. Such souls forever live
> In boundless measure of the love they give.
>   [*Elbert Hubbard's Scrap Book*, p. 15; Reporter]

Hon. George W. Peterson then said:

I took the examination for admission to the bar in September 1897. Judge Lees was a member of the board. The other members were Messrs. Knox, Southworth, Willard, Parsons, and Williams. It is a fine service, and the standard of admission to the profession that we love is in the keeping of the board. The fine impression then formed of Judge Lees always remained, and his life and work prompt this tribute to his memory. It is appropriate to be just in life as well as in memorial, and so on October 6, last year, when life to him shadowed to its close, I wrote Judge Lees as follows:

> I am grieved to learn that the condition of your health prompts your retirement from the Bench that you have adorned so well. In the entire history of the court there is no finer expression than is found in your opinions. Of course, the words of Judge Start always recur: The work of the Court "is the work of no one man. A procession of men have helped. [144 Minn. xlvi; Reporter]
>
> I express the sentiment of the Court to Mr. Justice Day, upon his retirement: "We sincerely hope that in your retirement and in a long evening of life you may find happiness, as well as you may, in your extended and honorable record of public service. [260 U.S. x; Reporter]

Of course, no good man courts eulogy, and least, Judge Lees. Life is its own panegyric; its own philippic.

Judges Mitchell, Start, and Lees, among other distinguished judges and lawyers, came from the same portion of the state. In good judgment, in the higher qualities of mind and soul, they serve and endure and are patient. Judges Mitchell, Start, and Lees were peers. Each was the equal of the other.

In the memorial in this Court to Judge Mitchell, Judge Start, speaking for the Court, said: "His manner was direct, simple, and unaffected. He was a man of the best abilities and of the weightiest character. His mental grasp was clear and incisive, his impulses honorable, his aims lofty, and his love of justice and truth supreme." [79 Minn. xlviii; Reporter]

In the memorial in this Court to Judge Start, Judge Lees, speaking for the Court, said:

No man ever sat here who was more concerned that cases should be correctly decided . . . He was solicitous that no fact or principle of law that might have a bearing upon the decision should be overlooked. He did not spare himself the labor of examining and considering the records and briefs in every case before the court. He was a tireless worker, wholly absorbed in his work . . .

Endowed by nature with an alert and vigorous mind and of a strong and resolute character, he impressed his convictions upon others to a marked degree. Of unfailing probity and with a deep sense of duty to which he was always true, he justly gained the respect and confidence of the public. [144 Minn. 1, li; Reporter]

What is said here of Judges Mitchell and Start applies equally to Judge Lees. In marked degree, he had courtesy, mental poise, and social justice; and to the bar he was an attentive listener upon the Bench. Genuine compliment is due the Court that named him a member of it. This Court is stronger that he sat, gave judgment, and wrote.

> His life was gentle, and the elements
> So mixed in him, that Nature might stand up
> And say to all the world—"This was a man."

Hon. S. D. Catherwood then said:

I enjoyed a personal acquaintance and the friendship of Edward Lees for many years, both before and after he became a member of this Court. I have visited with him personally. I have seen him at his duties in his law office. I have seen and heard him in court.

As a man he was sociable, genial, kindly. As a counselor he was patient, thorough, and sincere. He harkened to the story of the poor with the same fidelity that he counseled with the rich.

As an advocate he was skilful and sagacious. Judge Lees was not a noisy lawyer. In court in the trial of a lawsuit, he was watchful, keen, shrewd, conducting his client's cause with rare tact. In his trial work there was a total absence of browbeating or bombast. I regarded him as one of the most effective cross-examiners of a dangerous witness that I have ever seen in action in a court room.

His learning, his ability, and his experience made him especially valuable as a member of this Court. His appointment here was welcomed by unanimous approval of the Bench and Bar and of this state. His work has come up to our highest hopes. That his career should be ended while he was at the summit of his usefulness is one of the inscrutable things that finite minds are not able to understand. Paraphrasing that which in ancient days was said of one less worthy than our friend, we say, "He should have died hereafter."

Hon. John B. Sanborn, Judge of the United States District Court, District of Minnesota, then said:

It is now more than 20 years since I first met Judge Lees. He was at that time a member of the State Board of Law Examiners. I was an applicant for admission to the bar of this Court, and he took kindly interest in me at that time, an interest that I have never forgotten. I saw much of him from that day until he was appointed a Commissioner of this Court. After that I met him frequently. He was a delightful companion. He was always a gentleman, always courteous, always considerate of the feelings of others, always a loyal friend, and he never complained. I cannot now remember his ever having expressed an unkind or a bitter thought about any man. He had a delightful sense of humor, which remained with him until the end of his life. He was by virtue of his high sense of honor, his fine character, his understanding of human nature, his sympathy with human weakness, his lack of prejudice, because of his legal and scholastic attainments, a great lawyer and a great judge. He expressed himself clearly because he thought clearly and logically. His opinions ranked with those of Judge Gilfillan, Judge Mitchell, Judge Bunn, and the other great judges of this Court. When he was selected by this Court to serve as a Commissioner, he was more than appreciative of the honor. I know he considered it a privilege to serve with you. I know he enjoyed the friendships he made, and I feel happy in many respects the days that he spent with you were the happiest days of his life. Public service is its own reward. Its compensation consists of friendships, understanding, experience, memories, and the satisfaction of having performed a useful service.

Judge Lees had these compensations. He first erected his own monument and then wrote his own epitaph and delivered his own memorial by the fine things he did and the excellent life he lived. Nothing we can say here can add to or take away anything from his record. We cannot honor him, but in a sense we do honor ourselves by paying this last tribute of respect and affection to the memory of one member of our profession who by his conduct has left it better than when he entered it. It can be said of him:

> He scarce had need to doff his pride
>   or slough the dross of Earth—
> E'en as he trod that day to God so walked
>   he from his birth,
> In simpleness and gentleness and honor
>   and clean mirth.
>   [Kipling, *Verses*; Reporter]

Edward Lees has become a memory, a fine memory, a memory that those who knew him will carry with them until they too shall have gone. Our profession, this court, the state of Minnesota, and our common country have suffered an irreparable loss in the death of Judge Lees.

Judge O'Brien then said:

I have been handed the following tribute from Justice Quinn:

It is with profound regret that I am forced to say that I am unable to be present at the services to be held in the Court upon the life and character of our late friend and associate Edward Lees.

His manly features, the extended hand of encouragement and succor, the affable manner of the gentleman, coupled with the safe and salutary advice ever given, endeared him forever to his friends, neighbors, and associates. To each he was a brother—friend by nature. In him there was no counterfeit, no cunning.

During his residence at Winona, Judge Lees enjoyed a lucrative practice and soon became an active and leading citizen of the community. He was broadminded, genial, and considerate, yet firm in the discharge of his duties to his clients. His practice was unusually successful, not alone from his ability and learning but largely because he always lived and worked "with malice towards none, with charity for all." [Lincoln, Second Inaugural; Reporter] As a judge he exhibited a pure, deep, penetrating mind, respected the law, and believed in its enforcement. He performed his duties as a member of this Court with the very highest ideals of justice. His clear intellect and sound judgment inspired and held the complete confidence of his associates. His opinions seldom met with dissent; seldom did they require or receive a review.

Judge Taylor then said:

In speaking at the memorial for Chief Justice Start, Judge Lees took occasion to say:

> If Judge Start could speak, he would protest against praise of himself or his work, despite the fact that eulogy of the dead is the common thing. It would be his wish that whatever was said of him should be temperate in expression, and should not overdraw his virtues. [144 Minn. xlviii; Reporter]

In thus stating the wish of another, Judge Lees unquestionably gave expression to his own wish, and it is typical of the man. He would tolerate nothing that savored of show or pretense on his part and was inclined to depreciate his own merits.

It was my privilege to be associated with Judge Lees during his service on the Bench. He never slighted his work but gave the same painstaking care to every case, although to do so entailed long hours and placed a heavy strain upon a body weakened by pain and disease. When he took up a case for consideration, he forgot the parties and considered the case solely as presenting a problem that it was his duty to aid in solving. To its solution he directed the full powers of an unusually keen, alert, and well-trained mind. His opinions appear in thirty two volumes of the Minnesota Reports. They justly rank high. They are clear, exhaustive, and easily understood. They show a thorough examination of the authorities and a full understanding of the facts of the case and of the applicable law. They are such as we would expect from a man of Judge Lees' thoroughness, possessed of his ability to sift the essential from the nonessential unerringly. He believed that technicalities should never be allowed to stand in the way of a righteous result and was quick to detect and condemn fraud and trickery. He perceived the pivotal facts of a case and the conclusions to which they led with surprising quickness and certainty; and his opinions expressed in conference, though never advanced assertively,

were valued highly and are reflected in numberless decisions. He was never dogmatic, always welcomed suggestions, and was more than ready to admit any mistakes on his part.

Judge Lees possessed a keen sense of humor and often enlivened days of wearisome work by humorous remarks and suggestions but never in a manner that could be deemed offensive to anyone. He was one of the most even-tempered of men—serene and unruffled at all times and under all circumstances. During nine years of intimate association with him I never saw anything to indicate that he ever became irritated or impatient and never knew him to make an unkind or disparaging remark to or concerning anyone. His cheerful and genial disposition, his unvarying good nature and kindliness, and his consideration for others made it a pleasure to work with him and endeared him to all his associates.

Throughout his long and painful illness he was uniformly cheerful and always had a kind and cordial greeting for everyone. He faced his affliction with serene courage, never complained, and maintained his natural cheerfulness to the end—even after he must have known that the sands were running low. He was a man of high ideals, of spotless integrity, and in all the relations of life exemplified the highest type of manhood and citizenship.

He devoted his great abilities untiringly to the conscientious performance of every duty that devolved upon him. He was a profound lawyer and made an enviable record as a jurist. His associates of the Bench join in the encomiums pronounced by the members of the Bar and, in words too weak, wish to express their high regard for Judge Lees as a man and citizen, as a lawyer and judge and as a friend.

Chief Justice Wilson then said:

Judge Lees was a humble, kind man with strong convictions and the courage to support them. He was intensely devoted to duty. His ideals and co-operative conduct at all times met the admiration of those associated with him. He deserves all that has been said. He was indeed a splendid gentleman. The State has lost a valuable member of this Court. A great light has gone out. [174 Minn. xxxv]

Samuel B. Wilson

1873–1954
Chief Justice, 1923–1933

On May 15, 1956, at 1:30 P.M., the Court being assembled in the courtroom in the State Capitol, Chief Justice Roger L. Dell said:

The Court recognizes the president of the Minnesota State Bar Association, Mr. John M. Palmer.

Mr. Palmer then said:

This time has been graciously and appropriately set apart for proceedings to commemorate the lives, the characters, and the public service of four members of this Court who have passed away, namely: Chief Justice Samuel B. Wilson, Associate Justice Clifford L. Hilton, Associate Justice Julius J. Olson, and Associate Justice Theodore Christianson.

The Court has called upon the Minnesota State Bar Association as the representative of the Bar of this state to arrange for the presentation of memorials to perpetuate the memory of those distinguished members of the profession who served for many years on this Court. The Association is honored to respond to the call . . . Mr. William C. Blethen of Mankato . . . will deliver the memorial in honor of Chief Justice Samuel B. Wilson . . .

Mr. Blethen then presented the following memorial:

For a number of years it was my privilege to be closely associated with the late Samuel Bailey Wilson, and it is therefore a particular honor to be chosen to present the tribute of the Bar on this occasion. The Chief, as he was affectionately known by his friends, was a big man in every sense of the word—strong of physique, brilliant of mind, of powerful personality—yet he possessed a gentleness and an understanding of human frailties that won him devoted friends among

the weak and downtrodden as readily as among the mighty. With his passing Minnesota has lost one of its most distinguished citizens, the Court has lost an outstanding judge, and the Bar has lost one of the greatest advocates ever to appear in the Courts of this State.

Samuel Bailey Wilson was born at Price's Branch, Missouri, in 1873. Like so many of the men who have left their mark upon our Nation, he was poor, and whatever success he achieved he earned through his own efforts. He was educated in the public schools of Missouri, at the Mankato Normal School, and earned his legal degree at the University of Minnesota in 1896. Early in his career he served with distinction as County Attorney of Blue Earth County, and throughout his life he held many positions of public trust and civic responsibility in his community.

He is perhaps best known as Chief Justice of this Court for ten years from 1923 to 1933. He brought to the Court a wealth of trial experience. He understood to an exceptional degree the practical problems facing a trial lawyer in the conduct of a lawsuit, and this point of view was reflected repeatedly in his decisions. His opinions tended to be short, even terse in style, and while others might occasionally argue with his conclusions, no one ever had the least trouble in understanding what those conclusions were. He resigned from the Court in 1933 to return to the practice of law at Mankato, where he remained active until his death on January 24, 1954, at the age of eighty (80) years.

Aside from his profession, his devotion to his family, and his active participation in political and civic affairs, Judge Wilson found but little time for leisure pursuits. And as in everything else in his life, here too he was satisfied with nothing less than the best. Whether it was his herd of dairy cattle, an occasional round of golf, or a card game at his club, he approached everything he did with a zeal and an energy that never ceased to astound his associates.

Important as were his other accomplishments, it was as a general practitioner in the law that Judge Wilson found his greatest satisfaction. To him the practice of law was not only a way to make a living but was in itself a way of life. He loved the law with a passionate intensity rarely found in any profession. While he studied the law continuously throughout his life, his interest in it was not so much that of the scholar but rather in the application of the law to the lives of people, rich or poor, great and small. His opinions as a Judge will live as a part of the common law of our State, but he will live on even more surely in the lives of those who were influenced by contact with him. His counsel has helped dry the tears of many a bereaved family, has given hope to many who were down on their luck, has charted a new course for countless people who were hopelessly confused by personal or financial disaster, and has caused more than one businessman who was tempted to take a questionable course to face up squarely to his responsibilities.

Judge Wilson's greatest ability was as a trial lawyer. He was admirably equipped for the role of an advocate. Possessed of an unusually keen mind, he had the rare ability to cut through masses of evidence and confused testimony to reach the basic issues of a controversy with a speed and accuracy that could not but impress the most able opponent and utterly overwhelm the mediocre. He was a master-showman in a courtroom, gifted with that indefinable thing known as "color" and the ability to think best when pressed the hardest. Thunderous in invective, biting in sarcasm, flashing in wit, towering in righteous rage, yet patient and gentle with a timid witness or sympathetic with one in trouble, he could present a case not only with flawless logic but with a dramatic impact that would do credit to a Shakespeare or a George Bernard Shaw. He understood and deeply believed in our judicial system, often discoursing on the duty of the advocate to use every

honorable means in his power to present his client's cause while leaving the decision to an impartial judge and jury, who perform an equally important but decidedly different function.

His capacity for work was prodigious. I can see him as he would brief some difficult point of law, shutting himself in his library for hours, then suddenly throwing his door open to reveal an apparent confusion of books in wild disarray, only to dictate rapidly while turning unerringly from volume to volume and ending with an argument that would be the envy of us who toiled for days with scratchpad and pencil for a much less convincing result. I can recall cases that seemed utterly hopeless where in a matter of minutes his vast knowledge of the law would lead him to a spectacular but often simple and sure solution. Impatient with delay, sometimes hasty in temper, completely intolerant of slipshod effort, he was not the easiest man to work with, but as one grew to know him he commanded not only respect but an affection and devoted loyalty that few men ever earn.

With all his ability and the personal success he attained, the Chief was never too important to see the most unfortunate client, never too busy to lend advice and encouragement to a deserving young lawyer, and never too serious to enjoy a joke on himself. Some of his most enjoyable moments came in later years when opinions he had written while a member of this Court were cited against him in the course of a trial.

Judge Wilson's view of the high calling of the law may best be summarized in the advice I have heard him give to a new member of the profession. In his words: "The practice of law is like the practice of medicine or the ministry. Your door is open 24 hours of the day to any one who is in trouble, regardless of his reputation, his social standing, or his ability to pay for your services. It is your duty to hear his story and to use every honorable means to insure that his rights are protected."

His fellow members of the Bar can testify that he not only believed but lived by this code.

Truly Judge Wilson was intrusted by his Creator with many talents. Like the good servant of old, he used them diligently, and their return was manifold. May his example be an inspiration for us to do likewise.

The Chief was survived by his widow, Daisy Sheehan Wilson; a daughter, Phyllis Wilson Johnson; a daughter, Corol Wilson Blethen; and grandchildren, Bailey W. Blethen, Nan Blethen, Pamela Blethen, Jane Blethen, and Peter William Blethen. He was predeceased in death by a son, Samuel Bailey Wilson Jr., and a daughter, Nan Wilson.

Chief Justice Dell then said:

It is indeed fitting and right that we should assemble here today in memory of the departed justices who served as members of this Court and to record the respect, esteem, and affection in which they were held by the Bench and Bar alike. That these men who we memorialize today have justly earned and richly deserve their place in the history of this state, has been most ably pointed out by the memorials presented here this afternoon. Their work is finished and finished well, but our memory of them and what they have done will remain with us always.

I knew Chief Justice Wilson as a practicing lawyer of Mankato. He was a brilliant and outstanding trial lawyer with a boundless amount of energy and capacity for work. He had the faculty of being able to go directly to the point, to remove the wheat from the chaff, and he could usually be found on one side or the other in all of the important litigation in southwestern Minnesota. He brought to this Court that same energy and capacity. He was a man who insisted on getting things done. His opinions were strong, virile, and clear and will remain always as monuments to his work and industry. [246 Minn. xvii]

Royal A. Stone

1875–1942
Associate Justice, 1923–1942

In the afternoon of February 10, 1943, at two o'clock, the Court being assembled at the courtroom in the State Capitol, Chief Justice Henry M. Gallagher called upon James A. Garrity, President of the Minnesota State Bar Association.

Mr. Garrity then said:

The Bar of the State of Minnesota has recently lost by the death of Chief Justice John P. Devaney and Associate Justice Royal A. Stone two of its most distinguished and illustrious members. The State Bar Association, of which I am President and which I am here to represent, has thought fit that there be recorded in this high tribunal some proper and permanent memorial in recognition of the ability and virtues of our departed brothers.

It is truly meet and just that this great tribunal, over which Chief Justice John P. Devaney presided and of which Associate Justice Royal A. Stone was a member for many years, should specially assemble in their honor and join in tributes paid to their memory.

These men loved their work and I know tried to the best of their ability to discharge the sacred obligations placed upon their shoulders as members of this Court; and now in the words of Kipling it can be said:

> And only the Master shall praise us,
>   and only the Master shall blame;
> And no one shall work for money,
>   and no one shall work for fame,
> But each for the joy of working,
>   and each, in his separate star,
> Shall draw the Thing as he sees
>   It for the God of Things as They Are!

This Court has permitted the Minnesota State Bar Association the privilege of presenting these memorials . . . The Chairman of the Committee who has the memorial to former Associate Justice Royal A. Stone in charge for the Association is Montreville J. Brown, of St. Paul . . .

Mr. Montreville J. Brown then said:

Royal Augustus Stone, Associate Justice of the Supreme Court of Minnesota from May 25, 1923, until his death, died at Miller Hospital in St. Paul, Minnesota, on September 13, 1942.

Justice Stone came from pioneer stock. His parents, Herman Ward Stone and Polly Wells Stone, were natives of eastern Ontario. They came to Minnesota in 1856, locating at Belle Plaine, Scott County, where Mr. Stone engaged in the mercantile business for a year. After engaging in the flour milling business at Jordan, then returning to Belle Plaine and reentering the mercantile business, he purchased a flour mill at Le Sueur, Le Sueur County, and moved his family to Le Sueur. He operated the mill from 1871 to 1876. In 1876 he disposed of the mill and with his family located at Morris, Stevens County. After engaging in the mercantile business there for a time, he acquired a considerable tract of land south of Morris and took up farming. In 1879 he erected a flour mill alongside the Pomme de Terre River, which ran through the farm. A dam was constructed to furnish the necessary power. That same year he moved his family to the farm, having erected a commodious residence not a great distance from the mill. He operated the farm and the mill until his death. He and his wife passed away quite a number of years ago.

Justice Stone's father stuck pretty close to his private business, but he took an active interest in the affairs of the communities in which he lived. In 1877 he was elected to the State Legislature and in 1888 was Republican Presidential Elector at Large for Minnesota.

On June 26, 1875, while the Stones were living at Le Sueur, Justice Stone was born. He was just a year old when the family moved to Morris. A line of railroad had been completed from the Twin Cities as far as Morris just a few years before. There was little settlement to the north. It was in this pioneer country and on the frontier farm of his father that Justice Stone grew from infancy to young manhood. As a boy he did his share of the chores about the farm and in between chores attended the public schools at Morris. He passed through the grades and one year of high school and then entered the Academy at Carleton College at Northfield, Minnesota, where he completed his high school training. The following year, because of a crop failure, he was unable to continue with his schooling, and during that year he lived on the farm and studied law in the office of William C. Bicknell, then a practitioner at Morris. He entered the University of Minnesota in the fall of 1894, contemplating a course of study leading to B.A. and LL.B. degrees; but it was concluded that the family finances would not permit this, so young Stone transferred to Washington University at St. Louis, which was offering a two-year law course, and there he obtained his LL.B. degree in 1897.

Last spring Washington University at St. Louis invited Justice Stone to deliver the commencement address at its graduation exercises to be held in June and informed him that the University authorities had voted to confer the LL.D. on him at that time. He was deprived of this deserved honor because of the illness that eventually carried him away.

After completing his course at Washington University and taking and passing such examinations as were then required in Minnesota, he was admitted to the Minnesota Bar. He immediately opened an office at Morris and began the practice of law. This was early in the summer of 1897. At the outbreak of the Spanish-American War the next year, 1898, he volunteered and served through the war with the 15th Minnesota. At the close of war a year later, he was mustered out and at that time was Quartermaster Sergeant of Company C. He then returned to Morris and resumed the practice of law.

Justice Stone was successful at the Bar from the outset. His practice grew rapidly and by 1905 had ex-tended throughout the western half of the state and into the Dakotas. For a time he served as Village Attorney at Morris. During his practice at Morris he came in contact with Edward T. Young, then practicing law at Appleton, Minnesota. Mr. Stone so impressed Mr. Young with his ability that when Mr. Young became Attorney General of the State he appointed Mr. Stone one of his assistants. The appointment was made and accepted on March 30, 1905.

On August 14, 1901, he married Olive Whiting of Spring Valley, Minnesota, who survives him. Shortly after his appointment as Assistant Attorney General, Mr. and Mrs. Stone moved to St. Paul, where they thereafter made their home.

As Assistant Attorney General, Mr. Stone participated in cases of great importance to the State. His work in these cases gave him a deserved reputation as a lawyer of much ability.

He left the Attorney General's office in 1907 and, with Thomas D. O'Brien, formed the law firm of O'Brien & Stone with offices in St. Paul. Upon completion of his term as Attorney General, Mr. Young joined the firm, and the name was changed to O'Brien, Young & Stone. In 1909 Mr. O'Brien was appointed to the Supreme Court to fill the vacancy caused by the death of Justice Edwin A. Jaggard. He served for two years, during which time Mr. Young and Mr. Stone practiced under the firm name of Young & Stone, and then returned to practice with his former partners, again under the name of O'Brien, Young & Stone.

In 1917 Mr. Stone offered his services to his country in the World War and entered the First Officers Training Camp. He came out a Captain. As Commanding Officer of A Company, 349th Infantry, he trained his outfit at Camp Dodge, Iowa, until it left for France on August 1, 1918. To his great disappointment, he was left behind. He was promoted to the rank of Major and made Commanding Officer of the Third Battalion, 14th Infantry. When the Armistice came, he was transferred to the Inspector General's office in the War Department. He was discharged on July 21, 1919. Upon his discharge, General W. T. Wood wrote: "Major Stone's services in the Inspector General's Department have been meritorious and extremely valuable. He is an officer of discretion and sound judgment, and his discharge will be a loss to

269

this Department." He was given a reserve commission as a Lieutenant Colonel in the department and held the same until he resigned some years later.

Following his discharge, he returned to the practice of law in St. Paul, joining his old associates under the firm name of O'Brien, Young, Stone & Horn. He remained with the firm until May 25, 1923.

Judge Stone had much native ability. This, combined with hard work, consisting of a constant study of the law and its development to meet new conditions, painstaking, thorough, and exhaustive preparation of the cases that came to him for attention, made him an able all-round lawyer. But it was as a trial lawyer that he gained unusual prominence and success. He was a natural advocate and a skilled and forceful antagonist. He was easily outstanding in his profession.

On May 25, 1923, Governor J. A. O. Preus appointed him to the Supreme Court to fill the vacancy caused by the resignation of Justice Oscar Hallam. Following his appointment, he was elected in 1924, 1930, and 1936, and in 1942 was nominated as a candidate to succeed himself.

The appointment of Mr. Stone was regarded at the time and is still regarded as one of the best ever made to the Supreme Court. He was preeminently qualified for the high station by training, knowledge of the law, experience, and temperament. And Governor Preus gave expression not only to his own opinion but to the opinion of judges and lawyers throughout the State when he said upon making the appointment: "I regard Mr. Stone as one of the ablest attorneys in the State."

And in accepting the appointment, Mr. Stone did so with some inner misgivings. He said: "This is an offer for service no lawyer could very well decline. I appreciate the honor and will do my best to justify the Governor's confidence in me." That Justice Stone merited the Governor's confidence in him is now demonstrated by a record as an appellate judge that stands far above the average, a record outstanding and distinguished, a record that has materially added to the prestige and standing of Minnesota's high court amongst students of the law and courts throughout the country, and a record that must be the delight of those who were his associates on the bench.

Judge Stone was a Congregationalist and all his life took an active interest in the affairs of the church.

He was a member of the American Legion and from time to time served on its committees. He was sought after as a public speaker and delivered many addresses on a variety of subjects. He was a 32d Degree Mason and in 1933 served as Grand Orator of the Masonic Grand Lodge of Minnesota. He was a member of the Minnesota Historical Society and at the time of his death was serving as a member of the Executive Council of the Society. For some years he taught the subject of Contracts at the St. Paul College of Law. He was a member of the American Law Institute, and the American, State, and Ramsey County Bar Associations, and participated freely in the work of all these groups. So his life was full of service in many fields foreign to his work as a practicing lawyer and as a judge.

Probably because of his early environment, he was a lover of outdoor life. He liked fishing, and he made many a trip back to Morris to enjoy hunting for a day or so with old friends.

He liked people and enjoyed visiting with them. He was friendly, approachable, and affable, and people always enjoyed his company. Quite frequently on Friday noons he would have luncheon at the lawyers table at the St. Paul Athletic Club, and the conversation on those occasions was always lively and full of interest due in large part to his presence and participation. Judge Stone never failed to make lawyers feel that he was just a lawyer among them. He was liked as well as admired by lawyers generally.

The lawyers of the State honored him in 1923 by electing him President of the State Bar Association. He served with distinction and continued throughout his life to take a keen interest in the affairs of the Association.

His great contribution of service, of course, was as a member of the Supreme Court of the State.

The influence of his previous experience as an active practitioner upon Judge Stone's judicial career was evident throughout his service. At times, especially during his earlier years on the Bench, his aggressive mind and active experience as a practitioner made it hard for him to be patient with some of those who appeared before the Court. He was wont to go at once to the points that he deemed controlling, and his interruptions of counsel with pertinent questions enlivened many an otherwise dull argument. While such interruptions were less fre-quent during his later years of service, the lawyer who spent much time in rambling was suddenly confronted with a question that brought him face to face with the precise point in issue.

His opinions were vigorously critical of any un-ethical practice or conduct of counsel. The high plane on which he placed the practice of law was evident in many of his decisions.

His conception of the proper function and conduct of the lawyer in litigation disapproved of "making a mere game of the trial of a lawsuit."

He had profound respect and admiration for the trial lawyer and often expressed his belief that the ideal appellate court judge was as apt to be one who had been a successful and experienced trial lawyer, with a wide range of practice, as one who had had previous judicial experience. No one ever better justi-fied this view than Judge Stone himself.

An appellate judge is measured by his opinions. Justice Stone's opinions are models of concise and forceful language. To read some of them one must go beyond the use of legal terminology. He was a master of the use of English, and many a musty principle of law took on new life from the manner in which he stated it. He maintained to the end his habit of "calling things by their right names" as he saw them. He had the faculty of going directly to the point or points at issue in a case and of disposing of them without indulging in discussion of facts and law foreign to a decision of the case. He had an ana-lytical mind. He unerringly discriminated between essentials and nonessentials. His opinions show him to have been a deep student of the law, show that his knowledge of the law covered the entire field of the law, and show him to have had quite singular ability in stating rules and principles of law. Quite often he seemed to show discontent with the statement of a rule or principle in cases of long standing. On such occasions he had his own way of stating the rule or principle. But this was not because he thought the statement as originally made was not appropriate at the time made, but because he shared in the belief that case law needs, from time to time, some modi-fication with resultant restatement to meet changes wrought by social and economic development. His

pronouncements of the law constitute an important contributing factor in a development of recent years, still continuing, which may well be termed the mod-ernization of the common law. Justice Stone's opin-ions were highly regarded throughout the land, and through them he took high rank among the appellate judges of the country.

He had great respect for precedent, but he was by no means a "case-lawyer," and when he regarded a previous decision as erroneous he showed little re-luctance in overruling it. He was a legal student with a genuine love for the law as a science. He was a firm believer that, as humanity is constantly progressive, so must the law be constantly progressive. It was he who said: "Static or retrograde law cannot achieve justice." And he was not content just to make such a statement. He did his part as a member of the Court and also as a member of the American Law Institute and the American and Minnesota Bar Associations to make the law a progressive thing, a changing thing to meet new conditions requiring new legal concepts, in order that justice might be accomplished.

Courage was one of Judge Stone's outstanding characteristics, and this was no more evident than in his public career. Whether as Village Attorney, as As-sistant Attorney General, or as a Justice of the Su-preme Court, he never failed to do what he conceived to be the right thing to do. He was impervious to out-side influences. On which side is the right in this situ-ation? On which side is justice in this case? Answers to these questions were the objectives he constantly had in mind. If he concluded that, under the facts and the law applicable thereto in a given case, a decision must go against a person or a group or an organiza-tion with extensive influence, or be contrary to the popular notion at the time, courageously and without hesitation he decided according to his convictions. He was honest in every sense of that term, but in his work as a public servant and particularly as a judge he was, without a single deviation, intellectually honest. He was true always to his own conception of what was right. And in this day and age as never before we are in need of such men in public life. Public servants might well emulate the high ideals of Justice Stone to the ultimate good of those they serve, might well in the performance of their duties, whether in an executive, legislative, or judicial capacity, make it a rule at all times to do the right as conscience gives them to see the right.

Much more might well be said in extolling the virtues of Judge Stone as a man, as a citizen, as a lawyer, and as a judge. Suffice to say in conclusion that all through his life he was guided in all things by the highest and noblest of ideals; that he was intensely loyal to his country and showed this twice by volunteering his services in time of war; that as a lawyer he was an outstanding credit to the legal profession; and that as a judge he was just, profound, and able, and has left a record that stamps him as one of the greatest of a long line of distinguished judges who have served as members of the Supreme Court of the State.

May the example of his conscientious, faithful, and able performance of duty as a Judge be an inspiration to those who are and who are to become judicial servants of the State.

> Montreville J. Brown, Chairman
> G. Aaron Youngquist
> Rollo F. Hunt

The Honorable Carlton F. McNally, Judge of the District Court of Ramsey County, then said:

On behalf of the Judges of the District Court of Ramsey County, the following memorial to Justice Royal A. Stone is respectfully submitted:

Royal A. Stone was born in Le Sueur County in 1875, and except for his absence during the Spanish-American War and in World War I, his entire life was lived in and for the State of Minnesota. He was a product of Minnesota, his interests were here, and he had a deep affection for his native state.

We of the Ramsey County District Bench had a delightful association with him throughout the years. He was a frequent guest at our monthly dinner meetings and was a most enjoyable and stimulating companion in our discussions. Frequently, of course, the discussions involved the decisions of this Court and the difficulties of the trial court and, I believe, were beneficial to the members of both courts.

We knew Justice Stone as a lawyer, for he carried on his practice in St. Paul from 1907 to the time of his appointment to this Court in 1923. Those of our judges who were on the bench at the time Justice

Stone was practicing law say that they found him to be a profound lawyer and a persistent, persuasive, and powerful advocate, tireless in the interest of his client. He was a believer in preparedness and explored every angle of his client's cause and made, as well, a careful study of his opponent's resources and the moves that he could make.

A veteran of two wars, Justice Stone was a student of tactics, both military and legal. His training, ability, and earnestness made him a dangerous but honorable opponent.

He had a wide acquaintance with general literature and an accurate knowledge of the law. He was meticulous both in the use of the spoken and the written word and had an exceptional command and understanding of English.

In his preparation for the trial of cases from the day of the first interview with his client he would start the preparation of what would ultimately be a complete and comprehensive brief. His brief would be revised from day to day until at the time of trial very little needed to be added to it in the event of its later use as a brief on appeal. However, such was the thoroughness of his preparation that he was unusually successful both in the settlement of his cases out of court and in the winning of them in court.

He was fortunate in his choice of associates in the practice of law, and his ability and character "were improved by association with such men as Justice Thomas D. O'Brien, General E. T. Young, Dillon J. O'Brien, Edward S. Stringer, and A. E. Horn. He was fortunate in being a member of the Bar of Ramsey County and being in daily association with the members of that Bar.

As a judge he brought to his work a well-balanced judgment, a wide experience in the law including a country practice, a term as Assistant Attorney General, and a large city practice. He maintained that judicial temperament which enabled him to combine a fine legal discrimination and great legal learning with an alert sense of justice and a keen social vision. With him the merits of the cause ever outweighed considerations of technicalities or expediency. His judicial balance was never disturbed by public clamor, political pressure, or specious appeals for sympathy. He combined the cold neutrality of scholarly impartiality with an intimate knowledge of human strength and frailty. His decisions are his monument. Into them he has written his reverence of justice and his love of humanity.

Justice Stone was an intensely patriotic man and gave unstintingly of his time in the advancement of civic matters. He was a forceful, interesting, and instructive speaker, usually confining his speaking engagements to legal, civic, or patriotic subjects. He was a man who worked hard at everything—even at play. His strenuous ways and driving force were sometimes hard on his associates, but he always drove himself the hardest. Life with him was not easy, but it was fruitful and exciting.

He was a man of exceptional force of character. When he became interested in a subject his approach to it was never half-hearted but aggressive, and his interest continued until the subject was accomplished or exhausted. His whole life was spent in trying to improve the aspects of life in which he was interested, including the law. The lawyers of Minnesota are deeply indebted to his persevering pursuit of a better system of law.

Highly respected by everyone in St. Paul, he had built for himself here a lucrative practice. His appointment to the Supreme Court was accepted by him as a command and as an opportunity for further service in the field of law, but it was accomplished at a very substantial financial sacrifice.

I did have an opportunity to know Justice Stone intimately because of employment with him as a law student and law clerk from the time he formed a law firm with the late Justice Thomas D. O'Brien in 1907 until 1912, and I find pleasure in acknowledging Justice Stone's aid and counsel. His continued interest and advice during an entire lifetime have been a comfort and inspiration.

The last time I heard him speak was at the Ramsey County Bar memorial exercises, when he paid a tribute to Justice Pierce Butler. I thought then, as I do now, that the closing sentence of his remarks applied to himself—"We will do better as lawyers and judges if we remember his unswerving loyalty to convictions of professional and judicial duty."

Mr. Edward S. Stringer then said:

It was my very good fortune to become acquainted with Mr. Justice Stone very early in my professional career, shortly after I graduated from the law school. At that time he was a member of the staff of the Attorney General of this State, under the Honorable Edward T. Young. A few years later, for the first time, I was his opponent in litigation involving title to certain lands in northern Minnesota. At various times during the next ten years I found myself opposed to him. It was not until 1921 that I became a member of his law firm, which association continued until his appointment as a member of this Court. During the 35 years of our acquaintance, at first at times as his opponent, then as his partner and associate, and later while he was on the Bench of this Court, I came to know him well and to admire his character and his ability, and I felt that I was privileged to call him one of my best and closest friends. He was possessed of a personality so difficult adequately to portray that whatever is said is likely to fall below the level of what ought in fact to be said. I feel that on this occasion it would be better to pay tribute to him as a lawyer, as a man, and as a friend rather than as a Justice of this Court. His opinions, written as a member of this Court, covering a period of nearly 20 years from 1923 until the date of his death and inscribed upon the records of this Court, speak for themselves and clearly demonstrate his ability and clear thinking as a judge.

As a lawyer he was equally at home as an adviser in his office and as a trial lawyer. During the course of a busy professional career, he tried many cases before juries and before courts sitting without a jury, many of them of the utmost importance. He possessed a sound and clear knowledge of legal principles, and to the preparation and trial of his cases he brought the aid of a clear and comprehensive intellect and the power of analysis that attends a discriminating mind. He commanded the attention and respect of both court and jury, for they knew that what he said expressed his true belief and that he asked only what he believed his client was entitled to under the facts and the law.

I never saw him seek in court an unfair advantage. His manner toward his adversary was always considerate, courteous, and forbearing. He possessed the faculty of being firm in presenting his points while at the same time avoiding giving offense. He participated in none of the animosities that sometimes arise out of the trial of a case.

He had an alert and inquiring mind, and his persistency in exploring whatever question may have been involved in a case was untiring. He always sought the truth, and his interest as to the ultimate realities often led him into extensive reading upon the subject at hand, but he did not have the type of mind that accepted the opinions of others. He was essentially an original thinker; and while he eagerly sought the light that others could throw, his conclusions were independent and were his own.

His broad acquaintance with literature reflected itself in the fluency and the care with which he chose his words, not only in his opinions and occasionally in his addresses but in ordinary conversations. He was capable at times of eloquence, but he could and did usually express his ideas in simple language yet in a style so impressive that it never failed to hold attention.

There was in him a certain gentleness and sincerity that will always be remembered by those who had the privilege of his friendship. He lived and practiced the fundamental Christian virtues that were a part of his character. He never hesitated when occasion required to condemn what he deemed improper conduct, but his condemnation was directed to the act and not the person. He was ready to forgive the individual. His attitude toward others was kind, his judgment charitable, and his belief in the high average honesty of mankind was one of the foundation stones of his life. It was truly said that although he was able at times to employ the most withering sarcasm, it was not directed toward the humiliation of those with whom he disagreed but toward the destruction of what they advocated.

As a friend he displayed his finest qualities. To that relation he brought loyalty, companionship, and sympathy. Generosity he carried to a fault. In time of trouble he could always be counted on. He was not capable of effusive expressions of sympathy. In fact, on first acquaintance, he often appeared to be retiring, but this was all on the outside. His true inward feelings and character were indicated in the active and practical assistance he never failed to give.

The man whom we remember here lived a life of accomplishment, usefulness, and distinction. He pos-

sessed and conducted himself according to the highest ideals. Toward everything his attitude was wholesome. Never was he guided by any unworthy purpose or a dishonorable impulse. His attitude toward his fellow man was that of sympathy and charity.

Mr. Garrity then said:

I ask the Court's kind permission to read a letter addressed to the Chief Justice from the Honorable I. M. Olsen, a former member of this Court:

I regret that physical infirmities keep me confined to the house at the present time and prevent me from being with you at the memorial services for Chief Justice Devaney and Justice Stone on February 10.

My association with the two Justices, while serving with them on the Supreme Court, was most agreeable and cordial. They were both men of sterling character and outstanding ability and learning in our profession. I am indebted to each of them for many kind suggestions and aids in our work in the Court. They will always be remembered by me as dear friends whom it was my good fortune to meet and associate with in my journey through life.

Justice Holt then said:

I had the opportunity to work with Judge Stone as an associate for almost 20 years. Most of the time we had adjoining offices. There is no doubt in my mind that he was a man who will go down as one of the outstanding justices of this Court. He was positive in his character, and he had one characteristic that I sometimes envied him, and that was that he was so sure that he had arrived at the correct result. I think he seldom wrote an opinion where he tried to lessen the pang of defeat for either litigant or attorneys. He was always exacting of the conduct of attorneys and did not condone any of their loose practices. He gave considerable help to the whole court. No question would pass him without thorough examination, and I think that the State and the community [are] indebted to him for his work here. I agree with all that has been said of him, and I join in the tributes paid him.

Chief Justice Gallagher then said:

I will respond for the Court on behalf of Justice Stone.

Last June, when this Court recessed, we knew that in the fall we should be deprived of the assistance and companionship of our beloved Justice Holt because he had indicated his desire and intention to retire from active service. But to be deprived at the same time by death of the counsel and guidance of Justice Stone, who upon the retirement of Justice Holt would have become the senior Associate Justice of this Court, was a shock and a loss that we were ill prepared to bear.

Perhaps no member of the Court misses Justice Holt and Justice Stone more than I. Coming to the Court as a novice in judicial experience, I leaned heavily upon both of them. I shall not attempt to review the work of Justice Stone. It is a matter of record, well known to us all. Nor can I add to what the other speakers have said about his life, his ability, and his character. Those of us who served with him vouch for the truth of their glowing pronouncements.

Justice Stone was an outstanding member of this Court for about 20 years. He never failed to carry his share of the work and was always ready to assist any of his associates who needed help. As a profound student of the law, he brought to the court a depth and breadth of interpretation and vision that will leave its mark upon the work of the Court. He had the gift of making his views clear to others, giving at the same time the most careful study and attention to the opinions of his associates. If convinced of the soundness of their views, he would gracefully yield his position. But if he could not be persuaded to their ideas, he would stand his ground and often dissent—sometimes vigorously but always honorably and as a gentleman.

The fact that Justice Stone wore the robe of judicial office did not set him apart from his fellows or lessen his interest in their legal problems or in public affairs. His concern for good government was as great as his desire for the just administration of the law. He will long be remembered as an able judge, an upright citizen, and by the members of this Court with whom he served as a considerate and valuable associate. [213 Minn. xxx]

Ingerval M. Olsen

1861–1943
Commissioner, 1927–1930; Associate Justice, 1930–1936

On the morning of January 11, 1946, at ten o'clock, the Court being assembled in the courtroom in the State Capitol, Chief Justice Charles Loring said:

The Court is convened here today for the presentation of memorials to Mr. Justice I. M. Olsen and Mr. Justice Oscar Hallam. This session is at the request of the State Bar Association, and now the Court will recognize the president of that association, Mr. Donald D. Harries.

Mr. Harries then said:

This Court and the Bar of the State have lost from our ranks two of the foremost exemplars of the ideals of our profession. We are met today to do honor to their memory.

The record of their services to the State is of course their best memorial, and it is not easy for us afterward to review that service in the light of the circumstances and events that give it lasting vitality. As Winston Churchill has put it: "History, with its flickering lamp, stumbles along the trail of the past, trying to reconstruct its scenes, to revive its echoes, and kindle with pale gleams the passion of former days. What is the worth of all this?"

And he answers: "The only guide to a man is his conscience; the only shield to his memory is the rectitude and sincerity of his actions. It is very imprudent to walk through life without this shield, because we are so often mocked by the failure of our hopes and the upsetting of our calculations; but with this shield, however the fates may play, we march always in the ranks of honor."

In their practice at the Bar and in their judgments rendered from the bench of this Court, Mr. Justice Olsen and Mr. Justice Hallam bore this shield. The Bar of the State of Minnesota is therefore proud to move the Court to receive the tributes that we have

prepared to their memory, and for that purpose may I ask the Court to recognize, first, former Chief Justice Samuel B. Wilson of Mankato, who will present the memorial to Mr. Justice Olsen.

The Honorable Samuel B. Wilson then presented the following:

Mr. Justice Olsen was born in Lillehammer, Norway, on January 4, 1861. At four years of age, he came with his parents to America and located at St. Peter, Minnesota. They lived in the city of St. Peter until 1871, when the family moved onto a farm in Nicollet county, where Ingerval grew to manhood.

He graduated from the University of Minnesota in 1887. He was a member of the Psi Upsilon fraternity. He became a student and clerk in the law office of Ueland, Shores & Holt in Minneapolis. He then went to Duluth, where he was employed in an abstract office. He was next employed in the law office of Lind and Hagberg in New Ulm. He was admitted to the Bar in Minnesota on December 22, 1893. He then practiced law at Redwood Falls, and in June 1894 he moved to Sleepy Eye and became a member of the firm of Sommerville and Olsen, which continued until the fall of 1906. He served the city of Sleepy Eye two years as mayor and one year as city attorney.

In November 1906, Governor John A. Johnson appointed him to fill a vacancy on the district bench in the Ninth Judicial District. In that same month, at the general election, he was elected for a six-year term. He was reelected in 1912. He was not a candidate in 1918.

He then practiced law in New Ulm until November 1920. During a part of that period of time, he was in partnership with Attorney A. W. Mueller, under the firm name of Olsen and Mueller.

Another vacancy occurred in his district, and on or about the 1st day of February 1920 he accepted an appointment from Governor J. A. A. Burnquist to return to the district bench. He was again reelected district judge in November 1920 and also in 1926. He served in that capacity until October 1, 1927, when he was appointed by the Supreme Court as a commissioner of that court. While serving as a commissioner, he was appointed associate justice of the Supreme Court by Governor Theodore Christensen on November 20, 1930. He was elected to that office in November 1932. He retired from the Supreme Court on December 15, 1936, on account of ill health. He lived until June 26, 1943.

In June 1896, Justice Olsen was married to Miss Lida C. McBain, who survives him as do their two children, Harold M. Olsen, an investment broker of New York City, and Mrs. Ruth Olsen Reineke of Cincinnati, Ohio.

Justice Olsen lived in Sleepy Eye at the time he first went on the Bench and for a period of time thereafter. He later moved to New Ulm, where he resided until the time when he came to the Supreme Court.

Mr. Justice Olsen had a thorough knowledge of the law and the judicial principles that support our form of jurisprudence. His sympathetic kindness, his high character, his mental equilibrium, his grasp of the rules of law and of what by reason and logic the law ought to be, made him a wise and safe counsellor and an admirable jurist.

His was a judicial temperament. He was kind and considerate but firm and steadfast in his concept of duty, from which he never swerved. He . . . was fearless and did not bend to bias or prejudice; nor was he concerned with the consequences that the law imposed. He acted without rancor or bitterness. By study and experience he was mentally well equipped. He never spoke evil of anyone.

He was prompt, punctual, and *semper paratus*; yet to him, time was only relative. He was little aware of the good impression his presence always created.

While on the district bench, he appeared cold, distant, and unsociable, a silent man who spoke only when duty demanded. He left this impression with attorneys practicing before him—due largely to his sense of propriety—and also with employees about him. He perhaps so appeared to the public generally but not to his associates in the Supreme Court, nor to those who were near him. There he talked freely and without reservation. At heart, he had a warm personality. He was a calm, modest, plain man who accepted life simply. He was a great judge. He added to the Court's reputation, confidence, and dignity.

We quote the following from a resolution recently passed by the Bar Association of the Ninth. Judicial District: "No lawyer of whatever experience and accomplishments came before him in a difficult case without surprise and admiration at Judge Olsen's learning, which covered unusual and unexpected fields, and at his lucid and sure insight into legal principles. Of modest and retiring disposition, he was strong in his convictions and fearless in their statement and in their application to the cases that came before him. He was a patient and courteous judge, without undue pride of opinion."

Justice Olsen was always conscious of his civic duty and gave freely of his strength and ability to his local community. During World War I, he was active in promoting the sale of Liberty bonds, encouraging enlistments, and engaging in other activities. He was his county's director in the Minnesota Safety Commission.

He admired nature and enjoyed fishing and hunting. He apparently found his greatest pleasure in his legal work.

> S. B. Wilson, Chairman
> T. O. Streissguth
> James H. Hall

Mr. Harries then said:

Your Honors, both Mr. Justice Olsen and Mr. Justice Hallam, before ascending to the bench of this Court, were judges of the district courts of the State of Minnesota. The District Court Judges Association is a constituent member of the State Bar Association and is represented here by Judge Albert H. Enersen and Judge Albin S. Pearson, who wish to be heard on behalf of their association.

Judge Albert H. Enersen, of the Ninth Judicial District, then presented the following memorial to Justice I. M. Olsen on behalf of the District Court Judges Association:

June 26, 1943, marked the passing of one of Minnesota's most esteemed jurists, Ingerval M. Olsen. Born in Norway in 1861, he came to the United States in 1865, was admitted to the Bar of Minnesota in 1893, and thereafter established an enviable reputation for integrity, industry, and superior ability in the practice of his profession.

He was elected District Judge of the Ninth Judicial District in 1906. Then, as now, that district comprised the counties of Brown, Nicollet, Redwood, Lyon, and Lincoln. Politically a Republican, he ran as such in 1906, but following his election and all during his service on the Bench he abstained from participation in partisan politics and even expression of political opinion. He was happy when in 1912 the laws of the State were changed so as to provide that candidates for judicial positions file without party designation. He served a second six-year term following reelection in 1912 but in 1918 was not a candidate and resumed the practice of law in New Ulm. In 1920, however, he accepted reappointment as district judge to fill a vacancy and was elected later in that year.

Judge Olsen was elected to a final term on the district bench in 1926.

At Sleepy Eye he was a member of the Congregational Church, which membership he transferred to the First Congregational Church of New Ulm when he moved there in August 1913; he was a faithful attendant, and his son and daughter were given the full benefit of church atmosphere and Christian training.

Those who practiced before him remember vividly his honesty, his impartiality, his thoroughness, and untiring devotion to duty. On the Bench he was untouched by friendships, unswayed by personal sympathies, prejudices, or antagonisms. His charges to juries were models of good and concise English, invariably prepared by him carefully in advance in longhand. An outstanding Winona lawyer once said of one of Judge Olsen's charges: "That charge covers everything properly—as clear as crystal, as cold as ice."

Court work during his 19 years on the district bench was heavy, especially during the "ditching" years so well remembered by many members of the Bar. Judge Olsen, then the only judge in the district, never failed to meet the onerous demands upon him. He was never known to miss a term or to fail to keep an appointment.

A model of legal propriety himself, he was deeply interested in maintaining the high standards and traditions of the legal profession. His leadership contributed substantially to the high level of observance of the rules of professional conduct that has carried on throughout the State to the present day.

He was elevated to the Supreme Court of Minnesota in 1927 when appointed Court Commissioner. He was appointed an Associate Justice in 1930, and elected Associate Justice in November 1932, in which position he served until he retired in 1936. He distinguished himself there as one of the greatest jurists in the history of that eminent body. The same clarity, soundness, conciseness combined with thoroughness and the same integrity and industry that characterized his work on the district bench and that led to his selection as a member of our State's highest court are evident in the many opinions that bear his name.

Perhaps the greatest testimonial to his sterling qualities as a man, lawyer, and judge exists in the fact that those who knew him best, who practiced against him and practiced under him, mourn him most. They cherish his memory and, with it, the ideals for which he staunchly stood. The District Judges join with the lawyers of the entire State and his many friends everywhere in an expression of appreciation of Judge Olsen's great contribution to Minnesota jurisprudence, and of the ever-living example the memory of his character and leadership furnishes the members of Bench and Bar.

Albert H. Enersen, Chairman,
Marshall, Minnesota
G. E. Qvale,
Willmar, Minnesota
Frank Clague,
Redwood Falls, Minnesota
A. B. Gislason,
New Ulm, Minnesota

Chief Justice Loring then requested that there be incorporated into the memorial for Justice I. M. Olsen the following tribute prepared by William R. Mitchell of Tracy, Minnesota, who was unable to be present because of illness:

When I returned from France in 1919, I began to practice law at Tracy, Minnesota, and immediately became very well acquainted with Judge Olsen. Judge Olsen was, most certainly, very courteous. His honesty and integrity and his judicial temperament made him an ideal judge. He had a faculty of quickly grasping the fundamental facts and points upon which each case depended. Although he was firm in his conclusions, he always paid courteous attention to arguments presenting a contrary conclusion. The legal profession and Judge Olsen's family can be justly proud of the wonderful record he made as a lawyer and as a judge.

Commissioner Andrew Holt [on behalf of the court] then said:

In the history of this Court, five persons have had the unique distinction of being selected by the Court itself to become members thereof. They were Homer B. Dibell, Myron D. Taylor, Edward Lees, Ingerval M. Olsen, and Charles Loring, the present Chief Justice.

When illness compelled the genial and learned Lees to retire, Ingerval M. Olsen was selected by the Court as his successor. That the selection was a wise one is demonstrated by the memorials prepared by the committees and also by his work here.

Judge Olsen was graduated from the academic department of the University of Minnesota in 1887. I was a junior member of a law firm in Minneapolis from 1882 to 1894, and that firm had as clients Professor John Blegen of the Augsburg College and Seminary of Minneapolis, and his wife, a sister of Ingerval M. Olsen. From that condition of affairs, it happened that when Ingerval decided to make law his profession he applied to our firm for a place to study law, and my recollection is that he remained with us the better part of a year as a law student. His duties for the firm were not arduous, and his pay was small. I remember that. His work was, of course, well done. There was no fault found.

When he was selected and became a member of this Court, of course I was in daily contact with him in the consultation room and in his own chambers. He was always ready and willing to aid the Court in anything that came up. When he came to our law office, he was a serious-minded, quiet, studious young man, and that was characteristic of him all along. You will find no attempt to display his learning or his literary ability in his opinions. They state the issues on appeal clearly, and the arguments and conclusions are so clear and plain that there can be no misconstruction about the results. He was always pleasant and agreeable and never lost his temper in the consideration of any case or proposition that came up and was always ready to help in his chambers as well as in the consultation room.

I think the tribute that the committee has presented is merited, and we sincerely concur in it.

Chief Justice Loring then said:

These proceedings in which Bench and Bar participate in memory of departed judges afford us an opportunity to record the respect, the esteem, and the affection with which in their lifetimes we regarded our professional brethren. It is wise that we pause in the course of our active work to conduct such ceremonies. It emphasizes in our minds the fact that all that is of real value that a judge can leave behind is a fair name and a good reputation—the respect that we have for lives well spent in service to the State and to the profession. When a lawyer accepts a call to the Bench, he must reconcile himself to serving without hope or prospect of other reward.

Mr. Justice Olsen was a close friend of mine. We were commissioners together until appointed justices in November 1930. Our offices adjoined. He was a great judge—his opinions ranked with those of the best judges whoever sat on this bench. On the district bench, he had the reputation of being among the very best of our district judges. On that bench as on this, he seldom talked much. But he listened with unusual understanding. His counsel in conference was listened to with the respect that our high regard for his professional attainments insured. Off the bench, he was cordial, gracious, and companionable, as I, probably better than anyone outside his immediate family, had opportunity to realize.

The justices whose memories we honor today have added their names to the illustrious list of distinguished men who devoted a large share of their lives to the service of this State by their devotion to the cause of justice. [220 Minn. xxix]

Clifford L. Hilton

1866–1946
Associate Justice, 1928–1943

On May 15, 1956, at 1:30 P.M., the Court being assembled in the courtroom in the State Capitol, Chief Justice Roger L. Dell said:

The Court recognizes the president of the Minnesota State Bar Association, Mr. John M. Palmer.

Mr. Palmer then said:

This time has been graciously and appropriately set apart for proceedings to commemorate the lives, the characters, and the public service of four members of this Court who have passed away, namely: Chief Justice Samuel B. Wilson, Associate Justice Clifford L. Hilton, Associate Justice Julius J. Olson, and Associate Justice Theodore Christianson.

The Court has called upon the Minnesota State Bar Association as the representative of the Bar of this state to arrange for the presentation of memorials to perpetuate the memory of those distinguished members of the profession who served for many years on this Court . . . Mr. Cyrus A. Field of Fergus Falls will deliver the memorial in honor of Associate Justice Clifford L. Hilton.

Mr. Field then presented the following memorial:

Clifford L. Hilton was born in the state that he later loved and served so long and faithfully. He was born at Kenyon, Minnesota, on December 8, 1866, the son of Addison and Harriet Hilton. His parents moved to Fergus Falls, Minnesota, in 1879, where he grew to manhood and attended the public schools. He graduated from the High School in Fergus Falls in 1884. He went to our neighboring State of Wisconsin to study law and graduated from the University of Wisconsin in 1888 with a degree of Bachelor of Laws. That same year he was admitted to practice law in both Minnesota and Wisconsin. Mr. Hilton returned almost at

once to his home town of Fergus Falls, where he commenced the practice of law in 1888. On September 23, 1891, Mr. Hilton was united in marriage with Frances G. Moll. They had two children. A daughter, Jean Hilton, died in childhood, and Mr. and Mrs. Hilton established a memorial library room in one of the grade schools in Fergus Falls in her memory. A son, Bernard M. Hilton, lives in St. Paul.

Mr. Hilton was engaged in the active practice of law in Fergus Falls from 1888 to 1909. During that time, he was City Attorney of Fergus Falls from 1896 to 1898 and County Attorney of Otter Tail County from 1899 to 1909. In 1908, Mr. Hilton formed a partnership with Anton Thompson, and they practiced law together in Otter Tail County under the firm name of Hilton & Thompson. As we lawyers all well know, his partner, Mr. Thompson, later became Judge of the District Court in the Seventh Judicial District and enjoyed a long and highly renowned period of service on that Bench.

In 1909 Mr. Hilton came to the Capitol Building in St. Paul and remained there as a legal public servant, in one capacity or another, continuously from that date until his retirement in 1943, a period of 34 years.

From 1909 to 1917, Mr. Hilton was Assistant Attorney General and was Deputy Attorney General from April 1917 to March 1918. Attorney General Lyndon A. Smith died on March 8, 1918, and Governor Burnquist appointed Mr. Hilton as Attorney General of the State of Minnesota to fill that vacancy. History records an interesting event that occurred shortly after Mr. Hilton became Attorney General. The year of his appointment was the political campaign year of 1918. David H. Evans of Tracy filed as an independent candidate for Governor, with no designation of a political party accompanying his name. Evans had the backing of A. C. Townley of Non-Partisan League fame and [of] an association of members of the Minnesota Federation of Labor. Attorney General Hilton ruled that Mr. Evans' name could not be printed on the official ballot unless followed by the name of some party. To comply with that ruling, the name of "Farmer-Labor Party" was chosen.

Many hundreds of rulings were destined to be made during Mr. Hilton's tenure as Attorney General. The voters of the state returned him to that office for four consecutive terms, and he served as Attorney General of the state until his appointment to this Court.

Associate Justice James H. Quinn of Fairmont retired from this Court on December 31, 1927. On January 1, 1928, Governor Theodore Christianson appointed Clifford L. Hilton as an Associate Justice of this Honorable Court. Many of us had the honor and privilege of practicing before Justice Hilton and this Court during the succeeding fifteen years that Justice Hilton served the Court, the Bar, and the people of this state, so ably as a member of this Court. It was in that capacity that the author of this memorial knew Justice Hilton personally. It would be appropriate to note, parenthetically, that it was necessary to draw upon recorded history and other reliable sources for many of the events of Justice Hilton's life prior to his ascendency to the Supreme Court.

Justice Hilton's forthrightness, integrity, and legal ability are permanently implanted in the common law of this state in his many opinions reported in Volumes 173 to 215 of the Minnesota Reports. The voters of the state returned him to the office of Associate Justice for successive terms in 1928, 1934, and 1940. He retired from this Court and from active professional life, on May 1, 1943. He lived about three years after his retirement, during which time he maintained his home in St. Paul. Justice Hilton passed away on April 5, 1946, at Clearwater, Florida, while with his family there during the winter months. He was survived by his wife and son. Mrs. Hilton died on April 24, 1949, at St. Paul.

Both Justice and Mrs. Hilton were members of and active in the House of Hope Presbyterian Church in St. Paul. Justice Hilton was a member of the Minnesota State Bar Association and the American Bar Association. While he was Attorney General, he was President of the National Association of Attorneys General.

Justice Hilton had a long and distinguished legal and public career. He maintained a keen interest in state and national affairs and also in political trends and developments. The voters of the state endorsed his public service by large majorities on many occasions. In his long, continuous public service, Justice Hilton was never defeated at the polls. While he was in public office for many years, he always served in his chosen legal profession.

The life of Associate Justice Clifford L. Hilton has enriched the Judicial branch of the State Government, the legal profession generally, and, in a broader aspect the lives of the peoples of the State of Minnesota. It is indeed fitting that we should pay tribute to his memory today as a part of the permanent records of this Court.

Chief Justice Dell then said:

It is indeed fitting and right that we should assemble here today in memory of the departed justices who served as members of this Court and to record the respect, esteem, and affection in which they were held by the Bench and Bar alike. That these men who we memorialize today have justly earned and richly deserve their place in the history of this state has been most ably pointed out by the memorials presented here this afternoon. Their work is finished and finished well, but our memory of them and what they have done will remain with us always.

I best remember Associate Justice Clifford L. Hilton as Attorney General of this state, which office he filled with dignity and ability for several years. It was then that I had most of my contacts with him. He was a fine administrator and had that rare trait of being able to select the right man for a particular job. His assistant attorney generals were some of the best in the history of this state and the efficiency of his office as well as the opinions prepared by his staff were recognized for their worth by the Bench and Bar alike. There is little that could be added to the memorial prepared by Mr. Field. The highly efficient office that he maintained as Attorney General of this state as well as his work as an Associate Justice of this Court will always be remembered by the Bench and Bar alike. [246 Minn. xvii]

Charles Loring

1873–1961
Commissioner, 1930; Associate Justice, 1930–1944; Chief Justice, 1944–1953

On May 31, 1966, at 2 P.M., the Court being assembled in the courtroom in the State Capitol, Chief Justice Oscar R. Knutson said:

The Court recognizes the president of the Minnesota State Bar Association, Mr. James E. Montague.

Mr. Montague then said:

The Minnesota State Bar Association comprising more than 4,000 members of the Bar of this State is honored to participate in this proceeding to commemorate the memories of departed justices of this court who have died since proceedings in memory of departed justices were last held in this room. Since that time five justices have gone to their ultimate reward. Three of them were chief justices of this court and two were associate justices. All left their imprint on the law, on the profession, and on the state. In order that there may be a record of their lives, their personal characteristics, and their achievements, we ask the Court at this time to recognize members of the Bar of this State who will deliver memorials to these departed justices . . . Mr. William K. Montague of Duluth will deliver the memorial honoring Chief Justice Charles M. Loring.

Mr. Montague then presented the following:

For many years I admired greatly the late Chief Justice Charles Loring. As a boy in Crookston, I thought of him as a leading citizen of the community; as a young man, I worked for a year or two—back in 1913 and 1914—as a clerk and stenographer in his law office. As a practicing lawyer, I looked up to him as one of the leaders of his profession and later as an able Justice and Chief Justice of this Court. It is, therefore, a privilege for me to have the honor of presenting the memorial to him on this occasion.

Charles Loring, former Commissioner, Associ-

ate Justice, and Chief Justice of the Minnesota Supreme Court, was born on a farm in St. Croix County, Wisconsin, on November 26, 1873. He was the only child of Lyman Loring and Eugenie Hutchinson Loring.

His father was an early pioneer of this area. A native of Maine, he pushed steadily westward as government land was opened for cultivation. He located in Wisconsin in the 1850s. He served with distinction during the Civil War, returning to Wisconsin after its termination. In 1877 he and his family moved to Clay County, Minnesota, where they resided until 1890. They then moved to Missoula County, Montana, where he engaged in ranching until his death in 1898.

In Montana Judge Loring became an avid lover of ranch life and for many years afterwards still kept the saddle and lariat that he had used as a cowboy on his father's ranch.

From 1888 to 1891, he attended the State Teachers College at Moorhead and later the Phillips Exeter Academy. He then entered the University of Minnesota Law School and graduated as Bachelor of Laws in 1898. Following his graduation, he was admitted to the bar in Montana and practiced there for one year. He then returned to Minnesota, where he entered the law office of his cousin, Carroll A. Nye, later Judge of the Seventh Judicial District.

In 1900 he moved to Crookston and entered the law office of Halvor Steenerson, a long-time member of Congress from the Crookston district. That association was dissolved in 1905, and Loring entered into a law partnership with G. Aaron Youngquist, who later was Attorney General of Minnesota and Assistant United States Attorney General. They were both highly regarded by their fellow lawyers. They enjoyed a large practice together until 1918, when the offices were closed as both men entered the military service.

As I stated previously—in 1913 and 1914 I worked as a law clerk and stenographer in that office. I was impressed not only with Mr. Loring's ability but by the fact that he was highly regarded by other lawyers in that area, as evidenced by the frequency with which they consulted him on their legal problems. Of the legal matters handled by him during that period, my principal recollection is his representation of a large group of homesteaders, woodsmen, and farmers in the northern part of the state, who had been wiped out by a disastrous forest fire. Suits were commenced against a railroad company as being to blame for the fire, and very satisfactory settlements were made.

Judge Loring was married to Bertha Darrow, a very close friend of the Nye family, at Moorhead in 1900. She was a skilled pianist. At Crookston she and Judge Loring sponsored and promoted musical concerts and artistic exhibitions. They were recognized as community leaders. He was a great lover of automobiles and in those early days, at a time when decent highways were unknown, promoted automobile tours. He was also very interested in farming and owned a fairly large farm near Crookston.

During World War I, he was local Chairman of the Citizens Training Corps Association and a Captain and Major in the Minnesota Home Guard. In 1918 he accepted a commission as Major in the Judge Advocate's Division of the U.S. Army, serving in that capacity in Washington and in Ohio. Later as Lt. Colonel, in the Judge Advocate's Department, he served in the First Corps Area at Boston, in the U.S. Army Forces in China, and in the Hawaiian Department. While he served in these capacities with distinction, neither he nor Mrs. Loring enjoyed life in the Far East, and [they] were glad when his tour of duty there ended.

As evidence of the respect with which he was regarded in those capacities, the Judge Advocate General later wrote: "Mr. Loring served with me and under me for several years, and I feel that I can say of him that he is a lawyer of great ability, a man of entire integrity and of admirable judicial temperament."

In 1926 he retired from Army Service and returned to the practice of law at Crookston, where he was associated with John Haugen from 1926 to 1930. During that period, he served as Special Assistant to the U. S. Attorney in carrying out the provisions of the treaty between the United States and Canada for water levels in the Lake of the Woods area and in settling claims arising out of the raising of those levels.

On August 1, 1930, he was appointed as Commissioner of the Supreme Court of Minnesota and in November of that year was appointed Associate Justice of that Court. He was elected to that position in 1932 and re-elected in 1938. In January 1944, he was appointed Chief Justice of the Minnesota Supreme Court, a position he held until his retirement in July 1953.

Upon retirement, he moved to Tucson, Arizona, where he died on March 7, 1961, at the age of 87 years.

By his first wife, Judge Loring had two daughters—Genevieve, who predeceased him, and Helen (Mrs. Charles B. Bryant), who survived him. Some years after the death of his first wife, Judge Loring in March 1933 married Frances Nye, a relative of the Nye family group with which he had been associated at Moorhead. She died in 1964.

Besides his active practice of law and his work as Justice of the Supreme Court, Judge Loring took an active part in many civic fields. By religion, he was a Unitarian. He was a member of the Masonic Order. He was twice a member of the Minnesota Board of Law Examiners and for a time was president of that Board. In 1949, he was appointed to the Executive Council of the Conference of Chief Justices of the United States. In 1954, after retirement, he was named by President Eisenhower as Chairman of a three-member nationwide arbitration board set up to settle certain types of railway disputes.

I am sure that I express the views of all the members of the bar who appeared before Chief Justice Loring as well as the opinion of all of the Justices of this Court who served with him that he was a very distinguished member of this Court; that in his years of judicial service, he displayed the same high degree of legal ability, the same complete integrity, and the same judicial temperament for which he was praised by the Judge Advocate General of the Army upon his retirement from that service.

Chief Justice Knutson then said:

It is proper that we hold these memorial services for those who have served on this Court. Some of us have had the privilege of serving with most of those whom we honor today. All of them have served with distinction and have added much to the jurisprudence of this state and this nation. While the opinions they have written, which are to be found in our Minnesota Reports, are the best testimonial to their ability, their intellectual integrity, and their devotion to their work, it is fitting that we who survive them express our appreciation for what they have done. [273 Minn. xxi]

John P. Devaney

1882–1941
Chief Justice, 1933–1937

In the afternoon of February 10, 1943, at two o'clock, the Court being assembled at the courtroom in the State Capitol, Chief Justice Henry M. Gallagher called upon James A. Garrity, President of the Minnesota State Bar Association.

Mr. Garrity then said:

The Bar of the State of Minnesota has recently lost by the death of Chief Justice John P. Devaney and Associate Justice Royal A. Stone two of its most distinguished and illustrious members. The State Bar Association, of which I am President and which I am here to represent, has thought fit that there be recorded in this high tribunal some proper and permanent memorial in recognition of the ability and virtues of our departed brothers.

It is truly meet and just that this great tribunal, over which Chief Justice John P. Devaney presided and of which Associate Justice Royal A. Stone was a member for many years, should specially assemble in their honor and join in tributes paid to their memory.

These men loved their work and, I know, tried to the best of their ability to discharge the sacred obligations placed upon their shoulders as members of this Court; and now in the words of Kipling it can be said:

And only the Master shall praise us,
   and only the Master shall blame;
And no one shall work for money,
   and no one shall work for fame,
But each for the joy of working,
   and each, in his separate star,
Shall draw the Thing as he sees
   It for the God of Things as They Are!

This Court has permitted the Minnesota State Bar Association the privilege of presenting these memori-

als. The Chairman of the Committee who has the memorial to former Chief Justice John P. Devaney in charge for the Association is George B. Leonard, of Minneapolis . . .

Mr. George B. Leonard then presented the following memorial:

Chief Justice Devaney, having retired on February 15, 1937, died on Sunday, September 21, 1941, at the age of 59.

John Patrick Devaney, the youngest of eight children, was born in the village of Bristol, Worth County, Iowa, June 30, 1882. His parents, Patrick and Ellen Lavelle Devaney, were natives of Ireland. They came to the United States in their youth, before the Civil War.

His father, apprenticed to blacksmithing, followed his trade almost until his death at the age of 75, first in New York state, later in Louisiana, and lastly in Iowa. While in Louisiana, the elder Devaney joined the Confederate Army, with which he served for four years. In the early [18]70s, having met and married his wife at Buffalo, New York, he moved to Iowa and continued his trade as a village blacksmith, most of the time at Bristol. When his son John was eight years of age, the family moved to nearby Lake Mills in Iowa in order to afford the children a high school education.

At the age of 18, John, after graduating from high school, entered the University of Minnesota and completed the four-year course in the Liberal Arts College in 1905 with the B.A. degree. He graduated from the College of Law with the LL.B. degree in 1907 and received the LL.M. degree in the year 1908.

Magnetic personality, a quick and alert mind, driving power, and unbounded energy soon made young John a leader on the University campus. For two years he served as editor of the *Minnesota Daily,* and during most of his time at the University he held the lead as a skillful intercollegiate debater. For two years he taught rhetoric.

He began the practice of law in Minneapolis in 1907 in the office of George B. Leonard. Later, he became the junior partner of Stiles & Devaney, which was dissolved in 1916. Between 1920 and 1930, he was senior partner in the firm of Devaney & Edwards, specializing in the law of common carriers. This type of practice brought him in close contact with the chief farming and producing groups of the Northwest, with their needs and problems, and helped to shape the direction of his many later interests and activities.

From 1930 he practiced law by himself until the fall of 1933 when Governor Floyd B. Olson appointed him Chief Justice of the Supreme Court to fill the vacancy created by the resignation of Chief Justice Samuel B. Wilson. In the general election in 1934 he was elected to the same office. He served from September 4, 1933, until February 15, 1937, when he resigned and returned to private practice. On the Bench, John Devaney proved to be an able judge with an excellent knowledge of the law and abundant capacity for sensing essential facts and applying to them the legal principles involved. To him, law was not an end in itself but a means to render justice. His ability and character as a jurist were deservedly recognized by the Marquette and DePaul Universities when they conferred upon him the honorary degree of Doctor of Laws in the years 1935 and 1936, respectively.

While on the Bench, Judge Devaney acted as Chairman of the Minnesota Crime Commission, to the work of which he gave much of his time. The adoption by the Legislature of many of the Commission's recommendations is proof of the worth of his untiring efforts to improve the administration of criminal law in Minnesota.

Being sensitive by nature to the plight of the poor and being made more so by his early experiences in life, the pleas that came to the Pardon Board, of which he was a member as Chief Justice, by the children, wives, mothers, and friends of the imprisoned, sank deeply into his soul. He labored hard on records presented to the Board, patiently listened to every plea for a pardon, and interviewed applicants for pardon personally in the penal institutions they were confined in. The responsibilities as a member of the Board, coming as they did in addition to the duties of Chief Justice, bore heavily upon Judge Devaney.

On returning to private life, Judge Devaney was not content to devote himself solely to his practice. Pressing social and economic problems that agitated the public mind during the 1930s did not escape him. Urged by a desire to contribute to the improvement of existing conditions, he became one of the prime movers and organizers of the National Lawyers' Guild, which at a convention held in Washington, D.C., in February 1937, elected him as its first president. Great stress was laid by this organization on the protection and preservation of our Civil Liberties.

The outstanding quality of Chief Justice Devaney was his singular ability to sense the vital issue in any dispute, strip it of all nonessentials, and concentrate upon solving it, if need be, by the give-and-take method. He excelled as a mediator. In his later years he frequently served as the neutral arbitrator in industrial disputes, either by invitation of the employer and employee representatives or through appointment by public authority. President Roosevelt frequently appointed him mediator in such matters, notably as Chairman of the President's Emergency Board of Settlement of labor disputes in the Chicago, Great Western Railway, Pacific Electric Company, and Northland Greyhound Bus Lines.

He was generous. He was particularly solicitous of young men struggling to obtain an education. Few of them, after proving themselves worthy of help, went away empty-handed. His own experience served to remind him that a lift in time means much to a struggling youth.

He will be remembered for his broad sympathy and concern for the ordinary man, whose trials and difficulties to find a rightful place for himself in the ever-changing social structure of his time made a very strong appeal to him.

He had an abiding faith in the integrity of the ordinary man and his loyalty to our institutions. He had the firm conviction that, in teaching the man on the street to look upon the Constitution as his Constitution and the Bill of Rights as his Bill of Rights, no fear need be entertained for the future of the Nation. He carried his message directly to the people and invariably received good response. That his faith in the common man has been fully justified is demonstrated by the undivided support being given by rich and poor alike to the Nation's effort to win this war, so that a free life under the Constitution may be preserved.

He is survived by his wife, Mrs. Beatrice Langevin Devaney of Minneapolis, to whom he was married in 1919; his son, John Patrick Devaney, now serving with the U.S. Merchant Marine; his daughters, Beatrice and Sheila; a sister, Mrs. Nell Davlin of San Francisco, California; and his brother, Dr. William L. Devaney of Robbinsdale, Minnesota.

> George B. Leonard, Chairman
> Matthew M. Joyce
> Michael J. Doherty

The Honorable John B. Sanborn, Judge of the United States Circuit Court of Appeals for the Eighth Circuit, then said:

The difficulty of portraying accurately in words the character and qualities of a friend who has gone is like the difficulty that an artist must experience in attempting to paint a satisfactory portrait from memory or from some old photograph. While they live, we take our friends for granted. We do not stop to analyze their characteristics. We have general impressions about them, but when they have left us and we try to reproduce those impressions in the form of words, we find the picture blurred and unsatisfactory.

In paying my inadequate tribute to the memory of John P. Devaney, formerly Chief Justice of this Court, I shall try to avoid exaggeration, knowing as I do that he had too keen a sense of humor and too little personal pride to wish anyone to idealize him. My memory of him goes back to the early years of this century, when we were in the same class at the University of Minnesota. There are those here today who knew him more intimately than I did, but I doubt if there is anyone here who knew him longer.

John Devaney was always a companionable, lovable person with all of the qualities that are attractive. He had an agile and alert mind, a delightful sense of humor, a genial, kindly, and gentle disposition, the ability to talk interestingly, and the capacity to do well whatever he undertook. To these qualities,

coupled with industry and sound legal judgment, may be attributed his early and remarkable success as a lawyer. Perhaps his outstanding characteristic was his talent for dealing with highly controversial matters without creating antagonisms. His opponents in the trial of lawsuits showed the utmost confidence in his fairness and treated him more as a friend with whom they had a slight difference of opinion than as an antagonist. No matter how much those who knew him might disagree with his beliefs as to the law or as to politics or philosophy, their regard for him and his regard for them remained the same. He was intensely loyal to his friends and would, with no hope of reward, do anything to help them, without making them feel that they were under the slightest obligation to him. He had that rare faculty of knowing what he could do that would be of the greatest assistance; of doing it with effectiveness, and of quietly effacing himself after it was done.

John Devaney demonstrated what can be achieved in this country by those who are worthy. Starting without influence and with little aside from education, industry, and his own native ability, he had great success in his profession, occupied the highest judicial office in the State, and acquired a position of nationwide prominence. As Chief Justice he used his powers to maintain the high standing and reputation of this Court. He believed that only lawyers and judges of demonstrated fitness should occupy judicial position and that the efficient and impartial administration of justice is a matter of the most vital concern to every citizen.

For the meritorious service that he rendered to his chosen profession, to this Court, and to the people of this State, the name of John P. Devaney should be held in cherished memory.

Mr. [Dewitt] Clinton Edwards then said:

If the only purpose of our being here were to give some measure of comfort to members of families, there would be little occasion for me to speak. Members of Judge Devaney's family well know of our close friendship in his lifetime, and I am sure they know too how deeply I cherish an affectionate regard for his memory. But it is a privilege to be included among those who may on this occasion express their sentiments for your records.

Perhaps I knew Judge Devaney as well or better than anyone did, except his family. He had been practicing law about seven years when I first came to know him at the University during the college year of 1912–1913. That was when he presided at moot court sessions that we were expected to attend during my senior year in the Law School. When he was considering accepting appointment to this Court he reminded me rather drolly that that was his only previous judicial experience and he was doubtful whether it would be of much help.

The day after graduation I began the practice of law with a firm of which he was the junior partner. That firm had a large practice in the law of common carriers. He was then trying many cases. I recalled to one of the committee a few days ago an occurrence of that fall of 1913, and he suggested that I might appropriately relate it here. At the first jury term one of the cases on my office calendar was set for trial. I announced that fact to Mr. Devaney with some considerable trepidation and inquired of him what we were to do about it. "Well," he said, "you go down and try it, unless you think we ought to look for some young lawyer with more courage to try it for you." With passing years, I have remembered that conversation with a growing sense of grateful appreciation, though I must confess that that was not my reaction at the time.

To at once begin trying cases under his stimulating direction and watchful guidance was an opportunity indeed, because in that field and in negotiations he was at his very best. He had all the essential qualifications of the good trial lawyer and negotiator. Especially, he possessed a talent for yielding quickly and a discriminating capacity for yielding the unimportant but never the substantial rights of his client.

He withdrew from his firm in 1916 to open his own law office. Later, we formed a partnership that continued for ten years, beginning in the fall of 1920. Those earlier years of working for his firm and of our partnership association gave me the opportunity to know him very well.

Though he early acquired a fine reputation, he never acquired smugness. It is to his credit that he felt there was no need for any high-grade reputable lawyer to explain or apologize for his representation of

men injured in industry. He represented many, particularly in the railroad industry—always resourcefully, competently, and effectively. Lawyers of high grade representing industry have never asked more nor expected less than that from their adversaries. Among those whom he most frequently opposed in such matters were some of his closest personal friends.

He believed strongly in more thorough prelegal education for those who would become lawyers. It seemed to him that many who knew and understood accepted legal principles lacked the capacity properly to apply them. Greater ability to think, to reason, to rationalize he felt might have been attained had they been required extensively to pursue cultural, social, and economic studies. He thought too that lawyers so equipped obtain more enjoyment and profit out of their practice and the public greater benefits. Apart from that, he believed in cultural education for itself, for a greater enjoyment of life, and a better understanding of its problems. He put that theory into practice, and it was a source of great pride and satisfaction for him to note the progress and achievements of a number of young men whom he had assisted—young men preparing for law, for other professions, and for business.

But I should like to refer more particularly to those personal qualities that endeared him to his friends and associates. He was never opinionated nor self-sufficient. He did not regulate every proceeding by the standard of his own sole judgment. He sought counsel and thoughtfully gave consideration to the views of his associates or others with whom he consulted. In considering the views of others, he was always deferential, if not always in agreement, with them.

He had a genuinely sympathetic approach in moments of grief or sorrow. His were not the detached utterances of conventional platitudes but rather the happy faculty of saying or doing the things that make lighter one's burden, of making one feel and deeply appreciate his sympathetic understanding. He knew how to be helpful and comforting.

The mean, petty things of life were no part of his make-up. He was always one to emphasize the good qualities in others, never to accentuate the bad, nor to publish their faults and vices. Commenting one time about a mutual friend whose wit was often rather caustic and barbed, and still smarting from it, I had observed that it required a brilliant mind to think and say the things this chap could say in the trial of a lawsuit. Devaney agreed but added that it required a better mind to think them and not say them.

He was good company. He had a fine sense of humor and a rare wit. One might wish that this were the time and place to recall incidents that occurred during our association when his fine mind and keen wit had play, the latter always in that kindly way so characteristic of him. It is pleasant to recall that there never passed between us an unkind word. Those were years of delightful association and now of pleasant, lasting memory. For his many fine personal qualities, I shall best remember him.

Of humble origin, here was one who was instinctively a gentleman.

Justice Andrew Holt then said:

I have had the rare privilege of serving with and under five different Chief Justices of this Court. They have been men of outstanding ability as lawyers and all gentlemen possessed of the utmost kindness, which has been exhibited to their associates at all times.

I was a district judge when Judge Devaney began to practice law. My courtroom was at the corner of Fourth avenue and Fifth street in Minneapolis. He tried or was interested in several cases at which I presided, but I remember one occasion distinctly when he came into the courtroom to try a case against a railway company for damage to some fruit in transportation. He was associated with Mr. George C. Stiles, the attorney for the plaintiff, who took a seat at the counsel table. Mr. Devaney came in with a lot of books on his hip and sat down beside him. I was attracted to his neat appearance, his kindly smile and personality, and of course he won the case. I was impressed with him as a trial lawyer, and I would refer to him as a person somewhat similar to such men as W. W. McNair, E. M. Wilson, Nat Whelen, and J. O. Wheelwright. I realize that he did not enjoy the exacting duties of this Court. He was looking for some-

thing more active, and it did not surprise me when he resigned. I agree fully with what has been said of him by the gentlemen of the Bar Association committee, by Judge Sanborn, and by Mr. Edwards.

Justice Charles Loring [for the court] then said:

Your Memorial is a just and merited acknowledgment of the distinguished service rendered to this State by John P. Devaney as Chief Justice. He came to this court to fill the place vacated by the resignation of Chief Justice Samuel B. Wilson.

In the light cast by the exceptional services rendered by his distinguished predecessors, it was not an easy place to fill. However, Chief Justice Devaney's magnetic personality, his patience, his tolerance, and his perfect courtesy on all occasions to his associates and to the bar soon endeared him to bench and bar alike. To these fine qualities he added a mind so keen and alert as to instantly grasp the application of legal principles to a state of facts. He brought with him a wide experience at the bar, an experience that gave him that quality so necessary in a judge, the ability to apply the principles of jurisprudence to the problems presented—a faculty that can be acquired only by long experience at the bar. Well versed as he was in legal principles, his warm heart and deep human sympathy kept him always within the spirit of the law as distinguished from a legalistic view of it.

He had many friends whom he loved and who loved him, but when they came through the doors of the courtroom they presented only a problem in the administration of justice—not a problem in friendship or politics. Always his first loyalty was to the Court as an institution. He was jealous of its reputation and ready to make personal sacrifice to insure its high standing among the tribunals of the Nation.

He left us all with the warmest affection for him personally and with great admiration for his many fine qualities. To those of us who served with him the memory of that association will always be one of the pleasantest of our service on this Court. [213 Minn. xxx]

Julius J. Olson

1875–1955
Associate Justice, 1934–1948

On May 15, 1956, at 1:30 P.M., the Court being assembled in the courtroom in the State Capitol, Chief Justice Roger L. Dell said:

The Court recognizes the president of the Minnesota State Bar Association, Mr. John M. Palmer.

Mr. Palmer then said:

This time has been graciously and appropriately set apart for proceedings to commemorate the lives, the characters, and the public service of four members of this Court who have passed away, namely: Chief Justice Samuel B. Wilson, Associate Justice Clifford L. Hilton, Associate Justice Julius J. Olson, and Associate Justice Theodore Christianson.

The Court has called upon the Minnesota State Bar Association as the representative of the Bar of this state to arrange for the presentation of memorials to perpetuate the memory of those distinguished members of the profession who served for many years on this Court. The Association is honored to respond to the call . . . The Honorable Oscar R. Knutson, Associate Justice of this Court . . . will deliver the memorial in honor of Associate Justice Julius J. Olson.

The Honorable Oscar R. Knutson then presented the following memorial:

I suppose that a memorial of this kind should present as a verbal portrait of the man we honor and as such should be a frank appraisal of his work, his accomplishments, and his service to his fellow man. It should be a picture of him as he was and as he lived and worked and served. For the benefit of posterity it should leave a written memento of what manner of man he was. It should too, I suppose, be as impersonal as it is possible to make it.

Julius J. Olson was born on the Isle of Donna, off

the coast of northern Norway, on February 22, 1875. At the age of eight years, he and his parents immigrated to America and settled on a farm near Lake Park, in Becker County, where he attended grade school and grew to young manhood. He attended high school in Detroit Lakes, graduating in 1897. The same year he entered the Law School at the University of Minnesota, where he earned his own way, graduating in 1900. He was admitted to the Bar the same year and went first to Crookston, where he stayed only a short time, after which he went to Warren, where he became associated with the late Andrew Grindeland. In March 1903 a second judgeship was created for the Fourteenth Judicial District, and Grindeland was appointed to that position. Justice Olson then took over the practice and continued alone for some time, after which he formed a partnership with the late Rasmus Hage of Warren. In April 1927 this partnership was dissolved, and, after completion of law school in 1927, I had the good fortune of becoming associated with Justice Olson in the practice of law. In December 1930, Judge Grindeland retired from the bench. Nearly the entire Bar of the Fourteenth Judicial District requested the appointment of Judge Olson to fill the vacancy, and as a result he was so appointed at the close of the year by the late Governor Theodore Christianson. He was elected to that position in 1932. On March 5, 1934, he was appointed as an Associate Justice of the Supreme Court by the late Governor Floyd B. Olson to succeed the Honorable Homer B. Dibell. He served in that capacity until he was forced to retire in May 1948 because of ill health. In October 1950, he moved back to Warren, where he resided until his death on May 22, 1955. He is survived by his wife, Caroline, and one son, Sletten Olson, both of Warren, and a daughter, Katherine Staley, of Washington, D.C. Both son and daughter are engaged in the practice of law. Also surviving are two grandchildren and two brothers: Alfred of Fargo and Einar Olson Juel of Colorado Springs, Colorado, and one sister, Marie Jacobson, of Osakis, Minnesota.

During his lifetime Justice Olson served in many civic and professional capacities. In his local community he helped organize and was the first secretary of the Marshall County Agricultural Association. He served on the school board, was head of the County Red Cross during the First World War, and served in many other capacities. He was active in Bar association work and helped organize the Fourteenth Judicial District Bar Association, of which he was a Past President. He was for many years a member of the District, State, and American Bar Associations. For a number of years he served on the Board of Law Examiners.

As a lawyer, Justice Olson ranked among the best. His practice extended throughout the district in which he lived and elsewhere. He had an extensive knowledge of the law and an unusual memory. He understood rural people with whom he dealt as few are gifted to understand them. In a trial before a farmer jury he was a formidable opponent in any kind of a lawsuit. He argued many cases in this Court, and in appearing before a court, his knowledge of the law and manner of presentation brought him much success. His conduct in the courtroom was always exemplary—that of a gentleman—and his sense of fairness and display of courtesy toward the judge on the bench and witnesses alike won him many friends. On the other hand, once he was convinced that a witness was not telling the truth, his skill in cross-examination frequently shattered the composure of a witness and effectively destroyed the value of his testimony. Toward his clients he was scrupulously ethical in his dealings, and in his community as elsewhere it was known that his word was as good as his bond.

As a trial judge he probably was at his best. I think that he spent the happiest years of his professional life as a trial judge. Unfortunately, it was not a long time. He loved people, and in serving as a trial judge he felt that he was close to them and could be of service to

them. He had seen much of the hardship of life and had a broad understanding of people. He dealt with them as they are, not as he would have liked to make them. While he could be stern when the occasion demanded it, he had a sympathy for people who had not always had the best of life, and he knew how to temper justice with mercy. His verbal spanking of young people who had made a mistake, before he placed them on probation, was something which they never forgot, and yet he did it without rancor or any outward appearance of vindictiveness. In presiding over a trial he was patient, courteous, and understanding, but no one ever had to be in doubt as to who was running his courtroom. His decisions as trial judge were usually right. In the three and a half odd years that he served on the trial bench he was reversed by this Court only three times, in a day when there was much litigation and many appeals.

As a member of this Court, his opinions speak for themselves and are their own best memorial. About all that need be said about them is that he wrote as he lived. Here, again, he had only one guide to go by and that was intellectual honesty. His opinions are clear and straight to the point. They are based on his honest judgment, uninfluenced by politics, desire for personal acclaim, or prejudice or malice toward anyone. His only desire was to see that justice was done, as he saw it, regardless of who was involved in the litigation. While serving on this Court he missed the personal contact with people that he had formerly had as a lawyer and as a trial judge. He did not underestimate the great honor that the people of the state had conferred upon him, nor was he ungrateful for it, but he realized that the nature of the work on this bench is such that contact with people for one who comes here from a distance and leaves his intimate friends back home is bound to be somewhat limited. He was a hard worker and more than willing to carry his share of the load. While he realized the seriousness and the importance of the work of this Court, he maintained throughout his service here a sense of humor that kept him from setting himself above the people whose disputes he was called upon to decide. His sense of humor occasionally found its way even into his opinions. But through it all he never lost sight of the fact that even the cases that seem trivial to judges are important to the litigants involved and that each case deserves careful consideration.

As a man, Justice Olson was possessed of a rugged character. He had only one rule to live by and that was based on personal integrity. On matters involving integrity he was unyielding. He often said that there can be no compromise with what is right. He had no time for sham or deceit or pretentiousness and was quick to spot it. No one had to guess where he stood on any matter of importance. In his dealing with other people he was frank almost to a point where it became a fault, and yet he was patient and understanding of others and tempered his thinking with a knowledge that all did not react to everything as he did. His ready wit and earthy humor were known to all who came to know him intimately. Not only was he a good lawyer, an ideal trial judge, and an exemplary appellate justice, but on a hunting or fishing trip he was a most delightful companion. While it was known that he loved to hunt and fish, I think that it was the companionship of the group he was with that he loved the most. He was an ardent gardener, and his flower beds were not only beautiful but as carefully kept and free from extraneous weeds as his mental thinking. He took much pride in his garden at his home, and almost any evening in the spring or summer you could find him working in his garden. For many years he maintained a summer home on Lake Miltona, a short distance north of Alexandria, and one look at his premises and garden was sufficient to convince even the most skeptical that he spent little time loafing, even on vacation. Starting from a humble beginning as an immigrant boy, Justice Olson rose by hard work and unswerving loyalty to the code by which he lived to hold a position on the highest court in the service of his state. His life exemplifies that which has made America what it is, a land of opportunity for those who will to do what they may choose to do. It might well be said of him: "There was no guile in him—only a simplicity within, a humility of heart, a sense of humor that never failed him and always helped us."

Chief Justice Dell then said:

It is indeed fitting and right that we should assemble here today in memory of the departed justices who served as members of this Court and to record the respect, esteem, and affection in which they were held by the Bench and Bar alike. That these men who we memorialize today have justly earned and richly deserve their place in the history of this state, has been most ably pointed out by the memorials presented here this afternoon. Their work is finished and finished well, but our memory of them and what they have done will remain with us always.

In 1920, when I commenced to practice law in Fergus Falls, Associate Justice Julius J. Olson was then one of the outstanding lawyers in northern Minnesota. He was an excellent trial lawyer and possessed a most enviable reputation for his honesty, integrity, and fairness. After he became district judge I had the pleasure of trying several cases before him. And what a rare treat that was, for his knowledge of the law and the rules of evidence coupled with his keen desire to do complete justice assured every litigant in advance of the trial that he would get exactly what he was entitled to— nothing more and nothing less. His work on this Court was outstanding. Plain, blunt, and fair, his legal knowledge and wisdom known and respected by all his colleagues, his opinions stand out as among the best. He will live always in the hearts of the members of his profession who had the good fortune to know him. [246 Minn. xvii]

Harry H. Peterson

1890–1985
Associate Justice, 1936–1950

Harry H. Peterson was raised the middle child of seven in a rough-and-tumble St. Paul neighborhood. After surviving a sometimes pugilistic adolescence, he rented a room from Gustavus Loevinger, a former Ramsey County district judge, and entered the University of Minnesota Law School. He graduated *cum laude* in 1912. Justice Peterson recalled that he "had no money to spend, so I stayed home and studied." He married Mabel V. Norquist on June 28, 1916. They eventually had two children and four grandchildren.

After graduation from law school, Harry Peterson went to work as assistant Ramsey County attorney. He was said to be so dedicated that he once practiced law uninterrupted for 10 days with a ruptured appendix, finally showing up at the hospital under his own power. He served as the Ramsey County attorney from 1923 to 1926.

Once known as the "brain" of the original Farmer-Labor Party, he became the campaign manager for the "steely-eyed" William Mahoney, St. Paul's first "labor mayor." In 1932, Peterson became the successful Farmer-Labor endorsed candidate for state attorney general, and he was reelected in 1934 and again in 1936.

During the bitter depression of the 1930s, then Attorney General Peterson distinguished himself by drafting the Homestead Preferential Tax Act, a law that cut taxes for homeowners. He successfully guided the bill through the legislature and won all the substantial litigation that followed the passage of the bill into law. His office drafted the Minnesota Mortgage Moratorium Act, which provided the court's authority to postpone foreclosures until the homeowner had a chance to refinance. The Minnesota Supreme Court upheld the act's constitutionality in the landmark case *Blaisdell v. Home Bldg.*

& Loan Ass'n, 189 Minn. 142, 249 N.W. 334 (1933). Peterson appeared in Blaisdell as a "friend of the court" to help secure its vitality. Then, on appeal to the U.S. Supreme Court, Peterson appeared as counsel for the state and Blaisdell and successfully defended the act in *Home Bldg. & Loan Ass'n v. Blaisdell*, 290 U.S. 398 (1934).

He also drafted a law that permitted farmers victimized by the harsh dust-bowl conditions and the lack of an accessible source of credit to borrow money to feed their livestock.

Gov. Hjalmar Petersen, filling out the term of the recently deceased Gov. Floyd B. Olson, named Harry Peterson to the Minnesota Supreme Court in 1936. Justice Peterson was elected in 1938 and again in 1944. He resigned from the Minnesota Supreme Court in 1950 to run for governor and won the Democratic Farmer-Labor nomination against Orville Freeman, who was elected governor four years later. Justice Peterson lost the general election, however, to another former supreme court justice, Luther Youngdahl.

One of Justice Peterson's most interesting cases arose not during his tenure on the court but during the difficult 1950 gubernatorial campaign. He sought to be identified on the primary ballot as "former supreme court justice," as a way to be distinguished from two other candidates of the same last name. He obtained an attorney general's opinion supporting his request. A third candidate challenged the attorney general opinion in the court from which Justice Peterson had recently resigned. The supreme court did not grant the candidate's request to overturn the opinion of the attorney general.

After the election, Justice Peterson engaged in the private practice of law. He also acted as an associate dean and instructor at the Metropolitan College

293

of Law in Minneapolis. He founded and was dean of the Midwestern College of Law, which later became Hamline University Law School.

In a 1964 interview, Justice Peterson announced his intention to "practice law until I die—if I can."

This was one of the few life goals he was unable to attain. After a brilliant 56-year legal career, Justice Peterson retired at the age of 78. He died in 1985 in St. Paul at the age of 94.

—David S. Paull

Henry M. Gallagher

1885–1965
Chief Justice, 1937–1944

On May 31, 1966, at 2 P.M., the Court being assembled in the courtroom in the State Capitol, Chief Justice Oscar R. Knutson said:

The Court recognizes the president of the Minnesota State Bar Association, Mr. James E. Montague.

Mr. Montague then said:

The Minnesota State Bar Association comprising more than 4,000 members of the Bar of this State is honored to participate in this proceeding to commemorate the memories of departed justices of this court who have died since proceedings in memory of departed justices were last held in this room. Since that time five justices have gone to their ultimate reward. Three of them were chief justices of this court and two were associate justices. All left their imprint on the law, on the profession, and on the state. In order that there may be a record of their lives, their personal characteristics, and their achievements, we ask the Court at this time to recognize members of the Bar of this State who will deliver memorials to these departed justices. The Honorable Robert J. Sheran, an associate justice of this Court, will deliver the memorial honoring Chief Justice Henry M. Gallagher . . .

Justice Sheran then presented the following memorial:

On April 3, 1965, Henry M. Gallagher came to his death at Waseca, Minnesota, survived by his wife, Maude, his daughter Henrietta Gahler, and his brother, Judge Frank T. Gallagher of this court. One other daughter, Alice Toller, predeceased him.

He was born September 10, 1885, in Wilton Township, southwest of Waseca, Minnesota, the son of the late Bernard M. and Kathryn Barden Gallagher. Following his graduation from Waseca High School in 1905, he worked in the law office of the late John Moonan of Waseca, obtaining his legal education at Creighton University of Omaha, Nebraska, from which he graduated in 1910 with an LL.B. degree. That same year he commenced the practice of law at Waseca, Minnesota, first in partnership with Fred W. Senn, who later became district judge in the area, and then in partnership with G. P. Madden and his brother, Frank. Before his appointment as Chief Justice of the Minnesota Supreme Court in 1937 he had served as Waseca County Attorney, Waseca Municipal Judge, and as a member of the Waseca School Board, the Minnesota State Board of Law Examiners, and the Minnesota State Industrial Commission. He was elected by a large majority in 1938 and continued to serve as chief justice until January 3, 1944, when he resigned to resume the practice of law in Waseca and Mankato, Minnesota, where his partners included Charlotte Farrish and Miles Zimmerman. Three of his nephews, Daniel, Lawrence, and Michael Gallagher, are members of the legal profession in this state. He was a Director of Northern States Power from 1953 to 1963. His religious honors included designation as a Knight of St. Gregory.

This recitation of the attainments of Chief Justice Henry M. Gallagher serves principally to give the background in which his stature as judge and lawyer and his distinctive character can be recalled and appreciated.

He had an innate understanding of the law and the reasons for it. From this understanding came appreciation of the law's complexities; the never-ending need for examination and research of statute and precedent. He did not try to give and was not moved by the quick or flippant answer. "Let me think this over," he would say; and when he had done so, his opinions and advice were based solidly on the facts, the law, and common sense—blended in such a way as to make the complex seem simple and the prescribed course evidently right. Because these professional skills were combined with rare qualities of character, he will always be memorable as a jurist and lawyer.

While he devoted a considerable part of his life to civic affairs, he did so without ostentation. "Everyone," he often said, "owes something to his community besides the payment of taxes." For him, no more elaborate rationale was needed to explain his willingness always to be of public service.

He was, above all else, a person of great compassion and humility, finding his greatest satisfaction in the assistance of others. He was by nature a man of the highest personal rectitude, but never did he deplore or publicize another's faults. He seemed to be able to find the essential quality of goodness in everyone and to accord to each individual courtesy and respect regardless of his state or condition in life.

Henry Gallagher's philosophy is illustrated by a quotation that he kept always in his office, reading: "There are three sides to every question—your side, my side, and the right side." This saying epitomized his faith that men could, if they but would, find a common denominator of agreement for the adjustment of controversy and dispute. Committed to this principle, he enjoyed a disciplined and constructive life both personal and professional, at peace with his fellow men and with himself.

People of all kinds and backgrounds seemed to recognize his worth almost spontaneously, and he in turn could and did visit with a fellow townsman, or the president of the United States, or the operator of an elevator, or the editor of a newspaper, or a law clerk, or the president of a large corporate enterprise, or the bellhop at a hotel, or a United States Senator, or the relative of a convicted felon seeking a pardon or release—easily and simply—giving the same deferential attention to each of them. He had respect for greatness; he was unimpressed by grandeur.

I conclude this memorial by giving testimony based upon 25 years of close acquaintance with Henry M. Gallagher as his law clerk, his partner, and his close friend—a witness that can be condensed in this statement: During all of this term of regular and intimate association, I observed not one recallable incident, whatever the provocation, where he treated any person harshly, inconsiderately, or unfairly. He was indeed a good and gentle man.

Chief Justice Knutson then said:

It is proper that we hold these memorial services for those who have served on this Court. Some of us have had the privilege of serving with most of those whom we honor today. All of them have served with distinction and have added much to the jurisprudence of this state and this nation. While the opinions they have written, which are to be found in our Minnesota Reports, are the best testimonial to their ability, their intellectual integrity, and their devotion to their work, it is fitting that we who survive them express our appreciation for what they have done. [273 Minn. xxi]

Maynard E. Pirsig

1902–1997
Associate Justice, 1942

Maynard E. Pirsig was an influential figure in Minnesota jurisprudence, not only for his three-month-long term on the state supreme court in 1942 but also for the generations of legal scholars he influenced as a professor at the University of Minnesota and William Mitchell College of Law. He must have been proud of both jobs: Legend has it that if someone asked whether to call him professor or judge, he told them, "The judges call me professor, and the professors call me judge."

Maynard Pirsig was born on January 9, 1902, in Kossuth County, Iowa, near the Minnesota town of Elmore. The oldest of five children, he grew up speaking German until he started school in a one-room schoolhouse. He earned B.A. and LL.B. degrees from the University of Minnesota, where he served as a note editor for the *Minnesota Law Review* and was elected to the Order of the Coif.

In 1925, Pirsig turned down a job offer from the Minneapolis law firm of Dorsey & Whitney to become a Legal Aid attorney, supposedly because Legal Aid then paid more. He was the director of the Legal Aid Society for the six years from 1925 and 1931. Jeremy Lane, the director of Mid-Minnesota Legal Assistance, said that the minutes of the early Legal Aid board meetings demonstrate Pirsig's determination that Legal Aid exhibit the professionalism of a law firm. Legal Aid started as part of the Family Welfare Association, and when Pirsig's board considered sharing space with various charitable entities, he let it be known that he preferred to work for a law firm, not a social work agency. By the time Pirsig left Legal Aid in 1931, it had incorporated as an independent entity, and, of course, today there is no question that Legal Aid is a professional law firm.

Pirsig moved to the University of Minnesota, developed its clinic program, and taught there until 1970, when he was forced to retire. Preparing to teach a course in judicial administration, Pirsig studied law at Harvard University under Roscoe Pound and Felix Frankfurter and spent some time in England as a pupil in a barrister's chamber.

Pirsig also taught pleading, actions and equity, criminal law, evidence, insurance, and ethics. He served as dean from 1948 to 1955. After retiring from the university, he joined the faculty of William Mitchell College of Law, where he taught criminal law and procedure, professional responsibility, and comparative judicial administration until 1993.

As a professor and scholar, Pirsig was fairly "straight-laced" and "stringent," said William Mitchell's Prof. Kenneth F. Kirwin, who co-edited with Pirsig two editions of a casebook on professional responsibility. "He had high standards and he thought lawyers should as well," Kirwin recalled. Most students recalled him fondly, and Kirwin said that it was almost impossible for Pirsig to walk through an airport anywhere in the country without being greeted by a former student.

Minneapolis attorney Randall Tietjen remembered that as a student he didn't think he would like Pirsig's class in criminal law because the professor was too demanding: "He made it very clear the first night that he expected a high level of performance from the students," Tietjen recalled. "He said that he had nothing but contempt for any student who came to class unprepared. He chided some fellow in the front row for taking notes on loose pages of paper. Maynard told him he should use a bound notebook, something more permanent. He told us that he still had *his* criminal law notes from 1923, and he still used them." Tietjen and Pirsig became fast friends.

Pirsig was devoted to William Mitchell, said Prof. Michael K. Steenson. He recalled working late one night and seeing Pirsig dart in and out of the classrooms, so he followed him to see what he was up to. Pirsig was turning off the lights. Steenson picked up the habit: "Every time I flip a switch I say, 'Maynard, this one's for you.'"

Pirsig received an honorary doctorate of law from William Mitchell in 1981 and the University of Minnesota's Outstanding Achievement Award in 1985. He wrote numerous casebooks, treatises, and pieces for the *Minnesota Law Review*.

While these achievements were impressive, Pirsig's brief stint on the Minnesota Supreme Court in 1942 gave him a permanent place in the judicial history of the state. Incumbent Justice Royal A. Stone had run for reelection as one of nine candidates for two seats. Stone came in third in a September primary but died five days later. Gov. Harold Stassen appointed Pirsig to serve the remainder of Stone's term (before the turnover). The high court had to decide whether Stone's death necessitated a special election. The court ruled that it did not and allowed the November election to proceed as scheduled. Pirsig served until the newly elected justice took office, making the most of his time on the court. During his three-month tenure, the prolific justice wrote 11 majority opinions and five dissents, along with several concurrences.

Labeling a justice's philosophy based on his opinions is difficult, especially when there are only 11 of them. On at least one occasion Pirsig deferred to the legislature, though he thought it was wrong to impose a property tax on airplanes domiciled in Minnesota. "That question is more properly addressed to the legislature, whose prerogative and responsibility it is to enter into such considerations. The power to make a good law of necessity carries with it the power to make an unwise one," he wrote for the majority.

On the other hand, Pirsig also wrote in a case involving a dispute over utility assessments: "If a court is convinced of the justice of a cause, it cannot refuse to recognize and give effect to it merely because an applicable precedent or legal principle cannot be found. In the absence of authority, it must of its own develop and assert those legal principles which in its judgment will best serve the ends of justice in the case before it and in other like cases. Cases of the kind before us must stand on a footing of their own."

Concurrence by Pirsig in a workers' compensation case, *Gentle v. Northern States Power Co.*, proved influential. Pirsig wrote that a "common enterprise" should be found when the employees of two or more employers are engaged in a common activity—regardless of the common purposes of the employers. The law was tending in that direction, Pirsig wrote, and today it has arrived. The state supreme court aided its journey in *McCourtie v. U.S. Steel*, which wove the idea into its three-part test for common enterprise and wrote that Pirsig's earlier concurrence provided the "cornerstone" interpretation of the statute.

The court was not the only venue for Pirsig's service to the legal profession. At the national level he served on the National Conference of Commissioners on Uniform State Laws, U.S. Supreme Court Advisory Committees on Federal Rules of Civil Procedure and Criminal Procedure, and the U.S. Department of Labor's Industry Committee for Puerto Rico, which established minimum wages for Puerto Rican industries.

At the state level Pirsig served as secretary of the Minnesota Judicial Council and was a member of the Minnesota State Bar Association's Committee on the Youth Conservation Act, which was the beginning of jurisprudence emphasizing the treatment rather than the punishment of minors. He also served on the advisory committee for what then was the Minnesota Division of Employment and Security, on an advisory committee on the Minnesota Criminal Code, on the Rules of Criminal Procedure, and on a state commission on juvenile courts.

Pirsig was said to be avidly interested in almost everything in addition to the law. William Mitchell professor and former dean James Hogg recalled that Pirsig, starting when he was in his eighties, acquired at least five computers and was able to repair them himself.

Minneapolis attorney Allen I. Saeks recalled that Pirsig became interested in the commodities markets and estimated he made millions on his investments. Hogg also remembered that Pirsig sat at his broker's office watching the tickertape and researched everything about the commodities market, right down to the weather patterns in Russia. He was said to have the longest successful string of pork bellies trades in the country.

Tietjen said that Pirsig taught him how to grow old gracefully because all of Pirsig's life he practiced the habits of study, compassion, generosity, moderation, dignity, and humor, leading to the character that served him well as the years passed.

Pirsig published his last *Law Review* article in 1990, but he continued teaching at William Mitchell until 1993. At the time of his retirement it was widely believed he had taught longer than any other law professor in the United States and that he was the oldest person regularly teaching at any law school in the country.

Maynard E. Pirsig died on February 5, 1997. His wife of 54 years and one daughter died before him. He was survived by a daughter and a son.

—Barbara L. Jones

Thomas O. Streissguth

1889–1950
Associate Justice, 1942, 1944

On October 8, 1951, at 2:30 P.M., the Court being assembled in the courtroom in the State Capitol, Chief Justice Charles Loring said:

The Court recognizes the president of the Minnesota State Bar Association, Mr. Charles B. Howard.

Mr. Howard then said:

The Minnesota State Bar Association, representing three thousand lawyers of Minnesota, are delighted to have this opportunity to honor one of the distinguished lawyers of the state of Minnesota. We have asked that memorials be presented by two of our distinguished members. We have asked Mr. Henry N. Somsen Sr., of New Ulm, Minnesota, and the Honorable Harry H. Peterson, formerly a colleague on the Supreme Court, to present a memorial as such colleague on the Supreme Court. If the Court please, I would like to have the Court first recognize Mr. Henry N. Somsen, the dean of the Bar of New Ulm, who will speak for the Bar.

Mr. Henry N. Somsen then presented the following memorial:

This memorial is presented in behalf of the members of the Bench and Bar of the Ninth Judicial District as a token of the respect and esteem in which they held our late friend and associate Thomas Otto Streissguth. It was intended that this memorial should be presented to the Court by a beloved friend and colleague of Mr. Striessguth's, Mr. Henry H. Flor of New Ulm. Owing to his untimely death a few weeks ago, this plan was necessarily changed, and I was asked to take his place here today, which I do with a deep sense of duty and obligation, both to Mr. Streissguth and to Mr. Flor.

Thomas Otto Streissguth was born at Arlington, Sibley County, in this state, on February 27, 1889.

He died on December 21, 1950, age 61. He passed away shortly before midnight of that day and then started that long journey to an undiscovered country from whose bourne no traveler ever returns.

Mr. Streissguth was commonly and affectionately known as "Tom" to his brethren of the bar and to hundreds of friends and acquaintances. He was the son of Theodore and Katie Streissguth and was one of a family of nine children. The Streissguth home was a Christian home. The teachings of the Christian faith were truly exemplified and followed in the daily life of the family. They thoroughly pervaded the atmosphere of the home. Consideration one for the other, love and affection between the members of the family, and a high regard one for the other were present to a striking degree. The result was a family solidarity that was rare indeed—a condition that continues to this day. In the Streissguth family it was "all for one and one for all." This fine atmosphere in which Tom grew to manhood made a deep and lasting impression on his life and character that continued through his entire life.

Tom attended the public schools at Arlington. Upon his graduation from high school there, he entered Carleton College, where he remained for two years. He then went to the State University and obtained his Bachelor of Arts degree in that institution in 1908. He then took up the study of law at the University and received the Bachelor of Laws degree in 1910.

From that time until 1914, a period of four years, he was employed by the West Publishing Company of St. Paul and by the Callaghan Law Book Company of Chicago, where he was engaged in research work and the writing of text material. In 1914 he entered the practice of law at Redwood Falls, Minnesota, associating himself with that distinguished lawyer and gentleman, the Honorable Frank Clague. He remained there only a short time and then opened his own law office at Gaylord in his home county, where he remained until 1923. During that period, however, he answered the call to the flag and served almost two years in active military service. In 1923, he came to New Ulm and joined Alfred W. Mueller in the practice of his profession. That partnership continued until 1927, at which time Tom opened his own office in New Ulm. He was associated for a number of years with his brother-in-law, John Fordyce, under the name of Streissguth & Fordyce. In 1935 Mr. Fordyce went to Wisconsin, whereupon James Gislason became associated with Tom. This partnership was soon terminated by the tragic death of Mr. Gislason. The latter part of 1936 Judge S. P. Gislason became Tom's partner. That partnership was dissolved when Tom was appointed an Associate Justice of this Court in 1942. When his service on this Court ended, he resumed the practice of law at New Ulm. Soon afterward he entered into a partnership with Robert J. Berens. Later, Richard T. Rodenberg was admitted to the firm, which continued until Tom's death. A few months before he died, Tom was proud to welcome as an associate in his office his daughter, Janice, immediately following her admission to the bar of this state.

For a period of 18 years, from 1924 to 1942, Tom served as County Attorney of Brown county. He was fearless and untiring in his efforts to perform the duties of his office in the fullest measure. His reelection to this important office time and again is testimony of the high esteem in which the people of Brown county held his character and ability. As a prosecutor it may fairly be said that he was impartial and fair, as zealous in shielding the innocent as he was diligent and untiring in prosecuting those of whose guilt he was convinced.

On October 6, 1942, he was appointed an Associate Justice of our State Supreme Court by Governor Harold E. Stassen, and he was later appointed to the same position by Governor Edward Thye to fill a vacancy then existing in the Court. His work and accomplishments on the Supreme Court will be dealt with in another memorial being presented to this Court today.

I think it may fairly be said that Tom ranked in the top bracket of his profession. He was a student of the law and a most forceful advocate at the bar. He had a tremendous capacity for work. His counsel was widely sought not only by clients but by lawyers. He was in a true sense a lawyers' lawyer. His passing is a shocking loss to our local bar as well as to the bar of the entire state.

To terminate this memorial at this point would be a grave injustice, for Tom was more than a mere lawyer. He was a good citizen in the fullest sense of the word. He participated in all activities that promised to further the welfare of the community in which he lived, particularly in all matters pertaining to law and government. He came to the aid of his country in time of need. All these, and all other obligations of good citizenship, he met in full measure. He was a director and officer of the Brown County Historical Society, of the New Ulm Library Association, of the New Ulm Charter Commission, and of many, many other organizations—all calculated to promote the welfare of the community. He was not only a member but actively worked and promoted the interests in every possible way of all of these organizations. He was generous in supporting all of them and spared neither his time nor money in promoting their best interests.

In politics he was always a Republican. He was one of the organizers of the Young Republican League, was County Republican Chairman for a time, was a delegate to a Republican National Convention, and a candidate for the office of lieutenant governor of this state in 1932. When this country entered World War I, he promptly responded to his country's call, served faithfully, and rose to the rank of Captain in the Fourth Regiment of Field Artillery.

Tom had an intense interest in the welfare of the boys of the community. He was one of the leaders of the Boy Scouts organization of this area. By reason of his long contact with the Boy Scout movement and as an adult scouter, he firmly believed that no other institution in our country was so potent an influence in developing good citizenship and good character. He was a pillar of strength and support to the organization all through southwestern Minnesota. That Tom did give willingly and generously of his time and money to the support of the Boy Scout movement does not admit of any doubt. Tom was a very busy man. Many of us, including myself, often wondered how Tom could possibly find the time from his many other activities to do the work that he took upon himself to do in his support of the Boy Scout movement. Truly the boys of the New Ulm community have lost a great and a good friend.

Tom was married to Gladys Burnside, of Neenah, Wisconsin, in 1918. In passing on, he leaves her his widow; a son, Tom Jr., who is in public relations work at Geneva College, Beaver Falls, Pennsylvania; and a daughter, Janice, who, as previously mentioned, is a member of the bar in New Ulm and an associate in her father's former firm. He was a generous and indulgent husband and father.

Tom leaves a community wherein he was a trusted, gifted, and energetic leader. He leaves a bar that was proud to include him within its circle. He leaves a multitude of friends, all of whom have fond memories of Tom that will long continue. He leaves the boys of the New Ulm community, whose loyal and true friend he was. They are all better boys and will be better men because of his interest and friendship.

To his memory, there has been erected a monument much more worthwhile and more imposing than any granite column or marble mausoleum. That monument is a living monument—a better and finer generation of young American citizens.

May it please the Court, I respectfully ask that this Memorial be spread upon the minutes of the Court as a permanent record of the doings and accomplishments of our good friend and brother, Thomas Otto Streissguth.

Justice Peterson then said:

My brief remarks concerning Judge Streissguth's work as a justice of this Court shall be for the purpose of paying him a just tribute and perpetuating his memory rather than for that of appraisal and analysis of his judicial work. Our task is one of portraiture, and as has been observed on other similar occasions, it is one that can be done only imperfectly for the same reasons that an artist can portray but imperfectly from memory his subject.

Judge Streissguth's work as a justice of this Court demonstrates the truth of the assertion that the judge's personality determines what kind of a judge he is. Judge Streissguth was a very distinct personality. He was strong and compact physically and seemed to have almost boundless physical and mental energy. He had a very lively disposition and was not only aware of what transpired about him but also took an interest in events and persons. He was studious, industrious, thorough, and painstaking in everything he did.

He early acquired a wide range of learning in history, literature, criticism, and a smattering of music. His conversation was enlivened and adorned by allusions thereto to illustrate or emphasize points. His opinions as a justice of this Court sometimes referred thereto, as, for example, the reference in his dissent in *State v. Glenny*, 213 Minn. 177, 181, to Bacchus, Aphrodite, Olympus, and Cyprus of ancient Greek mythology; in *Thiede v. Town of Scandia Valley*, 217 Minn. 218, to the philosophers Hood and Paine; in *State v. The Crabtree Company*, 218 Minn. 36, to Tom Sawyer; in his dissent in *Berthiaume v. Christgau*, 218 Minn. 65, 71, to the singer Frank Sinatra; and so on in other opinions that he wrote.

Of a highly competitive nature, ardent, buoyant, intense, thorough, sanguine, and ambitious to be a successful lawyer, he followed a course that was bound not only to achieve that goal but also to fit him for the honor that was to be his as a justice of this Court. He devoted both his days and his nights to the practice of law. He mastered his cases. By the analysis of evidence in case after case, he became expert in the handling of fact questions that arise in the course of a busy practice. He clearly perceived the legal points involved in his practice and read and studied all the law in the books pertinent to such questions. The consequence was that his legal education continued from the time he entered the law school until his death; that he covered practically the entire field of the law, excepting, of course, such subjects as are unlikely to arise in the course of a country practice; and that he grew in legal stature with the passing of the years.

His was a country practice running the entire gamut of the law incident to such a practice. He was counsel in many important cases, some of which were of national importance. He engaged in stirring and exciting trials with lawyers of the highest standing and ability with a high measure of success. He was an able and effective advocate and no respecter of persons, whether they happened to be opposing counsel of high standing and ability or even the trial judge. This is not to say that he did not respect the presiding judge. He had a high conception of the functions and importance of the judicial office, which he believed was the instrumentality for doing justice here on earth. He believed that in the decision of cases courts should apply the law to the facts of the particular case without fear or favor so as to do exact justice as between man and man. He was a firm believer in our system of constitutional government and that it was the first duty of courts to apply constitutional principles so as not only to preserve our form of government but also the rights and privileges it guarantees to the citizen.

He not only was busy in the practice of law but also engaged in political activity, in which field he was energetic, resourceful, and determined. As a campaigner for his party—the Republican Party—he struck hard and telling blows. I know this of personal knowledge, for I felt the impact thereof in the state campaign of 1932 when he was the Republican candidate for Lieutenant Governor and I was the Farmer-Labor candidate for Attorney General. While he was a hard-hitting and strenuous contestant, he was withal humorous, kind, and sympathetic, and after the contest was over he bore no grudges. He viewed the issues involved objectively; his contests related to causes and not to personalities. Because he failed sometimes to make this clear and because his opponents thought he fought with vengeance and rancor, he was often misunderstood. Judge Streissguth enjoyed good and gracious living and the companionship of his fellow-men. His home in New Ulm radiated hospitality and friendship. He mingled with his fellow citizens and took part in the affairs of the community. The dominant group in New Ulm being of German extraction, much of the life and culture of the community was in the German tradition, which was characterized by a friendly and pleasant social intercourse with participation in food and drink to create a feeling of well being and satisfaction. This they called "Gemutlichkeit"—a state of being that must be experienced and enjoyed in order to be understood.

When Judge Streissguth came to this Court, he possessed, therefore, rare qualities of learning, experience, insight, common sense, industry, and temperament. The processes he daily applied in the practice of law in preparing his cases were the identical ones employed by this Court in the decision of cases. When he became a justice of the Court, he merely stepped from one side of the bar to the other. His prior training in the analysis of facts and the application of legal rules to established facts were a perfect preparation for the performance of his duties as an appellate judge. In short, when he came to this Court, he came as one prepared for the work—as a true journeyman and master of the craft, so to speak; as one equal to the responsibilities of the office; and when he took his seat on the bench it was as one among his peers.

While Judge Streissguth's term of service was short, he demonstrated high ability in his judicial work. His expertness in dealing with complicated fact situations stood him and the Court to good advantage in many cases, as, for example, in the case of *In re Restoration to Capacity of Masters,* 216 Minn. 553, involving the application of the principles of psychology and psychiatry in determining the mental capacity of a party. In the course of his service, he wrote for the Court several important cases in the field of public administrative law that determined important questions and that will serve as guides to the bench and bar as long as our system of government endures. Among such decisions were those of *State ex rel. Rockwell v. State Board of Education,* 213 Minn. 184; *Tepel v. Sima,* 213 Minn. 526; *State ex rel. Ging v. Board of Education,* 213 Minn. 550; *and Juster Bros. Inc. v. Christgau,* 214 Minn. 108. Other decisions written by him cover many legal subjects. All of them bear evidence of his grasp of the questions considered and decided, of thorough scholarship, and his purpose to do justice.

In the conferences of the justices, where the work of actually deciding the cases is done—work with which the members of this Court are familiar but the Bench and the Bar generally are not—Judge Streissguth's abilities in dealing with facts and applying principles of law thereto showed off to fine advantage. The supposition is that the Court derives strength from its membership—that the interaction and cooperation of several judges having equal authority and responsibility in the decision of all matters coming before it will bring to the process the learning, the insight, the judgment, the understanding, and the common sense of all and thus afford a surer basis for decision. Judge Streissguth made just such contributions. He mastered every case during his tenure. He was prepared to discuss them and thus contribute to the decisions written by his colleagues as well as his own. He was interesting and delightful in conference, for there he could use picturesque language and display his humor and kindness. A conference at which he was present was never dull. He, like his colleagues, rendered decisions of the entire Court and not, as has been sometimes asserted, "one man decisions."

Judge Streissguth was a valued member of this Court and a lovable friend and companion. His judicial work will endure forever as a perpetual memorial to his high ability, his integrity, and his devotion to the duties of the judicial office as an able and upright judge.

Mr. Everett L. Young, of New Ulm, Minnesota, then presented the following memorial on behalf of the Minnesota State County Attorneys Association:

The committee appointed by the President of the Minnesota County Attorneys Association presents before the Supreme Court the following Memorial for Thomas O. Streissguth, who died at New Ulm, Minnesota, on December 21, 1950:

Tom Streissguth, as he was best known to his friends and associates, was appointed County Attorney of Brown county by the Board of County Commissioners in the year 1924 and was reelected to that office four times. He served as County Attorney until October 1, 1942, at which time he resigned to accept an appointment to this Supreme Court.

After Tom entered his work as County Attorney he soon became one of the outstanding County Attorneys of this state. Tom, as a prosecutor, tried his cases vigorously and successfully. He was meticulous in the investigation and preparation of a case, brilliant and untiring in his trial work, and asked for and gave no quarter. Having entered upon the prosecution of a case where he was convinced of guilt, he was zealous in seeking conviction but always impartial and fair, would unhesitatingly urge dismissal when it appeared that one accused was apparently innocent. Tom believed that circumstances and environment were often a great factor in the failings of individuals, that it was human to err, and would often give of his time, efforts, and influence in an attempt to rehabilitate offenders, and on occasion was known to go before our Board of Parole to give information favorable to a prisoner to assist the board and prisoner to attempt rehabilitation.

Early in life Tom became a staunch supporter of youth organizations and particularly the Boy Scouts of America and his church. He was an adult Scouter and gave of his time and money toward facilities for Scout Camps in his territory of the State. The young people of his church now benefit through provisions made by Tom for them.

As County Attorney, Tom gave no less attention to the civil and administrative end of county business. He felt it his obligation as County Attorney not only to give legal advice to the Board of County Commissioners, the County Welfare Board, and the County Officers but to advise with them on policy as well.

During the remainder of his life after he became County Attorney, he rarely if ever missed a meeting of the State County Attorneys Association. He served as an officer of the County Attorneys Association for three years from 1925 through 1927, serving as President in the year 1927. Thereafter he served on many committees and in many advisory capacities. It may be said of Tom that he was a "regular fellow," never absent when there was work to be done or when something had been assigned to him. Because of his ability as prosecutor and his experience gained through his years of service, Tom's help and advice was often asked for and received by the younger county attorneys throughout the State. Tom was never stingy about his time if he could be helpful to other county attorneys.

The county attorneys of this state and members of the State County Attorneys Association were grieved by the death of their friend and associate, Tom Streissguth. At the annual meeting of the Association held on December 28, 1950, the Association halted proceedings, and in Convention Assembled the members stood for a moment of silence in memory of their departed brother. The death of Tom Streissguth was a great loss to our association and its members.

The Committee in preparing this Memorial has sought to confine itself to that phase of Tom's life which he spent as County Attorney. Much more could be said that would be repetitious because of other Memorials presented by the Bar.

We move that this Memorial be made a part of the permanent records of this Court.

> B. M. Heinzen
> Sidney P. Gislason
> George D. Erickson
> James Lynch
> A. L. McConville
> Robert G. Williamson
> Everett L. Young,
>   Committee

Chief Justice Loring then said:

Your memorial is a just and merited acknowledgment of the brief but distinguished service rendered to this state by Thomas O. Streissguth as a justice of this Court and also of his services as a member of the Bar and as a citizen of the state.

As you have stated, he served the people of this state twice, first to fill out the term of Mr. Justice Holt and second to fill the vacancy created when Chief Justice Henry Gallagher resigned and I was appointed his successor.

He brought with him the wide experience at the bar, as Judge Peterson has said, so necessary to equip a lawyer for a career on the bench. He was a tireless worker, as his excellent opinions demonstrated. I am sure that the quality of his work contributed much to the reputation of this Court. He was a most patriotic American. He served in the line in the first World War, but one of his great disappointments in life was his inability to pass the required physical examination to qualify him to accept a commission in the Judge Advocate General's Corps of the United States Army in the second World War.

He was a gracious and cordial person to be associated with. He won the affections and respect of all his colleagues on this Court. But I am sure that he was much happier in his active practice at the bar, where his wide acquaintance and high reputation won him a large clientele. We join with the Bar of this state in regret for his passing. [233 Minn. xxxi]

Luther W. Youngdahl

1896–1978
Associate Justice, 1943–1946

Any gallery of Minnesota's preeminent public servants must include Luther W. Youngdahl. He served as municipal and district court judge, associate justice of the state supreme court, governor, and federal district court judge for the District of Columbia. He is remembered as a person of high moral standards and deep religious faith, with a lifelong commitment to the principles of fairness and justice.

Luther W. Youngdahl was born in Minneapolis on May 29, 1896, the son of Swedish Lutheran emigrants. He graduated from South High School in Minneapolis before attending the University of Minnesota. After one year at the university, he joined the army to serve in World War I as a field artillery lieutenant. Upon his return from military service, he attended Gustavus Adolphus College, where he graduated in 1919 as a bachelor of arts. He obtained his law degree in 1921 from the Minnesota College of Law (now the William Mitchell College of Law). After admittance to the Minnesota bar, he served as assistant Minneapolis city attorney from 1921 to 1923 and as a law partner with former Judge C. M. Tifft from 1923 to 1930. In 1930 he was appointed to the Minneapolis municipal bench, where he served until he was elected a Hennepin County District Court judge in 1936. In 1942 he was elected an associate justice of the Minnesota Supreme Court.

Youngdahl was a highly regarded member of the state supreme court. During his tenure he wrote 79 majority opinions and five dissenting opinions. A review of his opinions reveals a justice who took a scholarly and principled approach to the law. He had a well-defined understanding of the individual liberties guaranteed by the U.S. Constitution. He understood the concept of separation of powers as shown in a dissent in which he sided with the ability of the legislature to establish prima facie evidence for proof of a crime. His opinions also display well-developed concepts of court procedure and the right to due process.[1]

Youngdahl's tenure came to a dramatic end with the Republican Party's "Ides of March" announcements in mid-March 1946. Many speculated that former Gov. Harold Stassen would return to Minnesota in 1946 to run against U.S. Senator Henrik Shipstead because Shipstead had voted against ratification of the United Nations charter. On March 14, 1946, Stassen announced that he would not run against Shipstead. Gov. Edward Thye then announced that he would challenge Shipstead—with Stassen's support. The following day, Youngdahl announced that he would leave the court to run for governor with the support of both Stassen and Thye. In November, Youngdahl easily won the election.

Youngdahl served with great distinction as Minnesota's 27th governor. He brought to that office his strong Swedish-Lutheran religious beliefs. He scoffed at those who referred to him as Minnesota's "Sunday-school governor" or as the "blue-nosed governor." Much of this criticism was the result of his effort to rid the state of its pernicious gambling problem. When Youngdahl became governor, a vast illegal gambling industry thrived in the state, an industry that benefited from indifferent law enforcement. In 1946 more than 8,500 one-armed bandits reportedly were "choking down coins in the state." Restaurants, bars, and country clubs profiting from the use of the illegal slot machines opposed reform. Law enforcement was generally indifferent to the illegal gambling operations, even if they took place in plain sight.[2]

Youngdahl, who grew up in a Lutheran/Swedish household that read the Bible and believed sin was something to avoid, pushed for the passage of antigambling legislation and chastised law enforcement for not upholding the law. In the process, he ignored critics who referred to him as a "Christian in politics." In 1947 Youngdahl succeeded in his fight for antigambling legislation and in persuading law enforcement to support the legislation vigorously. Youngdahl's actions led the *Des Moines Register* to write about the morally stoic governor to its north: "Youngdahl has a trait puzzling to professional politicians—he means what he says . . . the Minnesota record proves that old-fashioned morality can be still sold to the public."[3]

Former Minnesota Gov. Al Quie remembers Governor Youngdahl as having "a strong moral compass."[4] But this moral compass was not limited to the elimination of "sinful" activities such as gambling. After enacting his antigambling legislation, Youngdahl embarked upon what he called his "humanity agenda." He promoted reform of the mental health care system for which he received national recognition. During his second two-year term, Youngdahl launched a campaign that led to a new mental health law that became a model for the nation. He promoted initiatives to increase the funding for public education, improve conditions to troubled juveniles, and give returning veterans a financial boost.

Youngdahl also promoted equality among the races by working to eliminate segregation in the National Guard and to improve the status of American Indians. He stated: "All races must quickly learn to cooperate according to the principles of justice or perish," and he challenged the "dominant white governing group" in Minnesota to "set the example by correcting wrongs done to the Indian." In 1950, when the National Association of Retarded Children honored him for his work, Youngdahl revealed his commitment to all citizens of the state: "Our great democracy can be measured best by what it does for the least of its little citizens." Youngdahl's strong moral compass clearly pointed him in the direction of treating his fellow citizens with humanity.[5]

Republican activist Charles W. Arneson, an undergraduate and law student during Youngdahl's tenure as governor, recalled how impressive Youngdahl was in person. He was well over six feet tall. He had been a college football star and maintained the posture of an athlete. He had a ruddy complexion complemented by a full head of slightly graying hair. Arneson recounted that when Youngdahl walked into a room, he took immediate command of it. He was an excellent speaker, who liked to campaign. He loved to travel throughout the state and was as welcome at an Iron Range booyah as he was at a Lutheran church supper.

While some conservative Republicans criticized Youngdahl for being too liberal in his views, this criticism did not deter him from pushing his agenda for the state. When confronted with such, he often went directly to the people and won their support. He was so popular that, when he ran for reelection in 1950, he won with 60.7 percent of the vote.

Perhaps the most controversial episode in Youngdahl's life of public service involved his 1951 resignation as governor. Hubert H. Humphrey had been elected U.S. Senator in the Democratic landslide of 1948—a landslide that Youngdahl easily survived with a vote margin of more than 100,000 votes. Humphrey knew Youngdahl was the only Minnesota politician capable of challenging him for the Senate in 1954. Many thought Youngdahl would win reelection in 1952 and challenge Humphrey two years later. That all changed in September 1951. A contemporary recounting of that event appeared in *TIME Magazine*: "Last week Republican Youngdahl and Fair-Dealer Humphrey smiling side-by-side stepped out of President Truman's office and made an announcement that shook their state from border to border. The President had appointed Youngdahl a federal judge in the District of Columbia . . . With one round from his gun, Harry Truman had just about blown off the head of the Minnesota Republican Party. Slick Senator Humphrey, who had laid the gun on the target, could chuckle."[6]

Humphrey easily won reelection in 1954, leading many DFL candidates to victory. Only later did Youngdahl reveal that he resigned as governor only after his physician told him that he must start taking it easier because his inordinately high blood pressure could prove fatal.

As a federal judge in Washington, D.C., Youngdahl was at the center of prominent national issues. In 1952, at the height of the anti-Communist campaign of Senator Joseph McCarthy, Youngdahl dismissed as unconstitutional four of seven counts of the government's case against Far East expert Owen J. Lattimore. The government charged Lattimore, a Johns Hopkins University professor, with perjury, asserting that he lied to the U.S. Subcommittee on Internal Security when he said he was not a sympathizer or promoter of Communism. McCarthy claimed that Lattimore was a top Soviet Union agent. The U.S. Court of Appeals in Washington upheld Youngdahl's dismissal of two of the counts by 8–1 decisions but reinstated the other two counts he dismissed by 5–4 decisions.

In 1955 Youngdahl threw out a new indictment brought against Lattimore, and the government ultimately dropped its case. Youngdahl later said he was as proud of his action in the Lattimore case as of anything he had ever done: The "country came as close to being a dictatorship at the time as I hope we will ever come." He also said, "When public excitement runs high as to alien ideologies is a time when we must be particularly alert not to impair the ancient landmarks set up in the Bill of Rights." As a federal judge, Youngdahl built on the strong record of defending individual liberties that he had established as a state supreme court justice and governor.[7]

Youngdahl continued to serve as a federal judge until he took senior status in 1966; then he was active as a senior judge until the last month before his death at age 82 from cancer, at home, on June 21, 1978. Long a believer in the benefits of exercise, he hiked four miles a day until his early eighties. Youngdahl was survived by his wife, Irene Annette Engdahl, a daughter, and two sons. He is buried in section 30 of Arlington National Cemetery.

—Justice Paul H. Anderson

References

1. *State v. Kelly*, 15 N.W.2d 554 (Minn. 1944).

2. "Luther W. (Wallace) Youngdahl," www.mnhs.org/people/governors/gov/gov_29.htm, accessed March 6, 2008. T. W. Budig, "Gov. Luther W. Youngdahl Crusaded against Vast, Illegal Gambling Industry in Minnesota," see www.hometownsource.com/capitol/2004/december/8gambling.html, accessed March 6, 2008. Budig, *supra* note.

3. Robert W. Esbjornson, *A Christian in Politics: Luther W. Youngdahl: A Story of a Christian's Faith at Work in a Modern World* (Minneapolis: T. S. Denison, 1955). Budig, *supra* note.

4. Albert H. Quie was governor of Minnesota from 1979 to 1983. He was elected to the Minnesota Senate in 1954, where he served until February 18, 1958, when he was elected to the U.S. Congress. There he represented Minnesota's First Congressional District until 1979.

5. Clifford E. Clark, ed., *Minnesota in a Century of Change: The State and Its People since 1900* (St. Paul: Minnesota Historical Society Press, 1989). "A History of the National Association for Retarded Children, Inc.," www.thearc.org/netcommunity/page.aspx?&pid=272&srcid=270, accessed March 6, 2008.

6. "Call Me Judge," *Time Magazine*, July 16, 1951, www.time.com/time/magazine/article/0,9171,889066,00.html, accessed March 6, 2008.

7. "Luther W. Youngdahl: Second Lieutenant, United States Army, Governor of Minnesota—Federal Judge," www.arlingtoncemetery.net/lwyoungd.htm, accessed March 6, 2008. "Luther W. Youngdahl, Former Governor, Dies," *Minneapolis Star Tribune*, June 22, 1978, www.lawlibrary.state.mn.us/judges/memorials/YoungdahlObit.pdf, accessed March 6, 2008. *U.S. v. Lattimore*, 112 F.Supp 507, 518 (D.D.C. 1953) (Youngdahl, J., dissenting), *aff'd in part, rev'd in part, U.S. v. Lattimore*, 215 F.2d 847 (D.C. Cir. 1954).

Clarence R. Magney

1883–1962
Associate Justice, 1943–1953

On May 31, 1966, at 2 P.M., the Court being assembled in the courtroom in the State Capitol, Chief Justice Oscar R. Knutson said:

The Court recognizes the president of the Minnesota State Bar Association, Mr. James E. Montague.

Mr. Montague then said:

The Minnesota State Bar Association comprising more than 4,000 members of the Bar of this State is honored to participate in this proceeding to commemorate the memories of departed justices of this court who have died since proceedings in memory of departed justices were last held in this room. Since that time five justices have gone to their ultimate reward. Three of them were chief justices of this court and two were associate justices. All left their imprint on the law, on the profession, and on the state. In order that there may be a record of their lives, their personal characteristics, and their achievements, we ask the Court at this time to recognize members of the Bar of this State who will deliver memorials to these departed justices . . . The Honorable Edwin J. Kenny of Duluth, a Judge of the District Court, will deliver the memorial honoring Associate Justice Clarence R. Magney.

Judge Kenny then presented the following memorial:

My nearly twenty years of association with Judge Magney on the Bench of the Eleventh District and my rather close personal contacts with him through the years were such a rewarding experience that I am grateful for this opportunity to present this memorial and to have entered in the records of this Court a sincere, if inadequate, portrayal of his life and career.

Clarence R. Magney, of Swedish ancestry, was born to Reverend Jonas and Hilda Magney, in the Town of Trenton, Pierce County, Wisconsin. His family lived at various places in the St. Croix River area, where his father served different pastorates. His father was the first student enrolled at Gustavus Adolphus College at St. Peter. Clarence received his early education at Bayport and later entered and pursued his academic studies at Gustavus Adolphus, where he received the degree of Bachelor of Arts. He attended the Harvard Law School and received his Bachelor of Law Degree in 1908. He thus had fine academic and legal training. He studied law under such masters as Williston, Beale, Ames, and Roscoe Pound. Combined with his natural ability, this training fitted him to become what he was—a good lawyer and a good judge.

Upon graduation from law school and after passing the state bar examination, he went to Duluth and entered the law office of Jenswold & Jenswold. He remained there until 1917. In the meantime he had taken an active interest in civic affairs, always taking an independent and courageous stand on controversial issues such as local option on the liquor traffic and municipal ownership of public utilities. He ran for and was elected to the office of mayor in 1917 at the age of 34. His term of office as mayor embraced the duration of World War I, which created some problems not ordinarily arising in peace time. One of these problems was that of controlling the liquor traffic that was affecting defense work at the steel plant and shipyards. Minnesota had set up a state commission with wide powers, which prohibited the sale of liquor within a certain distance of a defense plant, but the liquor establishments at Oliver, just across the St. Louis River but in Wisconsin, flourished in the absence of such regulation. Mayor Magney made a special trip to Washington and through his efforts a

Federal law or regulation was adopted that controlled the situation on the Wisconsin side. During his term as mayor he was especially active in developing the city's park system, assuming the duties of park commissioner himself for a time. All in all, he was one of the best mayors if not the best in the city's history.

He entered the primary election for nomination as a candidate for election in 1920 to succeed retiring Judge J. D. Ensign as Judge of the District Court of the Eleventh District. Upon his nomination, he resigned as mayor and was elected to that position, taking office in January 1921. During his tenure as such judge, he exhibited all of the qualities usually considered characteristic of a good judge, so much so that he easily ranked with earlier and contemporaneous judges of that court who gave the bench of that district the reputation of being outstanding—notably Judges Cant, Dibell, Hughes, Fesler, and Freeman. He had a good sense of humor and enjoyed a good joke even if it was on himself, and many a time the corridor in the Court House rang with his hearty laughter. The work of the District Court involves a continual parade before it of all kinds of people, a great variety of controversies, and close contact with the lawyers, and I know that Judge Magney enjoyed all that.

On July 1, 1943, Judge Magney was appointed an Associate Justice of the Supreme Court. He continued as such until his retirement at the age of 70 in 1953. Upon retirement, he was appointed a Commissioner of the Supreme Court and served actively as such a part of each year until his death on May 14, 1962. His wife, the former Lillian Lundgren of Center City, having predeceased him, he left surviving three children: Mrs. Mary Miller of San Antonio, Texas; two sons, John H. residing in Minneapolis and Charles residing at Hopkins; one sister, Edla Magney of Minneapolis; two brothers, Gottlieb, a well-known Minneapolis architect, and Dr. F. H. Magney of Duluth.

As for his work on the Supreme Court, the other members of the Court, of course, were familiar with his industry and habits of work. But for others, the opinions written by him reflect very well his characteristics. Those opinions are for the most part short, concise, clear, and directly to the point. We all know that it requires skill and laborious work to epitomize long records and briefs and to express their substance and the court's conclusions in a fairly short opinion, and Judge Magney had the ability and disposition to do that. One of his associates has told me that he was a prodigious and meticulous worker, that he wrote all his opinions in longhand in the first instance, in order as he expressed it to keep them short and to keep from saying something he did not intend to say simply because it was easier to say too much than just enough.

He had deep sympathy for the unfortunate and a kindly understanding of the failings of his fellow man, which often lies at the bottom of litigation that reaches the high court. He was a deeply religious man and had an innate and inflexible standard of what is right and what is wrong. At the same time he had a profound respect for law and the necessity of upholding it in order that there might be stability in the rules by which we live. He performed his supreme court duties with the realization that all the cases that come to that court are of importance to the people involved and consequently were entitled to the best and most conscientious consideration the members of the court can give it.

So much for Judge Magney's professional career as lawyer and judge. The proper limits to a memorial address such as this do not permit as lengthy a review of his other interests and accomplishments as one might desire. But he was a many-sided man and pursued many activities.

He was a great out-of-doors man and particularly loved the area along the north shore of Lake Superior and adjacent thereto. I think he knew it better than any other person. But he was not content to enjoy it himself but took an active interest in preserving its natural advantages and making them available to the public. He was largely responsible for bringing about the acquisition by the state of many tracts of land that have been made into public state parks. One of these is at the mouth of the Brule River, which by act of the legislature in 1963 was named after him. A director of the state historical society has said that he was one of the nation's foremost park conservationists.

He was a great lover of beauty. This observation is not prompted by a comment that I am told a newspaper made in reporting the decision of the Supreme Court in an action wherein a young woman had sought and obtained a recovery because of the alleged loss of her good looks due to the use of a deleterious cosmetic preparation by a beautician. Judge Magney wrote the opinion sustaining the award, and the newspaper headline, I am told, read: "Judge Magney votes for beauty." But he did have an unusual aesthetic sense—an appreciation of beauty in nature and in art. Upon the walls of his chambers here there were hung many beautiful colored pictures of places in the north country. His beautiful home at the mouth of the Caribou River contained many fine art objects, including numerous native African wood carvings.

He was a world traveler. He shunned the beaten paths of tourists and took unusual trips. A visit to a brother, a missionary in Tanganyika in East Africa, stimulated his interest in Africa, and he made six subsequent trips there. On one occasion he took a trip 1,500 miles up the Congo on a freight boat. He evidently sensed the change that is now focusing attention on the emerging nations of that continent. He was in Capetown when he was stricken with the disease that caused his death shortly thereafter.

Having in mind this record of his life it is small wonder that in a popular poll conducted by the Minnesota Junior Chamber of Commerce in connection with the Centennial Celebration of the organization of the territorial government of the state, Judge Magney was named as one of the greatest living Minnesotans.

In conclusion let me say that Judge Magney was a fine character, an inspiration and example to bench and bar, and a splendid public servant, to whom the people of the state are indebted for his contribution to their welfare.

Chief Justice Knutson then said:

It is proper that we hold these memorial services for those who have served on this Court. Some of us have had the privilege of serving with most of those whom we honor today. All of them have served with distinction and have added much to the jurisprudence of this state and this nation. While the opinions they have written, which are to be found in our Minnesota Reports, are the best testimonial to their ability, their intellectual integrity, and their devotion to their work, it is fitting that we who survive them express our appreciation for what they have done. These memorials written by men who have been closely associated with our departed brethren on the bench will be spread on the Minutes of the Court and will be contained in an early copy of the Minnesota Reports—there to remain as a permanent testimonial to the high regard we have for all of them. [273 Minn. xxi]

Thomas F. Gallagher

1897–1985
Associate Justice, 1943–1967

Justice Thomas F. Gallagher had a long and distinguished career as a lawyer, politician, and jurist. During his rich and productive life, he gained the respect of the trial bar, was a founder of the modern two-party system in Minnesota, and served as a distinguished member of the Minnesota Supreme Court for nearly a quarter of a century.

A native Minnesotan, Thomas Gallagher was born in Faribault on November 24, 1897, the son of Patrick James and Helena McCall Gallagher. His maternal grandparents, John and Catherine McCall, had settled in Faribault in the early 1850s. His father, Patrick Gallagher, operated a successful contracting business in Faribault that engaged in public and private construction projects throughout the north central states and that continued to thrive under the ownership of Tom Gallagher's brothers, Luke and Robert.

Thomas Gallagher received his preliminary education in Faribault and, subsequently, at St. Thomas Academy in St. Paul. He continued his studies as an undergraduate at the University of Minnesota, where he received his bachelor of arts degree in 1919. His studies were interrupted for a time, however, when in 1918 he entered the armed forces to serve in World War I as a commissioned officer in the U.S. Field Artillery. Following the war, he earned a bachelor of laws degree from the University of Minnesota in June 1921. He was a member of the Alpha Sigma Phi, Phi Delta Phi, and Scabbard and Blade fraternities.

From 1921 until 1942, Thomas Gallagher was engaged in the private practice of law in Minneapolis. Initially associated with John E. Tappan, founder of the Investors Syndicate (later known as Investors Diversified Services, Inc.), in 1929, Gallagher opened his own law offices in Minneapolis. Gallagher had a general practice with emphasis on trial work as well as corporate, real estate, trust, and contract law.

On August 19, 1931, Thomas Gallagher married Elizabeth Jane Gillum of Minneapolis. They had four children surviving this union: sons Thomas Patrick, Michael John, and Robert Brian, and daughter, Sharon Elizabeth. The Gallaghers were married nearly 45 years, until Elizabeth's death in June 1976.

In addition to practicing law, Gallagher was active politically. In 1936, he campaigned throughout Minnesota in support of the reelection of President Franklin D. Roosevelt and Vice President John Nance "Cactus Jack" Garner. He made speeches from a sound trailer on the streets of more than 400 Minnesota cities and towns.

He was nominated as the Democratic candidate for governor in the 1938 primary election. Minnesota then operated under a three-party system: Democrats, Farmer-Laborites, and Republicans. Gallagher was defeated in the general election when the young Harold E. Stassen swept into office, the youngest governor in the history of Minnesota in the first of three successive terms.

In 1939 and 1940 Gallagher led an extensive drive that ultimately resulted in the merger of the Democrats and Farm-Laborites, which became the present-day Democratic Farm-Labor Party. In 1939, he served as vice chairman of the Democratic State Central Committee. He also served as a delegate-at-large from Minnesota at the 1940 Democratic National Convention in Chicago, which nominated Franklin D. Roosevelt for a historic third term as president. From 1939 to 1942, Gallagher's recommendations governed appointments to numerous federal positions in Minnesota. He was a close friend and confidant of the late Hubert H. Humphrey, as well as of J. Howard McGrath, James A. Farley, Edward P. Flynn, Robert E. Hannegan, and

Maurice Tobin, all of who served as cabinet members under Presidents Roosevelt or Truman.

Thomas Gallagher was elected to the Minnesota Supreme Court in 1942; he was the first Minnesotan elected to that office without previously having received a gubernatorial appointment to a judicial office. He was subsequently reelected in 1948 and 1954 as well as in 1960, when with more than 1.1 million votes he established a record for the largest number of votes cast for that office. He served on the court until his retirement in 1966.

During his service on the court, Justice Gallagher participated in approximately 5,000 decisions and wrote well over 600 opinions on behalf of the court. Practicing attorneys generally credited his opinions for their clarity and brevity. At the time of his retirement, the American Trial Lawyers Association presented Justice Gallagher with its national award for outstanding service in the judiciary at its national convention.

Justice Gallagher authored opinions on a wide array of subjects, some of which received particular recognition and acclaim. The distinguished Prof. Brainerd Currie of the University of Chicago ranked him among "the modern American judges whose work has contributed to the enlightenment and to the cause of justice and reason in the conflict of laws"— a group that included U.S. Supreme Court Justices Harlan F. Stone and Robert H. Jackson, as well as the legendary Roger J. Traynor of the California Supreme Court. Gallagher also authored noteworthy opinions on product liability, taxation, mineral rights, juvenile court proceedings, access to freeways, dram shop laws, and limitations on municipal zoning authority.

Justice Gallagher served as an arbitrator during the court's summer recesses. He acted as a referee at more than 130 railway arbitrations conducted under the jurisdiction of the National Mediation Board. In 1945, he served as chairman of the Board of Arbitration in the dispute between Twin City Rapid Transit Company and Amalgamated Association of Street, Electric Railway and Motor Coach Employees of America.

In 1946, Justice Gallagher declined a presidential appointment as U.S. member of the International Court for the trial of Japanese war criminals in Tokyo and to the war-crimes trials in Nuremberg, Germany.

Between 1948 and 1950, President Harry S. Truman appointed Justice Gallagher to serve successively on three presidential emergency boards created to avert railway strikes that threatened the national economy. These disputes involved the Grand Trunk Western Railroad at Detroit in 1948, the Texas and Pacific Railroad at Dallas in 1950, and the Atlantic and East Carolina and other railroads at Washington, D.C., in 1950. In 1948, Gallagher served as a neutral arbitrator in the dispute between National Airlines and the Airlines Pilots Association in Miami, Florida.

For seven years during the 1960s, Gallagher served as president of the Minnesota Safety Council. In that capacity, he conducted panels of judges, prosecutors, and law enforcement officials in each of Minnesota's judicial districts in work aimed at developing uniform judicial procedures and equitable penalties in traffic offenses. The American Automobile Association, the National Safety Council, and the Minnesota Trial Lawyers Association presented awards recognizing his work in the field of traffic and industrial safety.

Gallagher's law clerks during the time he was on the state supreme court included Walter F. Mondale—future Minnesota attorney general, U.S. senator, vice president, and ambassador to Japan—who recalled his clerking experience with great fondness. Vice President Mondale remembers being assigned a big case his first day on the job, whereupon he asked Justice Gallagher what he should do. Gallagher asked what kind of case it was and, when told that it was an insurance case, advised the young law clerk to "Look under 'I.'"

Justice Gallagher served as chairman of the Minnesota branch of the National Conference of Christians and Jews. He also served as judge advocate of the Fifth District American Legion and commander of Downtown Post No. 335. His work in the American Legion included conducting panels each year for the Boys' State program sponsored by the American Legion, in which he outlined the structure, conduct, and jurisdiction of the state and federal court systems. He also chaired the fund drive to construct a new boys' gymnasium for a Catholic orphanage in Minneapolis.

Justice Gallagher was a member of the American, Minnesota, and Hennepin County Bar Associations, the American Judicature Society, and the Minnesota Trial Lawyers Association. He was a member of the Minneapolis Athletic Club, the University of Minnesota Alumni Club, and the Minneapolis Amateur Chefs, as well as an honorary member of both the Minnesota Club and the University Club of St. Paul. In 1962, he was president and director of the University of Minnesota Law School Alumni Association.

Justice Gallagher died on March 3, 1985, in Minneapolis, at the age of 87. He was survived by his daughter, Sharon Walsh, who had married Col. Richard A. Walsh of the U.S. Air Force. Tragically, Colonel Walsh was listed as missing in action over Laos in 1969. Justice Gallagher was also survived by three sons: Thomas P. Gallagher, who served as a law clerk for his father, practices law in Minneapolis, and has been a labor arbitrator for 30 years; Michael J. Gallagher, who has since died, practiced law in Minneapolis and was an attorney with the Hennepin County Juvenile Division for many years; and Robert B. Gallagher, a specialist in herbal remedies who operates Present Moment Herbs and Books in south Minneapolis. Twelve grandchildren, including the third Thomas [C.] Gallagher to graduate from the University of Minnesota Law School, survive him, as well his sister, Helen Traughber, and his brother, Robert.

—Thomas H. Boyd

Leroy E. Matson

1896–1960
Associate Justice, 1945–1960

On May 31, 1966, at 2 P.M., the Court being assembled in the courtroom in the State Capitol, Chief Justice Oscar R. Knutson said:

The Court recognizes the president of the Minnesota State Bar Association, Mr. James E. Montague.

Mr. Montague then said:

The Minnesota State Bar Association comprising more than 4,000 members of the Bar of this State is honored to participate in this proceeding to commemorate the memories of departed justices of this court who have died since proceedings in memory of departed justices were last held in this room. Since that time five justices have gone to their ultimate reward. Three of them were chief justices of this court and two were associate justices. All left their imprint on the law, on the profession, and on the state. In order that there may be a record of their lives, their personal characteristics, and their achievements, we ask the Court at this time to recognize members of the Bar of this State who will deliver memorials to these departed justices . . . Mr. Arthur Sund Nelson of Minneapolis will deliver the memorial honoring Associate Justice Leroy E. Matson . . .

Mr. Nelson then presented the following memorial:

Every man's actions affect the lives of other people to some degree. Those men whose talents and opportunities lead them in the direction of the Bench have a great responsibility because their actions affect, directly or indirectly, the lives of everyone in the community. Leroy E. Matson, whose memorial I am honored to present at this service, was uniquely fitted to discharge this responsibility as Justice of the Minnesota Supreme Court because of his amazing self-discipline and his determination to give his profession the best in himself. This facet of his character burned so brightly one could not help but notice his dedication to excellence whether the task before him was cutting down a tree, outfitting a hunting trip, building a fish-cleaning house, playing a little joke on a close friend, serving a civic organization, or writing a Supreme Court opinion—in all things the execution was thorough.

A son of the North Country, he was born in Crookston on February 11, 1896, and raised on a farm at Saum in Beltrami County. He loved the wilderness, and his blue eyes twinkled at a chance to get out into the woods. In memories of my boyhood hunting days, I smile as I recall my Dad and Mat, a couple of 250-pounders, strong as horses, setting a pace no one else could match. They could eat as if food were going out of style, and many were the astounded waitresses in small northern towns who served them the largest steak dinner on the menu only to be called back again 15 minutes later and told to fix up two more just like the first!

Justice Matson graduated from Bemidji High School in 1916 and served 23 months with the United States First Infantry Division, spending much of that time overseas, during which he was injured in a gas attack. Attendance at the A.E.F. University of Beaune, France, was followed by the earning of Bachelor of Arts and Bachelor of Law degrees at the University of Minnesota in 1926. From that time until his election as Associate Justice of the Minnesota Supreme Court in 1944, he practiced law in Minneapolis with my father, Arthur T. Nelson, and others. His service on this court continued from 1944 until his death on February 28, 1960. During his many years of active practice and service on the Bench, Justice Matson contributed his time to many civic organizations. He served for many years as an advisory board member of the Minneapolis YMCA. For a while he engaged in teaching at the YMCA. He was chairman of the Judicial Council, a member of the Minnesota Constitutional Revision Commission, a board member of the American Swedish Institute, an honorary member of the Interracial Service Council, Past President of the Six O'clock Club of Minneapolis, member of the American Legion, and a member of the Gamma Eta Gamma and Delta Sigma Rho fraternities. He was also a member of the American and Minnesota Bar Associations and the American Judicature Society. As a Mason, Justice Matson was a former Grand Master of the Grand Lodge of Minnesota and during his tenure acted as co-chairman of the fund drive for the building of the Masonic Memorial Cancer Hospital at the University of Minnesota. He was a member of the Board of Directors of the Natural History Society of Minnesota and State President of the Izaak Walton League, reflecting his great interest in conservation.

The members of this court who were privileged to serve with Leroy have, I'm sure, been enriched by their association with him. Those who knew him well will recall the extraordinary sense of humor and the kindness that lay behind the serious surface of his face, as well as the smile that played at the corners of his mouth betraying the humor about to reveal itself.

I count the year served as his law clerk as one of the most demanding and instructive of my career. He expected much of me but much more of himself. He wrote his opinions, rewrote them—and rewrote them again in his constant search for excellence. More than once after getting home from the court after 7 P.M. and feeling somewhat abused, I would get a phone call about 9 P.M. from the Judge, who would ask me whether I had read a certain case that dealt with the issue we were researching. When I hadn't read it, he would suggest that perhaps I should—I did—bright and early the next morning!

His dedication to a job well done and his lack of tolerance for carelessness comes through clearly in parts of the memo he himself presented to me when I began service as his law clerk. This two-page document contained, among other directions, the following statements:

- When a case is before us, we work on it, regardless of hours, until it is finished. By following this procedure, we dispose of our work promptly. Please bear in mind that legal research is not done on a civil service basis; it is necessary to complete the work regardless of hours.

- We work Saturdays.

- If you are allergic to the regular devout and unfailing use of Shepards Citator, do not ask for the job. There is absolutely no excuse for citing or quoting any case which has not been carefully Shepardized. In quoting a statute or a decision, you are expected to be absolutely accurate. The court doesn't need help in being sloppy.

- All statements of the law must be made with definitiveness, clarity, and brevity. I am not interested in acquiring the help of a law clerk who has developed a capacity for sliding around the point. Each legal issue must be dealt with in a straightforward manner. It is necessary to keep in mind that the only excuse for writing a legal opinion is to provide practicing lawyers and trial judges with working tools. An opinion that is not clear and definite is of little use to the profession.

Those who are familiar with his work in this Court will recognize that he followed these standards and practiced what he preached.

Justice Matson is survived by his wife, Elsie H. Matson, his sister, Lillian Matson Rust, by former clients who benefit from the help he gave them as a practicing attorney, by his colleagues of the Bench and the Bar who admire his integrity and his determination to do his best, and by his many friends to whom a man of such strength and kindness is a source of faith in humanity.

Chief Justice Knutson then said:

It is proper that we hold these memorial services for those who have served on this Court. Some of us have had the privilege of serving with most of those whom we honor today. All of them have served with distinction and have added much to the jurisprudence of this state and this nation. While the opinions they have written, which are to be found in our Minnesota

Reports, are the best testimonial to their ability, their intellectual integrity, and their devotion to their work, it is fitting that we who survive them express our appreciation for what they have done. These memorials written by men who have been closely associated with our departed brethren on the bench will be spread on the Minutes of the Court and will be contained in an early copy of the Minnesota Reports—there to remain as a permanent testimonial to the high regard we have for all of them. [273 Minn. xxi]

William C. Christianson

1892–1985
Associate Justice, 1946

William C. Christianson's judicial career was marked most prominently not by his service on the Minnesota Supreme Court but by his work as a judge at the Nuremberg war crimes tribunal, presiding over the trials of Nazi war criminals following World War II, and by his long career as a Minnesota district court judge.

Christianson's career as a supreme court justice was brief, beginning in March 1946, when he was appointed by Gov. Edward Thye to replace then Associate Justice Luther Youngdahl, who resigned to run for governor. The electorate had little time to familiarize itself with Christianson before he had to stand for election. Frank T. Gallagher, the brother of the popular former Chief Justice Henry M. Gallagher, had a more familiar surname on the ballot. Frank T. Gallagher successfully eliminated Justice Christianson in a four-man field race, disqualifying Christianson from seeking the full six-year term for Associate Justice. His term on the Minnesota Supreme Court ended ten months later, in January 1947.

Born in Moody County, South Dakota, on a farm near the Minnesota-South Dakota line, Christianson attended high school at the Austin Academy, where he met his friend and future law partner C. H. Bentley. After college in Iowa, Christianson attended the University of Chicago Law School, from which he graduated in 1920. He then came to the Twin Cities, where he entered private practice. In 1923 Christianson and his friend Bentley opened a law practice in Red Wing in which Judge Christianson practiced until 1946, when he was appointed to the Minnesota Supreme Court.

While a practicing attorney in Red Wing, he held the offices of Red Wing city attorney and assistant Goodhue County attorney at the same time he con-

ducted a successful and prominent private practice.

In 1927, he married Myrtle LaVerna Lorentz, and they had one son, William L. Christianson, who is a lawyer currently practicing in Red Wing.

Judge Christianson was scholarly and hard working. In the short time he sat as a justice on the state supreme court, he was the author of 15 opinions. He enjoyed doing his own legal research and legal writing and was highly admired by his brethren on the court.

In 1947, Chief Justice Charles Loring recommended that Judge Christianson be considered for appointment as a judge on the Nuremberg Military Tribunal (NMT), formed to try Nazi war criminals. President Harry Truman appointed him to serve on that tribunal, and Judge Christianson considered that service the high point of his legal and judicial career. That year he was named as one of three judges to serve on the NMT panel trying a German industrialist, Friedrich Flick, who controlled the largest private steel-manufacturing business in Germany during World War II. Flick and two of his associates were found guilty of war crimes.

In a 1964 interview, Christianson described the legal basis for the trials as the violation of international law, which in several areas specifically outlawed aggressive war practices. These were the charges brought against the defendants at Nuremberg. He described the war crimes tribunal as a "landmark in jurisprudence." Christianson was also the presiding judge at the trial of Hitler's cabinet ministers, which lasted until the spring of 1949. Most of the 21 defendants, which included SS (Schutzstaffel or in English, "protect squadron") generals and directors of Nazi espionage programs, were convicted of planning aggressive war and other crimes. Judge Christianson characterized the import of the Nuremberg trials: "The trials are a step in the right direction in that they put an end to war as a sport of kings and make individuals responsible for their actions. The trials added to international law more than any other event in our time and strengthened the bulwarks of peace as the first postmortem to expose the rise to dictatorship and to show how a minority rises to power through terrorism and by attacking individual freedoms."

Christianson said that the Nuremberg trials helped establish in international law the principle that obeying the orders of military superiors was not an excuse for committing war crimes.

Upon his return to Minnesota in 1949, Christianson was appointed district court judge in the First Judicial District by Gov. Luther Youngdahl. Christianson described his cases and calendar there as "routine."

Perhaps his most noteworthy decision was his ruling against what was then the City of Bloomington when it attempted to annex Northern States Power Company-Black Dog, in what was then Burnsville township. The case went to the Supreme Court on appeal, and Judge Christianson's decision was affirmed. *Town Of Burnsville v. City Of Bloomington,* 268 Minn. 84, 128 N.W.2d 97 (1964).

Christianson retired in 1963 and was appointed by the state supreme court as a part-time judge to help out in the Hennepin County District Court. In his free time he spent time with and assisted the lawyers with legal research in his old law firm, Bentley and Christianson, where his son, William, was a partner.

Judge Christianson died in May 1985, at the age of 92.

—George L. May

Frank T. Gallagher

1887–1977

Associate Justice, 1947–1963

"A man is known by the company he keeps." That phrase, inserted into one of his most famous decisions,[1] aptly describes the man who sat for nearly 20 years as an associate justice and seven more years as a retired jurist with a well-regarded and active Minnesota Supreme Court. Justice Frank T. Gallagher enjoyed a distinguished career on the court; his prolific judicial legacy created precedents of enduring importance.

Francis ("Frank") Thomas Gallagher was born in Wilton Township in Waseca County, Minnesota on July 13, 1887. His parents were Bernard M. Gallagher and Catherine J. Barden. He grew up in a large family with surviving siblings Rose Ellen, Henry (who became chief justice of the Minnesota Supreme Court),[2] Bernard ("Ben," who became a physician), Robert (who became a dentist), and Joseph. The Gallagher boys were active in sports and played on the Waseca baseball team for many years. Baseball—along with a healthy appreciation for the Minnesota Gophers football team—remained an interest of Frank Gallagher throughout his life.

Gallagher graduated from Waseca High School in 1907. He entered the University of Minnesota in 1909 and graduated from its law school on June 12, 1913.

After completing his studies, Gallagher embarked on a career in sales. He worked for the Black Swan Company in Waseca, selling electric generators for farms until the early 1920s. Then he began selling insurance for the Equitable Life Assurance Society of the United States.

In 1929, Gallagher switched his career path and opened a law practice in Albert Lea, Minnesota. Shortly thereafter he joined his brother's law firm: Gallagher, Madden & Gallagher in Waseca. He remained in general practice at this firm for the next 25 years.

Frank Gallagher married Belle Clara Sparks and they had five children: Kathleen, Patricia, Thomas, Daniel, and Michael. Daniel and Michael both followed in their father's path. Daniel served as a Minnesota workers' compensation judge, and Michael was an attorney for the Office of the Minnesota Attorney General.

While practicing law and raising his family, Frank Gallagher served on the Waseca School Board for 13 years—both as a member and as its president. He did so even though his own children attended Sacred Heart parochial school because he believed in the importance of public schools for everyone. Gallagher was also a member of the Knights of Columbus Lodge, the Waseca Lions Club, and the Waseca Chamber of Commerce.

In 1946, Associate Justice Luther Youngdahl retired from the state supreme court to run for governor. Then Gov. Edward Thye appointed William C. Christianson to fill the unexpired portion of Justice Youngdahl's term on the court. This placed the seat in a contested election in the fall of 1946. Gallagher saw it as his opportunity to serve the state as a jurist and announced his plans to run for the position.

The Minnesota State Bar Association conducted a judicial plebiscite of its members to rank the contestants for the court. The results published in September of 1946 gave Frank almost a 100-point lead over the incumbent Justice Christianson. Frank went on to win the election.

During his tenures as an associate justice and a retired jurist, Gallagher authored nearly 600 opinions. His sons commented that he had limited outside interests because "his job was his hobby." Justice Gallagher thrived on the challenges presented by cases before the court. He gave considerable thought and energy to those cases—often discussing the issues with his sons. He lived and worked in the Twin Cities, returning on weekends and free times to home and family in Waseca, so that he could devote himself to the work of the court.

Gallagher's judicial efforts spanned all areas of the law. A review of his judicial opus shows he took great care to research the law thoroughly and craft opinions adapting a particular set of facts to the legal landscape as it developed—and sometimes pushing the landscape in a new direction.

Two of his most innovative decisions were in criminal cases. In *State v. Fearon,* 283 Minn. 90, 166 N.W.2d 720, 40 A.L.R.3d 312 (1969), Justice Gallagher considered whether a chronic alcoholic could be guilty of the crime of "voluntary drunkenness." Noting the developing medical and psychological literature that recharacterized alcoholism as a disease rather than as an act of moral turpitude, Justice Gallagher asked: "Can a person who is classed as a chronic alcoholic be said to drink by choice?" *Id.* at 95, 166 N.W.2d at 723. He answered that question in the negative, concluding that the overwhelming social, medical, and legislative evidence prompting a view that criminalizing alcoholism was bad policy, inconsistent with the language of Minnesota's criminal drunkenness statute, *Id.* at 97, 166 N.W.2d at 724.

Justice Gallagher's opinion for the court in *State v. Coursolle,* 255 Minn. 384, 97 N.W.2d 472, 75 A.L.R.2d 755 (1959), shows his willingness to move the criminal justice system in a new direction. The question presented was whether a rape conviction could stand given that the defendant's witnesses had attended the trial in manacles. (The witnesses had previously been convicted of the same rape for which the defendant was being tried). Gallagher's opinion recognized that the common law had long permitted a defendant, in the absence of a threat of violence or flight, to attend his trial free from shackles. The issue in the *Coursolle* case, however, was whether that common-law right extended to a defendant's witnesses. Justice Gallagher put it simply, "The old adage that 'a man is known by the company he keeps' could easily produce an inflammatory situ-

ation so far as the jury was concerned as a result of the accused's principal witnesses being handcuffed each day during the trial," *Id.* at 389, 97 N.W.2d at 476. The conviction was reversed.

Although he was willing to move the law within the boundaries of common-law development, Justice Gallagher was not willing to disregard statutory language—even when the facts were compelling. In *Witthun v. Durbahn,* 279 Minn. 437, 157 N.W.2d 360 (1968), he held to the language of the survival statute, noting its harsh consequences for the widowed plaintiff. The court was asked to overrule an earlier decision and "interpret" Minnesota's survival statute so that a widow could pursue a negligence action started by her husband before his death, from causes unrelated to the original tort. Justice Gallagher's opinion showed his sympathy for the plaintiff but declined to ignore the court's precedent or the plain language of the survival statute: "Regardless of the personal predilections of the court, it does 'not have the right to grant judgment in defiance of the statute,'" *Id.* at 440, 157 N.W.2d at 362. Gallagher's strong sentiments, however, plainly had some impact, as the legislature later amended the survival statute to permit a personal representative to continue a negligence action begun by the decedent before his death.

Gallagher's decisions were firmly grounded in his southern Minnesota roots. For example when the Mayo Clinic of Rochester sued a pharmacy for trademark infringement, his opinion recognized the importance of the clinic to the state.[3] The Mayo Clinic sought a permanent injunction against a Rochester pharmacy using the name Mayo or Mayo's in selling cosmetic and pharmaceutical products. The defendant had been incorporated by three persons, one by the name of Mayo L. Priebe Sr. The Mayo Clinic claimed that the pharmacy's use of the name Mayo or Mayo's was infringing and confusing. The court had to decide whether the defendant pharmacy could infringe when it used its incorporator's own name, which just happened to be identical to that of the clinic. Justice Gallagher wrote: "It would indeed seem naive for us to say . . . that anyone purchasing . . . a small container or bottle marked Mayo-Cin, Mayo's A-Wake Tablets, or Mayo's Lotion, Rochester, Minnesota, might not be deceived into believing that it was a product originating from the well-known Mayo Clinic of Rochester, Minnesota." The permanent injunction was affirmed.

Justice Gallagher is perhaps best known for a decision written early in his career on the court. In *Dart v. Pure Oil Co.,* 223 Minn. 526, 27 N.W.2d 555, 171 A.L.R. 885 (1947), he wrote the court's opinion in a negligence case in which none other than William L. Prosser provided a brief on behalf of one of the *amici curiae.* The court considered whether the statute governing the sale and delivery of volatile oils was designed to protect the general public or to protect a special class of persons unable to protect themselves. In the latter case, strict liability applies and contributory negligence by the injured party would not be available as a defense. In concluding that the statute was not special protective legislation, Justice Gallagher observed: "[T]he handling and use of volatile oils is of such an important and widespread nature and the potential dangers to the public at large resulting from its negligent handling is so general that we believe the statute was enacted for the general public, as well as for the users of such products," *Id.* at 540, 27 N.W.2d 562. *Dart* became the leading case for determining whether a statute was an "exceptional statute" which, when violated, would apply the concepts of negligence *per se.*

As the foregoing sample of his opinions shows, Justice Gallagher greatly contributed to Minnesota's tradition of a thoughtful judiciary.

—Katherine L. MacKinnon

References

1. *State v. Coursolle,* 225 Minn. 384, 389, 97 N.W.2d 472, 477 (1959).

2. Frank Gallagher's older brother, Henry M. Gallagher, was chief justice of the Minnesota Supreme Court from 1937 to 1944. Henry retired from the court before Frank's election to the court in 1946. They were the only brothers ever to serve on the court (albeit at different times). During Frank's tenure, an unrelated Gallagher, Thomas F., also served as an associate justice (1943–1967).

3. *Mayo Clinic v. Mayo's Drug and Cosmetic, Inc.,* 262 Minn. 101, 113 N.W.2d 852, 132 U.S.P.Q. (BNA) 691 (1962).

Oscar R. Knutson

1899–1981

Associate Justice, 1948–1962; Chief Justice, 1962–1973

The State of Minnesota owes a debt of gratitude to Chief Justice Oscar R. Knutson. Many of the reforms that took place in the state's legal system during the 25 years he served on the state supreme court can be attributed at least indirectly to him. The longtime jurist has often been called the father of the public defense system in Minnesota, and he was instrumental in the development of the court administrator's office and the mechanisms used to assure the accountability of judges in Minnesota.

Knutson overcame humble beginnings to realize those successes. He was born on October 9, 1899, in Superior, Wisconsin, and spent much of his childhood milking cows on his family's dairy farm. His parents had moved to the United States from Norway when they were just 20 years old. Knutson grew up speaking Norwegian, not learning English until he began grade school.

In 1916, Knutson moved with his parents and siblings to Warren, Minnesota, where they had purchased a grain farm. Rather than immediately returning to high school, he attended the Northwest School of Agriculture in Crookston, where students went to school six months of the year and worked on their family farms the remainder of the year.

Money was tight. Despite farming 200 acres of land, the family sold only $28 of grain the first year. Eventually, Knutson's parents went broke with the grain farm and moved back to Superior to try their hand at dairying again.

In the meantime, Knutson went back to high school, earning his diploma in 1920 and then enrolling in St. Olaf College in Northfield, Minnesota. At the time, Knutson had $50 in his pocket and no idea what he wanted to do with his life. He attended St. Olaf for a year, but his dishwashing job at the school wasn't enough to pay the bills, and he was forced to take some time off. Eventually, Knutson was able to go back to college; he attended the University of Minnesota for a year before obtaining an LL.B. from the university's law school in 1927.

Not knowing anything about law, Knutson made the decision to study it primarily because he had done some debate work and thought he was pretty good at it. He paid his expenses during law school by working as a chauffeur for a real estate salesman, earning $3.50 a week and—because his employer also owned a restaurant—one meal a day.

Knutson never let his money problems get him down; instead, his economic situation gave him empathy for others, especially those who were less fortunate—something that served him well as a lawyer and as a judge.

Following his graduation from law school, Knutson returned to Warren—where there were only seven lawyers—to practice law with Julius J. Olson, who was later appointed to the Minnesota Supreme Court. For the next 14 years, Knutson plied his trade in the small town, also becoming a member of the Minnesota and American Bar Associations and joining the American Judicature Society.

Times were still tough in Warren, and Knutson once probated an estate for a woman who paid him in eggs. He ate a lot of eggs that summer, eventually becoming so sick of them that he told his secretary that if any more eggs arrived she should send the woman her bill, marked "paid."

Knutson married Louise M. Halvorson on June 20, 1934, and had three children—twins Richard Henry and Robert Owen and a daughter, Anne Joyce. He saw little of his family, however, working from 7 A.M. until 10 P.M. most days, including weekends. Unable to afford a law clerk, he even did his own research and writing.

In addition to being active in the legal community, Knutson had a strong sense of civic duty. He served three terms as mayor of Warren, for $20 a year. As a mayor with a law degree, he ended up serving as the city's attorney too, doing all of its legal work for free. His other civic duties included serving as secretary, treasurer, and manager of the Warren Telephone Company and as chairman of the county chapter of the American Red Cross. He was also director of the Marshall County Agricultural Association, a member of the governing board of the Council of State Governments, and a director of both the University of Minnesota Alumni Association and the University of Minnesota Law Alumni Association.

In January 1941, Gov. Harold Stassen appointed Knutson to the district court bench, and Knutson was elected to the position the following year. Becoming a judge forced Knutson to give up many of his civic activities, including his job as mayor. But the civic-minded jurist wasn't content with merely doling out justice from the bench, and he eventually served as president of the Minnesota District Judges Association as well as of the national Conference of Chief Justices.

As one of just two trial judges in the 200-mile-wide district, Knutson handled work in 14 counties. That meant a lot of travel, which in Minnesota sometimes meant being in treacherous winter snowstorms.

Knutson served on the district court for seven years before being appointed to the state supreme court in 1948. Happy with his trial judge position, he didn't really want the appellate job, but Gov. Luther Youngdahl asked him to take it, so he agreed. While Knutson may not have wanted the position initially, once he committed to it, he gave it his best.

The appellate workload was heavy, and the staff was limited. When Knutson first joined the high court, he shared a secretary with another justice. Because his own time was limited, Knutson requested brevity—in briefing and in oral argument—from the lawyers who appeared before him. He wasn't afraid to ask questions when something wasn't covered in a brief or when an attorney overlooked an issue. And because he read every brief before hearing oral argument, he was always

prepared. Eventually, Knutson got his own secretary and even a law clerk to do much of the preliminary research necessary to decide a case.

In 1962, Gov. Elmer L. Andersen elevated Knutson to the court's top spot as chief justice, where he served for 10 years, 10 months, and 22 days. The high court justices differed on many opinions over the years Knutson served as chief, but they always got along well with each other.

Knutson believed that to be a good judge one must have patience and an understanding of people. His own door was always open to the public because he enjoyed talking to people and believed it was important to keep in close contact with those he served.

Knutson lost his wife Louise on January 28, 1955. He married again, however, on July 9, 1968, to Katherine (Kay) Anderson. He continued to serve as the state's top jurist until his retirement in 1973. But he wasn't really ready to leave, and he worked as a retired judge for yet another half-decade.

Knutson was a well-respected attorney, judge, and civic leader, and he made some impressive connections during his legal career. He became good friends with U.S. Supreme Court Chief Justice Warren Burger before Burger's appointment to the nation's highest court, and he was well acquainted with U.S. Supreme Court Associate Justice Harry Blackmun while Blackmun worked as an attorney for the Mayo Clinic.

One of Knutson's greatest accomplishments—and one for which he is often praised—was his role in the initiation of the public defender system in Minnesota. After the U.S. Supreme Court determined that every defendant had a right to a lawyer, Knutson went straight to the local bar association and said the ruling would bankrupt the state if the association didn't address the issue. He suggested setting up a formal system covering public defenders, and from there the idea blossomed. In 1965, the Minnesota Legislature created the Office of the State Public Defender and authorized the establishment of defender systems in the 10 judicial districts comprising the state judicial system.

Late in his life, Knutson suffered a stroke and lost his eyesight, thereafter causing him to rely heavily on his wife, Kay, to get around. He died on June 15, 1981, leaving a legacy that will endure for years to come.

—Michelle M. Lore

Theodore Christianson

1913–1955
Associate Justice, 1950–1955

On May 15, 1956, at 1:30 P.M., the Court being assembled in the courtroom in the State Capitol, Chief Justice Roger L. Dell said:

The Court recognizes the president of the Minnesota State Bar Association, Mr. John M. Palmer.

Mr. Palmer then said:

This time has been graciously and appropriately set apart for proceedings to commemorate the lives, the characters, and the public service of four members of this Court who have passed away, namely: Chief Justice Samuel B. Wilson, Associate Justice Clifford L. Hilton, Associate Justice Julius J. Olson, and Associate Justice Theodore Christianson.

The Court has called upon the Minnesota State Bar Association as the representative of the Bar of this state to arrange for the presentation of memorials to perpetuate the memory of those distinguished members of the profession who served for many years on this Court. The Association is honored to respond to the call. It has designated . . . The Honorable Warren E. Burger, Judge of the United States Court of Appeals for the District of Columbia . . . to deliver the memorial in honor of Associate Justice Theodore Christianson.

The Honorable Warren E. Burger then presented the following memorial:

The occasion for this sitting of the Court is to record permanently in its records what we designate as a memorial to one of the men who was a member of this Bar and a member of this Court, the Honorable Theodore Christianson.

Memorials are in a sense eulogies that recite the tributes of colleagues and friends, but our objective should be to give an appraisal, an evaluation, of the man—especially in relation to his work as a Justice of this great Court. And, since the whole man makes the judge, it is valuable to look back to see of what components the whole man was made.

In a country like ours, the people have many opportunities to see and evaluate the leaders of the Executive Branch and of the Legislative Branch. Most of the problems of the Executive Branch and of the law makers are close to our daily lives. But by tradition and by the very nature of the work of a court of last resort, its judges must work with tools and subjects not readily understood by the public generally and not such as to arouse public interest. So it is that as members of the Judiciary pass from the scene it is important that we take note in a special way of the lives and the character of the men entrusted with what Mr. Justice Frankfurter calls "the awful business of judging."

Seldom has this Court, or any court, numbered among its members a lawyer whose combination of talents fitted him so well for a life on the Bench as did the qualities of Justice Theodore Christianson. These qualities have been carefully discussed in other memorials of the Bar that have adequately covered his outstanding scholastic record, his activities as a student leader and later in public affairs, and his service as a Navy Officer in World War II. Rather than repeat what has been accurately and eloquently said by others, I would prefer on this occasion to look to some aspects of his life, his personality, his character and temperament, that in a special way explain him in the role he occupied as an Associate Justice of the Supreme Court of Minnesota—the youngest, I believe, ever to occupy that high place.

This man was reared in a tradition and an atmosphere of service to his fellow men. As a boy he went often with his father to hear him speak either as Governor of the state, or as one of its representatives in Congress, or in political campaigns. The excitement and the drama of hard-fought political debate was to him what the baseball field and fishing were to his contemporaries. That is not to suggest he was devoid of a love of sports and the outdoors but rather that, to the normal activities of boyhood that he enjoyed to the fullest, he added another experience. Early in life he learned that the glamour of public life and high political office has other aspects—of hard blows, of criticism and attack, and, for many, hard defeat. There could have been no better conditioner for a man who was first to test himself in the difficult school of trial advocacy and later in the exacting duties of an appellate court.

With some men, a close association with partisan politics and campaigns tends to make them narrow. Sometimes, but less often, such exposure may make a man completely philosophic or even cynical. With Theodore Christianson neither result occurred. He never lost his capacity to take sides and to be an ardent advocate for what he believed, but he was never narrow or sharp or partisan. At times his willingness to see the other person's point of view irritated his more partisan friends, who in their calmer moments of reflection admired this capacity to keep his mind open. To him most issues, most institutions, and most human beings were like Voltaire's symbolic statue of Man—composed of base metals, mud, and clay, and of diamonds and rare jewels and the purest of metals. His readiness to see the diamonds and rare metals in every human being has been emphasized in every memorial to him—and happily it did not await the occasion of a memorial to call forth these observations. His friends often commented on this quality in his lifetime, and many sought to emulate him.

As a trial lawyer he tried many cases, and inevitably, as all lawyers do, he lost some. Even when he felt deeply disappointed, it was not his custom to berate the judge or the jury or his opponent. His inquiry more often was a search for what he had done wrong or what he had failed to do to transmit his conviction on the case to the court or to the jurors. This critical self analysis aided in his very early development into an accomplished advocate.

This awareness of others and their views and their problems was perhaps the one trait that set him apart from most of his fellow human beings. His reaction to bad conduct of others was not to say "Look how he acts" but usually a thoughtful introspective query: "Why does he act that way?"

This sensitivity to the hidden and unseen in others, this search for good in everyone, is of course one of the highest and truest expressions of the Christian concept. And it was more than tolerance, which is passive; it was invariably an active search for the best aspect in every person and every situation. His mind seemed to have thousands of facets or pigeonholes for other human beings. It was not a cold or calculating study even though it was analytical. It had a warmth and compassion and a genuine urge to understand. I, in common surely with many of his other close friends, recall that he might on occasion pick up the thread of a conversation about another person discussed long before, when he would find some new link in the explanation of some act or some transaction or event concerning that person. His search was always for the best motives, for the best traits, and for the explanation most favorable to the other.

This concern for others manifested itself in many ways. He was constantly sensitive to opportunities to help advance others—to help them find occasions and opportunities where they could develop talents and abilities that he could see and that they often overlooked in themselves.

This warm and wonderful quality was one I personally observed on many occasions. Right today I can hear the very phrases he would use—"Now look, we've got to find some way to see that 'John' gets a chance to show what he can do." Often I found myself, on his urging, being one of the implements in this process—a consequence due primarily to his constant pressing of the point with all the warmth and vitality of his personality, operating in a way that permitted me no other course.

In his lifelong habit of speaking well of all men and of seeing the best in others, it might be suggested that our friend was heeding the gospel admonition of Matthew to "judge not" lest he be judged. But there was nothing negative in his attitude—his was, as I suggested, the positive desire of the prospector to find the rare metals and jewels in every person he knew.

The remarkable fact is that this quality did not prevent his being a highly effective advocate; it was a tempering as with fine steel, producing resilient strength rather than brittle weakness. It is fair to say that this resiliency of mind and sensitivity of spirit affected all his work as a lawyer and as a judge. In all these relationships the qualities I have mentioned not only endeared him to allies and opponents alike but tended to lift him above the very conflicts and struggles in which he took part. When he came to this Court at 37 he was actually a mature, seasoned lawyer—more mature than many men 15 or 20 years his senior—and the maturity was of a kind that gave him the detachment and objectivity essential in a really fine judge.

I hope I may be indulged a personal reference that illustrates his own attitude toward judicial work. We had been very close friends for over 20 years, and when I struggled with the decision whether to return to private law practice or go on the Bench, he was one of a very few friends in whom I confided. His reaction was prompt, and it was documented and presented like a fine appellate argument. Among other things, he said he had concluded after seven years on this Court that active general practitioners accustomed to trial work made the best appellate judges. "Trial lawyers," he said, "learn to take sides and the essence of judging is to take sides; the difference is that a judge takes sides after hearing all the arguments and evidence."

He emphasized that, while he found appellate work exacting, it had less of the day-to-day pressure that he had encountered as a lawyer.

It is not a reflection on his fine legal mind and his intuitively sound legal judgment to say that he had to drive himself at times. He would sometimes say that he was essentially lazy and that his pride and conscience kept him at work. It is of course more accurate to say that it was his really strong passion for truth and facts and justice that supplied the drive.

These drives never altered his capacity for pleasure in the companionship of his contemporaries or in the simple common pleasures of life. In fact, he transmitted his feeling for competition and for recreation into his work, and the solution of a difficult legal problem or completion of a trying opinion produced in him the same exhilaration that we would see when he caught the largest wall-eyed pike of the day.

His legal writing and his opinions as a member of the Supreme Court showed that he tended to be professionally and legally orthodox. He respected the limitations on scope of appellate review, partly no doubt because his wide trial experience taught him that cold records do not present the same picture that a trial judge sees. Likewise, he had a profound respect for the fundamental separation of powers, and he felt that the durability of our system of government depended on having each coordinate branch respect the powers of the others. More than most judges, he was capable of judicial self-restraint.

One of the compensations that he felt came to him to offset giving up a career in practice far more rewarding in a material sense, was the freedom to be with his family while his children grew up. Although he worked long hours, he found that life on the Bench freed him from much of the nervous tension that seems to be the constant companion of the practicing lawyer. Within a week of his death I spent with him one of the best days we ever shared together, fishing on the St. Croix with an expert guide. His enthusiasm for a catch of a limit of large wall-eyed pike was like that of a teenage boy on his first real fishing trip, and he at once talked of taking his family out with this same guide.

His colleagues of this Court have expressed and recorded their unbounded esteem for Theodore Christianson as an individual and as a lawyer and judge. They were themselves refreshed by his fresh buoyant enthusiasm for his work, his warm and friendly attitude toward his fellow judges, and the fact that he never lost his feeling of kinship with the lawyers who appeared before this Court. He always remembered that lawyers do not act for themselves but for others. He considered that it was the responsibility of lawyers to advocate and of judges to decide, and he expected partisan arguments rather than scholarly objective discourses. He knew the problems and burdens of the advocate and was always aware of the great disparity of power between the lawyer on the court and the lawyer facing the court. Few things brought a reaction of irritation from him so much as the spectacle of a judge who treated lawyers in an overbearing or arrogant manner. His relationship with new young lawyers was especially close. No judge could have been more ready to help, to put them at ease, and to smooth over the rough spots every young lawyer must encounter. Perhaps it was premature for a man barely 40, but he often said to his friends that he never wanted to lose his contact with younger men and their points of view. The life of every younger lawyer he worked with was richer for the contact.

The sudden and tragic termination of his life found him at the peak of his powers of mind and body, keenly enjoying companionship with his wife, Dorothy, and his two children, Sally and Theodore, at home and at ease with his work on this Court. He was often pressed to consider leaving the Bench for attractive opportunities in private practice and for pressing demands that he run for Governor or Senator or accept a high post in the Executive Branch of President Eisenhower's Administration. The call of public service was a strong one for him, but I am confident that he had finally resolved in his own mind to devote his life to the Judiciary. He had found genuine happiness and deep satisfaction in that work.

Life, as we know on reflection, is measured in more dimensions than simply calendar years. What is given into it, what it gives off, the impact of a life on its environment—and surely the influence on other human beings—all these things are more significant than years or time alone. Judged by these more vital and meaningful dimensions, Theodore Christianson lived a rich, full, and significant life, and the product of that life has enriched his community, his state, and in a very special way, this Court and the law.

It is a record that any man would be proud to have as his own.

Mr. Palmer then said:

Before closing the memorial services, I ask leave of the Court to present and file a resolution of the Law Alumni Association of the University of Minnesota honoring the memory of Associate Justice Christianson. At the time of his death, Mr. Justice Christianson was the president of the Alumni Association of his Law School. That position, coupled with his many years of interest and service to the Law School or our State University, made it appropriate for his fellow alumnae to commemorate his memory by special resolution.

So it is, that I now ask leave of the Court to deliver and file the resolution that was enacted by unanimous and rising vote at a meeting of the Law Alumni Association on April 26 of this year:

> BE IT RESOLVED by the members of the Law Alumni Association of the University of Minnesota in meeting assembled this 26th day of April 1956, that the recent death of Associate Justice Theodore Christianson of the Supreme Court of the State of Minnesota is a great loss to that Court, to this Association of which he was the President, and to the bench and bar of the entire state. He was an able judge whose brilliant mind, warm personality, and application to the study of the law brought distinction to his Law School, to his profession, and to the bench of this state.
>
> The Law Alumni Association of the University of Minnesota joins with the bench and bar of the state of Minnesota in honoring his memory and extending sympathy to his family and associates.
>
> Respectfully,
> Judge Walter F. Rogosheske,
> President
> Law Alumni Association
> of the University of Minnesota

Chief Justice Dell then said:

It is indeed fitting and right that we should assemble here today in memory of the departed justices who served as members of this Court and to record the respect, esteem, and affection in which they were held by the Bench and Bar alike. That these men who we memorialize today have justly earned and richly deserve their place in the history of this state has been most ably pointed out by the memorials presented here this afternoon. Their work is finished and finished well, but our memory of them and what they have done will remain with us always.

In the early hours of September 19th last, tragedy visited this Court and took from us our youngest and most beloved member. I knew Justice Theodore Christianson since he was a boy. He worked each summer at Dunnvilla in my home county of Otter Tail. I watched him grow from a boy into a man, from a student into a lawyer, and from a lawyer into a judge.

To know him was to love him. When he came to this Court he had only practiced law 13 years. When he died he had the complete confidence, respect, and admiration of every member of this Court. He was a tireless worker day and night and his opinions measure up to the best. Minnesota has lost a truly great judge and citizen. I want to here and now acknowledge my indebtedness to him and the indebtedness of all of the members of this Court who served with him, for his patience, his help and understanding, and above all for his kindness in making life just a little easier and a little more pleasant for all of us. We have lost a true friend, a very fine justice, and we shall ever mourn his loss. [246 Minn. xvii]

Roger L. Dell

1897–1966
Associate Justice, 1953; Chief Justice, 1953–1962

On May 31, 1966, at 2 P.M., the Court being assembled in the courtroom in the State Capitol, Chief Justice Oscar R. Knutson said:

The Court recognizes the president of the Minnesota State Bar Association, Mr. James E. Montague.

Mr. Montague then said:

The Minnesota State Bar Association comprising more than 4,000 members of the Bar of this State is honored to participate in this proceeding to commemorate the memories of departed justices of this court who have died since proceedings in memory of departed justices were last held in this room. Since that time five justices have gone to their ultimate reward. Three of them were chief justices of this court and two were associate justices. All left their imprint on the law, on the profession, and on the state. In order that there may be a record of their lives, their personal characteristics, and their achievements, we ask the Court at this time to recognize members of the Bar of this State who will deliver memorials to these departed justices . . . The Honorable Chester Rosengren of Fergus Falls, a Judge of the District Court, will deliver the memorial honoring Chief Justice Roger L. Dell.

Judge Rosengren then presented the following memorial:

It is with mixed emotions that I present this memorial in behalf of Roger L. Dell, formerly Associate Justice and also Chief Justice of this Court. I am grateful for being accorded the privilege of presenting the same, but simultaneously I mourn the death of my dear friend, my intimate adviser, and former partner.

Roger L. Dell was born July 19, 1897, at the Village of Bird Island, Minnesota, his parents being August T. and Ellen Dell. He attended school both in Bird Island and Shakopee, graduating from the High School of the latter city with the Class of 1916. Without attending any college or university for pre-law preparation, he enrolled in the St. Paul College of Law, graduating from that school in 1920.

He was admitted to the Bar of the State of Minnesota on October 7, 1920, and immediately commenced the practice of law at Fergus Falls, Minnesota, as an associate of one James E. Brown, subsequently becoming a partner of the latter, the firm being known as Brown and Dell. Mr. Brown died a short time thereafter, and Judge Dell continued to practice alone or with part-time associates or assistants until April of 1933 when Chester G. Rosengren became associated with him, they subsequently becoming partners, the firm being known as Dell and Rosengren. They were joined by Gerald S. Rufer in January 1947, who also subsequently became a partner, the firm name being changed to Dell, Rosengren and Rufer. Judge Dell remained the senior member of this firm until his appointment to this Court as Associate Justice on January 12, 1953. He was appointed Chief Justice of this Court on July 16, 1953. He terminated his tenure of such office in 1962 for personal reasons.

He was married twice, both wives predeceasing him. They were respectively, Marjory Webber Dell who died August 18, 1934, and Agnes Collier Dell who died December 17, 1964. Two brothers, Harold Dell and Kenneth Dell, both of whom were lawyers, also predeceased him. He had no children. He left surviving him a brother, Thomas Dell of New York City, New York, and a sister, Dorothy Graeber of Tulsa, Oklahoma.

He served briefly with the Armed Forces during World War I being located at Field Artillery Central

Officers Training School at Camp Zachary at Louisville, Kentucky.

The Bench and Bar of our state recognizes that Judge Dell was one of the last of the great advocates who practiced in our trial courts when the art of advocacy reached its zenith prior to the adoption of the Rules of Procedure designed to prevent surprise and to reduce the advantage of the ability and ingenuity of counsel. During this period he was recognized as a giant among the giants of the trial lawyers both in the civil and the criminal field, and some of his trials and exploits are now legendary. Because of his tremendous success as a trial lawyer, many of his admirers failed to credit him with his legal ability, judicial mind, and rare lucidity of legal analysis and thinking. Having almost literally lived with him for twenty years as a partner and through subsequent association, I can personally attest to the latter better than anyone else. However, his abilities other than as an advocate were immediately recognized after he became a member of this Court, and I think that his colleagues on this Court would be the first to acknowledge his outstanding judicial ability and temperament, his legal stature and capacity, his clarity of scholarly reasoning, and his complete judicial honesty.

Judge Dell was blessed with innate ability and keen legal mind, but these assets were abetted by a tremendous capacity for work. Time meant nothing to him in the preparation of his files and in representing clients. He was an indefatigable laborer in all phases of his profession. And when he became a member of this Court he brought all of those rare qualities with him, and immediately the Court and its functions became the object of his all-consuming interest and pride.

While a member of this Court he became one of our fine jurists and leaders. Under his aegis as Chief Justice the Court never had greater unity and solidarity. As a writer of opinions he was remarkable for his power of exposition, recognized for his erudition, respected for his conservative leadership, accepted for his courage, and followed because of his common-sense approach to problems. He was strong in his philosophy that the Court should not invade the province of the legislature, should not remake the common law, or should not revise the constitution. But he did recognize that imperceptible changes in conditions and mores necessarily made the law living and flexible. Coinciding with that philosophy was an amazing basic feeling and intuition for what the law should be. In retrospect, I remember innumerable times when a new factual situation was presented to him concerning which he had never read or heard any decision law. And his reasoned reaction under these circumstances was always, "I think this should be the answer"; and, inevitably research would either disclose the answer or it would appear in later decisions and sometimes many years later. He was a true disciple of Blackstone, by nature, training, and dedication.

Having worked hard all of his early life and later being entirely dedicated to his profession and busy with the management of his personal estate, he really never learned to play and relax. Almost his sole recreation other than reading, and he was a voracious reader, was shooting, either for game or as a competitive sport. He did not have much time to spend with this type of recreation, but nevertheless he brought to this sport the same concentration that characterized everything he did, and he enjoyed an enviable reputation for his shooting prowess on both a state and national level.

Niggardly as he was of his own time for personal relaxation and recreation, he was generous with both time and money in various philanthropic organizations and in connection with the affairs of the Episcopal Church and served without hesitation when requested. His death was a great loss to his church.

After his retirement from the Bench, he continued until the day of his death actively taking care of his personal affairs. With wonderful business acumen he alone amassed an estate large even by present standards. But he was not content to simply enjoy financial independence. Instead he embarked on what could be generally described as a one-man urban renewal project of the business area of Fergus Falls, Minnesota, well knowing that in the course of his ordinary anticipated span of life he would never receive a return of more than a fraction of his investment. But this again was consistent with the personality that made him an outstanding trial lawyer, a splendid jurist, and a leader of men.

The community in which he elected to practice his profession, the Bench and Bar of our great state, and the State of Minnesota suffered a great loss with his death, but they can profit from his memory and the contributions tangible and intangible that he made. He was the type of man envisioned by James Oliver when he wrote, "The world is blessed most by men who do things, and not by those who merely talk about them." Such is the memorial I now offer in behalf of the Honorable Roger L. Dell, deceased.

Chief Justice Knutson then said:

It is proper that we hold these memorial services for those who have served on this Court. Some of us have had the privilege of serving with most of those whom we honor today. All of them have served with distinction and have added much to the jurisprudence of this state and this nation. While the opinions they have written, which are to be found in our Minnesota Reports, are the best testimonial to their ability, their intellectual integrity, and their devotion to their work, it is fitting that we who survive them express our appreciation for what they have done. [273 Minn. xxi]

Martin A. Nelson

1889–1979
Associate Justice, 1953–1972

Martin Nelson's extensive life and career began in Hesper, Iowa, where he was born on February 21, 1889. He moved north to Minnesota when his family left Iowa, first to Mabel, Minnesota, then on to St. Paul. He was a graduate of Mechanic Arts High School in St. Paul. He later took pharmacy courses and became a registered pharmacist in 1912. In 1916, he received his bachelor of laws degree from the St. Paul College of Law (now William Mitchell) and began the practice of law in St. Paul.

At about this time, he took up the new and risky avocation of flying airplanes. He used his flying experience to become an aviator and an aviation instructor during World War I. After his discharge from the U.S. Army Air Force, he practiced law in Austin, Minnesota, from 1919 to 1944. There he met and married Merle and became the father of two children, Arthur Nelson and Enid Nelson (now Jesmer).

Active in the Republican Party, Nelson was a delegate to the Republican National Convention in 1928 and 1932. In 1934, he was the Republican nominee for governor, running unsuccessfully against Floyd B. Olson. Nelson's campaign in 1934, and his later unsuccessful campaign against Elmer Benson in 1936, were highlighted by his being one of the first candidates to fly himself to different areas of the state to campaign. In 1938, once again attempting to secure a spot on the Republican ticket, Nelson was defeated for the gubernatorial nomination by Harold Stassen, who went on to win the governorship.

Nelson was an early member of the American Legion, a devoted supporter of that institution, one frequently asked to speak to Legion audiences. He was active in Austin civic affairs and served on the Board of Trustees of St. Olaf Hospital for many years, including ten years as its president. An active attorney in local and state bar associations, he was appointed to the Mower County district bench by Gov. Edward Thye in 1944, was reelected in 1950, and served until he was appointed by Gov. C. Elmer Anderson to replace Associate Justice Roger L. Dell, who had become chief justice of the Minnesota Supreme Court in 1953.

Justice Nelson had a long and illustrious career as an associate justice of the state supreme court, being reelected to that position until his retirement in 1972. He possessed a wide range of knowledge in many different areas of the law and was the author of 546 opinions during his career on the court.

One of Justice Nelson's favorite opinions was the one he wrote in *Slezak v. Ousdigian*, 110 N.W.2d 1 (Minn. 1951), which held that members of the Minnesota Public Employee Retirement Association lacked legal standing to maintain a class-action suit against the association secretary. The decision was highly publicized and discussed in the press. Another of his prominent opinions was *Bruce v. Najarian*, 1 N.W.2d 282 (Minn. 1957), which discussed and clarified the role of the constitutional lien and its impact on real property owners. Finally, toward the end of his career, he was the author of *Head v. Special School District No. 1*, 182 N.W.2d 887 (Minn. 1970), which resulted in the legislature enacting meet-and-confer provisions and clarifying the instances in which strikes would be allowed under the Public Employment Relations Act.

After Justice Nelson's retirement from the court in 1972, he continued to live in St. Paul, until his death in 1979. His funeral at the Gloria Dei Lutheran Church in St. Paul was attended by his many friends and family, including several of his former law clerks; six of them were pallbearers.

—George L. May

William P. Murphy

1898–1986
Associate Justice, 1955–1972

"Mr. Justice Comes Home" the headline declared. St. Cloud native William P. Murphy received a hero's welcome when he returned for an official visit in 1956.

Not that Murphy had been away for long; he had been appointed to the Minnesota Supreme Court just one year earlier. But the Murphy family roots run deep in St. Cloud.

Public service does, too. Following in the footsteps of his father, one of St. Cloud's first city council members and a popular business owner, William Murphy became the face of justice during turbulent times.

Born July 6, 1898, Murphy graduated from Cathedral High School of St. Cloud in 1915. He later attended St. Thomas College (now the University of St. Thomas) and earned a law degree from the St. Paul College of Law (now William Mitchell). In 1922, Murphy returned home and ran his own practice for the duration of the Roaring Twenties and throughout the Great Depression.

He became an assistant U.S. attorney in 1939, and after the United States entered World War II, Murphy conducted criminal prosecutions for the Office of Price Administration (OPA), which set maximum prices for commodities and rationed essential supplies such as tires, gasoline, sugar, and meat.

In this capacity, according to the *St. Cloud Times*, Murphy handled a tire-rationing scandal that resulted in the conviction of three top OPA officials and the resignation of several others. He also took the fight to organized crime, leading an investigation in 1943 against the boxing bootlegger Sam Taran after federal agents seized $250,000 in black-market liquor from a St. Paul warehouse.

Murphy later served as an enforcement director for the price administration office and with the St. Paul law firm of Silver, Goff, Murphy, Ryan and Gottlich.

The death of Minnesota Supreme Court Justice Theodore Christianson in 1955 opened a seat on the bench and paved the way for Murphy's 17-year tenure in the state judiciary. Gov. Orville L. Freeman took only five days to name Christianson's successor, citing the need to avoid any 3–3 decisions on the court, reported the *St. Cloud Times*.

Of course, politics played a role, too. Although supreme court justices were appointed without party designation, the right-leaning court contained four Republican justices. The addition of Murphy made for three Democrats and more balance.

Concern about the makeup of the supreme court soon took a backseat to more a dramatic event—the meatpackers' strike in Albert Lea. The labor dispute pitted Wilson & Company against the United Packinghouse Workers. After officials from Albert Lea and Freeborn County warned of a high threat of violence, Freeman mustered the National Guard to keep the peace and close the plant. Wilson & Company sought a federal injunction against the plant closure, and the U.S. District Court in Minnesota ruled in favor of the company—at the same time criticizing the governor's use of the guard to shutter businesses. Author Cheri Register popularized the story in *Packinghouse Daughter* (MHS Press, 2000).

Meanwhile, in the state judiciary Freeman fought to save his Reorganization Act of 1955, which would have significantly expanded the commerce department's jurisdiction, along with that of nearly a dozen other state agencies. According to archival records stored with the Minnesota Historical Society, the DFL-controlled house had proposed the law and the Republican-led senate strongly opposed it. The law was hung up, however, by a minor variance between the document approved by the legislature and the one given the governor to sign. Litigation ensued, and *State ex rel. Foster v. Naftalin* was one of the earliest cases that Murphy confronted.

The law signed by the governor read: "The commissioner of administration after consultation with the auditor is empowered to formulate and prescribe a system of uniform records, accounts." As passed by the legislature, the law read, "The state auditor, with the advice and assistance of the commissioner of administration, is empowered to formulate and prescribe a system of uniform records, accounts."

The court ultimately declared the entire law unconstitutional—despite Murphy's dissent; legislative proceedings frequently reference the ruling.

Murphy served on the Minnesota Supreme Court until his retirement in 1972, issuing 419 majority opinions, three concurring opinions, and 21 dissents. He died April 25, 1986, in Hastings.

—Michael Krieger

Lee Loevinger

1913–2004
Associate Justice, 1960–1961

Lee Loevinger was an extraordinary lawyer. Not only was he successful in private practice, but he also worked for all three branches of government— as a legislative counsel, a state supreme court justice, a prosecuting attorney, and head of a federal administrative agency. His service as an associate justice on the Minnesota Supreme Court from 1960 to 1961 was the midpoint of a legal career that can only be described as remarkable.

Loevinger was born in St. Paul in 1913. His father, Gustavus Loevinger, helped organize the Farmer-Labor Party and served 25 years as a district court judge in Minnesota.

Loevinger graduated summa cum laude from the University of Minnesota in 1933, where he earned a reputation as a talented debater and had even convinced the student body to adopt the Oxford University debating society's antiwar resolution (though Loevinger abandoned this position a few years later). Loevinger continued his studies at the university and earned his law degree in 1936.

After law school, Loevinger practiced law in Kansas City, Missouri, and then served as the Minneapolis regional attorney for the National Labor Relations Board in New York.

In 1942, after a stint working in the antitrust division of the U.S. Department of Justice in Washington, Loevinger joined the U.S. Navy. He had assignments in North Africa and Europe while serving in World War II.

After the war, Loevinger spent several years in Minnesota, practicing law at the firm of Larson, Loevinger, Lindquist, Freeman and Fraser (now Lindquist & Vennum) and teaching as a visiting professor and lecturer at the University of Minnesota. He also spent a brief time in Washington serving as chief counsel to a subcommittee of the U.S. Senate Committee on Small Business.

In 1960, Gov. Orville Freeman, Loevinger's former partner, appointed Loevinger an associate justice of the Minnesota Supreme Court. For most, this would have been the capstone of a successful legal career. But for Loevinger it was just the beginning. He was just one year into his appointment, and he had authored just 19 majority opinions, when he got a call from President John F. Kennedy.

In 1961, Loevinger left the Minnesota Supreme Court for Washington to serve with Robert F. Kennedy as assistant attorney general in charge of the Antitrust Division of the U.S. Department of Justice. There, along with Robert Kennedy and Byron White, who later became a U.S. Supreme Court justice, Loevinger became part of the "exclusive triumvirate" of antitrust enforcement.

Loevinger believed strongly in his new line of work. Indeed, a few years earlier, he had told a Congressional committee that "the problems with which antitrust laws are concerned—the problems of distribution of power within society—are second only to the questions of survival in the face of threats of nuclear weapons in importance for our generation." He even told Robert Kennedy in a job interview, "I believe in antitrust almost as a secular religion."

Loevinger's passion for his work paid great dividends. In the 1963 case of *United States v. Philadelphia National Bank*, Loevinger successfully persuaded the Supreme Court to apply the Clayton Antitrust Act to commercial banks for the first time. All together, in his two years on the job, he approved a record 150 antitrust suits for prosecution.

In 1963, President Kennedy appointed Loevinger commissioner of the Federal Communications Commission. At the FCC, Loevinger's background in antitrust was evident. Rather than trying to control the programming available to television viewers, he advocated for "diversity of ownership and control" as a way to improve the program quality.

Loevinger's influence extended far beyond television. As perhaps his greatest accomplishment at the FCC, Loevinger originated the idea of emergency 911 calls. He pressed AT&T to implement a system allowing telephone users to summon help in the case of an emergency, even though the telephone conglomerate believed the technology was impractical.

Loevinger left the FCC in 1968 and joined the Washington law firm of Hogan & Hartson. There, he continued to practice antitrust law as well as federal administrative and communications law. He officially retired in 1985, but he maintained an office at the firm until his death.

Loevinger's retirement gave him the opportunity to pursue another interest—the study of science and technology. He was a founder and chairman of the American Bar Association's Section of Science and Technology Law and served as a liaison to the National Conference of Lawyers and Scientists, established jointly by the ABA and the American Association for the Advancement of Science.

Throughout his life, Loevinger was an avid writer. He authored some 150 published books and articles in the fields of law, economics, antitrust, and communications, and in his eighties he began publishing book reviews and articles about cosmology, the scientific study of the universe.

Loevinger died April 26, 2004, in Washington, D.C., as a result of complications from heart disease. He was 91 years old. Preceded in death by his wife, Ruth, a native of Glencoe, Minnesota, he was survived by a daughter, Barbara, sons Eric and Peter, and two grandchildren.

—Dan Piper

James C. Otis

1912–1993
Associate Justice, 1961–1982

During his time as a Minnesota Supreme Court justice, James C. Otis developed a reputation as an independent thinker, often providing the sole dissenting opinion in controversial decisions.

While his tendency to be a "lone wolf" on contentious issues sometimes ruffled feathers, the colleagues, employees, and lawyers who practiced in his court appreciated Otis's candor and his ability to see the nuances in legal issues.

James Cornish Otis was born in St. Paul on March 23, 1912, and he grew up on Summit Avenue with a brother and two sisters. During his childhood, Otis had aspirations of being a minister, but his family legacy pulled him in another direction. There were lawyers in his family going back to his great-grandfather, and so, after earning a bachelor's degree at Yale University, he moved back home and earned his law degree from the University of Minnesota.

In 1937, Otis joined the St. Paul law firm of Otis, Faricy, Burger and Moore, which his grandfather George L. Otis had founded in territorial Minnesota. Now known as Moore, Costello & Hart, the firm is the oldest continuing law firm in the state of Minnesota.

Otis practiced at the firm for 10 years, working not only with his father, James Sr.—who at the time was president of the Minnesota State Bar Association—but also with three uncles and with Warren Burger, who later became chief justice of the U.S. Supreme Court. Otis later described his early responsibilities as those of "a glorified law clerk," mainly the examination of real estate titles, but he went on to become a partner in the firm.

After a few years, Otis interrupted his law career to serve his country during World War II. Otis had a physical disability that kept him from being accepted into the military, so instead he served with the U.S.

Army Corps of Engineers starting in 1942; he returned to the firm in 1944.

Four years later, the death of Judge John Finehout opened a seat on the Ramsey County municipal court bench. Republican Gov. Luther Youngdahl appointed Otis to serve out the remainder of the term, and a judicial career was born.

After six years on the municipal court, Otis in 1954 was appointed a judge on the Ramsey County district court, again replacing a judge who had died—in this case, his uncle Kenneth Gray Brill.

Otis came to the state supreme court in 1961 at the age of 48, one of three relatively youthful judges appointed by Gov. Elmer L. Andersen. At the time of Otis's death in 1993, former Chief Justice Robert Sheran said Otis's depth of experience, which came from serving as a trial lawyer and a municipal and district judge, was unique for a supreme court justice.

"His age also was somewhat unusual," said Pat Leighton, who was an attorney at Otis, Faricy, Burger and Moore starting in 1958 and who knew Otis socially. "He was still a young man when he reached the supreme court."

During his 21-year stint on the high court Otis developed a reputation as someone who wasn't afraid to go against the grain. Many of his dissenting opinions were unpopular even among his fellow justices.

In a 1970 decision in *State v. Hoyt*, Otis was the only member to dissent when the court upheld the conviction of a pair of bookstore clerks in St. Paul for selling what the majority called "filth for the sake of filth." Otis dissented on the grounds that the greater issue of censorship was not adequately addressed.

In a case that gained national attention, he was again the sole dissenter when the supreme court upheld the conviction of a man arrested at the University of Minnesota for possession of a microscopic amount of marijuana. Following that case, the Minnesota Legislature reduced the penalty for possession of small amounts of marijuana.

Otis also wrote the well-known decision in *Reserve Mining Co. v. Herbst*, in which the court ruled that the taconite tailings the company had been dumping into Lake Superior could be deposited inland.

Otis was reluctant to toe the party line both inside and outside the courtroom. His son Todd, a former legislator and chairman of the DFL Party, said that although his father considered himself a Republican, he voted along Democratic lines. "He jokingly used to say that some people thought he was the Fidel Castro of Minnesota," said St. Paul attorney Peter H. Seed, who clerked for Otis in the mid-1960s, "because he was considered kind of a liberal Republican."

Despite his willingness to consider factors outside the letter of the law, Otis was scrupulous about policy. Leighton recalled that Otis was careful never to hear cases being tried by his old firm.

"If I had an argument and my case was coming up," recalled Leighton, "as soon as my case was called and I started walking forward to the counsel's tables, he would pack up his papers and leave."

Those who worked with Otis recalled him with fondness. Steve Swartz, a former Maslon Edelman Borman & Brand partner, clerked for Justice Lee Loevinger in the early 1960s, when Loevinger was called to Washington to serve as attorney general in charge of the U.S. Department of Justice Antitrust Division. Swartz was struck by the difference between Loevinger and his replacement, Otis.

"Loevinger was a very tough-minded, demanding fellow," Swartz remembered. "So it was quite a contrast to work for him first and then for Justice Otis, who was really a kind gentleman."

Seed recalled that Otis mentally accumulated a great deal of information before settling down to write an opinion. "Every judge has a different style in how he writes opinions," he said. "[Otis's] style was to have me write an exhaustive memorandum, and then he would read it carefully and sit down with me and his secretary, and working off the top of his head, he would dictate his opinion."

"He was very thorough about gathering information from wherever he could and working that into his opinions," Seed recalled. "He had a great talent for that."

After his initial appointment to the supreme court, Otis was elected to three more terms before he retired in 1982. He was a board member for Hamline University and helped start its law school. Both Hamline and William Mitchell College of Law offer scholarships in Otis's name.

Otis kept busy in retirement, serving on the Commission for the Bicentennial of the Constitution, presiding over a constitutional convention sponsored by the Minnesota State Bar Association, cochairing the Minnesota Judicial Center Public Education Commission, and refereeing lawyer-disciplinary proceedings and two election contests. He was also a trustee of the Amherst H. Wilder Foundation, Hamline University, and the Minnesota State Bar Foundation and a member of the American Judicature Society, the Institute of Judicial Administration, and the Nature Conservancy.

Outside the courtroom, Otis loved the outdoors and enjoyed spending time at a family cabin in Wisconsin. He loved skiing and hiking and got pleasure from both until the very end.

"I went on a two-week hiking trip to Norway, and as soon as I got back he wanted to hear all about it," said Seed. "Then he did it himself—and this was right about the time when he became sick. He went ahead and did it anyway."

Otis died of pneumonia on March 15, 1993, eight months after being diagnosed with a brain tumor. He was survived by his second wife, Constance, sons Todd and James, and a daughter, Emily.

On his death, colleagues and friends remembered a man who used his position to fight for justice and who was gracious and congenial away from the bench.

"He had the uncanny judgment about what's unfair," Walter Rogosheske, who served with Otis on the court for 20 years, told the *Minneapolis Star Tribune*. "If there was one appellate court judge I was going to be associated with, he would be it."

Pat Leighton referred to him as "truly a nice human being."

—Dan Heilman

Walter F. Rogosheske

1914–1998
Associate Justice, 1962–1980

Anyone fortunate enough to meet Associate Justice Walter F. Rogosheske immediately noticed his warmth, his ease, and his gentleness. With pipe in hand and a twinkle in his eye, he never failed to offer comfort, encouragement, and inspiration. Although his 30-year judicial career was remarkable, it did not fully define him. His service to the public as a lawyer, a legislator, and a leader in the bar was extraordinary. And it was always grounded in an abiding faith and deep love of family and friends.

Walter Rogosheske was born in Sauk Rapids, Minnesota, and he completed his high school education there. His father was in the creamery business and was active in Republican politics. His mother expected her sons to become educated in a profession—preferring for Walter the profession of dentistry. After attending the St. Cloud Teacher's College and Valparaiso University, he obtained a bachelor's degree from the University of Minnesota and chose to enter law school instead of dental school, at the university. His mother later acknowledged, at the time he joined the Minnesota Supreme Court, that he had made the right choice.

The year of his graduation from law school, Walter Rogosheske made two momentous decisions: he married Dorothy Heywood of Sartell, Minnesota, and he returned to Sauk Rapids to begin a solo law practice. As might be imagined, his return to Sauk Rapids received considerable local media attention. He was clearly a favorite son.

Barely three years into his practice, by this time in partnership with Benton County Attorney Arthur Benson, Rogosheske filed to seek election after the elderly representative of his district died. He won the primary against several opponents and the general election against the mayor of Foley, Minnesota. He had just turned 28 years of age.

Rogosheske caught the early attention of Speaker of the House Lawrence Hall of St. Cloud and enjoyed a rapid rise in leadership and responsibility. He became an advocate for public vocational education and rural school consolidation. When Rogosheske was reelected in 1947, Luther Youngdahl, a former justice of the state supreme court, became governor and enlisted him in an effort to rid the state of slot-machine gambling. For his efforts, Rogosheske was recognized as one of the "10 Most Valuable Legislators" by a large number of newspapers in the state.

Rogosheske's road to the bench developed quickly after he left the legislature. Governor Youngdahl appointed him chair of the Metropolitan Airport Commission, then involved in the development of the current Minneapolis/Saint Paul airport, despite Rogosheske's protest that he was afraid of planes. A year later, in 1950, the governor, using an early form of merit selection that relied on a plebiscite of the lawyers in the district, appointed Rogosheske to the Seventh District Court. Rogosheske indicated his willingness to be considered in the plebiscite but almost withdrew when he thought Fergus Falls attorney Roger Dell might want the job. Dell interviewed Rogosheske and at the conclusion said, "I think you ought to be the judge." Rogosheske was appointed at age 36. Dell later was appointed to the Minnesota Supreme Court and ultimately became chief justice. In small-world fashion, Rogosheske filled the vacancy created when Chief Justice Dell retired.

When Rogosheske was a district judge, the Minnesota District Judges Association called on him to lead its efforts in the legislature, focused on improving judicial pay and benefits. The association also asked him to become involved in the American Bar Association (ABA), in which he ultimately became a prominent national leader. While on the trial bench, Rogosheske responded to one of the first jury studies, conducted by the University of Chicago Law School. This put him in a position to lead the association's effort to create the first *Jury Instruction Guide* for Minnesota.

In 1962, Gov. Elmer L. Andersen surveyed the district presidents of the state bar association about who should fill the vacancy on the state supreme court caused by the retirement of Chief Justice Dell. Rogosheske received high praise in that process, won the appointment, and was sworn in by the new chief justice, Oscar Knutson, in open court; only his wife accompanied him, to hold his robe. After the oath, Rogosheske robed and joined the justices to hear his first case.

During Rogosheske's 18-year tenure on the supreme court, his authorship of opinions touched on virtually every major area of Minnesota law. Many of his decisions dealt with issues that would resurface years later. In *Port Authority of City of Saint Paul v. Fisher*, 145 N.W.2d 560 (1966), the authority sought a declaratory judgment approving the use of public financing to construct and lease back an industrial building for the benefit of a private manufacturing company on land previously acquired by condemnation. The issue was whether the legislative authorization of the financing satisfied the public purpose required by the Minnesota Constitution—"The legislature shall pass no . . . law . . . authorizing public taxation for a private purpose."

In announcing the court's approval of the project, Rogosheske wrote:

> If the lands in question were not marginal or if the building to be erected were not admittedly an industrial building, this would be evidence of an intent to serve a private purpose. The same would be true if accomplishing the reclamation of the lands could be achieved without public assistance or if the revenues derived from the proposed lease were insufficient to recoup acquisition costs. The evidence, however, is otherwise and supports the conclusion that only by leasing a publicly financed building can acquisition costs be recouped, productive use of the reclaimed

lands in question be accomplished, and such use of other tracts presumably be accelerated.

The issue addressed in *Fisher* recently became nationally prominent when the U.S. Supreme Court decided *Kelo v. City of New London, Conn.*, 545 U.S. 469 (2005). The court held that the city's plan to condemn privately owned property so as to spur economic redevelopment satisfied the "public use" requirement of the Fifth Amendment's "takings clause."

In *Sherlock v. Stillwater Clinic*, 260 N.W.2d 169 (1977), the state supreme court considered the validity of a medical malpractice claim for wrongful birth resulting from negligently performed sterilization. In what Rogosheske later described as his most difficult case, he wrote for the majority as follows:

> Most troublesome is the matter of allowing recovery for the costs of rearing a normal, healthy child. Ethical and religious considerations aside, it must be recognized that such costs are a direct financial injury to the parents, no different in immediate effect than the medical expenses resulting from the wrongful conception and birth of the child. Although public sentiment may recognize that to the vast majority of parents the long-term and enduring benefits of parenthood outweigh the economic costs of rearing a healthy child, it would seem myopic to declare today that those benefits exceed the costs as a matter of law.

Molloy v. Meier, 679 N.W.2d 711 (Minn. 2004), presented a similar issue, the court holding that a physician has the duty to inform parents of the possibility that any child they conceived suffers a genetic disorder.

While serving on the state's highest court, Rogosheske's involvement in the ABA increased dramatically. He became chair of the ABA's Committee on the Prosecution and Defense Functions, succeeding Warren Burger when the latter became chief justice of the U.S. Supreme Court. The committee published standards for prosecutorial conflicts of interest that became the basis for an ABA resolution recommending the appointment of special counsel to investigate the Watergate affair.

As his friends and former law clerks attest, Walter Rogosheske was devoted to his family. He and his wife, Dorothy, had five children—Paul, Mary, Thomas, James, and Mark. Walter generously invited his clerks to become a part of his extended family, frequently entertaining them at his home and including them in trips to the family cabin on Lake Alexander, near Little Falls. One law clerk commented, "My wife and I were made a part of his family—both his judicial clerkship family and his own personal family." Another summed him up this way: "While all of the good things that people were saying about him are true, he is almost but not quite a saint. Saints tend to make us uncomfortable. Walter Rogosheske is one of the most comfortable human beings in the world to be around. It is his ability to see his own foibles, to share them, to laugh at them, and to profit from them that makes this so."

—Justice Sam Hanson

C. Donald Peterson

1918–1987
Associate Justice, 1967–1986

Fewer than 5,000 votes may have kept C. Donald Peterson from becoming the first person in Minnesota history to serve in three capacities under the Minnesota State Constitution: as a legislator, a constitutional executive officer, and a justice of the supreme court. Nearly 30 years later, the person who received those 5,000 votes did, in fact, achieve that distinction. That irony was part of the life of one of the most highly regarded and important justices of the supreme court.

It started in 1962. Peterson was a two-term state legislator from Edina when he ran for lieutenant governor in 1962 as incumbent Republican Gov. Elmer L. Andersen's running mate. In those days, the positions of governor and lieutenant governor were voted upon separately, not together as a ticket. Two years later, Karl Rolvaag, along with A. M. (Sandy) Keith as his lieutenant governor, ran against Gov. Andersen and Peterson. It was a razor-edge election, with Rolvaag winning after a historic recount, by 91 votes. Keith, a state senator from Rochester at the time, defeated Peterson for lieutenant governor by fewer than 5,000 votes. Keith later served nearly a decade on the Minnesota Supreme Court, from 1989 to 1998, including eight years as chief justice. He was the first Minnesotan to serve in all three constitutional capacities: legislative, executive, and judicial.

Peterson made it to the supreme court much earlier; he was elected in the next cycle, in 1966, which ushered in nearly two decades of service with the high court until his retirement in 1986, a year before he died on December 19, 1987.

C. Donald Peterson was born 69 years earlier, on February 2, 1918, in Minneapolis. His parents were of Swedish stock and his father was a Swedish Covenant clergyman. He was reared in north Minneapolis and attended and graduated from Minnehaha Academy, a private school in the southern part of the city. The youngest of 10 children, formally named Carl, he used the appellation "C. Donald" later in life. He attended junior college in Chicago and graduated from the University of Minnesota in 1939 before obtaining his law degree from the University of Illinois in 1941.

Peterson was on active military duty for four years during World War II and was recalled to service during the Korean War. He served as a senior legal officer, presiding over major military trials and reviewing criminal appeals; he received the Bronze Star for heroic or meritorious achievement.

C. Donald Peterson married Gretchen Palen of Minneapolis, a performer in the Shipstad & Johnson Ice Follies, in 1952. Gretchen was the great-granddaughter of Ard Godfrey, the Minneapolis pioneer whose still-standing house is considered the first residence built in Minneapolis. They raised six children—Barbara, Mark, Craig, Polly, Todd, and Scott. Mark, Craig, and Polly are lawyers; Mark and Polly married lawyers. The oldest daughter, now Barbara Burwell, was Miss USA in 1976, and Polly was the second runner-up to Miss Teenage America.

After ending his military service and starting his family, Peterson entered private practice in the Twin Cities, primarily with the law firm then known as Howard, Peterson, LeFevere, Leffler, Hamilton & Pearson. Although his practice concentrated on representing employees and their interests in management-labor matters, he maintained good relationships with labor unions and their leaders, and many supported him in his later electoral campaigns. Highly regarded as a legislator, he was voted the most outstanding first-term representative, and in his second term he was selected assistant minority leader of the Conservative caucus. With some 250,000 constituents, his legislative district, encompassing numerous communities in the west and southwest portion of the Twin Cities, was the most populous in the state. His large constituency prompted his interest in reapportionment, which he considered his "single most legislative concern." Within a few years, the U.S. Supreme Court in a pair of landmark decisions adopted the "one-person, one-vote" standard leading to reapportionment of legislative bodies throughout the country. As a result of reapportionment, the suburban district that he represented now has 15 separate legislative representatives.

After his narrow loss in the lieutenant governor race in 1962, Peterson continued in private practice. Four years later, he ran for the state supreme court and was elected in a hard-fought contest that included an unusual legal proceeding. One of the other candidates sought to require identification on the ballot so that an opposing candidate, the son of a retiring justice, would not be confused with the outgoing justice himself, *Foley v. Donovan*, 274 Minn. 501, 144, N.W.2d 600 (1966). Peterson did not join the case but ultimately benefited from the court's ruling, which required the son to be identified as other than the incumbent. Peterson was elected for three more six-year terms before stepping down for health reasons in 1986.

Justice Peterson considered the next two decades on the supreme court to be the most "rewarding years of my professional life." His service on the court was prolific, and his work included 509 majority decisions, 123 concurrences, 70 dissents, and 109 per curiam opinions.

The decisions authored by Peterson include some of the most significant ones of the era. They began with *Rose v. Koch*, 278 Minn. 235, 154 N.W.2d 498 (1967), the first Minnesota case applying the *New York Times* standard of "actual malice" to a libel action brought by a state legislature against a publisher of a disparaging tract. His work in the case, along with the dissent in *Manhke v. Northwest Publications,*

Inc., 280 Minn. 328, 352 160 N.W.2d 1, 16 (1968), reflected his acumen in the First Amendment and led to a request for his help in launching the Minnesota News Council, an organization that hears complaints against the media, and to his serving as its first chair, from 1971 to 1981.

Peterson felt strongly about the organization, which still exists today, viewing it as "positive evidence that the [media] in our state were committed not only to being free, but at the same time, to being responsive and responsible." He regarded the media highly, and they reciprocated. One veteran reporter, Gwyneth Jones, who covered legal affairs during Peterson's tenure, stated that while she "often disagreed with him," she considered him "my favorite conservative."

Although he regarded himself as a practitioner of "judicial restraint," Justice Peterson was not reluctant to stray from precedent when he felt it was needed. For example, his opinion for the court in *Springrose v. Wilmore*, 292 Minn. 23, 192 N.W.2d 826 (1973) abrogated the absolute common-law defense of assumption risk in tort actions, ultimately leading to the comparative fault statute. Similarly, in *Baudette v. Frana*, 285 Minn. 366, 173 N.W.2d 416 (1969), his decision for the court ended the bar of interspousal immunity in tort claims.

Justice Peterson's experience in private practice involved little criminal law, but that became one of his favorite topics on the tribunal. He authored 169 opinions on criminal law matters, including *State v. Andrews*, 282 Minn. 528, (1969), which upheld plea bargaining in a multidefendant criminal case, and a pair of obscenity cases, *State v. Welke*, 298 Minn. 402, 216 N.W.2d 641 (1975), which reversed convictions because of the absence of a specific definition of "obscene," and *State v. Ray*, 292 Minn. 104, 193 N.W.2d 315 (1971), upholding an obscenity conviction under a statute that proscribed "indecent or lascivious exposure or use of the human body."

Although not a frequent dissenter, Justice Peterson wrote a final dissent that was one of his most striking. In *State by McClure v. Sports & Health Club*, 370 N.W.2d 844, 854 (Minn. 1985), he would have ruled in favor of the operator of a health club who demanded that his employees espouse his religious views, on grounds that the right of religious freedom enjoyed by a private business owner trumped the religious discrimination provision of the Human Rights Act.

Not only was Justice Peterson a judicial luminary but also his relations with others on the court were excellent. He served with 16 different justices, including three chief justices, and had good relations with all of them. Chief Justice Douglas K. Amdahl referred to Justice Peterson as a "thoughtful, gentle, articulate man who has a built-in compass which points towards fairness." Another chief with whom he served, Robert Sheran, praised him for his "unique contributions," which included opinions that were "distinctively well written . . . Peterson managed to disagree when he felt the need without ever becoming personal or disparaging."

While dealing with difficult and disputive issues, Peterson said he steered from conflict with his colleagues, refraining from "any lobbying or pressuring" because he thought that each "has a mind of his or her own, and each is able to decide the case on the merits as he or she sees fit." This action entitled him to observe that "we never get aggravated with each other and when we leave the court at the end of the day, we leave as friends."

—Marshall H. Tanick

Fallon Kelly

1907–1992
Associate Justice, 1970–1980

Associate Justice Fallon Kelly's 47-year legal career was marked by humble beginnings, by the practice of law with future governors, senators, state legislators, and judges, by service to the profession and to the community, and by his ever-present love of the law, meticulous attention to detail, and robust Irish sense of humor.

Born in Crookston, Minnesota, on September 13, 1907, Fallon was the only boy among the four Kelly children. His Irish-immigrant father was a registered pharmacist, but he chose to forego that profession in favor of better providing for the Kelly family as a traveling coffee-and-tea salesman. Fallon attended school in Crookston through the eighth grade, deciding as early as ten or 12 years of age to become a lawyer. He seems to have read a book about a lawyer who successfully defended a man unjustly accused of a crime. Kelly later recalled finishing the book and thinking "how great it would be if I could do something like that."

Kelly's early school achievement must have shown his great potential, for a kindly aunt from South Dakota generously agreed to pay his tuition, room, board, and expenses to attend four years of high school at St. Thomas Military Academy in St. Paul. Kelly graduated second in the class of 1926. Nearly 50 years later, in 1973, St. Thomas Academy presented Justice Kelly with its Edward G. Hames Alumni Award.

Kelly received an undergraduate degree from the University of Minnesota and went on to law school there, where he learned from the likes of the legendary William Prosser. Kelly's achievements at the University of Minnesota Law School were many. He was a member and editor of the *Minnesota Law Review*, a member of Grey Friars (a senior honor society), president of Phi Alpha Delta legal fraternity, presi-dent of the law school's senior class, and president of the All-University Council. Kelly graduated fifth in the law school class of 1933.

The new graduate left law school only to face the grim job market of the Great Depression. Kelly felt lucky to find work with the firm of Kyle & Kyle at the starting salary of $25 per month, a sum less than he had earned pumping gas to support himself through college. His fortune soon changed, however, when another young lawyer, Harold Stassen, began searching for an exceptional attorney to serve the growing practice of the firm Stassen & Ryan. Kelly was that exceptional attorney, and he joined Stassen & Ryan in 1935. Three years later, Stassen became the country's youngest governor ever, triggering a remarkable seven-decade run of political and judicial success for Stassen & Ryan and its successor firms, starting with Kelly & LeVander. The attorneys of these firms supplied two governors, two state supreme court justices, a U.S. Congressman, a U.S. Senator, a U.S. District Court judge, a state legislator, and the St. Paul city attorney.

Fallon Kelly and Mary Batchelder were married in Renville, Minnesota, in 1935. Despite the struggles of the depression, Kelly described their early years of marriage as "some of the happiest days of our lives . . . We were very easily pleased with the simple things in life." The Kellys had four children: Katharine, John, Anne, and Molly. In addition to raising their family, the Kellys shared many interests, including a love for hunting, which Mary introduced to her husband. Fallon Kelly also enjoyed other recreation like fishing and golfing. In 1949 he was the state badminton doubles champion. He also served as a trustee of St. John Vianney Church in South St. Paul and as commander of the Abner Rude American Legion Post.

346

And he loved laughter. Kelly had at the ready an enormous storehouse of Irish jokes for any willing listener. His lively sense of humor also proved useful in his practice, such as when he and his law colleagues were stymied in a roundtable discussion of how to handle a client's difficult legal problem. Kelly eased the tension and spurred a breakthrough when he suddenly blurted, "I think we should go out and consult a lawyer!"

During World War II, Kelly interrupted his legal career to serve as a lieutenant in the U.S. Navy. As a gunnery officer with a PBY (amphibious aircraft) squadron, Lieutenant Kelly engaged in patrol work, night bombing, and sea/air rescues. He spent nearly 27 months on duty in the Marshall Islands.

Upon his return from duty, Kelly resumed his private law practice until 1958, when President Dwight Eisenhower appointed him U.S. attorney for Minnesota. Kelly spent the next three years prosecuting high-profile criminal cases, many of which involved local underworld figures. Of particular notoriety was the case against Isadore (Kid Cann) Blumenfeld, a longtime local crime figure who had escaped prosecution in the 1930s, '40s, and '50s. Under Kelly's leadership, Kid Cann was charged with and convicted of transporting a person for immoral purposes, a crime that in later years has been described as human trafficking.

Kelly also successfully prosecuted the high-profile Hillcrest Bank robbery case, at the time the first St. Paul bank robbery in more than a quarter of a century. In addition to his successful prosecutions, Kelly's leadership brought written commendations from U.S. Attorney General William Rogers for case management success, including substantial reductions in the backlog of cases pending in the District of Minnesota.

When the Eisenhower administration ended, Kelly returned to private practice, this time founding the firm of Kelly, Segell, and Fallon. Again Kelly's firm produced judges. Of the three named partners, two (including Kelly) ascended to the bench.

In July 1970, Justice Fallon Kelly began ten years of service on the Minnesota Supreme Court. As he had in law practice, Kelly was meticulous in his attention to detail, often spending the extra effort to inform his decisions with what he called "pretty points of law." His judicial colleagues, however, admired Kelly for other things as well. Former Chief Justice Robert Sheran later said of Kelly, "I think the unique quality that Kelly brought to our court was that he combined business experience with a really high level of legal competence." And Justice Lawrence Yetka said of Kelly's service on the court, "I found him to be one of the most level-headed, honorable men I've served with on the court. He had an open mind. I don't think you can pay a higher compliment to a judge than to say he was open-minded."

Justice Kelly authored 262 majority decisions on behalf of the court. Among many of special note is *Zerby v. Warren*, 297 Minn. 134, 210 N.W.2d 58 (1973), a case that perhaps signaled the imposition of greater legal responsibility for those who provide dangerous substances to minors. In *Zerby*, the court imposed absolute liability for the illegal sale of glue to a minor, which had resulted in the death of an 11-year-old from sniffing. Another decision of special note is the 1980 case of *Continental Can Co. v. State of Minn.*, 297 N.W.2d 241 (Minn. 1980), a ruling that ushered in a new era of workplace protections. In a case that—amazingly—was the first of its kind in the country, Kelly wrote for the court that workplace sexual harassment is discriminatory and therefore illegal.

Justice Kelly was amazed by the heavy caseload the court faced in the 1970s, remarking that the only way to "cut down on the work of the supreme court effectively . . . is to have an intermediate court of appeals." The intermediate court began serving Minnesota three years after Kelly retired from the supreme court in 1980. But Kelly continued to serve even in retirement, accepting a temporary appointment to help reduce the backlog of cases in Hennepin, Ramsey, and Dakota Counties. True to his strengths, Kelly volunteered to tackle "the complicated, intricate cases."

Justice Fallon Kelly died on June 19, 1992. Who could have predicted, some 75 years earlier, how well served the legal profession and the State of Minnesota would be that a young boy from Crookston imagined "how great it would be" to become a lawyer?

—William M. Hart

Harry H. MacLaughlin

1927–2005
Associate Justice, 1972–1977

Associate Justice Harry H. MacLaughlin has been called a "brilliant jurist," and many would place him high on the list of outstanding members of the Minnesota Supreme Court. He was extraordinarily well prepared for each case, kept an open mind, and wrote decisive, clearly worded opinions. He found strong support in family and friends, to whom he was loyal and devoted. His great sense of humor was perhaps disarming for one so otherwise studious and precise.

Harry was born in 1927 in Breckenridge, Minnesota, to Grace and Harry MacLaughlin. He was raised in Wahpeton, North Dakota, where he completed high school. As for many men of his generation, World War II interrupted Harry's college education. He served as a yeoman in the U.S. Navy from 1945 to 1946, when he resumed his pursuit of a degree in business administration, earning a bachelor's degree in 1949 from the University of Minnesota.

After acquiring some business experience, Harry MacLaughlin returned to the University of Minnesota to study law. There he met and formed a lifelong friendship with Walter Mondale, who would become a Minnesota attorney general, a U.S. senator, vice president, and ambassador to Japan. Vice President Mondale has described Harry as "one of the most impressive, important jurists in Minnesota history." Many speculated that if Walter Mondale had been elected president, Harry would have been appointed to the U.S. Supreme Court. Another law school classmate, Mary Jeanne Coyne, followed Harry to the state supreme court, being appointed in 1982.

After graduating from law school, both MacLaughlin and Mondale became clerks to the Minnesota Supreme Court for the 1955–1956 term. The two served the pair of Gallaghers on the court—MacLaughlin clerking for Justice Frank Gallagher and Mondale clerking for Justice Thomas F. Gallagher. They were joined by a distinguished group of other law clerks who would also become leaders of the bar—Sherman Winthrop, Roger Pauly, Gilbert Harries, John Engberg, Allen Saeks, and John Hetlund.

After his clerkship ended in 1956, MacLaughlin practiced law with Mondale at the firm of Larson, Loevinger, Lindquist, Freeman & Fraser (later to become Lindquist & Vennum). A year later, MacLaughlin and Mondale established the separate firm of MacLaughlin & Mondale. That firm became MacLaughlin & Harstad when Mondale became state attorney general. During these early years of practice MacLaughlin also served as a law instructor at the William Mitchell College of Law, where he was recognized for his scholarship and teaching ability.

Harry MacLaughlin married Mary Jean Shaffer in 1958, and they had two sons, David and Douglas. He was an adoring family man and especially treasured the time he spent with the family at his cabin in Alexandria.

Gov. Wendell R. Anderson appointed MacLaughlin to the Minnesota Supreme Court in 1972; there he authored more than 160 opinions. Notable among them was *Nieting v. Blondell*, 235 N.W.2d 597 (1975), in which the court announced that the common law doctrine of sovereign immunity of the state with respect to tort claims was abolished, subject to any appropriate action taken by the legislature. MacLaughlin wrote:

> One of the paramount interests of the members of an organized and civilized society is that they be afforded protection against harm to their persons, properties, and characters. The logical extension of that interest is that, if harm is wrongfully inflicted upon an individual in such a society, he should have

an opportunity to obtain a reasonable and adequate remedy against the wrongdoer, either to undo the harm inflicted or to provide compensation therefore. If the state is properly to serve the public interest, it must strive, through its laws, to achieve the goals of protecting the people and of providing them with adequate remedies of injuries wrongfully inflicted upon them. So long as the state fails to do so, it will be functioning in conflict with the public interest and the public good.

Although MacLaughlin was an infrequent dissenter, he did write concise and pointed dissents on issues controlled by the U.S. Constitution, perhaps foretelling his future as a federal judge. Two cases stand out. In *State v. Lebewitz,* 202 N.W.2d 648 (1972), he reluctantly concluded, contrary to the majority, that a pornographic movie was not obscene and that the exhibition of it was constitutionally protected under the First Amendment. In *Schwartz v. Talmo,* 205 N.W.2d 318 (1973) he again differed from the majority when he concluded that an amendment to the Worker's Compensation laws, to exclude all work-related suicides from coverage under the act, was a violation of the Fourteenth Amendment's requirement of equal protection.

President Jimmy Carter appointed MacLaughlin to the U.S. District Court in Minnesota in 1977, inter-rupting MacLaughlin's service on the state supreme court. MacLaughlin took his oath of office at the White House, where his friend Walter Mondale officiated. MacLaughlin's term on the federal bench was both distinguished and extensive. He took senior status in 1992 but continued to serve on the court until his death in 2005, having served 28 years as a federal judge after seven years on the Minnesota Supreme Court.

During his time on the federal district court, MacLaughlin frequently served as a guest lecturer at the University of Minnesota Law School. In 1995, the regents of the University of Minnesota honored him with the university's Outstanding Achievement Award. Earlier in 1983, *The American Lawyer* named him the best judge in the federal Eighth Circuit.

David Lillehaug, one of MacLaughlin's former law clerks, who would become U.S. attorney for Minnesota, observed that Harry MacLaughlin "walked fast, talked fast, and ruled fast." He was decisive and fair and especially well suited to complex civil litigation because of his depth of knowledge of business law.

Harry MacLaughlin died on May 3, 2005, at the age of 78. He is deeply missed by family, friends, and colleagues.

—Justice Sam Hanson

George M. Scott

1922–2006
Associate Justice, 1973–1987

Associate Justice Scott's "unusual and lucky career" was marked by a profound dedication to the principles of American democracy. When others wondered whether there were too many lawyers, he observed that Americans did not learn enough about the founding fathers and the workings of American democracy, suggesting that "everybody should go to law school."

George M. Scott was born in Clark township, New Jersey, on September 14, 1922, the youngest of eight children in a home without running water, gas, or electricity. His father was an Irish immigrant from a farm "40 miles by hay wagon out of Dublin." The Great Depression of the 1930s marked Scott's childhood. He observed mass unemployment and the problems of organizing workers and thought government could do more for people—a sentiment that clearly stayed with him through some 33 years of public service.

Before Scott had a chance to pursue his ambition, Japan attacked Pearl Harbor, and the United States entered World War II. The ambitious young man volunteered and was inducted into the service in May 1942. He was sent to the University of Minnesota, where he studied engineering as part of the Army Specialized Training Program—part of the plan for rebuilding after the war. There he met Joyce Hughes, whom he would later marry, and her father, a prominent Minneapolis lawyer. After two years of study, the college program ended because young single men were needed on the battlefield. After "rather perfunctory training," Scott landed in Normandy with the 44th Infantry Division as part of the D-Day invasion, reaching the Rhine River when Strasbourg was taken four months later. He was close to Italy's northern border by the time hostilities ceased in Europe on May 8, 1945.

The battle-hardened troops, Scott among them, were sent home for a 30-day furlough before their scheduled deployment to the South Pacific for the invasion of Japan. Joyce Hughes went to the New Jersey coast to join Scott's family in welcoming him home. During the furlough, Scott learned the atom bomb had been dropped on Hiroshima. "The war," he said, "ended while we sat on the beach."

Scott wanted to go back to college right away, but there were so many servicemen going to school that the University of Minnesota required a one-year delay before he could return. Scott was in too big a hurry to wait that long, so he applied to other schools. He went to the first that had room for him immediately—the University of Tennessee in Knoxville. Once he had three years of pre-law credits, Scott was accepted at New York University Law School. By then he planned to marry Joyce Hughes and move to Minnesota. When her father died suddenly, he changed his law school plans, moved to Minneapolis, got married, and enrolled at the Minneapolis-Minnesota College of Law, which later became William Mitchell.

Never afraid of hard work, Scott spent his days working at a law firm as an investigator and his nights in law school. During this time that he picked up the "habit," as he called it, of getting up at 4 A.M., which stayed with him throughout his career. The time between 4 A.M. and 7 A.M., he said, is an "excellent, quiet, alert time." By the time Scott entered practice in October 1951, he and Joyce had three sons. Having witnessed the effects of polio in his own neighborhood, Scott became actively involved with the National Foundation for Infantile Paralysis–March of Dimes, meeting Dr. Jonas Salk and even digging with him the first shovel of dirt for his institute.

After law school, Scott and his friend Douglas Amdahl, future chief justice of the Minnesota Supreme Court, formed the law firm of Amdahl & Scott. By 1954, the Scotts were both active participants in the DFL Party. When Miles Lord, their neighbor, was elected state attorney general, George Scott became deputy attorney general, assigned to the Minnesota Highway Department to implement the interstate highway system. Every condemnation case had to be tried to a jury, with no settlements out of court, to avoid any opportunity for corruption. Scott acquired a great deal of trial experience in a short time.

In 1955, Scott was to move on to another job in public service—that of Hennepin County attorney. When the position became vacant, Scott was appointed and immediately found himself trying and winning a sensational murder case against A. Arnold Axelrod, M.D., accused of sexually molesting and murdering a patient. The case was thoroughly covered by the national press and even abroad. For Scott it was just the beginning of what he called a "very unusual and lucky career." In 18 years as Hennepin County attorney, personally trying as many cases as possible, Scott never lost a case.

Scott was recognized as a leader in his field. He became president of the Minnesota County Attorney Association in 1960 and president of the National District Attorney Association in 1964. During this period, he remained active in the DFL, going as a delegate to the Democratic National Convention in Los Angeles, where he voted for John F. Kennedy when Hubert Humphrey's bid for the nomination was unsuccessful. Scott managed Humphrey's successful campaign for a third term in the U.S. Senate.

Scott made substantive contributions to the law during the critical period of the 1960s. As he described it, we were "going through a crisis in this country as we had before. Every once in a while this democracy gets a little shaky." There were riots, and there was dissatisfaction with the lack of equality. Perhaps during this period Scott adopted the saying for which he became well known: "There must be change so that things can remain the same."

Scott spoke often of the 1930s and the 1960s as two periods during which American democracy was shaky and needed change within to avoid revolution and another form of government altogether. Scott considered Chief Justice Earl Warren of the U.S. Supreme Court to be the leader of the 1960s' "revolution in constitutional and criminal law" and a "strict conformist" to the law, especially in his application of the Fourteenth Amendment. *Plessy v. Ferguson*, 163 U.S. 537 (1896), a decision that had "grated on [Scott's] innards," was finally corrected.

As Hennepin County attorney, Scott read decisions handed down from the U.S. Supreme Court every Friday. They did not, however, always give clear guidance as to their implementation. Many prosecutors balked at the Supreme Court's directives, but Scott decided they had to be implemented immediately. He pioneered procedures with no statutory basis and no precedent. He opened files to the defendants, conducted plea negotiations in open court, and developed other fair procedures. American Bar Association president Lewis F. Powell, later a U.S. Supreme Court Justice, appointed Scott to a task force for standards of criminal justice. The procedures Scott had developed in Hennepin County were adopted and became the "omnibus hearing." Later, as a justice of the Minnesota Supreme Court, Scott was a key participant in Minnesota's adoption of rules that have since been copied in many other states.

In 1969, Scott was urged to run for governor. He did not get the DFL nomination and instead supported Wendell Anderson in his successful campaign for the office. A few years later, in 1973, Governor Anderson appointed Scott to the newly expanded Minnesota Supreme Court, where he became justice "number 9." By the time he retired in 1987, the court of appeals was in existence, and the supreme court again had only seven justices.

In 14 years on the court, Justice Scott authored 415 majority opinions. Among his most important was *State v. Knaffla*, 243 N.W.2d 737 (Minn. 1976), allowing a criminal defendant at least one right of review. Another was *Anderson v. Stream*, 295 N.W.2d 595 (Minn. 1980), establishing a reasonable parent standard in tort actions by children against their parents. A personal favorite of Justice Scott's was *Kossak v. Stalling*, 277 N.W.2d 30 (Minn. 1979), in which the court held that when a city had actual notice of an accident, a one-year commencement-of-suit requirement was invalid as a denial of equal protection.

An avid poet, Justice Scott often commemorated occasions with poetry, and he liked to deliver his case reports to the court in verse. Cynthia M. Johnson, his first clerk and later supreme court commissioner, recalled that he spent much time with each clerk, "asking for little but subtly demanding the best or more." She described his greatest contribution to the confer-

ence process as "his strong belief in the vitality of the constitution and his persuasive analysis of the practical consequences of any decision which would issue."

Justice George M. Scott died on May 25, 2006, survived by his wife, four sons, and a daughter. He had risen, as his brother said, "from poor and disadvantaged beginnings" to become Minnesota's one and only justice "number 9."

—Monica Kelley and Christine Kain

Glenn E. Kelley

1921–1992
Associate Justice, 1981–1990

Glenn E. Kelley enjoyed at least three distinguished careers—as a trial lawyer, a district court judge, and an associate justice on the Minnesota Supreme Court. He enjoyed the challenge at every level, and he observed the significant changes occurring in the legal profession over the more than 40 years of his legal career. Born into a family of educators, Glenn was at home in the study of the law. He commented that he enjoyed the fact that American law has its roots in so much history and that it requires consideration of philosophy, economics, sociology, and all human endeavor—subjects that were a lifelong interest.

Glenn Kelley was born in St. Edward, Nebraska, in 1921. His father was the superintendent of schools, and his mother was a former schoolteacher. When his father earned a doctorate in education, the family moved to Aberdeen, South Dakota, and his father became a college professor. Glenn graduated from high school in Aberdeen and in 1943 received a bachelor of science degree from what became Northern State College (and later, Northern State University) in Aberdeen.

Immediately after college, Kelley joined the U.S. Army Air Corps, and in 1944, as a first lieutenant, he joined the 379th Bomber Group, Eighth Air Force, as a navigator-bombardier on B-17 Flying Fortresses operating from Kimbolton, England. On his third mission over Germany his plane, struck by flak, lost two engines; ground fire over Belgium disabled a third engine, and the aircraft was forced to ditch in the English Channel. The crew escaped with minor injuries, was rescued by a British coastal patrol craft, and returned to England. After a short recuperation, Lt. Kelley was flying again; he completed another eight missions and survived a midair collision before being rotated to the United States for training on the new B-

29, which later led the assault on Japan. The war ended before that assignment did, and Lt. Kelley, awarded a Purple Heart and the Air Medal with oak leaf clusters, was mustered out in time to enroll at the University of Michigan Law School in the fall of 1945.

Upon receipt of his law degree in 1948, Kelley, with his wife Margaret ("Peggy"), whom he had married in 1946, moved to Austin, Minnesota, where he joined the firm later known as Alderson, Catherwood, Kelley and Ondov. For the next 22 years Kelley practiced with that firm; he later estimated that in those years 95 percent of his practice was in litigation. His trial practice focused primarily on insurance defense, railroad defense, and the representation of the Hormel Company. He became active in the American Bar Association and frequently authored articles on tort law for the torts and insurance section of the American Bar Association. Kelley was active in the community, where he served as president of the Mower County and Third Judicial District Bar Associations and, it was said, occasionally enjoyed a round or two of golf.

In 1969, Gov. Harold LeVander appointed Glenn Kelley a district judge in the Third Judicial District. The Kelleys, now including young Glenn, David, and Anne, moved to Winona, the site of the judge's chambers. Congenial relations with the bar, court personnel, litigants, and the general public and a marked accessibility to all with business before the court marked Kelley's service on the bench. He was a fair, practical, thoughtful, and respected trial court judge. He presided over several prominent trials, including a murder case involving a Winona businessman charged with hiring a gunman from Illinois to murder his wife. Donald Howard, the businessman, was tried in Dakota County after a change of venue, and Judge Kelley presided at the trial. The publicity was intense, from the early pretrial proceedings until the jury returned a guilty verdict on February 15, 1978. The jury deliberated over 11 hours and asked the judge to repeat many of the critical instructions. Kelley continued to receive correspondence from Howard, his parents, and his two daughters, years after announcing a life sentence. He always responded, though he could only say that a life sentence means "life" and that there was nothing further he could do.

Just over ten years later, in 1981, Gov. Al Quie, filling a vacancy created by the resignation of Justice Robert Sheran, appointed Judge Kelley to the Minnesota Supreme Court. Justice Kelley served on that court for ten years, retiring on disability to deal with cancer in 1990. He died in Woodbury, Minnesota, in 1992.

In private comments, Justice Kelley allowed that the state supreme court was a monastery compared to the rough and tumble of the trial courts. That ecclesiastical aura did not, however, extend to infallibility, as within a few days of the announcement of his appointment, the court released an opinion reversing the decision in a case he had tried. In that case, Judge Kelley had found that an innocent intervener in a bar-room brawl did not lose the protection of his homeowner's insurance policy for injuries he had caused, under the "intentional act" exclusion of the policy. The supreme court, however, found that the swing of a fist was an intentional act, hence no coverage: reversed.

Justice Kelley's judicial philosophy might be characterized as conservative, practical, seasoned by his years on the trial bench, and scrupulously fair. In *Hunt v. Regents of the University of Minnesota*, a medical malpractice case, he dissented from the majority opinion on a series of procedural and evidentiary rulings. While the majority found errors in the trial not of sufficient gravity to require reversal of the trial

court, Justice Kelley, no doubt drawing upon his experience in the courtroom, wrote that the lower court verdict should be reversed. The errors found would have influenced the jury, perhaps a point not as apparent to those members of the court who had not served or practiced as long in the trial courts.

In a 1985 case that attracted much notoriety, *State v. Soto,* Justice Kelley wrote for a majority of the court that the phrase "human being" in the vehicular homicide statute did not include an unborn fetus: "It is not within our judicial province, under the guise of interpretation, to hold that the words 'human being' as used in the [Minnesota vehicular homicide statue] encompass a viable eight-and-one-half-month-old fetus. The enactment of criminal laws, the scope of those laws, and the sanctions for their violation, are solely within the legislative function and province."

As might be expected, some roundly criticized the decision as an example of judicial rigor mortis, the triumph of semantics over reason, but the legislature, pursuant to Justice Kelley's invitation, promptly enacted criminal statutes relating to "fetal homicide." The separation of powers was an important judicial principle for Justice Kelley.

Kelley was a jurist learned in the law, seasoned by experience in the trial courts, and well aware of the limitations of judicial power, and its proper exercise. But as one former law clerk observed, the key to understanding Justice Kelley was his incredible character: "[I] am convinced that much of his success as a lawyer, a trial court judge, and ultimately as an associate justice on the supreme court can be attributed to his remarkable personality, which was down-to-earth, unpretentious, reasonable, fair, and caring. The one thing that personified this more than anything else was his well-worn briefcase, which was symbolic of his long-lasting and meaningful affection for people, the law, and above all, justice."

—Norman R. Carpenter

M. Jeanne Coyne

1926–1998
Associate Justice, 1982–1996

Although Justice M. Jeanne Coyne was the only woman to graduate in her law school class, her firm's only woman lawyer for 22 of her 25 years of practice, and one of the first women to serve on Minnesota's highest court, she would not want to be remembered as a "trailblazer." She once observed, "Although I was always aware of being a lawyer and a woman, I never practiced law as a 'woman lawyer' . . . My goal was to be the best lawyer that I could be and to serve my clients and the community well." This dedication to excellence served her well. She became first among many, achieving distinction as a brilliant lawyer and judge.

Mary Jeanne Coyne was born on December 7, 1926. She lived in a modest bungalow at 55th and Pillsbury in Minneapolis, which she once said was like being "at the end of the world—it was all cornfields beyond that." Her father, Vincent Coyne, worked for the railroad. Her mother was a traditional homemaker, who was heard to say that Mary Jeanne was difficult to raise because she "argued about everything." During high school, Mary Jeanne showed special aptitude in physics, chemistry and math. She attributed the school's intensive Latin course to developing her rigorous study habits and her appreciation for the English language. She graduated as salutatorian.

Lacking money for college, Coyne started work as a messenger for Marquette National Bank. She was promoted to head teller for the mortgage department when she turned 18. At the time, she was told that no other bank in Minneapolis had even a teller younger than 25. Later, she began work as a mortgage closer and studied accounting at night at the University of Minnesota. Her work brought her into contact with

Elsie Wolf, a real estate lawyer, who inspired her to study law. Coyne later observed that it was "a great shock to my parents."

Coyne began law school at the age of 25, in the "2-4" program, in which she was allowed to complete her undergraduate studies in two years and then spend four years in law school. She completed all of her pre-law courses in just one year with an A average. Although she was clearly academically gifted, her first year at law school was especially challenging. She was one of only four women entering the class in 1953. One professor's practice was to question students one by one, going down the row. Every day he would skip her as if she did not exist.

Another professor had an opposite but equally disconcerting approach. He questioned her for the entire hour of class for three days in a row. The dean's office advised her that she would never graduate if she continued to work the number of hours she was working. Yet she not only graduated, she also acted as associate editor of the *Minnesota Law Review* and clerked for Minnesota Supreme Court Justice Leroy E. Matson during her final year of law school. She graduated second in her class. Among her 180 classmates were the future vice president, Walter Mondale, Judge Harry MacLaughlin, Minnesota Attorney General Douglas Head, and Judge William Canby of the Ninth Circuit Court of Appeals. Coyne was named to the Order of the Coif.

After law school, Coyne was hired by Meagher, Geer, Markham, Anderson, Adamson, Flaskamp & Brennan (now Meagher & Geer), where she remained for the next 25 years. During that time, her excellent work and deep respect for the law led many to call her a "lawyer's lawyer." She eventually became the firm's managing partner. Her practice was focused on civil litigation, where her aptitude and interest in math and science made her the candidate for cases involving malfunctioning airplane propellers, blueprints, and pharmaceuticals. She was a born contender: when the governor asked what she liked most about practicing law, she replied: "Winning." Nevertheless, she eventually broadened her practice to include business and corporate law.

From the beginning of her career, Coyne focused on appellate practice, and she appeared in the Minnesota Supreme Court in more than a hundred cases. Her first argument before that court was in the fall of 1957, barely three months after she began practice. She said, "I will long remember that argument—in that case, I had the dubious honor of having the court overturn a long-established rule of law to rule against me." She liked appellate practice, she said, because it exposed her to a broad range of civil litigation. She also felt that appellate work allowed her to participate on the cutting edge of important legal questions. She prepared rigorously for argument, pursuing details tenaciously.

No matter how busy she was with her work at the firm, she found time to mentor those who aspired to a career in the law—law students as well as the young lawyers at Meagher Geer. Dick Bland, a Meagher Geer lawyer, remembered that Coyne always took the time to review his written work, complimenting what he had done well and offering advice on how to improve. Gary Hoch, another lawyer at the firm, said Coyne had particular interest in others who, like her, had come to the law after doing other work. The firm started a scholarship at the University of Minnesota in her name, with the hope that it would help just such students.

After 25 years of practice, then Gov. Al Quie called on Coyne to serve on the state's highest court. The decision to leave the many friends among her colleagues and clients was not easy, however. She explained, "The law's been very good to me, and I feel that I owe it something, and I owe the public something. I'm here to serve the law and the public, and I try very hard to do that and to do it as well as I can."

On the day Coyne met with the state's Judicial Merit Selection Commission in 1982, a longtime judge asked why she wanted to join the high court: She said: "I'm not sure I do. The pay is not that great. The job has so much power it scares me. But I think I'd be a darn good judge." She was sworn in on September 1, 1982. Ironically, she took Justice Matson's seat on the bench.

Through her tenure on the court, Coyne became known and respected for her intelligence, integrity, and clarity of thought. She issued many highly regarded opinions, particularly in insurance law and family law. She was also recognized for her criminal law opinions. Former Chief Justice A. M. (Sandy) Keith observed that she had "written some of the finest criminal law decisions of any judge, some victories for the prosecution, some for the defense—all examples of judging in its finest." In the courtroom, Justice Coyne was known for grilling lawyers on case history and on the court's previous decisions.

Her judicial philosophy was conservative in that she felt that the court should refrain from making social policy and generally should lag behind society, changing only when society had changed. This philosophy sprang from respect for the other branches of government and the constitutional separation of powers principle. She felt that in some cases the court had decided policy issues better left to the legislature. An example was Justice Coyne's decision to join the minority in the *Bloom* DNA testing case. Relative to *Bloom*, she observed that criminal cases should not become a battle of hired experts and that statistics could lie.

She recognized, however, when it was time to change the law. One of her most important opinions, in *Nardini v. Nardini*, 414 N.W.2d 184 (Minn. 1987), brought about a dramatic change to then-existing family law. The *Nardini* decision created a framework for valuing closely held businesses in traditional marriages. Justice Coyne felt that the decision was justified because men in their midfifties, who were at the height of their success, simply were unable to recognize how a woman's earning power diminished when she was out of the job market during a long marriage.

Justice Coyne retired as a justice after 14 years in October 31, 1996. Her resignation letter said that consistency and the need to envision the effect of cases in the future had been the driving forces in her work as a justice. When asked about her career and the impact of being a woman on the bench, she said, "A wise old man and a wise old woman often reach the same conclusion." She noted: "My viewpoint may have been different from a man's on some things, but I believe that this just offered another dimension to whatever I was doing."

Throughout her career, she was actively involved with many organizations, both legal and nonlegal, including the National Association of Women Judges and the National Association of Women Lawyers, for which she served as recording secretary and treasurer. She was also a charter member of Minnesota Women Lawyers. She served as a member of the Minnesota Lawyers Professional Responsibility Board and the Board of Directors of the University of Minnesota Law Alumni Association. She was a member of the Board of Conciliation and the Board of Arbitration of the Archdiocese of St. Paul and Minneapolis.

Coyne had many interests outside the law. She loved classical music, having studied piano at the MacPhail Center for Music for many years. She was a longtime member of the Minneapolis Golf Club and also enjoyed gardening. She was especially proud of her peonies. She was a long time member of Christ the King Catholic Church.

Coyne said she would like to be remembered "as a judge who has a passionate respect for the law and who really tried to maintain a consistent, analytical perspective on the law of a very moderate variety with a view toward the long-term effect of whatever decision we were making." Certainly we will remember her for that but also because she was a brilliant lawyer and jurist, a mentor of young lawyers, and a friend. She died on August 6, 1998, at the age of 71. *Minnesota Law & Politics* has since named Coyne to its "Legal Hall of Fame," as one of the hundred most influential attorneys in the state's history.

—Mary R. Vasaly

Peter S. Popovich

1920–1996
Associate Justice, 1987–1989; Chief Justice, 1989–1990

During his long and distinguished judicial career, Peter S. Popovich had the distinction of serving at different points as chief judge of the Minnesota Court of Appeals and as chief justice of the Minnesota Supreme Court.

The son of Yugoslavian immigrants, Popovich learned the value of hard work at an early age. He was born in Crosby, Minnesota, in 1920 and grew up in Chisholm, Minnesota. He took on household tasks such as cooking and cleaning after his mother, a teacher, died when he was 13. His father worked in the iron mines before becoming a Chisholm city official.

"In the Iron Range, the emphasis was on education," Popovich pointed out in a 1988 interview. "Education was the key to getting ahead. More than once I heard my father say, 'Get an education. They can't take that away from you.'"

Popovich sold candy bars out of the trunk of his car and worked other odd jobs, such as being a dance instructor, to put himself through Hibbing Junior College, the University of Minnesota, and the St. Paul College of Law (now William Mitchell College of Law). He obtained his law degree in 1947 and co-founded the Peterson and Popovich law firm in St. Paul, where he practiced for 36 years.

Popovich had a bout with polio shortly after law school, resulting in a three-month hospitalization. Throughout his life he remained grateful to the March of Dimes for providing financial assistance during this period, and he frequently spoke about that organization.

Popovich lost his first bid for a legislative seat in 1950 but went on to serve in the Minnesota House of Representatives from 1953 to 1963. During his first year in office he was named "Outstanding Freshman Legislator"; he was later named "Most Effective House Member."

"I just love the legislative process—negotiating and drafting bills, negotiating compromises," Popovich once said.

One of his legacies as a legislator was the Minnesota Open Meeting Law, as noted *Minneapolis Star Tribune* reporter Margaret Zack in Popovich's March 30, 1996, obituary: "He remained an effective and aggressive advocate for openness in government and free speech issues . . . But Popovich will be remembered best for making the Minnesota Court of Appeals a model of efficiency."

Gov. Rudy Perpich tapped Popovich, a personal friend and fellow iron ranger, to head the court of appeals when it was first created in 1983. Popovich soon earned a reputation as a demanding and hardworking chief judge who believed in meeting deadlines and avoiding delays. Under his watch, the court of appeals was held up as a national model for efficiency.

In November 1987, Popovich became the first jurist from the Iron Range to serve on the state's high court when Perpich elevated his old friend. On February 1, 1989, Popovich became the court's 17th chief justice, a position he occupied until November 1990, when he reached mandatory retirement age. Popovich had a reputation as a moderate and free thinker on the bench.

After retiring from the judiciary, Popovich joined the Minneapolis law firm of Briggs and Morgan, where he practiced until 1996. He died of multiple organ failure on March 29, 1996, at the age of 75. Popovich was survived by his second wife, Gail, his four children, and three stepchildren.

Throughout his tenure on the bench, Popovich was known for his meticulous attention to detail.

"As the first chief justice of the Minnesota Court of Appeals, Peter Popovich had the unique opportunity to structure an intermediate appellate court," noted Minnesota Supreme Court Chief Justice A. M. Keith not long after Popovich retired from the high court. "Consistent with his work habits, he read all the literature on the subject, attended seminars, and consulted with judges and administrative experts from around the country. When the court of appeals began operations in 1983, Chief Judge Popovich and five colleagues had in place policies and procedures that enabled the court to immediately take charge of its caseload."

Popovich acknowledged during a 1983 interview that he could be stubborn and demanding, but he also pointed out that his drive was only one part of his character. "I know the pangs and trauma other people feel. I'm warm. I've got a sense of humor," he said. "You live but once. You've got to do what you think."

Providing a personal perspective on Popovich, one of his former law clerks, Bryan J. Leary, told the following anecdote from when the high court moved its home into the Minnesota Judicial Center:

> I did not look forward to moving day, and when that sweltering August day arrived, I learned that barely a dent had been made in packing the Chief's mountains of paper and memorabilia. The Chief remained undaunted, determined that things would be business as usual by the next day. Thus, I was not surprised to see the Chief rummaging through the legal cargo late that afternoon, preparing for upcoming cases. As I passed his door in the late afternoon, the Chief beckoned me into his office. "What is the first thing you saw as you came through this door?" he demanded as I entered. Sheepishly, I pointed to the window sill directly in front of where I stood. "Good," said the Chief as he removed his wife's picture from a box and placed it gingerly where I had pointed. He then turned, grinned, and said that he wanted the picture to be the first thing people saw when they entered his office.

While his tenure as supreme court chief justice was relatively brief, Popovich brought the same work ethic to that court that he was known for throughout his career. He also genuinely liked the job. "Other chief justices may have been more famous, or stayed in the position longer, or authored more opinions, but it would be hard to find an individual who enjoyed being chief justice more than Peter S. Popovich," wrote two of his former law clerks, Jeff Shorba and Jean Whitney in tribute.

Among Popovich's accomplishments on the high court was establishing the Minnesota Court Information Office to assist the public and the media in understanding how the court system works. He also headed a task force that created uniform rules for the state's ten judicial districts.

Numerous sources report Popovich lived by the motto "Justice delayed is justice denied." His hard work, drive, and dedication proved instrumental in establishing an intermediate appellate court in Minnesota and earned him a key place in the state's judicial history. As of this writing, he remains the only individual in Minnesota to have served as chief of both its appellate courts.

—Mark A. Cohen

Minnesota Supreme Court: Table of Succession

	Chief Justice	First Associate Justice	Second Associate Justice	Third Associate Justice	Fourth Associate Justice	Fifth Associate Justice	Sixth Associate Justice	Seventh Associate Justice	Eighth Associate Justice
Justices of the Minnesota Territorial Supreme Court									
1845[1]	Aaron Goodrich 1849–1851	David Cooper 1849–1853	Bradley B. Meeker 1849–1853						
1850	Jerome Fuller 1851–1852								
	Henry Z. Hayner 1851–1852								
	William H. Welch 1853–1858	Andrew G. Chatfield 1853–1857	Moses Sherburne 1853–1857						
1855		Rensselaer R. Nelson 1857–1858	Charles E. Flandrau 1857–1858						
Justices of the Minnesota Supreme Court									
1855[2]	Lafayette Emmett 1858–1865	Isaac Atwater 1858–1864	Charles E. Flandrau 1858–1864						
1860		Thomas Wilson 1864–1865	Samuel J. R. McMillan 1864–1874						
1865	Thomas Wilson 1865–1869	John M. Berry 1865–1887							
	James Gilfillan 1869–1870								
1870	Christopher G. Ripley 1870–1874								
	Samuel J. R. McMillan 1874–1875		George B. Young 1874–1875						
1875	James Gilfillan 1875–1894		F. R. E. Cornell 1875–1881						
1880[3]			Daniel A. Dickinson 1881–1893	Greenleaf Clark 1881–1882	William Mitchell 1881–1900				
				Charles E. Vanderburgh 1882–1894					
1885		Loren W. Collins 1887–1904							

360

	Chief Justice	First Associate Justice	Second Associate Justice	Third Associate Justice	Fourth Associate Justice	Fifth Associate Justice	Sixth Associate Justice	Seventh Associate Justice	Eighth Associate Justice
1890			Daniel Buck 1894–1899	Thomas Canty 1894–1899					
1895	Charles M. Start 1895–1913		Calvin L. Brown 1899–1913						
1900		Wallace B. Douglas 1904–1905		Charles L. Lewis 1900–1912	John A. Lovely 1900–1905				
1905		Edwin A. Jaggard 1905–1911			Charles B. Elliott 1905–1909				
					Thomas D. O'Brien 1909–1911				
1910		George L. Bunn 1911–1913		Philip E. Brown 1912–1915	David F. Simpson 1911–1912				
4	Calvin L. Brown 1913–1923	Oscar Hallam 1913–1923	George L. Bunn 1913–1918		Andrew Holt 1912–1942	Commissioner Homer B. Dibell 1913–1918	Commissioner Myron D. Taylor 1913–1930		
1915				Albert Schaller 1915–1917					
			Homer B. Dibell 1918–1934	James H. Quinn 1917–1928		Commissioner Edward Lees 1918–1927			
1920	Samuel B. Wilson 1923–1933	Royal A. Stone 1923–1942							
1925				Clifford L. Hilton 1928–1943		Commissioner Ingerval M. Olsen 1927–1930	Commissioner Charles Loring 1930–1930		
1930⁵	John P. Devaney 1933–1937		Julius J. Olson 1934–1948			Ingerval M. Olsen 1930–1936	Charles Loring 1930–1944		
1935	Henry M. Gallagher 1937–1944					Harry H. Peterson 1936–1950			
1940		Maynard E. Pirsig 1942–1942			Thomas O. Streissguth 1942–1942				
	Charles Loring 1944–1953	Luther W. Youngdahl 1943–1946		Clarence R. Magney 1943–1953	Thomas F. Gallagher 1943–1967		Thomas O. Streissguth 1944–1944		
1945		William C. Christianson 1946–1946					Leroy E. Matson 1945–1960		
		Frank T. Gallagher 1947–1963	Oscar R. Knutson 1948–1962						

	Chief Justice	First Associate Justice	Second Associate Justice	Third Associate Justice	Fourth Associate Justice	Fifth Associate Justice	Sixth Associate Justice	Seventh Associate Justice	Eighth Associate Justice
1950	Roger L. Dell 1953–1962			Roger L. Dell 1953–1953		Theodore Christianson 1950–1955			
1955				Martin A. Nelson 1953–1972		William P. Murphy 1955–1972			
1960	Oscar R. Knutson 1962–1973		Walter F. Rogosheske 1962–1980				Lee Loevinger 1960–1961		
		Robert J. Sheran 1963–1970					James C. Otis 1961–1982		
1965					C. Donald Peterson 1967–1986				
1970[6]	Robert J. Sheran 1973–1981	Fallon Kelly 1970–1980		John J. Todd 1972–1985		Harry H. MacLaughlin 1972–1977		Lawrence R. Yetka 1973–1993	George M. Scott 1973–1987
1975		Douglas K. Amdahl 1980–1981				Rosalie E. Wahl 1977–1994			
1980[7]	Douglas K. Amdahl 1981–1989	Glenn E. Kelley 1981–1990	John E. Simonett 1980–1994				M. Jeanne Coyne 1982–1996		
1985				Seat Eliminated in 1985 by Retirement	Seat Eliminated in 1986 by Retirement				Peter S. Popovich 1987–1989
	Peter S. Popovich 1989–1990								A.M. Keith 1989–1990
1990	A.M. Keith 1990–1998	Esther M. Tomljanovich 1990–1998				Edward C. Stringer 1994–2002		Alan C. Page 1993–Current	Sandra S. Gardebring 1991–1998
			Paul H. Anderson 1994–Current						
1995							Kathleen A. Blatz 1996–1998		
	Kathleen A. Blatz 1998–2006	Russell A. Anderson 1998–2006					James H. Gilbert 1998–2004		Joan Ericsen Lancaster 1998–2002
2000						Sam Hanson 2002–2008	G. Barry Anderson 2004–Current		Helen M. Meyer 2002–Current
2005	Russell A. Anderson 2006–Current	Lorie Skjerven Gildea 2006–Current				Christopher J. Dietzen 2008–Current			
2010									

References

1. The first Minnesota Territorial Supreme Court was established in 1849. Organic Act, ch. 121, § 9, 9 Stat. 403, 406 (1849). It consisted of a chief justice and two associate justices, who held four-year terms. Id.

2. When Minnesota became a state in 1858, it brought with it an elected three-member supreme court. The Constitution provided for a court consisting of one chief justice and two associate justices. Minn. Const. of 1857, art. VI, § 2. The justices were to hold seven-year terms. Id. § 3.

3. The legislature expanded the size of the court from three to five members in 1881. Act of Mar. 7, 1881, ch. 141, 1881 Minn. Laws 184. In 1883 the length of term was reduced to six years by constitutional amendment. Act of Mar. 1, 1883, ch. 3, § 1, 1883 Minn. Laws 7, 8.

4. In 1913, the legislature authorized the appointment of two supreme court commissioners. The commissioners had the same qualifications, duties, tenure, and salary as justices, though a different method of appointment. The act specified that the offices would be abolished when the court was increased from five to seven justices. Act of Mar. 12, 1913, ch. 62, 1913 Minn. Laws 53–54.

5. In 1930, Minnesota voters amended the constitution to increase the court from five to seven members. Act of Mar. 9, 1929, ch. 430, § 1, 1929 Minn. Laws 676, 676–77.

6. In 1972, the constitution was amended to expand the membership of the court from seven to nine. Minn. Const. art. VI, § 2 ("The supreme court consists of one chief judge and not less than six nor more than eight associate judges as the legislature may establish.").

7. In 1982 the legislature placed on the ballot a constitutional amendment authorizing the creation of an intermediate court of appeals. Act of Mar. 22, 1982, ch. 501, 1982 Minn. Laws 569. The reduction in the membership of the supreme court from nine to seven occurred by attrition of the first two members to retire.

Index of Names

Numbers in *italics* indicate a photo of and/or the start of a memorial for the individual named. Authors of the newly written memorials, justices, members of the bar, and others in public life are listed below. Family members who do not fit those categories are not listed but may be found in the justice memorials.